Pathophysiology, Diagnosis and Treatment of Autism Spectrum Disorder

Pathophysiology, Diagnosis and Treatment of Autism Spectrum Disorder

Editor: Harold Herrera

AMERICAN
MEDICAL PUBLISHERS
www.americanmedicalpublishers.com

AMERICAN
MEDICAL PUBLISHERS
www.americanmedicalpublishers.com

Cataloging-in-Publication Data

Pathophysiology, diagnosis and treatment of autism spectrum disorder / edited by Harold Herrera.
p. cm.
Includes bibliographical references and index.
ISBN 979-8-88740-365-6
1. Autism spectrum disorders. 2. Autism spectrum disorders--Pathophysiology. 3. Autism spectrum disorders--Diagnosis.
4. Autism spectrum disorders--Treatment. 5. Developmental disabilities. I. Herrera, Harold.
RC553.A88 P38 2023
616.858 82--dc23

American Medical Publishers,
41 Flatbush Avenue,
1st Floor, New York,
NY 11217, USA

ISBN 979-8-88740-365-6 (Hardback)

Contents

Preface

Autism refers to a neurodevelopmental disorder characterized by difficulties in social communication along with confined and repetitive behaviors. It is thought to be caused by a combination of genetic and environmental factors. The factors that can increase the likeliness of autism during pregnancy include fetal growth restriction, infections, autoimmune diseases, and various toxins like alcohol, air pollution, and cocaine. Diagnosis of these disorders is done on the basis of the behavior and not through cause or mechanism. There does not exist any known treatment for these disorders but various interventions can be helpful. Skill building, and behavioral, educational and psychological interventions can be utilized to facilitate people with autism disorders, which help them in living their life independently. This book is a compilation of chapters that discuss the most pathophysiology, diagnosis and treatment of autism spectrum disorder. It is a vital tool for all researching and studying this medical condition.

This book has been the outcome of endless efforts put in by authors and researchers on various issues and topics within the field. The book is a comprehensive collection of significant researches that are addressed in a variety of chapters. It will surely enhance the knowledge of the field among readers across the globe.

It gives us an immense pleasure to thank our researchers and authors for their efforts to submit their piece of writing before the deadlines. Finally in the end, I would like to thank my family and colleagues who have been a great source of inspiration and support.

Editor

1

Genetic Causes and Modifiers of Autism Spectrum Disorder

Lauren Rylaarsdam and Alicia Guemez-Gamboa*

Department of Physiology, Feinberg School of Medicine, Northwestern University, Chicago, IL, United States

***Correspondence:**
Alicia Guemez-Gamboa
alicia.guemez@northwestern.edu

Autism Spectrum Disorder (ASD) is one of the most prevalent neurodevelopmental disorders, affecting an estimated 1 in 59 children. ASD is highly genetically heterogeneous and may be caused by both inheritable and *de novo* gene variations. In the past decade, hundreds of genes have been identified that contribute to the serious deficits in communication, social cognition, and behavior that patients often experience. However, these only account for 10–20% of ASD cases, and patients with similar pathogenic variants may be diagnosed on very different levels of the spectrum. In this review, we will describe the genetic landscape of ASD and discuss how genetic modifiers such as copy number variation, single nucleotide polymorphisms, and epigenetic alterations likely play a key role in modulating the phenotypic spectrum of ASD patients. We also consider how genetic modifiers can alter convergent signaling pathways and lead to impaired neural circuitry formation. Lastly, we review sex-linked modifiers and clinical implications. Further understanding of these mechanisms is crucial for both comprehending ASD and for developing novel therapies.

Keywords: autism spectrum disorder, genetic modifiers, CNV, epigenetics, gene-environment interaction

INTRODUCTION

Autism was first described by Kanner (1943) in a detailed report of 11 children with similar unusual tendencies. Intriguing common symptoms such as improper facilitation of language, indifference to other people, and obsessive interests can clearly be discerned while reading Kanner's thorough patient history. Twenty-three years later, the first epidemiological study of autism estimated prevalence to be 4.5 per 10,000 individuals. Estimates have since increased drastically to 1 in 59 individuals affected, with at least three times as many males diagnosed as females (Loomes et al., 2017). This significant increase in prevalence is partially attributable to both increase in awareness and evolvement of Diagnostic and Statistical Manual of Mental Disorders (DSM) criteria, from a childhood form of schizophrenia in 1952, to a core diagnosis covering a spectrum of disorders in the present (Zeldovich, 2018). The changing landscape of factors required for diagnosis makes it difficult to quantify the actual increase in prevalence.

According to the current DSM-5 criteria, only two core features make up an autism spectrum disorder (ASD) diagnosis: (1) persistent deficits in social communication and social interaction across multiple contexts; and (2) restricted, repetitive patterns of behavior, interests, or activities (Lai et al., 2014). Because of the broad nature of these definitions, an ASD diagnosis often co-occurs with other conditions. Motor abnormalities (79%), gastrointestinal problems (up to 70%), epilepsy (up to 30%), intellectual disability (45%), and sleep disorders (50–80%) are common examples (Lai et al., 2014). Language disorders are frequently co-occurring and were even included in the DSM-IV criteria.

Since autism's identification as a diagnosis, the medical and scientific community have put immense effort into determining the risk factors and etiology. In Kanner's original assessment, he makes the unfortunate observation that in addition to patients having highly intelligent parents, "One other fact stands out prominently. In the whole group, there are very few really warm-hearted fathers and mothers" (Kanner, 1943). Thankfully, this "Refrigerator Mother" theory of autism was quickly disproved. ASD is now understood to be a disease of complex interaction between genetics and the environment, with heritability estimates ranging from 40 to 80% (Chaste and Leboyer, 2012). Extensive genetic studies have revealed hundreds of genes linked to autism. Epidemiological investigations have begun to elucidate which environmental factors might be contributing to risk, but there is a lot left to understand about how they interact with genetic predisposition to contribute to ASD etiology.

As is often the case with complex diseases, individuals with similar pathogenic variants may have drastically varying phenotypes. For example, people with duplications of proximal 15q range from unaffected to severely disabled (Cook et al., 1997; Bolton et al., 2001). Genetic modifiers - factors that modulate the expression of other genes - likely exist when individuals with the same pathogenic variant present on opposite ends of the spectrum. In this review, we will discuss what is presently known about the genetic landscape of ASD, then look at potential modifiers including copy number variation (CNV), double-hit mutations, epigenetic influences, and sex-linked effects.

GENETICS OF ASD

Identification of Candidate ASD Risk Genes

Following the classification of autism by Kanner, research efforts were undertaken to determine the disease etiology. Though it was initially assumed to be of environmental origin, an improved understanding of the role of genetics in human health soon suggested otherwise. In 1977, Folstein and Rutter (1977) conducted twin studies upon the observation that incidence among siblings was 50× higher than average. They found that monozygotic twins were more likely to share a diagnosis than dizygotic twins, suggesting a genetic influence. Bailey et al. (1995) supported this finding, documenting 60% concordance for monozygotic twins versus no concordant dizygotic pairs. In addition, risk of a child having ASD was found to be proportional to the percentage of the genome they shared with an affected sibling or parent (Constantino et al., 2010; Risch et al., 2014; Sandin et al., 2014). By the turn of the century, ASD was established to have some genetic component, though which genes were involved remained a mystery.

Early karyotype studies documenting chromosomal abnormalities began to shed light on which regions of the genome were involved (Gillberg and Wahlström, 1985). Additional susceptibility loci screens implicated regions on chromosome 7q, 1p, 3q, 16p, and 15q (IMGSAC, 1998; Barrett et al., 1999; Buxbaum et al., 2001; International Molecular Genetic Study of Autism Consortium [IMGSAC], 2001; Liu et al., 2001; Auranen et al., 2002; Lamb et al., 2002; Shao et al., 2003; Risch et al., 2014). However, to investigate at gene-level resolution, early studies had to use the candidate approach. Hypothesized targets included genes from suspected chromosomal regions that played a critical role in neurodevelopment, such as homeobox (*Hox*) family or *Wnt* genes. Unsurprisingly, many early studies using this method were largely inconclusive (Krebs et al., 2002; Lamb et al., 2002; Talebizadeh et al., 2002; Zhang et al., 2002). Starting in 2001, the candidate approach experienced moderate success with findings supporting reelin (*RELN*), aristaless related homeobox (*Arx*), methyl-CpG binding protein 2 (*MeCP2*), neuroligin 3 (*NLGN3*), neuroligin 4 (*NLGN4*), tuberous sclerosis complex 2 (*TSC2*), and ubiquitin protein ligase E3A (*UBE3A*)'s involvement in ASD etiology (Persico et al., 2001; Strømme et al., 2002; Carney et al., 2003; Jamain et al., 2003; Serajee et al., 2003; Jiang et al., 2004).

In the early 2000s, the advent of high throughput sequencing revolutionized genetic research and enabled investigators to study ASD on a genome-wide level. Sequencing technology quickly confirmed that the etiology of ASD was multigenic and highly heterogeneous, with very few of the same pathogenic variants present in a significant percentage of afflicted individuals. It is now known that the average case is a product of many susceptibility-increasing variations. Only a handful of ASD-related diseases have monogenic causes, such as Rett syndrome, fragile X syndrome, tuberous sclerosis, and Schuurs–Hoeijmakers syndrome (Artuso et al., 2011; Stern et al., 2017; Woodbury-Smith and Scherer, 2018). Dozens of large-scale genetic studies have since been conducted on ASD patients and their families, leading to hundreds of risk genes being identified. While these proteins have diverse functions, a majority of reproducible hits come from two broad classes of proteins: those involved in synapse formation, and those involved in transcriptional regulation and chromatin-remodeling pathways (De Rubeis et al., 2014).

Synapse-related risk genes include those encoding cell-adhesion proteins such as neuroligins, neurexins, and cadherins; synaptic vesicle cycling proteins synapsin-1 (SYN1) and synapsin-2 (SYN2); ion transport proteins such as sodium voltage-gated channel alpha subunit 2 (SCN2A), calcium voltage-gated channel subunit alpha1 E (CACNA1E), calcium voltage-gated channel auxiliary subunit beta 2 (CACNB2), potassium voltage-gated channel subfamily Q members 3 and 5 (KCNQ3 and KCNQ5), potassium voltage-gated channel subfamily D member 2 (KCND2), glutamate receptor signaling protein SH3 and multiple ankyrin repeat domains 3 (SHANK3), synaptic Ras GTPase activating protein 1 (SYNGAP1), and gamma-aminobutyric acid type A receptor gamma3 subunit (GABRG3) (Jamain et al., 2003; Durand et al., 2012; Schmunk and Gargus, 2013; Giovedí et al., 2014; Stessman et al., 2017). *In vivo* data supports the implication of synapse pathology and abnormal neural network formation in ASD.

Additional susceptibility loci impact transcription of other proteins through various mechanisms. For example, multiple studies have found an increased *de novo* mutation load in regulatory elements of ASD risk genes in patients

(Turner et al., 2016, 2017; Short et al., 2018). The broad class of susceptibility genes that impacts transcription and chromatin-remodeling pathways includes *MeCP2, UBE3A*, chromodomain helicase DNA binding protein 8 (*CHD8*), activity dependent neuroprotector homeobox (*ADNP*), pogo transposable element derived with ZNF domain (*POGZ*), fragile X mental retardation protein (*FMRP*), and RNA binding forkhead box (*RBFOX*) genes (Carney et al., 2003, p. 2; Samaco et al., 2005; De Rubeis et al., 2014; Stessman et al., 2017; Tran et al., 2019). These pathogenic variants have the potential to induce extremely widespread effects. For example, Tran et al. (2019) recently showed that *FMRP* and fragile X related protein 1 (*FXRP1*) mutations can result in abnormal RNA-editing enzyme activity, resulting in a global bias for adenosine-to-inosine hypoediting in ASD brains. Diverse phenotypes that may result are further discussed in the epigenetics section.

Somatic Mosaicism and ASD Risk

Disease-causing variations were conventionally thought to be familial/inherited and present in every cell in the body. However, the role of somatic mosaicism, which is the result of a post-zygotic DNA mutation, is increasingly being recognized as crucial to various neurodevelopmental diseases including autism (Poduri et al., 2013; Ronemus et al., 2014; D'Gama and Walsh, 2018). During neurogenesis, each progenitor gives rise to roughly five single nucleotide variants (SNV) per day as the brain rapidly develops (Bae et al., 2018; D'Gama and Walsh, 2018). Studies estimate that of *de novo* pathogenic variations, roughly 5–7% are postzygotic, though estimates of up to 22% have been reported (Acuna-Hidalgo et al., 2015; Freed and Pevsner, 2016; Krupp et al., 2017; Lim et al., 2017). Most mutations are harmless, but variations in exons can be extremely detrimental. Pathogenic somatic variations have been connected to ASD, Rett syndrome, tuberous sclerosis, intellectual disability, schizophrenia, and many other disorders (Clayton-Smith et al., 2000; Bourdon et al., 2001; Qin et al., 2010; Gilissen et al., 2014; Acuna-Hidalgo et al., 2015; Tyburczy et al., 2015; Freed and Pevsner, 2016; Dou et al., 2017; Doyle et al., 2017; Krupp et al., 2017; D'Gama and Walsh, 2018).

Until recently, our understanding of somatic mosaicism in ASD was restricted primarily to case reports (Oliveira et al., 2003; Sauter et al., 2003; Papanikolaou et al., 2006; Havlovicova et al., 2007; Yurov et al., 2007; Castermans et al., 2008; Kakinuma et al., 2008; Vorstman et al., 2011). Several recent investigations of whole exome-sequencing (WES) data from large cohorts have been instrumental in shaping our understanding of the role of somatic mosaicism, which is currently estimated to account for roughly 3–5% of simplex ASD cases (Freed and Pevsner, 2016; Krupp et al., 2017). Lim et al. (2017) used WES analysis of 5,947 ASD-affected families and determined that somatic variations in autistic individuals were more likely to be in critical exons than variations in control siblings. Interestingly, they found that the pathogenic variants had enhanced expression in the amygdala, an area critical for emotional response and social awareness (Rasia-Filho et al., 2000). In another large WES study, new risk genes identified were enriched in the cerebellum, which suggests potential coordination difficulty that could be related to gait disorders common in autistic children (Dou et al., 2017). Freed and Pevsner (2016) analyzed 2,388 families and identified an ascertainment bias for pathogenic mosaic variations in ASD individuals relative to unaffected siblings. These large-scale sequencing studies of post-zygotic mutations have both confirmed previously implicated candidate genes, such as *SCN2A*, in addition to revealing dozens of new risk genes and establishing somatic mosaicism as a significant factor in ASD etiology (Lim et al., 2017).

CNVs Contribute to ASD Susceptibility

Copy number variations (CNVs) are submicroscopic structural variants in chromosomes that include duplications, deletions, translocations, and inversions, sometimes stretching several kilobases (Marshall et al., 2008). CNV can either be inherited or arise *de novo* (Thapar and Cooper, 2013). Many genes may be affected with these changes, but not all are necessarily drivers of disease. Studies have found a higher load of rare, genic CNVs in autistic individuals, implicating these variants in ASD pathology (Sebat et al., 2007; Pinto et al., 2010; Pizzo et al., 2019). CNV is now understood as an extremely important contributing factor in ASD susceptibility, and current estimates postulate that these variations directly cause roughly 10% of ASD cases (Geschwind, 2011).

Studies of how individual CNVs contribute to ASD have been done for more frequent structural variants, such as 16p11.2 duplications. The majority of the 25 genes in this region are highly active during nervous system development and are critical for proper formation (Blaker-Lee et al., 2012). While the alteration of many genes involved in development suggests a mechanism for the diverse symptoms observed in ASD, Golzio et al. (2012) reported that only one gene in the 16p11.2 region, potassium channel tetramerization domain containing 13 (*KCTD13*), seems to be the major driver for neuropsychiatric disease. Duplications or deletions of this gene are thought to affect synaptic transmission through altered regulation of Ras homolog family member A (*RHOA*) (Escamilla et al., 2017). However, Escamilla et al. (2017) also hypothesized that *KCTD13* deletions alone are not likely to be sufficient for disease. Mouse models suggest another gene in the 16p11.2 region as a driver of disease – mitogen-activated protein kinase 3 (*MAP3*) – with deletions resulting in altered cortical cytoarchitecture and reduced brain size (Pucilowska et al., 2015). Likely, the real driver of disease in 16p11.2 duplications or deletions is not from just one gene, but an interaction of all 25 contributing to susceptibility. Iyer et al. (2018) systematically investigated interaction between genes in the 16p11.2 region, using RNAi in *Drosophila* to test 565 pairwise knockdowns. In addition to 24 modifying interactions discovered between pairs of genes within the 16p11.2 region, they also found 46 interactions between 16p11.2 genes and others involved in neurodevelopment (Iyer et al., 2018). This strongly suggests that modifying interactions within CNVs result in the complex phenotypes observed and may not be elucidated from studies with single genes, a phenomenon that is likely true for other CNV regions in addition to 16p11.2.

The disease mechanisms of other CNVs are less frequently studied due to the paucity of commonly affected regions. Even the most prevalent ASD-associated CNVs, such as 15q11-13 as well as 16p11.2, are only present in roughly 1% of autism cases (Kumar et al., 2008; Marshall et al., 2008; Weiss et al., 2008; Marshall and Scherer, 2012). In addition, there are no known CNVs with complete penetrance; studies that find CNVs with significant correlation to ASD often detect non-ASD carriers, or ASD siblings without the variant (Marshall et al., 2008). One useful approach in the midst of this heterogeneity is to assess common functional networks affected. Repeatedly, studies have shown that autistic individuals have deletions in synaptic genes, such as *SHANK3*, dipeptidyl peptidase-like 10 (*DPP10*), neuroligins, and neurexins (The Autism Genome Project Consortium et al., 2007; Marshall et al., 2008; Glessner et al., 2009; Pinto et al., 2010, 2014; Marshall and Scherer, 2012). Other common functional gene sets with rare CNVs include those involved in cell proliferation and development, chromatin regulation, and ubiquitin pathways (Glessner et al., 2009; Pinto et al., 2010, 2014).

With certain CNVs, copy number dosage appears to affect disease phenotype. For example, Horev et al. (2011) observed a dose-dependent effect and change in brain structure in mice with 16p11.2 deletions and duplications, but this effect is not as established in humans (Kumar et al., 2008). Another study investigating CNV in the locus containing the *UBE3A* gene also report a positive correlation between duplication and autistic traits in mice, as well as decreased glutamatergic synaptic transmission (Smith et al., 2011). In humans, Stefansson et al. (2014) analyzed a 15q11.2 CNV region of autistic individuals and found two brain areas with dose-dependent structural and functional effects. Interestingly, some non-ASD/schizophrenic controls who were diagnosed with dyslexia and dystaxia also exhibited the same structural changes (Stefansson et al., 2014). In another study with humans, Girirajan et al. (2013) reported a dose-dependent effect from their microarray analysis with identified CNVs in ASD-associated genes, finding a positive correlation between duplication size increase and autism severity increase, but no correlation between duplication size and non-verbal IQ. CNV are often critical and complex contributors to ASD risk, but patients with similar structural variants may have highly variable phenotypes. Following sections will discuss how non-causative modifiers play an important role in modulating CNV pathogenicity.

Epigenetic Regulation and ASD

Genes with epigenetic-modulating functions are highly involved in ASD susceptibility. A recent review of 215 candidate genes estimated that 19.5% are epigenetic regulators, suggesting the potential for diverse disease phenotypes from few pathogenic variants (Duffney et al., 2018). Another study suggested that risk genes with high penetrance were typically located in the nucleus and involved in modulation of expression, or tied to the protein-protein interaction network essential in guiding CNS developmental patterning (Casanova et al., 2016). Twin studies particularly demonstrate the profound ways epigenetics can modulate disease phenotype; for example, a study of 50 pairs of monozygotic twins discordant for ASD reported numerous autism-associated differentially methylated regions, with methylation patterns at some CpG sites common to symptom groups (Wong et al., 2014).

Though the scientific and medical community still has a great deal to learn about epigenetic modulation of ASD, patterns have emerged from large-scale epigenomic studies. Susceptibility loci often include genes involved in methylation such as *KMT2C*, lysine methyltransferase 5B (*KMT5B*), and lysine demethylase 6B (*KDM6B*); chromatin remodeling proteins including MeCP2, CHD8, and POGZ; RNA-binding/splicing proteins such as FMRP and the RBFOX family, post-translational modification proteins like UBE3A, mindbomb E3 ubiquitin protein ligase 1 (MIB1); or transcription factors like ADNP and additional sex combs like 3 (ASXL3) (De Rubeis et al., 2014). Targets of these proteins can range from few to hundreds, and often include pathways previously implicated in autism, such as synaptic formation. To demonstrate how mutations in a single epigenetic regulator can modify many other risk genes, we will look more in depth at two key susceptibility genes: *MeCP2* and *UBE3A*.

MeCP2 is a chromatin modifier that is consistently implicated in ASD. In a healthy individual, the binding action of MeCP2 has been shown to regulate many genes with synaptic function, such as *GABRB3*, brain derived neurotrophic factor (*BDNF*), distal-less homeobox 5 (*DLX5*), insulin like growth factor binding protein 3 (*IGFBP3*), cyclin dependent kinase like 1 (*CDKL1*), protocadherin beta 1 (*PCDHB1*), protocadherin 7 (*PCDH7*), and lin-7 homolog A (LIN7A) (Samaco et al., 2005; Kubota and Mochizuki, 2016). It also serves post-translational functions (Cheng and Qiu, 2014). In addition, MeCP2 is the rate-limiting factor in regulating glutamatergic synapse formation during development, which implicates its involvement in yet another important aspect of ASD pathology (Chao et al., 2007). MeCP2 is shown to be reduced in the frontal cortex of ASD individuals due to increased methylation of its promoter (Samaco et al., 2005; Nagarajan et al., 2006, 2008).

UBE3A, an E3 ubiquitin protein ligase, is a second important epigenetic regulator strongly implicated in ASD pathology. It is modulated by MeCP2, but can be causative on its own (Samaco et al., 2005, p. 2). *UBE3A* lies in the chromosomal region 15q11-13, which is commonly duplicated in autism. Dose-dependent effects have been positively correlated with reduced excitatory synaptic transmission, delay of first word, and psychomotor regression (Guffanti et al., 2011; Smith et al., 2011; Xu et al., 2018). The mechanism of UBE3A's pathological activity can be hypothesized based on its function as a ubiquitin ligase, which targets proteins for degradation, but research is still revealing exactly how these dose-dependent impairments occur. Lee et al. (2014) identified four proteosome-related proteins that were direct substrates of UBE3A. Overexpression of *UBE3A* and one of its substrates, proteasome 26S subunit, non-ATPase 4 (*Rpn10*), led to increased accumulation of ubiquitinated proteins, suggesting a proteostatic imbalance. Proteosome health has been strongly implicated in dendritic spine outgrowth, linking UBE3A with one of the key pathologies observed in autism (Hamilton et al., 2012; Puram et al., 2013). Its involvement in Wnt signaling could also cause significant perturbation during development (Yi et al., 2017). *MeCP2* and *UBE3A* are just two examples of how one altered gene can have extremely far-reaching effects.

Large-scale epigenetic studies have also helped achieve a broader picture of epigenetic mis-regulation in ASD. Sun et al. (2016) conducted a histone acetylome-wide association study on 257 post-mortem prefrontal and temporal cortex samples. Surprisingly, they found that >68% of both syndromic and idiopathic cases shared a common acetylome signature at roughly 5,000 enhancer regions (Sun et al., 2016). Intriguingly, a SHANK3 mouse model of autism displayed rescued behavioral phenotypes when treated with a potent histone deacetylase inhibitor, reinforcing the role of epigenetics in ASD (Qin et al., 2018). Ladd-Acosta and coworkers measured over 485,000 CpG loci in post-mortem brain tissue from 40 individuals and identified four differentially methylated regions. Three sites were found in cortical tissue: the proline rich transmembrane protein 1 (*PRRT1*) 3' UTR, promoter regions of tetraspanin 32 (*TSPAN32*), and *C11orf21*. The last site, an alternative promoter for succinate dehydrogenase complex flavoprotein subunit A pseudogene 3 (*SDHAP3*), was found in cerebellar tissue (Ladd-Acosta et al., 2014). Affected pathways implied in these studies and others include synaptic transmission, immune function, ion transport, and GABAergic genes (Nardone and Elliott, 2016; Sun et al., 2016; Andrews et al., 2017; Zhubi et al., 2017).

Mor et al. (2015) took a different approach, using small RNA sequencing data and correlating results to genome-wide DNA methylation data to find dysregulated miRNAs. miRNAs that were found to be significantly expressed in the ASD brain were linked to synaptic function, consistent with data from numerous other studies. They also discovered a link to the oxytocin receptor (*OXTR*) gene, suggesting attenuated *OXTR* expression in the autistic brain. This finding was supported by a study that found fetal membranes from preterm birth had hypermethylated *OXTR*, potentially linking an environmental risk factor to a pathological mechanism (Behnia et al., 2015). Another risk gene with epigenetic functions is engrailed homeobox 2 (*EN2*), a homeobox gene with an unusual methylation pattern in ASD that has been hypothesized to cause abnormal cerebellar Purkinje growth (James et al., 2013). The list of ASD risk genes with epigenetic functions is vast, suggesting a mechanism by which few mutations can result in widespread misregulation of gene expression. Because of this, genes with epigenetic functions and their substrates may be promising targets of therapies. For example, mutations in *FMRP*, a chromatin remodeler, result in widespread gene expression abnormalities, but a recent study found that inhibition of FMRP target bromodomain containing 4 (*BRD4*) alleviated many of the disease characteristics (Korb et al., 2017). Proteins with epigenetic-regulating function may also be key targets of disease modifiers, a concept that will be discussed later in this review.

ASD Risk Genes Overlap With Other Diseases

Large-scale sequencing studies of major psychiatric diseases have revealed extensive overlap in risk loci, challenging the classification of these conditions as distinctive disorders. In 2013, the Cross-Disorder Group of the Psychiatric Genomics Consortium (PGC) conducted a massive study with 33,332 cases and 27,888 controls in order to identify pathogenic variants shared between ASD, schizophrenia, bipolar disorder, ADHD, and major depressive disorder (Cross-Disorder Group of the Psychiatric Genomics Consortium, 2013; Cross-Disorder Group of the Psychiatric Genomics Consortium et al., 2013). In addition to establishing varying degrees of pair-wise crossover, they found loci that reached genome-wide significance for all five disorders near the following genes: inter-alpha-trypsin inhibitor heavy chain 3 (*ITIH3*), arsenite methyltransferase (*AS3MT*), calcium voltage-gated channel subunit alpha1 C (*CACNA1C*), and *CACNB2*. Glessner et al. (2017) have also conducted a large-scale meta-analysis of structural variants across the same diseases and correlated structural variants in the loci of dedicator of cytokinesis 8 (*DOCK8*) and KN motif and ankyrin repeat domains 1 (*KANK1*) with all five conditions. Schork et al. (2019) recently hypothesized that abnormal gene regulation in radial glia and interneurons during mid-gestation is a mechanism of shared risk, after using GWAS to identify susceptibility loci in genes including phosphodiesterase 1A (*PDE1A*), protein phosphatase 1 regulatory inhibitor subunit 1C (*PPP1R1C*), *RHOA*, immunoglobulin superfamily member 11 (*IGSF11*), and sortilin related VPS10 domain containing receptor 3 (SORC3).

Studies also report shared susceptibility genes across a more restricted set of psychiatric diseases. For example, ASD, intellectual disability (ID), and schizophrenia have been found to share risk loci in FMRP targets, *CHD5*, *CHD8*, *SCN2A*, and neurexin 1 (NRXN1) (Iossifov et al., 2014; Wang et al., 2019). Wang et al. (2019) also found commonalities across ASD, ID, and bipolar disorder with increased incidence of *de novo* pathogenic variants in periodic circadian regulator 1 (*PER1*) and lysine methyltransferase 2C (*KMT2C*). Khanzada et al. (2017) found 23 susceptibility genes common to ASD, bipolar disorder, and schizophrenia including dopamine receptor D2 (*DRD2*), cholinergic receptor nicotinic alpha 7 subunit (*CHRNA7*), 5-hydroxytryptamine receptor 2A (*HTR2A*), solute carrier family 6 member 3 (*SLC6A3*), and tryptophan hydroxylase 2 (*TPH2*). Hit genes were primarily involved in dopamine and serotonin homeostasis, suggesting a potential mechanism for abnormal emotional regulation observed across all three disorders (Khanzada et al., 2017). The immense crossover revealed in these studies intriguingly suggests some level of shared etiology across psychiatric conditions, despite having clinically distinct presentations.

Of the four other diseases assessed in the PGC study, the most highly correlated disease to ASD was schizophrenia (Cross-Disorder Group of the Psychiatric Genomics Consortium et al., 2013). Previous epidemiological studies had suggested their linkage, reporting increased risk of ASD in children with schizophrenic parents and significant co-morbidity of child-onset schizophrenia and autism (Rapoport et al., 2009; Sullivan et al., 2012). A follow-up report to the 2013 PGC study estimated genetic correlation between the two diseases to be 23%, with shared risk loci including several genes involved in neurodevelopment, such as forkhead box P1 (*FOXP1*), exostosin glycosyltransferase 1 (*EXT1*), astrotactin 2 (*ASTN2*), mono-ADP ribosylase 2 (*MACROD2*), and histone deacetylase 4

(*HDAC4*) (The Autism Spectrum Disorders Working Group of The Psychiatric Genomics Consortium, 2017). In addition to susceptibility genes involved in neurodevelopment, other studies have also reported shared susceptibility in genes affecting chromatin remodeling, oxidative stress response, and lipid metabolism (McCarthy et al., 2014; Lim et al., 2017).

Many studies have also found a significant correlation between autistic and ADHD scored traits. This includes a study of autistic symptoms in ADHD probands and siblings, autistic trait correlation in an ADHD twin sample, and an association between autistic and ADHD traits in the general population (Reiersen et al., 2007; Ronald et al., 2008; Mulligan et al., 2009; Stergiakouli et al., 2017). Nijmeijer et al. (2010) identified five specific genetic loci that were associated with ASD traits in children with ADHD: 7q36, 16p13, 18p11, 15q24, and 12q24. A study investigating the overlap of pathological structural variants in ADHD and ASD found significant overlap in genes related to a wide variety of processes, including the nicotinic receptor signaling pathway and cell division (Martin et al., 2014). The shared heritability of ASD and ADHD is still being explored, and is further discussed in a review by Rommelse et al. (2010).

Since ASD is a multigenic and highly heterogeneous disease that often co-occurs with other conditions, it can be difficult to distinguish which genes truly have overlapping risk for multiple psychiatric conditions, and which variations are responsible for the common disease phenotypes. For example, the ubiquitin ligase gene *UBE3A* is implicated in both autism and Angelman Syndrome, a condition distinct from ASD but with similar symptoms, such as movement and speech defects. Interestingly, Angelman Syndrome is generally associated with *UBE3A* deletions, while ASD can be caused by duplications – yet the same individual can be diagnosed with both syndromes (Peters et al., 2004; Williams et al., 2010; Smith et al., 2011; Kalsner and Chamberlain, 2015; Yi et al., 2015). Another example is intellectual disability, which co-occurs with autism in roughly 45% of cases (Lai et al., 2014). Multiple studies have found that ASD and intellectual disability share risk loci (Pinto et al., 2010; McCarthy et al., 2014), but overlapping phenotypes are a potentially confounding factor. Similarly, other risk genes for ASD are epigenetic regulators whose effectors are associated with different diseases (Samaco et al., 2005; Pinto et al., 2010; Michaelson et al., 2017). The interaction and overlap between psychiatric disorders is complex, and much is left to discern regarding shared disease mechanisms.

MODIFIERS IN ASD

Genetic Modifiers

Though significant progress has been made in determining genetic causes of ASD, many aspects of how pathogenic variants regulate genetic susceptibility remain unknown. Individuals with the same variants can have widely heterogeneous disease presentations and levels of disability. Presence of second modulating variants that may interact with other susceptibility loci are one possible explanation of this heterogeneity. This "second hit" could be somatic – a phenomenon first proposed to cause disease by Alfred Knudson in the context of retinoblastomas – or in the germline, a "two-locus model" previously explored in conditions such as Hirschprung disease (Knudson, 1971; Fisher and Scambler, 1994; McCallion et al., 2003). To date, genetic evidence supporting a multiplex theory of autism has primarily been found for germline second-hits. Studies with CNVs will be discussed first, followed by a brief overview of known modulating SNPs. These investigations of how non-causative variants may modify the ASD phenotype are challenging to undertake, as few autistic individuals have the same pathogenic variants. In addition, there is not yet a complete understanding of which CNVs and SNPs are pathogenic in ASD.

One way to circumvent these issues is to investigate an autism subtype with a monogenic cause, such as Rett Syndrome. Artuso et al. (2011) used this strategy and identified 15 "likely" and 14 "unlikely" modulators of the RTT phenotype based on array comparative genome hybridization with eight RTT subjects. Another valuable approach is to assess monozygotic twins with a discordant phenotype. Several studies have assessed potential differences in CNVs or epigenetic regulation in discordant monozygotic twins, revealing potential methylation pattern differences in one case and anomalies in the 2p25.3 region in another (Bruder et al., 2008; Kunio et al., 2013; Rio et al., 2013). However, a study involving 100 twin pairs failed to find differences in CNVs that could explain the discordant phenotypes (Stamouli et al., 2018). The authors still acknowledge postzygotic mosaicism as a potential modifier and encourage more studies to help develop a clearer understanding of CNV modulating activity.

A handful of reports also exist of putative modifying CNVs in polygenic ASD cases with unrelated subjects. For example, Girirajan et al. (2012) found that children with two CNVs not known to be pathological were eight times more likely to be diagnosed with developmental delay than controls. In the same year, a study of *SHANK2* pathogenic variants found abnormalities in both individuals with neuropsychiatric disease and controls, suggesting the presence of additional variants in order to cause disease. Three of the patients with *de novo SHANK2* mutations were also found to have deletions of *CHRNA7* and cytoplasmic FMR1 interacting protein 1 (*CYFIP1*) – both previously implicated in ASD – supporting a "multiple-hit" model of autism (Leblond et al., 2012). *CHRNA7* was also suggested as a potential modifier in an earlier study by Szafranski et al. (2010). Barber et al. (2013) provided further support for a multiple-loci model of ASD upon finding that patients with 16p12.1 duplications had a more severe phenotype when a second large CNV was present. Included in these hypothesized modifier regions were genes G protein regulated inducer of neurite outgrowth 2 (*GPRIN2*) – previously implicated as a modifier in the study by Artuso et al. (2011) – and steroid sulfatase (*STS*), which was formerly thought to be non-causative (Li et al., 2010). More recently, an analysis of 20,226 patient records revealed 19 patients with CNVs in contactin 6 (*CNTN6*), a gene hypothesized to be involved in neurodevelopmental disorders including ASD (Repnikova et al., 2019). The authors were not able to find any significant genotype-phenotype relationships and concluded that CNV in *CNTN6* were likely benign or modifying, but not causative of disease.

In addition to CNVs, there may be thousands of smaller pathogenic variants – such as SNPs and indels – that also modulate severity. For example, in a study of developmental delay, individuals that only carried a specific 16p12.1 microdeletion had a less severe phenotype than individuals with random second variants (Girirajan et al., 2010). One study of individuals with 22q11.2 deletion syndrome – all haploinsufficient for an mGluR network gene – found that 20% who were co-diagnosed with autism had second-hit pathogenic variants, while only 2% of 22q11DS individuals without autism had second hits (Wenger et al., 2016). Bonnet-Brilhault et al. (2016) assessed a family affected with ID and ASD due to *NLGN4X* pathogenic variants and found that individuals with ASD – but not ID or controls – had second-hit variants in glycine receptor beta (*GRLB*) and ankyrin 3 (*ANK3*). Additional evidence may exist, but GWAS and WES studies have tended to focus on causative susceptibility loci. Therefore, other variants which are not causative by themselves are not often emphasized or even reported. The emerging study of all types of genetic modifiers is a relatively recent development, and continuing advancements in sequencing technology, analyzing software, and expansion of databases should lay the framework for significant advancements in the near future.

Epigenetics and the Environment

Autism susceptibility is currently estimated to be 40–80% genetic. Environmental factors – likely acting through epigenetic regulation as the major mechanism – presumably compromise the remainder of the risk. Hundreds of potential environmental factors have been suggested to contribute to risk, such as increased parental age (especially paternal), maternal complications or infections during pregnancy, or prenatal exposure to anticonvulsants (Rasalam et al., 2005; Kong et al., 2012; O'Roak et al., 2012; Ohkawara et al., 2015). In-depth reviews of these findings can be found elsewhere (Gardener et al., 2009; Chaste and Leboyer, 2012; Liu et al., 2016; Karimi et al., 2017; Modabbernia et al., 2017; Bölte et al., 2019). In this review, we will only discuss the epigenetic modifying effects of valproic acid – an anticonvulsant – as one example of the widespread modifications that an environmental factor can induce. Valproic acid has been hypothesized to modify gene expression through histone deacetylase inhibition activity and is sometimes used to induce an autistic phenotype in animal models (Kataoka et al., 2013). Examples of its far-reaching effects include apoptotic cell death in the neocortex, decreased proliferation in the ganglionic eminence, increased homeobox A1 (*HOXA1*) expression, abnormal serotonergic differentiation via Achaete-Scute family BHLH transcription factor 1 (*ASCL1*) silencing, disrupted serotonin homeostasis in the amygdala, dendritic spine loss, reduced prefrontal dopaminergic activity, and disruption of the glutamatergic/GABAergic balance (Stodgell et al., 2006; Dufour-Rainfray et al., 2010; Kataoka et al., 2013; Wang et al., 2013; Jacob et al., 2014; Takuma et al., 2014; Hara et al., 2015; Iijima et al., 2016; Mahmood et al., 2018).

In more thorough studies of the mechanism of action, Go et al. (2012) found that rats exposed to valproic acid *in utero* presented enhanced proliferation of neural progenitors and delayed neurogenesis by upregulating *Wnt1* expression and activating the GSK-3β/β-catenin pathway, leading to macrocephaly. Another study found that valproic acid increased BDNF by two transcriptional mechanisms involving *MeCP2* and tissue plasminogen activator (tPA). This increase in BDNF is proposed to alter neurite outgrowth, impairing synapse formation (Ko et al., 2018). Finally, Kolozsi et al. (2009) observed a downregulation of *NLGN3* – a highly implicated autism risk gene involved in synapse formation – in both hippocampal and somatosensory cortex of valproate-exposed mice. Examples of other proposed environmentally modulated mechanisms of ASD risk exist, but the literature supporting valproic acid is an excellent example of the heterogeneous effects one environmental factor can induce. Further research is strongly needed to determine how the environment modulates ASD risk.

Clearly, epigenetics can have a profound impact on the transcriptome of an organism. Pathogenic variants in even one epigenetic-regulating gene or effects from the environment can cause widespread gene dysregulation. Epigenetic modulators can themselves be causative of disease, but they may also exacerbate or ameliorate the disease phenotype by influencing expression of risk genes. More genome-wide studies are needed to understand the common ASD epigenome, and whether certain epigenetic markings might be protective or detrimental to individuals who are genetically susceptible. In addition, more studies are needed to decipher epigenetics as a link between environmental risk factors and genetic susceptibility. There is a possibility that certain environmental factors could have protective epigenetic effects, providing potential avenues for therapy.

Sex-Linked Modifiers

It is well established that ASD affects males at much higher rates than females. The reasons for this are not yet completely clear. Some studies argue that differential expression between genders may result in an under-diagnosis of females, as males tend to present more external behavior (e.g., aggression or increased repetitive behavior) and females tend to present more internal behavior (e.g., depression and avoiding demands) (Werling and Geschwind, 2013). While this may contribute to the rates of diagnosis, other possibilities include that the female sex is protective and/or males are particularly vulnerable. This may be due to influence from hormones, genetics, or other unknown factors. The genetically heterogeneous nature of ASD makes it likely that all these elements are involved – sex bias varies drastically based on factors such as which CNVs are causative or which comorbidities are present, suggesting diverse means by which a sex bias may occur (Amiet et al., 2008; Polyak et al., 2015). Potential mechanisms of sex-specific modulation will be discussed briefly, although more thorough reviews are available elsewhere (Ferri et al., 2018).

Multiple studies argue that the female sex is protective toward ASD susceptibility (Robinson et al., 2013; Pinto et al., 2014). For example, the average mutational burden in diagnosed females is much higher than in males, suggesting that males have a lower mutational burden threshold (Jacquemont et al., 2014; Desachy et al., 2015). Another study by Robinson et al. (2013) investigated nearly 10,000 dizygotic autistic twin pairs and

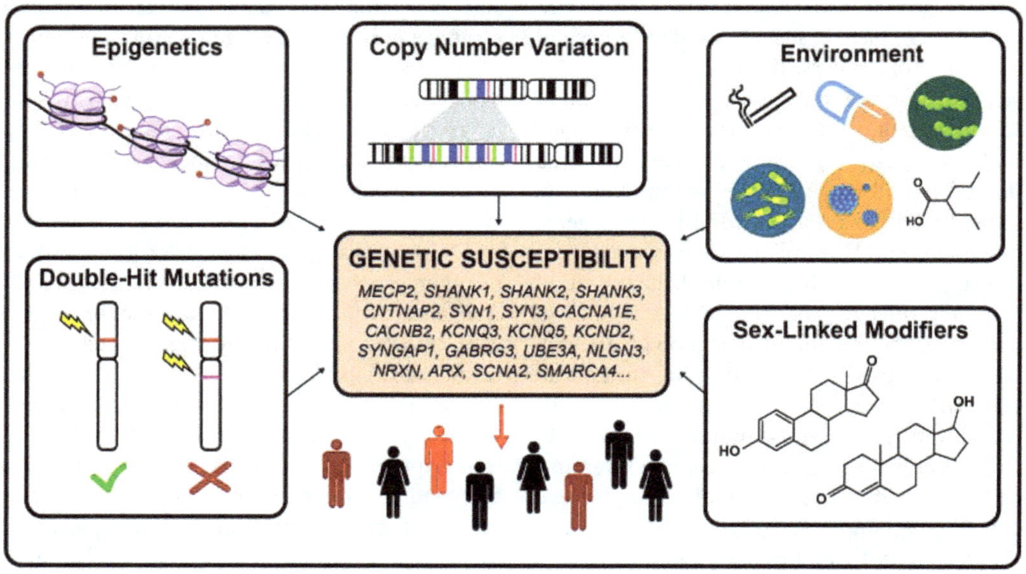

FIGURE 1 | Genetic modifiers in autism spectrum disorder. Autism is estimated to be 40–80% heritable. However, both genetic and non-genetic factors modulate the penetrance of risk genes, resulting in a highly heterogeneous disease phenotype for similar pathogenic variants. Examples of genetic modulators include CNV, epigenetics, and double-hit mutations. Examples of non-genetic modifiers include environmental exposures and sex-linked modifiers.

found that siblings of female probands had significantly worse symptoms than siblings of male probands. Many investigations have also found that unaffected mothers may carry the same mutation as their affected male children. One particularly well-documented example for this is the 15q11-13 duplication (Cook et al., 1997; Schroer et al., 1998; Gurrieri et al., 1999; Boyar et al., 2001). This region codes for $GABA_A$ receptors, which is supported by the observation of perturbed GABA signaling in ASD (Al-Otaish et al., 2018). The discovery that estrogens rescue ASD phenotypes in both zebrafish and mouse models of autism is an especially convincing piece of evidence for the female protective theory (Macrì et al., 2010; Hoffman et al., 2016).

It is also possible that the female sex is not protective, but males are particularly vulnerable. Three studies of gene expression patterns noted males generally had a higher expression of genes implicated in ASD, such as chromatin regulators and genes related to immune involvement (Ziats and Rennert, 2013; Shi et al., 2016; Werling et al., 2016). A study with rat models of ASD reported male-specific downregulation of *MeCP2* leading to abnormal glutamate activity, providing another potential mechanism for male-specific vulnerability (Kim et al., 2016). Interestingly, multiple studies have found decreased levels of aromatase – an enzyme that catalyzes the conversion of testosterone to estradiol – in the brains of adolescent ASD individuals (Sarachana et al., 2011; Crider et al., 2014). Decreased aromatase has also been associated with decreased RAR-related orphan receptor A (*RORA*), an ASD-associated gene that is oppositely regulated by male and female hormones (Nguyen et al., 2010; Sarachana et al., 2011). Hu et al. (2015) found a much stronger correlation between *RORA* expression and that of its targets in the cortex of male mice relative to female mice, suggesting that RORA-deficient males may have greater dysregulation of genes than females.

Of course, there may also be a combination of female-specific protective and male-specific deleterious effects. For example, Jung et al. (2018) recently assessed sexually dimorphic traits in a $CHD8^{+/N2373K}$ mouse model of autism. While male mice demonstrated abnormal social behaviors such as isolation-induced self-grooming, female behavior was similar to controls. Neuronal excitability was also enhanced in males and suppressed in females. Transcriptomes were distinct, with female mice revealing an enrichment for ECM molecules, likely providing a protective effect.

A likely mechanism of divergent modulation is from differential effects of sex hormones, which have been hypothesized to play an important role in ASD pathology for both males and females (Baron-Cohen et al., 2005, 2015; Whitehouse et al., 2010; Honk et al., 2011; Ferri et al., 2018). For example, testosterone and estrogen have been shown to have contrasting effects on the immune system (Lenz et al., 2013; Roved et al., 2017), which has been repeatedly shown to play a pathological role in ASD (Estes and McAllister, 2015; Koyama and Ikegaya, 2015; Kim et al., 2017; McCarthy and Wright, 2017; Nadeem et al., 2019). Schwarz et al. (2011) analyzed biomarkers from individuals with Asperger's syndrome and found 24 male-specific and 17 female-specific hits, including many immune-related molecules. Spine density, another phenotype strongly implicated in autism (Comery et al., 1997; Irwin et al., 2001; Hutsler and Zhang, 2010; Durand et al., 2012; Takuma et al., 2014; Tang et al., 2014; Liu et al., 2017a,b; Soltani et al., 2017), is also affected by testosterone (Hatanaka et al., 2015). Key molecules involved in neurotransmission such as GABA, glutamate, serotonin, and BDNF are all implicated in ASD and modulated by sex hormones (Kim et al., 2016, p. 2; Saghazadeh and Rezaei, 2017; Al-Otaish et al., 2018; Edwards et al., 2018; Ferri et al., 2018; Garbarino et al., 2018; Zieminska et al., 2018). It is not yet clear whether the majority of differences between male and female presentation of ASD arise from differential regulatory actions of sex hormones or from other modifiers, but the presence of a sexually dimorphic phenotype is well established. Future research will likely elucidate a clearer picture of the identity and mechanisms of sex-specific modifiers.

CLINICAL IMPLICATIONS AND FUTURE PERSPECTIVES

When autism was first described, it was hypothesized to be an environmentally caused disease. Decades of research have since revealed that autism is a highly heterogeneous and extremely complex genetic condition. Even though great progress had been made in identifying hundreds of risk genes, very little is known about the different types of modifiers that may exacerbate or ameliorate disease severity. Such modifiers could include epigenetics, sex-linked modifiers, CNVs, double-hit mutations, or environmental factors (see **Figure 1**).

It may take many more decades of research before the scientific community has an accurate picture of how these modulators contribute to the etiology of ASD. However, this understanding is critical for the development of effective therapies. Due to the extremely diverse genetic phenotype of patients, personalized medicine may be a future avenue for maximally effective treatment. A condensed series of genetic tests – such as a microarray with identified risk loci – could be an expedient and cost-effective solution to determining genetic etiology. Alternatively, therapies may be developed to address convergent disease phenotypes that encompass multiple genetic etiologies, such as neuronal hyperexcitability and abnormal synaptic function. Autism research has come astonishingly far in just a half a century. There is much more work to be done, but continued investigation will eventually lead to a cohesive understanding of the interplay between causative genetic factors and disease modifiers in the etiology of ASD.

AUTHOR CONTRIBUTIONS

LR contributed to writing the main text and gathering all references. AG-G contributed to editing the manuscript drafts and providing insight into structure and material that should be included.

FUNDING

This work was supported by start-up funds from the Feinberg School of Medicine, Northwestern University.

REFERENCES

Acuna-Hidalgo, R., Bo, T., Kwint, M. P., van de Vorst, M., Pinelli, M., Veltman, J. A., et al. (2015). Post-zygotic point mutations are an underrecognized source of *De Novo* genomic variation. *Am. J. Hum. Genet.* 97, 67–74. doi: 10.1016/j.ajhg.2015.05.008

Al-Otaish, H., Al-Ayadhi, L., Bjørklund, G., Chirumbolo, S., Urbina, M. A., and El-Ansary, A. (2018). Relationship between absolute and relative ratios of glutamate, glutamine and GABA and severity of autism spectrum disorder. *Metab. Brain Dis.* 33, 843–854. doi: 10.1007/s11011-018-0186-6

Amiet, C., Gourfinkel-An, I., Bouzamondo, A., Tordjman, S., Baulac, M., Lechat, P., et al. (2008). Epilepsy in autism is associated with intellectual disability and gender: evidence from a meta-analysis. *Biol. Psychiatry* 64, 577–582. doi: 10.1016/j.biopsych.2008.04.030

Andrews, S. V., Ellis, S. E., Bakulski, K. M., Sheppard, B., Croen, L. A., Hertz-Picciotto, I., et al. (2017). Cross-tissue integration of genetic and epigenetic data offers insight into autism spectrum disorder. *Nat. Commun.* 8:1011. doi: 10.1038/s41467-017-00868-y

Artuso, R., Papa, F. T., Grillo, E., Mucciolo, M., Yasui, D. H., Dunaway, K. W., et al. (2011). Investigation of modifier genes within copy number variations in Rett syndrome. *J. Hum. Genet.* 56, 508–515. doi: 10.1038/jhg.2011.50

Auranen, M., Vanhala, R., Varilo, T., Ayers, K., Kempas, E., Ylisaukko-oja, T., et al. (2002). A genomewide screen for autism-spectrum disorders: evidence for a major susceptibility locus on chromosome 3q25-27. *Am. J. Hum. Genet.* 71, 777–790. doi: 10.1086/342720

Bae, T., Tomasini, L., Mariani, J., Zhou, B., Roychowdhury, T., Franjic, D., et al. (2018). Different mutational rates and mechanisms in human cells at pregastrulation and neurogenesis. *Science* 359, 550–555. doi: 10.1126/science.aan8690

Bailey, A., Le Couteur, A., Gottesman, I., Bolton, P., Simonoff, E., Yuzda, E., et al. (1995). Autism as a strongly genetic disorder: evidence from a British twin study. *Psychol. Med.* 25, 63–77. doi: 10.1017/s0033291700028099

Barber, J. C. K., Hall, V., Maloney, V. K., Huang, S., Roberts, A. M., Brady, A. F., et al. (2013). 16p11.2–p12.2 duplication syndrome; a genomic condition differentiated from euchromatic variation of 16p11.2. *Eur. J. Hum. Genet.* 21, 182–189. doi: 10.1038/ejhg.2012.144

Baron-Cohen, S., Auyeung, B., Nørgaard-Pedersen, B., Hougaard, D. M., Abdallah, M. W., Melgaard, L., et al. (2015). Elevated fetal steroidogenic activity in autism. *Mol. Psychiatry* 20, 369–376. doi: 10.1038/mp.2014.48

Baron-Cohen, S., Knickmeyer, R. C., and Belmonte, M. K. (2005). Sex differences in the brain: implications for explaining autism. *Science* 310, 819–823. doi: 10.1126/science.1115455

Barrett, S., Beck, J. C., Bernier, R., Bisson, E., Braun, T. A., Casavant, T. L., et al. (1999). An autosomal genomic screen for autism. Collaborative linkage study of autism. *Am. J. Med. Genet.* 88, 609–615. doi: 10.1002/(sici)1096-8628(19991215)88:6<609::aid-ajmg7>3.0.co;2-l

Behnia, F., Parets, S. E., Kechichian, T., Yin, H., Dutta, E. H., Saade, G. R., et al. (2015). Fetal DNA methylation of autism spectrum disorders candidate genes: association with spontaneous preterm birth. *Am. J. Obstet. Gynecol.* 212:533.e1-e9. doi: 10.1016/j.ajog.2015.02.011

Blaker-Lee, A., Gupta, S., McCammon, J. M., De Rienzo, G., and Sive, H. (2012). Zebrafish homologs of genes within 16p11.2, a genomic region associated with brain disorders, are active during brain development, and include two deletion dosage sensor genes. *Dis. Model. Mech.* 5, 834–851. doi: 10.1242/dmm.009944

Bölte, S., Girdler, S., and Marschik, P. B. (2019). The contribution of environmental exposure to the etiology of autism spectrum disorder. *Cell. Mol. Life Sci.* 76, 1275–1297. doi: 10.1007/s00018-018-2988-4

Bolton, P. F., Dennis, N. R., Browne, C. E., Thomas, N. S., Veltman, M. W. M., Thompson, R. J., et al. (2001). The phenotypic manifestations of interstitial duplications of proximal 15q with special reference to the autistic spectrum disorders. *Am. J. Med. Genet.* 105, 675–685. doi: 10.1002/ajmg.1551

Bonnet-Brilhault, F., Alirol, S., Blanc, R., Bazaud, S., Marouillat, S., Thépault, R.-A., et al. (2016). GABA/Glutamate synaptic pathways targeted by integrative genomic and electrophysiological explorations distinguish autism from intellectual disability. *Mol. Psychiatry* 21, 411–418. doi: 10.1038/mp.2015.75

Bourdon, V., Philippe, C., Bienvenu, T., Koenig, B., Tardieu, M., Chelly, J., et al. (2001). Evidence of somatic mosaicism for a MECP2 mutation in females with Rett syndrome: diagnostic implications. *J. Med. Genet.* 38, 867–871. doi: 10.1136/jmg.38.12.867

Boyar, F. Z., Whitney, M. M., Lossie, A. C., Gray, B. A., Keller, K. L., Stalker, H. J., et al. (2001). A family with a grand-maternally derived interstitial duplication of proximal 15q. *Clin. Genet.* 60, 421–430. doi: 10.1034/j.1399-0004.2001.600604.x

Bruder, C. E. G., Piotrowski, A., Gijsbers, A. A. C. J., Andersson, R., Erickson, S., Diaz, et al. (2008). Phenotypically concordant and discordant monozygotic twins display different DNA copy-number-variation profiles. *Am. J. Hum. Genet.* 82, 763–771. doi: 10.1016/j.ajhg.2007.12.011

Buxbaum, J. D., Silverman, J. M., Smith, C. J., Kilifarski, M., Reichert, J., Hollander, E., et al. (2001). Evidence for a susceptibility gene for autism on chromosome 2 and for genetic heterogeneity. *Am. J. Hum. Genet.* 68, 1514–1520. doi: 10.1086/320588

Carney, R. M., Wolpert, C. M., Ravan, S. A., Shahbazian, M., Ashley-Koch, A., Cuccaro, M. L., et al. (2003). Identification of MeCP2 mutations in a series of females with autistic disorder. *Pediatr. Neurol.* 28, 205–211. doi: 10.1016/s0887-8994(02)00624-0

Casanova, E. L., Sharp, J. L., Chakraborty, H., Sumi, N. S., and Casanova, M. F. (2016). Genes with high penetrance for syndromic and non-syndromic autism typically function within the nucleus and regulate gene expression. *Mol. Autism* 7:18. doi: 10.1186/s13229-016-0082-z

Castermans, D., Thienpont, B., Volders, K., Crepel, A., Vermeesch, J. R., Schrander-Stumpel, C. T., et al. (2008). Position effect leading to haploinsufficiency in a mosaic ring chromosome 14 in a boy with autism. *Eur. J. Hum. Genet.* 16, 1187–1192. doi: 10.1038/ejhg.2008.71

Chao, H.-T., Zoghbi, H. Y., and Rosenmund, C. (2007). MeCP2 controls excitatory synaptic strength by regulating glutamatergic synapse number. *Neuron* 56, 58–65. doi: 10.1016/j.neuron.2007.08.018

Chaste, P., and Leboyer, M. (2012). Autism risk factors: genes, environment, and gene-environment interactions. *Dialogues Clin. Neurosci.* 14, 281–292.

Cheng, T.-L., and Qiu, Z. (2014). MeCP2: multifaceted roles in gene regulation and neural development. *Neurosci. Bull.* 30, 601–609. doi: 10.1007/s12264-014-1452-6

Clayton-Smith, J., Watson, P., Ramsden, S., and Black, G. (2000). Somatic mutation in MECP2 as a non-fatal neurodevelopmental disorder in males. *Lancet* 356, 830–832. doi: 10.1016/S0140-6736(00)02661-1

Comery, T. A., Harris, J. B., Willems, P. J., Oostra, B. A., Irwin, S. A., Weiler, I. J., et al. (1997). Abnormal dendritic spines in fragile X knockout mice: maturation and pruning deficits. *Proc. Natl. Acad. Sci. U.S.A.* 94, 5401–5404. doi: 10.1073/pnas.94.10.5401

Constantino, J. N., Zhang, Y., Frazier, T., Abbacchi, A. M., and Law, P. (2010). Sibling recurrence and the genetic epidemiology of autism. *Am. J. Psychiatry* 167, 1349–1356. doi: 10.1176/appi.ajp.2010.09101470

Cook, E. H., Lindgren, V., Leventhal, B. L., Courchesne, R., Lincoln, A., Shulman, C., et al. (1997). Autism or atypical autism in maternally but not paternally derived proximal 15q duplication. *Am. J. Hum. Genet.* 60, 928–934.

Crider, A., Thakkar, R., Ahmed, A. O., and Pillai, A. (2014). Dysregulation of estrogen receptor beta (ERβ), aromatase (CYP19A1), and ER co-activators in the middle frontal gyrus of autism spectrum disorder subjects. *Mol. Autism* 5:46. doi: 10.1186/2040-2392-5-46

Cross-Disorder Group of the Psychiatric Genomics Consortium (2013). Identification of risk loci with shared effects on five major psychiatric disorders: a genome-wide analysis. *Lancet* 381, 1371–1379. doi: 10.1016/S0140-6736(12)62129-1

Cross-Disorder Group of the Psychiatric Genomics Consortium, Lee, S. H., Ripke, S., Neale, B. M., Faraone, S. V., Purcell, S. M., et al. (2013). Genetic relationship between five psychiatric disorders estimated from genome-wide SNPs. *Nat. Genet.* 45, 984–994. doi: 10.1038/ng.2711

De Rubeis, S., He, X., Goldberg, A. P., Poultney, C. S., Samocha, K., Cicek, A. E., et al. (2014). Synaptic, transcriptional and chromatin genes disrupted in autism. *Nature* 515, 209–215. doi: 10.1038/nature13772

Desachy, G., Croen, L. A., Torres, A. R., Kharrazi, M., Delorenze, G. N., Windham, G. C., et al. (2015). Increased female autosomal burden of rare copy number variants in human populations and in autism families. *Mol. Psychiatry* 20, 170–175. doi: 10.1038/mp.2014.179

D'Gama, A. M., and Walsh, C. A. (2018). Somatic mosaicism and neurodevelopmental disease. *Nat. Neurosci.* 21, 1504–1514. doi: 10.1038/s41593-018-0257-3

Dou, Y., Yang, X., Li, Z., Wang, S., Zhang, Z., Ye, A. Y., et al. (2017). Postzygotic single-nucleotide mosaicisms contribute to the etiology of autism spectrum disorder and autistic traits and the origin of mutations. *Hum. Mutat.* 38, 1002–1013. doi: 10.1002/humu.23255

Doyle, G. A., Crist, R. C., Karatas, E. T., Hammond, M. J., Ewing, A. D., Ferraro, T. N., et al. (2017). Analysis of LINE-1 elements in DNA from postmortem brains of individuals with Schizophrenia. *Neuropsychopharmacology* 42, 2602–2611. doi: 10.1038/npp.2017.115

Duffney, L. J., Valdez, P., Tremblay, M. W., Cao, X., Montgomery, S., McConkie-Rosell, A., et al. (2018). Epigenetics and autism spectrum disorder: a report of an autism case with mutation in H1 linker histone HIST1H1E and literature review. *Am. J. Med. Genet. B Neuropsychiatr. Genet.* 177, 426–433. doi: 10.1002/ajmg.b.32631

Dufour-Rainfray, D., Vourc'h, P., Le Guisquet, A.-M., Garreau, L., Ternant, D., Bodard, S., et al. (2010). Behavior and serotonergic disorders in rats exposed prenatally to valproate: a model for autism. *Neurosci. Lett.* 470, 55–59. doi: 10.1016/j.neulet.2009.12.054

Durand, C. M., Perroy, J., Loll, F., Perrais, D., Fagni, L., Bourgeron, T., et al. (2012). SHANK3 mutations identified in autism lead to modification of dendritic spine morphology via an actin-dependent mechanism. *Mol. Psychiatry* 17, 71–84. doi: 10.1038/mp.2011.57

Edwards, K. A., Madden, A. M. K., and Zup, S. L. (2018). Serotonin receptor regulation as a potential mechanism for sexually dimorphic oxytocin dysregulation in a model of Autism. *Brain Res.* 1701, 85–92. doi: 10.1016/j.brainres.2018.07.020

Escamilla, C. O., Filonova, I., Walker, A. K., Xuan, Z. X., Holehonnur, R., Espinosa, F., et al. (2017). *Kctd13* deletion reduces synaptic transmission via increased RhoA. *Nature* 551, 227–231. doi: 10.1038/nature24470

Estes, M. L., and McAllister, A. K. (2015). Immune mediators in the brain and peripheral tissues in autism spectrum disorder. *Nat. Rev. Neurosci.* 16, 469–486. doi: 10.1038/nrn3978

Ferri, S. L., Abel, T., and Brodkin, E. S. (2018). Sex differences in autism spectrum disorder: a review. *Curr. Psychiatry Rep.* 20:9. doi: 10.1007/s11920-018-0874-2

Fisher, E., and Scambler, P. (1994). Human haploinsufficiency — one for sorrow, two for joy. *Nat. Genet.* 7, 5–7. doi: 10.1038/ng0594-5

Folstein, S., and Rutter, M. (1977). Genetic influences and infantile autism. *Nature* 265, 726–728. doi: 10.1038/265726a0

Freed, D., and Pevsner, J. (2016). The contribution of mosaic variants to autism spectrum disorder. *PLoS Genet.* 12:e1006245. doi: 10.1371/journal.pgen.1006245

Garbarino, V. R., Gilman, T. L., Daws, L. C., and Gould, G. G. (2018). Extreme enhancement or depletion of serotonin transporter function and serotonin availability in autism spectrum disorder. *Pharmacol. Res.* 140, 85–99. doi: 10.1016/j.phrs.2018.07.010

Gardener, H., Spiegelman, D., and Buka, S. L. (2009). Prenatal risk factors for autism: a comprehensive meta-analysis. *Br. J. Psychiatry J. Ment. Sci.* 195, 7–14. doi: 10.1192/bjp.bp.108.051672

Geschwind, D. H. (2011). Genetics of autism spectrum disorders. *Trends Cogn. Sci.* 15, 409–416. doi: 10.1016/j.tics.2011.07.003

Gilissen, C., Hehir-Kwa, J. Y., Thung, D. T., van de Vorst, M., van Bon, B. W. M., Willemsen, M. H., et al. (2014). Genome sequencing identifies major causes of severe intellectual disability. *Nature* 511, 344–347. doi: 10.1038/nature13394

Gillberg, C., and Wahlström, J. (1985). Chromosome abnormalities in infantile autism and other childhood psychoses: a population study of 66 cases. *Dev. Med. Child Neurol.* 27, 293–304. doi: 10.1111/j.1469-8749.1985.tb04539.x

Giovedí, S., Corradi, A., Fassio, A., and Benfenati, F. (2014). Involvement of synaptic genes in the pathogenesis of autism spectrum disorders: the case of synapsins. *Front. Pediatr.* 2:94. doi: 10.3389/fped.2014.00094

Girirajan, S., Dennis, M. Y., Baker, C., Malig, M., Coe, B. P., Campbell, C. D., et al. (2013). Refinement and discovery of new hotspots of copy-number variation associated with autism spectrum disorder. *Am. J. Hum. Genet.* 92, 221–237. doi: 10.1016/j.ajhg.2012.12.016

Girirajan, S., Rosenfeld, J. A., Coe, B. P., Parikh, S., Friedman, N., Goldstein, A., et al. (2012). Phenotypic heterogeneity of genomic disorders and rare copy-number variants. *N. Engl. J. Med.* 367, 1321–1331. doi: 10.1056/NEJMoa1200395

Girirajan, S., Rosenfeld, J. A., Cooper, G. M., Antonacci, F., Siswara, P., Itsara, A., et al. (2010). A recurrent 16p12.1 microdeletion supports a two-hit model for severe developmental delay. *Nat. Genet.* 42, 203–209. doi: 10.1038/ng.534

Glessner, J. T., Li, J., Wang, D., March, M., Lima, L., Desai, A., et al. (2017). Copy number variation meta-analysis reveals a novel duplication at 9p24 associated with multiple neurodevelopmental disorders. *Genome Med.* 9:106. doi: 10.1186/s13073-017-0494-1

Glessner, J. T., Wang, K., Cai, G., Korvatska, O., Kim, C. E., Wood, S., et al. (2009). Autism genome-wide copy number variation reveals ubiquitin and neuronal genes. *Nature* 459, 569–573. doi: 10.1038/nature07953

Go, H. S., Kim, K. C., Choi, C. S., Jeon, S. J., Kwon, K. J., Han, S.-H., et al. (2012). Prenatal exposure to valproic acid increases the neural progenitor cell pool and induces macrocephaly in rat brain via a mechanism involving the GSK-3β/β-catenin pathway. *Neuropharmacology* 63, 1028–1041. doi: 10.1016/j.neuropharm.2012.07.028

Golzio, C., Willer, J., Talkowski, M. E., Oh, E. C., Taniguchi, Y., Jacquemont, S., et al. (2012). KCTD13 is a major driver of mirrored neuroanatomical phenotypes of the 16p11.2 copy number variant. *Nature* 485, 363–367. doi: 10.1038/nature11091

Guffanti, G., Lievers, L. S., Bonati, M. T., Marchi, M., Geronazzo, L., Nardocci, N., et al. (2011). Role of UBE3A and ATP10A genes in autism susceptibility region 15q11-q13 in an Italian population: a positive replication for UBE3A. *Psychiatry Res.* 185, 33–38. doi: 10.1016/j.psychres.2010.04.057

Gurrieri, F., Battaglia, A., Torrisi, L., Tancredi, R., Cavallaro, C., Sangiorgi, E., et al. (1999). Pervasive developmental disorder and epilepsy due to maternally derived duplication of 15q11-q13. *Neurology* 52, 1694–1697.

Hamilton, A. M., Oh, W. C., Vega-Ramirez, H., Stein, I. S., Hell, J. W., Patrick, G. N., et al. (2012). Activity-dependent growth of new dendritic spines is regulated by the proteasome. *Neuron* 74, 1023–1030. doi: 10.1016/j.neuron.2012.04.031

Hara, Y., Takuma, K., Takano, E., Katashiba, K., Taruta, A., Higashino, K., et al. (2015). Reduced prefrontal dopaminergic activity in valproic acid-treated mouse autism model. *Behav. Brain Res.* 289, 39–47. doi: 10.1016/j.bbr.2015.04.022

Hatanaka, Y., Wada, K., and Kabuta, T. (2015). Abnormal instability, excess density, and aberrant morphology of dendritic spines in prenatally testosterone-exposed mice. *Neurochem. Int.* 85–86, 53–58. doi: 10.1016/j.neuint.2015.04.008

Havlovicova, M., Novotna, D., Kocarek, E., Novotna, K., Bendova, S., Petrak, B., et al. (2007). A girl with neurofibromatosis type 1, atypical autism and mosaic ring chromosome 17. *Am. J. Med. Genet. A* 143A, 76–81. doi: 10.1002/ajmg.a.31569

Hoffman, E. J., Turner, K. J., Fernandez, J. M., Cifuentes, D., Ghosh, M., Ijaz, S., et al. (2016). Estrogens suppress a behavioral phenotype in Zebrafish mutants of the autism risk gene, CNTNAP2. *Neuron* 89, 725–733. doi: 10.1016/j.neuron.2015.12.039

Horev, G., Ellegood, J., Lerch, J. P., Son, Y.-E. E., Muthuswamy, L., Vogel, H., et al. (2011). Dosage-dependent phenotypes in models of 16p11.2 lesions found in autism. *Proc. Natl. Acad. Sci. U.S.A.* 108, 17076–17081. doi: 10.1073/pnas.1114042108

Hu, V. W., Sarachana, T., Sherrard, R. M., and Kocher, K. M. (2015). Investigation of sex differences in the expression of RORA and its transcriptional targets in the brain as a potential contributor to the sex bias in autism. *Mol. Autism* 6:7. doi: 10.1186/2040-2392-6-7

Hutsler, J. J., and Zhang, H. (2010). Increased dendritic spine densities on cortical projection neurons in autism spectrum disorders. *Brain Res.* 1309, 83–94. doi: 10.1016/j.brainres.2009.09.120

Iijima, Y., Behr, K., Iijima, T., Biemans, B., Bischofberger, J., and Scheiffele, P. (2016). Distinct defects in synaptic differentiation of neocortical neurons in response to prenatal valproate exposure. *Sci. Rep.* 6:27400. doi: 10.1038/srep27400

IMGSAC (1998). Full genome screen for autism with evidence for linkage to a region on chromosome 7q | human molecular genetics | oxford academic. *Hum. Mol. Genet.* 7, 571–578. doi: 10.1093/hmg/7.3.571

International Molecular Genetic Study of Autism Consortium [IMGSAC] (2001). A genomewide screen for autism: strong evidence for linkage to chromosomes 2q, 7q, and 16p. *Am. J. Hum. Genet.* 69, 570–581. doi: 10.1086/323264

Iossifov, I., O'Roak, B. J., Sanders, S. J., Ronemus, M., Krumm, N., Levy, D., et al. (2014). The contribution of *de novo* coding mutations to autism spectrum disorder. *Nature* 515, 216–221. doi: 10.1038/nature13908

Irwin, S. A., Patel, B., Idupulapati, M., Harris, J. B., Crisostomo, R. A., Larsen, B. P., et al. (2001). Abnormal dendritic spine characteristics in the temporal and visual cortices of patients with fragile-X syndrome: a quantitative examination. *Am. J. Med. Genet.* 98, 161–167. doi: 10.1002/1096-8628(20010115)98:2<161::AID-AJMG1025>3.0.CO;2-B

Iyer, J., Singh, M. D., Jensen, M., Patel, P., Pizzo, L., Huber, E., et al. (2018). Pervasive genetic interactions modulate neurodevelopmental defects of the autism-associated 16p11.2 deletion in *Drosophila melanogaster*. *Nat. Commun.* 9:2548. doi: 10.1038/s41467-018-04882-6

Jacob, J., Ribes, V., Moore, S., Constable, S. C., Sasai, N., Gerety, S. S., et al. (2014). Valproic acid silencing of ascl1b/Ascl1 results in the failure of serotonergic differentiation in a zebrafish model of fetal valproate syndrome. *Dis. Model. Mech.* 7, 107–117. doi: 10.1242/dmm.013219

Jacquemont, S., Coe, B. P., Hersch, M., Duyzend, M. H., Krumm, N., Bergmann, S., et al. (2014). A higher mutational burden in females supports a "female protective model" in neurodevelopmental disorders. *Am. J. Hum. Genet.* 94, 415–425. doi: 10.1016/j.ajhg.2014.02.001

Jamain, S., Quach, H., Betancur, C., Råstam, M., Colineaux, C., Gillberg, I. C., et al. (2003). Mutations of the X-linked genes encoding neuroligins NLGN3 and NLGN4 are associated with autism. *Nat. Genet.* 34, 27–29. doi: 10.1038/ng1136

James, S. J., Shpyleva, S., Melnyk, S., Pavliv, O., and Pogribny, I. P. (2013). Complex epigenetic regulation of Engrailed-2 (EN-2) homeobox gene in the autism cerebellum. *Transl. Psychiatry* 3:e232. doi: 10.1038/tp.2013.8

Jiang, Y.-H., Sahoo, T., Michaelis, R. C., Bercovich, D., Bressler, J., Kashork, C. D., et al. (2004). A mixed epigenetic/genetic model for oligogenic inheritance of autism with a limited role for UBE3A. *Am. J. Med. Genet. A* 131, 1–10. doi: 10.1002/ajmg.a.30297

Jung, H., Park, H., Choi, Y., Kang, H., Lee, E., Kweon, H., et al. (2018). Sexually dimorphic behavior, neuronal activity, and gene expression in Chd8-mutant mice. *Nat. Neurosci.* 21, 1218–1228. doi: 10.1038/s41593-018-0208-z

Kakinuma, H., Ozaki, M., Sato, H., and Takahashi, H. (2008). Variation in GABA-A subunit gene copy number in an autistic patient with mosaic 4 p duplication (p12p16). *Am. J. Med. Genet. B Neuropsychiatr. Genet.* 147B, 973–975. doi: 10.1002/ajmg.b.30663

Kalsner, L., and Chamberlain, S. J. (2015). Prader-Willi, Angelman, and 15q11-q13 duplication syndromes. *Pediatr. Clin. North Am.* 62, 587–606. doi: 10.1016/j.pcl.2015.03.004

Kanner, L. (1943). Autistic disturbances of affective contact. *Nerv. Child* 2, 217–250.

Karimi, P., Kamali, E., Mousavi, S. M., and Karahmadi, M. (2017). Environmental factors influencing the risk of autism. *J. Res. Med. Sci.* 22:27. doi: 10.4103/1735-1995.200272

Kataoka, S., Takuma, K., Hara, Y., Maeda, Y., Ago, Y., and Matsuda, T. (2013). Autism-like behaviours with transient histone hyperacetylation in mice treated prenatally with valproic acid. *Int. J. Neuropsychopharmacol.* 16, 91–103. doi: 10.1017/S1461145711001714

Khanzada, N. S., Butler, M. G., and Manzardo, A. M. (2017). GeneAnalytics pathway analysis and genetic overlap among autism spectrum disorder, bipolar disorder and schizophrenia. *Int. J. Mol. Sci.* 18:E527. doi: 10.3390/ijms18030527

Kim, H.-J., Cho, M.-H., Shim, W. H., Kim, J. K., Jeon, E.-Y., Kim, D.-H., et al. (2017). Deficient autophagy in microglia impairs synaptic pruning and causes social behavioral defects. *Mol. Psychiatry* 22, 1576–1584. doi: 10.1038/mp.2016.103

Kim, K. C., Choi, C. S., Kim, J.-W., Han, S.-H., Cheong, J. H., Ryu, J. H., et al. (2016). MeCP2 modulates sex differences in the postsynaptic development of the valproate animal model of autism. *Mol. Neurobiol.* 53, 40–56. doi: 10.1007/s12035-014-8987-z

Knudson, A. G. (1971). Mutation and cancer: statistical study of retinoblastoma. *PNAS* 68, 820–823. doi: 10.1073/pnas.68.4.820

Ko, H. M., Jin, Y., Park, H. H., Lee, J. H., Jung, S. H., Choi, S. Y., et al. (2018). Dual mechanisms for the regulation of brain-derived neurotrophic factor by valproic acid in neural progenitor cells. *Korean J. Physiol. Pharmacol.* 22, 679–688. doi: 10.4196/kjpp.2018.22.6.679

Kolozsi, E., Mackenzie, R. N., Roullet, F. I., deCatanzaro, D., and Foster, J. A. (2009). Prenatal exposure to valproic acid leads to reduced expression of synaptic adhesion molecule neuroligin 3 in mice. *Neuroscience* 163, 1201–1210. doi: 10.1016/j.neuroscience.2009.07.021

Kong, A., Frigge, M. L., Masson, G., Besenbacher, S., Sulem, P., Magnusson, G., et al. (2012). Rate of *de novo* mutations and the importance of father's age to disease risk. *Nature* 488, 471–475. doi: 10.1038/nature11396

Korb, E., Herre, M., Zucker-Scharff, I., Gresack, J., Allis, C. D., and Darnell, R. B. (2017). Excess translation of epigenetic regulators contributes to fragile X syndrome and is alleviated by Brd4 inhibition. *Cell* 170, 1209.e20–1223.e20. doi: 10.1016/j.cell.2017.07.033

Koyama, R., and Ikegaya, Y. (2015). Microglia in the pathogenesis of autism spectrum disorders. *Neurosci. Res.* 100, 1–5. doi: 10.1016/j.neures.2015.06.005

Krebs, M. O., Betancur, C., Leroy, S., Bourdel, M. C., Gillberg, C., Leboyer, M., et al. (2002). Absence of association between a polymorphic GGC repeat in the 5' untranslated region of the reelin gene and autism. *Mol. Psychiatry* 7, 801–804. doi: 10.1038/sj.mp.4001071

Krupp, D. R., Barnard, R. A., Duffourd, Y., Evans, S. A., Mulqueen, R. M., Bernier, R., et al. (2017). Exonic mosaic mutations contribute risk for autism spectrum disorder. *Am. J. Hum. Genet.* 101, 369–390. doi: 10.1016/j.ajhg.2017.07.016

Kubota, T., and Mochizuki, K. (2016). Epigenetic effect of environmental factors on autism spectrum disorders. *Int. J. Environ. Res. Public. Health* 13:E504. doi: 10.3390/ijerph13050504

Kumar, R. A., KaraMohamed, S., Sudi, J., Conrad, D. F., Brune, C., Badner, J. A., et al. (2008). Recurrent 16p11.2 microdeletions in autism. *Hum. Mol. Genet.* 17, 628–638. doi: 10.1093/hmg/ddm376

Kunio, M., Yang, C., Minakuchi, Y., Ohori, K., Soutome, M., Hirasawa, T., et al. (2013). Comparison of genomic and epigenomic expression in monozygotic twins discordant for rett syndrome. *PLoS One* 8:e66729. doi: 10.1371/journal.pone.0066729

Ladd-Acosta, C., Hansen, K. D., Briem, E., Fallin, M. D., Kaufmann, W. E., and Feinberg, A. P. (2014). Common DNA methylation alterations in multiple brain regions in autism. *Mol. Psychiatry* 19, 862–871. doi: 10.1038/mp.2013.114

Lai, M.-C., Lombardo, M. V., and Baron-Cohen, S. (2014). Autism. *Lancet* 383, 896–910. doi: 10.1016/S0140-6736(13)61539-1

Lamb, J. A., Parr, J. R., Bailey, A. J., and Monaco, A. P. (2002). Autism. *NeuroMol. Med.* 2, 11–28. doi: 10.1385/NMM:2:1:11

Leblond, C. S., Heinrich, J., Delorme, R., Proepper, C., Betancur, C., Huguet, G., et al. (2012). Genetic and functional analyses of SHANK2 mutations suggest a multiple hit model of autism spectrum disorders. *PLoS Genet.* 8:e1002521. doi: 10.1371/journal.pgen.1002521

Lee, S. Y., Ramirez, J., Franco, M., Lectez, B., Gonzalez, M., Barrio, R., et al. (2014). Ube3a, the E3 ubiquitin ligase causing Angelman syndrome and linked to autism, regulates protein homeostasis through the proteasomal shuttle Rpn10. *Cell. Mol. Life Sci.* 71, 2747–2758. doi: 10.1007/s00018-013-1526-7

Lenz, K. M., Nugent, B. M., Haliyur, R., and McCarthy, M. M. (2013). Microglia are essential to masculinization of brain and behavior. *J. Neurosci.* 33, 2761–2772. doi: 10.1523/JNEUROSCI.1268-12.2013

Li, F., Shen, Y., Köhler, U., Sharkey, F. H., Menon, D., Coulleaux, L., et al. (2010). Interstitial microduplication of Xp22.31: causative of intellectual disability or benign copy number variant? *Eur. J. Med. Genet.* 53, 93–99. doi: 10.1016/j.ejmg.2010.01.004

Lim, E. T., Uddin, M., De Rubeis, S., Chan, Y., Kamumbu, A. S., Zhang, X., et al. (2017). Rates, distribution and implications of postzygotic mosaic mutations in autism spectrum disorder. *Nat. Neurosci.* 20, 1217–1224. doi: 10.1038/nn.4598

Liu, J., Nyholt, D. R., Magnussen, P., Parano, E., Pavone, P., Geschwind, D., et al. (2001). A genomewide screen for autism susceptibility loci. *Am. J. Hum. Genet.* 69, 327–340. doi: 10.1086/321980

Liu, S., Zhou, L., Yuan, H., Vieira, M., Sanz-Clemente, A., Badger, J. D., et al. (2017a). A rare variant identified within the GluN2B C-Terminus in a patient with autism affects NMDA receptor surface expression and spine density. *J. Neurosci.* 37, 4093–4102. doi: 10.1523/JNEUROSCI.0827-16.2017

Liu, X., Campanac, E., Cheung, H.-H., Ziats, M. N., Canterel-Thouennon, L., Raygada, M., et al. (2017b). Idiopathic autism: cellular and molecular phenotypes in pluripotent stem cell-derived neurons. *Mol. Neurobiol.* 54, 4507–4523. doi: 10.1007/s12035-016-9961-8

Liu, Z., Li, X., Zhang, J.-T., Cai, Y.-J., Cheng, T.-L., Cheng, C., et al. (2016). Autism-like behaviours and germline transmission in transgenic monkeys overexpressing MeCP2. *Nature* 530, 98–102. doi: 10.1038/nature16533

Loomes, R., Hull, L., and Mandy, W. P. L. (2017). What is the male-to-female ratio in autism spectrum disorder? A systematic review and meta-analysis. *J. Am. Acad. Child Adolesc. Psychiatry* 56, 466–474. doi: 10.1016/j.jaac.2017.03.013

Macrì, S., Biamonte, F., Romano, E., Marino, R., Keller, F., and Laviola, G. (2010). Perseverative responding and neuroanatomical alterations in adult heterozygous reeler mice are mitigated by neonatal estrogen administration. *Psychoneuroendocrinology* 35, 1374–1387. doi: 10.1016/j.psyneuen.2010.03.012

Mahmood, U., Ahn, S., Yang, E.-J., Choi, M., Kim, H., Regan, P., et al. (2018). Dendritic spine anomalies and PTEN alterations in a mouse model of VPA-induced autism spectrum disorder. *Pharmacol. Res.* 128, 110–121. doi: 10.1016/j.phrs.2017.08.006

Marshall, C. R., Noor, A., Vincent, J. B., Lionel, A. C., Feuk, L., Skaug, J., et al. (2008). Structural variation of chromosomes in autism spectrum disorder. *Am. J. Hum. Genet.* 82, 477–488. doi: 10.1016/j.ajhg.2007.12.009

Marshall, C. R., and Scherer, S. W. (2012). Detection and characterization of copy number variation in autism spectrum disorder. *Methods Mol. Biol.* 838, 115–135. doi: 10.1007/978-1-61779-507-7_5

Martin, J., Cooper, M., Hamshere, M. L., Pocklington, A., Scherer, S. W., Kent, L., et al. (2014). Biological overlap of attention-deficit/hyperactivity disorder and autism spectrum disorder: evidence from copy number variants. *J. Am. Acad. Child Adolesc. Psychiatry* 53, 761.e26–770.e26. doi: 10.1016/j.jaac.2014.03.004

McCallion, A. S., Stames, E., Conlon, R. A., and Chakravarti, A. (2003). Phenotype variation in two-locus mouse models of Hirschsprung disease: tissue-specific interaction between Ret and Ednrb. *PNAS* 100, 1826–1831. doi: 10.1073/pnas.0337540100

McCarthy, M. M., and Wright, C. L. (2017). Convergence of sex differences and the neuroimmune system in autism spectrum disorder. *Biol. Psychiatry* 81, 402–410. doi: 10.1016/j.biopsych.2016.10.004

McCarthy, S. E., Gillis, J., Kramer, M., Lihm, J., Yoon, S., Berstein, Y., et al. (2014). *De novo* mutations in schizophrenia implicate chromatin remodeling and support a genetic overlap with autism and intellectual disability. *Mol. Psychiatry* 19, 652–658. doi: 10.1038/mp.2014.29

Michaelson, J. J., Shin, M.-K., Koh, J.-Y., Brueggeman, L., Zhang, A., Katzman, A., et al. (2017). Neuronal PAS domain proteins 1 and 3 are master regulators of neuropsychiatric risk genes. *Biol. Psychiatry* 82, 213–223. doi: 10.1016/j.biopsych.2017.03.021

Modabbernia, A., Velthorst, E., and Reichenberg, A. (2017). Environmental risk factors for autism: an evidence-based review of systematic reviews and meta-analyses. *Mol. Autism* 8:13. doi: 10.1186/s13229-017-0121-4

Mor, M., Nardone, S., Sams, D. S., and Elliott, E. (2015). Hypomethylation of miR-142 promoter and upregulation of microRNAs that target the oxytocin receptor gene in the autism prefrontal cortex. *Mol. Autism* 6:46. doi: 10.1186/s13229-015-0040-1

Mulligan, A., Anney, R. J. L., O'Regan, M., Chen, W., Butler, L., Fitzgerald, M., et al. (2009). Autism symptoms in attention-deficit/hyperactivity disorder: a familial trait which correlates with conduct, oppositional defiant, language and motor disorders. *J. Autism Dev. Disord.* 39, 197–209. doi: 10.1007/s10803-008-0621-3

Nadeem, A., Ahmad, S. F., Attia, S. M., Al-Ayadhi, L. Y., Al-Harbi, N. O., and Bakheet, S. A. (2019). Dysregulated enzymatic antioxidant network in peripheral neutrophils and monocytes in children with autism. *Prog. Neuropsychopharmacol. Biol. Psychiatry* 88, 352–359. doi: 10.1016/j.pnpbp.2018.08.020

Nagarajan, R. P., Hogart, A. R., Gwye, Y., Martin, M. R., and LaSalle, J. M. (2006). Reduced MeCP2 expression is frequent in autism frontal cortex and correlates with aberrant MECP2 promoter methylation. *Epigenetics* 1, e1–e11.

Nagarajan, R. P., Patzel, K. A., Martin, M., Yasui, D. H., Swanberg, S. E., Hertz-Picciotto, I., et al. (2008). MECP2 promoter methylation and X chromosome inactivation in autism. *Autism Res.* 1, 169–178. doi: 10.1002/aur.24

Nardone, S., and Elliott, E. (2016). The interaction between the immune system and epigenetics in the etiology of autism spectrum disorders. *Front. Neurosci.* 10:329. doi: 10.3389/fnins.2016.00329

Nguyen, A., Rauch, T. A., Pfeifer, G. P., and Hu, V. W. (2010). Global methylation profiling of lymphoblastoid cell lines reveals epigenetic contributions to autism spectrum disorders and a novel autism candidate gene, RORA, whose protein product is reduced in autistic brain. *FASEB J.* 24, 3036–3051. doi: 10.1096/fj.10-154484

Nijmeijer, J. S., Arias-Vásquez, A., Rommelse, N. N. J., Altink, M. E., Anney, R. J. L., Asherson, P., et al. (2010). Identifying loci for the overlap between attention-deficit/hyperactivity disorder and autism spectrum disorder using a genome-wide QTL linkage approach. *J. Am. Acad. Child Adolesc. Psychiatry* 49, 675–685. doi: 10.1016/j.jaac.2010.03.015

Ohkawara, T., Katsuyama, T., Ida-Eto, M., Narita, N., and Narita, M. (2015). Maternal viral infection during pregnancy impairs development of fetal serotonergic neurons. *Brain Dev.* 37, 88–93. doi: 10.1016/j.braindev.2014.03.007

Oliveira, G., Matoso, E., Vicente, A., Ribeiro, P., Marques, C., Ataíde, A., et al. (2003). Partial tetrasomy of chromosome 3q and mosaicism in a child with autism. *J. Autism Dev. Disord.* 33, 177–185.

O'Roak, B. J., Vives, L., Girirajan, S., Karakoc, E., Krumm, N., Coe, B. P., et al. (2012). Sporadic autism exomes reveal a highly interconnected protein network of *de novo* mutations. *Nature* 485, 246–250. doi: 10.1038/nature10989

Papanikolaou, K., Paliokosta, E., Gyftodimou, J., Kolaitis, G., Vgenopoulou, S., Sarri, C., et al. (2006). A case of partial trisomy of chromosome 8p associated with autism. *J. Autism Dev. Disord.* 36, 705–709. doi: 10.1007/s10803-006-0104-3

Persico, A. M., D'Agruma, L., Maiorano, N., Totaro, A., Militerni, R., Bravaccio, C., et al. (2001). Reelin gene alleles and haplotypes as a factor predisposing to autistic disorder. *Mol. Psychiatry* 6, 150–159. doi: 10.1038/sj.mp.4000850

Peters, S. U., Beaudet, A. L., Madduri, N., and Bacino, C. A. (2004). Autism in Angelman syndrome: implications for autism research. *Clin. Genet.* 66, 530–536. doi: 10.1111/j.1399-0004.2004.00362.x

Pinto, D., Delaby, E., Merico, D., Barbosa, M., Merikangas, A., Klei, L., et al. (2014). Convergence of genes and cellular pathways dysregulated in autism spectrum disorders. *Am. J. Hum. Genet.* 94, 677–694. doi: 10.1016/j.ajhg.2014.03.018

Pinto, D., Pagnamenta, A. T., Klei, L., Anney, R., Merico, D., Regan, R., et al. (2010). Functional impact of global rare copy number variation in autism spectrum disorders. *Nature* 466, 368–372. doi: 10.1038/nature09146

Pizzo, L., Jensen, M., Polyak, A., Rosenfeld, J. A., Mannik, K., Krishnan, A., et al. (2019). Rare variants in the genetic background modulate cognitive and developmental phenotypes in individuals carrying disease-associated variants. *Genet. Med.* 21, 816–825. doi: 10.1038/s41436-018-0266-3

Poduri, A., Evrony, G. D., Cai, X., and Walsh, C. A. (2013). Somatic mutation, genomic variation, and neurological disease. *Science* 341:1237758. doi: 10.1126/science.1237758

Polyak, A., Rosenfeld, J. A., and Girirajan, S. (2015). An assessment of sex bias in neurodevelopmental disorders. *Genome Med.* 7:94. doi: 10.1186/s13073-015-0216-215

Pucilowska, J., Vithayathil, J., Tavares, E. J., Kelly, C., Karlo, J. C., and Landreth, G. E. (2015). The 16p11.2 deletion mouse model of autism exhibits altered cortical progenitor proliferation and brain cytoarchitecture linked to the *ERK MAPK* pathway. *J. Neurosci.* 35, 3190–3200. doi: 10.1523/JNEUROSCI.4864-13.2015

Puram, S. V., Kim, A. H., Park, H.-Y., Anckar, J., and Bonni, A. (2013). The ubiquitin receptor S5a/Rpn10 links centrosomal proteasomes with dendrite development in the mammalian brain. *Cell Rep.* 4, 19–30. doi: 10.1016/j.celrep.2013.06.006

Qin, L., Ma, K., Wang, Z.-J., Hu, Z., Matas, E., Wei, J., et al. (2018). Social deficits in Shank3-deficient mouse models of autism are rescued by histone deacetylase (HDAC) inhibition. *Nat. Neurosci.* 21, 564–575. doi: 10.1038/s41593-018-0110-8

Qin, W., Chan, J. A., Vinters, H. V., Mathern, G. W., Franz, D. N., Taillon, B. E., et al. (2010). Analysis of TSC cortical tubers by deep sequencing of TSC1, TSC2, and KRAS demonstrates that small second hit mutations in these genes are rare events. *Brain Pathol. Zurich Switz* 20, 1096–1105. doi: 10.1111/j.1750-3639.2010.00416.x

Rapoport, J., Chavez, A., Greenstein, D., Addington, A., and Gogtay, N. (2009). Autism spectrum disorders and childhood-onset schizophrenia: clinical and biological contributions to a relation revisited. *J. Am. Acad. Child Adolesc. Psychiatry* 48, 10–18. doi: 10.1097/CHI.0b013e31818b1c63

Rasalam, A. D., Hailey, H., Williams, J. H. G., Moore, S. J., Turnpenny, P. D., Lloyd, D. J., et al. (2005). Characteristics of fetal anticonvulsant syndrome associated autistic disorder. *Dev. Med. Child Neurol.* 47, 551–555. doi: 10.1017/s0012162205001076

Rasia-Filho, A. A., Londero, R. G., and Achaval, M. (2000). Functional activities of the amygdala: an overview. *J. Psychiatry Neurosci.* 25, 14–23.

Reiersen, A. M., Constantino, J. N., Volk, H. E., and Todd, R. D. (2007). Autistic traits in a population-based ADHD twin sample. *J. Child Psychol. Psychiatry* 48, 464–472. doi: 10.1111/j.1469-7610.2006.01720.x

Repnikova, E. A., Lyalin, D. A., McDonald, K., Astbury, C., Hansen-Kiss, E., Cooley, L. D., et al. (2019). CNTN6 copy number variations: uncertain clinical significance in individuals with neurodevelopmental disorders. *Eur. J. Med. Genet.* doi: 10.1016/j.ejmg.2019.02.008 [Epub ahead of print].

Rio, M., Royer, G., Gobin, S., de Blois, M., Ozilou, C., Bernheim, A., et al. (2013). Monozygotic twins discordant for submicroscopic chromosomal anomalies in 2p25.3 region detected by array CGH. *Clin. Genet.* 84, 31–36. doi: 10.1111/cge.12036

Risch, N., Hoffmann, T. J., Anderson, M., Croen, L. A., Grether, J. K., and Windham, G. C. (2014). Familial recurrence of autism spectrum disorder: evaluating genetic and environmental contributions. *Am. J. Psychiatry* 171, 1206–1213. doi: 10.1176/appi.ajp.2014.13101359

Robinson, E. B., Lichtenstein, P., Anckarsäter, H., Happé, F., and Ronald, A. (2013). Examining and interpreting the female protective effect against autistic behavior. *Proc. Natl. Acad. Sci. U.S.A.* 110, 5258–5262. doi: 10.1073/pnas.1211070110

Rommelse, N. N. J., Franke, B., Geurts, H. M., Hartman, C. A., and Buitelaar, J. K. (2010). Shared heritability of attention-deficit/hyperactivity disorder and autism spectrum disorder. *Eur. Child Adolesc. Psychiatry* 19, 281–295. doi: 10.1007/s00787-010-0092-x

Ronald, A., Simonoff, E., Kuntsi, J., Asherson, P., and Plomin, R. (2008). Evidence for overlapping genetic influences on autistic and ADHD behaviours in a community twin sample. *J. Child Psychol. Psychiatry* 49, 535–542. doi: 10.1111/j.1469-7610.2007.01857.x

Ronemus, M., Iossifov, I., Levy, D., and Wigler, M. (2014). The role of *de novo* mutations in the genetics of autism spectrum disorders. *Nat. Rev. Genet.* 15, 133–141. doi: 10.1038/nrg3585

Roved, J., Westerdahl, H., and Hasselquist, D. (2017). Sex differences in immune responses: hormonal effects, antagonistic selection, and evolutionary consequences. *Horm. Behav.* 88, 95–105. doi: 10.1016/j.yhbeh.2016.11.017

Saghazadeh, A., and Rezaei, N. (2017). Brain-derived neurotrophic factor levels in autism: a systematic review and meta-analysis. *J. Autism Dev. Disord.* 47, 1018–1029. doi: 10.1007/s10803-016-3024-x

Samaco, R. C., Hogart, A., and LaSalle, J. M. (2005). Epigenetic overlap in autism-spectrum neurodevelopmental disorders: MECP2 deficiency causes reduced expression of UBE3A and GABRB3. *Hum. Mol. Genet.* 14, 483–492. doi: 10.1093/hmg/ddi045

Sandin, S., Lichtenstein, P., Kuja-Halkola, R., Larsson, H., Hultman, C. M., and Reichenberg, A. (2014). The familial risk of autism. *JAMA* 311, 1770–1777. doi: 10.1001/jama.2014.4144

Sarachana, T., Xu, M., Wu, R.-C., and Hu, V. W. (2011). Sex hormones in autism: androgens and estrogens differentially and reciprocally regulate RORA, a novel candidate gene for autism. *PLoS One* 6:e17116. doi: 10.1371/journal.pone.0017116

Sauter, S., von Beust, G., Burfeind, P., Weise, A., Starke, H., Liehr, T., et al. (2003). Autistic disorder and chromosomal mosaicism 46,XY[123]/46,XY,del(20)(pter -> p12.2)[10]. *Am. J. Med. Genet. A* 120A, 533–536. doi: 10.1002/ajmg.a.20089

Schmunk, G., and Gargus, J. J. (2013). Channelopathy pathogenesis in autism spectrum disorders *Front. Genet.* 4:222. doi: 10.3389/fgene.2013.00222

Schork, A. J., Won, H., Appadurai, V., Nudel, R., Gandal, M., Delaneau, O., et al. (2019). A genome-wide association study of shared risk across psychiatric disorders implicates gene regulation during fetal neurodevelopment. *Nat. Neurosci.* 22, 353–361. doi: 10.1038/s41593-018-0320-0

Schroer, R. J., Phelan, M. C., Michaelis, R. C., Crawford, E. C., Skinner, S. A., Cuccaro, M., et al. (1998). Autism and maternally derived aberrations of chromosome 15q. *Am. J. Med. Genet.* 76, 327–336. doi: 10.1002/(sici)1096-8628(19980401)76:4<327::aid-ajmg8>3.0.co;2-m

Schwarz, E., Guest, P. C., Rahmoune, H., Wang, L., Levin, Y., Ingudomnukul, E., et al. (2011). Sex-specific serum biomarker patterns in adults with Asperger's syndrome. *Mol. Psychiatry* 16, 1213–1220. doi: 10.1038/mp.2010.102

Sebat, J., Lakshmi, B., Malhotra, D., Troge, J., Lese-Martin, C., Walsh, T., et al. (2007). Strong association of *De Novo* copy number mutations with autism. *Science* 316, 445–449. doi: 10.1126/science.1138659

Serajee, F., Nabi, R., Zhong, H., and Mahbubul, H. (2003). Association of INPP1, PIK3CG, and TSC2 gene variants with autistic disorder: implications for phosphatidylinositol signalling in autism. *J. Med. Genet.* 40:e119. doi: 10.1136/jmg.40.11.e119

Shao, Y., Cuccaro, M. L., Hauser, E. R., Raiford, K. L., Menold, M. M., Wolpert, C. M., et al. (2003). Fine mapping of autistic disorder to chromosome 15q11-q13 by use of phenotypic subtypes. *Am. J. Hum. Genet.* 72, 539–548. doi: 10.1086/367846

Shi, L., Zhang, Z., and Su, B. (2016). Sex biased gene expression profiling of human brains at major developmental stages. *Sci. Rep.* 6:21181. doi: 10.1038/srep21181

Short, P. J., McRae, J. F., Gallone, G., Sifrim, A., Won, H., Geschwind, D. H., et al. (2018). *De novo* mutations in regulatory elements in neurodevelopmental disorders. *Nature* 555, 611–616. doi: 10.1038/nature25983

Smith, S. E. P., Zhou, Y.-D., Zhang, G., Jin, Z., Stoppel, D. C., and Anderson, M. P. (2011). Increased gene dosage of ube3a results in autism traits and decreased glutamate synaptic transmission in mice. *Sci. Transl. Med.* 3:103ra97. doi: 10.1126/scitranslmed.3002627

Soltani, A., Lebrun, S., Carpentier, G., Zunino, G., Chantepie, S., Maïza, A., et al. (2017). Increased signaling by the autism-related Engrailed-2 protein enhances dendritic branching and spine density, alters synaptic structural matching, and exaggerates protein synthesis. *PLoS One* 12:e0181350. doi: 10.1371/journal.pone.0181350

Stamouli, S., Anderlid, B.-M., Willfors, C., Thiruvahindrapuram, B., Wei, J., Berggren, S., et al. (2018). Copy number variation analysis of 100 twin pairs enriched for neurodevelopmental disorders. *Twin Res. Hum. Genet.* 21, 1–11. doi: 10.1017/thg.2017.69

Stefansson, H., Meyer-Lindenberg, A., Steinberg, S., Magnusdottir, B., Morgen, K., Arnarsdottir, S., et al. (2014). CNVs conferring risk of autism or schizophrenia affect cognition in controls. *Nature* 505, 361–366. doi: 10.1038/nature12818

Stergiakouli, E., Davey Smith, G., Martin, J., Skuse, D. H., Viechtbauer, W., Ring, S. M., et al. (2017). Shared genetic influences between dimensional ASD and ADHD symptoms during child and adolescent development. *Mol. Autism* 8:18. doi: 10.1186/s13229-017-0131-2

Stern, D., Cho, M. T., Chikarmane, R., Willaert, R., Retterer, K., Kendall, F., et al. (2017). Association of the missense variant p.Arg203Trp in PACS1 as a cause of intellectual disability and seizures. *Clin. Genet.* 92, 221–223. doi: 10.1111/cge.12956

Stessman, H. A. F., Xiong, B., Coe, B. P., Wang, T., Hoekzema, K., Fenckova, M., et al. (2017). Targeted sequencing identifies 91 neurodevelopmental disorder risk genes with autism and developmental disability biases. *Nat. Genet.* 49, 515–526. doi: 10.1038/ng.3792

Stodgell, C. J., Ingram, J. L., O'Bara, M., Tisdale, B. K., Nau, H., and Rodier, P. M. (2006). Induction of the homeotic gene Hoxa1 through valproic acid's teratogenic mechanism of action. *Neurotoxicol. Teratol.* 28, 617–624. doi: 10.1016/j.ntt.2006.08.004

Strømme, P., Mangelsdorf, M. E., Scheffer, I. E., and Gécz, J. (2002). Infantile spasms, dystonia, and other X-linked phenotypes caused by mutations in Aristaless related homeobox gene, ARX. *Brain Dev.* 24, 266–268. doi: 10.1016/s0387-7604(02)00079-7

Sullivan, P. F., Magnusson, C., Reichenberg, A., Boman, M., Dalman, C., Davidson, M., et al. (2012). Family history of schizophrenia and bipolar disorder as risk factors for autism. *Arch. Gen. Psychiatry* 69, 1099–1103. doi: 10.1001/archgenpsychiatry.2012.730

Sun, W., Poschmann, J., Cruz-Herrera del Rosario, R., Parikshak, N. N., Hajan, H. S., Kumar, V., et al. (2016). Histone acetylome-wide association study of autism spectrum disorder. *Cell* 167, 1385.e11–1397.e11. doi: 10.1016/j.cell.2016.10.031

Szafranski, P., Schaaf, C. P., Person, R. E., Gibson, I. B., Xia, Z., Mahadevan, S., et al. (2010). Structures and molecular mechanisms for common 15q13.3 *Microduplications* involving CHRNA7: benign or pathological? *Hum. Mutat.* 31, 840–850. doi: 10.1002/humu.21284

Takuma, K., Hara, Y., Kataoka, S., Kawanai, T., Maeda, Y., Watanabe, R., et al. (2014). Chronic treatment with valproic acid or sodium butyrate attenuates novel object recognition deficits and hippocampal dendritic spine loss in a mouse model of autism. *Pharmacol. Biochem. Behav.* 126, 43–49. doi: 10.1016/j.pbb.2014.08.013

Talebizadeh, Z., Bittel, D., Miles, J., Takahashi, N., Wang, C., Kibiryeva, N., et al. (2002). No association between HOXA1 and HOXB1 genes and autism spectrum disorders (ASD). *J. Med. Genet.* 39:e70. doi: 10.1136/jmg.39.11.e70

Tang, G., Gudsnuk, K., Kuo, S.-H., Cotrina, M. L., Rosoklija, G., Sosunov, A., et al. (2014). Loss of mTOR-dependent macroautophagy causes autistic-like synaptic pruning deficits. *Neuron* 83, 1131–1143. doi: 10.1016/j.neuron.2014.07.040

Thapar, A., and Cooper, M. (2013). Copy number variation: what is it and what has it told us about child psychiatric disorders? *J. Am. Acad. Child Adolesc. Psychiatry* 52, 772–774. doi: 10.1016/j.jaac.2013.05.013

The Autism Genome Project Consortium, P., Paterson, A. D., Zwaigenbaum, L., Roberts, W., Brian, J., et al. (2007). Mapping autism risk loci using genetic linkage and chromosomal rearrangements. *Nat. Genet.* 39, 319–328. doi: 10.1038/ng1985

The Autism Spectrum Disorders Working Group of The Psychiatric Genomics Consortium (2017). Meta-analysis of GWAS of over 16,000 individuals with autism spectrum disorder highlights a novel locus at 10q24.32 and a significant overlap with schizophrenia. *Mol. Autism* 8:21. doi: 10.1186/s13229-017-0137-9

Tran, S. S., Jun, H.-I., Bahn, J. H., Azghadi, A., Ramaswami, G., Van Nostrand, E. L., et al. (2019). Widespread RNA editing dysregulation in brains from autistic individuals. *Nat. Neurosci.* 22, 25–36. doi: 10.1038/s41593-018-0287-x

Turner, T. N., Coe, B. P., Dickel, D. E., Hoekzema, K., Nelson, B. J., Zody, M. C., et al. (2017). Genomic patterns of *de novo* mutation in simplex autism. *Cell* 171, 710.e12–722.e12. doi: 10.1016/j.cell.2017.08.047

Turner, T. N., Hormozdiari, F., Duyzend, M. H., McClymont, S. A., Hook, P. W., Iossifov, I., et al. (2016). Genome sequencing of autism-affected families reveals disruption of putative noncoding regulatory DNA. *Am. J. Hum. Genet.* 98, 58–74. doi: 10.1016/j.ajhg.2015.11.023

Tyburczy, M. E., Jozwiak, S., Malinowska, I. A., Chekaluk, Y., Pugh, T. J., Wu, C.-L., et al. (2015). A shower of second hit events as the cause of multifocal renal cell carcinoma in tuberous sclerosis complex. *Hum. Mol. Genet.* 24, 1836–1842. doi: 10.1093/hmg/ddu597

Honk, J., Schutter, D. J., Bos, P. A., Kruijt, A.-W., Lentjes, E. G., and Baron-Cohen, S. (2011). Testosterone administration impairs cognitive empathy in women depending on second-to-fourth digit ratio. *Proc. Natl. Acad. Sci. U.S.A.* 108, 3448–3452. doi: 10.1073/pnas.1011891108

Vorstman, J., van Daalen, E., Jalali, G., Schmidt, E., Pasterkamp, R., de Jonge, M., et al. (2011). A double hit implicates DIAPH3 as an autism risk gene. *Mol. Psychiatry* 16, 442–451. doi: 10.1038/mp.2010.26

Wang, C.-C., Lin, H.-C., Chan, Y.-H., Gean, P.-W., Yang, Y. K., and Chen, P. S. (2013). 5-HT1A-receptor agonist modified amygdala activity and amygdala-associated social behavior in a valproate-induced rat autism model. *Int. J. Neuropsychopharmacol.* 16, 2027–2039. doi: 10.1017/S1461145713000473

Wang, W., Corominas, R., and Lin, G. N. (2019). *De novo* mutations from whole exome sequencing in neurodevelopmental and psychiatric disorders: from discovery to application. *Front. Genet.* 10:258. doi: 10.3389/fgene.2019.00258

Weiss, L. A., Shen, Y., Korn, J. M., Arking, D. E., Miller, D. T., Fossdal, R., et al. (2008). Association between microdeletion and microduplication at 16p11.2 and Autism. *N. Engl. J. Med.* 358, 667–675. doi: 10.1056/NEJMoa075974

Wenger, T. L., Kao, C., McDonald-McGinn, D. M., Zackai, E. H., Bailey, A., Schultz, R. T., et al. (2016). The role of mGluR copy number variation in genetic and environmental forms of syndromic autism spectrum disorder. *Sci. Rep.* 6:19372. doi: 10.1038/srep19372

Werling, D. M., and Geschwind, D. H. (2013). Sex differences in autism spectrum disorders. *Curr. Opin. Neurol.* 26, 146–153. doi: 10.1097/WCO.0b013e32835ee548

Werling, D. M., Parikshak, N. N., and Geschwind, D. H. (2016). Gene expression in human brain implicates sexually dimorphic pathways in autism spectrum disorders. *Nat. Commun.* 7:10717. doi: 10.1038/ncomms10717

Whitehouse, A. J. O., Maybery, M. T., Hart, R., Mattes, E., Newnham, J. P., Sloboda, D. M., et al. (2010). Fetal androgen exposure and pragmatic language ability of girls in middle childhood: implications for the extreme male-brain theory of autism. *Psychoneuroendocrinology* 35, 1259–1264. doi: 10.1016/j.psyneuen.2010.02.007

Williams, C. A., Driscoll, D. J., and Dagli, A. I. (2010). Clinical and genetic aspects of Angelman syndrome. *Genet. Med.* 12, 385–395. doi: 10.1097/GIM.0b013e3181def138

Wong, C. C. Y., Meaburn, E. L., Ronald, A., Price, T. S., Jeffries, A. R., Schalkwyk, L. C., et al. (2014). Methylomic analysis of monozygotic twins discordant for autism spectrum disorder and related behavioural traits. *Mol. Psychiatry* 19, 495–503. doi: 10.1038/mp.2013.41

Woodbury-Smith, M., and Scherer, S. W. (2018). Progress in the genetics of autism spectrum disorder. *Dev. Med. Child Neurol.* 60, 445–451. doi: 10.1111/dmcn.13717

Xu, X., Li, C., Gao, X., Xia, K., Guo, H., Li, Y., et al. (2018). Excessive UBE3A dosage impairs retinoic acid signaling and synaptic plasticity in autism spectrum disorders. *Cell Res.* 28, 48–68. doi: 10.1038/cr.2017.132

Yi, J. J., Berrios, J., Newbern, J. M., Snider, W. D., Philpot, B. D., Hahn, K. M., et al. (2015). An autism-linked mutation disables phosphorylation control of UBE3A. *Cell* 162, 795–807. doi: 10.1016/j.cell.2015.06.045

Yi, J. J., Paranjape, S. R., Walker, M. P., Choudhury, R., Wolter, J. M., Fragola, G., et al. (2017). The autism-linked UBE3A T485A mutant E3 ubiquitin ligase activates the Wnt/β-catenin pathway by inhibiting the proteasome. *J. Biol. Chem.* 292, 12503–12515. doi: 10.1074/jbc.M117.788448

Yurov, Y. B., Vorsanova, S. G., Iourov, I. Y., Demidova, I. A., Beresheva, A. K., Kravetz, V. S., et al. (2007). Unexplained autism is frequently associated with low-level mosaic aneuploidy. *J. Med. Genet.* 44, 521–525. doi: 10.1136/jmg.2007.049312

Zeldovich, L. (2018). *The Evolution of 'Autism' as a Diagnosis, Explained.* Available at: https://www.spectrumnews.org/news/evolution-autism-diagnosis-explained/(accessed December 4, 2018).

Zhang, H., Liu, X., Zhang, C., Mundo, E., Macciardi, F., Grayson, D. R., et al. (2002). Reelin gene alleles and susceptibility to autism spectrum disorders. *Mol. Psychiatry* 7, 1012–1017. doi: 10.1038/sj.mp.4001124

Zhubi, A., Chen, Y., Guidotti, A., and Grayson, D. (2017). Epigenetic regulation of RELN and GAD1 in the frontal cortex (FC) of autism spectrum disorder (ASD) subjects. *Int. J. Dev. Neurosci.* 62, 63–72. doi: 10.1016/j.ijdevneu.2017.02.003

Ziats, M. N., and Rennert, O. M. (2013). Sex-biased gene expression in the developing brain: implications for autism spectrum disorders. *Mol. Autism* 4:10. doi: 10.1186/2040-2392-4-10

Zieminska, E., Toczylowska, B., Diamandakis, D., Hilgier, W., Filipkowski, R. K., Polowy, R., et al. (2018). Glutamate, glutamine and GABA levels in rat brain measured using MRS, HPLC and NMR methods in study of two models of autism. *Front. Mol. Neurosci.* 11:418. doi: 10.3389/fnmol.2018.00418

2

Functional and Structural Impairments in the Perirhinal Cortex of a Mouse Model of CDKL5 Deficiency Disorder Are Rescued by a TrkB Agonist

Elisa Ren[1†], Vincenzo Roncacé[2†], Stefania Trazzi[1†], Claudia Fuchs[1], Giorgio Medici[1], Laura Gennaccaro[1], Manuela Loi[1], Giuseppe Galvani[1], Keqiang Ye[3], Roberto Rimondini[4], Giorgio Aicardi[2,5] and Elisabetta Ciani[1]**

[1] Department of Biomedical and Neuromotor Sciences, University of Bologna, Bologna, Italy, [2] Department for Life Quality Studies, University of Bologna, Bologna, Italy, [3] School of Medicine, Emory University, Atlanta, GA, United States, [4] Department of Biomedical and Clinical Sciences, University of Bologna, Bologna, Italy, [5] Interdepartmental Center "Luigi Galvani" for Integrated Studies of Bioinformatics, Biophysics and Biocomplexity, University of Bologna, Bologna, Italy

***Correspondence:**
Giorgio Aicardi
giorgio.aicardi@unibo.it
Elisabetta Ciani
elisabetta.ciani@unibo.it

† These authors have contributed equally to this work

Cyclin-dependent kinase-like 5 (CDKL5) deficiency disorder (CDD) is a severe X-linked neurodevelopmental encephalopathy caused by mutations in the *CDKL5* gene and characterized by early-onset epilepsy and intellectual and motor impairments. No cure is currently available for CDD patients, as limited knowledge of the pathology has hindered the development of therapeutics. *Cdkl5* knockout (KO) mouse models, recently created to investigate the role of CDKL5 in the etiology of CDD, recapitulate various features of the disorder. Previous studies have shown alterations in synaptic plasticity and dendritic pattern in the cerebral cortex and in the hippocampus, but the knowledge of the molecular substrates underlying these alterations is still limited. Here, we have examined for the first time synaptic function and plasticity, dendritic morphology, and signal transduction pathways in the perirhinal cortex (PRC) of this mouse model. Being interconnected with a wide range of cortical and subcortical structures and involved in various cognitive processes, PRC provides a very interesting framework for examining how CDKL5 mutation leads to deficits at the synapse, circuit, and behavioral level. We found that long-term potentiation (LTP) was impaired, and that the TrkB/PLCγ1 pathway could be mechanistically involved in this alteration. PRC neurons in mutant mice showed a reduction in dendritic length, dendritic branches, PSD-95-positive puncta, GluA2-AMPA receptor levels, and spine density and maturation. These functional and structural deficits were associated with impairment in visual recognition memory. Interestingly, an *in vivo* treatment with a TrkB agonist (the 7,8-DHF prodrug R13) to trigger the TrkB/PLCγ1 pathway rescued defective LTP, dendritic pattern, PSD-95 and GluA2-AMPA receptor levels, and restored visual recognition memory in *Cdkl5* KO mice. Present findings demonstrate a critical role of TrkB signaling in the synaptic development alterations due to CDKL5 mutation, and suggest the possibility of TrkB-targeted pharmacological interventions.

Keywords: CDKL5, synaptic plasticity, TrkB, PLCγ1, dendritic pattern, GluA2, perirhinal cortex, rett syndrome

INTRODUCTION

Cyclin-dependent kinase-like 5 (CDKL5) deficiency disorder (CDD) is a rare encephalopathy characterized by early-onset intractable epileptic seizures, severe intellectual disability, gross motor impairment, stereotypies, visual impairments and autistic-like features (Kalscheuer et al., 2003; Weaving et al., 2004; Bahi-Buisson et al., 2008; Bahi-Buisson and Bienvenu, 2012; Moseley et al., 2012; Paine et al., 2012; Stalpers et al., 2012; Fehr et al., 2013). CDD is caused by mutations in the X-linked gene, *CDKL5*, a member of a highly conserved family of serine-threonine kinases (Tao et al., 2004). To date, several different mutations have been described in the *CDKL5* gene, mainly located within the CDKL5 catalytic domain (Kilstrup-Nielsen et al., 2012; Das et al., 2013; Fehr et al., 2013), suggesting that impaired CDKL5 kinase activity plays an important role in the pathogenesis of CDD (Tao et al., 2004; Bahi-Buisson et al., 2012).

No cure is currently available for CDD patients, as limited knowledge of the pathology has hindered the development of therapeutics. *Cdkl5* knockout (KO) mice (Wang et al., 2012; Amendola et al., 2014; Okuda et al., 2017) have recently been created to investigate the role of CDKL5 in the etiology of CDD. *Cdkl5* KO mice recapitulate different features of CDD, exhibiting severe impairment in learning and memory, visual and respiratory deficits, and motor stereotypies (Wang et al., 2012; Amendola et al., 2014; Fuchs et al., 2014, 2015; Mazziotti et al., 2017). The neuropathology of CDD points to arrested neuronal development rather than neurodegeneration or severe malformation of nervous tissue. Reduced neuronal branching and spine density have been observed in the visual and somatosensory cortex (Della Sala et al., 2016; Pizzo et al., 2016), and in the hippocampal region (Amendola et al., 2014; Fuchs et al., 2014) of *Cdkl5* KO mice. In addition, immunocytochemical studies have demonstrated alterations in synaptic connectivity, which might lead to an excitation-inhibition imbalance (Pizzo et al., 2016; Sivilia et al., 2016). Together, these observations have led to the suggestion that there is an overall reduction in the number of synaptic inputs to neurons in the CDKL5-deficient brain. It has been shown that CDKL5 is localized at excitatory synapses (Ricciardi et al., 2012) where it binds to the scaffolding postsynaptic density protein 95 (PSD-95) and to the synaptic cell adhesion molecule NGL-1 (Ricciardi et al., 2012; Zhu et al., 2013). Cdkl5 deficiency in primary hippocampal neurons leads to deranged expression of the GluA2 subunit of alpha-amino-3-hydroxy-5-methyl-4-isoxazole propionic acid receptors (GluA2-AMPAR), and it is probable that this prompts an alteration of synaptic functions (Tramarin et al., 2018).

To date, only a few studies have investigated the functional consequences of these changes at the synaptic level (Della Sala et al., 2016; Okuda et al., 2017; Tang et al., 2017). Long-term potentiation (LTP) is the most widely studied form of synaptic plasticity in the mammalian nervous system. It provides a neuronal substrate for learning and memory and is impaired in several models of psychiatric and neurologic disorders. LTP was found to be altered in opposing ways in two brain regions of *Cdkl5* KO mice: it was strongly reduced in the somatosensory cortex (Della Sala et al., 2016) and slightly increased in the hippocampal CA1 region (Okuda et al., 2017). The latter effect appears to be mediated by upregulation of GluN2B-containing NMDA receptors (Okuda et al., 2017). Interestingly, the ablation of Cdkl5 expression specifically from forebrain glutamatergic neurons leads to impairment in hippocampal neuronal maturation, synaptic function, and impairment in hippocampal-dependent learning and memory (Tang et al., 2017). Despite this well-documented evidence, knowledge of the molecular substrates underlying CDKL5-related alterations in synaptic plasticity is still limited.

The perirhinal cortex (PRC) is located at the boundary between the medial temporal lobe and the ventral visual pathway. It has several interconnections with a wide range of cortical and subcortical structures and is involved in various cognitive processes. In particular, it plays an essential role in visual recognition memory, that is critical to the ability to record events and to guide prospective behavior (Kealy and Commins, 2011; Suzuki and Naya, 2014; Brown and Banks, 2015). A previous study has shown that male *Cdkl5* KO mice tested in a sociability protocol are more interested than littermate controls in a novel object (Wang et al., 2012). This might suggest that visual recognition memory is not affected by CDKL5 mutation, but a novel object recognition (NOR) test is required to exclude this possibility.

Perirhinal cortex has never been investigated in *Cdkl5* KO mice. Here we provide evidence for LTP impairment, associated with reduced dendritic length, dendritic branches, PSD-95-positive puncta, GluA2-AMPA receptor levels, and spine density and maturation. Data obtained in a four-object NOR indicate that also visual recognition memory is impaired. Notably, most of these alterations, including LTP and visual recognition memory impairments, were rescued by triggering the TrKB/PLCγ1 pathway using the 7,8-DHF prodrug R13.

MATERIALS AND METHODS

Colony

The mice were produced by crossing *Cdkl5* KO +/− females with *Cdkl5* KO Y/− males (Amendola et al., 2014). Littermate controls were used for all experiments. Animals were karyotyped using PCR on genomic DNA as previously described (Amendola et al., 2014). The day of birth was designated as postnatal day (P) zero and animals with 24 h of age were considered as 1-day-old animals (P1). Mice were housed three to five per cage on a 12-h light/dark cycle in a temperature-controlled environment with food and water provided *ad libitum*. Experiments were performed in accordance with the European Communities Council Directive of 24 November 1986 (86/609/EEC) for the use of experimental animals, and were approved by the Italian Ministry of Public Health (approval n 114/2018-PR). All efforts were made to minimize animal suffering and to keep the number of animals used to a minimum.

Experimental Protocol

Experiments were carried out on a total of 85 *Cdkl5* −/Y and 70 *Cdkl5* +/Y mice. Treated *Cdkl5* −/Y and *Cdkl5* +/Y mice received a daily intraperitoneal injection (at 9–10 am) of R13 (7,8-DHF prodrug (Chen et al., 2018), 5.0 mg/kg in vehicle: PBS with 1% DMSO) or vehicle from P35 to P50. The dosage of 5.0 mg/kg R13 (7,8-DHF) was chosen on the basis of previous *in vivo* studies (Jang et al., 2010; Liu et al., 2010; Andero et al., 2011, 2012; Devi and Ohno, 2012), which demonstrated central TrkB activation enhanced neurogenesis and related behavioral changes in rodents treated with systemic 7,8-DHF administration. Intraperitoneal administration was chosen since prolonged oral gavage administration was stressful and harmful for *Cdkl5* KO mice. At the end of the treatment, (P50) mice were sacrificed for electrophysiological or histological analyses or behavioral testing.

Electrophysiology

Preparation of horizontal brain slices (400 μm-thick, including the PRC, the entorhinal cortex and the hippocampus), electrophysiological recording of evoked field excitatory postsynaptic potentials (fEPSP), measurements of fEPSP amplitude and calculation of paired-pulse ratio (PPR) were performed as previously reported (Ziakopoulos et al., 1999; Aicardi et al., 2004; Roncacé et al., 2017) and are described in detail in the online **Supplementary Data.** Theta burst stimulation (TBS; four trains every 15 s, each train comprising 10 bursts of 5 pulses at 100 Hz, inter-burst interval 150 ms) (Ziakopoulos et al., 1999) was used to induce LTP. Synaptic plasticity was further investigated by delivering four consecutive TBS stimulations at 15-min intervals (Weng et al., 2011).

Immunohistochemistry

Some animals were deeply anesthetized and transcardially perfused with ice cold phosphate-buffered saline (PBS, 100 mM, pH 7.4), followed by a 4% solution of paraformaldehyde in PBS. The right hemisphere was cut with a freezing microtome into 30 μm-thick coronal sections.

Synaptic Terminals

One out of four sections (3–6 per mouse) of the PRC was used for immunohistochemistry. Free-floating sections were stained overnight at 4°C with the primary antibodies post-synaptic density protein 95 (1:1000, anti-PSD-95 rabbit polyclonal Ab, Abcam, Cambridge, United Kingdom) or glutamate vesicular transporter 1 (1:500, anti-VGlut1 rabbit polyclonal Ab, Thermo Scientific), and then stained in fluorescent secondary antibody (Cy3-conjugated anti-rabbit secondary antibody 1:200; Jackson ImmunoResearch Laboratories Inc., West Grove, PA, United States) for 2 h at room temperature. For quantification of synaptic puncta, images immunoprocessed for PSD-95 and VGlut1 were acquired with a Leica TCS SL confocal microscope. In each section four images from the PRC were captured and the density of individual puncta exhibiting VGlut1 or PSD-95 immunoreactivity was evaluated as previously described (Guidi et al., 2013).

P-PLCγ1 Intensity

Horizontal brain slices were cut from both hemispheres, and LTP was induced in the PRC by TBS as described above and in online **Supplementary Data** (Electrophysiology). Ten minutes after TBS, the slices were fixed in a 4% solution of paraformaldehyde in PBS, then cryoprotected in 15–20% sucrose. Brain slices were cut using a freezing microtome into 30 μm-thick transversal sections. Free-floating sections were stained overnight at 4°C with the primary antibodies P-PLCγ1 (1:500, anti-P-PLCγ (Y783) rabbit polyclonal Ab, Cell Signaling Technology, Danvers, MA, United States), and then stained in fluorescent secondary antibody (Cy3-conjugated anti-rabbit secondary antibody 1:200; Jackson ImmunoResearch Laboratories, Inc., West Grove, PA, United States) for 2 h at room temperature. Nuclei were counterstained with Hoechst-33342 (Sigma-Aldrich) and fluorescence images were acquired at the same intensity. To assess P-PLCγ1 cytoplasmic intensity a cytoplasmic area was traced and the Cy3-staining corresponding to the P-PLCγ1 signal was quantified by determining the mean intensity of positive (bright) pixels inside this area. The intensity of the cytoplasmic signal was normalized to the background outside the same cell by calculating the ratio between the intensity of cytoplasmic versus extra cellular signal.

Golgi Staining

Golgi staining, measurement of the dendritic tree, and dendritic spine analysis and calculation were performed as previously reported (Guidi et al., 2013; Risher et al., 2014), and are described in detail in the online **Supplementary Data**.

Western Blotting

In order to obtain samples of the PRC in isolation, it was micro-dissected from slices (400 μm-thick) taken at the same levels as those used for electrophysiological recording. In homogenates of the PRC of P50 mice, total proteins were obtained as previously described (Trazzi et al., 2011) and the antibodies used are listed in **Supplementary Table**. For TrkB, PLCγ1, and Erk phosphorylation levels, membranes were probed with the antibody for the phosphorylated form of the analyzed protein, stripped with the Restore^{TM} Stripping Buffer (Thermo Fisher Scientific) following manufacturer's instructions, and then re-probed with the antibody for the un-phosphorylated form of the same protein. Densitometric analysis of digitized images was carried out with ChemiDoc XRS Imaging Systems and Image LabTM Software (Bio-Rad Laboratories, Hercules, CA, United States).

Behavioral Testing

The animal behavioral test was performed by operators blind to genotype and treatment. Mice were allowed to habituate to the testing room for at least 1 h before the test, and testing was always performed at the same time of day. The test was performed in an open field-arena (50 × 50 cm) and the behavior of the mice was monitored using a video camera placed above the center of the arena. The experiments were scored using EthoVision XT ver. 14 software (Noldus, Netherlands). Test chambers were cleaned with 70% ethanol between test subjects.

Pretraining Habituation

The animals were habituated in the open field arena without stimuli for 2 days before the commencement of the behavioral testing. Each animal was placed in the center of the arena and allowed to freely explore the open field for 20 min.

Novel Object Preference Task

The procedure involved a familiarization phase, followed by a preference test phase (**Supplementary Figure 1A**). In the familiarization phase (10 min duration), each animal was placed in the same arena (of the pre-training habituation), in which four copies of the same object (a plastic tube, too heavy for the animal to displace; objects 1–4) were located near the four corners of the arena (15 cm from each adjacent wall). After 1 h delay, during which one of the four objects (object 1) was replaced by a novel object (a wooden cube; objects 2–4 remained in the same positions), the animal was returned to the arena for the preference test phase (10 min duration; **Supplementary Figure 1A**).

Behavioral Measures

Exploration behavior was defined as the animal directing its nose toward the object at a distance $\leq$ 2 cm or touching it with the nose, while turning around or sitting on the object was not considered as an exploration. Discrimination among the objects was calculated using the Exploratory Preference Index, i.e., the percentage of time spent exploring any of the four objects over the total time spent exploring the four objects (Wang et al., 2007). Therefore, a preference index of above 25% indicates the preference for an object. Data obtained from the 10 min of the test period are presented.

Statistical Analysis

Results are presented as the mean $\pm$ standard error of the mean (SE). Statistical testing was performed using the two-tailed Student's *t*-test or two-way ANOVA with genotype (*Cdkl5* −/Y, *Cdkl5* +/Y) and treatment (R13, vehicle) as factors, followed by Fisher's LSD or the Tukey *post hoc* test. For categorical data, that is, percentages of spines, we used a chi-squared test. A probability level of $p < 0.05$ was considered to be statistically significant.

RESULTS

LTP Is Impaired in the Perirhinal Cortex of *Cdkl5* KO Mice

To evaluate possible differences in PRC functional connectivity between *Cdkl5* −/Y and wild-type (+/Y) mice, we compared fEPSPs evoked in layers II–III of the PRC by stimuli applied in the same layers (**Figure 1A**). Stimulus-response curves (input-output relationships) obtained from *Cdkl5* −/Y slices were not significantly different from those of wild-type mice over a wide range of stimulus intensities (**Figure 1B**). Thus, the basic properties of synaptic function in response to single stimuli appear to be unaltered by *Cdkl5* deletion. This conclusion is strengthened by the observation that the slices from *Cdkl5* −/Y and wild-type (+/Y) mice exhibited a similar relationship between the magnitude of the afferent volley ("non-synaptic" component of the response) and the magnitude of the synaptic response (**Figure 1C**). Also the responses to paired stimuli obtained in slices from *Cdkl5* −/Y mice were not significantly different from those of wild-type mice (**Figure 1D**), suggesting that *Cdkl5* deletion does not affect short-term synaptic plasticity.

To evaluate the possibility that *Cdkl5* deletion may affect long-term synaptic plasticity, we induced LTP in layers II–III of the PRC using TBS, i.e., short trains of 100 Hz pulses delivered at theta (5 Hz) frequency. We found that the magnitude of TBS-induced LTP was significantly smaller in slices from *Cdkl5* −/Y mice (**Figures 2A,B**). **Figure 2B** shows that 55–60 min after TBS the LTP magnitude was 165 $\pm$ 3.1% in slices from wild-type (+/Y) mice, and only 139.0 $\pm$ 1.6% in slices from *Cdkl5* −/Y mice. Further investigation of synaptic plasticity was conducted by delivering four consecutive TBS stimulations at 15-min intervals, in order to reveal possible saturation effects. **Figures 2C,D** show that the four TBS stimulations induced a significantly smaller progressive increase of LTP magnitude in slices from *Cdkl5* −/Y mice compared to slices from wild-type (+/Y) mice, revealing a saturation effect after the second stimulation (+/Y: 151.3 $\pm$ 2.1%, 180.8 $\pm$ 2.5%, 203.7 $\pm$ 3.3% and 221.4 $\pm$ 4.2%; −/Y: 131.7 $\pm$ 1.2%, 150.7 $\pm$ 1.8%, 153.6 $\pm$ 2.3% and 161.5 $\pm$ 3.3% of baseline response; **Figure 2D**).

TrkB/PLCγ1 Signaling Is Impaired in the Perirhinal Cortex of *Cdkl5* KO Mice

A previous study in the PRC has shown that TBS elicits a large increase in brain-derived neurotrophic factor (BDNF) secretion, which is necessary for LTP induction (Aicardi et al., 2004). As shown in **Figure 3A**, BDNF acts on TrkB receptors leading to dimerization and autophosphorylation of tyrosine residues at position Tyr515 and Tyr816. Phosphorylation and recruitment of adaptors at position 515 activate Erk and Akt pathways, which promote survival and growth of neurons and other cells through Ras or GRB-associated binder G1 (GAB1). Phosphorylation at position 816 recruits and activates phospholipase Cγ1 (PLCγ1), which results in the generation of inositol-1,4,5-triphosphate and diacylglycerol, leading to synaptic plasticity and dendritic maturation (Minichiello et al., 2002; Gartner et al., 2006; Minichiello, 2009).

To investigate the molecular mechanisms underlying TBS-induced LTP impairment, we first analyzed the levels of TrkB phosphorylation using Western blot in tissue homogenates isolated from the PRC. *Cdkl5* −/Y mice showed no differences in the P-TrkB(Tyr515) or total TrkB protein levels (**Figures 3B,D**). On the contrary, we found a significantly lower level of P-TrkB(Tyr816) protein in *Cdkl5* −/Y mice compared to wild-type (+/Y) mice (**Figures 3B,D**). No significant differences in BDNF protein level were observed (**Figures 3C,D**), suggesting a specific effect of *Cdkl5* deletion on the autophosphorylation process at position Tyr816 of TrkB, rather than on BDNF availability. We then examined the main downstream effectors of the TrkB pathway. Predictably, we found a significantly lower PLCγ1 phosphorylation in the PRC of *Cdkl5* KO mice in comparison with wild-type mice, whereas no

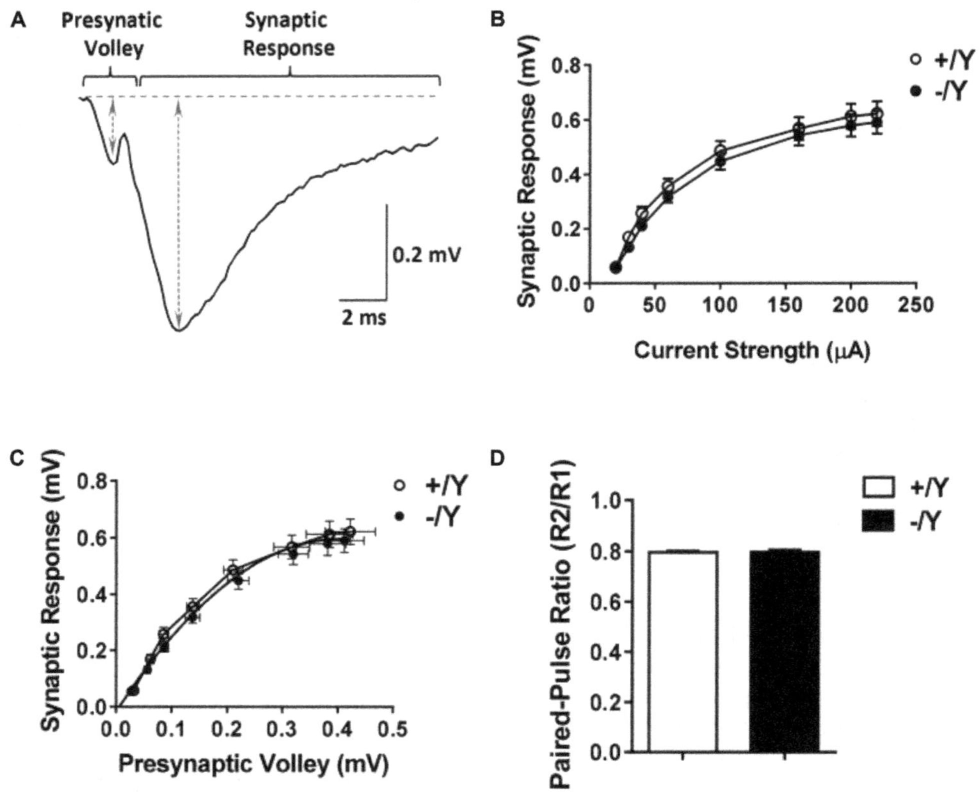

FIGURE 1 | Input-output relations and responses to paired-pulse stimulation in the perirhinal cortex (PRC) of *Cdkl5* +/Y and *Cdkl5* −/Y mice. **(A)** Example of the response evoked in layers II/III of the PRC by stimulation of layers II/III. The double-headed arrows indicate how the magnitude of the presynaptic volley and synaptic response were measured. **(B)** Magnitude of the synaptic response as a function of the stimulus strength in P50 *Cdkl5* +/Y (*n* = 16; 10 animals) and *Cdkl5* −/Y (*n* = 21; 10 animals) mice. **(C)** Magnitude of the synaptic response as a function of the magnitude of the presynaptic volley. **(D)** Ratio of the synaptic responses (R2/R1) evoked by a pair of stimuli with an interpulse interval of 200 ms in P50 *Cdkl5* +/Y (*n* = 11; 9 animals) and *Cdkl5* −/Y (*n* = 9; 9 animals) mice. Values represent mean ± SE.

significant differences in Erk and Akt phosphorylation were observed (**Figures 3C,D**).

Impaired PLCγ1 Phosphorylation and LTP in the Perirhinal Cortex of *Cdkl5* KO Mice Are Rescued by Treatment With the TrkB Agonist R13

In order to investigate whether TrkB/PLCγ1 signaling alteration underlies LTP impairment in *Cdkl5* KO mice, we quantified P-PLCγ1 cellular intensity in PRC slices from *Cdkl5* KO and wild-type mice before and after TBS. **Figures 4A–C** show that 10 min after TBS, PLCγ1 phosphorylation was increased in PRC slices from both *Cdkl5* and wild-type mice. Interestingly, PLCγ1 phosphorylation after TBS was still significantly lower in *Cdkl5* KO slices than in wild-type slices.

In order to investigate the effect of chronic activation of TrkB/PLCγ1 signaling in *Cdkl5* KO mice, we treated *Cdkl5* −/Y mice for 15 days with R13, a prodrug of 7,8-dihydroxyflavone (7,8-DHF) (Chen et al., 2018). 7,8-DHF is a potent molecular TrkB agonist that specifically binds to the TrkB receptor extra cellular domain. A recent study in striatal neurons has shown that it acts through selective phosphorylation of the 816 residue of TrkB, leading to activation of the PLCγ1 pathway (Garcia-Diaz Barriga et al., 2017). Accordingly, we found that R13 treatment increased PLCγ1 phosphorylation levels but not P-Erk levels in both *Cdkl5* and wild-type mice (**Figures 4D,E**), suggesting a selective action of 7,8-DHF on the TrkB(Y816)-PLCγ1 pathway also in the PRC.

Interestingly, R13 treatment restored LTP in *Cdkl5* −/Y mice (**Figures 5A–D**), suggesting a critical role of TrkB/PLCγ1 signaling in the defective synaptic plasticity. R13 treatment affected neither LTP in *Cdkl5* +/Y mice (**Figures 5A–D**) nor basal synaptic transmission (input-output responses; responses to paired stimuli) in *Cdkl5* −/Y and *Cdkl5* +/Y mice (not shown). Vehicle treatment did not affect any functional parameter considered in *Cdkl5* −/Y and *Cdkl5* +/Y mice (**Figures 5A–D**).

Alteration of Dendritic Pattern in the Perirhinal Cortex of *Cdkl5* KO Mice Is Rescued by Treatment With the TrkB Agonist R13

BDNF/TrkB signaling participates in the regulation of dendritic differentiation, and in the formation and maturation of dendritic

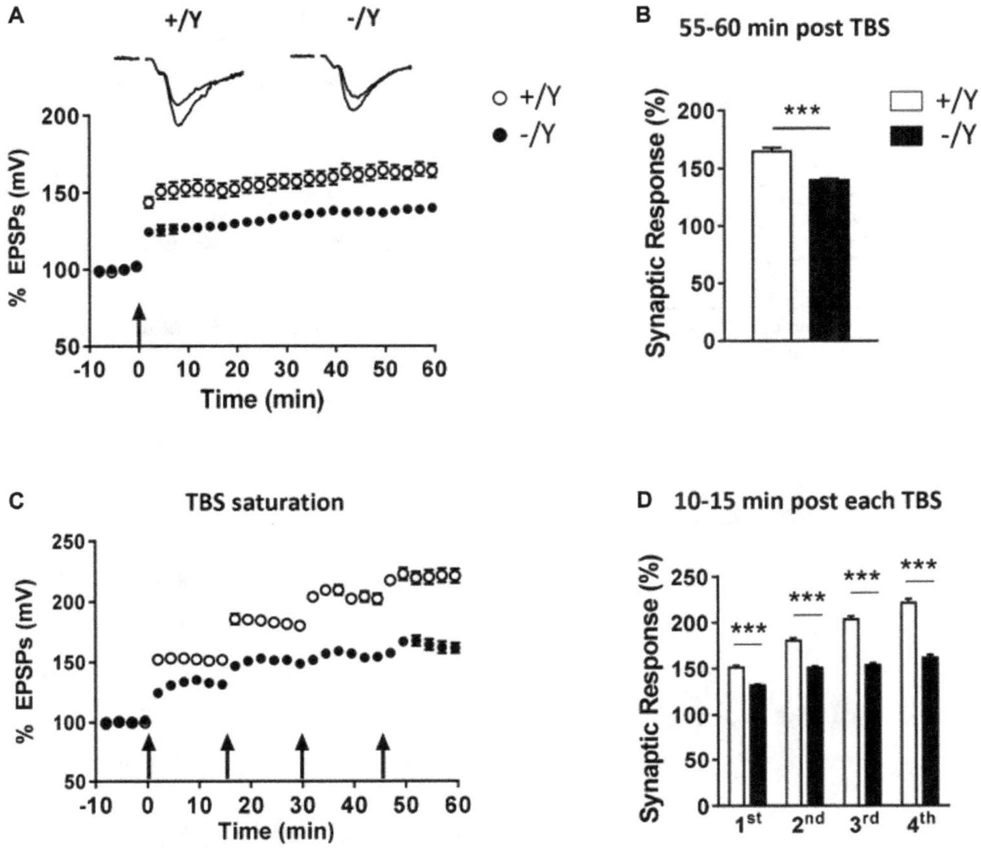

FIGURE 2 | LTP in the perirhinal cortex of *Cdkl5* +/Y and *Cdkl5* −/Y mice. **(A)** Amplitude of the synaptic responses evoked before and after theta burst stimulation (TBS; four trains every 15 s, each train comprising 10 bursts of 5 pulses at 100 Hz, inter-burst interval 150 ms). Here and in the following panels **(B–D)**, the amplitude of the responses is expressed as a percentage of the average amplitude of responses recorded 10 min before LTP induction. Here, and in panel C, the arrows indicate the time of delivery of the TBS. The traces at the top are examples of responses recorded before, and 55–60 min after, LTP induction. **(B)** The histograms indicate the averaged amplitude of the responses recorded 55–60 min after TBS. Same data as in **(A)**. Recordings were carried out in slices from P50 *Cdkl5* +/Y ($n = 9$; 5 animals) and *Cdkl5* −/Y ($n = 11$; 9 animals) mice. **(C)** Amplitude of the synaptic response evoked before and after four consecutive TBS stimulations delivered at 15-min intervals. **(D)** The histograms indicate the averaged amplitude of the responses recorded 10–15 min after each TBS. Same data as in **(C)**. Recordings were carried out in slices from P50 *Cdkl5* +/Y ($n = 7$; 7 animals) and *Cdkl5* −/Y ($n = 7$; 7 animals) mice. ***$p < 0.001$ (Student's two-tailed t-test).

spines during postnatal development (Chapleau et al., 2009). Abnormalities in dendritic and synaptic differentiation are thought to underlie altered synaptic function and network connectivity, thus contributing to the impaired neuronal function. Previous studies in *Cdkl5* −/Y mice have shown a reduction in dendritic pattern in granule cells and CA1 pyramidal neurons of the hippocampal region (Fuchs et al., 2015; Trazzi et al., 2016).

In order to establish whether these alterations also occur in PRC neurons, we examined apical and basal dendritic branches of layer II-III PRC neurons in Golgi-stained brain sections (**Figure 6A**). We found that both basal and apical dendrites were shorter (**Figure 6B**), and there was a reduced number of branches (**Figure 6C**) in PRC neurons of *Cdkl5* −/Y compared to *Cdkl5* +/Y mice. Interestingly, R13 treatment restored dendritic length and number of branches in *Cdkl5* −/Y mice, but had no effect in control mice (+/Y) (**Figures 6B,C**). **Figure 6D** shows that the difference in number of branches was significant in the fourth and fifth order in apical dendrites, and in the second, third, and fourth order in basal dendrites; moreover, it shows a lack of branches of the seventh order in basal dendrites. All these defects were corrected by R13 treatment. These results indicate that activation of the TrkB/PLCγ1 pathway restores the dendritic pattern of the PRC neurons in *Cdkl5* −/Y mice. Vehicle treatment did not affect any morphological parameter considered in *Cdkl5* −/Y and *Cdkl5* +/Y mice (**Figures 6B–D**).

Alteration of Dendritic Spine Density in the Perirhinal Cortex of *Cdkl5* KO Mice Is Rescued by Treatment With the TrkB Agonist R13

In Golgi-stained brain sections we examined spine density in the apical and basal dendritic branches of layer II-III neurons of the PRC. PRC neurons had a reduced spine density in both basal and apical dendrites in untreated *Cdkl5* −/Y mice in comparison with wild-type (+/Y) mice (**Figures 7A,B**). *Cdkl5* −/Y mice treated with R13 underwent a restoration of spine

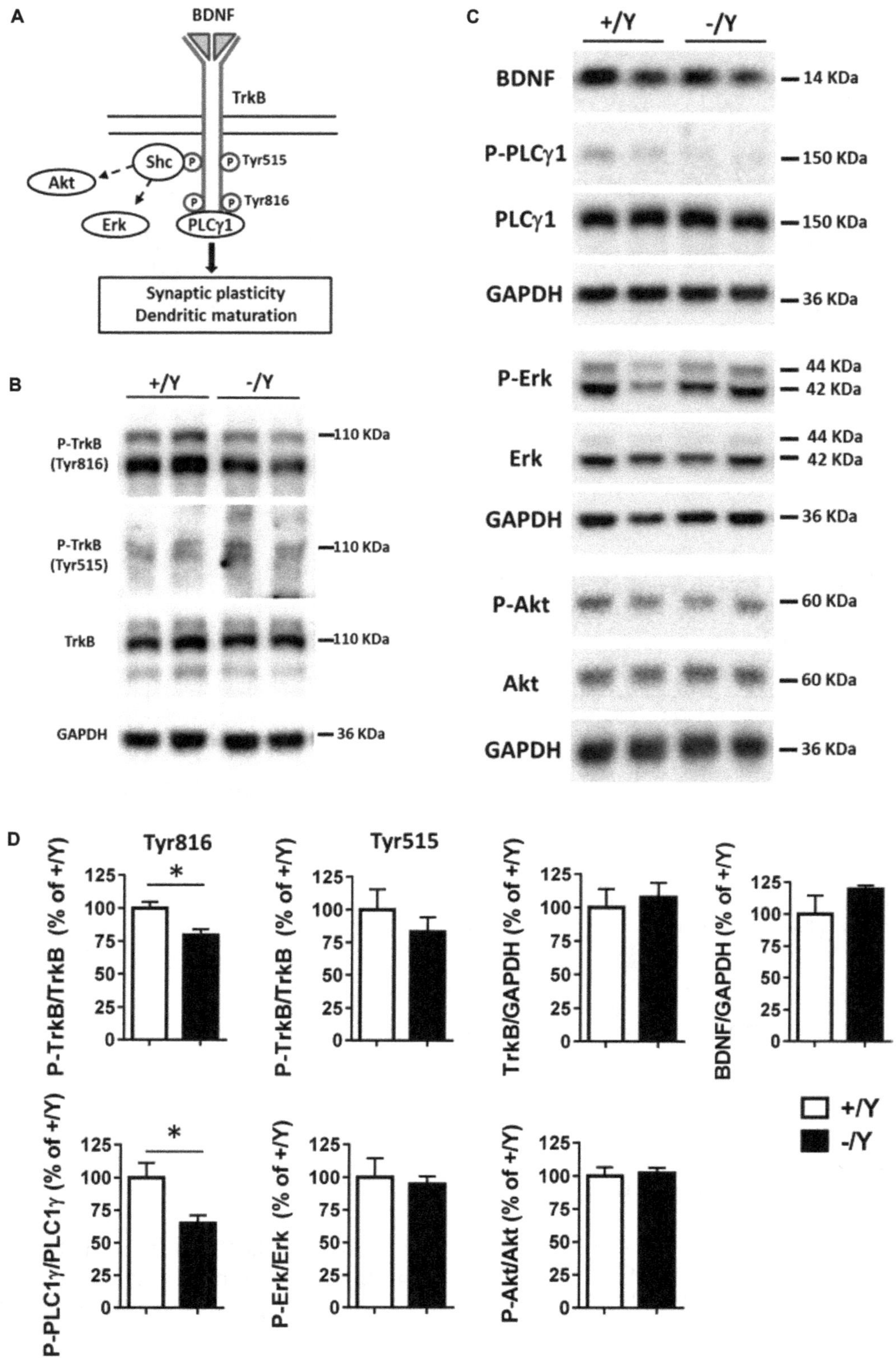

FIGURE 3 | TrkB signaling pathways in the perirhinal cortex of *Cdkl5* +/Y and *Cdkl5* −/Y mice. **(A)** Diagram of brain-derived neurotrophic factor (BDNF) and TrkB signaling pathways. BDNF binds to the extra cellular domain of TrkB forming homodimers to activate downstream intracellular signaling cascades, including Shc/Erk, Shc/Akt, and phospholipase C (PLC) γ1 pathways. **(B)** Western blots examples of P-TrkB (Tyr816 and Tyr515) and TrkB in PRC homogenates of P50 *Cdkl5* +/Y and *Cdkl5* −/Y mice. **(C)** Western blot examples of BDNF, P-PLCγ1 (Tyr783), PLCγ1, P-Erk, Erk, P-Akt (Ser437), Akt and GAPDH levels in PRC homogenates of P50 *Cdkl5* +/Y and *Cdkl5* −/Y mice. **(D)** The histograms show western blot analysis of samples as in B,C. Phosphoprotein levels were normalized to corresponding

(Continued)

FIGURE 3 | Continued
total protein levels, and total protein levels were normalized to GAPDH (*Cdkl5* +/Y *n* = 5; *Cdkl5* +/Y *n* = 5). Data are expressed as % of those obtained in *Cdkl5* +/Y mice. Values represent mean ± SE. **p* < 0.05 (Student's two-tailed *t*-test).

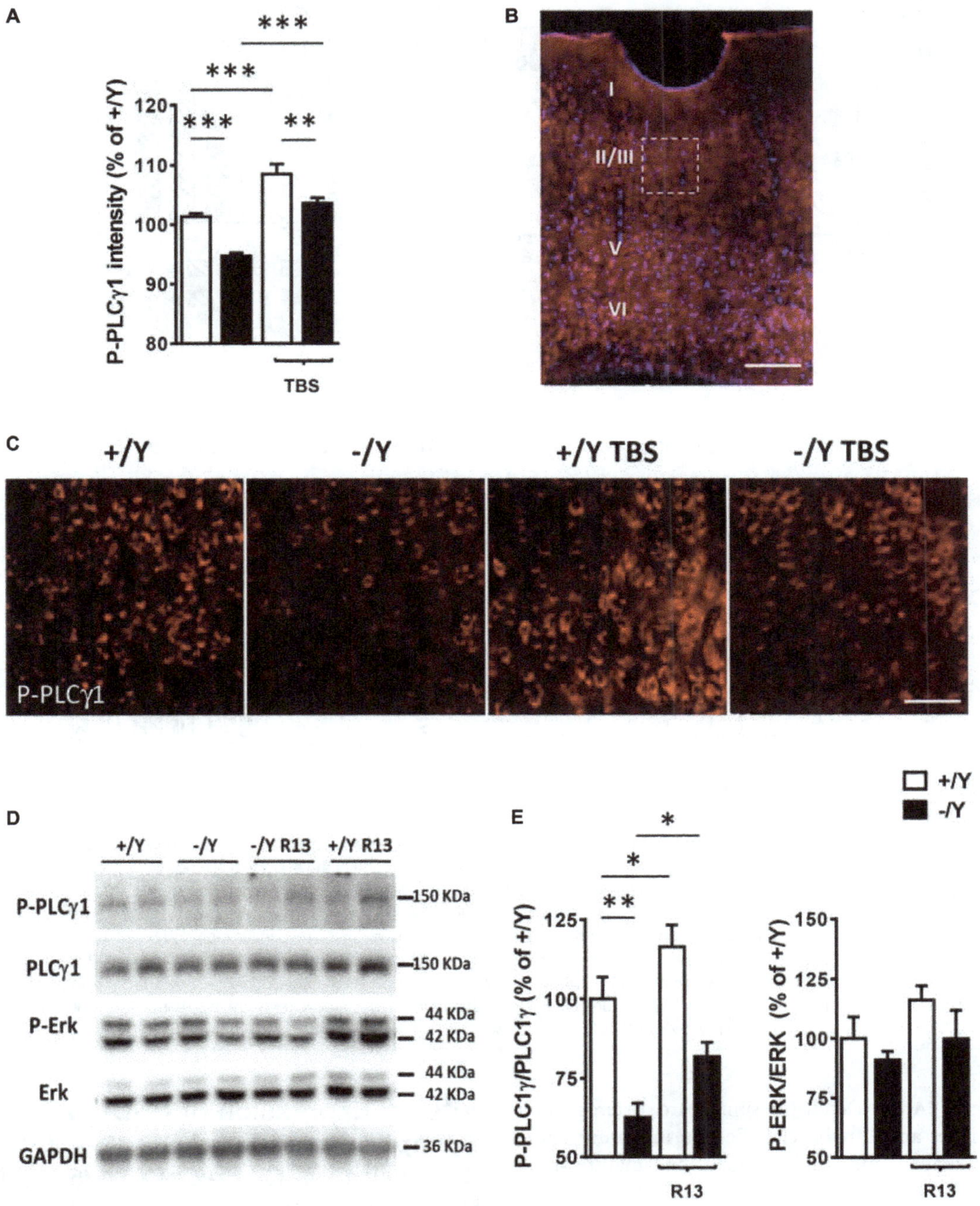

FIGURE 4 | Effect of TBS or treatment with R13 on TrkB/ PLCγ1 signaling in the perirhinal cortex of *Cdkl5* −/Y mice. **(A)** Quantification of P-PLCγ1 signal intensity in PRC slices before and after theta burst stimulation (TBS; four trains every 15 s, each train comprising 10 bursts of 5 pulses at 100 Hz, inter-burst interval 150 ms) of *Cdkl5* +/Y (*n* = 4) and *Cdkl5* −/Y (*n* = 4) mice. **(B)** A representative image of PRC processed for fluorescent P-PLCγ1 immunostaining (red) of a wild-type (+/Y) mouse. Nuclei are stained with Hoechst (blue). The dotted box indicates the region shown at a higher magnification in **(C)**. Scale bar = 50 μm. Roman numerals indicate PRC cytoarchitectonic layers. **(C)** Representative images of layer II-III PRC neurons of *Cdkl5* +/Y and *Cdkl5* −/Y PRC slices as in **(A)**. **(D,E)** Quantification of PLCγ1 and Erk phosphorylation levels before and after treatment with R13. *Cdkl5* −/Y and *Cdkl5* +/Y mice were treated for 15 days (5 mg/Kg IP) from postnatal day 35 (P35) to 50 (P50), the day of sacrifice. Western blot examples **(D)** and analyses **(E)** of P-PLCγ1 (Tyr783), PLCγ1, P-Erk and Erk levels in PRC homogenates of vehicle-treated *Cdkl5* +/Y (*n* = 5) and *Cdkl5* −/Y (*n* = 5) mice, and R13-treated *Cdkl5* +/Y (*n* = 6) and *Cdkl5* −/Y (*n* = 6) mice. Values represent mean ± SE. **p* < 0.05; ***p* < 0.01; ****p* < 0.001 (Fisher's LSD test after two-way ANOVA).

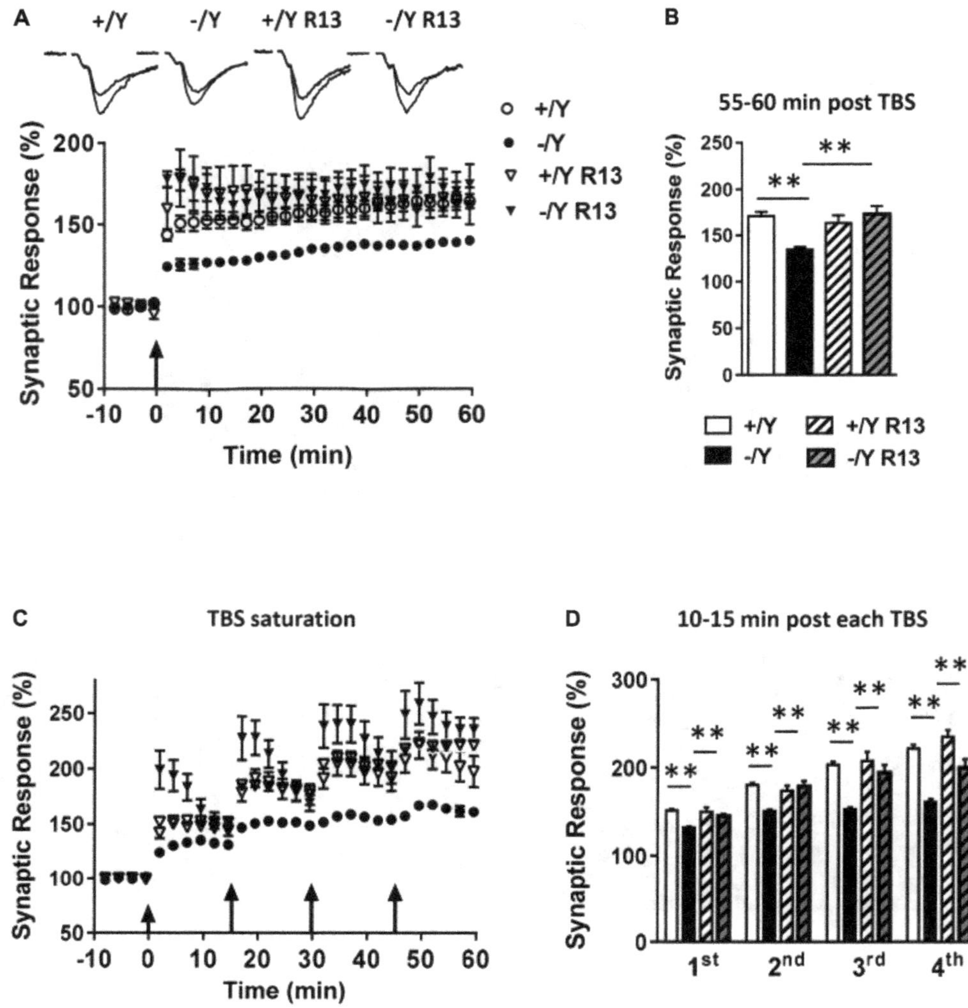

FIGURE 5 | Effect of treatment with R13 on LTP in the perirhinal cortex of *Cdkl5* −/Y mice. **(A)** Amplitude of the synaptic responses evoked before and after TBS. Here, and in the following panels **(B–D)**, the amplitude of the responses is expressed as a percentage of the average amplitude of responses recorded 10 min before TBS. The traces at the top are examples of responses recorded before, and 55–60 min after, TBS. Here, and in panel C, the arrows indicate the time of TBS delivery. Recordings were carried out in slices from P50 vehicle-treated *Cdkl5* +/Y (n = 13; 7 animals) and *Cdkl5* −/Y (n = 13; 6 animals), and R13-treated *Cdkl5* +/Y (n = 6; 4 animals) and *Cdkl5* −/Y (n = 7; 7 animals) mice. **(B)** The histograms indicate the averaged amplitude of the responses recorded 55–60 min after TBS. Same data as in **(A)**. **(C)** Amplitude of the synaptic responses evoked before and after four consecutive TBS stimulations delivered at 15-min intervals. Recordings were carried out in slices from P50 vehicle-treated *Cdkl5* +/Y (n = 6; 6 animals) and *Cdkl5* −/Y (n = 7; 7 animals), and R13-treated *Cdkl5* +/Y (n = 7; 4 animals) and *Cdkl5* −/Y (n = 6; 6 animals) mice. **(D)** The histograms indicate the averaged amplitude of the responses recorded 10–15 min after each TBS. Same data as in **(C)**. Values represent mean ± SE. *$p < 0.05$; **$p < 0.01$ (Tukey test after two-way ANOVA).

density (**Figures 7A,B**). Dendritic spines are heterogeneous in size and shape, and can be classified as immature spines (filopodia, thin-shaped, and stubby-shaped) and mature spines (mushroom and cup shapes) (Risher et al., 2014). Separate counts of different classes of dendritic spines revealed that PRC neurons of *Cdkl5* −/Y mice had a higher percentage of immature spines and a reduced percentage of mature spines compared to *Cdkl5* +/Y mice (**Figure 7C**). Treatment with R13 improved the balance between immature and mature spines (**Figure 7C**), suggesting that activation of the TrkB/PLCγ1 pathway improves PRC dendritic spine maturation. Vehicle treatment did not affect spine density in *Cdkl5* −/Y and *Cdkl5* +/Y mice (**Figures 7A,B**).

Altered Expression of PSD-95 Positive Synaptic Puncta and GluA2-AMPAR in the Perirhinal Cortex of *Cdkl5* KO Mice Is Rescued by Treatment With the TrkB Agonist R13

Most excitatory synapses in the mature mammalian brain occur on spines in which postsynaptic density protein 95 (PSD-95) clusters are localized. Evaluation of PSD-95 immunoreactivity showed a strong reduction in the number of PSD-95-positive puncta in the PRC of *Cdkl5* −/Y mice (**Figures 8A,B**), which is consistent with the reduced number of mature spines (**Figure 7C**) and suggests loss of excitatory synaptic contacts. To clarify

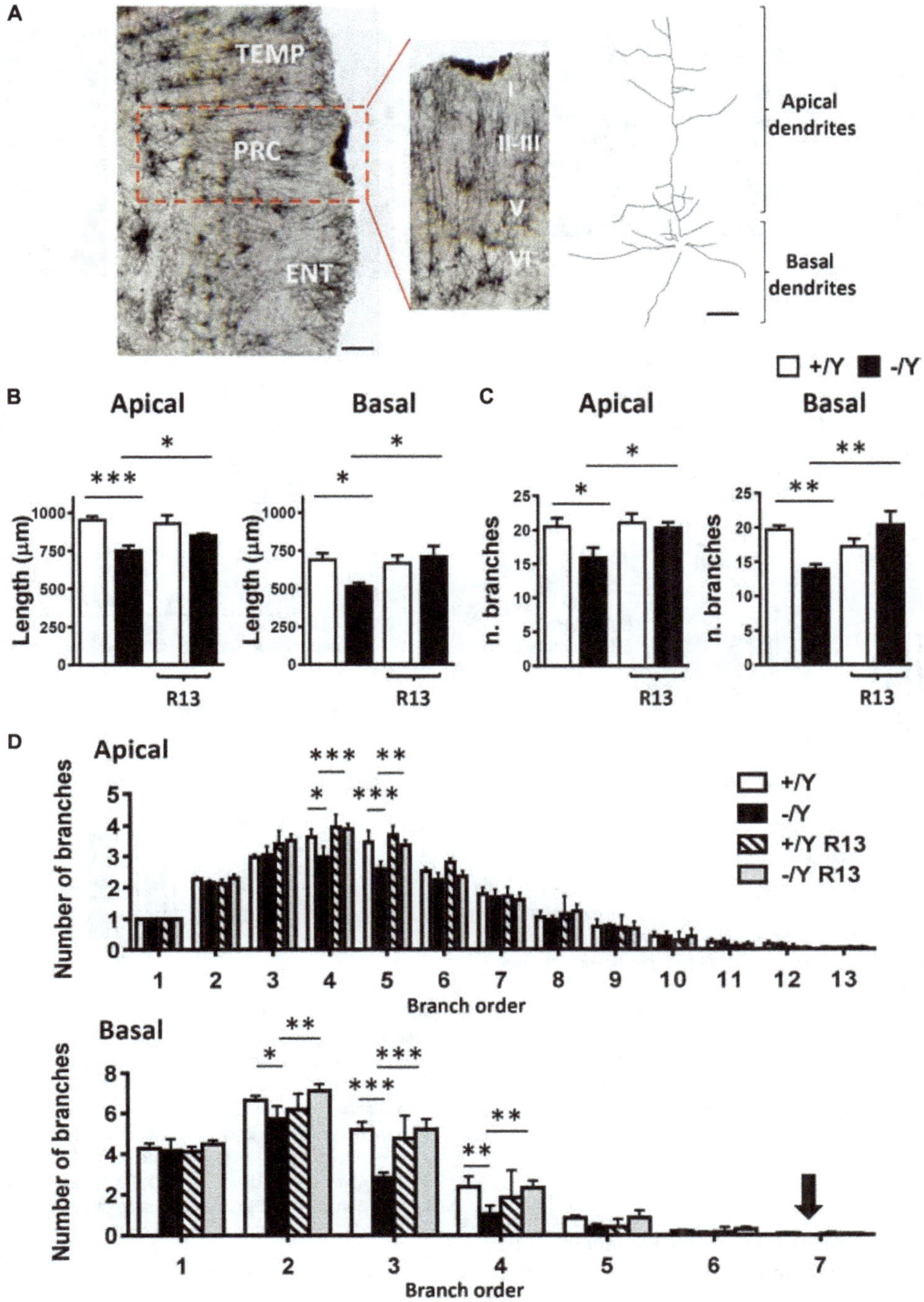

FIGURE 6 | Effect of treatment with R13 on dendritic morphology in the perirhinal cortex of *Cdkl5* −/Y mice. **(A)** Example of Golgi-stained section at the level of the PRC of a P50 *Cdkl5* −/Y mouse (panel on the left; scale bar = 100 μm). The central panel shows a higher magnification of the area enclosed in the red square. Roman numerals indicate PRC cytoarchitectonic layers. The panel on the right shows an example of the apical and basal dendritic tree of a Golgi-stained PRC neuron from layers II-III (scale bar = 30 μm). **(B)** Apical and basal mean total dendritic length of layer II-III PRC neurons of vehicle-treated P50 *Cdkl5* +/Y ($n = 4$) and *Cdkl5* −/Y ($n = 4$) mice, and R13-treated P50 *Cdkl5* +/Y ($n = 4$) and *Cdkl5* −/Y ($n = 5$) mice. **(C)** Mean number of dendritic segments of the apical and basal dendrites of layer II-III PRC neurons in the same mice as in **(B)**. **(D)** Mean number of apical and basal branches of the different orders of vehicle-treated *Cdkl5* +/Y ($n = 4$) and *Cdkl5* −/Y ($n = 4$) mice, and R13-treated *Cdkl5* −/Y ($n = 5$) mice. The numbers on the X axis indicate the branch order. The arrow indicates the absence of branches in *Cdkl5* −/Y mice. Values in **(B–D)** represent mean ± SE. *$p < 0.05$; **$p < 0.01$; ***$p < 0.001$ (Fisher's LSD test after two-way ANOVA).

this issue, we examined the immunoreactivity for the vesicular glutamate transporter-1 (VGlut1), a marker of glutamatergic (excitatory) terminals. We found no difference in the number of VGlut1-positive immunoreactive puncta between *Cdkl5* −/Y and wild-type mice (**Figures 8A,C**), indicating a similar number of glutamatergic terminals in the PRC. Treatment with R13 restored

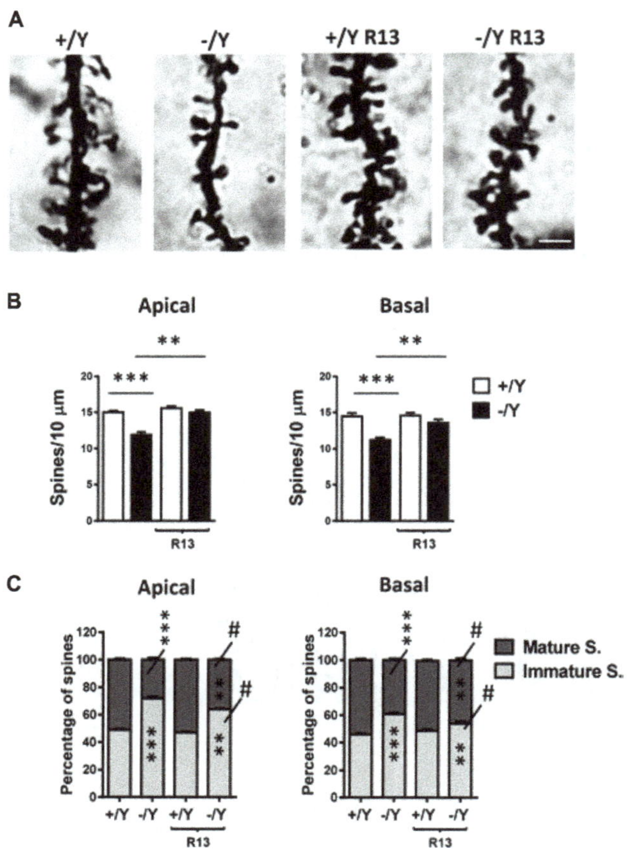

FIGURE 7 | Effect of treatment with R13 on dendritic spines in the perirhinal cortex of *Cdkl5* −/Y mice. **(A)** Images of Golgi-stained dendritic branches of layer II-III perirhinal neurons of a P50 *Cdkl5* +/Y and a *Cdkl5* −/Y mouse, and of a *Cdkl5* −/Y mouse treated with R13. Scale bar = 1.5 μm. **(B)** Dendritic spine density (number of spines per 10 μm) in apical and basal dendrites from vehicle-treated *Cdkl5* +/Y ($n = 4$) and *Cdkl5* −/Y ($n = 4$) mice, and *Cdkl5* +/Y ($n = 4$) and *Cdkl5* −/Y ($n = 4$) mice treated with R13. **(C)** Percentage of immature and mature spines in relation to the total number of protrusions of layer II-III perirhinal neurons in mice as in **(B)**. Values represent mean ± SE. $^{**}P < 0.01$; $^{***}P < 0.001$; $^{\#}p < 0.01$ compared to untreated *Cdkl5* −/Y mice in **(C)** [data in **(B)** Fisher's LSD test after two-way ANOVA; data in **(C)** Chi-squared test].

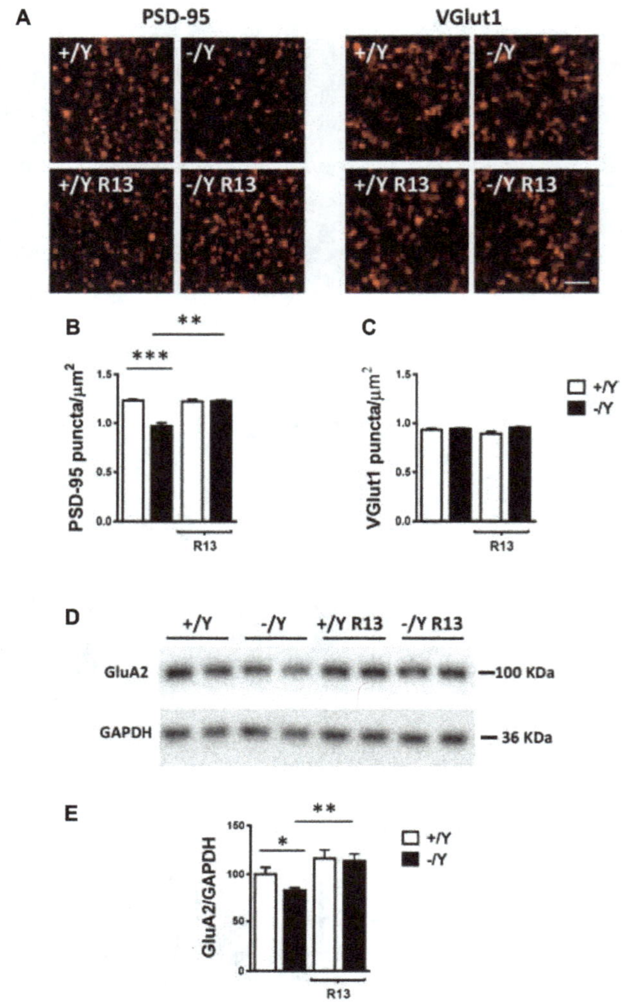

FIGURE 8 | Effect of treatment with R13 on neuronal connectivity in the perirhinal cortex of *Cdkl5* −/Y mice. **(A)** Representative fluorescence image of a PRC section processed for PSD-95 or VGlut1 immunoreactivity, showing examples of PSD-95 and VGlut1 immunoreactive puncta. Scale bar: 3 μm. **(B,C)** Number of fluorescent puncta per μm^2 exhibiting PSD-95 **(B)** or VGlut1 **(C)** immunoreactivity in layers II-III of the PRC of vehicle-treated P50 *Cdkl5* +/Y ($n = 4$) and *Cdkl5* −/Y ($n = 4$) mice, and P50 *Cdkl5* +/Y ($n = 4$) and *Cdkl5* −/Y ($n = 4$) mice treated with R13. **(D,E)** Western blot analysis of GluA2-AMPA levels in PRC homogenates of vehicle-treated P50 *Cdkl5* +/Y ($n = 6$) and *Cdkl5* −/Y ($n = 6$) mice and R13-treated P50 *Cdkl5* −/Y ($n = 5$) mice. Values represent mean ± SE. $^{*}p < 0.05$; $^{**}p < 0.01$; $^{***}p < 0.001$ (data in **(B,C)** Fisher's LSD test after two-way ANOVA; data in **(E)** Student's two-tailed *t*-test).

the number of PSD-95-positive immunoreactive puncta in *Cdkl5* −/Y mice, but did not affect immunoreactivity for PSD-95 in *Cdkl5* +/Y mice (**Figures 8A,B**) or for VGlut1 in *Cdkl5* +/Y and *Cdkl5* −/Y mice (**Figures 8A,C**). Vehicle treatment did not affect immunoreactivity for PSD-95 or VGlut1 in *Cdkl5* +/Y and *Cdkl5* −/Y mice (**Figures 8A,C**).

The TrkB/PLCγ1 pathway is involved in diverse postsynaptic events, such as the modulation of AMPAR expression and trafficking, which in turn contributes to synaptic plasticity (Jang et al., 2013). As previously observed in hippocampal neurons (Tramarin et al., 2018), we found a lower expression of GluA2-AMPAR in the PRC of *Cdkl5* −/Y mice in comparison with wild-type mice (**Figures 8D,E**). Notably, GluA2-AMPAR levels in *Cdkl5* −/Y mice were rescued by treatment with R13 (**Figures 8D,E**).

Altered Visual Recognition Memory in *Cdkl5* KO Mice Is Rescued by Treatment With the TrkB Agonist R13

In the rodent brain, PRC plays an essential role in visual object recognition memory, that can be evaluated using the NOR test. A 4-object NOR test was performed in an open-field arena, preceded by a 2-day habituation phase (**Supplementary Figure 1A**). During the familiarization phase, animals normally show equal preference for the objects that are placed in an arena, while they exhibit a higher preference for the new object during the subsequent test phase. Discrimination among the objects (Preference Index) was calculated by taking into account the percentage of time spent exploring any of the four objects over the total time spent exploring the objects. As expected, the preference index in wild-type (+/Y) mice was significantly larger for the novel object during the test phase (**Figures 9A,B**). However, we did not observe any increase in preference index in *Cdkl5* −/Y mice (**Figure 9B**), indicating a deficit in remembering the identity of an object in an open field. Interestingly, treatment with R13 rescued visual recognition memory in *Cdkl5* −/Y mice (**Figure 9B**). R13 treatment did not affect locomotor activity in *Cdkl5* −/Y or *Cdkl5* +/Y mice (**Supplementary Figure 1B**); nor was it able to further increase the preference index in *Cdkl5*+/Y mice (**Figure 9B**).

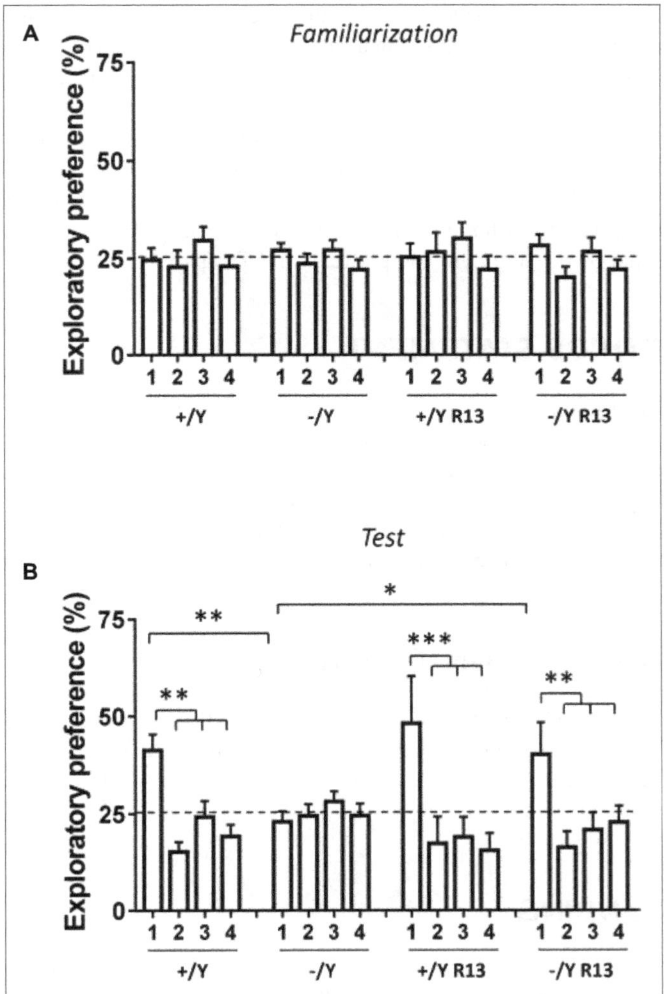

FIGURE 9 | Effect of treatment with R13 on novel object recognition memory in *Cdkl5* -/Y mice. **(A)** Familiarization phase. Percentage of time spent exploring the four identical objects during the familiarization phase (10 min duration) of vehicle-treated *Cdkl5* −/Y (*n* = 13) and *Cdkl5* +/Y (*n* = 13) mice, and R13-treated *Cdkl5* −/Y (*n* = 9) and *Cdkl5* +/Y (*n* = 9) mice.
(B) Exploratory Preference Test phase (one hour after the familiarization phase, 10 min duration). Percentage of time spent exploring new object 1 (that replaced the previous object 1) and the previous identical objects 2–4. Same mice as in **(A)**. Values represent mean ± SE. *$p < 0.05$; **$p < 0.01$; ***$p < 0.001$ (Fisher's LSD test after two-way ANOVA).

DISCUSSION

Functional and Morphological Impairments in the Perirhinal Cortex of *Cdkl5* KO Mice

Our results indicate that the magnitude of LTP is reduced in the PRC of *Cdkl5* KO mice, consistently with the strong reduction previously observed in the somatosensory cortex (Della Sala et al., 2016). To investigate the molecular mechanisms underlying LTP reduction, we analyzed some elements of the signaling cascade activated by BDNF. Previous studies in the hippocampus have shown that the PLCγ1 pathway mediated by TrkB plays a predominant role in LTP (Minichiello et al., 2002), whereas the Erk/Akt pathway is of lesser, if of any, importance (Korte et al., 2000). Accordingly, we found a lower PLCγ1 phosphorylation in the PRC of *Cdkl5* KO mice in comparison with wild-type mice, and no significant differences in Erk and Akt phosphorylation. This evidence suggests that the TrkB/PLCγ1 pathway plays a critical role in the observed alteration of LTP in the PRC.

Brain-derived neurotrophic factor levels were not reduced in *Cdkl5* KO mice, suggesting a specific effect of *Cdkl5* deletion on the autophosphorylation process at position Tyr816, rather than on BDNF availability.

At variance with the results obtained in the PRC (present data) and somatosensory cortex (Della Sala et al., 2016), LTP was previously found to be slightly increased in the hippocampal CA1 region of *Cdkl5* KO mice (Okuda et al., 2017), suggesting that CDKL5 action might be region-specific. These conflicting results might also be explained, at least in part, by different sensitivity to LTP inducing protocols, TBS [present data, and (Della Sala et al., 2016)] versus HFS (Okuda et al., 2017).

Previous studies in *Cdkl5* KO mice have shown reduced neuronal branching accompanied by reduced spine density and maturation in the hippocampus, in the visual cortex, and in the somatosensory cortex (Amendola et al., 2014; Fuchs et al., 2014; Della Sala et al., 2016; Pizzo et al., 2016; Trazzi et al., 2016). Accordingly, we found that PRC neurons of *Cdkl5* KO mice are characterized by a shorter dendritic length, a reduced number of branches, a lower spine density and a higher percentage of immature spines. Moreover, we observed a reduced number of PSD-95 immunoreactive puncta in dendritic spines. Since PSD-95 localization in the spine correlates with activity-driven synapse stabilization (Ehrlich et al., 2007), the decreased number of PSD-95 puncta in *Cdkl5* KO mice correlates with the observed increased number of immature spines. Evaluation of the number of presynaptic excitatory terminals (VGlut1 immunopositive puncta) showed no difference between *Cdkl5* KO and wild-type mice, in accordance with the observation that basic properties of synaptic function are unaltered in the PRC (present data) and in the hippocampus (Okuda et al., 2017). As observed in hippocampal neurons (Tramarin et al., 2018), we found a lower expression of GluA2-AMPAR in the PRC of *Cdkl5* −/Y mice. Most neuronal AMPARs contain this critical subunit, but in certain restricted neuronal populations and under certain physiological or pathological conditions, AMPARs that lack this subunit are expressed. This subunit determines many of the major biophysical properties of AMPARs (including Ca^{2+} permeability, single-channel conductance, and receptor kinetics), strongly influences receptor assembly and trafficking, and plays pivotal roles in various forms of synaptic plasticity (Isaac et al., 2007). In particular, GluA2-AMPAR is required for spine changes during synaptic plasticity (Asrar and Jia, 2013). Thus, it is reasonable to suppose that the lower expression of GluA2-AMPAR in the PRC might play a role in the impaired functional and morphological synaptic plasticity observed in the PRC of *Cdkl5* −/Y mice.

Visual recognition memory is the ability to judge the prior occurrence of stimuli and is fundamental to our ability to record events and to guide prospective behavior. Studies in humans and animals indicate that PRC plays an essential role in recognition memory and familiarity discrimination for individual items (Kealy and Commins, 2011; Suzuki and Naya, 2014; Brown and Banks, 2015). Our finding that short-term object recognition memory is impaired in *Cdkl5* KO mice is in line with the observed neuroanatomical defects and LTP impairment in the PRC. This behavioral evidence suggests that specific PRC defects may contribute, along with hippocampal impairments, to poor memory performance in individuals with CDD.

Treatment With the TrkB Agonist R13 Rescues Functional and Morphological Impairments in the Perirhinal Cortex of *Cdkl5* KO Mice

The natural flavonoid 7,8-DHF, a potent small molecular TrkB agonist, displays beneficial effects on the brain in health and disease (Spencer, 2008; Williams and Spencer, 2012; Roncacé et al., 2017), but has only modest oral bioavailability and a moderate pharmacokinetic profile. To efficiently mimic the actions of BDNF, we used the recently synthesized 7,8-DHF prodrug R13, which is hydrolyzed into 7,8-DHF in liver microsomes and is characterized by a longer half-life and a higher plasma concentration, and higher brain exposure (Chen et al., 2018). We found that treatment with R13 activated TrkB/PLCγ1 signaling, rescued the impaired TBS-induced LTP, restored dendritic pattern as well as PSD-95 and GluA2-AMPAR levels, and improved the balance between immature and mature spines in PRC neurons of *Cdkl5* KO mice. Importantly, restoration of morphological and synaptic impairments leaded to recovery of PRC-dependent visual recognition memory in *Cdkl5* KO mice.

In wild type +/Y mice, treatment with R13 caused an activation of TrkB/PLCγ1 signaling in the PRC (**Figure 4D**), which, however, did not induce effects on PRC neuroanatomy or synaptic function and, consequently, on behavior. The finding that treatment with R13 has relatively scarce or no effects in normal animals is in line with a previous evidence (Garcia-Diaz Barriga et al., 2017) and suggests that TrkB/PLCγ1 signaling activation may help brain development under abnormal, but not normal, brain conditions.

Indeed, an increasing body of evidence suggests that PLCγ1 plays a pivotal role in the regulation of synaptic plasticity and maturation; in particular, PLCγ1 signaling is required for structural and functional changes in spine actin, PSD scaffolding, and AMPAR trafficking (Horne and Dell'Acqua, 2007). Consistent with its critical role, abnormal expression and activation of PLCγ1 has been observed in various brain disorders (Jang et al., 2013).

CONCLUSION

In conclusion, present results provide the first evidence for morphological and functional impairments in the PRC of *Cdkl5* KO mice, associated with a deficit in visual recognition memory. The TrkB agonist R13 rescued most of these alterations, including LTP and visual recognition memory impairments, by triggering the TrkB/PLCγ1 pathway. If R13 induced a widespread positive effect in other brain areas, it might represent a promising candidate for a targeted therapeutic strategy aimed at restoring synaptic development and plasticity in CDD patients.

ETHICS STATEMENT

Experiments were performed in accordance with the European Communities Council Directive of 24 November 1986 (86/609/EEC) for the use of experimental animals, and were approved by the Italian Ministry of Public Health (approval in 114/2018-PR). All efforts were made to minimize animal suffering and to keep the number of animals used to a minimum.

AUTHOR CONTRIBUTIONS

EC, GA, ST, and VR designed the study. ER, VR, ST, CF, GM, LG, ML, and GG performed the experiments. ER, VR, ST, and RR analyzed the data. KY executed the R13 synthesis. EC and GA wrote the manuscript.

FUNDING

This work was supported by the Telethon Foundation (Grant No. GGP15098 to EC) and by the Italian parent association "CDKL5 insieme verso la cura."

REFERENCES

Aicardi, G., Argilli, E., Cappello, S., Santi, S., Riccio, M., Thoenen, H., et al. (2004). Induction of long-term potentiation and depression is reflected by corresponding changes in secretion of endogenous brain-derived neurotrophic factor. *Proc. Natl. Acad. Sci. U.S.A.* 101, 15788–15792. doi: 10.1073/pnas.0406960101

Amendola, E., Zhan, Y., Mattucci, C., Castroflorio, E., Calcagno, E., Fuchs, C., et al. (2014). Mapping pathological phenotypes in a mouse model of CDKL5 disorder. *PLoS One* 9:e91613. doi: 10.1371/journal.pone.0091613

Andero, R., Daviu, N., Escorihuela, R. M., Nadal, R., and Armario, A. (2012). 7,8-dihydroxyflavone, a TrkB receptor agonist, blocks long-term spatial memory impairment caused by immobilization stress in rats. *Hippocampus* 22, 399–408. doi: 10.1002/hipo.20906

Andero, R., Heldt, S. A., Ye, K., Liu, X., Armario, A., and Ressler, K. J. (2011). Effect of 7,8-dihydroxyflavone, a small-molecule TrkB agonist, on emotional learning. *Am. J. Psychiatry* 168, 163–172. doi: 10.1176/appi.ajp.2010.10030326

Asrar, S., and Jia, Z. (2013). Molecular mechanisms coordinating functional and morphological plasticity at the synapse: role of GluA2/N-cadherin interaction-mediated actin signaling in mGluR-dependent LTD. *Cell. Signal.* 25, 397–402. doi: 10.1016/j.cellsig.2012.11.007

Bahi-Buisson, N., and Bienvenu, T. (2012). CDKL5-related disorders: from clinical description to molecular genetics. *Mol. Syndromol.* 2, 137–152.

Bahi-Buisson, N., Nectoux, J., Rosas-Vargas, H., Milh, M., Boddaert, N., Girard, B., et al. (2008). Key clinical features to identify girls with CDKL5 mutations. *Brain* 131(Pt 10), 2647–2661. doi: 10.1093/brain/awn197

Bahi-Buisson, N., Villeneuve, N., Caietta, E., Jacquette, A., Maurey, H., Matthijs, G., et al. (2012). Recurrent mutations in the CDKL5 gene: genotype-phenotype relationships. *Am. J. Med. Genet. A* 158A, 1612–1619. doi: 10.1002/ajmg.a.35401

Brown, M. W., and Banks, P. J. (2015). In search of a recognition memory engram. *Neurosci. Biobehav. Rev.* 50, 12–28. doi: 10.1016/j.neubiorev.2014.09.016

Chapleau, C. A., Larimore, J. L., Theibert, A., and Pozzo-Miller, L. (2009). Modulation of dendritic spine development and plasticity by BDNF and vesicular trafficking: fundamental roles in neurodevelopmental disorders associated with mental retardation and autism. *J. Neurodev. Disord.* 1, 185–196. doi: 10.1007/s11689-009-9027-6

Chen, C., Wang, Z., Zhang, Z., Liu, X., Kang, S. S., Zhang, Y., et al. (2018). The prodrug of 7,8-dihydroxyflavone development and therapeutic efficacy for treating Alzheimer's disease. *Proc. Natl. Acad. Sci. U.S.A.* 115, 578–583. doi: 10.1073/pnas.1718683115

Das, D. K., Mehta, B., Menon, S. R., Raha, S., and Udani, V. (2013). Novel mutations in cyclin-dependent kinase-like 5 (CDKL5) gene in Indian cases of Rett syndrome. *Neuromolecular Med.* 15, 218–225. doi: 10.1007/s12017-012-8212-z

Della Sala, G., Putignano, E., Chelini, G., Melani, R., Calcagno, E., Michele Ratto, G., et al. (2016). Dendritic spine instability in a mouse model of CDKL5 disorder is rescued by insulin-like growth factor 1. *Biol. Psychiatry* 80, 302–311. doi: 10.1016/j.biopsych.2015.08.028

Devi, L., and Ohno, M. (2012). 7,8-dihydroxyflavone, a small-molecule TrkB agonist, reverses memory deficits and BACE1 elevation in a mouse model of Alzheimer's disease. *Neuropsychopharmacology* 37, 434–444. doi: 10.1038/npp.2011.191

Ehrlich, I., Klein, M., Rumpel, S., and Malinow, R. (2007). PSD-95 is required for activity-driven synapse stabilization. *Proc. Natl. Acad. Sci. U.S.A.* 104, 4176–4181. doi: 10.1073/pnas.0609307104

Fehr, S., Wilson, M., Downs, J., Williams, S., Murgia, A., Sartori, S., et al. (2013). The CDKL5 disorder is an independent clinical entity associated with early-onset encephalopathy. *Eur. J. Hum. Genet.* 21, 266–273. doi: 10.1038/ejhg.2012.156

Fuchs, C., Rimondini, R., Viggiano, R., Trazzi, S., De Franceschi, M., Bartesaghi, R., et al. (2015). Inhibition of GSK3beta rescues hippocampal development and learning in a mouse model of CDKL5 disorder. *Neurobiol. Dis.* 82, 298–310. doi: 10.1016/j.nbd.2015.06.018

Fuchs, C., Trazzi, S., Roberta, T., Viggiano, R., De Franceschi, M. E., et al. (2014). Loss of Cdkl5 impairs survival and dendritic growth of newborn neurons by altering AKT/GSK-3beta signaling. *Neurobiol. Dis.* 70, 53–68. doi: 10.1016/j.nbd.2014.06.006

Garcia-Diaz Barriga, G., Giralt, A., Anglada-Huguet, M., Gaja-Capdevila, N., Orlandi, J. G., Soriano, J., et al. (2017). 7,8-dihydroxyflavone ameliorates cognitive and motor deficits in a Huntington's disease mouse model through specific activation of the PLCgamma1 pathway. *Hum. Mol. Genet.* 26, 3144–3160. doi: 10.1093/hmg/ddx198

Gartner, A., Polnau, D. G., Staiger, V., Sciarretta, C., Minichiello, L., Thoenen, H., et al. (2006). Hippocampal long-term potentiation is supported by presynaptic and postsynaptic tyrosine receptor kinase B-mediated phospholipase Cgamma signaling. *J. Neurosci.* 26, 3496–3504. doi: 10.1523/JNEUROSCI.3792-05.2006

Guidi, S., Stagni, F., Bianchi, P., Ciani, E., Ragazzi, E., Trazzi, S., et al. (2013). Early pharmacotherapy with fluoxetine rescues dendritic pathology in the Ts65Dn mouse model of down syndrome. *Brain Pathol.* 23, 129–143. doi: 10.1111/j.1750-3639.2012.00624.x

Horne, E. A., and Dell'Acqua, M. L. (2007). Phospholipase C is required for changes in postsynaptic structure and function associated with NMDA receptor-dependent long-term depression. *J. Neurosci.* 27, 3523–3534. doi: 10.1523/JNEUROSCI.4340-06.2007

Isaac, J. T., Ashby, M. C., and McBain, C. J. (2007). The role of the GluR2 subunit in AMPA receptor function and synaptic plasticity. *Neuron* 54, 859–871. doi: 10.1016/j.neuron.2007.06.001

Jang, H. J., Yang, Y. R., Kim, J. K., Choi, J. H., Seo, Y. K., Lee, Y. H., et al. (2013). Phospholipase C-gamma1 involved in brain disorders. *Adv. Biol. Regul.* 53, 51–62. doi: 10.1016/j.jbior.2012.09.008

Jang, S. W., Liu, X., Yepes, M., Shepherd, K. R., Miller, G. W., Liu, Y., et al. (2010). A selective TrkB agonist with potent neurotrophic activities by 7,8-dihydroxyflavone. *Proc. Natl. Acad. Sci. U.S.A.* 107, 2687–2692. doi: 10.1073/pnas.0913572107

Kalscheuer, V. M., Tao, J., Donnelly, A., Hollway, G., Schwinger, E., Kubart, S., et al. (2003). Disruption of the serine/threonine kinase 9 gene causes severe X-linked infantile spasms and mental retardation. *Am. J. Hum. Genet.* 72, 1401–1411. doi: 10.1086/375538

Kealy, J., and Commins, S. (2011). The rat perirhinal cortex: a review of anatomy, physiology, plasticity, and function. *Prog. Neurobiol.* 93, 522–548. doi: 10.1016/j.pneurobio.2011.03.002

Kilstrup-Nielsen, C., Rusconi, L., La Montanara, P., Ciceri, D., Bergo, A., Bedogni, F., et al. (2012). What we know and would like to know about CDKL5 and its involvement in epileptic encephalopathy. *Neural Plast.* 2012:728267. doi: 10.1155/2012/728267

Korte, M., Minichiello, L., Klein, R., and Bonhoeffer, T. (2000). Shc-binding site in the TrkB receptor is not required for hippocampal long-term potentiation. *Neuropharmacology* 39, 717–724. doi: 10.1016/s0028-3908(99)00273-7

Liu, X., Chan, C. B., Jang, S. W., Pradoldej, S., Huang, J., He, K., et al. (2010). A synthetic 7,8-dihydroxyflavone derivative promotes neurogenesis and exhibits potent antidepressant effect. *J. Med. Chem.* 53, 8274–8286. doi: 10.1021/jm101206p

Mazziotti, R., Lupori, L., Sagona, G., Gennaro, M., Della Sala, G., Putignano, E., et al. (2017). Searching for biomarkers of CDKL5 disorder: early-onset visual impairment in CDKL5 mutant mice. *Hum. Mol. Genet.* 26, 2290–2298. doi: 10.1093/hmg/ddx119

Minichiello, L. (2009). TrkB signalling pathways in LTP and learning. *Nat. Rev. Neurosci.* 10, 850–860. doi: 10.1038/nrn2738

Minichiello, L., Calella, A. M., Medina, D. L., Bonhoeffer, T., Klein, R., and Korte, M. (2002). Mechanism of TrkB-mediated hippocampal long-term potentiation. *Neuron* 36, 121–137. doi: 10.1016/s0896-6273(02)00942-x

Moseley, B. D., Dhamija, R., Wirrell, E. C., and Nickels, K. C. (2012). Historic, clinical, and prognostic features of epileptic encephalopathies caused by CDKL5 mutations. *Pediatr. Neurol.* 46, 101–105. doi: 10.1016/j.pediatrneurol.2011.11.007

Okuda, K., Kobayashi, S., Fukaya, M., Watanabe, A., Murakami, T., Hagiwara, M., et al. (2017). CDKL5 controls postsynaptic localization of GluN2B-containing NMDA receptors in the hippocampus and regulates seizure susceptibility. *Neurobiol. Dis.* 106, 158–170. doi: 10.1016/j.nbd.2017.07.002

Paine, S. M., Munot, P., Carmichael, J., Das, K., Weber, M. A., Prabhakar, P., et al. (2012). The neuropathological consequences of CDKL5 mutation. *Neuropathol. Appl. Neurobiol.* 38, 744–747. doi: 10.1111/j.1365-2990.2012.01292.x

Pizzo, R., Gurgone, A., Castroflorio, E., Amendola, E., Gross, C., Sassoe-Pognetto, M., et al. (2016). Lack of Cdkl5 disrupts the organization of excitatory and inhibitory synapses and parvalbumin interneurons in the primary visual cortex. *Front. Cell Neurosci.* 10:261. doi: 10.3389/fncel.2016.00261

Ricciardi, S., Ungaro, F., Hambrock, M., Rademacher, N., Stefanelli, G., Brambilla, D., et al. (2012). CDKL5 ensures excitatory synapse stability by reinforcing NGL-1-PSD95 interaction in the postsynaptic compartment and is impaired in patient iPSC-derived neurons. *Nat. Cell Biol.* 14, 911–923. doi: 10.1038/ncb2566

Risher, W. C., Ustunkaya, T., Singh Alvarado, J., and Eroglu, C. (2014). Rapid golgi analysis method for efficient and unbiased classification of dendritic spines. *PLoS One* 9:e107591. doi: 10.1371/journal.pone.0107591

Roncacé, V., Burattini, C., Stagni, F., Guidi, S., Giacomini, A., Emili, M., et al. (2017). Neuroanatomical alterations and synaptic plasticity impairment in the perirhinal cortex of the Ts65Dn mouse model of Down syndrome. *Neurobiol. Dis.* 106, 89–100. doi: 10.1016/j.nbd.2017.06.017

Sivilia, S., Mangano, C., Beggiato, S., Giuliani, A., Torricella, R., Baldassarro, V. A., et al. (2016). CDKL5 knockout leads to altered inhibitory transmission in the cerebellum of adult mice. *Genes Brain Behav.* 15, 491–502. doi: 10.1111/gbb.12292

Spencer, J. P. (2008). Flavonoids: modulators of brain function? *Br. J. Nutr.* 99(E Suppl. 1), ES60–ES77. doi: 10.1017/S0007114508965776

Stalpers, X. L., Spruijt, L., Yntema, H. G., and Verrips, A. (2012). Clinical phenotype of 5 females with a CDKL5 mutation. *J. Child Neurol.* 27, 90–93. doi: 10.1177/0883073811413832

Suzuki, W. A., and Naya, Y. (2014). The perirhinal cortex. *Annu. Rev. Neurosci.* 37, 39–53. doi: 10.1146/annurev-neuro-071013-014207

Tang, S., Wang, I. J., Yue, C., Takano, H., Terzic, B., Pance, K., et al. (2017). Loss of CDKL5 in glutamatergic neurons disrupts hippocampal microcircuitry and leads to memory impairment in mice. *J. Neurosci.* 37, 7420–7437. doi: 10.1523/JNEUROSCI.0539-17.2017

Tao, J., Van Esch, H., Hagedorn-Greiwe, M., Hoffmann, K., Moser, B., Raynaud, M., et al. (2004). Mutations in the X-linked cyclin-dependent kinase-like 5 (CDKL5/STK9) gene are associated with severe neurodevelopmental retardation. *Am. J. Hum. Genet.* 75, 1149–1154. doi: 10.1086/426460

Tramarin, M., Rusconi, L., Pizzamiglio, L., Barbiero, I., Peroni, D., Scaramuzza, L., et al. (2018). The antidepressant tianeptine reverts synaptic AMPA receptor defects caused by deficiency of CDKL5. *Hum. Mol. Genet.* 27, 2052–2063. doi: 10.1093/hmg/ddy108

Trazzi, S., Fuchs, C., Viggiano, R., De Franceschi, M., Valli, E., Jedynak, P., et al. (2016). HDAC4: a key factor underlying brain developmental alterations in CDKL5 disorder. *Hum. Mol. Genet.* 25, 3887–3907. doi: 10.1093/hmg/ddw231

Trazzi, S., Mitrugno, V. M., Valli, E., Fuchs, C., Rizzi, S., Guidi, S., et al. (2011). APP-dependent up-regulation of Ptch1 underlies proliferation impairment of neural precursors in Down syndrome. *Hum. Mol. Genet.* 20, 1560–1573. doi: 10.1093/hmg/ddr033

Wang, D., Noda, Y., Zhou, Y., Mouri, A., Mizoguchi, H., Nitta, A., et al. (2007). The allosteric potentiation of nicotinic acetylcholine receptors by galantamine ameliorates the cognitive dysfunction in beta amyloid25-35 i.c.v.-injected mice: involvement of dopaminergic systems. *Neuropsychopharmacology* 32, 1261–1271. doi: 10.1038/sj.npp.1301256

Wang, I. T., Allen, M., Goffin, D., Zhu, X., Fairless, A. H., Brodkin, E. S., et al. (2012). Loss of CDKL5 disrupts kinome profile and event-related potentials leading to autistic-like phenotypes in mice. *Proc. Natl. Acad. Sci. U.S.A.* 109, 21516–21521. doi: 10.1073/pnas.1216988110

Weaving, L. S., Christodoulou, J., Williamson, S. L., Friend, K. L., McKenzie, O. L., Archer, H., et al. (2004). Mutations of CDKL5 cause a severe neurodevelopmental disorder with infantile spasms and mental retardation. *Am. J. Hum. Genet.* 75, 1079–1093. doi: 10.1086/426462

Weng, S. M., McLeod, F., Bailey, M. E., and Cobb, S. R. (2011). Synaptic plasticity deficits in an experimental model of rett syndrome: long-term potentiation saturation and its pharmacological reversal. *Neuroscience* 180, 314–321. doi: 10.1016/j.neuroscience.2011.01.061

Williams, R. J., and Spencer, J. P. (2012). Flavonoids, cognition, and dementia: actions, mechanisms, and potential therapeutic utility for Alzheimer disease. *Free Radic. Biol. Med.* 52, 35–45. doi: 10.1016/j.freeradbiomed.2011.09.010

Zhu, Y. C., Li, D., Wang, L., Lu, B., Zheng, J., Zhao, S. L., et al. (2013). Palmitoylation-dependent CDKL5-PSD-95 interaction regulates synaptic targeting of CDKL5 and dendritic spine development. *Proc. Natl. Acad. Sci. U.S.A.* 110, 9118–9123. doi: 10.1073/pnas.1300003110

Ziakopoulos, Z., Tillett, C. W., Brown, M. W., and Bashir, Z. I. (1999). Input- and layer-dependent synaptic plasticity in the rat perirhinal cortex in vitro. *Neuroscience* 92, 459–472. doi: 10.1016/s0306-4522(98)00764-7

3

Myosin XVI Regulates Actin Cytoskeleton Dynamics in Dendritic Spines of Purkinje Cells and Affects Presynaptic Organization

*Mona Katrin Roesler[1], Franco Luis Lombino[1], Sandra Freitag[1], Michaela Schweizer[2], Irm Hermans-Borgmeyer[3], Jürgen R. Schwarz[1], Matthias Kneussel[1] and Wolfgang Wagner[1]**

[1] *Department of Molecular Neurogenetics, Center for Molecular Neurobiology Hamburg, University Medical Center Hamburg-Eppendorf, Hamburg, Germany,* [2] *Electron Microscopy Unit, Center for Molecular Neurobiology Hamburg, University Medical Center Hamburg-Eppendorf, Hamburg, Germany,* [3] *Transgenic Animal Unit, Center for Molecular Neurobiology Hamburg, University Medical Center Hamburg-Eppendorf, Hamburg, Germany*

Correspondence:
Wolfgang Wagner
wolfgang.wagner@zmnh.uni-hamburg.de

The actin cytoskeleton is crucial for function and morphology of neuronal synapses. Moreover, altered regulation of the neuronal actin cytoskeleton has been implicated in neuropsychiatric diseases such as autism spectrum disorder (ASD). Myosin XVI is a neuronally expressed unconventional myosin known to bind the WAVE regulatory complex (WRC), a regulator of filamentous actin (F-actin) polymerization. Notably, the gene encoding the myosin's heavy chain (*MYO16*) shows genetic association with neuropsychiatric disorders including ASD. Here, we investigated whether myosin XVI plays a role for actin cytoskeleton regulation in the dendritic spines of cerebellar Purkinje cells (PCs), a neuronal cell type crucial for motor learning, social cognition and vocalization. We provide evidence that both myosin XVI and the WRC component WAVE1 localize to PC spines. Fluorescence recovery after photobleaching (FRAP) analysis of GFP-actin in cultured PCs shows that *Myo16* knockout as well as PC-specific *Myo16* knockdown, lead to faster F-actin turnover in the dendritic spines of PCs. We also detect accelerated F-actin turnover upon interference with the WRC, and upon inhibition of Arp2/3 that drives formation of branched F-actin downstream of the WRC. In contrast, inhibition of formins that are responsible for polymerization of linear actin filaments does not cause faster F-actin turnover. Together, our data establish myosin XVI as a regulator of the postsynaptic actin cytoskeleton and suggest that it is an upstream activator of the WRC-Arp2/3 pathway in PC spines. Furthermore, ultra-structural and electrophysiological analyses of *Myo16* knockout cerebellum reveals the presence of reduced numbers of synaptic vesicles at presynaptic terminals in the absence of the myosin. Therefore, we here define myosin XVI as an F-actin regulator important for presynaptic organization in the cerebellum.

Keywords: Purkinje cell, dendritic spine, actin cytoskeleton, autism spectrum disorder, *Myo16*, WAVE, Arp2/3, synaptic vesicles

---

Abbreviations: ASD, autism spectrum disorder; DIV, days *in vitro*; F-actin, filamentous actin; FRAP, fluorescence recovery after photobleaching; mEPSCs, miniature excitatory postsynaptic currents; miR, microRNA; PCs, Purkinje cells; PFs, parallel fibers; RNAi, inhibitory RNA; WRC, WAVE regulatory complex.

INTRODUCTION

Synaptic development, function and plasticity depend on a functional neuronal actin cytoskeleton (Cingolani and Goda, 2008; Hotulainen and Hoogenraad, 2010; Konietzny et al., 2017). F-actin is enriched at presynaptic terminals and within postsynaptic dendritic spines, small cellular protrusions on which excitatory synapses are found (Matus et al., 1982; Cingolani and Goda, 2008; Honkura et al., 2008; Korobova and Svitkina, 2010; Rust and Maritzen, 2015). F-actin comprises a meshwork of branched and linear filaments and provides structural support to dendritic spines. Moreover, it serves as track for actin-based myosin motors, some of which deliver cargos needed for postsynaptic plasticity (Wagner et al., 2011a; Kneussel and Wagner, 2013). A large fraction of the actin cytoskeleton in dendritic spines is highly dynamic and undergoes continuous turnover ("treadmilling"), i.e., cycles of nucleation of new filaments, their elongation by polymerization, filament severing and depolymerization (Star et al., 2002; Pollard and Borisy, 2003; Chazeau and Giannone, 2016; Konietzny et al., 2017). Importantly, the regulation of actin dynamics appears to be fundamental for processes associated with learning and memory such as structural and functional synaptic plasticity (Matus, 2000; Honkura et al., 2008; Kasai et al., 2010; MacGillavry et al., 2013; Rust and Maritzen, 2015; Hlushchenko et al., 2016; Basu and Lamprecht, 2018; Borovac et al., 2018).

Myosin XVI is a neuronally expressed, vertebrate-specific unconventional myosin (Patel et al., 2001; Yokoyama et al., 2011; Cameron et al., 2013). There are indications that the myosin might be involved in actin cytoskeleton regulation. The myosin XVI heavy chain (MYO16, also known as NYAP3) is an F-actin-binding protein with an N-terminal ankyrin repeat domain that binds protein phosphatase 1 catalytic subunits, followed by a myosin motor domain that, in mammals, is likely impaired in its ability to hydrolyze ATP (Patel et al., 2001; Cameron et al., 2007; Kengyel et al., 2015). Via its tail domain, MYO16 binds phosphoinositide 3-kinase (PI3K) and the WRC, an upstream regulator of Arp2/3-dependent actin filament nucleation (Yokoyama et al., 2011). MYO16/NYAP3 and two proteins that resemble the myosin's tail domain (NYAP1, NYAP2) are thought to function redundantly via bridging WRC-PI3K association in order to regulate neurite outgrowth (Yokoyama et al., 2011). Notably, both WRC and Arp2/3 are key factors that drive actin dynamics in hippocampal dendritic spines (Spence and Soderling, 2015; Chazeau and Giannone, 2016).

The WRC constitutes a heteropentameric complex consisting of WAVE1 (or its orthologs WAVE2, WAVE3), CYFIP1 (also known as SRA1; or its ortholog CYFIP2/PIR121), NCKAP1 (also known as NAP1, HEM2; or its ortholog HEM1), ABI1 (or its orthologs ABI2, ABI3) and HSPC300 (also known as BRICK1) (Takenawa and Suetsugu, 2007; Bisi et al., 2013). Activation of the WRC is a multistep process that involves binding to the small GTPase Rac1, and results in exposure of the VCA domain of WAVE (Lebensohn and Kirschner, 2009; Chen et al., 2010). Once exposed, the VCA domain binds and activates Arp2/3. The seven subunit Arp2/3 complex catalyzes the nucleation of new filaments from the side of pre-existing ones, thereby promoting formation of a branched F-actin meshwork (Rotty et al., 2013).

Genetic approaches demonstrated the importance of WRC- and Arp2/3-mediated actin dynamics for synaptic structure and function. Ablation of WRC components leads to abnormal F-actin turnover in hippocampal spines and to changes in spine density and morphology (Grove et al., 2004; Kim Y. et al., 2006; Hazai et al., 2013; Pathania et al., 2014; Njoo et al., 2015). Loss of WAVE1 furthermore causes deficits in synaptic plasticity, learning, and memory (Soderling et al., 2003, 2007). Moreover, genetic disruption of Arp2/3 alters F-actin dynamics in hippocampal spines, structural spine plasticity, and AMPA receptor recruitment into synapses (Hotulainen et al., 2009; Kim et al., 2013; Spence et al., 2016). Many more factors are known that control actin dynamics in hippocampal spines and impact synaptic plasticity, including further Arp2/3 regulators (Mikhaylova et al., 2018; Parkinson et al., 2018), non-muscle myosin IIb (Rex et al., 2010; Koskinen et al., 2014), and post-translational modification of actin subunits (Bertling et al., 2016). Finally, formins have been detected at the tip of finger-like protrusions growing out from hippocampal spine heads (Hotulainen et al., 2009; Chazeau et al., 2014). Similar to Arp2/3, formins drive *de novo* formation of actin filaments that are, however, linear and lead to the formation of elongated protrusions such as filopodia.

Interestingly, several genes linked to an increased risk of developing ASD encode actin regulators (Joensuu et al., 2018). This includes the genes encoding WRC components CYFIP1 and NCKAP1, two established myosin XVI protein interaction partners (Wang et al., 2009; Yokoyama et al., 2011; Chang et al., 2013; Joensuu et al., 2018). ASD is a complex neuropsychiatric disease characterized by deficits in social interaction and communication, with motor coordination problems as a frequent comorbidity (Wang et al., 2014; de la Torre-Ubieta et al., 2016). Strikingly, ASD-like phenotypes in mouse models can be reverted by manipulating actin regulators (Dolan et al., 2013; Duffney et al., 2015). Therefore, it has been suggested that alterations in F-actin dynamics are one of the important pathological features in ASD (Spence and Soderling, 2015; Lin et al., 2016; Yan et al., 2016; Borovac et al., 2018; Hlushchenko et al., 2018; Joensuu et al., 2018). Notably, genetic evidence links also *MYO16* to an increased risk of developing ASD (Wang et al., 2009; Chang et al., 2013; Liu et al., 2015) and other neuropsychiatric disorders (Rodriguez-Murillo et al., 2014; Kao et al., 2016).

MYO16 occurs in cerebellar PCs (Patel et al., 2001; Cameron et al., 2013), central signal integrators that provide the only output from the cerebellar cortex. Their dendrites project into the cerebellar molecular layer and receive excitatory synaptic input via dendritic spines from axons termed PFs (granule cell axons) and climbing fibers (CFs). PCs are crucial for motor coordination and motor learning (Ito, 2001; Schonewille et al., 2010). However, recent research demonstrates that PCs are also important for social cognition, language and vocalization (Tsai et al., 2012; Fujita-Jimbo and Momoi, 2014; Peter et al., 2016; Sokolov et al., 2017). Interestingly, malfunction of the cerebellum and PCs has been linked to ASD and ASD-like phenotypes in mice (Wang et al., 2014; de la Torre-Ubieta et al., 2016). For example,

PC-specific knockout of ASD genes *Shank2* or *Tsc1* causes social interaction deficits in mice (Tsai et al., 2012; Peter et al., 2016). Thus, cerebellar PCs appear to be a highly relevant cell type for studying the role of ASD-related genes such as *Myo16*.

Notably, little is known about F-actin regulation in the dendritic spines of PCs, compared to hippocampal neurons. PCs express WRC components, the formin Daam1, and the Arp2/3-formin coordinator MTSS1 (Soderling et al., 2003; Saarikangas et al., 2015; Kawabata Galbraith et al., 2018). However, whether and how the WRC, Arp2/3, and formins affect F-actin turnover in PC spines has not been examined directly. Remarkably, PCs also harbor specific F-actin regulators such as espin and delphilin that are not found in other neurons (Miyagi et al., 2002; Sekerkova et al., 2003). Thus, actin dynamics might be regulated in a unique manner in PC dendritic spines.

The aim of the present study was to obtain insight into the role of myosin XVI in neuronal cells. Given the known interaction of MYO16 with the actin regulator WRC, and considering that several genes associated with ASD encode actin regulators, we hypothesized that myosin XVI is involved in regulating dendritic spine F-actin and, possibly, synaptic structure and function.

RESULTS

Generation and Initial Characterization of *Myo16* Knockout Mice

To investigate the role of MYO16 in the brain, we generated two mouse lines that carry constitutive *Myo16* knockout alleles (*Myo16*^{em2}, *Myo16*^{em3}; **Figures 1A,B**). Western blot analyses confirmed the absence of myosin XVI heavy chain in homozygous *Myo16*$^{-/-}$ mice of both lines (**Figure 1C**). Since *Myo16* is expressed in cerebellum (Patel et al., 2001; Cameron et al., 2007; see also **Figure 1C**), we examined the anatomical organization of this structure in *Myo16*$^{-/-}$ knockout mice. Nissl staining of cerebellar sections did not reveal gross abnormalities regarding foliation and the organization of layers (**Figure 1D**). Moreover, immuno-fluorescence labeling for the presynaptic marker VGLUT1 did not expose gross deficits in terms of presence of PF terminals in the molecular layer (**Figure 1E**). Given the genetic association of *MYO16* with ASD, we also examined the *in situ* localization of Shank2 and neuroligin-2, two proteins that are strongly linked to ASD and that form postsynaptic clusters at excitatory and inhibitory synapses of PCs, respectively (Zhang et al., 2015; Ha et al., 2016; Peter et al., 2016). Quantification of Shank2 clusters (**Figure 1F**) and neuroligin-2 clusters (**Figure 1G**) within the cerebellar molecular layer showed that cluster density is unaltered in the absence of myosin XVI. Finally, we characterized protein levels and subcellular distribution of postsynaptic molecules in *Myo16*$^{-/-}$ knockout cerebellum (**Figures 1H,I**). We focused on excitatory synapse proteins (AMPA receptor subunits GluA1 and GluA2, scaffolding molecule PSD-95) and on inhibitory synapse proteins (GABA$_A$ receptor subunit α1, neuroligin-2). All of these proteins are present in cerebellum, including postsynaptically in PCs (Briatore et al., 2010; Yamasaki et al., 2011; Zhang et al., 2015). Using differential fractionation of cerebellar extracts, we generated a crude extract (S1), a membrane-enriched fraction (P2) and a fraction enriched for synaptosomal proteins (SYP) (**Figure 1H**). Quantification of GluA1, GluA2, PSD-95, GABA$_A$ α1, and neuroligin-2 amounts showed that the levels of these synaptic proteins in S1, P2, and SYP fractions are not significantly changed in the absence of myosin XVI, compared to littermate control (**Figure 1I**). Together, this indicates that gross anatomical organization, as well as expression and localization of selected synaptic proteins, are unaltered in the cerebellum of *Myo16* knockout mice.

Myosin XVI Localizes to Purkinje Cell Dendritic Spines

In order to obtain insight into the subcellular locations at which endogenous myosin XVI might act, we determined its distribution using fractionation of cerebellar extracts (**Figure 2A**). MYO16 was detected in crude extracts (S1), but also in the membrane-enriched and synaptosomal fractions (P2, SYP), suggesting the possibility that the myosin localizes at or close to synapses. Successful enrichment of membranes and synaptosomes in P2 and SYP fractions was verified via PSD-95 enrichment and loss of tubulin subunit alpha-Tubulin-4A (**Figure 2A**). Since MYO16 is present in cerebellar PCs (Patel et al., 2001; Cameron et al., 2007), we further examined its subcellular location in this cell type. We made use of heterogeneous cerebellar cultures transfected with PC-specific expression plasmids as described (Wagner et al., 2011b) (see section "Materials and Methods"). Observation of live PCs expressing a red-fluorescent cell volume marker and GFP-tagged myosin XVI heavy chain (GFP-MYO16) showed that the myosin accumulates in essentially all dendritic spines (**Figures 2B,C**). Time-lapse movies of PC dendrites revealed that the GFP-MYO16 clusters change their shape over time (**Supplementary Movie S1**). These dynamic morphology changes were reminiscent of F-actin in the dendritic spines of live PCs (**Figures 2D,E**; see also **Supplementary Movie S2**), as visualized via F-tractin (Johnson and Schell, 2009). Indeed, GFP-MYO16 and F-tractin co-localized in spines of live PCs (**Figure 2F**; see also **Supplementary Movie S3**). Thus, the myosin XVI heavy chain localizes to the postsynaptic, F-actin rich spines of cerebellar PCs.

Purkinje Cell Spine F-Actin Turnover Is Faster in the Absence of Myosin XVI

Given the localization of MYO16 to PC spines, combined with the known ability of the myosin to bind the WRC (Yokoyama et al., 2011), we wondered whether the myosin is involved in regulating actin polymerization in spines. In order to monitor F-actin turnover in dendritic spines of *Myo16*$^{-/-}$ PCs, the beta isoform of actin was tagged with monomeric GFP (GFP-actin) and expressed in cultured PCs. GFP-actin is widely used to monitor F-actin dynamics and turnover in hippocampal and cortical spines (e.g., Star et al., 2002; Okamoto et al., 2007; Hotulainen et al., 2009; Rex et al., 2010; Koskinen et al., 2012, 2014; Kim et al., 2013; Chazeau et al., 2015; Chen et al., 2015). As anticipated, GFP-actin accumulated in the spines of live PCs (**Figure 3A**). To

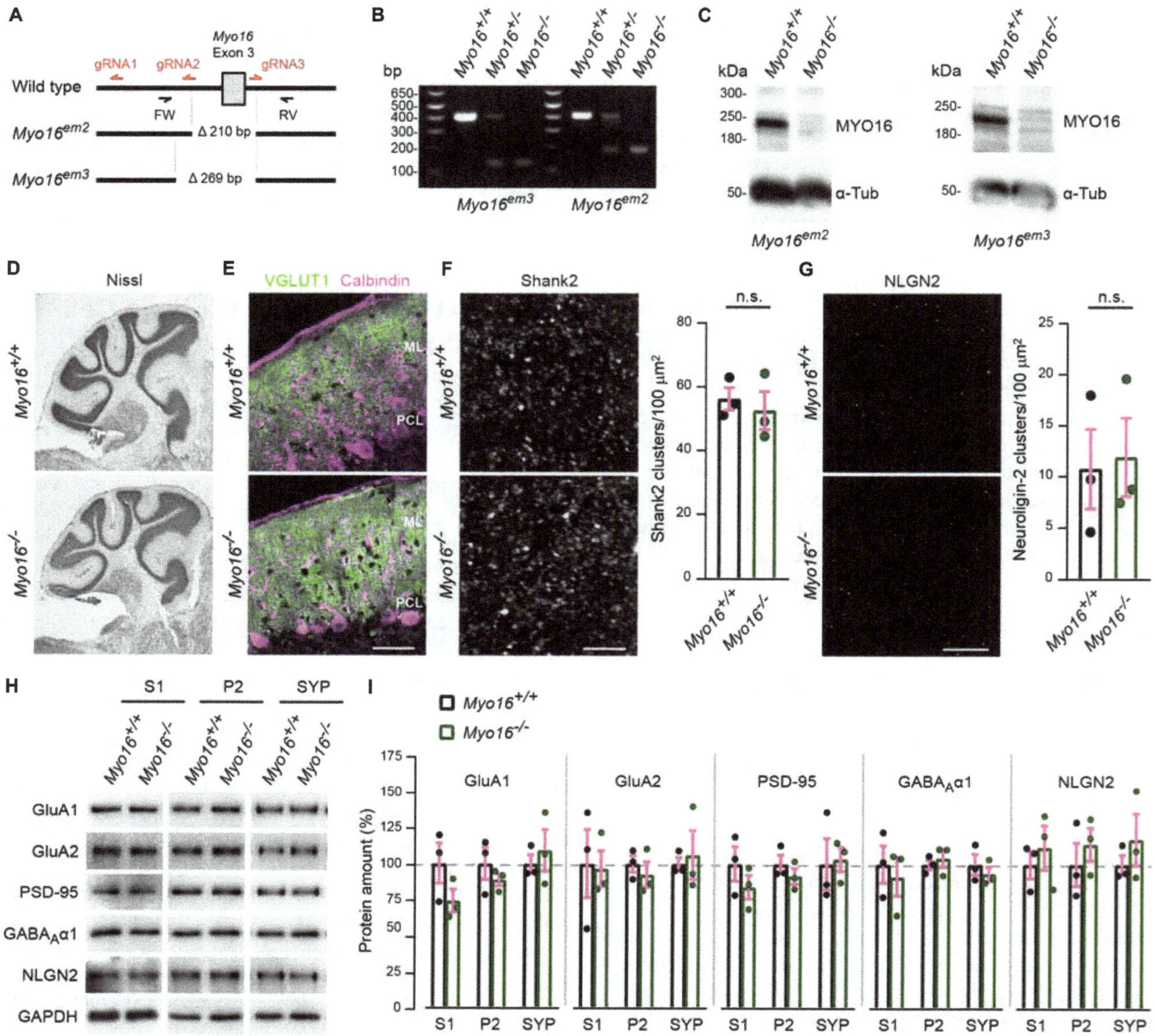

FIGURE 1 | Generation and initial characterization of *Myo16* knockout mice. **(A)** Overview of CRISPR/Cas9-mediated creation of *Myo16* knockout mice (see section "Materials and Methods" for details). Guide RNA sequences are indicated in red (gRNA1-3). Mouse lines carrying deletions of 210 bp ($Myo16^{em2}$) and 269 bp ($Myo16^{em3}$) were obtained, with both deletions comprising exon 3 of *Myo16*. Genotyping primers indicated (FW, RV). **(B)** Identification of mice that are hetero- or homozygous carriers of the $Myo16^{em3}$ and $Myo16^{em2}$ alleles via PCR genotyping using FW and RV primers. Shown is an agarose gel on which the obtained DNA fragments were separated. **(C)** Absence of MYO16 protein in cerebellum extracts of homozygous $Myo16^{em2}$ and $Myo16^{em3}$ mice. Western blot analysis was performed using cerebellar extracts from 11 day old wild-type ($Myo16^{+/+}$) and homozygous knockout ($Myo16^{-/-}$) mice. Antibodies against MYO16 (pre-adsorbed as described in section "Materials and Methods") and α-Tubulin (α-Tub; loading control) were used. **(D)** Nissl staining of sagittal cerebellar sections from adult wild-type ($Myo16^{+/+}$) and $Myo16^{em3}$ knockout ($Myo16^{-/-}$) mice. **(E)** Sagittal cerebellar sections from adult wild-type ($Myo16^{+/+}$) and $Myo16^{em3}$ knockout ($Myo16^{-/-}$) mice immuno-fluorescently labeled with antibodies against VGLUT1 (PF terminal marker) and Calbindin-D-28K (Purkinje cell marker). ML, molecular layer; PCL, Purkinje cell layer. Scale bar, 50 µm. **(F)** Sagittal sections of the cerebellar molecular layer from adult $Myo16^{+/+}$ and $Myo16^{em3}$ knockout mice ($Myo16^{-/-}$) were immuno-fluorescently labeled with antibodies against Shank2. Graph depicts number of Shank2 clusters per 100 µm² as mean ± SEM (magenta), $n = 3$ (single data points represent mice analyzed), no significant differences detected (n.s.; Student's *t*-test; see section "Materials and Methods"). Scale bar, 5 µm. **(G)** Sagittal sections of the cerebellar molecular layer from adult $Myo16^{+/+}$ and $Myo16^{em3}$ knockout mice ($Myo16^{-/-}$) were immuno-fluorescently labeled with antibodies against neuroligin-2 (NLGN2). Graph depicts number of NLGN2 clusters per 100 µm² as mean ± SEM (magenta), $n = 3$ (single data points represent mice analyzed), no significant differences detected (n.s.; Student's *t*-test). Scale bar, 20 µm. **(H,I)** Cerebellar extracts of 25 week old $Myo16^{+/+}$ and $Myo16^{em3}$ knockout mice ($Myo16^{-/-}$) were subjected to subcellular fractionation. S1, P2, and SYP fractions were analyzed by Western blot using the indicated antibodies. In **(I)**, quantification of the indicated proteins from Western blots of S1, P2, and SYP fractions of $Myo16^{+/+}$ and $Myo16^{-/-}$ mice is shown. Graphs depict protein amount after normalization to GAPDH loading control, as percentage of the mean protein amount in the respective $Myo16^{+/+}$ fraction. Bars represent mean values ($n = 3$; data points represent mice analyzed) ± SEM (magenta), no significant differences were detected when comparing protein amounts between the same fraction (S1, P2, or SYP) of $Myo16^{+/+}$ and $Myo16^{-/-}$ mice (n.s.; Student's *t*-test).

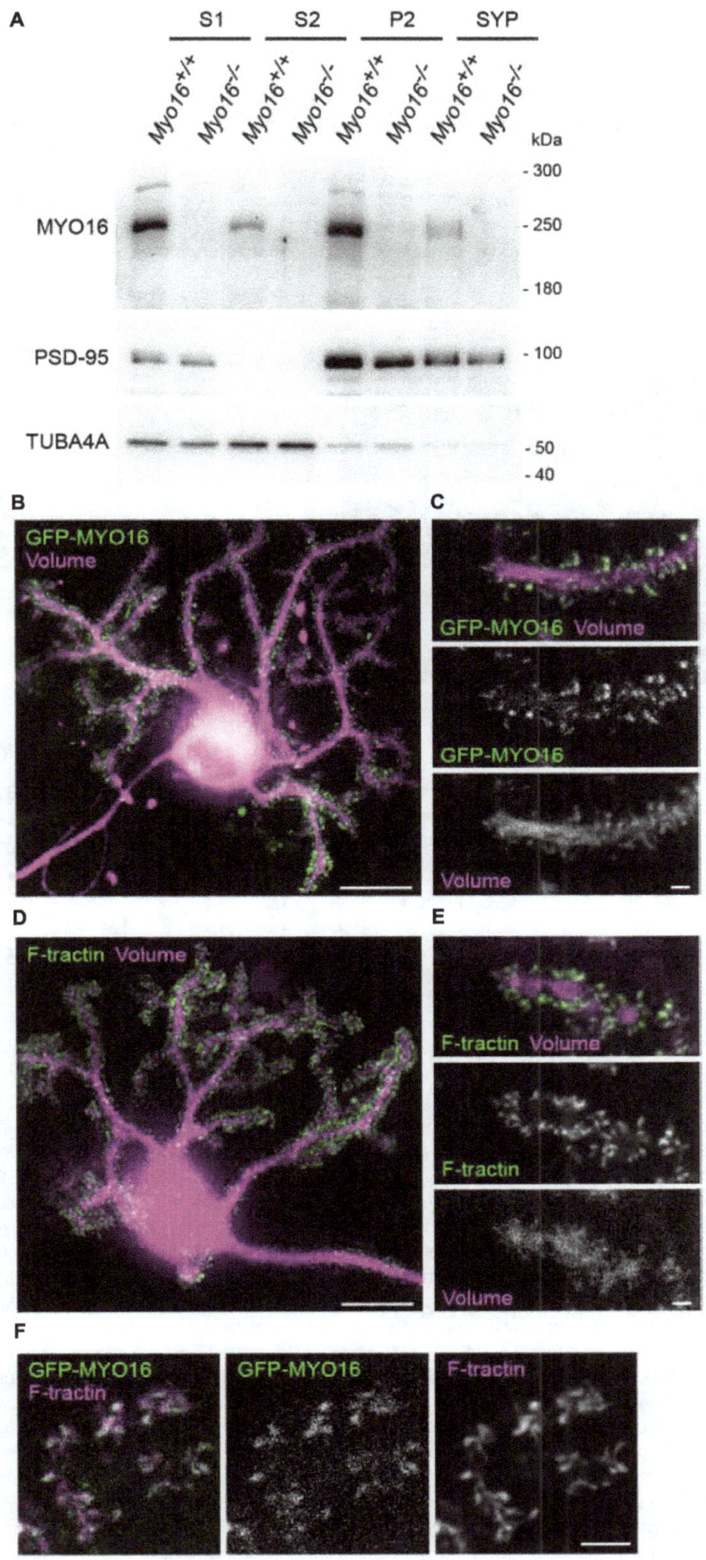

FIGURE 2 | MYO16 localizes to the synaptosomal fraction and to Purkinje cell dendritic spines. **(A)** Cerebellar extracts of 3–4 week old *Myo16*$^{+/+}$ and *Myo16*^{em2} knockout mice (*Myo16*$^{-/-}$) were subjected to subcellular fractionation. S1, S2, P2, and SYP fractions were analyzed by Western blotting using antibodies against MYO16 (pre-adsorbed), PSD-95 (marker for membrane/synaptosomes), and alpha-Tubulin 4A (TUBA4A; marker for loss of cytosolic components). Note that specific MYO16 signal is present in P2 and SYP fractions (n = 3 experiments). **(B)** GFP-tagged myosin XVI heavy chain accumulates within the dendritic spines of Purkinje

(Continued)

FIGURE 2 | Continued
cells (PCs). Cultured live PC at 14 DIV and co-transfected with *L7/Pcp-2* promoter plasmids for PC-specific expression of mGFP-MYO16 (green) and FusionRed (volume marker; magenta). Shown is a maximum projection of a *Z*-stack of images recorded using spinning disk confocal microscopy. Scale bar, 20 μm. **(C)** Dendrite branch of a live PC at 14 DIV transfected as in **(B)**. Shown are images of a single *Z*-plane recorded using spinning disk confocal microscopy. Images correspond to a frame of a time-lapse movie (**Supplementary Movie S1**). Scale bar, 2 μm. **(D)** Cultured live PC at 15 DIV and co-transfected with *L7/Pcp-2* promoter plasmids encoding the live cell F-actin marker F-tractin (green) and FusionRed (volume marker; magenta). Shown is a maximum projection of a *Z*-stack of images recorded using spinning disk confocal microscopy. Scale bar, 20 μm. **(E)** Dendrite branch of a live PC at 15 DIV transfected as in **(D)**. Shown are images of a single *Z*-plane recorded using spinning disk confocal microscopy. Images correspond to a frame of a time-lapse movie (**Supplementary Movie S2**). Scale bar, 2 μm. **(F)** Dendritic spines of a live PC at 15 DIV co-transfected with plasmids encoding mGFP-MYO16 (green) and F-tractin (magenta). Shown are spinning disk confocal images of a single *Z*-plane that correspond to a frame in a time-lapse movie (**Supplementary Movie S3**). Scale bar, 5 μm.

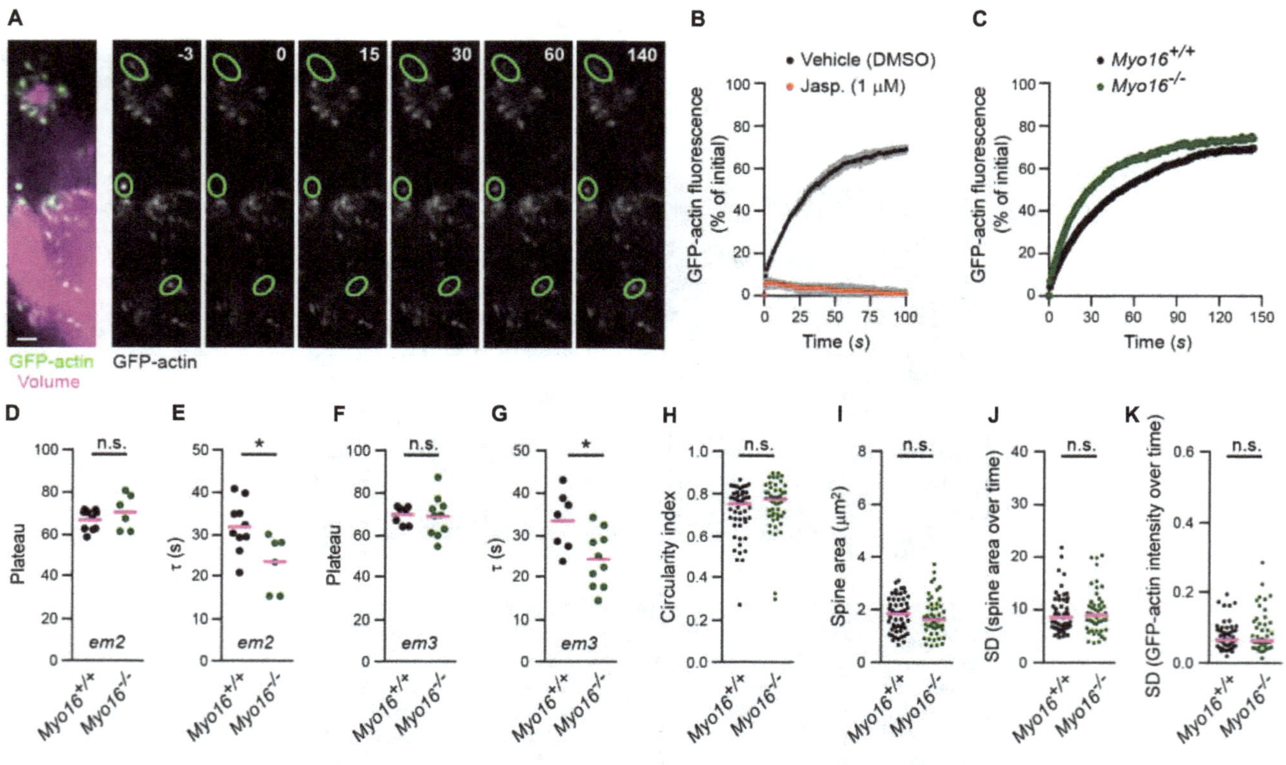

FIGURE 3 | *Myo16* knockout leads to accelerated F-actin turnover in Purkinje cell dendritic spines. **(A)** FRAP analysis of GFP-actin in PC spines. Left, Dendrite branches of a live PC at 14 DIV, co-transfected with *L7/Pcp-2* promoter plasmids encoding GFP-actin (green) and volume marker FusionRed (magenta). Shown is an image recorded using spinning disk confocal microscopy. Scale bar, 2 μm. Right, Example of a FRAP experiment. Images of GFP-actin taken before and after bleaching are shown, time is indicated (seconds). Green ovals highlight bleached spines. Images correspond to frames of a time-lapse movie (**Supplementary Movie S4**). **(B)** FRAP analysis of GFP-actin in spines of PCs treated with 1 μM jasplakinolide (Jasp.; red) or with vehicle (0.1% [v/v] DMSO; black). Cells were co-transfected with *L7/Pcp-2* promoter plasmids encoding GFP-actin and volume marker as in **(A)**. Graph depicts recovery of GFP-actin fluorescence intensity in spines over time (s) relative to the bleached fluorescence intensity. Data points represent mean (n = 3 independent experiments per condition) ± SD (gray). **(C)** FRAP analysis of GFP-actin in spines of $Myo16^{em2}$ knockout PCs ($Myo16^{-/-}$) and $Myo16^{+/+}$ littermate PCs co-transfected as in **(A)**. Graph depicts recovery of GFP-actin fluorescence intensity in spines, data points represent the mean of a representative experiment (see section "Materials and Methods"). **(D)** GFP-actin FRAP recovery plateau in spines of $Myo16^{em2}$ knockout PCs ($Myo16^{-/-}$) and $Myo16^{+/+}$ littermate PCs. Data show plateau values obtained as described in section "Materials and Methods" from independent experiments (n = 6–10; magenta line indicates mean); p value determined using Student's t-test. **(E)** GFP-actin FRAP recovery time constant (τ) in spines of $Myo16^{em2}$ knockout PCs ($Myo16^{-/-}$) and $Myo16^{+/+}$ littermate PCs. Data are τ values obtained as described in section "Materials and Methods" from independent experiments (n = 6–10; magenta line indicates mean); p value determined using Student's t-test. **(F,G)** As in **(D,E)**, but using $Myo16^{em3}$ knockout PCs ($Myo16^{-/-}$) and $Myo16^{+/+}$ littermate PCs (n = 7–10). **(H)** Circularity index of spines of $Myo16^{em2}$ knockout PCs ($Myo16^{-/-}$) and $Myo16^{+/+}$ littermate PCs expressing GFP-actin and volume marker. Value of 1.0 corresponds to perfectly circular shape, lower values indicate elongated shape. Data points represent single spines, magenta line indicates median; p value determined using Mann–Whitney test. **(I)** Apparent area covered by single spines of $Myo16^{em2}$ knockout PCs ($Myo16^{-/-}$) and $Myo16^{+/+}$ littermate PCs expressing GFP-actin and volume marker. Data points represent single spines, magenta line indicates median; p value determined using Student's t-test. **(J)** Spine area changes over time of $Myo16^{em2}$ knockout PCs ($Myo16^{-/-}$) and $Myo16^{+/+}$ littermate PCs expressing GFP-actin and volume marker. Data points represent standard deviation (SD) of the relative area change of single spines over 150 s, magenta line indicates median; p value determined using Mann–Whitney test. **(K)** Change of GFP-actin fluorescence intensity over time in spines of $Myo16^{em2}$ knockout PCs ($Myo16^{-/-}$) and $Myo16^{+/+}$ littermate PCs expressing GFP-actin and volume marker. Data points represent SD of the relative fluorescence change of single spines over 150 s, magenta line indicates median. For reason of comparability with the other figures, a single data point of $Myo16^{-/-}$ lying above the *Y*-axis limit is not shown; p value determined using Mann–Whitney test. $^{*}p < 0.05$; $^{**}p < 0.01$; $^{***}p < 0.001$; $^{****}p < 0.0001$; n.s., not significant.

assess the turnover of GFP-actin in single PC spines, we used FRAP (**Figure 3A**; see also **Supplementary Movie S4**). To verify that FRAP of GFP-actin reveals the turnover of actin filaments in PC spines (as opposed to diffusion of GFP-actin monomers into spines), cells were treated with the F-actin stabilizing drug jasplakinolide (1 μM) (Bubb et al., 1994; Cramer, 1999). As expected, while GFP-actin fluorescence recovered in spines of vehicle-treated cells following bleaching, recovery was almost entirely blocked upon jasplakinolide treatment (**Figure 3B**). This confirms that the observed fluorescence recovery reflects formation of new F-actin in PC spines.

To determine whether myosin XVI is required for F-actin turnover, we performed FRAP analysis of GFP-actin in spines of $Myo16^{-/-}$ PCs ($Myo16^{em2}$ allele; **Figure 3C**). The plateau of fluorescence recovery indicates the fraction of F-actin that undergoes turnover (referred to as the mobile F-actin pool), while the recovery time constant (τ) is a measure of F-actin turnover rate in spines (Star et al., 2002). Our analyses did not reveal a significant difference regarding the mobile pool of spine F-actin when comparing $Myo16^{-/-}$ to wild-type littermate PCs (71 vs. 67%, respectively; **Figure 3D**). However, F-actin turnover rate was significantly faster (i.e., τ was smaller) in $Myo16^{-/-}$ PC spines compared to control (τ = 23 s vs. τ = 32 s, respectively; **Figure 3E**). We independently confirmed these results using PCs from the knockout mouse line carrying the $Myo16^{em3}$ allele (**Figures 3F,G**). Therefore, F-actin turnover in PC spines is accelerated upon *Myo16* knockout.

Since the actin cytoskeleton is a crucial determinant of spine shape (Hotulainen and Hoogenraad, 2010), we also monitored whether overall morphology and dynamics of spines are changed in $Myo16^{-/-}$ PCs. Using images of unbleached spines recorded during the GFP-actin FRAP experiments, a spine circularity index was determined as a measure for spine shape (**Figure 3H**). Moreover, we monitored spine area (an indirect measure of spine size; **Figure 3I**), relative spine area size changes over 2.5 min (**Figure 3J**), and relative changes of actin fluorescence intensity in spines over time (**Figure 3K**). None of these parameters were significantly different in $Myo16^{-/-}$ PCs when compared to wild-type. Thus, overall morphology and dynamics of PC spines appear to be normal in the absence of myosin XVI.

Myosin XVI Acts Within Purkinje Cells to Regulate Spine F-Actin Turnover

Myosin XVI might affect F-actin turnover directly via acting in PC spines. Alternatively, altered F-actin dynamics in $Myo16^{-/-}$ PCs might be of non-cell autonomous origin such as altered presynaptic input from granule cells. Thus, to determine whether the myosin is required within PCs, we performed PC-specific *Myo16* knockdown. First, we identified RNAi sequences that, when embedded in a miR backbone, knockdown *Myo16* expression (**Figure 4A**). Compared to control levels, the independent knockdown sequences *Myo16* KD3 and *Myo16* KD5 significantly reduced GFP-MYO16 expression to 33% and 28%, respectively (**Figure 4B**). Following a previously used strategy (Alexander and Hammer, 2016), these knockdown sequences as well as a reporter (FusionRed) were placed under control of the *L7/Pcp-2* promoter (**Figure 4C**) which drives PC-specific expression in cerebellar cultures (Wagner et al., 2011b). Expression of the *Myo16* KD3, *Myo16* KD5 or scrambled miR knockdown constructs in the analyzed PCs was verified via monitoring FusionRed.

Fluorescence recovery after photobleaching analysis of GFP-actin showed that, similar to the situation in $Myo16^{-/-}$ PCs, the two independent PC-specific *Myo16* knockdown constructs both caused a significantly faster turnover of F-actin in spines compared to scrambled control (*Myo16* KD3, τ = 21 s; *Myo16* KD5, τ = 19 s; Scrambled, τ = 28 s), while the mobile pool of F-actin remained unchanged (**Figures 4D–G**). Moreover, as in case of $Myo16^{-/-}$ PCs, no consistent changes in terms of overall morphology and dynamics of spines were observed upon *Myo16* knockdown (**Figures 4H–K**). Therefore, both global *Myo16* knockout and PC-specific *Myo16* knockdown lead to an identical phenotype, i.e., accelerated F-actin turnover in PC-spines. Since GFP-MYO16 targets to PC spines (**Figure 2**), this indicates that the myosin functions at the postsynaptic side to attenuate spine F-actin turnover.

Faster F-Actin Turnover in Purkinje Cell Spines Upon WRC Inhibition

The WRC is an activator of Arp2/3-mediated F-actin polymerization (Bisi et al., 2013) and a well-established interaction partner of myosin XVI (Yokoyama et al., 2011). Therefore, we asked whether also the WRC is important for actin cytoskeleton dynamics in dendritic spines of PCs. We first determined whether the WRC-subunit WAVE1 localizes to PC spines *in situ*. We employed an anti-WAVE1 antibody that detects a band of expected size in cerebellar extracts (**Figure 5A**). Immuno-fluorescence labeling of wild-type cerebellum confirmed (Soderling et al., 2003) the presence of WAVE1 in PCs and revealed partial co-localization with PC spines (**Figure 5B**). Immuno-electron microscopy showed that WAVE1 is present at pre- and postsynaptic sites within the cerebellar molecular layer (**Figure 5C**, $Myo16^{+/+}$ panels). In spines, predominantly the postsynaptic density was labeled (**Figure 5C**, left $Myo16^{+/+}$ panel). In cerebellum of $Myo16^{-/-}$ mice, no obvious difference in WAVE1 labelling was observed (**Figure 5C**, $Myo16^{-/-}$ panels). Thus, WAVE1 is present in PC spines, and myosin XVI is not essential for WAVE1 targeting to spines.

To interfere with WRC function, we made use of a well-characterized dominant-negative version of WAVE1 that lacks the C-terminal VCA domain (WAVE1ΔVCA) and thus is unable to activate Arp2/3 (Miki et al., 1998; Kim H.J. et al., 2006; Pils et al., 2012). To selectively target the PCs in heterogeneous cerebellar culture, WAVE1ΔVCA was expressed under control of the *L7/Pcp-2* promoter. GFP-actin FRAP analysis revealed that WAVE1ΔVCA leads to a significantly smaller mobile F-actin pool in PC spines (FRED-WAVE1ΔVCA:

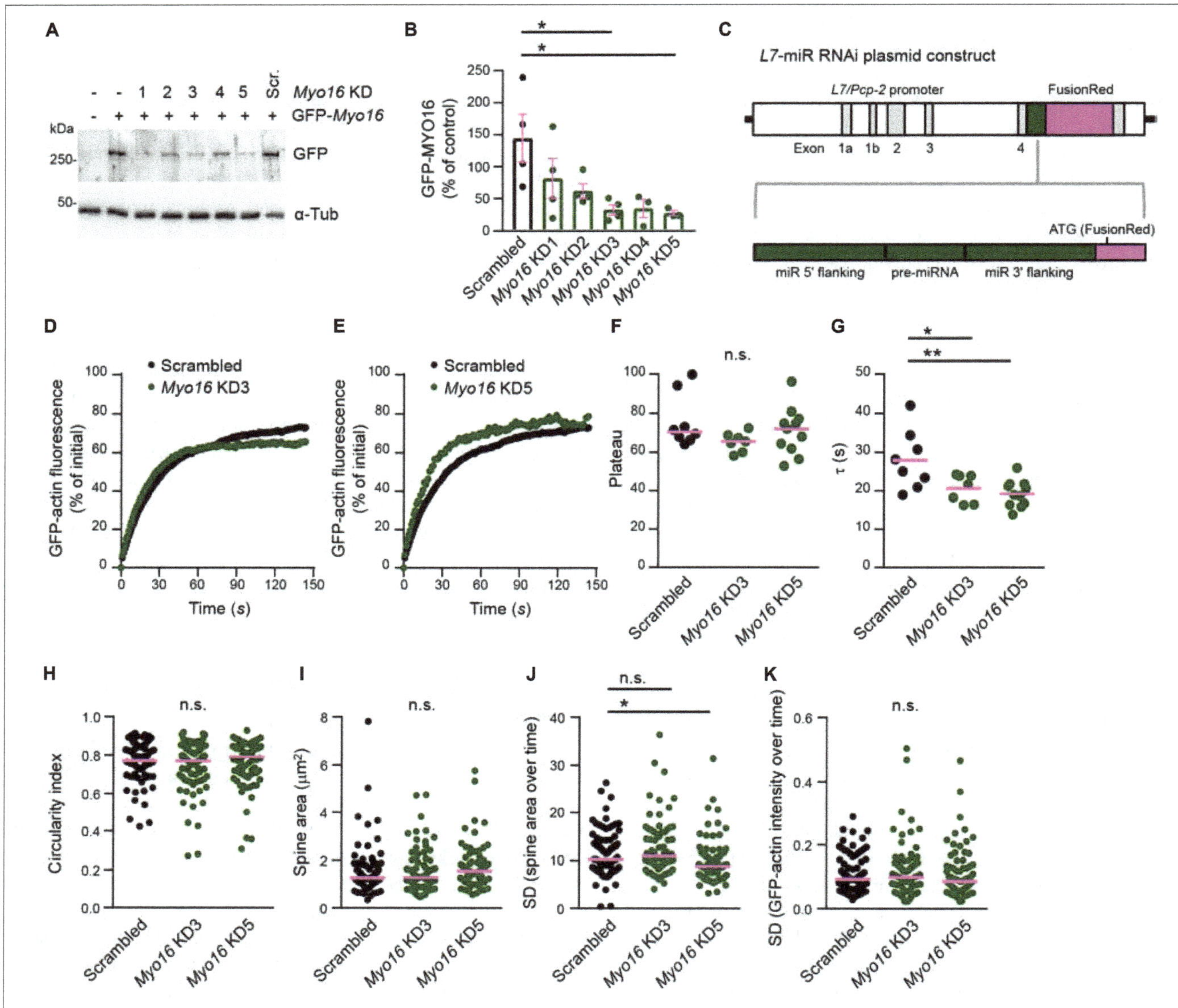

FIGURE 4 | Purkinje cell-specific *Myo16* knockdown leads to accelerated F-actin turnover in dendritic spines. **(A,B)** Identification of *Myo16* miR RNAi knockdown constructs. **(A)** Western blot analysis of HEK293 cells co-transfected with a plasmid encoding mGFP-tagged mouse MYO16 and pcDNA™6.2-GW/EmGFP-miR plasmids carrying the indicated knockdown sequences (*Myo16* KD1–KD5) or scrambled control (Scr.). For control, untransfected cells (first lane) and cells transfected only with plasmid encoding mGFP-*Myo16* were used. Antibodies against GFP and α-Tubulin (α-Tub; loading control) were used. **(B)** Quantification of GFP-MYO16 protein amount upon co-transfection with *Myo16* knockdown constructs KD1–KD5 or scrambled control. Graph depicts GFP-MYO16 signals normalized to tubulin signals and expressed as percentage of control (i.e., cells transfected with GFP-MYO16 plasmid only). Bars indicate mean values ($n = 3$–4; data points represent experiments) ± SEM (magenta); p values determined using Kruskal–Wallis test ($p = 0.0321$) followed by Dunn's multiple comparisons test. **(C)** Schematic representation of plasmids for expressing *Myo16* KD3, *Myo16* KD5 or scrambled sequence (*pre-miRNA*) and flanking miR sequences (green) together with FusionRed as a reporter for RNAi expression (magenta) under control of the PC-specific *L7/Pcp-2* promoter. **(D,E)** FRAP analysis of GFP-actin in spines of wild-type PCs transfected with *L7/Pcp-2* promoter plasmids carrying *Myo16* KD3, *Myo16* KD5, or scrambled sequence and FusionRed (reporter for knockdown construct expression). Cells were co-transfected with a plasmid encoding GFP-actin. Graphs depict recovery of GFP-actin fluorescence intensity in spines, data points represent the mean of a representative experiment. For clarity, recovery curves of *Myo16* KD3 **(D)** and *Myo16* KD5 **(E)** are compared to the same scrambled control but shown in separate graphs. **(F)** GFP-actin FRAP recovery plateau in spines of PCs transfected as described in **(D,E)**. Data are plateau values obtained from independent experiments ($n = 7$–11; magenta line indicates median); p value determined using Kruskal–Wallis test. **(G)** GFP-actin FRAP recovery time constant (τ) in spines of PCs transfected as described in **(D,E)**. Data are τ values from independent experiments ($n = 7$–11; magenta line indicates mean); p values determined using one-way ANOVA ($p = 0.0038$) followed by Tukey's multiple comparisons test. **(H)** Circularity index of spines of PCs transfected as described in **(D,E)**. Data points represent single spines, magenta line indicates median; p value determined using Kruskal–Wallis test. **(I)** Apparent area covered by single spines of PCs transfected as described in **(D,E)**. Data points represent single spines, magenta line indicates median; p value determined using Kruskal–Wallis test. **(J)** Spine area changes over time of PCs transfected as described in **(D,E)**. Data points represent SD of the relative area change of single spines over 150 s, magenta line indicates median; p values determined using Kruskal–Wallis test ($p = 0.0008$) followed by Dunn's multiple comparisons test. **(K)** Change of GFP-actin fluorescence intensity over time in spines of PCs transfected as described in **(D,E)**. Data points represent SD of the relative fluorescence change of single spines monitored over 150 s, magenta line indicates median. For reasons of comparability with the other figures, a single data point of *Myo16* KD5 lying above the *Y*-axis limit is not shown; p value determined using Kruskal–Wallis test. $^{*}p < 0.05$; $^{**}p < 0.01$; $^{***}p < 0.001$; $^{****}p < 0.0001$; n.s., not significant.

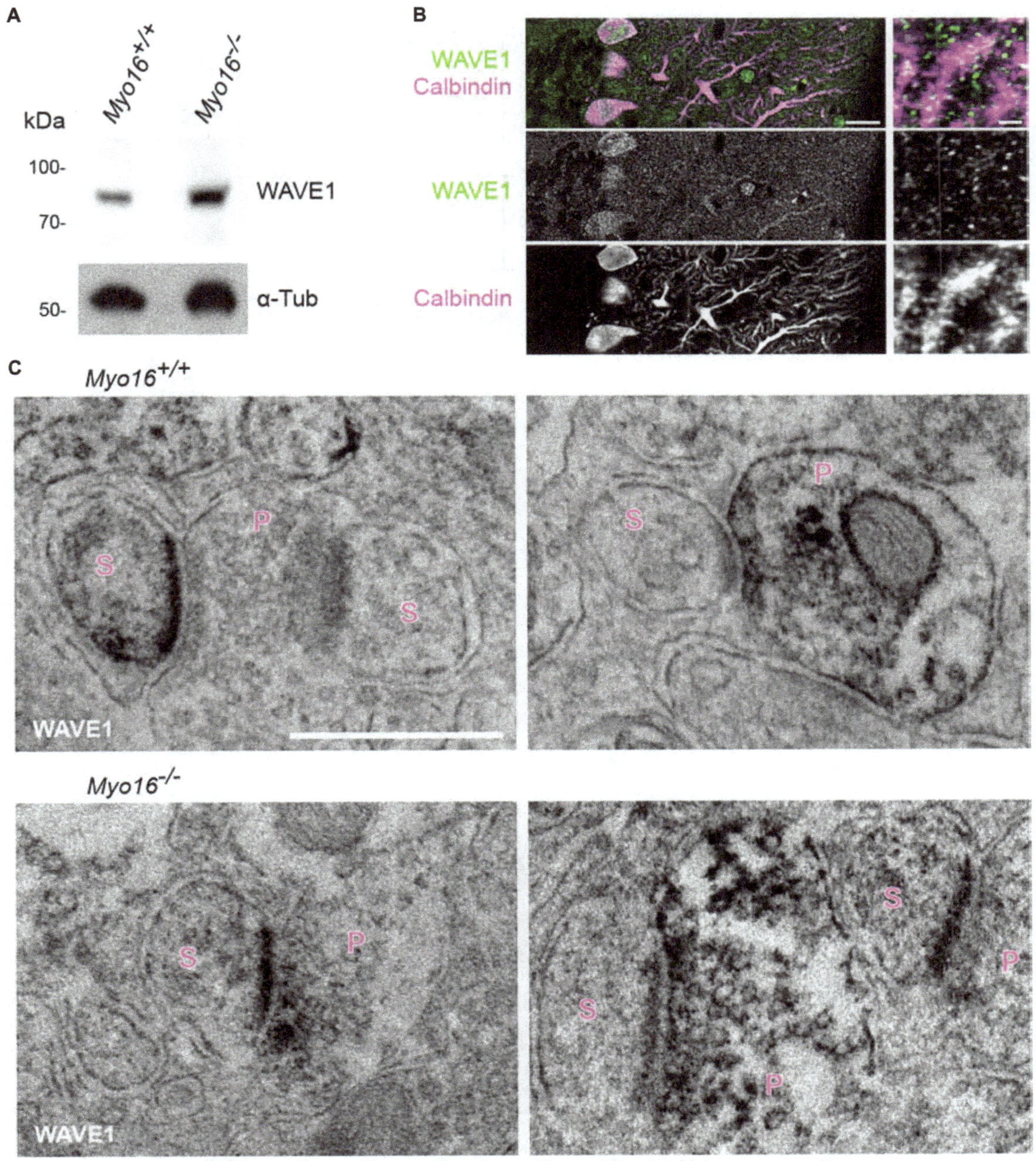

FIGURE 5 | WAVE1 localizes to Purkinje cell spines and to presynaptic terminals in the cerebellar molecular layer. **(A)** Western blot analysis of cerebellar extracts from 11 day old wild-type (*Myo16*$^{+/+}$) and *Myo16*^{em3} knockout (*Myo16*$^{-/-}$) mice. Antibodies against WAVE1 and α-Tubulin (α-Tub; loading control) were used. **(B)** WAVE1 partially co-localizes with PC spines. Confocal images of cerebellar sections from adult wild type mice immuno-fluorescently labeled with antibodies against WAVE1 and Calbindin-D-28K. Right panels are zoom-in images depicting the molecular layer. Scale bars, 20 μm (right panels); 2 μm (left panels). **(C)** Immuno-electron microscopy of cerebellar sections from adult wild-type mice (*Myo16*$^{+/+}$; upper panels) and *Myo16*^{em3} knockout mice (*Myo16*$^{-/-}$; lower panels) using WAVE1 antibody and DAB labeling. Black precipitate indicates presence of WAVE1. Left panels depict examples of PC spines positive for WAVE1, right panels are examples of presynaptic terminals positive for WAVE1. S, spine; P, presynaptic bouton. Scale bar, 500 nm.

plateau at 63%; FRED control: plateau at 70%; **Figures 6A,B**). Moreover, the mobile pool displayed faster turnover (FRED-WAVE1ΔVCA, τ = 27 s; FRED control, τ = 32 s; **Figure 6C**). Therefore, interference with the WRC within PCs phenocopies both *Myo16* knockout and knockdown in accelerating F-actin turnover in spines.

Analyses of PCs expressing GFP-actin showed furthermore that WAVE1ΔVCA leads to changes in spine morphology. Compared to control, spines of PCs that express WAVE1ΔVCA were more elongated and larger (**Figures 6D,E,H**; see also **Supplementary Movies S5, S6**). In addition, WAVE1ΔVCA attenuated size changes and actin intensity fluctuation in PC

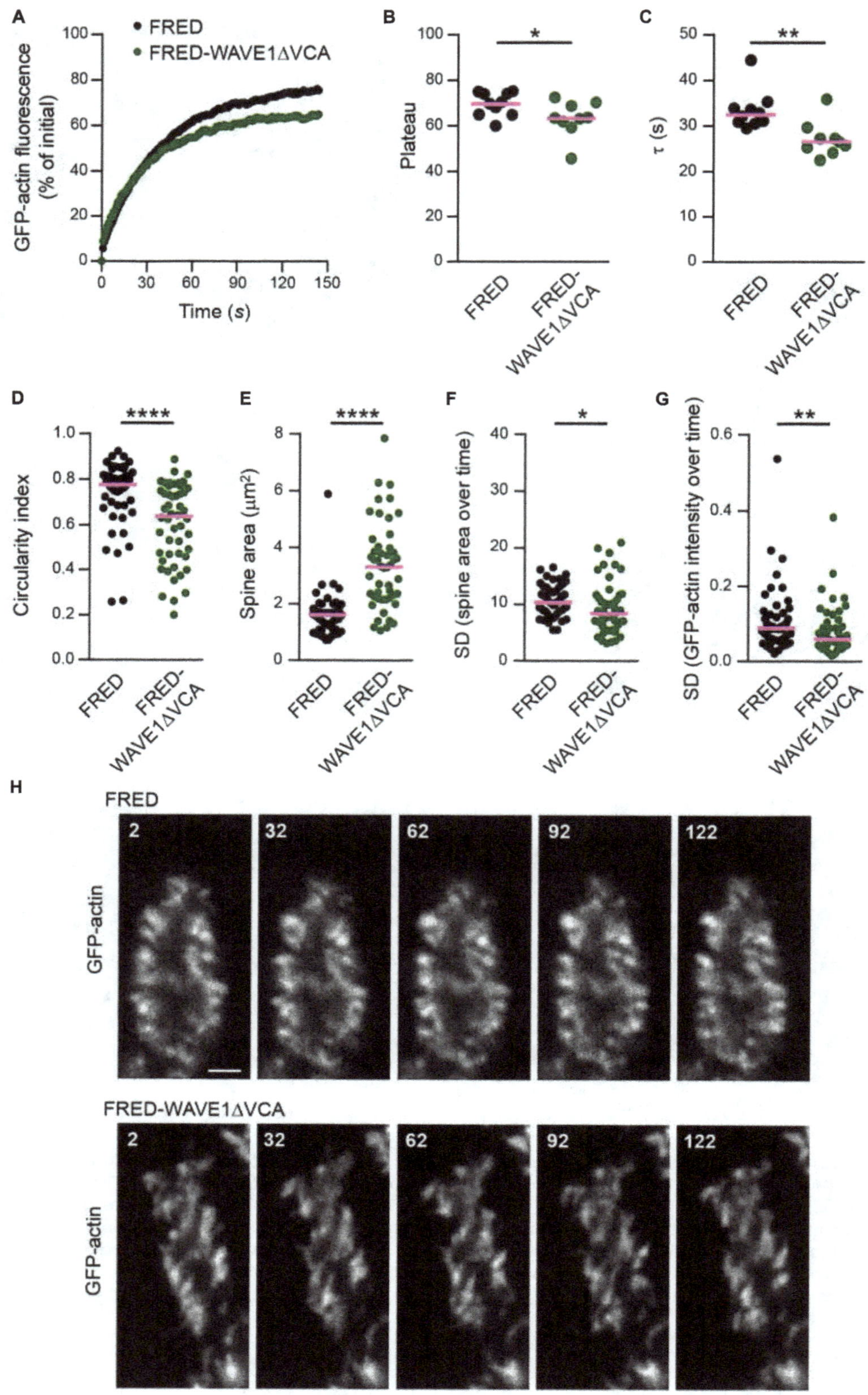

FIGURE 6 | WAVE1 ΔVCA leads to accelerated F-actin turnover and a decreased dynamic F-actin pool in Purkinje cell dendritic spines. **(A)** FRAP analysis of GFP-actin in spines of wild-type PCs transfected with *L7/Pcp-2* promoter plasmids encoding either FusionRed-tagged WAVE1 lacking the VCA domain (FRED-WAVE1 ΔVCA) or FusionRed alone (FRED). Cells were co-transfected with a plasmid encoding GFP-actin. Graph depicts recovery of GFP-actin fluorescence intensity in spines, data points represent the mean of a representative experiment. **(B)** GFP-actin FRAP recovery plateau in spines of PCs transfected

(Continued)

FIGURE 6 | Continued
as described in **(A)**. Data represent plateau values obtained from independent experiments (n = 9–10; magenta line indicates mean); p value determined using Student's t-test. **(C)** GFP-actin FRAP recovery time constant (τ) in spines of PCs transfected as described in **(A)**. Data represent τ values obtained from independent experiments (n = 9–10; magenta line indicates median); p value determined using Mann–Whitney test. **(D)** Circularity index of spines of PCs transfected as in **(A)**. Data points represent single spines, magenta line indicates median; p value determined using Mann–Whitney test. **(E)** Apparent area covered by single spines of spines of PCs transfected as in **(A)**. Data points represent single spines, magenta line indicates median; p value determined using Mann–Whitney test. **(F)** Spine area changes over time of PCs transfected as described in **(A)**. Data points represent SD of the relative area change of single spines over 150 s, magenta line indicates median; p value determined using Mann–Whitney test. **(G)** Change of GFP-actin fluorescence intensity over time in spines of PCs transfected as described in **(A)**. Data points represents SD of the relative fluorescence change of single spines over 150 s, magenta line indicates median; p value determined using Mann–Whitney test. **(H)** Examples of spines of PCs transfected as described in **(A)**. GFP-actin was visualized by spinning disk confocal microscopy (see also **Supplementary Movies S5**, **S6**). Time is indicated in seconds. Scale bar, 2 μm. $^*p < 0.05$; $^{**}p < 0.01$; $^{***}p < 0.001$; $^{****}p < 0.0001$; n.s., not significant.

spines over time (**Figures 6F,G**). This indicates that the WRC promotes circular spine shape and favors spine dynamics in PCs.

Arp2/3 Inhibition, but Not Formin Inhibition, Accelerates F-Actin Turnover in PC Spines

Since Arp2/3 is the downstream target of the WRC (Takenawa and Suetsugu, 2007; Bisi et al., 2013), reduced Arp2/3 activation might be the cause of accelerated F-actin turnover upon WRC inhibition (**Figure 6C**). To determine whether Arp2/3 plays a role for F-actin turnover in PC spines, cells were acutely exposed to CK-666, a well-established small molecule inhibitor of Arp2/3 (Nolen et al., 2009), before performing FRAP analysis of GFP-actin (**Figure 7A**). Similar as for WRC inhibition, spines of PCs treated with 200 μM CK-666 displayed a significantly smaller mobile F-actin pool (CK-666, plateau at 43%; vehicle control, plateau at 65%; **Figures 7B,C**). Moreover, like when interfering with the WRC or with myosin XVI, turnover of the mobile F-actin pool was significantly faster upon CK-666 treatment (CK-666, τ = 20 s; vehicle control, τ = 30 s; **Figure 7D**). Together, our data indicate that the WRC-Arp2/3 pathway determines the relative level of mobile F-actin in PC spines and attenuates its turnover time.

We next tested whether also manipulation of actin polymerization factors unrelated to Arp2/3 results in accelerated F-actin turnover in PC spines. For this purpose, cells were acutely treated with SMIFH2 (40 μM), an inhibitor of formin-mediated actin filament nucleation and elongation (Rizvi et al., 2009). Similar to interference with WRC-Arp2/3, this led to a significantly smaller mobile F-actin pool compared to vehicle control (SMIFH2, plateau at 40%; **Figures 7B,C**). Thus, formin activity is required for F-actin dynamics in PC spines. Notably, however, the turnover time of the dynamic pool was not reduced compared to control (SMIFH2, τ = 29 s; **Figure 7D**). Moreover, the effects of CK-666 and SMIFH2 on mobile pool size of F-actin were additive, with both blockers leading to a significantly reduced plateau compared to CK-666 alone (CK-666+SMIFH2, plateau at 30%; **Figure 7C**). Therefore, WRC-Arp2/3 and formins appear to act in parallel pathways influencing F-actin dynamics in PC spines, with WRC-Arp2/3 – but not formins – attenuating F-actin turnover rate.

Since myosin XVI attenuates F-actin turnover rate in PC spines (**Figures 3**, **4**) and binds to the WRC (Yokoyama et al., 2011), the myosin might act through the WRC-Arp2/3 pathway. If this is the case, *Myo16* knockout may not have an additive effect on actin dynamics upon Arp2/3 inhibition. Indeed, neither the mobile pool of spine F-actin nor its turnover rate was significantly different in spines of CK-666-treated $Myo16^{-/-}$ PCs when compared to CK-666-treated littermate, wild-type PCs (**Figures 7E,F**). This argues for myosin XVI regulating F-actin turnover rate in PC spines via Arp2/3.

Finally, we examined whether acute exposure to the Arp2/3 or formin inhibitors changes overall spine morphology or dynamics (**Figures 7G–O**). Similar to WRC inhibition (**Figure 6D**) or long-term (24 h) treatment with CK-666 (Kawabata Galbraith et al., 2018), short-term Arp2/3 inhibition led to a significantly more elongated spine shape (**Figure 7G**). Moreover, CK-666 treatment resulted in increased spine size (**Figure 7H**). Size changes of PC spines or actin intensity changes in spines over 2.5 min were not significantly affected by Arp2/3 inhibition (**Figures 7I,J**). This indicates that the WRC-Arp2/3 pathway promotes a circular spine shape in PCs, consistent with Arp2/3 driving the formation of a non-uniformly oriented, branched actin meshwork (Chazeau and Giannone, 2016). In contrast, acute formin inhibition affected PC spine morphology and dynamics differently (**Figures 7K–O**). Unlike CK-666, SMIFH2 did not lead to spine elongation (**Figure 7K**) but significantly reduced relative spine size changes and actin fluorescence intensity changes in spines over time (**Figures 7M,N**). Similar to CK-666 treatment, PC spines adopted a larger area upon exposure to SMIFH2 (**Figure 7L**). Therefore, unlike Arp2/3, formin activity is needed to promote fluctuations of PC spine size and actin content.

Altered Synaptic Structure and Transmission in the Cerebellum of *Myo16* Knockout Mice

Having established that myosin XVI regulates actin dynamics in cerebellar PCs, we examined in more detail whether synapses formed on PC spines are structurally altered in $Myo16^{-/-}$ mice *in situ*. First, using electron microscopy images of the middle third of the molecular layer, we quantified the number of asymmetric synapses per μm^2 (**Figure 8A**). No difference in the density of these excitatory synapses that mainly represent PF-PC synapses was detected. Consistent with the finding that spine size of cultured $Myo16^{-/-}$ PCs is unaltered (**Figure 3I**), also spine head area of molecular layer synapses measured from electron microscopy images was unaltered (**Figures 8B,C**).

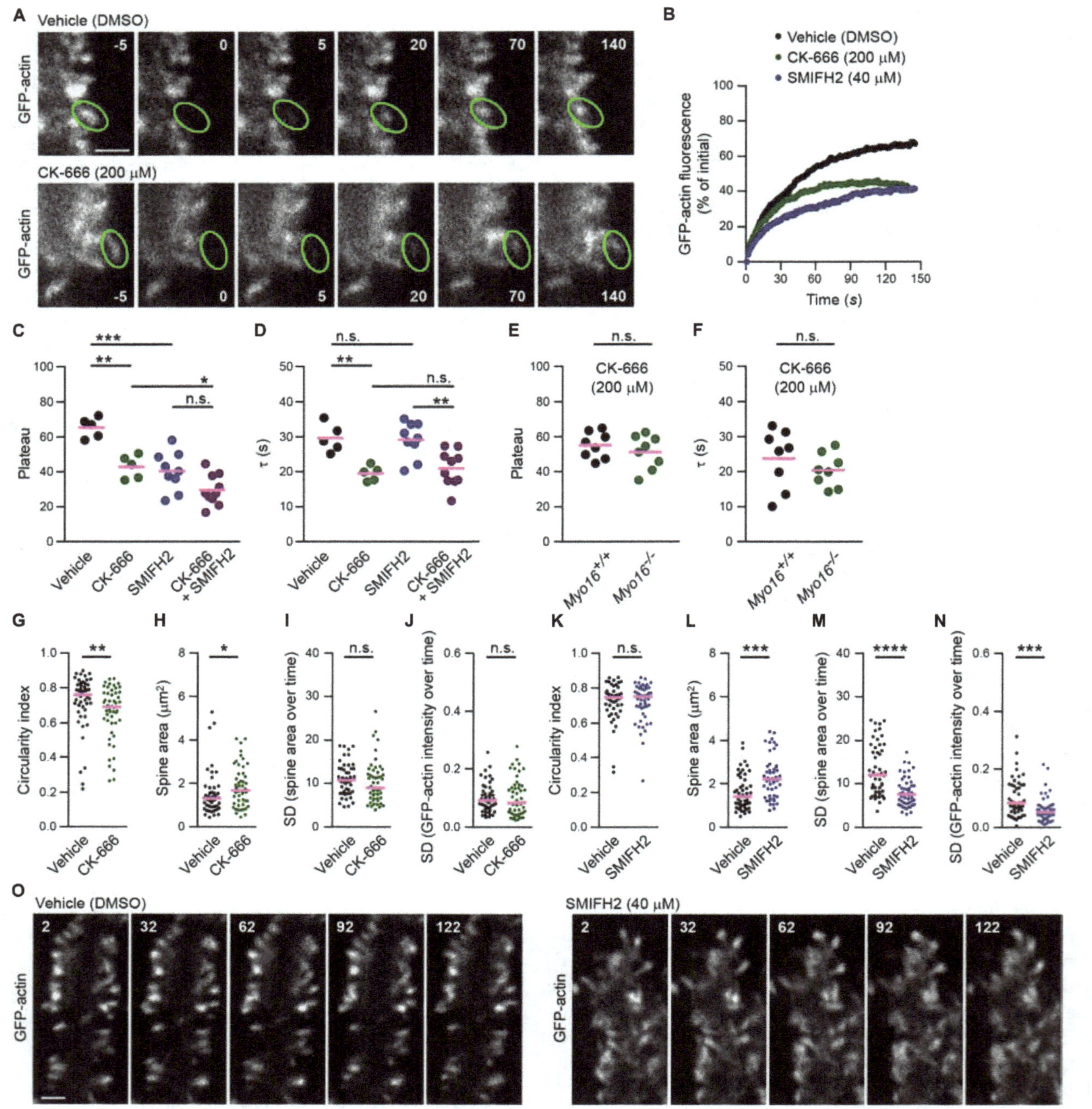

FIGURE 7 | Arp2/3 inhibition, but not formin inhibition, accelerates F-actin turnover in PC spines. **(A)** Examples of GFP-actin FRAP in PC spines in the absence or presence of Arp2/3 inhibitor CK-666. Wild-type PCs were co-transfected with *L7/Pcp-2* promoter plasmids encoding GFP-actin and volume marker FusionRed. Shown are images depicting GFP-actin and recorded using spinning disk confocal microscopy. Upper row, vehicle-treated control (0.4% [v/v] DMSO). Lower row, treated with CK-666 (final concentration, 200 μM). Time before and after bleaching is indicated (seconds). Green ovals highlight bleached spines. Scale bar, 2 μm. **(B)** FRAP analysis of GFP-actin in spines of PCs co-transfected as in **(A)** and treated with CK-666 (200 μM; green), formin inhibitor SMIFH2 (40 μM; blue), or vehicle (black). Graph depicts recovery of GFP-actin fluorescence intensity in spines, data points represent the mean of a representative experiment. **(C)** GFP-actin FRAP recovery plateau in spines of PCs transfected as in **(A)** and treated with CK-666, SMIFH2, CK-666 + SMIFH2, or vehicle. Data are plateau values obtained from independent experiments (n = 5–10; magenta line indicates mean); p values determined using one-way ANOVA ($p < 0.0001$) followed by Sidak's multiple comparisons test. **(D)** GFP-actin FRAP recovery time constant (τ) in spines of PCs transfected as in **(A)** and treated with CK-666, SMIFH2, CK-666 + SMIFH2, or vehicle. Data are τ values obtained from independent experiments (n = 5–10; magenta line indicates mean); p values determined using one-way ANOVA ($p = 0.0003$) followed by Sidak's multiple comparisons test. **(E)** GFP-actin FRAP recovery plateau in spines of $Myo16^{em2}$ knockout PCs ($Myo16^{-/-}$) and $Myo16^{+/+}$ littermate PCs transfected as in **(A)** and treated with CK-666. Data represent plateau values obtained from independent experiments (n = 8; magenta line indicates mean); p value determined using Student's t-test. **(F)** GFP-actin FRAP recovery time constant (τ) in spines of $Myo16^{em2}$ knockout PCs ($Myo16^{-/-}$) and $Myo16^{+/+}$ littermate PCs transfected as in **(A)** and treated with CK-666. Data represent plateau values obtained from independent experiments (n = 8; magenta line indicates mean); p value determined using Student's t-test. **(G)** Circularity index of spines of PCs treated with CK-666 or vehicle and transfected as in **(A)**. Data points

(Continued)

FIGURE 7 | Continued

represent single spines, magenta line indicates median; p value determined using Mann–Whitney test. **(H)** Apparent area covered by single spines of PCs treated with CK-666 or vehicle and transfected as in **(A)**. Data points represents single spines, magenta line indicates median; p value determined using Mann–Whitney test. **(I)** Spine area changes over time of PCs treated with CK-666 or vehicle and transfected as in **(A)**. Data points represent SD of the relative area change of single spines monitored over 150 s, magenta line indicates median; p value determined using Mann–Whitney test. **(J)** Change of GFP-actin fluorescence intensity over time in spines of PCs treated with CK-666 or vehicle and transfected as in **(A)**. Data points represent the SD of the relative fluorescence change of single spines monitored over 150 s, magenta line indicates median; p value determined using Mann–Whitney test. **(K)** Circularity index of spines of PCs transfected as in **(A)** and treated with SMIFH2 (blue; final concentration, 40 μM) or with vehicle (0.2% [v/v] DMSO; black). Data points represent single spines, magenta line indicates median; p value determined using Mann–Whitney test. **(L)** Apparent area covered by single spines of PCs treated with SMIFH2 or vehicle and transfected as in **(A)**. Data points represent single spines, magenta line indicates median; p value determined using Mann–Whitney test. **(M)** Spine area changes over time of PCs treated with SMIFH2 or vehicle and transfected as in **(A)**. Data points represent SD of the relative area change of single spines monitored over 150 s, magenta line indicates median; p value determined using Mann–Whitney test. **(N)** Change of GFP-actin fluorescence intensity over time in spines of PCs treated with SMIFH2 or vehicle and transfected as in **(A)**. Data point represent SD of the relative fluorescence change of single spines monitored over 150 s, magenta line indicates median; p value determined using Mann–Whitney test. **(O)** Examples of spines of PCs treated with SMIFH2 or vehicle and transfected as described in **(A)**. GFP-actin was visualized by spinning disk confocal microscopy. Time is indicated in seconds. Scale bar, 2 μm. $^*p < 0.05$; $^{**}p < 0.01$; $^{***}p < 0.001$; $^{****}p < 0.0001$; n.s., not significant.

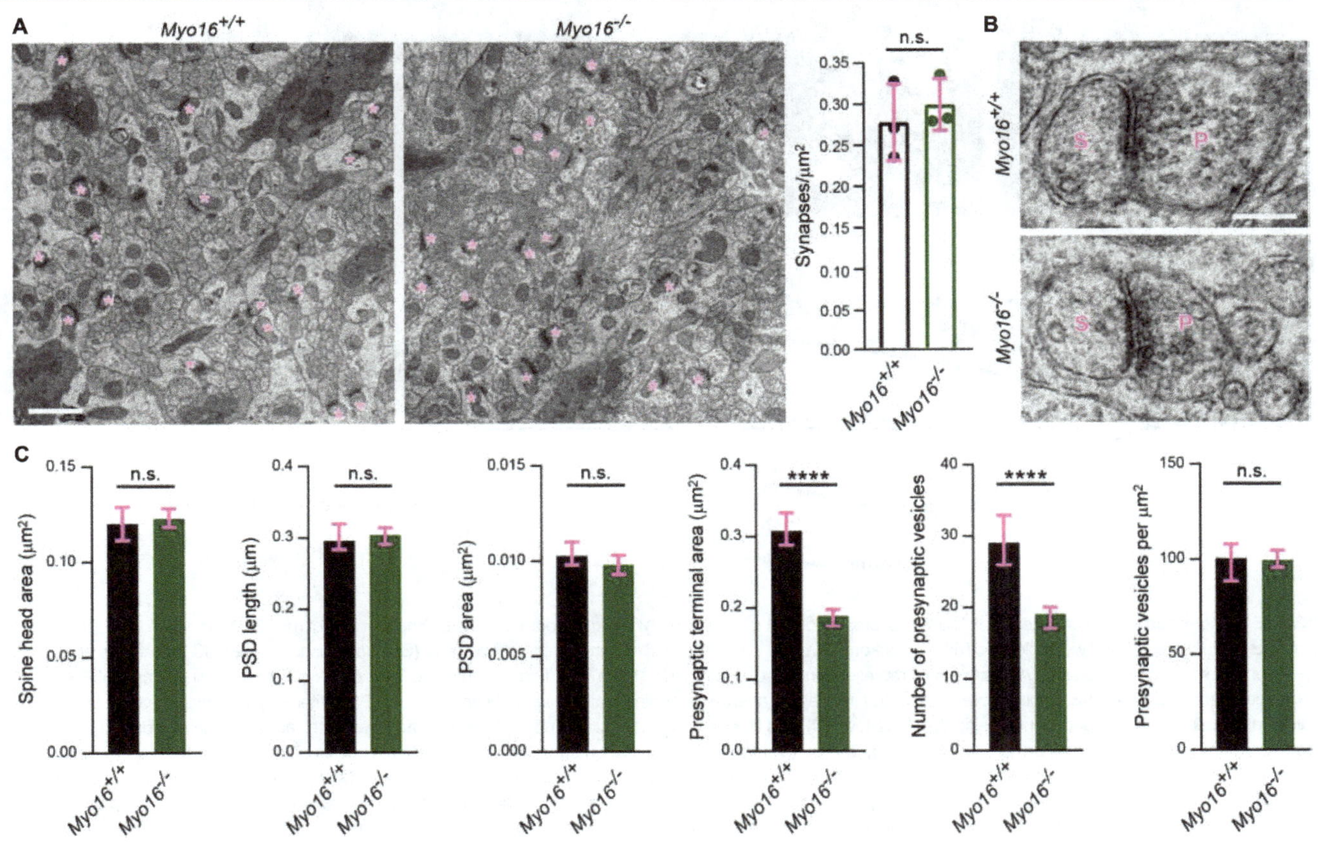

FIGURE 8 | Ultrastructural analysis reveals altered presynaptic organization in the cerebellar molecular layer of *Myo16*$^{-/-}$ knockout mice. **(A)** Electron microscopy images of the middle one third of the cerebellar molecular layer of adult male *Myo16*^{em3} knockout (*Myo16*$^{-/-}$) and *Myo16*$^{+/+}$ littermate control mice were surveyed for asymmetric synapses (indicated by magenta asterisks). Graph shows number of synapses per μm^2; bars indicate mean ± SEM (magenta), n = 3 (single data points represent mice analyzed), no significant differences detected (n.s.; p value determined using Student's t-test). Scale bar, 1 μm. **(B)** Representative electron microscopy images of cerebellar molecular layer synapses of adult male *Myo16*^{em3} knockout (*Myo16*$^{-/-}$) and *Myo16*$^{+/+}$ littermate mice. S, spine; P, presynaptic bouton. Scale bar, 250 nm. **(C)** Quantitative analysis of morphological parameters of cerebellar molecular layer synapses of *Myo16*$^{-/-}$ and *Myo16*$^{+/+}$ mice. Data are shown as median ± 95% confidence interval (magenta), n = 236 synapses (*Myo16*$^{+/+}$) and 380 (*Myo16*$^{-/-}$); p values determined using Mann–Whitney tests. $^*p < 0.05$; $^{**}p < 0.01$; $^{***}p < 0.001$; $^{****}p < 0.0001$; n.s., not significant.

Moreover, PSD length, PSD area and presynaptic vesicle density were unchanged at these synapses (**Figures 8B,C**). Strikingly, however, the area of presynaptic axon terminals and the absolute number of synaptic vesicles per terminal were dramatically reduced in the molecular layer of *Myo16*$^{-/-}$ cerebellum. Therefore, myosin XVI appears to be important for presynaptic ultrastructure and synaptic vesicle numbers at PF-PC synapses.

Both altered postsynaptic actin dynamics and the ultrastructural abnormalities at presynaptic terminals observed

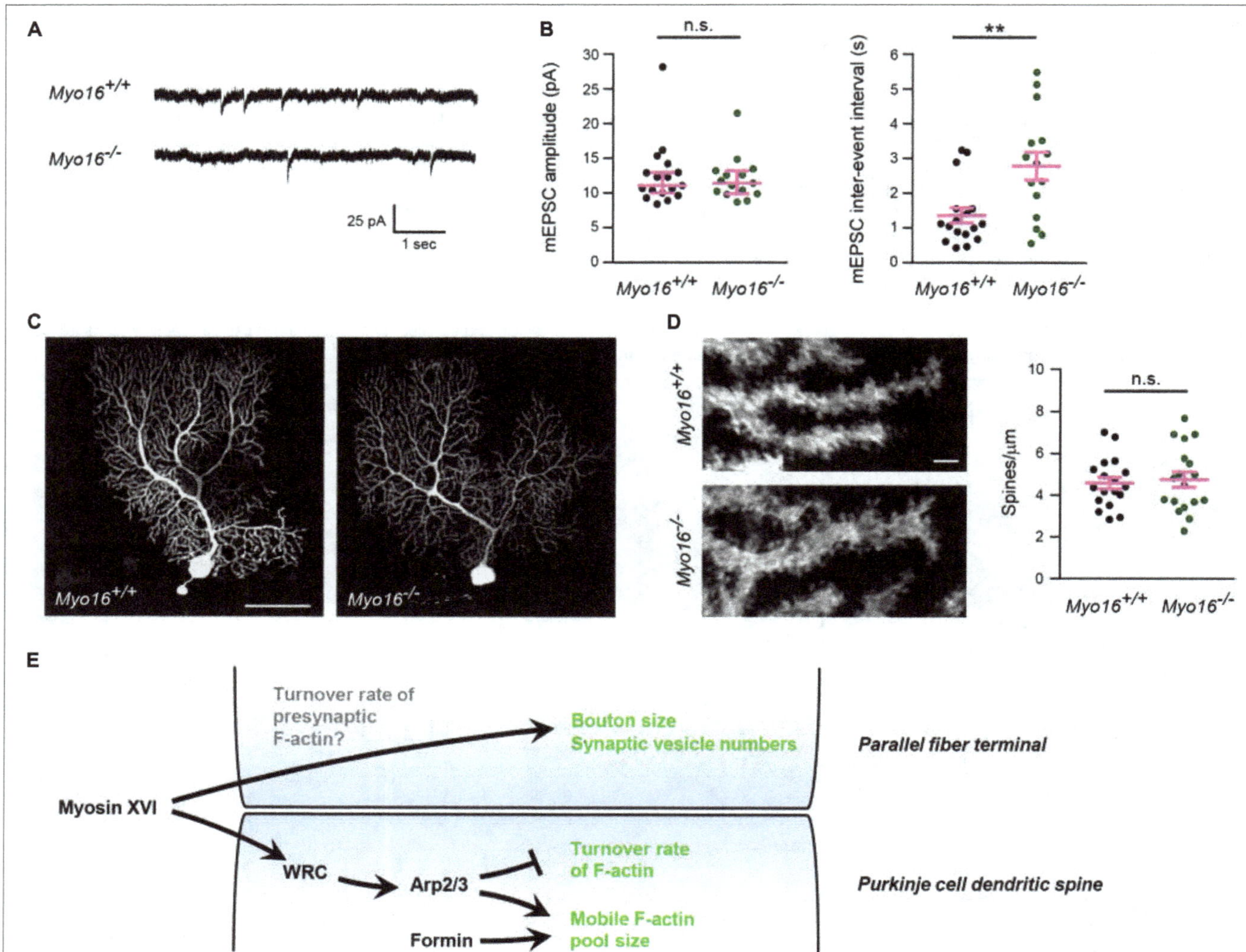

FIGURE 9 | Increased inter-event interval of AMPA receptor-mediated mEPSCs in *Myo16* knockout PCs. **(A)** Example traces of mEPSC measurement from PCs in acute cerebellar slices of 3–4 week old $Myo16^{em3}$ knockout ($Myo16^{-/-}$) and $Myo16^{+/+}$ littermate control mice. **(B)** Quantification of mEPSC amplitudes and inter-event intervals measured as in **(A)**. Data points represent analyzed PCs ($Myo16^{+/+}$: $n = 17$ from seven mice; $Myo16^{-/-}$: $n = 15$ from nine mice). mEPSC amplitude: median ± 95% confidence interval is indicated (magenta); *p* value determined using Mann–Whitney test. mEPSC inter-event interval: mean ± SEM is indicated (magenta); *p* value determined using Welch's *t*-test. **(C)** PCs filled with biocytin during mEPSC measurement were stained and visualized using confocal microscopy. Images show *Z*-stack projections. Scale bar, 50 μm. **(D)** Higher magnification images of PC dendrites with spines obtained as in **(C)**. Scale bar, 2 μm. Graph depicts number of spines per μm dendrite. Data points represent analyzed PCs, mean ± SEM is indicated (magenta); *p* value determined using Student's *t*-test. **(E)** Model of the role of myosin XVI at PF-PC synapses. In PC dendritic spines, myosin XVI is required for the attenuation of F-actin turnover. We propose that the myosin functions by promoting WRC activation which, in turn, activates Arp2/3-mediated branched F-actin formation. In addition to WRC and Arp2/3, also formins promote F-actin mobility in PC spines. However, interference with myosin XVI, WRC, and Arp2/3, but not with formins, accelerates F-actin turnover rate, consistent with formins acting in a separate pathway. At the presynaptic side, loss of myosin XVI leads to reduced numbers of synaptic vesicles and terminals of apparently reduced size. This may be a consequence (i) of a role of the myosin at the presynaptic side (e.g., in F-actin turnover) or (ii) of the postsynaptic changes in $Myo16^{-/-}$ PCs. $^{*}p < 0.05$; $^{**}p < 0.01$; $^{***}p < 0.001$; $^{****}p < 0.0001$; n.s., not significant.

in the absence of myosin XVI might affect the function of PF-PC synapses. To test whether *Myo16* knockout alters synaptic transmission onto PCs, we measured spontaneous AMPA receptor-mediated mEPSCs from PCs in acute cerebellar slices (**Figure 9A**). No difference in the peak amplitude of mEPSCs was observed when comparing $Myo16^{-/-}$ and wild-type littermate PCs (**Figure 9B**), suggesting that synaptic AMPA receptor content is unchanged. In contrast, the mEPSC inter-event interval was significantly longer in $Myo16^{-/-}$ PCs (**Figure 9B**). Such a reduced frequency of mEPSCs may arise from a reduced number of synapses formed on the PCs. However, no gross abnormalities in dendritic arborization of the analyzed PCs was observed (**Figure 9C**). Moreover, spine density on $Myo16^{-/-}$ PCs was unaltered (**Figure 9D**), and the density of excitatory molecular layer synapses was unchanged in $Myo16^{-/-}$ cerebellum (**Figure 8A**). Therefore, the increase in mEPSC inter-event interval provides further support for a reduced number

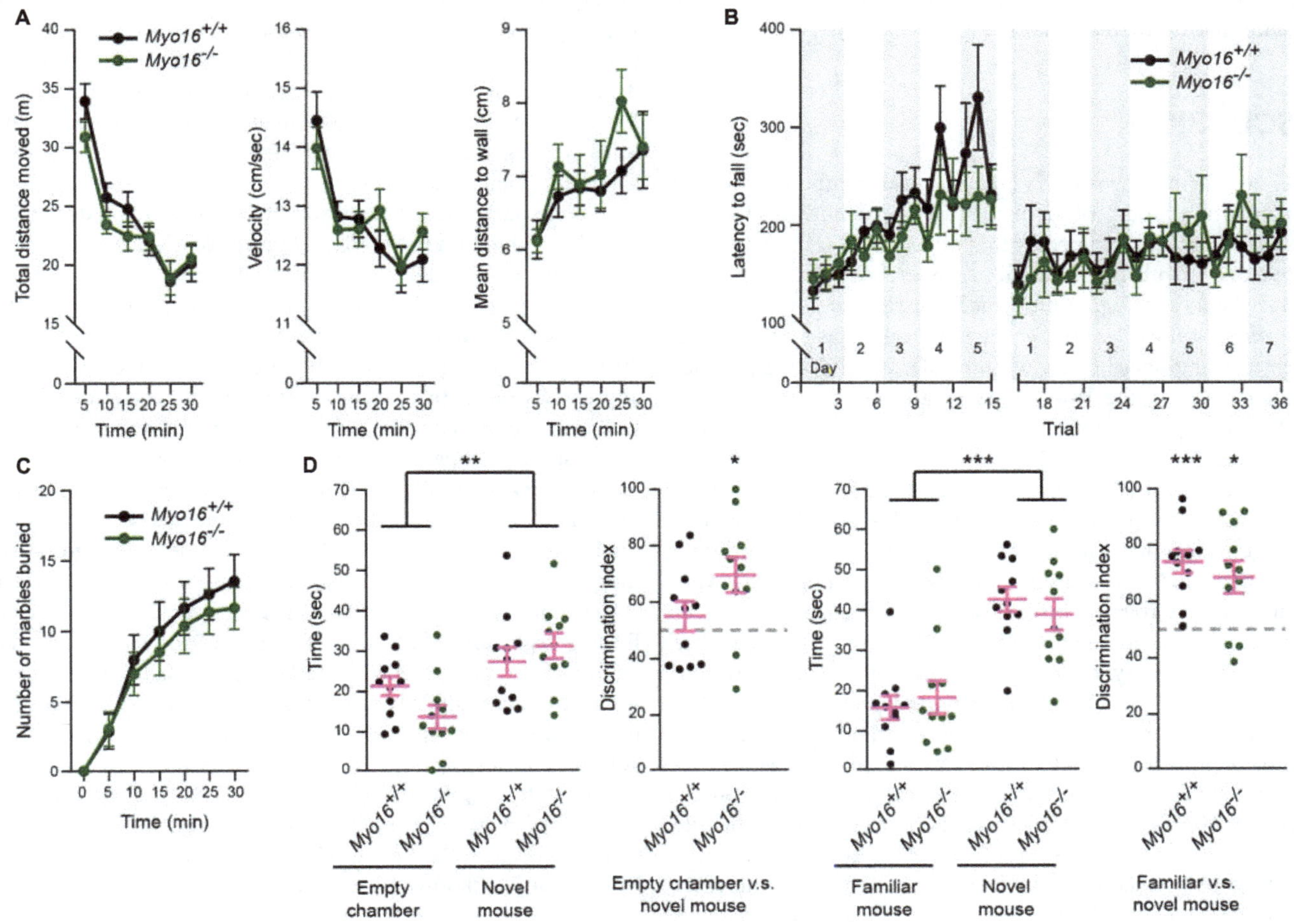

FIGURE 10 | Comparable performance of *Myo16*^{em3} knockout (*Myo16*$^{-/-}$) and *Myo16*$^{+/+}$ littermate control mice in a behavior test survey. **(A)** In the open field test, both genotypes showed similar locomotor habituation to the paradigm as indicated by the decrease in distance moved (genotype: $p = 0.42$), decreased mean velocity (genotype: $p = 0.88$) and an increased mean distance to wall (less thigmotaxis) (genotype: $p = 0.47$) over a 30 min test duration. **(B)** Latency to fall from an accelerating rotarod revealed significant increase of duration over trials ($p < 0.001$) with no effect of genotype ($p = 0.77$). **(C)** Both genotypes show similar performance in marble burying ($p = 0.61$). **(D)** Time exploring an empty cup vs. a novel mouse, or a familiar vs. a novel mouse during the first 2 min of a social recognition test. Mice spent more exploration time with the novel mouse vs. the empty cup ($p < 0.01$, no effect of genotype: $p = 0.17$) and more time investigating the novel mouse vs. the familiar mouse (choice: $p < 0.001$, no effect of genotype: $p = 0.82$). The discrimination index showed a significant preference of *Myo16*$^{-/-}$ but not the *Myo16*$^{+/+}$ mice for the novel mouse over the empty chamber ($p < 0.05$; $p = 0.372$, respectively) and a significant preference of both genotypes for the novel over the familiar mouse ($p < 0.05$; $p < 0.001$, respectively). Values represent mean ± SEM (**A–D**: repeated measures ANOVA, Discrimination index: one-sample *t*-test, test value: 50). *Myo16*$^{-/-}$ and *Myo16*$^{+/+}$ mice: $n = 11$ each. *$p < 0.05$; **$p < 0.01$; ***$p < 0.001$; ****$p < 0.0001$; n.s., not significant.

of presynaptic vesicles at PC synapses in *Myo16* knockout cerebellum (**Figures 8B,C**).

Myo16 Knockout Mice Show Comparable Performance to Controls in Motor- and Social Interaction-Tests

Given the synaptic roles of myosin XVI identified so far (**Figure 9E**), we examined whether *Myo16*$^{-/-}$ mice display behavioral abnormalities. In the open field test (**Figure 10A**), *Myo16*$^{-/-}$ mice were indistinguishable from wild-type littermate controls in terms of locomotor activity (total distance moved, velocity) and regarding a measure of anxiety (mean distance to wall). Since we found that MYO16 is important for F-actin dynamics in cerebellar PCs and that synaptic organization in the cerebellum is altered in *Myo16*$^{-/-}$ mice, we next monitored the motor learning ability of the knockout mice. In the accelerating rotarod test, both *Myo16*$^{-/-}$ and wild-type control mice improved their performance over the first five test days, without differing significantly between genotypes (**Figure 10B**). Therefore, mice lacking myosin XVI perform similar to wild-type controls in this test for motor learning. Given the genetic association of *MYO16* and ASD, we also examined *Myo16*$^{-/-}$ mice for behaviors altered in mouse models of ASD. A marble burying test did not reveal differences in repetitive behavior of *Myo16*$^{-/-}$ mice compared to littermate controls (**Figure 10C**). Moreover, a social interaction test did not reveal deficits of *Myo16*$^{-/-}$ mice in their ability to discriminate between an empty chamber or a novel mouse, or between a familiar and a novel mouse (**Figure 10D**). Therefore, at least this limited set of behavioral assays did not reveal gross abnormalities in mouse behavior upon *Myo16* knockout.

DISCUSSION

Here, we define myosin XVI as a novel component of the regulatory machinery of actin turnover in dendritic spines of cerebellar PCs, and we uncover that myosin XVI is important for normal presynaptic organization in the cerebellum.

Our results shed light on the mechanisms that govern F-actin turnover in spines of PCs, a neuronal cell type implicated in motor learning, social behavior and ASD. We show that, similar to other neurons, the WRC-Arp2/3 pathway is crucial for the regulation of postsynaptic actin turnover in PCs. Interference with either WRC or Arp2/3 led to a reduced mobile pool and faster F-actin turnover in spines (FRAP- and PC spine measurement-results are summarized in **Table 1**). Notably, our observation that acute inhibition of Arp2/3 accelerates turnover rate in dendritic spines is consistent with the finding that CK-666 increases retrograde actin flow rates at the leading edge of neuronal growth cones (Yang et al., 2012). In comparison, diverse outcomes for postsynaptic F-actin turnover upon interfering with Arp2/3 or WRC have been reported previously for other neurons. For example, sparse *in vivo* knockout of the Arp2/3 subunit *ArpC3* in a subset of hippocampal neurons leads to a reduced mobile pool and slower recovery (Kim et al., 2013). Moreover, WAVE1 knockdown was found to reduce the mobile pool of F-actin in cortical spines (Njoo et al., 2015). In contrast, heterozygous knockout of the WRC subunit *Cyfip1* increases the mobile pool while leaving the recovery rate of spine F-actin unchanged (Pathania et al., 2014).

While Arp2/3 drives the formation of a non-uniformly oriented F-actin meshwork, formins promote the formation of linear actin filaments. We show that formins are also crucial for actin cytoskeleton dynamics in PC dendritic spines, as formin inhibition dramatically reduces the size of the mobile F-actin pool (**Table 1**). The effect of SMIFH2 on mobile pool size being additive to CK-666 supports the view that formins promote F-actin dynamics in a pathway parallel to Arp2/3. Moreover, in contrast to Arp2/3, inhibition of formins leaves F-actin turnover rate in PC spines unchanged but dampens spine size fluctuations. Finally, PC spines become more elongated upon interfering with Arp2/3 or WRC (**Table 1**), consistent with formin-mediated polymerization of linear F-actin remaining. Along this line, depletion of MTSS1, a positive regulator of Arp2/3-mediated F-actin formation and negative regulator of formin DAAM1, also leads to longer PC spines (Saarikangas et al., 2015; Kawabata Galbraith et al., 2018).

We measured an increased size of PC spines upon dominant-negative inhibition of WRC (**Figure 6E**) and upon acute inhibition of Arp2/3 or formins (**Figures 7H,L**). This is surprising, given that in hippocampal neurons Arp2/3 is essential for the development of bigger, mature spines (Spence et al., 2016). In part, the distinct outcome may be due to different approaches taken (e.g., acute inhibition vs. genetic depletion). However, we propose that differences in the inherent properties of PC spines compared to hippocampal spines are also a major factor. For example, PC spines form independently of presynaptic input following an intrinsic program (Sotelo, 1978). Moreover, unlike hippocampal spines, PC spines do not undergo drastic morphological changes during plasticity (Sdrulla and Linden, 2007). Finally, in addition to WRC and Arp2/3, also specific F-actin regulators exist in PCs that are not found in other neurons (Miyagi et al., 2002; Sekerkova et al., 2003). Increased PC spine size might affect second messenger signaling within these microcompartements, leading to alteration in synaptic plasticity at PF-PC synapses.

Our data suggest a model where myosin XVI activates the WRC-Arp2/3 pathway in PC spines in order to affect F-actin turnover (**Figure 9E**). First, *Myo16* depletion via knockout or PC-specific knockdown phenocopies interference with the WRC-Arp2/3 pathway in terms of accelerated F-actin turnover rate in PC spines (**Table 1**). Second, there was no additive effect of *Myo16* knockout on F-actin turnover upon CK-666 treatment (**Figures 7E,F**), indicating that the myosin acts through Arp2/3. Third, the model is also supported by the known physical interaction of myosin XVI with the WRC (Yokoyama et al., 2011) and by the localization of both GFP-MYO16 and the WRC component WAVE1 to PC spines (**Figures 2, 5**). In contrast to interference with WRC and Arp2/3, however, depletion of myosin XVI did not alter the relative size of the mobile F-actin pool and spine circularity (**Table 1**). This is consistent with the existence of alternative, myosin XVI-independent ways of

TABLE 1 | Summary of GFP-actin FRAP and morphology/dynamics of Purkinje cell dendritic spines.

	Myo16 knockout	*Myo16* knockdown	WAVE1ΔVCA (WRC inhibition)	CK-666 (Arp2/3 inhibition)	SMIFH2 (formin inhibition)	CK-666 + SMIFH2
GFP-actin FRAP plateau*	–	–	↓	↓	↓	↓↓
GFP-actin FRAP tau	↓	↓	↓	↓	–	↓
Spine circularity	–	–	↓	↓	–	n.d.
Spine area	–	–	↑	↑	↑	n.d.
Spine area changes over time	–	–	↓	–	↓	n.d.
GFP-actin intensity changes in spines over time	–	–	↓	–	↓	n.d.

**Red arrows indicate significant decrease relative to control; green arrows indicate significant increase relative to control; black line indicates no change; n.d., not determined.*

activating WRC-Arp2/3. Similar to certain synaptic scaffolding proteins (e.g., IRSp53, nArgBP2; Takenawa and Suetsugu, 2007; Lee et al., 2016) and transmembrane proteins (e.g., neuroligins, protocadherins; Chen et al., 2014), myosin XVI might recruit the WRC at specific sites and facilitate its local activation. Nevertheless, our data argue against a general requirement of the myosin for localizing the WRC to spines, as WAVE1 is still present in spines of *Myo16* knockout cerebellum *in situ*. Myosin XVI might also function by bringing PP1c and/or PI3K in close proximity to the WRC in PC spines, thereby helping to regulate the local phosphorylation status – and thus activity – of the WRC.

Genetic ablation of Arp2/3 and WRC components leads to deficits in hippocampal synaptic transmission and to behavior deficits (Soderling et al., 2003, 2007; Kim et al., 2013; Spence et al., 2016). Therefore, also disrupted postsynaptic F-actin turnover caused by *Myo16* knockout may result in altered synaptic targeting of neurotransmitter receptors or altered spine morphology. However, our analyses did not reveal changes in PC spine density or spine morphology upon *Myo16* knockout. Moreover, subcellular fractionation and measurement of mEPSC amplitudes under basal activity indicate that synaptic AMPA receptor numbers are normal in the absence of myosin XVI. Notably, it has been suggested that the late phase of long-term depression in PCs requires actin polymerization (Smith-Hicks et al., 2010). Thus, while we did not detect alterations in postsynaptic morphology or function in *Myo16*$^{-/-}$ cerebellum, it is possible that myosin XVI-dependent actin turnover in PC spines specifically affects synaptic plasticity at PF-PC synapses. Importantly, the absence of a deficit in the rotarod test does not rule out that PC-dependent motor learning impairment is present in *Myo16* knockout mice and may be detected using other tests (compare e.g., with Ha et al., 2016).

Both ultrastructural analysis of the cerebellar molecular layer and mEPSC measurements pointed toward a striking presynaptic deficit at *Myo16*$^{-/-}$ PF-PC synapses. While synapse density was unchanged, a longer mEPSCs inter-event interval was observed, consistent with less spontaneous fusion events of synaptic vesicles in the absence of myosin XVI. This corroborates the reduction in presynaptic vesicle numbers visualized via electron microscopy. Notably, F-actin is also enriched at presynaptic sites, and presynaptic actin dynamics are thought to play a role for synaptic vesicle fusion (Rust and Maritzen, 2015). Moreover, *Wave1* knockout leads to altered morphology of axon terminals (Hazai et al., 2013), and we observed that WAVE1 localizes presynaptically at molecular layer synapses (**Figure 5C**). This raises the possibility that myosin XVI regulates actin dynamics at the presynaptic side to promote normal terminal size and synaptic vesicle numbers (**Figure 9E**). Future experiments will need to test this possibility.

Interference with the regulation of F-actin dynamics may lead to behavioral alterations. For example, *Wave1* knockout mice display motor coordination problems (Soderling et al., 2003). Moreover, an acute requirement of Arp2/3 activity for fear memory formation was demonstrated by microinjecting CK-666 into the lateral amygdala of live rats during fear conditioning (Basu et al., 2016). Since we observed altered F-actin turnover in PC spines and altered synaptic transmission onto PCs upon *Myo16* knockout, we carried out an initial behavioral characterization of *Myo16*$^{-/-}$ mice. Notably, while common variations at the *MYO16* locus are associated with ASD (Wang et al., 2009), it is not known if *Myo16* kockout mimics the effect of these alleles. Nevertheless, we included tests for ASD-like behavior. We did not detect phenotypes of *Myo16*$^{-/-}$ mice regarding locomotion activity, cerebellum-dependent motor learning, repetitive behavior and social interaction. This suggests that more elaborate future experiments will be needed to determine whether myosin XIV and/or actin turnover play a role for cerebellum-dependent functions such as motor learning or social behavior. Importantly, genetic evidence also indicates links of *MYO16* to schizophrenia (Rodriguez-Murillo et al., 2014) and to bipolar disorder (Kao et al., 2016). Moreover, epigenetic changes at the *MYO16* locus have been detected in depressed patients (Gross et al., 2017) and following learning tasks in mice (Koberstein et al., 2018). Together, this underscores the significance of determining in the future whether myosin XVI is crucial for the function of neuronal circuitry *in vivo*, and whether this involves regulation of F-actin dynamics.

MATERIALS AND METHODS

Plasmids

Prefix "pL7" denotes plasmids carrying the PC-specific *L7* (*Pcp-2*) promoter (Oberdick et al., 1990). Plasmids pL7-mGFP, pL7-mCherry and pL7-mGFP-F-tractin (i.e., pL7-ITPKA-9-52-mGFP) were described previously (Wagner et al., 2011a,b). pL7-ITPKA-9-52-mCherry is identical to pL7-ITPKA-9-52-mGFP except mGFP being replaced by mCherry. To generate pL7-FusionRed for expressing a red fluorescent volume marker in PCs, the FusionRed ORF (Shemiakina et al., 2012) was released from pFusionRed-C vector (#FP411, Evrogen, RU) using NheI, BglII restriction enzymes and ligated with vector backbone obtained by NheI, BglII digest of pL7-mGFP. Plasmid pL7-mGFP-actin was created by inserting a BglII, BamHI fragment encoding human β-actin from pPA-TagRFP-actin (#FP813, Evrogen, RU) in proper orientation into the BglII-site of pL7-mGFP. To generate plasmid pL7-FRED-WAVE1ΔVCA encoding WAVE1 lacking the VCA domain and fused at its N-terminus to FusionRed, a 1503 bp DNA fragment containing mouse *Wasf1* sequence (XM_006512932.2, nucleotides 468 to 1955) flanked by a BglII site at the 5′-end and a stop codon and SalI site at the 3′-end (i.e., 5′-agatct-CCGTTGGTG...AGTGACGCA-tgagtcgac, *Wasf1* sequence in upper case letters) was synthesized (Eurofins Genomics GmbH), digested with BglII and SalI, and ligated with vector backbone obtained by BglII, SalI digest of pL7-FusionRed. Plasmid pL7-mGFP-Myo16 encodes myosin XVI full length heavy chain (XP_006508842.1) fused at its N-terminus to GFP and corresponds to *Mus musculus Myo16* transcript variant X2 (XM_006508779.3) nucleotides 658-6417 cDNA inserted at the BglII, SalI sites of pL7-mGFP. Plasmid pCMV-mGFP-Myo16 was constructed by releasing a 6520 bp fragment comprising the mGFP-Myo16 sequence via NheI, BamHI digest from pL7-mGFP-Myo16. This fragment was ligated into the vector backbone obtained by NheI, BamHI digestion of pFusionRed-C. To construct plasmids for CRISPR/Cas9 sgRNA expression, the web-based tools CRISPRdirect[1], Optimized CRISPR design[2] and CCTop[3] were used to identify guide RNA (gRNA) target sequences flanking *Myo16* exon 3 (5′-TGCTTCAACTCTTGAAGGAGGGGGCAGATCCACA CACTCTCGTGTCCTCAGGAGGGTCTTTGCTACACCTG-3′) on chromosome 8. The selected gRNA target sequences (plus their PAM sequence in lower case letters) were TGCAATTTGCGAAGACCTAC-tgg (gRNA1), ACAATAGCTGTAGGGGCCGT-ggg (gRNA2) and AAGGGCCACGTAGTAACACC-tgg (gRNA3). 5′-phosphorylated oligonucleotides comprising the gRNA target sequence and its reverse complement (see **Table 2**) were annealed and ligated into the backbone of the pUC57-sgRNA expression vector (Shen et al., 2014) obtained by BsaI digestion, resulting in plasmids pUC57-M16upEx3-sgRNA, pUC57-M16up2Ex3-sgRNA, and pUC57-M16dwEx3-sgRNA. The pUC57-sgRNA expression vector was a gift from Xingxu Huang (Addgene plasmid #51132; RRID: Addgene_51132)[4]. Plasmids for expressing *Myo16* miRNA knockdown constructs under control of *CMV* promoter were termed pcDNA^{TM}6.2-GW/EmGFP-miR-*Myo16*-KD1, -KD2, -KD3, -KD4, -KD5 and -scrambled, and were constructed as follows: Target sequences were selected using Invitrogen's web-based RNAi Designer tool and mouse *Myo16* cDNA sequence BC151049.1. Five predicted perfect candidate target sequences (KD1–KD5) and a scrambled control (KD1 scrambled)[5] were chosen (see **Table 3**) and inserted into pcDNA^{TM}6.2-GW/EmGFP-miR using the BLOCK-iT^{TM} Pol II miR RNAi Expression Vector Kit (K4935-00, Invitrogen/Thermo Fisher Scientific) according the manufacturer's instructions. For this purpose, complementary oligonucleotides were annealed (KD1 forward, KD1 reverse, etc., see **Table 2**). Based on a previously described approach (Alexander and Hammer, 2016), we created plasmids expressing miRNA knockdown constructs under *L7* promoter control. Toward that end, DNA fragments containing the KD/scrambled sequence embedded in the miRNA backbone were PCR amplified from the respective pcDNA^{TM}6.2-GW/EmGFP-miR-*Myo16*-KD/scrambled plasmids using oligonucleotides L7sc_F and L7sc_R (**Table 2**). NheI and NotI-digested PCR fragments were inserted into the NotI/NheI sites of pL7-FusionRed to create pL7-miR-*Myo16* KD3 FRED, pL7-miR-*Myo16* KD5 FRED, and pL7-miR-*Myo16* scrambled FRED. Constructs were verified via restriction digests and sequencing.

Antibodies

A polyclonal MYO16 antibody (25104-1-AP, Proteintech) was employed. Before usage, the antibody solution was incubated

[1]https://crispr.dbcls.jp/
[2]http://crispr.mit.edu/
[3]https://crispr.cos.uni-heidelberg.de/
[4]http://n2t.net/addgene:51132
[5]https://www.genscript.com/tools/create-scrambled-sequence

TABLE 2 | Oligonucleotides used in this study.

Name	Sequence (5′ to 3′)
gRNA1-fw	taggTGCAATTTGCGAAGACCTAC
gRNA1-rv	aaacGTAGGTCTTCGCAAATTGCA
gRNA2-fw	taggACAATAGCTGTAGGGGCCGT
gRNA2-rv	aaacACGGCCCCTACAGCTATTGT
gRNA3-fw	taggAAGGGCCACGTAGTAACACC
gRNA3-rv	aaacGGTGTTACTACGTGGCCCTT
FW1	ATCGTGGGCAAGGGTTAATG
RV1	GCGAGCTGAGACTTGACATTC
FW2	CACGTAACAGGTTTGGGCACAAAG
RV2	TAGCGACACCTGTCACCTGAAATG
KD1 forward	TGCTGTGCTGAAGCCAATTACATTCAGTTTTGGCCACTGACTGACTGAATGTATGGCTTCAGCA
KD1 reverse	CCTGTGCTGAAGCCATACATTCAGTCAGTCAGTGGCCAAAACTGAATGTAATTGGCTTCAGCAC
KD2 forward	TGCTGTAGTGCAGTGAACTGAATGTCGTTTTGGCCACTGACTGACGACATTCATCACTGCACTA
KD2 reverse	CCTGTAGTGCAGTGATGAATGTCGTCAGTCAGTGGCCAAAACGACATTCAGTTCACTGCACTAC
KD3 forward	TGCTGTACACACTCTGTTTGCTCTTGGTTTTGGCCACTGACTGACCAAGAGCACAGAGTGTGTA
KD3 reverse	CCTGTACACACTCTGTGCTCTTGGTCAGTCAGTGGCCAAAACCAAGAGCAAACAGAGTGTGTAC
KD4 forward	TGCTGAGTAATGTCTGCCAGAGATTTGTTTTGGCCACTGACTGACAAATCTCTCAGACATTACT
KD4 reverse	CCTGAGTAATGTCTGAGAGATTTGTCAGTCAGTGGCCAAAACAAATCTCTGGCAGACATTACTC
KD5 forward	TGCTGATAAGAGCCACTGAGCTTCGTGTTTTGGCCACTGACTGACACGAAGCTGTGGCTCTTAT
KD5 reverse	CCTGATAAGAGCCACAGCTTCGTGTCAGTCAGTGGCCAAAACACGAAGCTCAGTGGCTCTTATC
Scrambled FW	TGCTGatactcattatcgacggacatGTTTTGGCCACTGACTGACATGTCCGTATAATGAGTAT
Scrambled RV	CCTGatactcattatacggacatGTCAGTCAGTGGCCAAAACATGTCCGTCGATAATGAGTATC
L7sc_F	ATTAGCGGCCGCTAAGCACTTCGTGGCCGTC
L7sc_R	TAAAGCTAGCCCCGGTAAACAAGGTACACTC

TABLE 3 | *Myo16* knockdown target sequences.

Name	Sequence (5′ to 3′)
KD1	TGAATGTAATTGGCTTCAGCA
KD2	GACATTCAGTTCACTGCACTA
KD3	CAAGAGCAAACAGAGTGTGTA
KD4	AAATCTCTGGCAGACATTACT
KD5	ACGAAGCTCAGTGGCTCTTAT
Scrambled	ATGTCCGTCGATAATGAGTAT

overnight at 4°C with 2% (w/v) brain powder prepared from *Myo16*$^{-/-}$ mice to block unspecific interactions. Subsequently, the mixture was centrifuged (30,000 × *g*, 30 min, 4°C) and the supernatant was used at a dilution of 1:600 for Western blot detection. To prepare the knockout brain powder, brains were washed in 0.8% NaCl before adding 1 ml buffer A (1 mM EGTA, 100 mM MES, 0.5 mM $MgCl_2$, pH 6.5 with NaOH) per 1 mg brain tissue and homogenization with Potter S Homogenizer (Sartorius AG). After centrifugation (150,000 × g, 1 h, 4°C), the pellet was resuspended in acetone. After 10 min of stirring, the precipitate was let sink down, mixed with fresh acetone and stirred again. After another repeat with fresh acetone, the mixture was filtered to recover the precipitate. After drying overnight, the brain powder was stored at -80°C. In addition, the following antibodies were used in this study at the indicated dilutions (WB, Western blot; IHC, immuno-histochemistry; IEM, immuno-electron microscopy): anti-α-Tubulin (mouse, clone DM1A, T9026, Sigma-Aldrich; WB 1:1,000 – 1:10,000), anti-TUBA4A (rabbit, 177479, Abcam, WB 1:2,000-1:5,000), anti-GFP (rabbit, G1544, Sigma-Aldrich; WB 1:250 – 1:500), anti-WAVE1 (rabbit, WP1731, ECM Biosciences; WB 1:1,000, IHC 1:100, IEM 1:100), anti-Calbindin-D-28K (mouse, C9848, Sigma-Aldrich; IHC 1:200), anti-GluA1 (rabbit, AB1504, Millipore, WB 1:500), anti-GluA2 (mouse, MAB397, Millipore, WB 1:500), anti-PSD-95 (mouse, MA-1-046, Thermo, WB 1:500), anti-$GABA_A$ alpha1 (guinea pig, 224205, Synaptic Systems, WB 1:500), anti-NLGN2 (rabbit, 129203, Synaptic Systems, WB 1:500, IHC 1:300), anti-GAPDH (mouse, GTX28245, Genetex, WB 1:1,000-1:2,500), anti-VGLUT1 (guinea pig, AB5905, Millipore, IHC 1:200), anti-Shank2 (rabbit, 162202, Synaptic Systems, IHC 1:300), peroxidase-conjugated anti-rabbit (donkey, 711-036-152, Jackson Immuno Research; WB 1:10,000), peroxidase-conjugated anti-mouse (donkey, 715-036-151, Jackson Immuno Research; WB 1:10,000), Alexa488-conjugated anti-rabbit (711-545-152, Jackson Immuno Research; IHC 1:1,000), Alexa546-conjugated anti-mouse (A11029, Invitrogen/Thermo Fisher Scientific; IHC 1:1,000), and biotinylated anti-rabbit IgG (BA-1000, Vector Laboratories, IEM 1:1,000).

Mice, Genotyping

Wild type (WT) mice were C57BL/6J (B6). Two novel mouse lines carrying distinct *Myo16* knockout alleles and termed B6-*Myo16*^{em2Hhtg}/J ("S line"; 210 bp deletion) and B6-*Myo16*^{em3Hhtg}/J ("L line"; 269 bp deletion) were generated using CRISPR/Cas9. Both deletions comprise exon 3 of *Myo16* and are thus predicted to lead to a premature stop codon after 77 amino acid residues of MYO16. Plasmids pUC57-M16upEx3-sgRNA, pUC57-M16up2Ex3-sgRNA, and pUC57-M16dwEx3-sgRNA, encoding sgRNA1, sgRNA2, and sgRNA3, respectively, under control of the *T7* promoter, were linearized with DraI and used for *in vitro* transcription using the HiScribe™ T7 High Yield RNA Synthesis Kit (E2040S, New England Biolabs) according to the manufacturer's instructions. Transcripts were subsequently purified with the MEGAclear™ Transcription Clean-Up Kit (AM1908, ThermoFisher Scientific) according to the manufacturer's instructions. Pronuclear injection into 1-cell stage embryos obtained from superovulated C57BL6/J mice was performed according to standard protocols using 5 ng/μl for each sgRNA and 16 ng/μl Cas9 protein (M0641T, New England Biolabs). Injected embryos were implanted into F1 foster mothers (C57BL6/J x CBA). PCR genotyping (see below) and sequencing of PCR products identified a founder mouse (#43) that carried both mutant alleles and inherited either one or the other allele, giving rise to both the S and L lines. Gross observation did not reveal phenotypic differences between WT, S and L lines. Moreover, brain size of homozygous *Myo16* knockout mice was indistinguishable from WT littermates (distance Bregma to Lambda, *Myo16*$^{+/+}$: 6.4 ± 0.7 mm, *Myo16*$^{-/-}$: 7.8 ± 1.3 mm; brain area, *Myo16*$^{+/+}$: 88.5 ± 14.6 mm^2, *Myo16*$^{-/-}$: 114.1 ± 34.6 mm^2; cerebellar area: *Myo16*$^{+/+}$: 23.3 ± 3.3 mm^2, *Myo16*$^{-/-}$: 26.7 ± 7.3 mm^2; mean ± SD, $n = 3$; p = n.s., Student's *t*-test). PCR genotyping was performed to distinguish among absence, heterozygous presence or homozygous presence of the *Myo16* knockout alleles. Genomic DNA was obtained by digesting tail biopsies or, for neuronal cultures, embryo tissue with QuickExtract™ DNA Extraction Solution (Epicentre) for 30 min at 65°C, followed by incubation for 10 min at 97°C. PCR was performed using primers FW2 and RV2 (see **Table 2**), Taq DNA Polymerase (Roche # 04728874001), and reaction conditions of 94°C for 2 min; 35 times repeat of (94°C for 10 s, 67°C for 20 s, 72°C for 10 s); followed by 72°C for 3 min. DNA fragments were separated on 1.2–2.0% agarose gels and imaged using a UV transillumination/digital camera system (INTAS Science Imaging Instruments). *Myo16* knockout alleles yield a 191 bp (S line) or 132 bp (L line) fragment, the WT allele yields a 401 bp fragment (**Figure 1B**). Alternatively, PCR was performed as above, but using primers FW1 and RV1 (see **Table 2**), and reaction conditions of 94°C for 2 min; 35 times repeat of (94°C for 10 s, 68°C for 20 s, 72°C for 25 s); followed by 72°C for 5 min. Here, *Myo16* knockout alleles yield a 519 bp (S line) or 460 bp (L line) fragment, the WT allele yields a 729 bp fragment. Homozygous *Myo16* knockout mice (*Myo16*$^{-/-}$ mice) were obtained by mating heterozygous mice. Absence of MYO16 protein in *Myo16*$^{-/-}$ mice was confirmed by Western blot using pre-adsorbed anti-MYO16 antibody and extracts of cerebellum (**Figure 1C**) and hippocampus of young and adult mice.

Protein Extracts, Fractionation, and Western Blot Analyses

For detection of MYO16 and WAVE1 in cerebellar crude extracts (**Figures 1C, 5A**), single cerebella were lysed in ice cold lysis buffer (150 mM NaCl, 1% IGEPAL® CA-630 [I8896,

Sigma-Aldrich], 50 mM Tris–Cl pH8.0, protease inhibitors [cOmplete™ Protease Inhibitor Cocktail; #04693116001, Roche]) using 12 strokes with Potter S Homogenizer (Sartorius AG). The homogenate was centrifuged at 600 × g for 10 min, 4°C and the supernatant was mixed with 20% (v/v) loading dye (5% β-mercaptoethanol, 0.02% bromophenol blue, 30% glycerol, 10% sodium dodecyl sulfate [SDS], 250 mM Tris–Cl pH 6.8) and denatured (10 min, 97°C).

Subcellular fractionation of cerebellar extracts (**Figures 1H,I**) to yield a crude extract (S1), a membrane-enriched fraction (P2), a cytosolic fraction (S2), and a synaptosomal fraction (SYP) was carried out by lysing a complete cerebellum in Sucrose 1 buffer (320 mM sucrose, 1 mM $NaHCO_3$, 1 mM $MgCl_2$, 500 μM $CaCl_2$, 1 μM PMSF) in the presence of EDTA-free protease inhibitors (cOmplete Tablets, EASYpack, 04693132001, Roche) and phosphatase inhibitors (PhosSTOP, EASYpack, 04906837001, Roche), by potterization in 2 ml teflon tubes at 800 rpm and 12 strokes. S1 post-nuclear fraction was obtained by centrifugation of the total lysate at 1,400 × *g* for 10 min at 4°C. A fraction of S1 was conserved for further analysis and the rest was centrifugated at 13,800 × g for 10 min at 4°C to obtain S2 soluble and P2 membranous fractions. S2 fraction was conserved and P2 was resuspended in Sucrose 2 buffer (320 mM sucrose, 1 mM $NaHCO_3$). P2 was shaken for 20-30 min at 4°C. Sucrose gradient for synaptosomal purification was achieved by sequentially adding three distinct layers of 1.2 M, 1 M, and 0.8 M sucrose in the presence of $NaHCO_3$. A part of the P2 fraction was conserved for analysis and 400 μl were placed on top of the gradient and centrifugated at 22,000 rpm using SW40 Ti rotor for 2 h at 4°C. Synaptosomes were isolated from the interface between 1.2 and 1 M fractions of the gradient using a 1 ml syringe. In order to assess myosin XVI localization in synaptosomes (**Figure 2A**), an identical protocol was used, however, omitting phosphatase inhibitors and PMSF from sucrose buffer 1 and, occasionally, $NaHCO_3$ from sucrose gradient. Protein concentration was quantified with Pierce™ BCA Protein Assay kit (#23227, Thermo Fisher Scientific), and identical amounts of proteins were mixed with loading dye and denatured as above.

Cerebellar crude extracts and fractions were separated via standard SDS-PAGE using 6–15% gels. Spectra™ Multicolor High Range Protein Ladder (26625, Thermo Fischer Scientific) and BlueStar Plus prestained protein markers (MWP04 and MWP03, Nippon Genetics) were used as size standards. Proteins were transferred onto methanol-activated polyvinylidene difluoride membranes (PVDF; Immobilon-P, #IPVH00010, Merck Millipore) using transfer buffer 1 (39 mM glycine, 48 mM Tris–Cl pH 8.3, 0.037% SDS, 20% [v/v] methanol) and semi-dry blotter V20-SDB (SCIE-PLAS, Cambridge, United Kingdom) for 2 h or transfer buffer 2 (25 mM Tris–Cl pH 8.3, 192 mM glycine and 20% [v/v] methanol) and wet blotting via Mini-Protean Tetra Cell system (Biorad). Subsequently, the membrane was blocked with TBST (20 mM Tris–Cl pH 7.6, 150 mM NaCl, 0.1% Tween20) containing 5% (w/v) non-fat dry milk or 3% bovine serum albumin (BSA) for 1 h at room temperature (RT). Incubations with primary and horse-radish peroxidase-coupled secondary antibodies were also carried out in blocking solution.

For *Myo16* knockdown in HEK cells, HEK293 cells (CRL-1573, ATCC) grown in DMEM, high glucose, GlutaMAX™ Supplement (61965026, ThermoFisher Scientific) containing 20% serum to a density of ~75% were co-transfected using the calcium phosphate method (Gromova et al., 2018) with plasmid pCMV-mGFP-Myo16 and a knockdown plasmid (pcDNA™6.2-GW/EmGFP-miR-*Myo16*-KD1, -KD2, -KD3, -KD4, -KD5, or -scrambled), as indicated. Cells were harvested 48 h after transfection and lysed on ice by pipetting up and down in PBS (137 mM NaCl, 2.7 mM KCl, 10 mM Na_2HPO_4, 1.8 mM KH_2PO_4, pH 7.4) containing 1% Triton X-100, protease inhibitors (cOmplete™, EDTA-free Protease Inhibitor Cocktail; #04693132001, Roche) and phosphatase inhibitors (PhosSTOP™; #04906845001, Roche). After centrifugation at 1,000 × g for 5 min at 4°C, the supernatant was removed and protein concentration was quantified with Pierce™ BCA Protein Assay kit (#23227, Thermo Fisher Scientific). Identical amounts of protein were separated via SDS-PAGE using 8–15% gels. Western blots were performed as above except that loading dye contained 10% β-mercaptoethanol, size standard was Precision Plus Protein™ Dual Color Standard (1610374, Biorad), and wet blotting was used with transfer buffer 2.

Chemiluminiscence detection was performed using Immobilon Western HRP Substrate (#WBKLS0500, Merck Millipore) and CCD camera-based ChemoStar ECL detection system (ChemoCam Imager ECL Typ HR 16-3200, INTAS Science Imaging Instruments, Göttingen, GER). Signals were quantified using Fiji image processing software (Schindelin et al., 2012).

Dissociated Cerebellar Cultures Containing Purkinje Cells

Preparation and transfection of cerebellar cultures containing PCs was done as described (Wagner et al., 2011b), with minor modifications. Briefly, C57BL/6J X C57BL/6J or $Myo16^{\pm}$ X $Myo16^{\pm}$ matings were used to obtain E17-18 mouse embryos from females after euthanization with CO_2 and cervical dislocation. Embryonic brains were isolated in ice-cold modified Hank's balanced salt solution (MHS; HBSS without calcium and magnesium, Gibco™ 14170088, Thermo Fisher Scientific) and treated individually during the whole procedure. In case of *Myo16* knockout cultures, $Myo16^{-/-}$, $Myo16^{\pm}$ and $Myo16^{+/+}$ brains were distinguished using PCR genotyping using embryo head tissue while the isolated brains were stored in Hibernate™-E medium (Gibco™ A1247601, Thermo Fisher Scientific) up to 6 h. The cerebellar primordium was minced and digested for 20 min at 30°C using 7 U papain (P3125, Sigma-Aldrich). After addition of heat-inactivated fetal bovine serum (FBS; Gibco™ 10082139, Thermo Fisher Scientific), cells were triturated in MHS containing 12 mM $MgSO_4$ (M2643, Sigma-Aldrich) and 5 U/ml DNAse I (Roche 04716728001, Sigma-Aldrich) and filtered through a nylon mesh (180 μm pore size, #NY8H04700, Millipore). After a wash in MHS, all cells from one cerebellum were nucleofected in a single reaction using Mouse Neuron Nucleofector® Kit (VPG-1001; Lonza; nucleofection program O-003) according to manufacturer's instructions. The transfected cells were then mixed with untransfected cells from one WT cerebellum resuspended in 300 μl DFM (see below) supplemented with 10% (v/v) FBS. DFM consisted of Dulbecco's Modified Eagle's Medium/Nutrient Mixture F-12 Ham (D6434, Sigma-Aldrich) supplemented with 1x GlutaMAX (Gibco^{TM} 35050-038; Thermo Fisher Scientific), 100 μM putrescine dihydrochloride (P5780, Sigma-Aldrich), 30 nM Na_2SeO_3 (S5261, Sigma-Aldrich), 40 nM progesterone (P7556, Sigma-Aldrich), 0.77 nM L-3,3′,5-tri-iodothyronine (T2877, Sigma-Aldrich), 2 μM cytosine β-D-arabinofuranoside (C6645, Sigma-Aldrich), 200 μg/ml apo-transferrin (T1147, Sigma-Aldrich), 100 μg/ml BSA (A3156, Sigma-Aldrich), and 20 μg/ml insulin (I0516; Sigma-Aldrich). The whole cell mixture was plated onto the glass surface (14 mm diameter) of a single glass bottom dish (D35-14-1.5-N, Invitro Scientific) coated with poly-L-ornithine hydrobromide (P4638, Sigma-Aldrich), thus resulting in a single culture of transfected cells per cerebellum. Cultures were kept in an incubator (37°C, 5% CO_2, saturated humidity). At 1.5 h after plating, 1.8 ml DFM containing 5 μg/ml gentamicin (Gibco^{TM} 15710049; Thermo Fisher Scientific) were added per dish, and 4–36 h after plating 1.5 ml of culture medium were replaced with fresh DFM/gentamicin. Subsequently 1 ml of medium was replaced by fresh DFM/gentamicin once per week.

Live Cell Microscopy

Cultured PCs were observed using a spinning disk confocal microscope (Visitron Systems GmbH) consisting of an inverted microscope (Nikon Ti-E) equipped with a spinning disk (Yokogawa), solid state lasers (405, 488, 561, and 647 nm), a 100× objective, EM-CCD cameras (Hamamatsu Photonics), autofocus system (Nikon TI-ND6-PFS), a multi-point FRAP/photo-activation module (VisiFRAP, Visitron Systems GmbH), and an incubation chamber for controlled environmental conditions (37°C, 5% CO_2). During imaging, cultures were kept in their conditioned growth medium. Images shown in **Figures 2B,D** were obtained by recording *Z*-stacks (0.3 μm *Z*-plane distance) and subjecting them to noise removal (de-noise, low pass filter; VisiView® software, Visitron Systems GmbH). Maximum projections were generated and stitched using Fiji/MosaicJ (Thevenaz and Unser, 2007; Schindelin et al., 2012). Images shown in **Figures 2C,E,F**, as well as **Supplementary Movies S1–S3** were obtained recording at a frame rate of 0.5/s, followed by noise removal (de-noise, low pass filter; VisiView® software, Visitron Systems GmbH). Subsequently images were processed in Fiji (Schindelin et al., 2012) using bleach correction (histogram matching) and generation of a three frame rolling average image.

Fluorescence Recovery After Photobleaching

To measure F-actin turnover in PC spines, FRAP experiments were performed with cultured PCs expressing GFP-actin at 14–15 DIV using the spinning disk microscope with a 100× objective. Images were obtained using 488 nm excitation and an exposure time of 500 ms. In each trial, following five frames of starting point recording (frame rate of 1/s), the GFP-actin fluorescence signal of six single spines on a PC was bleached by directing 405 nm laser light to a circular region (12 pixel diameter) placed on the spine (∼2 s total bleach time for six spines). Imaging was resumed immediately after and continued for 145 s at a frame rate of 1/s. If indicated, the following compounds were added to the culture medium prior to carrying out FRAP recordings: jasplakinolide (#420127-50UG, Merck; added to final concentration of 1 μM; FRAP performed 10–60 min after addition), CK-666 (#3950, Tocris Bioscience; added to final concentration of 200 μM; FRAP performed within 90 min after addition), SMIFH2 (S4826, Sigma-Aldrich; added to final concentration of 40 μM; FRAP performed 5–50 min after addition, as with combination of SMIFH2 and CK-666).

GFP-actin fluorescence intensity signal in bleached spines was quantified using Fiji (Schindelin et al., 2012; Schneider et al., 2012). Intensity was measured from a region of constant size encompassing the spine throughout the duration of the experiment. To determine recovery of the bleached fluorescence signal, the intensity measured in each frame was reduced by the intensity remaining in the first frame after bleaching, yielding baseline-corrected intensity values F_b. To correct for overall bleaching during the experiment, F_b was multiplied with a bleach factor (y) calculated for each trial and time point, yielding bleach-corrected intensity values (F_{bc}). To obtain y, fluorescence intensity in each frame was measured from part of the cell that included only spines not targeted by FRAP bleaching. After background correction of the measured intensities, bleach factor y was determined for each time point using Excel (Microsoft) by fitting a curve described by the exponential equation

$$y = at^b$$

(a and b, fitted variables; t, time) to the values obtained by dividing the initial, background-corrected intensity by the background-corrected intensity at each time point. The mean of F_{bc} (the bleach-corrected intensity values) before FRAP bleaching was normalized to 100% (F_0), and F_{bc} values at each time point after bleaching were expressed relative to F_0 (GFP-actin fluorescence,% of initial), yielding the fluorescence recovery curve. For each independent experiment (i.e., for each culture of transfected PCs derived from an individual embryo), a mean recovery curve was calculated from the recovery curves of roughly 50 spines on average, with up to six curves originating from a single FRAP trial. To calculate plateau and time constant τ of GFP-actin fluorescence intensity recovery in spines, the mean recovery curves from each experiment were fitted to the equation

$$y = P(1 - exp(-kx))$$

y, GFP-actin fluorescence intensity; x, time; P, plateau; k, inverse of τ. In case a mean recovery curve showed an intensity decrease of more than five percentage points at any time during the recovery phase, the values following the pre-decrease maximum value were ignored when fitting the equation. If this led to less than 70 s of recovery time that could be fitted, the data were excluded entirely from analysis. Cells that were immotile and stiff (i.e., apparently dead) during FRAP recording were also excluded from analyses. Spines were excluded if the fluorescence signal was oversaturated, if the spine overlapped with another spine during the 150 s of recording, or if the fluorescence signal was not bleached close to background level.

Spine Morphology and Dynamics of Live PCs

The following parameters were determined using Fiji and the time-lapse movies of GFP-actin recorded during the FRAP experiments. 50 spines (five spines from ten PCs) that were not FRAP-bleached were analyzed for each condition. The area covered by randomly selected, individual spines was determined in each frame by selecting a threshold at the level of dendritic shaft GFP-actin signal intensity, followed by an automatic creation of a smoothened region of interest (ROI) around the above-threshold spine GFP-actin signal in each frame. The "spine area" was determined by averaging the ROI area of the first three frames (1 s recording interval) for each spine. The variation of the spine area during 2.5 min (150 frames of recording), denoted as "SD (area over time)," is the standard deviation of the relative area (% of initial) over 150 frames, with the average area of the first three frames representing 100%. A circularity index (CI) was calculated from the ROI using the formula

$$CI = \frac{4\pi a}{p^2}$$

(a, area; p, perimeter) (Rubio et al., 2011) and is given as the average value of the first three frames (1 s recording interval) for each spine. The variation of the GFP-actin signal intensity in spines during 2.5 min (150 frames of recording), denoted as "SD (intensity over time)," is the standard deviation of the relative fluorescence intensity (% of initial) over 150 frames, with the average intensity of the first 20 frames representing 100%. Spine GFP-actin signal intensity was determined for each frame by measuring the integrated intensity within the above determined ROI, followed by background subtraction, bleaching correction and calculation of a 20 frame rolling average intensity value.

Immuno-Histochemistry and Immuno-Electron Microscopy

For WAVE1 immuno-histochemistry (**Figure 5B**), ~6 month old adult mice were anesthetized by a mixture of ketanest and rompun and transcardially perfused with 4% paraformaldehyde (PFA) in phosphate-buffer (PB). Brains were post-fixed in PFA/PB (overnight, 4°C) before 50 μm vibratome sections were cut. Brain sections were washed in PBS, incubated for 10 min in 0.5% (w/v) $NaBH_4$ in PBS, washed again in PBS, and blocked for 30 min in PBS containing 10% (v/v) horse serum (HS), 0.3% (w/v) BSA and 0.3% (v/v) Triton X-100. Sections were then incubated with primary antibodies diluted in carrier (PBS containing 1% HS, 0.2% BSA and 0.3% Triton X-100) for 24 h at 4°C with gentle agitation, washed in PBS, and incubated for 2 h with secondary antibodies diluted in carrier. After wash in PBS, sections were mounted on glass slides using ProLong^{TM} Gold Antifade Mountant (P36930; Thermo Fisher Scientific), imaged on an Olympus FV1000 confocal laser scanning microscope (60× objective; 0.8 μm Z-plane thickness).

Similarily, for immuno-histochemistry shown in **Figures 1D–G**, 19–26 week old mice were perfused as above. Postfixation was carried out for 48 h, followed by cryoprotection of the brains in 30% Sucrose/PBS. Brains were frozen in TissueTek at -80°C and 40 mm thick sagittal sections were obtained with a cryostat (Cryostar NX70, Thermo Scientific). For staining, sections were washed in PBS and permeabilized 20 min in presence of PBS/0.5% Triton X-100 at RT. Subsequently, sections were washed three times in PBS and blocked with blocking buffer (PBS/10% goat serum/1% BSA) for 1–2 h at RT. Primary antibodies were diluted in Ab incubation buffer (PBS/3% goat serum, 1% BSA/0.05% Triton X-100) and incubated over night in a wet chamber at 4°C before washing the sections three times in PBS, followed by incubation with the secondary antibodies in Ab incubation buffer (1–2 h at RT). After three washes, sections were mounted using Aqua Poly/Mount (18606-20, Polysciences, Inc.) and observed using confocal laser scanning microscopy as above.

Images were processed and analyzed using Fiji (Schindelin et al., 2012). Shank2 clusters were manually counted in a ~432 um^2 square area within three sections of the cerebellar molecular layer (identified via calbindin staining) for each animal. NLGN2 clusters were counted in a ~6000 um^2 square area spanning the whole molecular layer in five sections per animal using the "Analyze Particles" function.

For Nissl staining, sections were delipidized in ethanol with increasing concentration (70, 95, and 100%) followed by submersion in xylen (30 s per step). Rehydration was performed following the opposite order ending in H_2O for 4 min. After 3–4 min incubation in cresyl violet stain (0.1% cresyl violet acetate, 2.5% glacial acetic acid) sections were rinsed with dH_2O for 1 min and 6–7 times in 70% ethanol. Subsequently, a differentiation step was carried out by alternating between 95% ethanol and 95% ethanol with 10% acetic acid. Sections were then dehydrated with consecutive 30 s washes in 95% ethanol, 100% ethanol and xylen before covered with entellan. Images were taken with a stereomicroscope (Stemi 2000C, Zeiss, GER).

For ultrastructural electron microscopy (**Figure 8**), 40 week old anesthetized mice that previously underwent behavioral testing (see below) were transcardially perfused with 4% PFA (postfixed in a mixture of 4%PFA and 1% glutaraldehyde) in 0.1 M PB at pH 7.4. Similarly, for immuno-electron microscopy (**Figure 5C**), 38 week old mice were transcardially perfused with a mixture of 4% PFA and 0.1% glutaraldehyde in 0.1 M PB at pH 7.4. Brains were removed and 100 μm thick sagittal sections were cut with a Vibratom (Leica VT 1000S). Thereafter, pre-embedding immuno-electron microscopy was performed as follows: Sections were cryoprotected in 2.3M sucrose and subjected to two cycles of freeze-thaw in liquid nitrogen to aid penetration of immunoreagents into tissue. After rinsing in PBS, sections were incubated with PBS containing 10% HS and 0.2% BSA for 15 min, before being incubated with primary antibody in PBS containing 1% HS and 0.2% BSA overnight. Cells were washed with PBS, then incubated with biotinylated secondary antibody in PBS containing 1% HS and 0.2% BSA for 90 min. After rinsing, they were incubated with ABC (Vector Labs) diluted 1:100 in PBS for 90 min. Sections were washed in PBS and reacted in diaminobenzidine (DAB)-H_2O_2 solution

(Sigma, St. Louis, United States) for 10 min. Thereafter sections were rinsed three times in 0.1 M sodium cacodylate buffer (pH 7.2–7.4) (Sigma-Aldrich, Buchs, Switzerland) and incubated with 1% osmium tetroxide (Science Services, Munich, Germany) in cacodylate buffer for 20 min on ice. The osmication of sections was followed by dehydration through ascending ethyl alcohol concentration steps and rinsed twice in propylene oxide (Sigma-Aldrich, Buchs, Switzerland). Infiltration of the embedding medium was performed by immersing the tissue first in a mixture of 2:1 of propylene oxide and Epon (Carl Roth, Karlsruhe, Germany), then in a 1:1 mixture, and finally in neat Epon and hardened at 60°C for 48 h. Ultrathin sections (60 nm) were collected and analyzed with an EM902 transmission electron microscope (Zeiss, Germany) equipped with a CCD in lens 2K digital camera and running the ImageSP software (Tröndle, Moorenweis, Germany).

Quantification of synaptic parameters from electron microscopy images was performed using Fiji. For counting molecular layer synapse numbers, 7.086 μm × 7.086 μm images were obtained with 12,000× magnification. 25 consecutive images of the middle third area of the molecular layer were analyzed for each animal, with a total of three animals per genotype. Synapses were counted if they showed a uninterupted outline of the pre- and postsynaptic specialization, ER structure and PSD in spine head and an opposing presynaptic terminal with vesicles. For analyzing spine and presynaptic structural properties, images of the cerebellar molecular layer were taken using 20,000× magnification. Synapses were identified using the same criteria as before.

Cerebellar Slice Electrophysiology and Biocytin Staining of PCs

Mice used for electrophysiological measurements were 3–4 weeks old. After decapitation of mice under isoflurane anesthesia, the brain was removed into ice-cold slicing medium containing (in mM) 240 sucrose, 2.5 Na_2HPO_4, 2 $MgSO_4$, 26 $NaHCO_3$, 10 D-glucose, and 1 $CaCl_2$ which was carbonated continuously (95% O_2, 5% CO_2). 200 μm thick sagittal slices of the cerebellum were cut using a vibratome (Leica CT1200S) and left for incubation in artificial cerebrospinal fluid (ACSF) containing (in mM) 124 $NaCl_2$, 5 KCl, 1.25 $NaHPO_4$, 2 $MgSO_4$, 26 $NaHCO_3$, 20 D-glucose and 2 $CaCl_2$ for 1 h at 37°C and constant carbonation. mEPSCs were measured at 34°C and in the presence of 100 μM picrotoxin (P1675, Sigma-Aldrich), 50 μM (2R)-amino-5-phosphonovalecric acid (D-APV; 79055-68-8, Tocris) and 1 μM tetrodotoxin (TTX; 1078, Tocris). Whole-cell patch clamp recordings were performed with an EPC10 amplifier (HEKA Electronics, Lamprecht, Germany). PCs were visualized using a research Zeiss Axioskop 2 FS plus microscope equipped with a 40x objective. Recording electrodes of 4–5 MΩ, 1.5 mm outer diameter and 0.87 mm inner diameter (1810016, Hilgenberg) were filled with intracellular solution containing (in mM) 120 K-gluconate, 9 KCl, 10 KOH, 3.48 $MgCl_2$, 4 NaCl, 10 HEPES, 4 Na_2ATP, 0.4 Na_3GTP, 17.5 sucrose and 1 mg/ml biocytin (3349, Tocris) (pH 7.25–7.35 with an osmolality of 295 ± 5). Recordings were excluded from analysis if the noise level exceeded 10 pA. Slices with successfully measured cells were fixed after recording in Histofix (P087.6, Roth), washed with PBS and permeabilized in PBS/0.2% Triton. 20% [w/v] BSA was added for blocking. For staining, Alexa Fluor® 488 streptavidin conjugate (S32354, Invitrogen/Thermo Fisher Scientific) was diluted in PBS/20% BSA (1:1,000). Slices were mounted in Aqua Poly/Mount (18606-20, Polysciences, Inc.) and imaged using a confocal laser scanning microscope (Olympus FV1000) equipped with a 60× objective (488 nm laser line for excitation, 0.2 μm *Z*-plane thickness). Deconvolution was performed using AutoQant (100 deconvolution cycles; Media Cybernetics Inc.). To determine spine density, Imaris filament tracer and Imaris 8.4.1 spine module (Imaris Bitplane) were used.

Mouse Behavior Analyses

All behavior experiments were performed with a cohort of males of the B6-$Myo16^{em3Hhtg}/J$ line backcrossed to C57BL/6J for at least five generations. Heterozygous mice were bred in house to obtain naïve, age-matched $Myo16^{+/+}$ (11 individuals) and $Myo16^{-/-}$ (11 individuals) mice for the experiments. Weight did not differ significantly between groups. Animals were housed in groups of littermates (3–5 individuals per cage) in an acclimatized animal vivarium (21 ± 1°C, relative humidity 55 ± 5%) under a 12 h:12 h reversed light/dark cycle and were tested during dark hours. The mice had *ad libitum* access to food and water. At the beginning of the experiments, animals were between 9 and12 weeks old. All experiments were performed blind to genotype.

Open Field

The open field apparatus consisted of four identical square (50×50×50 cm) arenas made of white polyvinyl foam material. Four lamps were installed that provided even lightning (50 lux) in each arena and a video camera that was mounted directly above the apparatus. The videos were transmitted to a computer running Ethovision tracking software (Version XT8.5, Noldus Technology, Netherlands). Up to 4 mice were tested at the same time, counterbalanced across genotypes but blind to the experimenter. The mice were introduced to one corner of the arena and were allowed to explore undisturbed for 30 min. Total distance moved, velocity and mean distance to the wall were analyzed in 5 min consecutive time bins.

Rotarod

The Ugo Basile Model 47600 (Comerio, VA, Italy) accelerating rotarod for mice was used. The testing area was illuminated diffusely with 30 lux white light. A digital camera was located close to the apparatus to capture videos. The test was performed in two steps. For habituation, up to five subjects were tested simultaneously and placed on the rotating drum at a baseline speed of four rounds per minute (rpm) for up to 180 s. Two trials were performed with an inter-trial interval of 50–60 min. On the same day, three trials were performed for each subject with the speed increasing linearly for 4 min from 4 to 40 rpm. Animals were allowed to stay on the rotating drum for up to 600 s with an inter trial interval of 50–60 min. On the next 5 days each subject was tested in three trials per day of accelerating speed as described above, however, the inter-trial interval was shortened to 10–15 min. The latency to fall was measured. Two capture a second time window, the same animals performed the task again 5 weeks later for seven consecutive days.

Marble Burying Test

Two 26×42 cm cages, filled 6 cm high with fine fresh bedding material were used. Cages were closed with a plastic plate leaving space for air circulation. On the bedding, 20 marbles were placed in a regular pattern, covering the whole area. The apparatus was illuminated by diffuse light of 30 lux. A digital camera was located close to the apparatus to capture videos. Each mouse was introduced into the cage and allowed to explore freely for 30 min. Between subjects, the bedding was stirred thoroughly, pressed down to have a plane surface and marbles were again placed on top. The marbles buried were counted manually in 5 min time bins.

Social Interaction Test

The social interaction test was performed in a white, compartmentalized box made out of polyvinyl foam material. The box had the dimensions of 61 × 37 cm and was divided twice, resulting in three linked compartments: left (22 × 37 cm), center (17 × 37 cm), and right (22 × 37 cm), with doors in between. In the outer compartments, a round chamber (12 cm diameter, 13 cm high) with a heavy lid was placed. The apparatus was illuminated with 30 lux and a digital camera was mounted directly above the setup. Videos were transmitted to a computer running Ethovision tracking software (Version XT8.5, Noldus Technology, Netherlands) equipped with three-point (nose, body center, and tail) detection settings. After 5 min of habituation in the center compartment, doors were opened and mice were allowed to move freely between all three compartments. Active exploration was scored when the nose of the test mouse was detected within a distance of 2 cm to the round chambers. A WT mouse unknown to the test mouse (novel mouse) was present in one chamber, whereas the second chamber was empty. After 10 min a second, unfamiliar WT mouse (novel mouse) was placed in the empty chamber and the test mouse was allowed to explore for another 10 min. In the first part of the test, time spent with the novel mouse compared to the empty chamber was analyzed. In the second part, the time spent with unfamiliar mouse compared to familiar mouse was analyzed. Discrimination index was calculated as time spent with "novel mouse" divided by the time spent with "empty chamber" and "novel mouse" multiplied by 100 (part 1), or time spent with "novel mouse" divided by the time spent with "familiar mouse" and "novel mouse" (part 2) multiplied by 100.

Statistics

Analyses were performed using Prism 7.04 (GraphPad Software, Inc.). All data sets were subjected to Shapiro-Wilk normality test. When comparing two groups fulfilling the normality test, p values were obtained using Student's t-test (if variance in data sets was the same according to F test) or using t-test with Welch's correction (if variance in data sets was different according to F test). When comparing two groups not fulfilling the normality test, exact p values were obtained using Mann–Whitney test. For comparison of more than two groups that all fulfill the normality test, the presence of significant differences was first evaluated using ordinary one-way ANOVA, followed by Dunnett's, Tukey's or Sidak's multiple comparisons test against the control values. For comparison of more than two groups that not all fulfill the normality test, the presence of significant differences was first evaluated using ordinary Kruskal-Wallis test, followed by Dunn's multiple comparisons test against the control values. Significance values are indicated in the figures as $^{*}p < 0.05$; $^{**}p < 0.01$; $^{***}p < 0.001$; $^{****}p < 0.0001$; n.s., not significant. For behavior analyses, data were analyzed using IBM SPSS Statistics (SPSS Inc., Chicago, IL, United States, Version 22). The statistical tests are indicated in the figure legends of each experiment. For statistical significance a type I error rate of $p = 0.05$ was defined, all tests were performed two tailed. For analyzing data measured in different time bins, repeated measures ANOVA with genotype as between subject factor and time (bins) as within subject factor was carried out, followed by a Bonferroni *post hoc* test whenever appropriate.

ETHICS STATEMENT

This study was carried out in accordance with the recommendations of the European Community Council Directive (2010/63/EU) and the procedures used were approved by the City of Hamburg (Behörde für Gesundheit und Verbraucherschutz, Lebensmittelsicherheit und Veterinärwesen).

AUTHOR CONTRIBUTIONS

WW conceptualized the work and wrote the original draft. All authors contributed to the methodology and wrote, reviewed, and edited the manuscript. MR, FL, SF, MS, and WW contributed to the investigation and formal analysis. IH-B and MK contributed to the resources. MK and WW acquired the funding. SF, JS, and WW supervised the work.

FUNDING

This work was supported by the Deutsche Forschungsgemeinschaft (DFG, German Research Foundation) projects FOR2419 WA3716/1-1 (to WW), FOR2419 KN556/11-1 and FOR2419 KN556/11-2 (to MK).

ACKNOWLEDGMENTS

We thank Martijn Schonewille and Gerco Beekhof for advice regarding cerebellar slice electrophysiology, Pirta Hotulainen for critical reading of the manuscript, and Sabine Hoffmeister-Ullerich, Sarah Homann, Peggy Putthoff, Chudamani Raithore, and Hille Voß for excellent technical support.

SUPPLEMENTARY MATERIAL

MOVIE S1 | Movie depicting GFP-MYO16 (green) in dendritic spines of live Purkinje cells (volume marker; magenta). Time indicated in min:sec; scale bar, 2 μm. Related to **Figure 2C**.

MOVIE S2 | Movie depicting F-actin (F-tractin probe; green) in dendritic spines of live Purkinje cells (volume marker; magenta). Time indicated in min:sec; scale bar, 2 μm. Related to **Figure 2E**.

MOVIE S3 | Movie depicting GFP-MYO16 (green) and F-actin (F-tractin probe; magenta) in dendritic spines of live Purkinje cells. Time indicated in min:sec; scale bar, 2 μm. Related to **Figure 2F**.

MOVIE S4 | Movie depicting an example for FRAP analysis of GFP-actin in Purkinje cell spines. Green circles indicate bleached spines. Time indicated in min:sec; scale bar, 2 μm. Related to **Figure 3A**.

MOVIE S5 | Movie depicting GFP-actin in dendritic spines of live Purkinje cells transfected with control plasmid (pL7-FRED). Time indicated in min:sec; scale bar, 2 μm. Related to **Figure 6H**.

MOVIE S6 | Movie depicting GFP-actin in dendritic spines of live Purkinje cells transfected with a plasmid encoding a dominant-negative version of WAVE1 (pL7-FRED-WAVE1 ΔVCA). Time indicated in min:sec; scale bar, 2 μm. Related to **Figure 6H**.

REFERENCES

Alexander, C. J., and Hammer, J. A. III (2016). Optimization of cerebellar purkinje neuron cultures and development of a plasmid-based method for purkinje neuron-specific, miRNA-mediated protein knockdown. *Methods Cell Biol.* 131, 177–197. doi: 10.1016/bs.mcb.2015.06.004

Basu, S., Kustanovich, I., and Lamprecht, R. (2016). Arp2/3 and VASP are essential for fear memory formation in lateral amygdala. *eNeuro* 3:ENEURO.0302-16.2016. doi: 10.1523/eneuro.0302-16.2016

Basu, S., and Lamprecht, R. (2018). The role of actin cytoskeleton in dendritic spines in the maintenance of long-term memory. *Front. Mol. Neurosci.* 11:143. doi: 10.3389/fnmol.2018.00143

Bertling, E., Englund, J., Minkeviciene, R., Koskinen, M., Segerstrale, M., Castren, E., et al. (2016). Actin tyrosine-53-phosphorylation in neuronal maturation and synaptic plasticity. *J. Neurosci.* 36, 5299–5313. doi: 10.1523/JNEUROSCI.2649-15.2016

Bisi, S., Disanza, A., Malinverno, C., Frittoli, E., Palamidessi, A., and Scita, G. (2013). Membrane and actin dynamics interplay at lamellipodia leading edge. *Curr. Opin. Cell Biol.* 25, 565–573. doi: 10.1016/j.ceb.2013.04.001

Borovac, J., Bosch, M., and Okamoto, K. (2018). Regulation of actin dynamics during structural plasticity of dendritic spines: signaling messengers and actin-binding proteins. *Mol. Cell Neurosci.* 91, 122–130. doi: 10.1016/j.mcn.2018.07.001

Briatore, F., Patrizi, A., Viltono, L., Sassoè-Pognetto, M., and Wulff, P. (2010). Quantitative organization of GABAergic synapses in the molecular layer of the mouse cerebellar cortex. *PLoS One* 5:e12119. doi: 10.1371/journal.pone.0012119

Bubb, M. R., Senderowicz, A. M., Sausville, E. A., Duncan, K. L., and Korn, E. D. (1994). Jasplakinolide, a cytotoxic natural product, induces actin polymerization and competitively inhibits the binding of phalloidin to F-actin. *J. Biol. Chem.* 269, 14869–14871.

Cameron, R. S., Liu, C., Mixon, A. S., Pihkala, J. P., Rahn, R. J., and Cameron, P. L. (2007). Myosin16b: the COOH-tail region directs localization to the nucleus and overexpression delays S-phase progression. *Cell Motil. Cytoskeleton* 64, 19–48. doi: 10.1002/cm.20162

Cameron, R. S., Liu, C., and Pihkala, J. P. (2013). Myosin 16 levels fluctuate during the cell cycle and are downregulated in response to DNA replication stress. *Cytoskeleton* 70, 328–348. doi: 10.1002/cm.21109

Chang, S. C., Pauls, D. L., Lange, C., Sasanfar, R., and Santangelo, S. L. (2013). Sex-specific association of a common variant of the XG gene with autism spectrum disorders. *Am. J. Med. Genet. B Neuropsychiatr. Genet.* 162B, 742–750. doi: 10.1002/ajmg.b.32165

Chazeau, A., Garcia, M., Czondor, K., Perrais, D., Tessier, B., Giannone, G., et al. (2015). Mechanical coupling between transsynaptic N-cadherin adhesions and actin flow stabilizes dendritic spines. *Mol. Biol. Cell* 26, 859–873. doi: 10.1091/mbc.E14-06-1086

Chazeau, A., and Giannone, G. (2016). Organization and dynamics of the actin cytoskeleton during dendritic spine morphological remodeling. *Cell Mol. Life Sci.* 73, 3053–3073. doi: 10.1007/s00018-016-2214-1

Chazeau, A., Mehidi, A., Nair, D., Gautier, J. J., Leduc, C., Chamma, I., et al. (2014). Nanoscale segregation of actin nucleation and elongation factors determines dendritic spine protrusion. *EMBO J.* 33, 2745–2764. doi: 10.15252/embj.201488837

Chen, B., Brinkmann, K., Chen, Z., Pak, C. W., Liao, Y., Shi, S., et al. (2014). The WAVE regulatory complex links diverse receptors to the actin cytoskeleton. *Cell* 156, 195–207. doi: 10.1016/j.cell.2013.11.048

Chen, J. H., Kellner, Y., Zagrebelsky, M., Grunwald, M., Korte, M., and Walla, P. J. (2015). Two-Photon correlation spectroscopy in single dendritic spines reveals fast actin filament reorganization during activity-dependent growth. *PLoS One* 10:e0128241. doi: 10.1371/journal.pone.0128241

Chen, Z., Borek, D., Padrick, S. B., Gomez, T. S., Metlagel, Z., Ismail, A. M., et al. (2010). Structure and control of the actin regulatory WAVE complex. *Nature* 468, 533–538. doi: 10.1038/nature09623

Cingolani, L. A., and Goda, Y. (2008). Actin in action: the interplay between the actin cytoskeleton and synaptic efficacy. *Nat. Rev. Neurosci.* 9, 344–356. doi: 10.1038/nrn2373

Cramer, L. P. (1999). Role of actin-filament disassembly in lamellipodium protrusion in motile cells revealed using the drug jasplakinolide. *Curr. Biol.* 9, 1095–1105. doi: 10.1016/s0960-9822(99)80478-3

de la Torre-Ubieta, L., Won, H., Stein, J. L., and Geschwind, D. H. (2016). Advancing the understanding of autism disease mechanisms through genetics. *Nat. Med.* 22, 345–361. doi: 10.1038/nm.4071

Dolan, B. M., Duron, S. G., Campbell, D. A., Vollrath, B., Shankaranarayana Rao, B. S., Ko, H. Y., et al. (2013). Rescue of fragile X syndrome phenotypes in Fmr1 KO mice by the small-molecule PAK inhibitor FRAX486. *Proc. Natl. Acad. Sci. U.S.A.* 110, 5671–5676. doi: 10.1073/pnas.1219383110

Duffney, L. J., Zhong, P., Wei, J., Matas, E., Cheng, J., Qin, L., et al. (2015). Autism-like deficits in Shank3-Deficient mice are rescued by targeting actin regulators. *Cell Rep.* 11, 1400–1413. doi: 10.1016/j.celrep.2015.04.064

Fujita-Jimbo, E., and Momoi, T. (2014). Specific expression of FOXP2 in cerebellum improves ultrasonic vocalization in heterozygous but not in homozygous Foxp2 (R552H) knock-in pups. *Neurosci. Lett.* 566, 162–166. doi: 10.1016/j.neulet.2014.02.062

Gromova, K. V., Muhia, M., Rothammer, N., Gee, C. E., Thies, E., Schaefer, I., et al. (2018). Neurobeachin and the Kinesin KIF21B are critical for endocytic recycling of NMDA receptors and regulate social behavior. *Cell Rep.* 23, 2705–2717. doi: 10.1016/j.celrep.2018.04.112

Gross, J. A., Pacis, A., Chen, G. G., Drupals, M., Lutz, P. E., Barreiro, L. B., et al. (2017). Gene-body 5-hydroxymethylation is associated with gene expression changes in the prefrontal cortex of depressed individuals. *Transl. Psychiatry* 7:e1119. doi: 10.1038/tp.2017.93

Grove, M., Demyanenko, G., Echarri, A., Zipfel, P. A., Quiroz, M. E., Rodriguiz, R. M., et al. (2004). ABI2-deficient mice exhibit defective cell migration, aberrant dendritic spine morphogenesis, and deficits in learning and memory. *Mol. Cell Biol.* 24, 10905–10922. doi: 10.1128/mcb.24.24.10905-10922.2004

Ha, S., Lee, D., Cho, Y. S., Chung, C., Yoo, Y. E., Kim, J., et al. (2016). Cerebellar Shank2 regulates excitatory synapse density, motor coordination, and specific repetitive and anxiety-like behaviors. *J. Neurosci.* 36, 12129–12143. doi: 10.1523/jneurosci.1849-16.2016

Hazai, D., Szudoczki, R., Ding, J., Soderling, S. H., Weinberg, R. J., Sotonyi, P., et al. (2013). Ultrastructural abnormalities in CA1 hippocampus caused by deletion of the actin regulator WAVE-1. *PLoS One* 8:e75248. doi: 10.1371/journal.pone.0075248

Hlushchenko, I., Khanal, P., Abouelezz, A., Paavilainen, V. O., and Hotulainen, P. (2018). ASD-Associated de novo mutations in five actin regulators show both shared and distinct defects in dendritic spines and inhibitory synapses in cultured hippocampal neurons. *Front. Cell Neurosci.* 12:217. doi: 10.3389/fncel.2018.00217

Hlushchenko, I., Koskinen, M., and Hotulainen, P. (2016). Dendritic spine actin dynamics in neuronal maturation and synaptic plasticity. *Cytoskeleton* 73, 435–441. doi: 10.1002/cm.21280

Honkura, N., Matsuzaki, M., Noguchi, J., Ellis-Davies, G. C., and Kasai, H. (2008). The subspine organization of actin fibers regulates the structure and plasticity of dendritic spines. *Neuron* 57, 719–729. doi: 10.1016/j.neuron.2008.01.013

Hotulainen, P., and Hoogenraad, C. C. (2010). Actin in dendritic spines: connecting dynamics to function. *J. Cell Biol.* 189, 619–629. doi: 10.1083/jcb.201003008

Hotulainen, P., Llano, O., Smirnov, S., Tanhuanpaa, K., Faix, J., Rivera, C., et al. (2009). Defining mechanisms of actin polymerization and depolymerization during dendritic spine morphogenesis. *J. Cell Biol.* 185, 323–339. doi: 10.1083/jcb.200809046

Ito, M. (2001). Cerebellar long-term depression: characterization, signal transduction, and functional roles. *Physiol. Rev.* 81, 1143–1195. doi: 10.1152/physrev.2001.81.3.1143

Joensuu, M., Lanoue, V., and Hotulainen, P. (2018). Dendritic spine actin cytoskeleton in autism spectrum disorder. *Prog. Neuropsychopharmacol. Biol. Psychiatry* 84, 362–381. doi: 10.1016/j.pnpbp.2017.08.023

Johnson, H. W., and Schell, M. J. (2009). Neuronal IP3 3-kinase is an F-actin-bundling protein: role in dendritic targeting and regulation of spine morphology. *Mol. Biol. Cell* 20, 5166–5180. doi: 10.1091/mbc.E09-01-0083

Kao, C. F., Chen, H. W., Chen, H. C., Yang, J. H., Huang, M. C., Chiu, Y. H., et al. (2016). Identification of susceptible loci and enriched pathways for Bipolar II Disorder using genome-wide association studies. *Int. J. Neuropsychopharmacol.* 19:yw064. doi: 10.1093/ijnp/pyw064

Kasai, H., Fukuda, M., Watanabe, S., Hayashi-Takagi, A., and Noguchi, J. (2010). Structural dynamics of dendritic spines in memory and cognition. *Trends Neurosci.* 33, 121–129. doi: 10.1016/j.tins.2010.01.001

Kawabata Galbraith, K., Fujishima, K., Mizuno, H., Lee, S. J., Uemura, T., Sakimura, K., et al. (2018). MTSS1 regulation of actin-nucleating formin DAAM1 in dendritic filopodia determines final dendritic configuration of purkinje cells. *Cell Rep.* 24, 95–106.e9. doi: 10.1016/j.celrep.2018.06.013

Kengyel, A., Becsi, B., Konya, Z., Sellers, J. R., Erdodi, F., and Nyitrai, M. (2015). Ankyrin domain of myosin 16 influences motor function and decreases protein phosphatase catalytic activity. *Eur. Biophys. J.* 44, 207–218. doi: 10.1007/s00249-015-1015-z

Kim, H. J., DiBernardo, A. B., Sloane, J. A., Rasband, M. N., Solomon, D., Kosaras, B., et al. (2006). WAVE1 is required for oligodendrocyte morphogenesis and normal CNS myelination. *J. Neurosci.* 26, 5849–5859. doi: 10.1523/jneurosci.4921-05.2006

Kim, Y., Sung, J. Y., Ceglia, I., Lee, K. W., Ahn, J. H., Halford, J. M., et al. (2006). Phosphorylation of WAVE1 regulates actin polymerization and dendritic spine morphology. *Nature* 442, 814–817. doi: 10.1038/nature04976

Kim, I. H., Racz, B., Wang, H., Burianek, L., Weinberg, R., Yasuda, R., et al. (2013). Disruption of Arp2/3 results in asymmetric structural plasticity of dendritic spines and progressive synaptic and behavioral abnormalities. *J. Neurosci.* 33, 6081–6092. doi: 10.1523/JNEUROSCI.0035-13.2013

Kneussel, M., and Wagner, W. (2013). Myosin motors at neuronal synapses: drivers of membrane transport and actin dynamics. *Nat. Rev. Neurosci.* 14, 233–247. doi: 10.1038/nrn3445

Koberstein, J. N., Poplawski, S. G., Wimmer, M. E., Porcari, G., Kao, C., Gomes, B., et al. (2018). Learning-dependent chromatin remodeling highlights noncoding regulatory regions linked to autism. *Sci. Signal.* 11:eaan6500. doi: 10.1126/scisignal.aan6500

Konietzny, A., Bar, J., and Mikhaylova, M. (2017). Dendritic actin cytoskeleton: structure, functions, and regulations. *Front. Cell Neurosci.* 11:147. doi: 10.3389/fncel.2017.00147

Korobova, F., and Svitkina, T. (2010). Molecular architecture of synaptic actin cytoskeleton in hippocampal neurons reveals a mechanism of dendritic spine morphogenesis. *Mol. Biol. Cell* 21, 165–176. doi: 10.1091/mbc.E09-07-0596

Koskinen, M., Bertling, E., and Hotulainen, P. (2012). Methods to measure actin treadmilling rate in dendritic spines. *Methods Enzymol.* 505, 47–58. doi: 10.1016/B978-0-12-388448-0.00011-5

Koskinen, M., Bertling, E., Hotulainen, R., Tanhuanpaa, K., and Hotulainen, P. (2014). Myosin IIb controls actin dynamics underlying the dendritic spine maturation. *Mol. Cell Neurosci.* 61C, 56–64. doi: 10.1016/j.mcn.2014.05.008

Lebensohn, A. M., and Kirschner, M. W. (2009). Activation of the WAVE complex by coincident signals controls actin assembly. *Mol. Cell* 36, 512–524. doi: 10.1016/j.molcel.2009.10.024

Lee, S. E., Kim, Y., Han, J. K., Park, H., Lee, U., Na, M., et al. (2016). nArgBP2 regulates excitatory synapse formation by controlling dendritic spine morphology. *Proc. Natl. Acad. Sci. U.S.A.* 113, 6749–6754. doi: 10.1073/pnas.1600944113

Lin, Y. C., Frei, J. A., Kilander, M. B., Shen, W., and Blatt, G. J. (2016). A subset of autism-associated genes regulate the structural stability of neurons. *Front. Cell Neurosci.* 10:263. doi: 10.3389/fncel.2016.00263

Liu, Y. F., Sowell, S. M., Luo, Y., Chaubey, A., Cameron, R. S., Kim, H. G., et al. (2015). Autism and intellectual disability-associated KIRREL3 interacts with neuronal proteins MAP1B and MYO16 with potential roles in neurodevelopment. *PLoS One* 10:e0123106. doi: 10.1371/journal.pone.0123106

MacGillavry, H. D., Song, Y., Raghavachari, S., and Blanpied, T. A. (2013). Nanoscale scaffolding domains within the postsynaptic density concentrate synaptic AMPA receptors. *Neuron* 78, 615–622. doi: 10.1016/j.neuron.2013.03.009

Matus, A. (2000). Actin-based plasticity in dendritic spines. *Science* 290, 754–758. doi: 10.1126/science.290.5492.754

Matus, A., Ackermann, M., Pehling, G., Byers, H. R., and Fujiwara, K. (1982). High actin concentrations in brain dendritic spines and postsynaptic densities. *Proc. Natl. Acad. Sci. U.S.A.* 79, 7590–7594. doi: 10.1073/pnas.79.23.7590

Mikhaylova, M., Bar, J., van Bommel, B., Schatzle, P., YuanXiang, P., Raman, R., et al. (2018). Caldendrin directly couples postsynaptic calcium signals to actin remodeling in dendritic spines. *Neuron* 97, 1110–1125. doi: 10.1016/j.neuron.2018.01.046

Miki, H., Suetsugu, S., and Takenawa, T. (1998). WAVE, a novel WASP-family protein involved in actin reorganization induced by Rac. *EMBO J.* 17, 6932–6941. doi: 10.1093/emboj/17.23.6932

Miyagi, Y., Yamashita, T., Fukaya, M., Sonoda, T., Okuno, T., Yamada, K., et al. (2002). Delphilin: a novel PDZ and formin homology domain-containing protein that synaptically colocalizes and interacts with glutamate receptor delta 2 subunit. *J. Neurosci.* 22, 803–814. doi: 10.1523/jneurosci.22-03-00803.2002

Njoo, C., Agarwal, N., Lutz, B., and Kuner, R. (2015). The cannabinoid receptor CB1 interacts with the WAVE1 complex and plays a role in actin dynamics and structural plasticity in neurons. *PLoS Biol.* 13:e1002286. doi: 10.1371/journal.pbio.1002286

Nolen, B. J., Tomasevic, N., Russell, A., Pierce, D. W., Jia, Z., McCormick, C. D., et al. (2009). Characterization of two classes of small molecule inhibitors of Arp2/3 complex. *Nature* 460, 1031–1034. doi: 10.1038/nature08231

Oberdick, J., Smeyne, R. J., Mann, J. R., Zackson, S., and Morgan, J. I. (1990). A promoter that drives transgene expression in cerebellar purkinje and retinal bipolar neurons. *Science* 248, 223–226. doi: 10.1126/science.2109351

Okamoto, K., Narayanan, R., Lee, S. H., Murata, K., and Hayashi, Y. (2007). The role of CaMKII as an F-actin-bundling protein crucial for maintenance of dendritic spine structure. *Proc. Natl. Acad. Sci. U.S.A.* 104, 6418–6423. doi: 10.1073/pnas.0701656104

Parkinson, G. T., Chamberlain, S. E. L., Jaafari, N., Turvey, M., Mellor, J. R., and Hanley, J. G. (2018). Cortactin regulates endo-lysosomal sorting of AMPARs via direct interaction with GluA2 subunit. *Sci. Rep.* 8:4155. doi: 10.1038/s41598-018-22542-z

Patel, K. G., Liu, C., Cameron, P. L., and Cameron, R. S. (2001). Myr 8, a novel unconventional myosin expressed during brain development associates with the protein phosphatase catalytic subunits 1alpha and 1gamma1. *J. Neurosci.* 21, 7954–7968. doi: 10.1523/jneurosci.21-20-07954.2001

Pathania, M., Davenport, E. C., Muir, J., Sheehan, D. F., Lopez-Domenech, G., and Kittler, J. T. (2014). The autism and schizophrenia associated gene CYFIP1 is critical for the maintenance of dendritic complexity and the stabilization of mature spines. *Transl. Psychiatry* 4:e374. doi: 10.1038/tp.2014.16

Peter, S., Ten Brinke, M. M., Stedehouder, J., Reinelt, C. M., Wu, B., Zhou, H., et al. (2016). Dysfunctional cerebellar Purkinje cells contribute to autism-like behaviour in Shank2-deficient mice. *Nat. Commun.* 7:12627. doi: 10.1038/ncomms12627

Pils, S., Kopp, K., Peterson, L., Delgado Tascon, J., Nyffenegger-Jann, N. J., and Hauck, C. R. (2012). The adaptor molecule Nck localizes the WAVE complex to promote actin polymerization during CEACAM3-mediated phagocytosis of bacteria. *PLoS One* 7:e32808. doi: 10.1371/journal.pone.0032808

Pollard, T. D., and Borisy, G. G. (2003). Cellular motility driven by assembly and disassembly of actin filaments. *Cell* 112, 453–465. doi: 10.1016/s0092-8674(03)00120-x

Rex, C. S., Gavin, C. F., Rubio, M. D., Kramar, E. A., Chen, L. Y., Jia, Y., et al. (2010). Myosin IIb regulates actin dynamics during synaptic plasticity and memory formation. *Neuron* 67, 603–617. doi: 10.1016/j.neuron.2010.07.016

Rizvi, S. A., Neidt, E. M., Cui, J., Feiger, Z., Skau, C. T., Gardel, M. L., et al. (2009). Identification and characterization of a small molecule inhibitor of formin-mediated actin assembly. *Chem. Biol.* 16, 1158–1168. doi: 10.1016/j.chembiol.2009.10.006

Rodriguez-Murillo, L., Xu, B., Roos, J. L., Abecasis, G. R., Gogos, J. A., and Karayiorgou, M. (2014). Fine mapping on chromosome 13q32-34 and brain expression analysis implicates MYO16 in schizophrenia. *Neuropsychopharmacology* 39, 934–943. doi: 10.1038/npp.2013.293

Rotty, J. D., Wu, C., and Bear, J. E. (2013). New insights into the regulation and cellular functions of the ARP2/3 complex. *Nat. Rev. Mol. Cell Biol.* 14, 7–12. doi: 10.1038/nrm3492

Rubio, M. D., Johnson, R., Miller, C. A., Huganir, R. L., and Rumbaugh, G. (2011). Regulation of synapse structure and function by distinct myosin II motors. *J. Neurosci.* 31, 1448–1460. doi: 10.1523/JNEUROSCI.3294-10.2011

Rust, M. B., and Maritzen, T. (2015). Relevance of presynaptic actin dynamics for synapse function and mouse behavior. *Exp. Cell Res.* 335, 165–171. doi: 10.1016/j.yexcr.2014.12.020

Saarikangas, J., Kourdougli, N., Senju, Y., Chazal, G., Segerstrale, M., Minkeviciene, R., et al. (2015). MIM-Induced membrane bending promotes dendritic spine initiation. *Dev. Cell* 33, 644–659. doi: 10.1016/j.devcel.2015.04.014

Schindelin, J., Arganda-Carreras, I., Frise, E., Kaynig, V., Longair, M., Pietzsch, T., et al. (2012). Fiji: an open-source platform for biological-image analysis. *Nat. Methods* 9, 676–682. doi: 10.1038/nmeth.2019

Schneider, C. A., Rasband, W. S., and Eliceiri, K. W. (2012). NIH Image to ImageJ: 25 years of image analysis. *Nat. Methods* 9, 671–675. doi: 10.1038/nmeth.2089

Schonewille, M., Belmeguenai, A., Koekkoek, S. K., Houtman, S. H., Boele, H. J., van Beugen, B. J., et al. (2010). Purkinje cell-specific knockout of the protein phosphatase PP2B impairs potentiation and cerebellar motor learning. *Neuron* 67, 618–628. doi: 10.1016/j.neuron.2010.07.009

Sdrulla, A. D., and Linden, D. J. (2007). Double dissociation between long-term depression and dendritic spine morphology in cerebellar Purkinje cells. *Nat. Neurosci.* 10, 546–548. doi: 10.1038/nn1889

Sekerkova, G., Loomis, P. A., Changyaleket, B., Zheng, L., Eytan, R., Chen, B., et al. (2003). Novel espin actin-bundling proteins are localized to Purkinje cell dendritic spines and bind the Src homology 3 adapter protein insulin receptor substrate p53. *J. Neurosci.* 23, 1310–1319. doi: 10.1523/jneurosci.23-04-01310.2003

Shemiakina, I. I., Ermakova, G. V., Cranfill, P. J., Baird, M. A., Evans, R. A., Souslova, E. A., et al. (2012). A monomeric red fluorescent protein with low cytotoxicity. *Nat. Commun.* 3:1204. doi: 10.1038/ncomms2208

Shen, B., Zhang, W., Zhang, J., Zhou, J., Wang, J., Chen, L., et al. (2014). Efficient genome modification by CRISPR-Cas9 nickase with minimal off-target effects. *Nat. Methods* 11, 399–402. doi: 10.1038/nmeth.2857

Smith-Hicks, C., Xiao, B., Deng, R., Ji, Y., Zhao, X., Shepherd, J. D., et al. (2010). SRF binding to SRE 6.9 in the Arc promoter is essential for LTD in cultured Purkinje cells. *Nat. Neurosci.* 13, 1082–1089. doi: 10.1038/nn.2611

Soderling, S. H., Guire, E. S., Kaech, S., White, J., Zhang, F., Schutz, K., et al. (2007). A WAVE-1 and WRP signaling complex regulates spine density, synaptic plasticity, and memory. *J. Neurosci.* 27, 355–365. doi: 10.1523/jneurosci.3209-06.2006

Soderling, S. H., Langeberg, L. K., Soderling, J. A., Davee, S. M., Simerly, R., Raber, J., et al. (2003). Loss of WAVE-1 causes sensorimotor retardation and reduced learning and memory in mice. *Proc. Natl. Acad. Sci. U.S.A.* 100, 1723–1728. doi: 10.1073/pnas.0438033100

Sokolov, A. A., Miall, R. C., and Ivry, R. B. (2017). The cerebellum: adaptive prediction for movement and cognition. *Trends Cogn. Sci.* 21, 313–332. doi: 10.1016/j.tics.2017.02.005

Sotelo, C. (1978). Purkinje cell ontogeny: formation and maintenance of spines. *Prog. Brain Res.* 48, 149–170. doi: 10.1016/s0079-6123(08)61021-3

Spence, E. F., Kanak, D. J., Carlson, B. R., and Soderling, S. H. (2016). The Arp2/3 complex is essential for distinct stages of spine synapse maturation, including synapse unsilencing. *J. Neurosci.* 36, 9696–9709. doi: 10.1523/JNEUROSCI.0876-16.2016

Spence, E. F., and Soderling, S. H. (2015). Actin out: regulation of the synaptic cytoskeleton. *J. Biol. Chem.* 290, 28613–28622. doi: 10.1074/jbc.R115.655118

Star, E. N., Kwiatkowski, D. J., and Murthy, V. N. (2002). Rapid turnover of actin in dendritic spines and its regulation by activity. *Nat. Neurosci.* 5, 239–246. doi: 10.1038/nn811

Takenawa, T., and Suetsugu, S. (2007). The WASP-WAVE protein network: connecting the membrane to the cytoskeleton. *Nat. Rev. Mol. Cell Biol.* 8, 37–48. doi: 10.1038/nrm2069

Thevenaz, P., and Unser, M. (2007). User-friendly semiautomated assembly of accurate image mosaics in microscopy. *Microsc. Res. Tech.* 70, 135–146. doi: 10.1002/jemt.20393

Tsai, P. T., Hull, C., Chu, Y., Greene-Colozzi, E., Sadowski, A. R., Leech, J. M., et al. (2012). Autistic-like behaviour and cerebellar dysfunction in Purkinje cell Tsc1 mutant mice. *Nature* 488, 647–651. doi: 10.1038/nature11310

Wagner, W., Brenowitz, S. D., and Hammer, J. A. III (2011a). Myosin-Va transports the endoplasmic reticulum into the dendritic spines of Purkinje neurons. *Nat. Cell Biol.* 13, 40–48. doi: 10.1038/ncb2132

Wagner, W., McCroskery, S., and Hammer, J. A. III (2011b). An efficient method for the long-term and specific expression of exogenous cDNAs in cultured Purkinje neurons. *J. Neurosci. Methods* 200, 95–105. doi: 10.1016/j.jneumeth.2011.06.006

Wang, K., Zhang, H., Ma, D., Bucan, M., Glessner, J. T., Abrahams, B. S., et al. (2009). Common genetic variants on 5p14.1 associate with autism spectrum disorders. *Nature* 459, 528–533. doi: 10.1038/nature07999

Wang, S. S., Kloth, A. D., and Badura, A. (2014). The cerebellum, sensitive periods, and autism. *Neuron* 83, 518–532. doi: 10.1016/j.neuron.2014.07.016

Yamasaki, M., Miyazaki, T., Azechi, H., Abe, M., Natsume, R., Hagiwara, T., et al. (2011). Glutamate receptor δ2 is essential for input pathway-dependent regulation of synaptic AMPAR contents in cerebellar Purkinje cells. *J. Neurosci.* 31, 3362–3374. doi: 10.1523/JNEUROSCI.5601-10.2011

Yan, Z., Kim, E., Datta, D., Lewis, D. A., and Soderling, S. H. (2016). Synaptic actin dysregulation, a convergent mechanism of mental disorders? *J. Neurosci.* 36, 11411–11417. doi: 10.1523/jneurosci.2360-16.2016

Yang, Q., Zhang, X. F., Pollard, T. D., and Forscher, P. (2012). Arp2/3 complex-dependent actin networks constrain myosin II function in driving retrograde actin flow. *J. Cell Biol.* 197, 939–956. doi: 10.1083/jcb.201111052

Yokoyama, K., Tezuka, T., Kotani, M., Nakazawa, T., Hoshina, N., Shimoda, Y., et al. (2011). NYAP: a phosphoprotein family that links PI3K to WAVE1 signalling in neurons. *EMBO J.* 30, 4739–4754. doi: 10.1038/emboj.2011.348

Zhang, B., Chen, L. Y., Liu, X., Maxeiner, S., Lee, S. J., Gokce, O., et al. (2015). Neuroligins sculpt cerebellar purkinje-cell circuits by differential control of distinct classes of synapses. *Neuron* 87, 781–796. doi: 10.1016/j.neuron.2015.07.020

4

Altered Behaviors and Impaired Synaptic Function in a Novel Rat Model With a Complete *Shank3* Deletion

*Tian-Jia Song [1,2,3], Xing-Yu Lan [1,2,3], Meng-Ping Wei [4,5], Fu-Jun Zhai [1,2,3], Tobias M. Boeckers [6], Jia-Nan Wang [1,2,3], Shuo Yuan [1,2,3], Meng-Ying Jin [1,2,3], Yu-Fei Xie [1,2,3], Wan-Wen Dang [1,2,3], Chen Zhang [4,5], Michael Schön [6], Pei-Wen Song [7], Mei-Hong Qiu [7], Ya-Yue Song [8], Song-Ping Han [9], Ji-Sheng Han [1,2,3] and Rong Zhang [1,2,3]**

[1]Department of Neurobiology, School of Basic Medical Sciences, Peking University, Beijing, China, [2]Neuroscience Research Institute, Peking University, Beijing, China, [3]Key laboratory for Neuroscience, Ministry of Education/National Health and Family Planning Commission, Peking University, Beijing, China, [4]State Key Laboratory of Membrane Biology, School of Life Sciences, Peking University-IDG/McGovern Institute for Brain Research, Peking University, Beijing, China, [5]Department of Neurobiology, Capital Medical University, Beijing, China, [6]Institute for Anatomy and Cell Biology, Ulm University, Ulm, Germany, [7]Department of Neurobiology, School of Basic Medical Sciences, Fudan University, Shanghai, China, [8]School of Basic Medical Sciences, Tianjin Medical University, Tianjin, China, [9]Wuxi HANS Health Medical Technology Co., Ltd., Wuxi, China

Correspondence:
Rong Zhang
zhangrong@bjmu.edu.cn

Mutations within the *Shank3* gene, which encodes a key postsynaptic density (PSD) protein at glutamatergic synapses, contribute to the genetic etiology of defined autism spectrum disorders (ASDs), including Phelan-McDermid syndrome (PMS) and intellectual disabilities (ID). Although there are a series of genetic mouse models to study *Shank3* gene in ASDs, there are few rat models with species-specific advantages. In this study, we established and characterized a novel rat model with a deletion spanning exons 11–21 of *Shank3*, leading to a complete loss of the major SHANK3 isoforms. Synaptic function and plasticity of *Shank3*-deficient rats were impaired detected by biochemical and electrophysiological analyses. *Shank3*-depleted rats showed impaired social memory but not impaired social interaction behaviors. In addition, impaired learning and memory, increased anxiety-like behavior, increased mechanical pain threshold and decreased thermal sensation were observed in *Shank3*-deficient rats. It is worth to note that *Shank3*-deficient rats had nearly normal levels of the endogenous social neurohormones oxytocin (OXT) and arginine-vasopressin (AVP). This new rat model will help to further investigate the etiology and assess potential therapeutic target and strategy for *Shank3*-related neurodevelopmental disorders.

Keywords: Shank3, Phelan-McDermid syndrome, autism spectrum disorders, intellectual disabilities, social memory, pain threshold, oxytocin, vasopressin

INTRODUCTION

The *Shank3* gene is a member of the *Shank* gene family and encodes the SHANK3 protein, a key postsynaptic density (PSD) molecule at glutamatergic synapses (Naisbitt et al., 1999). SHANK3 is a scaffolding protein that interacts directly or indirectly with multiple glutamate receptors and the actin cytoskeleton critical for normal synaptic function and contains several specific protein domains, including an ANK (ankyrin repeats) domain, a SH3 (Src homology 3) domain, a PDZ (PSD95/Discs large/zona-occludens-1) domain, a proline-rich domain containing Homer binding regions and a SAM (sterile alpha motif) domain (Boeckers et al., 1999; Baron et al., 2006; Boeckers, 2006; Grabrucker et al., 2011).

Mutations within the *Shank3* gene are known to cause autism spectrum disorders (ASDs), which are characterized by impaired social interaction, communication skills and repetitive or restricted interests and behaviors. Haploinsufficiency of *Shank3* caused by a deletion or mutation accounts for up to 0.69% of autistic patients (Leblond et al., 2014). A specific form of a *Shank3*-dependent developmental disorder is Phelan-McDermid syndrome (PMS), which is also known as 22q13.3 deletion syndrome, with a deletion or single mutation in one copy of the *Shank3* gene (Wilson et al., 2003). PMS is characterized by intellectual disability (ID), developmental delays, absent or delayed speech, neonatal hypotonia and motor impairments, and autism or autistic-like behaviors are present in more than 80% of PMS patients (Soorya et al., 2013). Notably, many forms of ASDs present comorbidities, including ID (Polyak et al., 2015), attention deficits, hyperactivity (ADHD), anxiety (Croen et al., 2015), sensory-perceptual anomalies, pain insensitivity or self-injurious behaviors (Allely, 2013). In this respect, *Shank3* mutations play a key role in ID and cognitive impairments; for example, 1.7% of Chinese unexplained ID patients have 22q13 deletions (Gong et al., 2012). To further understand the etiology, the underlying neurobiological mechanisms and potential novel therapeutics, *Shank3*-related animal models need to be established and characterized.

Because of available and convenient genetic technologies, genetically modified mouse models are widely used despite several limitations of the species. To date, a series of mouse strains with *Shank3* deletions of different exons (Δe4–7, Δe4–9, Δe13–16, Δe9, Δe11, and Δe21) and a *Shank3* complete knockout mouse model have been established (Bozdagi et al., 2010; Bangash et al., 2011; Peca et al., 2011; Wang et al., 2011, 2016; Schmeisser et al., 2012; Yang et al., 2012; Kouser et al., 2013; Duffney et al., 2015; Lee et al., 2015). As expected, the *Shank3* mutation has been proven to affect synaptic proteins, synaptic morphology and related function in these *Shank3*-deficient mouse models. Most of these mice have been shown to have autistic-like behaviors, including impaired social and communication behaviors, increased repetitive behavior, and other phenotypes related to comorbidities, including anxiety behavior, deficits in learning and memory, impaired motor coordination ability and so on (Bozdagi et al., 2010; Bangash et al., 2011; Peca et al., 2011; Wang et al., 2011; Schmeisser et al., 2012; Yang et al., 2012; Kouser et al., 2013; Duffney et al., 2015; Lee et al., 2015; Wang et al., 2016). With some species-specific advantages compared to mouse models, genetically modified rat models make it possible to perform more complex and broader behavioral tests and to investigate related mechanisms in more precise brain regions of the larger brain. In addition, for pharmacological investigations and drug testing, rats are the prototypical animal model. However, to the best of our knowledge, only one *Shank3*-deficient rat model has been reported with impaired social memory and deficits in attention (Harony-Nicolas et al., 2017). In this study, a deletion was introduced in exon 6, which led to the disruption of the isoform-specific expression of SHANK3 (Harony-Nicolas et al., 2017). Interestingly, the *Shank3*-deficient rat model showed normal social interaction and self-grooming behaviors, which is different from those of *Shank3*-deficient mouse models. Therefore, more *Shank3* genetically modified rat models carrying different mutations need to be established and characterized, which may help to more comprehensively understand *Shank3* function, species-specific phenotype differences and the phenotypical diversity of clinical manifestations observed by clinicians and researchers; additionally, an animal model with a complete *Shank3* deletion can mimic the majority of patients carrying deletions of the entire *Shank3* gene in PMS (Soorya et al., 2013).

Oxytocin (OXT) and arginine-vasopressin (AVP) are two neuropeptides synthesized in the supraoptic nucleus (SON) and paraventricular nucleus (PVN) of the hypothalamus and are related to social interaction, social memory and anxiety in mammals (Harony and Wagner, 2010). Acute OXT treatment could improve impaired long-term social memory and nonsocial attention deficits in the *Shank3*-deficient rat model (Harony-Nicolas et al., 2017). Similar to the impact of OXT on this *Shank3*-deficient rats, the facilitation effect of OXT and AVP on social behavior has been observed in normal mice and rats (Lukas et al., 2011), low socially interacting rats (Zhang et al., 2015) and some genetic animal models (Jin et al., 2007; Gigliucci et al., 2014; Penagarikano et al., 2015). Interestingly, an impaired OXT/AVP system has been reported in autistic patients (Zhang et al., 2016) and some autistic animal models (Zhang et al., 2017); however, thus far, we know little about the endogenous OXT/AVP system in *Shank3*-deficient animal models.

In our present study, we established and characterized a novel rat model with a complete *Shank3* deletion, which adds to the existing *Shank3*-deficient rat model and can be compared with other *Shank3*-deficient animal models. It can also further help to understand the etiology and assess potential therapeutics of related neurodevelopmental disorders based on rat-specific advantages.

MATERIALS AND METHODS

Generation of *Shank3* Knockout Rats

The *Shank3* knockout rat, in which the *Shank3* gene has been deleted from exon 11 to exon 21, was generated by the introduction of two sgRNAs with Cas9 to induce repair of the resultant two DSBs by NHEJ with a deletion of the intervening DNA sequence (Yang et al., 2013). Briefly, two sgRNAs were designed to target a region upstream of exon 11 or downstream of exon 21 of *Shank3*. For each targeting site, candidate guide RNAs were designed by the CRISPR design tool[1] and screened for on-target activity. Then, the Cas9 mRNA and sgRNAs were transcribed *in vitro* using the MEGAshortscript T7 Transcription kit (AM1354, Invitrogen)

[1] http://crispr.mit.edu

and purified using the MEGAclear Transcription Clean-Up kit (AM1908, Invitrogen). Sprague-Dawley (SD) rat strains were used as embryo donors and pseudopregnant foster mothers. Superovulated female SD rats mated with SD stud males, and fertilized embryos were collected from the ampullae of the superovulated female SD rats. Different concentrations of Cas9 mRNA and sgRNAs were mixed and coinjected into the cytoplasm of one-cell stage fertilized eggs. After injection, surviving zygotes were transferred into oviducts of SD females to generate chimeras. Finally, positive SD founder rats mated to produce F1 heterozygous breeder pairs carrying approximately 26 kb deletions with the removal of the *Shank3* exon 11–21. The generation of *Shank3* knockout rats was conducted by Beijing Biocytogen Co. Ltd., Beijing, China.

Genotypes were determined by PCR of rat tail DNA using the primers F1 (CTGTTGGCTGAGCCTGGCATAGAG) and R1 (GCTGGAAAGAAACAACGAGAGCCAG) for the WT allele (559 base pairs) and the primers F2 (TTGTGCACTGCCTAT GTTGACCACT) and R2 (TAGGCGAGAGAAGATGGTGTG ATTTCC) for the mutant allele (688 base pairs).

Animal Husbandry and Care

Male SD rats from heterozygous breeder pairs were used in all experiments. The rats were housed 3–5 per cage and maintained on a 12:12 h light/dark cycle (light on at 07:00 AM) with free access to food and water. All animal experimental procedures were approved by the Animal Care and Use Committee of Peking University (ethics approval ID, LA2015204) and in accordance with the U.S. National Institutes of Health Guide for the Care and Use of Laboratory Animals.

Behavior Test

For all behavior tests, all genotypes were tested on the same day in a randomized order. Five- to six-week-old male rats were used for behavior testing unless otherwise stated. To minimize the impacts of repeated testing and handling, no more than four behavioral tests were performed in each cohort of rats.

Developmental Milestones

The rats were tested for developmental milestones from postnatal day (PND) 2 to 21. The parameters of physical developmental milestones included body weight, pinna detachment, incisor eruption and eye-opening. For each genotype, the number of pups that achieved these developmental goals were recorded.

Pup Separation-Induced Ultrasonic Vocalizations Test

A pup separation-induced ultrasonic vocalizations (USVs) test was performed on PND7 as previously described (Xu et al., 2015). Briefly, a pup was randomly chosen and was gently removed from the home cage and then transported to a clear plastic chamber (39 cm × 25 cm × 20 cm) on a heating pad (37°C) in a separate room. For each pup, the USVs were collected for 5 min by a condenser microphone (CM16/CMPA, Avisoft Bioacoustics, Germany) suspended approximately 25 cm above the base of the chamber with an amplifier (AUSG-116H, Avisoft Bioacoustics, Germany) set at a sampling rate of 250 kHz. After recording, the sound files were transferred to the sound analysis software SASLab Pro (Avisoft Bioacoustics, Germany) for fast Fourier transform with a 125 kHz low-pass filter. The classification algorithm of USVs was set as previously described (Li et al., 2011). The number and duration of each type of USVs were analyzed.

Juvenile Reciprocal Social Interaction Test

A juvenile reciprocal social interaction test was performed on PND 24–26 during the dark period of the light cycle under dim red illumination. Juvenile rats were habituated to the test arena (39 cm × 25 cm × 20 cm) for 15 min, and then an unfamiliar, age-matched, same-sex partner was introduced. The subject rat and the partner were allowed to move freely and videotaped for 10 min. The amount of time of total interactions was analyzed by a highly trained observer blinded to the genotype according to the parameters of social behaviors as previously described (Vanderschuren et al., 1995a,b).

Three-Chamber Test

A three-chamber test was performed on PND 35–42 during the dark period under dim red illumination. The apparatus using for testing was a rectangular, Plexiglas box divided into three chambers (40 cm × 34 cm × 24 cm), with the side chambers each connected to the middle chamber by a corridor (10 cm × 10 cm × 15 cm). The test consisted of three phases, named the adaptive phase, phase 1 and phase 2, according to previous studies with minor modifications (Zhang et al., 2015). During the adaptive phase, the subject rat was allowed to explore the entire apparatus freely for 5 min. During phase 1, an age- and sex-matched unfamiliar model rat was locked in a small cage made of stainless-steel wires as a social stimulus and then placed in one of the side chambers, and an identical but empty cage was placed in the other side chamber. The subject rat was allowed to explore the entire apparatus with the corridor opened and interact with the model rat for 10 min. During phase 2, another age- and sex-matched unfamiliar model rat was introduced to the empty cage as a novel social stimulus. The subject rat was also allowed to explore the entire apparatus and interact with the familiar and novel model rats for 10 min. The entire apparatus was cleaned with 75% ethanol after each trial concluded to eliminate the impact of residual rat odors. The amount of time spent in each of the three chambers was recorded automatically, and the rats were videotaped. The amount of time spent sniffing the wire cage was analyzed by a highly trained observer blinded to the genotype as closely social interaction time.

Self-Grooming Test

Repetitive behavior was analyzed by a self-grooming test during the dark period under dim red illumination in an empty cage (39 cm × 25 cm × 20 cm). The test consisted of a 10 min habituation and a followed 10 min test. The test session was videotaped, and the amount of time spent self-grooming was evaluated by a trained observer blinded to the genotype.

Olfactory Habituation/Dishabituation Test

Responses to nonsocial and social odors were analyzed by an olfactory habituation/dishabituation test (OHDT) during the dark period under dim red illumination as previously described with some modifications (Janssen et al., 2001; Li et al., 2015). The experiment was conducted in an acrylic cage (31 cm × 19 cm × 13 cm) with fresh bedding and a square metal gauze top. The test began with a 5 min familiarization followed by 15 sequential 2 min odor presentations with 1 min intervals. The odors consisted of three nonsocial odors, including water, almond (1:10 dilution, DJ-2372, Zhejiang Dahaojia Co., Ltd., Zhejiang, China) and vanilla (1:10 dilution, DJ-2301, Zhejiang Dahaojia Co., Ltd., Zhejiang, China) and two social odors, including social odor 1 (collected in the home cage consisting of three adult male rats without bedding) and social odor 2 (collected from adult female rats). Each odor, which was pipetted on a filter paper (70 mm diameter) placed on top of the gauze, was presented continuously three times. Sequences of three identical odor presentations evaluated habituation to the same smell. Switching to different odor presentations evaluated dishabituation to a new odor. The amount of time spent sniffing the odorized filter was quantitated by an observer blinded to the genotype.

Open Field Test

Anxiety behavior and spontaneous activity were evaluated in an acrylic box (100 cm × 100 cm × 40 cm) and videotaped by an overhead camera. Subject rats were initially placed in the center of the test arena and allowed to explore the arena freely for 10 min. Videos from each rat were processed using SMART software (v2.5.21, Panlab Harvard Apparatus). The amount of time spent in the peripheral zones of the open field was recorded as indices of anxiety-like behaviors. The total distances traveled in the open field were analyzed as indices of spontaneous activity.

Novel Object Recognition Test

Learning and memory were assessed by a novel object recognition test during the dark period under dim red illumination as performed in previous studies with some modifications (Ishikawa et al., 2014; Pyndt Jørgensen et al., 2015). Two days before the test, a subject rat was placed in the test arena (60 cm × 40 cm × 40 cm) for 10 min of habituation. During the training phase on the 3rd day, the rat was allowed to explore two identical objects in the arena for 20 min. After 1 h, during the test phase, in which one of the two objects was replaced by a new object (with a similar size but with different colors and shapes), the rat was introduced into the arena once again, allowed to explore freely for 10 min and videotaped. Then, the time spent exploring each of the two objects was measured by an observer blinded to the genotype. Object exploration behavior was defined as the nose of the rat touching the object or being oriented toward the object within 2 cm of it as previously described (Wang et al., 2011).

Von Frey Test

A von Frey test was used to assess the mechanical pain threshold of rats. Briefly, rats were restrained in transparent Lucite cubicles on an elevated metal mesh floor for 30 min to acclimate and then tested for the paw withdrawal threshold with calibrated von Frey filaments (bending forces ranging from 0.4 to 15 g) using the Dixon up-down method. The left hindpaw of a rat was stimulated perpendicularly to the central plantar surface, and withdrawal was determined if the rat lifted its paw. Finally, the withdrawal threshold was calculated and regarded as the index of the mechanical pain threshold.

Hot Plate Test

A hot plate test was used to detect the thermal pain threshold of rats. The apparatus consisted of a solid aluminum plate, which was heated and maintained at a constant temperature, confined by a transparent and removable Perspex cylinder. The temperature of the hot plate was set 53 ± 0.5°C. After a rat was placed on the hot plate surface, the amount of time for the rat to lick or lift its paw or jump off of the hot plate was defined as the paw withdrawal latency reflecting the temperature sensation. A cutoff time of 40 s was set to avoid tissue damage. The subject rat was tested three times with 15 min intervals and the mean of three recordings was reported as the final withdrawal latency.

Rotarod Test

Motor ability was analyzed by a rotarod test. Two days before the test, a subject rat was introduced into the apparatus for habituation (4 rpm). On the third day, during the test phase, the rat was introduced into the apparatus (4-40 rpm over 5 min) and was subjected to three trials with 15 min intervals. The latency to fall was recorded as the index of motor coordination and balance. The mean of three recordings was reported.

Hang Wire Test

A rat was placed midway on a horizontal metal gauze (1 mm diameter), which was held at a height of approximately 30 cm above the floor. After the subject rat crawled for a moment, the metal gauze was rotated 180 degrees, and the rat was allowed to hang. The latency to fall was recorded over 1 min; the test was performed three times per animal, and the results were averaged.

Golgi Staining

Golgi staining was conducted in 5-week-old rats using a Hito Golgi-Cox OptimStainTM kit (HTKNS1125, Hitobiotec) according to the manufacturer's instructions. Briefly, the brain was removed and transferred into a mixture of impregnation solution containing equal volumes of solution 1 and solution 2 at room temperature for 2 weeks in the dark. Then, brain tissue was transferred into solution 3 at 4°C for 24–72 h in the dark. Coronal sections (150 μm) were prepared with a freezing microtome (Leica-1950, Germany). The sections were stained using solutions 4 and 5 after mounting the sections onto the slides. Finally, the stained sections were imaged using a microscope (Olympus BX43, Tokyo, Japan) equipped with a 100× oil immersion lens. A researcher blinded to the genotype analyzed the spine density in the hippocampus using ImageJ (Wayne Rasband, National Institutes of Health, Bethesda, MD, USA). For each rat, nine different neurons were quantified from three slides. The spine density from three segments (70 μm) was averaged to provide a single value for each neuron.

Electrophysiology

Slice Preparation

Hippocampal brain slices were prepared from 5- to 6-week-old male wild-type or *Shank3* knockout rats as previously described

(Wei et al., 2016). Briefly, the rat brain was quickly removed and placed in ice-cold dissection solution (10 mM glucose, 213 mM sucrose, 1 mM NaH_2PO_4, 0.5 mM $CaCl_2$, 5 mM $MgCl_2$, 3 mM KCl and 26 mM $NaHCO_3$, pH 7.4). Transverse slices were cut in ice-cold dissection solution on a vibrating blade microtome (Leica VT-1,200s, Wetzlar, Germany). The slices were moved to a chamber containing artificial cerebrospinal fluid (ACSF; 10 mM glucose, 2 mM NaH_2PO_4, 125 mM NaCl, 2.6 mM $CaCl_2$, 1.3 mM $MgCl_2$, 5 mM KCl, and 26 mM $NaHCO_3$, pH 7.4, gassed with 95% O_2 and 5% CO_2) and incubated for 1 h at room temperature before recording.

Slice Electrophysiology

During recordings, slices were mounted on the stage of an upright microscope (Olympus BX51WI, Tokyo, Japan) and constantly perfused with ACSF using a gravity-driven perfusion system with a speed of 2 mL/min. The internal solution contained 145 mM KCl, 5 mM NaCl, 5 mM EGTA, 4 mM MgATP, 0.3 mM Na_2GTP, 10 mM Hepes and 5 mM QX314 with the pH adjusted to 7.2 and an osmolarity of 305. Whole-cell recordings were conducted by adding 100 μM PTX (1128, Tocris) to ACSF (for the recording of evoked excitatory postsynaptic currents (EPSCs) mediated by AMPARs). The stimulus was delivered to Schaffer collaterals through a concentric bipolar electrode (CBBEB75, FHC, Bowdoin, ME, USA). For the recording of evoked EPSCs mediated by NMDARs, 100 μM PTX (1128, Tocris) and 10 μM CNQX (C127, Sigma) were added to ACSF, and the recordings were performed by holding the membrane potential at +40 mV. The stimulation intensity was 100 μA in evoked EPSCs recordings. Microelectrodes filled with ACSF (3–5 MΩ) were used to record field excitatory postsynaptic potentials (fEPSPs) from the stratum radiatum of the CA1 region. The stimulation intensity in fEPSPs recordings was defined as 60% of the maximum response. An EPC10 Patch Clamp Amplifier (HEKA, Lambrecht, Germany) was used to record the fEPSPs, and the values were calculated by measuring the onset (a 30–70% rising phase) slope of the fEPSP. For LTP recordings, we recorded a 20 min baseline followed by performing theta-burst stimulation [TBS; five episodes of stimulation delivered at 0.1 Hz, where each episode contained 10 stimuli trains of five pulses (100 Hz) delivered at 5 Hz] to induce LTP. Synaptic responses were collected every 15 s, and the data were analyzed by averaging four responses.

Quantitative Immunoblot Analysis

Subcellular Fractionation

The brains of 6- to 8-week-old rats were removed quickly and separated into four regions, including the cortex, hippocampus, striatum and cerebellum. Brain tissues were homogenized with a motorized tissue grinder (G50, Coyote Bioscience, Campbell, CA, USA) at 3,000 rpm in buffer 1 [10 mM HEPES (pH 7.4), 2 mM EDTA, 5 mM sodium orthovanadate, 30 mM sodium fluoride, 20 mM β-glycerolphosphate, and protease inhibitor cocktail (Roche)]. The total homogenates were centrifuged at 500× *g* for 5 min at 4°C to remove nuclei, extracellular matrix and cell debris. The supernatant was collected and centrifuged at 10,000× *g* for 15 min at 4°C to separate the crude membrane fraction pellet 2 (P2). P2 was resuspended in 300–500 μl buffer 2 [50 mM HEPES (pH 7.4), 2 mM EDTA, 2 mM EGTA, 5 mM sodium orthovanadate, 30 mM sodium fluoride, 20 mM β-glycerolphosphate, 1% Triton-X-100, and protease inhibitor cocktail (Roche)] and centrifuged at 20,000× *g* for 80 min at 4°C to obtain pellet 3 (P3). P3 (Triton X-100 insoluble PSD fraction) was resuspended in 50 μl buffer 3 [50 mM Tris (pH 9), 5 mM sodium orthovanadate, 30 mM sodium fluoride, 20 mM β-glycerolphosphate, 1% NaDOC, and protease inhibitor cocktail (Roche)] and frozen in liquid nitrogen for storage at −80°C.

Western Blot Analysis

The total protein concentration was determined by Bradford assay using a Detergent Compatible Bradford Protein Assay kit (P0006C, Beyotime) according to the manufacturer's instructions. For western blot analysis, equal amounts of 5–15 μg total homogenate (abbreviated to H_0) and the PSD fraction (abbreviated to PSD) were loaded on the gels, transferred on a nitrocellulose membrane, and the membranes were blocked in 5% skim milk powder blocking solution using standard protocols. The membranes were subsequently incubated with primary antibodies on a horizontal shaker at 4°C overnight. After incubation, the membranes were further incubated with HRP-conjugated secondary antibodies on a horizontal shaker for 1 h at room temperature. Finally, the signals were visualized using an ECL Plus kit (PE0010, Solarbio). For quantification, the gray value of each band was analyzed by Quantity One software (Bio-Rad Laboratories, Irvine, CA, USA) and normalized to the gray value of β-actin. For SHANK proteins, different isoforms were all involved in the quantification. The following antibodies were used for western blot analysis: anti-SHANK1 (1:1,000 dilution, NB300–166, Neuromab), anti-SHANK2 (1:1,000 dilution, homemade from The Boeckers Lab, against amino acids 826–1259 of rat ProSAP1/ SHANK2), anti-C-term SHANK3 (1:2,500 dilution, homemade from The Boeckers Lab, against both amino acids 781–1009 and amino acids 1260–1392 of rat ProSAP2/SHANK3), anti-N-term SHANK3 (1:500 dilution, homemade from The Boeckers Lab, against the first 120 N-terminal amino acids of rat SHANK3), anti-PSD-95 (1:500 dilution, AB2723, Abcam), anti-Homer1b/c (1:1,000 dilution, 160022, sysy), anti-GluR1 (1:1,000 dilution, AB1504, Millipore), anti-GluR2 (1:1,000 dilution, MAB397, Millipore), anti-NR1 (1:1,000 dilution, 556308BD, Biosciences), anti-NR2A (1:2,000 dilution, 07–632, Millipore), and anti-β-actin (1:1,000 dilution, TA-09, ZSGB-BIO).

Brain Tissue Collection

For immunohistochemical analysis, 6- to 7-week-old rats were transcardially perfused with 0.9% saline solution and fixed with 4% paraformaldehyde solution (pH 7.2). Then, the brain was removed and postfixed in 4% paraformaldehyde solution (pH 7.2) overnight and cryoprotected in 15% sucrose solution at 4°C for 48 h followed by 30% sucrose solution for 5 days. Serial sections (30 μm each) were prepared using a freezing Microtome

(Leica-1950, Germany) and stored at −20°C *in situ* hybridization protective solution.

For analysis of the mRNA levels of OXT, AVP and their receptors, the brain was quickly removed from 6- to 7-week-old rats and frozen in liquid nitrogen with embedding medium. According to the Paxinos and Watson Rat Brain Atlas, bilateral micropunches (1 mm in diameter for PVN and 1.5 mm for others) were obtained from the following regions using a freezing Microtome (Leica-1950, Germany): the PVN and SON of the hypothalamus, basolateral nucleus of the amygdala (BLA), central nucleus of the amygdala (CeA), medial nucleus of the amygdala (MeA) and the lateral septum [LS; (PVN: Bregma −0.60 to −1.92 mm, SON: Bregma −0.48 to −1.72 mm, BLA: Bregma −1.72 to −3.60 mm, CeA: Bregma −1.72 to −3.00 mm, MeA: Bregma −1.72 to −3.60 mm, and LS: Bregma 0.96 to −0.12 mm)].

Immunohistochemistry

To estimate OXT- and AVP-immunoreactive cells in the PVN and SON, target sections were chosen and preincubated in 0.3% H_2O_2 for 15 min at 37°C to eliminate endogenous peroxidase activity. After preincubation in 0.3% H_2O_2, floating sections were incubated in blocking buffer containing 10% goat serum and 0.3% Triton X-100 in 0.01 M PBS (pH 7.2) for 60 min at 37°C and then incubated with specific primary antibodies at 37°C for 2 h followed by 4°C for 24–48 h. The following primary antibodies were used: anti-OXT (1:2,000 dilution, AB2078, Abcam) and anti-AVP (1:2,000 dilution, AB39363, Abcam). For OXT- and AVP-reactive cells determination, the sections were incubated with the enzyme-labeled secondary antibody from the DAB staining kit (PV-6001, ZSGB-BIO) at room temperature for 1 h and then stained by the DAB staining method using this kit. Finally, the floating sections were attached to a glass slide under a coverslip with mounting medium and imaged using a microscope (Leica DMI400B, Wetzlar, Germany) with a camera for counting. OXT- and AVP-immunoreactive cells were identified as cells containing brown immunoreactive deposits (OXT and AVP) in the nuclei. The total number of OXT- and AVP-immunoreactive cells were counted unilaterally in the PVN and SON from six sections between Bregma −0.8 and −2.1 mm by researchers blinded to the genotype using ImageJ (Wayne Rasband, National Institutes of Health, Bethesda, MD, USA).

Real-Time Quantitative PCR

Total mRNA was extracted from the brain tissue micropunches using TRIzol reagent (Invitrogen, Carlsbad, CA, USA) according to the manufacturer's instructions. The RNA sample was digested with DNase (Promega, Madison, WI, USA) to remove DNA contamination. Then, cDNA was synthesized from the sample using a PrimeScript RT-PCR kit (TaKaRa, Dalian, China). Expression levels of the target genes (OXT, AVP, OXTR, and V1aR) and the endogenous control gene (β-actin) were analyzed by real-time quantitative PCR using TaqMan® Gene Expression Assays (assay ID: OXT—Rn00564446_g1, AVP—Rn00690189_g1, OXTR—Rn00563503_m1, V1aR—Rn00583910_m1, β-actin—Rn00667869_m1). The RT PCR procedure was performed in an optical 96-well reaction plate in duplicate on a 7500 RT PCR System (Applied Biosystems, Foster City, CA, USA) under standard amplification conditions as follows: 2 min at 50°C, 10 min at 95°C, 40 cycles of 15 s at 95°C and 1 min at 60°C. Finally, the data were transformed using the ΔΔCT method with β-actin as the reference gene and normalized to the wild-type samples for comparison.

Statistics

IBM SPSS Statistics 19 (SPSS Inc., Chicago, IL, USA) and GraphPad Prism 5.0 (GraphPad Software Inc., San Diego, CA, USA) was used for statistical analyses and generating graphs. For the comparisons, parametric tests including *t*-tests and one-way analysis of variance (ANOVA) were used if the data were normally distributed (distribution tested by the Shapiro-Wilk normality test), and nonparametric approaches, including the Wilcoxon test and Kruskal-Wallis test, were used for data with a nonnormal distribution. Pearson's chi-squared test was used to assess rank variables. For all data, the results were expressed as the mean ± standard error of the mean (SEM), and $P < 0.05$ (two-tailed) was considered statistically significant.

RESULTS

Generation of *Shank3*-Deficient Rats

Shank3-deficient rats were generated using the CRISPR/Cas9 approach. As shown in the genomic structure of *Shank3*, two sgRNAs were designed to target the upstream region of exon 11 and the downstream region of exon 21 in the *Shank3* gene (**Figure 1A**). The region spanning these two targeting sites (approximately 26 kb) were deleted, including the SH3 domain, the PDZ domain and the proline-rich region. All subject rats used in the experiments were from heterozygous breeder pairs. The offspring genotypes were identified by PCR with rat tail DNA. For the WT allele, the PCR product was 559 base pairs, and for the mutant allele, the PCR product was 688 base pairs.

To analyze the expression of the SHANK3 protein, western blotting was performed with an antibody targeted against the proline-rich domain of SHANK3. The results showed that there were not any SHANK3 isoforms in *Shank3* knockout rats and low expression levels (approximately 64%) in heterozygous rats (**Figure 1B**). Another antibody targeted against the N-terminal amino acids of SHANK3 was also used, and the results showed that the full-length SHANK3 protein was completely absent in *Shank3* knockout rats and expressed to a lesser extent (approximately 53%) in heterozygous rats (**Figure 1B**). To confirm the expression of the SHANK3 protein in different brain regions, total homogenate (H_0) and isolated PSD fractions were all analyzed from the hippocampus, cortex, striatum and cerebellum. The results showed that there was no expression of full-length SHANK3 protein in all samples from the hippocampus, cortex and striatum of *Shank3* knockout rats and a reduced expression level in samples of heterozygous rats (**Supplementary Figure S1**). For the short isoform of SHANK3 in the cerebellum,

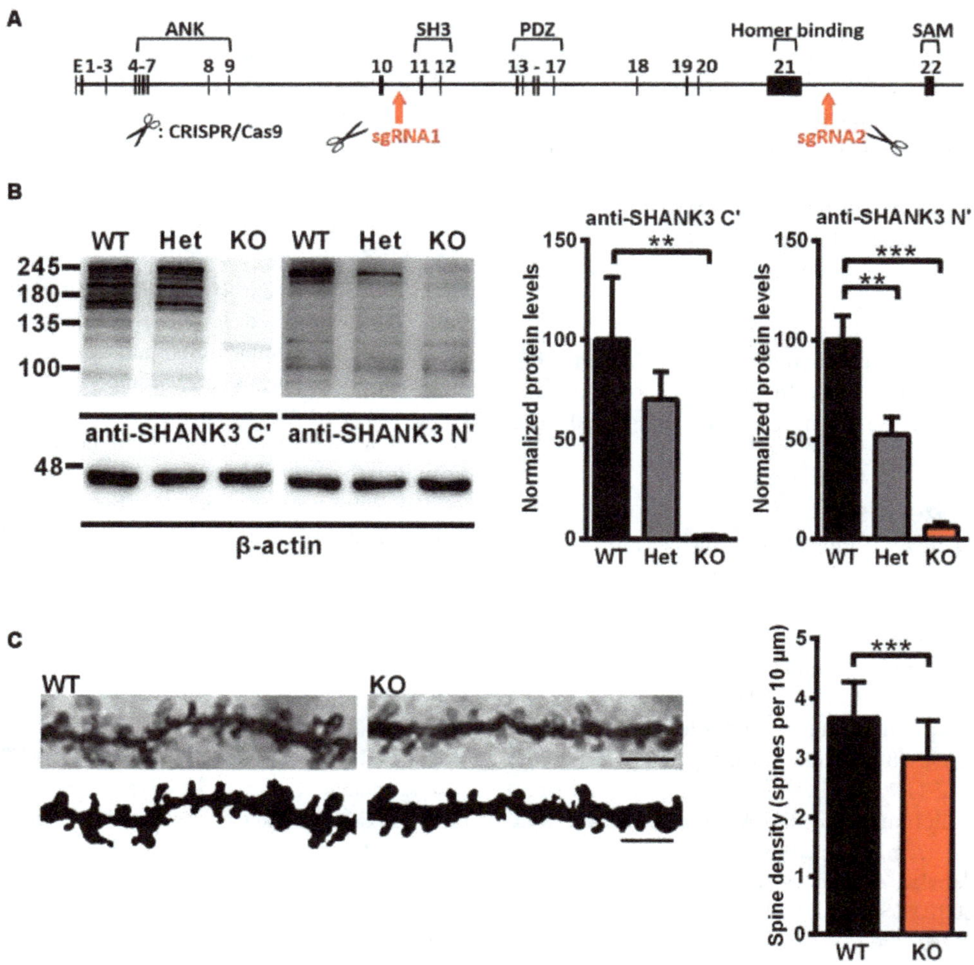

FIGURE 1 | Generation of *Shank3*-deficient rats and reduced spine density in *Shank3* knockout rats. **(A)** Targeting strategy for the *Shank3* gene. The top schematic shows the genomic structure of the *Shank3* gene. The arrows indicate the targeting site of the CRISPR/Cas9 system. **(B)** Representative immunoblots of SHANK3 in hippocampal postsynaptic density (PSD) fractions probed with two anti-SHANK3 antibodies directed against the C-terminus or N-terminus (left panel). Quantification of the SHANK3 expression levels normalized to β-actin [right panel; WT, $n = 5$; Het, $n = 5$–6; KO, $n = 6$; one-way analysis of variance (ANOVA) with Dunnett's multiple comparisons test]. **(C)** Representative images of dendritic spines from hippocampal neurons (scale bar: 10 μm; left panel) and quantification of spine density (right panel; $n = 3$ rats for each genotype, nine neurons per rat; unpaired t-test). Data are presented as the mean ± standard error of the mean (SEM). $^{**}P < 0.01$; $^{***}P < 0.001$.

there was also no expression in *Shank3* knockout rats (**Supplementary Figure S1**).

Reduced Spine Density in *Shank3*-Deficient Rats

Over 90% of excitatory synapses in the brain are located on dendritic spines (Gray, 1959), which undergo dramatic changes during development. We analyzed the dendritic spine density in the hippocampus by Golgi staining on PND35, at the time that spinogenesis was nearly completed (Bian et al., 2015). In *Shank3* knockout rats, the spine density was significantly decreased compared to that of the wild-type littermates ($Shank3^{+/+}$: 3.668 ± 0.1161/10 μm; $Shank3^{-/-}$: 3.006 ± 0.1191/10 μm; $n = 9$ neurons from three rats per genotype, $P < 0.001$; **Figure 1C**), which indicated impaired spinogenesis in the hippocampus of the *Shank3* knockout rats.

Altered Synaptic Proteins in *Shank3*-Deficient Rats

To examine synaptic protein alterations in *Shank3*-deficient rats, we performed quantitative immunoblot analysis for a series of proteins interacting with SHANK3 at the PSD, including SHANK family proteins (SHANK1 and SHANK2), scaffolding proteins (PSD-95 and Homer) and several glutamate receptor subunits (GluR1, GluR2, NR1 and NR2A). Total homogenate (H_0) and isolated PSD fractions were analyzed from the hippocampus, striatum, cortex and cerebellum of 6- to 8-week-old rats. In PSD fractions, the expression levels of Homer and GluR1 were significantly lower in the striatum of *Shank3* knockout rats compared to those in the wild-type controls (16.02 ± 2.864% of $Shank3^{+/+}$ for Homer, $P < 0.001$; 62.01 ± 4.369% of $Shank3^{+/+}$ for GluR1, $P < 0.05$; $n = 5$–6 per genotype; **Figure 2C**). The expression levels of PSD-95, Homer

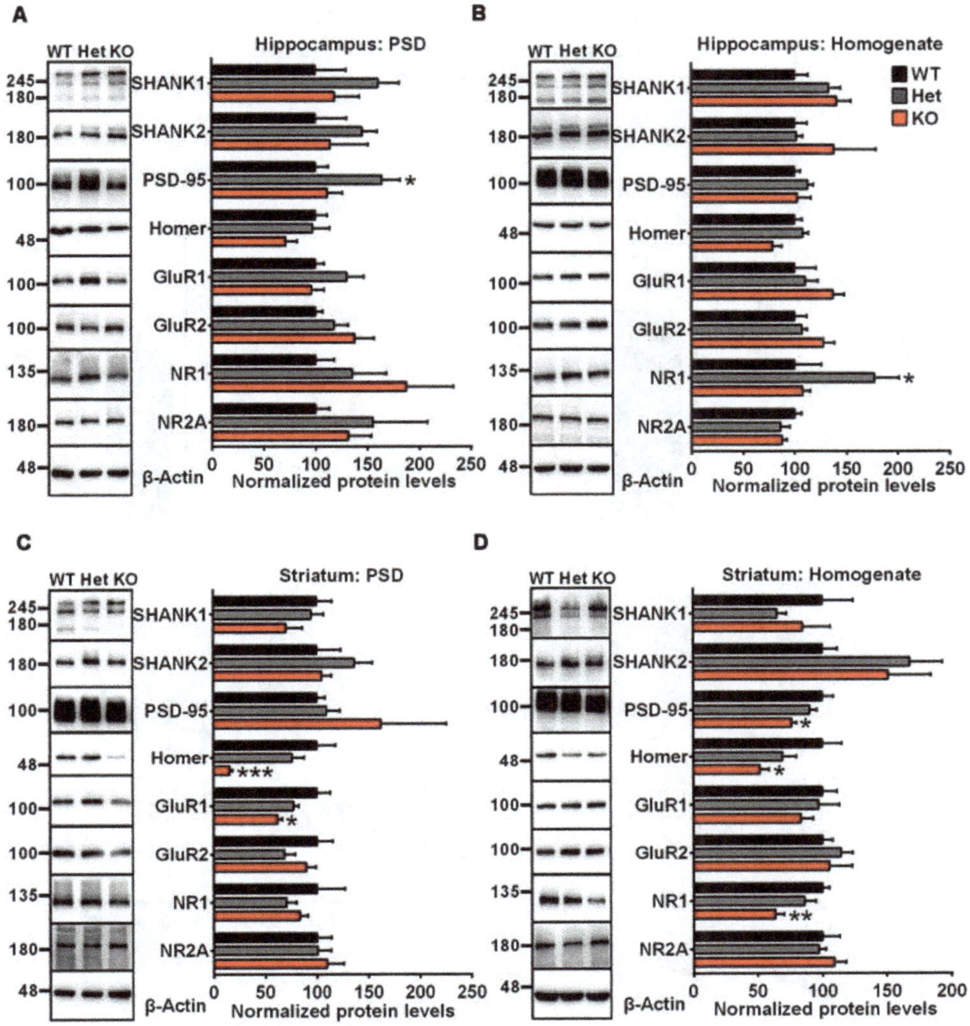

FIGURE 2 | Altered synaptic proteins in PSD fractions and total homogenates from the hippocampus and striatum of *Shank3*-deficient rats. **(A)** Representative immunoblots of PSD fractions from the hippocampus probed with different antibodies as indicated (left panel). Quantification of the corresponding protein expression levels normalized to β-actin (right panel). **(B)** Representative immunoblots of total homogenates from the hippocampus probed with different antibodies as indicated (left panel). Quantification of the corresponding protein expression levels normalized to β-actin (right panel). **(C)** Representative immunoblots of PSD fractions from the striatum probed with different antibodies as indicated (left panel). Quantification of the corresponding protein expression levels normalized to β-actin (right panel). **(D)** Representative immunoblots of total homogenates from the striatum probed with different antibodies as indicated (left panel). Quantification of the corresponding protein expression levels normalized to β-actin (right panel; WT, $n = 5$; Het, $n = 5–6$; KO, $n = 6$; one-way ANOVA with Dunnett's multiple comparisons test). Data are presented as the mean ± SEM. *$P < 0.05$; **$P < 0.01$; ***$P < 0.001$.

and NR1 were also significantly reduced in homogenates from the striatum of *Shank3* knockout rats compared with wild-type control samples (76.27 ± 3.863% of $Shank3^{+/+}$ for PSD-95, $P < 0.05$; 51.86 ± 7.439% of $Shank3^{+/+}$ for Homer, $P < 0.05$; 63.73 ± 6.608% of $Shank3^{+/+}$ for NR1, $P < 0.01$; $n = 5–6$ per genotype; **Figure 2D**). We observed that the expression level of PSD-95 was significantly increased in the hippocampal PSD fraction of heterozygous rats (164.2 ± 17.68% of $Shank3^{+/+}$, $P < 0.05$; $n = 5–6$ per genotype; **Figure 2A**), and the expression level of NR1 significantly increased in the hippocampal homogenate fraction of heterozygous rats (177.4 ± 23.63% of $Shank3^{+/+}$, $P < 0.05$; $n = 5–6$ per genotype; **Figure 2B**). The expression level of NR1 was significantly reduced in PSDs from the cerebellum of heterozygous rats (59.59 ± 8.231% of $Shank3^{+/+}$, $P < 0.05$; $n = 5–6$ per genotype; **Supplementary Figure S2C**). No genotype differences were observed for synaptic proteins in homogenate and PSDs from the cortex and homogenate from the cerebellum (**Supplementary Figures S2A,B,D**). These results above indicated altered synaptic proteins in *Shank3*-deficient rats.

Impaired Synaptic Function and Plasticity in *Shank3*-Deficient Rats

Whole-cell patch clamp and extracellular field recordings in acute hippocampal slices were recruited to analyze the influence of *Shank3* deficiency on synaptic function and plasticity. The amplitude of AMPARs-mediated but not NMDARs-mediated evoked EPSCs was significantly reduced in *Shank3* knockout rats (*Shank3*$^{+/+}$: 108.6 ± 17.55 pA, n = 16 neurons from three rats; *Shank3*$^{-/-}$: 63.74 ± 11.84 pA, n = 17 neurons from three rats; P < 0.05; **Figures 3A,B**). Furthermore, we analyzed fEPSP in the CA1 region, and the input-output curves demonstrated a significantly decreased fEPSP slope in *Shank3* knockout rats (*Shank3*$^{+/+}$: n = 6 slices from three rats;

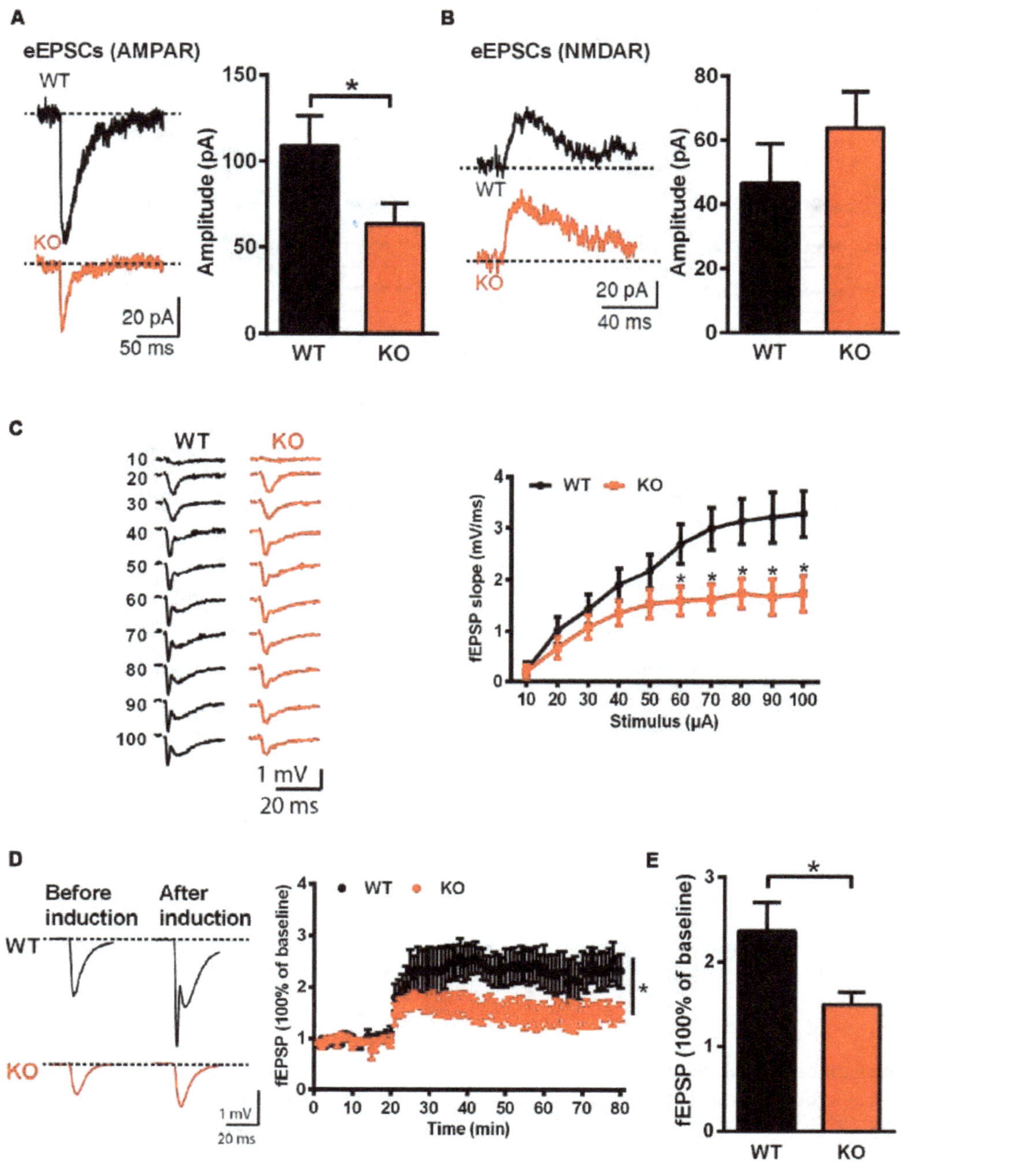

FIGURE 3 | Impaired hippocampal glutamatergic synaptic transmission and long-term potentiation (LTP) in *Shank3*-deficient rats. **(A)** Evoked excitatory postsynaptic currents (EPSCs) mediated by AMPAR in CA1 pyramidal cells. The sample traces of individual recordings (left panel) and the average amplitude of all eEPSCs (right panel; WT, n = 16 neurons from three rats; KO, n = 17 neurons from three rats; unpaired t-test). **(B)** Evoked EPSCs mediated by NMDAR in CA1 pyramidal cells. The sample traces of individual recordings (left panel) and the average amplitude of all eEPSCs (right panel; WT, n = 23 neurons from four rats; KO, n = 29 neurons from four rats; unpaired t-test). **(C)** Input-output curves for basal synaptic transmission in CA1. The sample traces of individual recordings (left panel) and the average fEPSP slope (right panel; WT, n = 6 slices from three rats; KO, n = 7 slices from three rats; unpaired t-test). **(D)** LTP induced by theta-burst stimulation (TBS) in CA1. The sample traces before and after LTP induction (left panel) and the average time plot (right panel; WT, n = 6 slices from three rats; KO, n = 8 slices from three rats; two-way ANOVA). **(E)** The mean fEPSP slope averaged 50–60 min after LTP induction (WT, n = 6 slices from three rats; KO, n = 8 slices from three rats; unpaired t-test). Data are presented as the mean ± SEM. *P < 0.05.

Shank3$^{-/-}$: $n = 7$ slices from three rats; $P < 0.05$; **Figure 3C**). In addition to deficits in basal synaptic transmission, long-term potentiation (LTP) induced by theta-burst stimulation (TBS) was also reduced in *Shank3* knockout rats (last 10 min: *Shank3*$^{+/+}$: 237.1 ± 33.50% of baseline, $n = 6$ slices from three rats; *Shank3*$^{-/-}$: 150.0 ± 14.97% of baseline, $n = 8$ slices from three rats; $P < 0.05$; **Figures 3D,E**). These results above showed impaired synaptic function and plasticity in *Shank3*-deficient rats.

Normal Social Interaction Behavior but Impaired Social Memory and Impaired Learning and Memory in *Shank3*-Deficient Rats

A series of behavioral tests were performed to determine the phenotype of *Shank3*-deficient rats. To determine whether the *Shank3* mutation impacts basic developmental processes in rats, developmental milestones were evaluated, including body weight, pinna detachment, incisor eruption and eye-opening. There were no significant genotype differences in the above-mentioned measures or general health (**Supplementary Figure S3**). We also observed no genotype differences in pup separation-induced USVs on PND7 (data not shown) and reciprocal social interaction behaviors (data not shown).

Social interaction behaviors and social memory were examined by a three-chamber test. In phase 1 of the three chamber test, when the subject rat was exposed to a social stimulus and a nonsocial stimulus simultaneously, *Shank3*-deficient and wild-type rats both spent more time in the compartment containing the social stimulus (data not shown) or in close interaction with the social partner (**Figure 4A**), which showed normal social interaction behaviors and social preferences in *Shank3*-deficient rats. In phase 2 of the three chamber test, a novel social partner was introduced, when the subject rat was exposed to a social and a novel social stimulus simultaneously. Wild-type rats showed a preference for the novel social partner, which was indicated by the increase in the amount of time spent in the compartment containing the novel social stimulus (data not shown) and the amount of time spent in close interaction with the novel

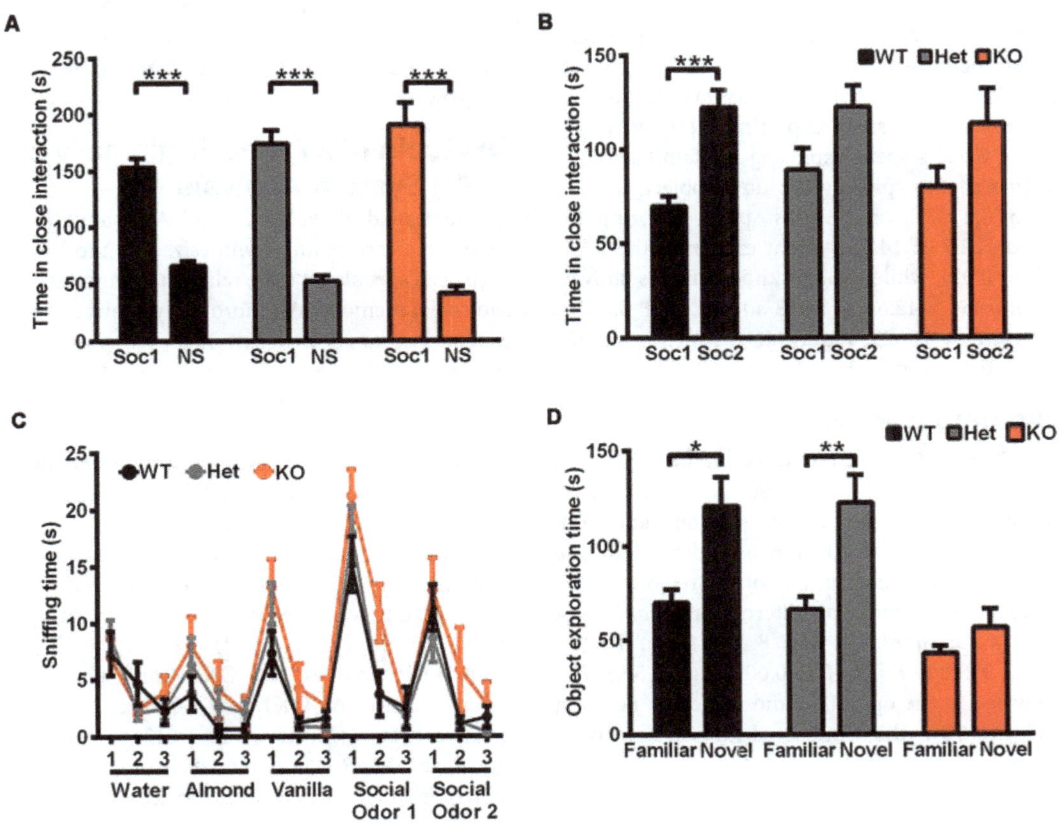

FIGURE 4 | *Shank3*-deficient rats exhibited normal social interaction behavior but impaired social memory and impaired learning and memory. **(A)** The amount of time spent investigating either the social (Soc1) or nonsocial (NS) stimulus in phase 1 of the three-chamber test (WT, $n = 19$, paired *t*-test; Het, $n = 24$, paired *t*-test; KO, $n = 10$, paired *t*-test). **(B)** The amount of time spent investigating either the familiar social (Soc1) or novel social (Soc2) stimulus in phase 2 of the three-chamber test (WT, $n = 19$, paired *t*-test; Het, $n = 24$, paired *t*-test; KO, $n = 10$, paired *t*-test). **(C)** The amount of time spent sniffing a sequence of identical or novel odors in the olfactory habituation/dishabituation test (OHDT; $n = 9$ rats for each genotype). **(D)** The amount of time spent investigating either the familiar or novel object in the novel object recognition test (WT, $n = 10$, Wilcoxon test; Het, $n = 18$, Wilcoxon test; KO, $n = 17$, Wilcoxon test). Data are presented as the mean ± SEM. $^{*}P < 0.05$; $^{**}P < 0.01$; $^{***}P < 0.001$.

social partner (69.42 ± 5.134 s spent in close interaction with the familiar social partner and 122.1 ± 9.124 s spent in close interaction with the novel social partner, $n = 19$, $P < 0.0001$; **Figure 4B**). However, *Shank3*-deficient rats did not show social novelty recognition, as indicated by a similar amount of time spent in the two compartments (data not shown) and the similar amount of time spent in close interaction with the two social partners (*Shank3*$^{+/-}$: 88.83 ± 11.79 and 122.2 ± 11.18 s, respectively, $n = 24$, $P = 0.1006$; *Shank3*$^{-/-}$: 79.90 ± 10.09 and 113.4 ± 18.33 s, respectively, $n = 10$, $P = 0.2157$; **Figure 4B**), indicating impaired social memory in *Shank3*-deficient rats.

Since olfactory ability is important for the social memory of rodents (Wacker and Ludwig, 2012), olfactory habituation/dishabituation was tested in three genotype groups. For nonsocial and social odor cues, both *Shank3*-deficient and wild-type rats showed olfactory habituation and dishabituation, as indicated by the decreased amount of time spent in sniffing the three sequences of the same odors and increased amount of time spent in sniffing the different odors (**Figure 4C**). Therefore, the deficits in social novelty recognition of *Shank3*-deficient rats may not be due to olfactory ability.

Cognitive performance was examined by a novel object recognition test. After a novel object was introduced to replace one of the familiar objects, wild-type and heterozygous rats showed preference for the novel object, which was indicated by the increased amount of time spent exploring the novel object (*Shank3*$^{+/+}$: 69.8 ± 6.955 s spent exploring the familiar object and 120.9 ± 15.19 s spent exploring the novel object, $n = 10$, $P < 0.05$; *Shank3*$^{+/-}$: 66.06 ± 6.976 s spent exploring the familiar object and 122.7 ± 14.55 s spent exploring the novel object, $n = 18$, $P < 0.01$), while *Shank3* knockout rats showed no preference (*Shank3*$^{-/-}$: 42.65 ± 3.918 and 56.35 ± 9.823 s, respectively, $n = 17$, $P = 0.3529$; **Figure 4D**), which suggested impaired learning and memory in *Shank3* knockout rats.

Increased Anxiety Behavior and Pain Threshold in *Shank3*-Deficient Rats

Rats were tested in an open field to analyze their total activity and anxiety-like behavior. *Shank3* heterozygous and knockout rats exhibited increased anxiety behavior, as indicated by the increased amount of time spent in the outer region of the open field compared with wild-type littermates (*Shank3*$^{+/+}$: 546.4 ± 6.498 s, $n = 13$; *Shank3*$^{+/-}$: 576.8 ± 3.456 s, $n = 18$; *Shank3*$^{-/-}$: 581.4 ± 9.220 s, $n = 10$; $P < 0.001$; **Figure 5A**). The total distances traveled in the open field did not differ between the genotypes (**Figure 5B**), which indicated normal activity in *Shank3*-deficient rats.

Since increased pain threshold and hypotonia have been reported in patients with *Shank3* mutations as frequent comorbidities, we conducted relevant behavior tests. The rotarod test showed that there were no differences in the latency to fall between the different genotypes (**Figure 5C**), which indicated normal motor coordination in *Shank3*-deficient rats. Neuromuscular strength and equilibrium were analyzed in the hang wire test, and *Shank3*-deficient rats exhibited no change compared to wild-type littermates (**Figure 5D**).

The von Frey test showed significant increases in paw withdrawal threshold to punctate mechanical stimuli of *Shank3* heterozygous and knockout rats (*Shank3*$^{+/+}$: 6.812 ± 1.206 g, $n = 13$; *Shank3*$^{+/-}$: 12.07 ± 1.229 g, $n = 11$; *Shank3*$^{-/-}$: 11.76 ± 1.011 g, $n = 13$; $P < 0.05$; **Figure 5E**), indicating their increased mechanical pain threshold. The hot plate test was performed at 53°C, and the results showed that *Shank3* knockout rats displayed significantly increased paw withdrawal latency (*Shank3*$^{+/+}$: 8.025 ± 0.5168 s, $n = 23$; *Shank3*$^{+/-}$: 9.200 ± 0.4393 s, $n = 18$; *Shank3*$^{-/-}$: 9.893 ± 0.6453 s, $n = 19$; $P < 0.05$; **Figure 5F**), which suggested a reduction in temperature sensation.

Self-Grooming Behavior and Skin Lesions in *Shank3*-Deficient Rats

Furthermore, repetitive behavior was analyzed in the self-grooming behavior test and the results showed that there was no genotype difference (**Figure 6A**), which only suggested that the self-grooming behaviors of 5- to 6-week-old *Shank3*-deficient rats were normal in this 10-min test. However, we observed skin lesions on the back of the neck in a few of the *Shank3*-deficient rats housed together that are not entirely explained at the moment (**Figure 6B**). Notably, the skin lesions were also observed in *Shank3*-deficient rats housed alone (**Figures 6C,D**), which was speculated to be related to excessive self-grooming behaviors or self-injurious behaviors.

Oxytocin (OXT) and Arginine-Vasopressin (AVP) System Analysis

As mentioned above, OXT and AVP are considered as social factors that are mainly synthesized in the PVN and SON and have been speculated to be related to mammalian social behavior and social memory. We thoroughly analyzed the OXT and AVP system in *Shank3*-deficient rats. We observed no significant genotype differences in the number of OXT-immunoreactive cells and AVP-immunoreactive cells in the PVN and SON (**Figures 7A,B**). Similarly, we also observed no significant differences in the mRNA expression levels of OXT and AVP in the PVN and SON between *Shank3*-deficient rats and their wild-type littermates (**Figures 7C,D**).

In mammals, there are three different receptors for AVP, including V1a, V1b, and V2; among them, the V1a receptor is the predominant form in the brain (Harony and Wagner, 2010; Manning et al., 2012). The amygdala and LS are two brain nuclei that express OXTR and V1aR and mediate the central actions of OXT and AVP on social behaviors and social memory (Lukas et al., 2013). Therefore, we analyzed OXTR and V1aR expression levels in these two nuclei. In three subregions of the amygdala, including the basolateral nucleus of the amygdala (BLA), the central nucleus of the amygdala (CeA) and the medial nucleus of the amygdala (MeA), the mRNA expression levels of OXTR and V1aR did not differ between the genotypes (**Figures 7E,F**). However, in the LS, we observed significantly increased OXTR mRNA expression levels (135.8 ± 11.04% of *Shank3*$^{+/+}$, $n = 13–15$ per genotype, $P < 0.01$) and unchanged V1aR mRNA expression levels in *Shank3* knockout rats (**Figures 7G,H**).

DISCUSSION

Shank3 mutations contribute to the genetic etiology of ASDs and *Shank3* is the major causative gene in the heterozygous deletion of the long arm of chromosome 22q, called PMS. In our present study, we established and thoroughly characterized a novel rat model with a complete *Shank3* deletion. Since alternative splicing of the *Shank3* gene has been reported (Wang et al., 2011), we confirmed that the full-length SHANK3 protein and major SHANK3 isoforms were disrupted completely in knockout rats using different SHANK3 antibodies, which is in contrast with other isoform-specific mutant mouse models and the rat model with a local deletion of exon 6 (Bozdagi et al., 2010; Peca et al., 2011; Wang et al., 2011; Schmeisser et al., 2012; Lee et al., 2015). This novel rat model with a complete *Shank3* deletion can likely better mimic the majority of patients carrying deletions of the entire *Shank3* gene in PMS (Soorya et al., 2013).

A series of biochemical analyses were also performed to examine whether SHANK family proteins and SHANK3-interacting proteins are altered in *Shank3* knockout rats. We did not find changes in other SHANK family proteins, which suggests that there no potential compensatory mechanisms related to other SHANK family proteins. The expression levels of other scaffolding proteins and glutamatergic receptors, including PSD-95, Homer, GluR1 and NR1, were altered, especially in the striatum. The striatum, which mediates components of rodent social behaviors and is related to parts of cognitive and sensorimotor abilities (Brielmaier et al., 2012), has previously been identified as one of the dysfunctional brain regions implicated in autism. In particular, it has been confirmed that the striatum is involved in repetitive behaviors in both autistic patients and animal models (Peca et al., 2011; Langen et al., 2014; Rothwell et al., 2014). Moreover, SHANK3 is the most abundant SHANK family member expressed in the striatum but not in other brain regions (Peca et al., 2011), which

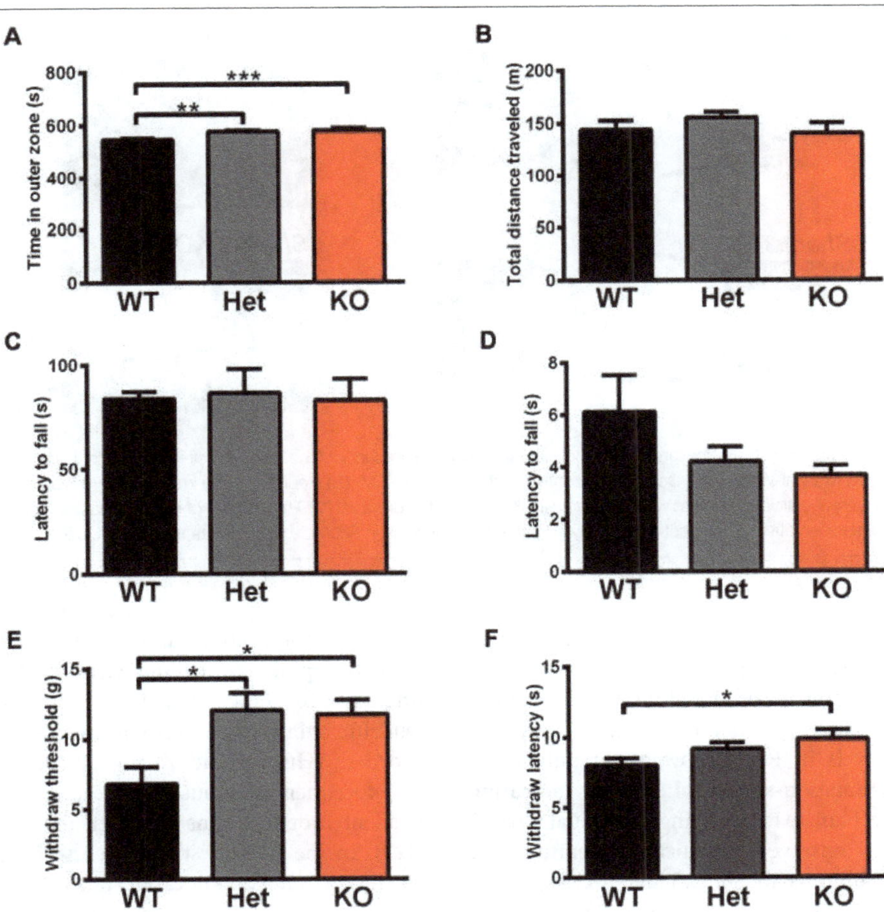

FIGURE 5 | *Shank3*-deficient rats exhibited increased anxiety behavior and an increased pain threshold. **(A)** The amount of time spent close to the chamber walls in the open field test (WT, $n = 13$; Het, $n = 18$; KO, $n = 10$; Kruskal-Wallis test with Dunn's multiple comparisons test). **(B)** Total distance traveled in the open field test (WT, $n = 13$; Het, $n = 18$; KO, $n = 10$; Kruskal-Wallis test). **(C)** The latency to fall from the rotarod in the rotarod test (WT, $n = 18$; Het, $n = 8$; KO, $n = 11$; one-way ANOVA). **(D)** The latency to fall in the hang wire test (WT, $n = 12$; Het, $n = 7$; KO, $n = 12$; Kruskal-Wallis test). **(E)** The withdrawal threshold in the von Frey test for punctate mechanical pain sensitivity (WT, $n = 13$; Het, $n = 11$; KO, $n = 13$; Kruskal-Wallis test with Dunn's multiple comparisons test). **(F)** The withdrawal latency in the hot plate test for heat sensitivity at 53°C (WT, $n = 23$; Het, $n = 18$; KO, $n = 19$; Kruskal-Wallis test with Dunn's multiple comparisons test). Data are presented as the mean ± SEM. $^{*}P < 0.05$; $^{**}P < 0.01$; $^{***}P < 0.001$.

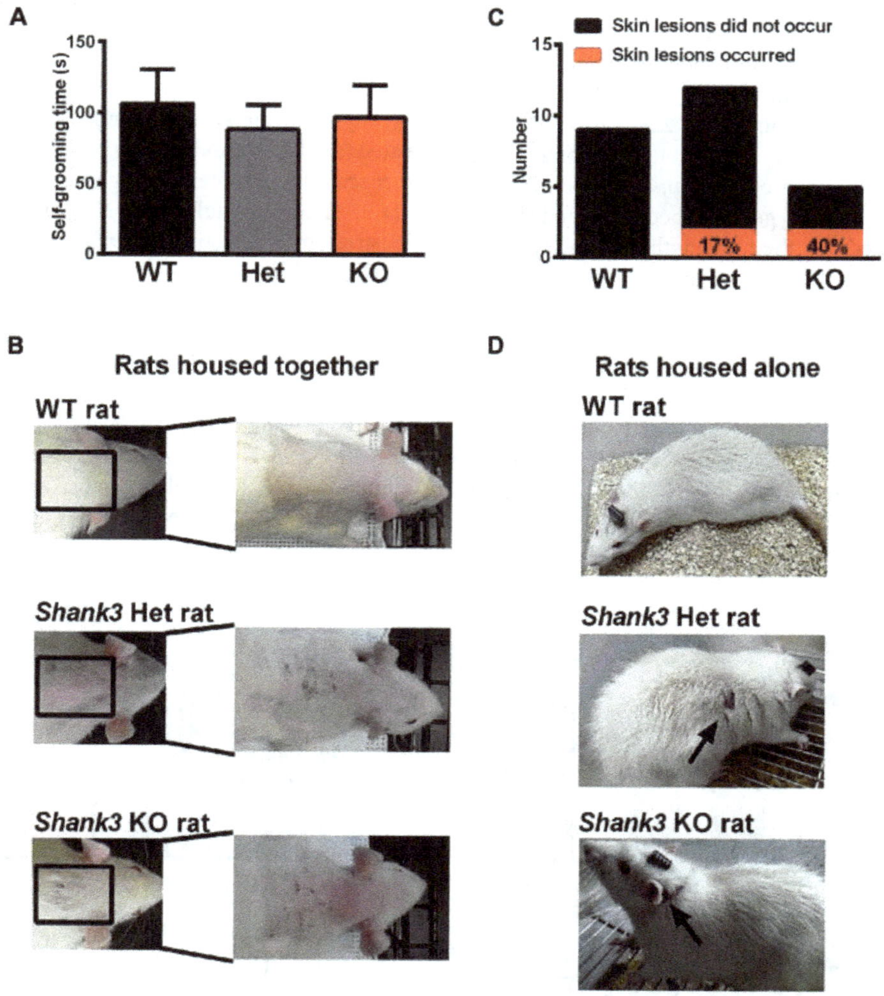

FIGURE 6 | Self-grooming behavior and skin lesions in *Shank3*-deficient rats. **(A)** The amount of time spent in self-grooming in the self-grooming behavior test (WT, $n = 12$; Het, $n = 13$; KO, $n = 11$; Kruskal-Wallis test). Data are presented as the mean ± SEM. **(B)** Representative images of wild-type rats and skin lesions on the back of the neck in a few of *Shank3*-deficient rats that were housed with 3–5 total rats per cage. **(C)** The number of skin lesions that occurred or did not occur in rats that were housed alone. **(D)** Representative photographs of wild-type rats and skin lesions in *Shank3*-deficient rats that were housed alone.

might explain why *Shank3* deficiency has a greater impact on the striatum. The altered molecular composition of *Shank3* knockout synapses confirmed the important role of SHANK3 as a scaffolding protein at PSDs. Compared to other *Shank3*-deficient animal models carrying different mutations, changes in protein expression levels in PSDs showed not only brain region-specific but also mutation-specific alterations, indicating complex biochemical mechanisms underlying individual *Shank3* mutations. Notably, we observed significant alterations of PSD95 and NMDAR1 subunits in *Shank3* heterozygous rats. This result could indicate that any alteration of *Shank3* levels (50% reduction in this study) might modulate the composition of PSDs. This is especially intriguing since human *Shank3* mutations are solely heterozygous disease entities. However, the molecular mechanism explaining these changes is far from being fully understood.

At glutamatergic synapses, SHANK3 interacts with multiple glutamate receptor subunits and the actin-based cytoskeleton as a scaffolding protein, and it is therefore critical for synaptic morphology and synaptic transmission. Normal dendritic spines contribute significantly to regular synaptic function and efficient neural circuit wiring, while altered dendritic spines often occur in individuals with autism-related disorders (Hutsler and Zhang, 2010; Tang et al., 2014), and in experimental mouse models, including some *Shank3*-deficient mouse strains (Peca et al., 2011; Wang et al., 2011, 2017). In the present study, we also observed decreased spine density in *Shank3* knockout rats, suggesting impaired spine formation, which may lead to impaired synaptic function and plasticity eventually. To this end, we analyzed synaptic function and plasticity, especially in the hippocampus. Basal synaptic transmission and LTP were both reduced in *Shank3* knockout rats. Therefore, we confirmed the effect of the *Shank3* mutation on glutamatergic synaptic function and plasticity. Impaired learning and memory formation, as well as impaired social memory, might also be consistent

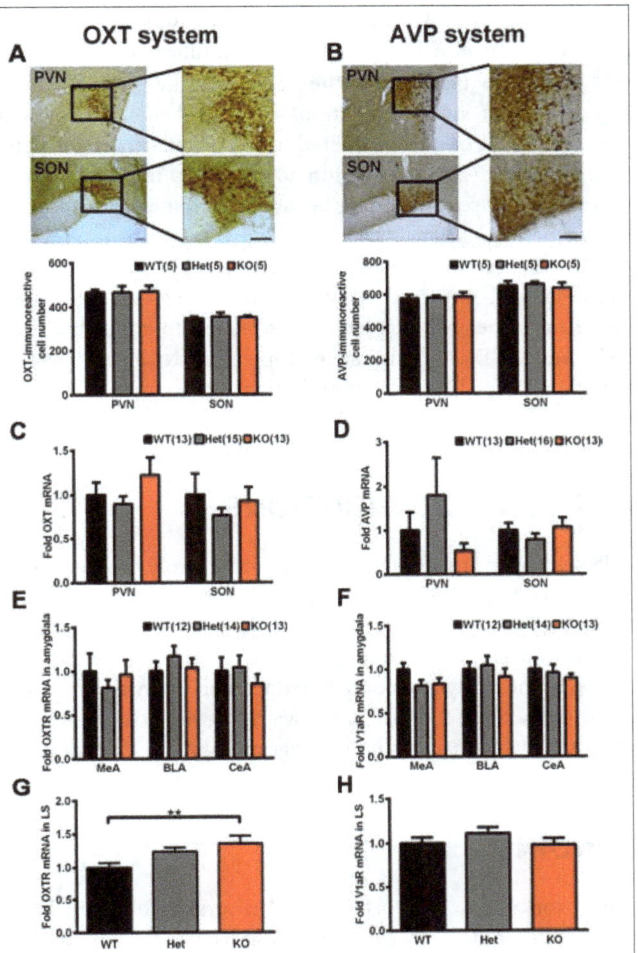

FIGURE 7 | The oxytocin (OXT)/arginine-vasopressin (AVP) system in *Shank3*-deficient rats. **(A)** Representative photomicrograph of OXT-positive cells in the paraventricular nucleus (PVN) and supraoptic nucleus (SON; scale bar: 100 μm) and quantification of the number of OXT-immunoreactive cells in the PVN and SON (n = 5 rats for each genotype, six slices per rat; one-way ANOVA). **(B)** Representative photomicrograph of AVP-positive cells in the PVN and SON (scale bar: 100 μm) and quantification of the number of AVP-immunoreactive cells in the PVN and SON (n = 5 rats for each genotype, six slices per rat; one-way ANOVA). **(C)** mRNA expression levels of OXT in the PVN and SON (WT, n = 13–14; Het, n = 15–17; KO, n = 13–15; one-way ANOVA and Kruskal-Wallis test). **(D)** mRNA expression levels of AVP in the PVN and SON (WT, n = 13–14; Het, n = 16–17; KO, n = 12–15; Kruskal-Wallis test). **(E)** mRNA expression levels of OXTR in three subregions of the amygdala (MeA, BLA, and CeA; WT, n = 12; Het, n = 14; KO, n = 13; one-way ANOVA and Kruskal-Wallis test). **(F)** mRNA expression levels of V1aR in three subregions of the amygdala (MeA, BLA, and CeA; WT, n = 12; Het, n = 14; KO, n = 13; one-way ANOVA). **(G)** mRNA expression levels of OXTR in the lateral septum (LS; WT, n = 13; Het, n = 15; KO, n = 13; one-way ANOVA with Dunnett's multiple comparisons test). **(H)** mRNA expression levels of V1aR in the LS (WT, n = 13; Het, n = 15; KO, n = 13; one-way ANOVA). Data are presented as the mean ± SEM. $^{**}P < 0.01$.

with dysfunctions in synaptic function and plasticity in the hippocampal formation.

Prompted by the crucial role of *Shank3* in synaptic function and the genetic etiology of ASDs and PMS, many *Shank3*-deficient mouse models carrying different mutations have been established. A spectrum of behavioral phenotypes, including impaired social behaviors and increased repetitive behavior, which are regarded as core symptoms of ASDs, have been described. Moreover, impaired learning and memory formation as well as increased anxiety behavior as comorbidities, have been identified (Bozdagi et al., 2010; Bangash et al., 2011; Peca et al., 2011; Wang et al., 2011; Yang et al., 2012; Kouser et al., 2013; Duffney et al., 2015). Subsequently, a rat model with a local deletion of exon 6 of *Shank3* was established, and normal social behavior but impaired social memory and attention were observed (Harony-Nicolas et al., 2017). Another *Shank3*-deficient nonhuman primate model with altered neurogenesis has also been reported (Zhao et al., 2017). In our present study, we did not find aberrant social interaction behaviors in *Shank3*-deficient rats, which have been identified in a majority of *Shank3*-deficient mouse models. These discrepancies may be attributed to species-specific differences, different genetic backgrounds, different targeting sites in the *Shank3* gene, different ages of animals used in behavioral tests and different paradigms of behavioral tests. Heterogeneity in clinical symptoms among patients with PMS and ASD and normal social behaviors performed by some of the patients with PMS should also be considered (Scheeren et al., 2012; Soorya et al., 2013). The normal levels of OXT and AVP in the hypothalamus and the normal levels of OXTR and V1aR in the amygdala might be one of the reasons for normal social behavior. To the best of our knowledge, the endogenous OXT/AVP system was explored for the first time in a *Shank3*-deficient animal model. Nevertheless, similar to different behavioral defects in *Shank3*-deficient animal models, we speculated that changes in the OXT/AVP system can also vary among different models and contribute to phenotypes related to social interaction. These results also suggest that there are independent pathways responding to social novelty recognition and social interaction ability, even in the same gene knockout condition.

In this genetically modified rat model, we observed impaired social memory indicated by deficits in social novelty recognition. Olfaction plays an important role in social recognition in rodents (Wacker and Ludwig, 2012), and social recognition tests make use of the natural tendency of animals toward the olfactory investigation of novel conspecifics (Bielsky and Young, 2004). Typically, OHDTs are performed as a control task. Impaired social behavior with normal olfactory ability has also been reported in *Shank3*-deficient mice with a deletion of exons 4 through 9 (Bozdagi et al., 2010). In this study, normal olfactory ability suggested that dysfunctions in other complex and elaborate mechanisms of processing social stimuli and memory led to impaired social memory in *Shank3*-deficient rats. OXT and AVP also play an important role in social memory, which can act on a variety of brain regions to facilitate social recognition and modulate subsequent behavioral responses (Wacker and Ludwig, 2012). Among these, the LS is thought to be crucial for the mediation of social recognition (van der Kooij and Sandi, 2012). However, analysis of OXTR and V1aR expression levels in the LS showed increased mRNA expression levels of OXTR even with normal synthetic levels of OXT. Currently, we cannot explain exactly the impaired social memory and the divergent changes of the OXT/AVP system. The involvement of acetylcholine, norepinephrine, dopamine, serotonin and estrogen in social memory has also been reported (van der Kooij and Sandi, 2012; Ervin et al., 2015). In addition, secretin can increase the acquisition of social recognition in an OXTR-dependent manner (Takayanagi et al., 2017). Therefore, we doubt that there are any cross-mediating mechanisms. The various neurotransmitter systems committed to social memory and the interactions between other neurotransmitters and the OXT/AVP system should be further analyzed. Notably, the facilitatory effect of OXT administration on a variety of social behaviors has been reported not only in humans (Domes et al., 2007; Guastella et al., 2008; Hurlemann et al., 2010) but also in rodents (Lukas et al., 2011). In particular, the improved effect of OXT treatment on social memory and attention has been observed in a *Shank3*-deficient rat model with a deletion in exon 6 (Harony-Nicolas et al., 2017). Combining these results from studies of humans and animals with normal or impaired social behavior, we can infer that there is an ameliorative effect of OXT on social memory even with a normal OXT/AVP system. Therefore, whether the OXT treatment can improve the defective behaviors in this *Shank3*-deficient rat should also be further studied.

Cognitive disabilities, anxiety, sensory-perceptual anomalies and pain insensitivity are common comorbidities in patients with ASD and PMS (Allely, 2013; Soorya et al., 2013; Croen et al., 2015; Polyak et al., 2015). Analogously, we observed impaired learning and memory, increased anxiety behavior, an increased baseline mechanical pain threshold and reduced temperature sensation in *Shank3*-deficient rats. Impaired learning and memory and increased anxiety behavior have often been reported in a majority of *Shank3*-deficient mouse models (Bozdagi et al., 2010; Bangash et al., 2011; Peca et al., 2011; Wang et al., 2011; Yang et al., 2012; Kouser et al., 2013; Duffney et al., 2015). Impaired heat hyperalgesia in inflammatory and neuropathic pain and the interaction between SHANK3 and transient receptor potential subtype V1 (TRPV1) have been reported in *Shank3* knockout mice with a deletion of exons 4–22, however, there was no change in the baseline thermal and mechanical sensitivity in this mouse model as we observed (Han et al., 2016). Incorporating these findings, *Shank3* mutation may underlie pain deficits in *Shank3*-related ASD and PMS through some mechanisms that include the interaction with TRPV1 but are not limited to.

Notably, to understand the results of the behavioral tests in our present study, limitations of some behavioral tests for rats should also be considered. In particular, the detection of muscle and motor function using other methods and the observation of self-grooming behavior in home cages should be further performed.

Overall, the *Shank3*-deficient rat model established in this study showed impaired synaptic function as expected, and a spectrum of behavioral phenotypes related to comorbidities in PMS and ASDs, which make it possible to assess potential therapeutics for PMS, ASDs and other developmental disorders using this model.

AUTHOR CONTRIBUTIONS

T-JS conceived and designed the study and wrote the manuscript. T-JS, X-YL and M-PW performed the experiments and analyzed the data. F-JZ, J-NW, SY, M-YJ, Y-FX, W-WD, P-WS and Y-YS helped to perform the experiments. RZ, J-SH, and S-PH helped to design the study and contributed to analysis with constructive discussions. RZ, TB, MS, CZ and M-HQ reviewed and edited the manuscript and made valuable suggestions. All authors approved the final version.

FUNDING

This work was supported by University of Ulm-Peking University Health Science Center Joint Center for Neuroscience fund (BMU20160563), National key research and development program (2016YFC0105501), National Basic Research Program of China (2017YFA0105201) and National Science Foundation of China (31670842).

ACKNOWLEDGMENTS

We thank Dr. Yong-hui Jiang, Dr. Feng-Yan Sun and Dr. Xin-Chun Jin for advice and comments on the manuscript.

REFERENCES

Allely, C. S. (2013). Pain sensitivity and observer perception of pain in individuals with autistic spectrum disorder. *ScientificWorldJournal* 2013:916178. doi: 10.1155/2013/916178

Bangash, M. A., Park, J. M., Melnikova, T., Wang, D., Jeon, S. K., Lee, D., et al. (2011). Enhanced polyubiquitination of Shank3 and NMDA receptor in a mouse model of autism. *Cell* 145, 758–772. doi: 10.1016/j.cell.2011.03.052

Baron, M. K., Boeckers, T. M., Vaida, B., Faham, S., Gingery, M., Sawaya, M. R., et al. (2006). An architectural framework that may lie at the core of the postsynaptic density. *Science* 311, 531–535. doi: 10.1126/science.1118995

Bian, W. J., Miao, W. Y., He, S. J., Qiu, Z., and Yu, X. (2015). Coordinated spine pruning and maturation mediated by inter-spine competition for cadherin/catenin complexes. *Cell* 162, 808–822. doi: 10.1016/j.cell.2015.07.018

Bielsky, I. F., and Young, L. J. (2004). Oxytocin, vasopressin and social recognition in mammals. *Peptides* 25, 1565–1574. doi: 10.1016/j.peptides.2004.05.019

Boeckers, T. M. (2006). The postsynaptic density. *Cell Tissue Res.* 326, 409–422. doi: 10.1007/s00441-006-0274-5

Boeckers, T. M., Winter, C., Smalla, K. H., Kreutz, M. R., Bockmann, J., Seidenbecher, C., et al. (1999). Proline-rich synapse-associated proteins ProSAP1 and ProSAP2 interact with synaptic proteins of the SAPAP/GKAP family. *Biochem. Biophys. Res. Commun.* 264, 247–252. doi: 10.1006/bbrc.1999.1489

Bozdagi, O., Sakurai, T., Papapetrou, D., Wang, X., Dickstein, D. L., Takahashi, N., et al. (2010). Haploinsufficiency of the autism-associated Shank3 gene leads to deficits in synaptic function, social interaction, and social communication. *Mol. Autism* 1:15. doi: 10.1186/2040-2392-1-15

Brielmaier, J., Matteson, P. G., Silverman, J. L., Senerth, J. M., Kelly, S., Genestine, M., et al. (2012). Autism-relevant social abnormalities and cognitive deficits in engrailed-2 knockout mice. *PLoS One* 7:e40914. doi: 10.1371/journal.pone.0040914

Croen, L. A., Zerbo, O., Qian, Y., Massolo, M. L., Rich, S., Sidney, S., et al. (2015). The health status of adults on the autism spectrum. *Autism* 19, 814–823. doi: 10.1177/1362361315577517

Domes, G., Heinrichs, M., Michel, A., Berger, C., and Herpertz, S. C. (2007). Oxytocin improves "mind-reading" in humans. *Biol. Psychiatry* 61, 731–733. doi: 10.1016/j.biopsych.2006.07.015

Duffney, L. J., Zhong, P., Wei, J., Matas, E., Cheng, J., Qin, L., et al. (2015). Autism-like deficits in shank3-deficient mice are rescued by targeting actin regulators. *Cell Rep.* 11, 1400–1413. doi: 10.1016/j.celrep.2015.04.064

Ervin, K. S., Lymer, J. M., Matta, R., Clipperton-Allen, A. E., Kavaliers, M., and Choleris, E. (2015). Estrogen involvement in social behavior in rodents: rapid and long-term actions. *Horm. Behav.* 74, 53–76. doi: 10.1016/j.yhbeh.2015.05.023

Gigliucci, V., Leonzino, M., Busnelli, M., Luchetti, A., Palladino, V. S., D'Amato, F. R., et al. (2014). Region specific up-regulation of oxytocin receptors in the opioid oprm1$^{-/-}$ mouse model of autism. *Front. Pediatr.* 2:91. doi: 10.3389/fped.2014.00091

Gong, X., Jiang, Y. W., Zhang, X., An, Y., Zhang, J., Wu, Y., et al. (2012). High proportion of 22q13 deletions and SHANK3 mutations in Chinese patients with intellectual disability. *PLoS One* 7:e34739. doi: 10.1371/journal.pone.0034739

Grabrucker, A. M., Schmeisser, M. J., Schoen, M., and Boeckers, T. M. (2011). Postsynaptic ProSAP/Shank scaffolds in the cross-hair of synaptopathies. *Trends Cell Biol.* 21, 594–603. doi: 10.1016/j.tcb.2011.07.003

Gray, E. G. (1959). Electron microscopy of synaptic contacts on dendrite spines of the cerebral cortex. *Nature* 183, 1592–1593. doi: 10.1038/1831592a0

Guastella, A. J., Mitchell, P. B., and Dadds, M. R. (2008). Oxytocin increases gaze to the eye region of human faces. *Biol. Psychiatry* 63, 3–5. doi: 10.1016/j.biopsych.2007.06.026

Han, Q., Kim, Y. H., Wang, X., Liu, D., Zhang, Z. J., Bey, A. L., et al. (2016). SHANK3 deficiency impairs heat hyperalgesia and TRPV1 signaling in primary sensory neurons. *Neuron* 92, 1279–1293. doi: 10.1016/j.neuron.2016.11.007

Harony, H., and Wagner, S. (2010). The contribution of oxytocin and vasopressin to mammalian social behavior: potential role in autism spectrum disorder. *Neurosignals* 18, 82–97. doi: 10.1159/000321035

Harony-Nicolas, H., Kay, M., Hoffmann, J. D., Klein, M. E., Bozdagi-Gunal, O., Riad, M., et al. (2017). Oxytocin improves behavioral and electrophysiological deficits in a novel Shank3-deficient rat. *Elife* 6:e18904. doi: 10.7554/elife.18904

Hurlemann, R., Patin, A., Onur, O. A., Cohen, M. X., Baumgartner, T., Metzler, S., et al. (2010). Oxytocin enhances amygdala-dependent, socially reinforced learning and emotional empathy in humans. *J. Neurosci.* 30, 4999–5007. doi: 10.1523/JNEUROSCI.5538-09.2010

Hutsler, J. J., and Zhang, H. (2010). Increased dendritic spine densities on cortical projection neurons in autism spectrum disorders. *Brain Res.* 1309, 83–94. doi: 10.1016/j.brainres.2009.09.120

Ishikawa, H., Yamada, K., Pavlides, C., and Ichitani, Y. (2014). Sleep deprivation impairs spontaneous object-place but not novel-object recognition in rats. *Neurosci. Lett.* 580, 114–118. doi: 10.1016/j.neulet.2014.08.004

Janssen, E., Göhlen, B., Behrens, D., Richter, K., and Zavazava, N. (2001). Allogeneic recombinant soluble MHC class I molecules modify urinary odor cues in rats. *Physiol. Behav.* 72, 107–114. doi: 10.1016/s0031-9384(00)00389-9

Jin, D., Liu, H. X., Hirai, H., Torashima, T., Nagai, T., Lopatina, O., et al. (2007). CD38 is critical for social behaviour by regulating oxytocin secretion. *Nature* 446, 41–45. doi: 10.1038/nature05526

Kouser, M., Speed, H. E., Dewey, C. M., Reimers, J. M., Widman, A. J., Gupta, N., et al. (2013). Loss of predominant Shank3 isoforms results in hippocampus-dependent impairments in behavior and synaptic transmission. *J. Neurosci.* 33, 18448–18468. doi: 10.1523/JNEUROSCI.3017-13.2013

Langen, M., Bos, D., Noordermeer, S. D., Nederveen, H., van Engeland, H., and Durston, S. (2014). Changes in the development of striatum are involved in repetitive behavior in autism. *Biol. Psychiatry* 76, 405–411. doi: 10.1016/j.biopsych.2013.08.013

Leblond, C. S., Nava, C., Polge, A., Gauthier, J., Huguet, G., Lumbroso, S., et al. (2014). Meta-analysis of SHANK mutations in autism spectrum disorders: a gradient of severity in cognitive impairments. *PLoS Genet.* 10:e1004580. doi: 10.1371/journal.pgen.1004580

Lee, J., Chung, C., Ha, S., Lee, D., Kim, D. Y., Kim, H., et al. (2015). Shank3-mutant mice lacking exon 9 show altered excitation/inhibition balance, enhanced rearing, and spatial memory deficit. *Front. Cell. Neurosci.* 9:94. doi: 10.3389/fncel.2015.00094

Li, J., Chai, A., Wang, L., Ma, Y., Wu, Z., Yu, H., et al. (2015). Synaptic P-Rex1 signaling regulates hippocampal long-term depression and autism-like social behavior. *Proc. Natl. Acad. Sci. U S A* 112, E6964–E6972. doi: 10.1073/pnas.1512913112

Li, M., He, W., and Heupel, K. (2011). Administration of clozapine to a mother rat potentiates pup ultrasonic vocalization in response to separation and re-separation: contrast with haloperidol. *Behav. Brain Res.* 222, 385–389. doi: 10.1016/j.bbr.2011.03.062

Lukas, M., Toth, I., Reber, S. O., Slattery, D. A., Veenema, A. H., and Neumann, I. D. (2011). The neuropeptide oxytocin facilitates pro-social behavior and prevents social avoidance in rats and mice. *Neuropsychopharmacology* 36, 2159–2168. doi: 10.1038/npp.2011.95

Lukas, M., Toth, I., Veenema, A. H., and Neumann, I. D. (2013). Oxytocin mediates rodent social memory within the lateral septum and the medial amygdala depending on the relevance of the social stimulus: male juvenile versus female adult conspecifics. *Psychoneuroendocrinology* 38, 916–926. doi: 10.1016/j.psyneuen.2012.09.018

Manning, M., Misicka, A., Olma, A., Bankowski, K., Stoev, S., Chini, B., et al. (2012). Oxytocin and vasopressin agonists and antagonists as research tools and potential therapeutics. *J Neuroendocrinol* 24, 609–628. doi: 10.1111/j.1365-2826.2012.02303.x

Naisbitt, S., Kim, E., Tu, J. C., Xiao, B., Sala, C., Valtschanoff, J., et al. (1999). Shank, a novel family of postsynaptic density proteins that binds to the NMDA receptor/PSD-95/GKAP complex and cortactin. *Neuron* 23, 569–582. doi: 10.1016/s0896-6273(00)80809-0

Peca, J., Feliciano, C., Ting, J. T., Wang, W., Wells, M. F., Venkatraman, T. N., et al. (2011). Shank3 mutant mice display autistic-like behaviours and striatal dysfunction. *Nature* 472, 437–442. doi: 10.1038/nature09965

Penagarikano, O., Lazaro, M. T., Lu, X. H., Gordon, A., Dong, H., Lam, H. A., et al. (2015). Exogenous and evoked oxytocin restores social behavior in the Cntnap2 mouse model of autism. *Sci. Transl. Med.* 7:271ra278. doi: 10.1126/scitranslmed.3010257

Polyak, A., Kubina, R. M., and Girirajan, S. (2015). Comorbidity of intellectual disability confounds ascertainment of autism: implications for genetic diagnosis. *Am. J. Med. Genet. B Neuropsychiatr. Genet.* 168, 600–608. doi: 10.1002/ajmg.b.32338

Pyndt Jørgensen, B., Krych, L., Pedersen, T. B., Plath, N., Redrobe, J. P., Hansen, A. K., et al. (2015). Investigating the long-term effect of subchronic phencyclidine-treatment on novel object recognition and the association between the gut microbiota and behavior in the animal model of schizophrenia. *Physiol. Behav.* 141, 32–39. doi: 10.1016/j.physbeh.2014.12.042

Rothwell, P. E., Fuccillo, M. V., Maxeiner, S., Hayton, S. J., Gokce, O., Lim, B. K., et al. (2014). Autism-associated neuroligin-3 mutations commonly impair striatal circuits to boost repetitive behaviors. *Cell* 158, 198–212. doi: 10.1016/j.cell.2014.04.045

Scheeren, A. M., Koot, H. M., and Begeer, S. (2012). Social interaction style of children and adolescents with high-functioning autism spectrum disorder. *J. Autism Dev. Disord.* 42, 2046–2055. doi: 10.1007/s10803-012-1451-x

Schmeisser, M. J., Ey, E., Wegener, S., Bockmann, J., Stempel, A. V., Kuebler, A., et al. (2012). Autistic-like behaviours and hyperactivity in mice lacking ProSAP1/Shank2. *Nature* 486, 256–260. doi: 10.1038/nature11015

Soorya, L., Kolevzon, A., Zweifach, J., Lim, T., Dobry, Y., Schwartz, L., et al. (2013). Prospective investigation of autism and genotype-phenotype correlations in 22q13 deletion syndrome and SHANK3 deficiency. *Mol. Autism* 4:18. doi: 10.1186/2040-2392-4-18

Takayanagi, Y., Yoshida, M., Takashima, A., Takanami, K., Yoshida, S., Nishimori, K., et al. (2017). Activation of supraoptic oxytocin neurons by secretin facilitates social recognition. *Biol. Psychiatry* 81, 243–251. doi: 10.1016/j.biopsych.2015.11.021

Tang, G., Gudsnuk, K., Kuo, S. H., Cotrina, M. L., Rosoklija, G., Sosunov, A., et al. (2014). Loss of mTOR-dependent macroautophagy causes autistic-like synaptic pruning deficits. *Neuron* 83, 1131–1143. doi: 10.1016/j.neuron.2014.07.040

van der Kooij, M. A., and Sandi, C. (2012). Social memories in rodents: methods, mechanisms and modulation by stress. *Neurosci. Biobehav. Rev.* 36, 1763–1772. doi: 10.1016/j.neubiorev.2011.10.006

Vanderschuren, L. J., Stein, E. A., Wiegant, V. M., and Van Ree, J. M. (1995a). Social isolation and social interaction alter regional brain opioid receptor binding in rats. *Eur. Neuropsychopharmacol.* 5, 119–127. doi: 10.1016/0924-977x(95)00010-m

Vanderschuren, L. J., Stein, E. A., Wiegant, V. M., and Van Ree, J. M. (1995b). Social play alters regional brain opioid receptor binding in juvenile rats. *Brain Res.* 680, 148–156. doi: 10.1016/0006-8993(95)00256-p

Wacker, D. W., and Ludwig, M. (2012). Vasopressin, oxytocin, and social odor recognition. *Horm. Behav.* 61, 259–265. doi: 10.1016/j.yhbeh.2011.08.014

Wang, X., Bey, A. L., Katz, B. M., Badea, A., Kim, N., David, L. K., et al. (2016). Altered mGluR5-Homer scaffolds and corticostriatal connectivity in a Shank3 complete knockout model of autism. *Nat. Commun.* 7:11459. doi: 10.1038/ncomms11459

Wang, W., Li, C., Chen, Q., van der Goes, M. S., Hawrot, J., Yao, A. Y., et al. (2017). Striatopallidal dysfunction underlies repetitive behavior in Shank3-deficient model of autism. *J. Clin. Invest.* 127, 1978–1990. doi: 10.1172/jci87997

Wang, X., McCoy, P. A., Rodriguiz, R. M., Pan, Y., Je, H. S., Roberts, A. C., et al. (2011). Synaptic dysfunction and abnormal behaviors in mice lacking major isoforms of Shank3. *Hum. Mol. Genet.* 20, 3093–3108. doi: 10.1093/hmg/ddr212

Wei, W., Song, Y., Fan, X., Zhang, S., Wang, L., Xu, S., et al. (2016). Simultaneous recording of brain extracellular glucose, spike and local field potential in real time using an implantable microelectrode array with nano-materials. *Nanotechnology* 27:114001. doi: 10.1088/0957-4484/27/11/114001

Wilson, H. L., Wong, A. C., Shaw, S. R., Tse, W. Y., Stapleton, G. A., Phelan, M. C., et al. (2003). Molecular characterisation of the 22q13 deletion syndrome supports the role of haploinsufficiency of SHANK3/PROSAP2 in the major neurological symptoms. *J. Med. Genet.* 40, 575–584. doi: 10.1136/jmg.40.8.575

Xu, X. J., Zhang, H. F., Shou, X. J., Li, J., Jing, W. L., Zhou, Y., et al. (2015). Prenatal hyperandrogenic environment induced autistic-like behavior in rat offspring. *Physiol. Behav.* 138, 13–20. doi: 10.1016/j.physbeh.2014.09.014

Yang, M., Bozdagi, O., Scattoni, M. L., Wöhr, M., Roullet, F. I., Katz, A. M., et al. (2012). Reduced excitatory neurotransmission and mild autism-relevant phenotypes in adolescent Shank3 null mutant mice. *J. Neurosci.* 32, 6525–6541. doi: 10.1523/JNEUROSCI.6107-11.2012

Yang, H., Wang, H., Shivalila, C. S., Cheng, A. W., Shi, L., and Jaenisch, R. (2013). One-step generation of mice carrying reporter and conditional alleles by CRISPR/Cas-mediated genome engineering. *Cell* 154, 1370–1379. doi: 10.1016/j.cell.2013.08.022

Zhang, H. F., Dai, Y. C., Wu, J., Jia, M. X., Zhang, J. S., Shou, X. J., et al. (2016). Plasma oxytocin and arginine-vasopressin levels in children with autism spectrum disorder in china: associations with symptoms. *Neurosci. Bull.* 32, 423–432. doi: 10.1007/s12264-016-0046-5

Zhang, H. F., Li, H. X., Dai, Y. C., Xu, X. J., Han, S. P., Zhang, R., et al. (2015). Electro-acupuncture improves the social interaction behavior of rats. *Physiol. Behav.* 151, 485–493. doi: 10.1016/j.physbeh.2015.08.014

Zhang, R., Zhang, H. F., Han, J. S., and Han, S. P. (2017). Genes related to oxytocin and arginine-vasopressin pathways: associations with autism spectrum disorders. *Neurosci. Bull.* 33, 238–246. doi: 10.1007/s12264-017-0120-7

Zhao, H., Tu, Z., Xu, H., Yan, S., Yan, H., Zheng, Y., et al. (2017). Altered neurogenesis and disrupted expression of synaptic proteins in prefrontal cortex of SHANK3-deficient non-human primate. *Cell Res.* 27, 1293–1297. doi: 10.1038/cr.2017.95

5

Urine Organic Acids as Potential Biomarkers for Autism-Spectrum Disorder in Chinese Children

Qiao Chen[1†], You Qiao[1†], Xin-jie Xu[2], Xin You[1,3,4] and Ying Tao[5*]*

[1] Department of Rheumatology and Clinical Immunology, Peking Union Medical College Hospital, Chinese Academy of Medical Sciences & Peking Union Medical College, Beijing, China, [2] Central Research Laboratory, Department of Scientific Research, Peking Union Medical College Hospital, Chinese Academy of Medical Sciences and Peking Union Medical College, Beijing, China, [3] Key Laboratory of Rheumatology and Clinical Immunology, Ministry of Education, Beijing, China, [4] Autism Special Fund, Peking Union Medical Foundation, Beijing, China, [5] Institute of Artificial Intelligence, Ping An Technology (Shenzhen) Ltd., Beijing, China

***Correspondence:**
Xin You
youxin@pumch.cn
Ying Tao
taoying7001@139.com

† These authors have contributed equally to this work

Autism spectrum disorder (ASD) is a neurodevelopmental disorder that lacks clear biological biomarkers. Existing diagnostic methods focus on behavioral and performance characteristics, which complicates the diagnosis of patients younger than 3 years-old. The purpose of this study is to characterize metabolic features of ASD that could be used to identify potential biomarkers for diagnosis and exploration of ASD etiology. We used gas chromatography-mass spectrometry (GC/MS) to evaluate major metabolic fluctuations in 76 organic acids present in urine from 156 children with ASD and from 64 non-autistic children. Three algorithms, Partial Least Squares-Discriminant Analysis (PLS-DA), Support Vector Machine (SVM), and eXtreme Gradient Boosting (XGBoost), were used to develop models to distinguish ASD from typically developing (TD) children and to detect potential biomarkers. In an independent testing set, full model of XGBoost with all 76 acids achieved an AUR of 0.94, while reduced model with top 20 acids discovered by voting from these three algorithms achieved 0.93 and represent a good collection of potential ASD biomarkers. In summary, urine organic acids detection with GC/MS combined with XGBoost algorithm could represent a novel and accurate strategy for diagnosis of autism and the discovered potential biomarkers could be valuable for future research on the pathogenesis of autism and possible interventions.

Keywords: autism spectrum disorder, biomarker, urine organic acids, Chinese, metabolomics, diagnosis

INTRODUCTION

Autism spectrum disorder (ASD) is a developmental disorder characterized by impaired communication and social behavior, as well as displays of restricted and repetitive behavior (Keller and Persico, 2003). Although the pathogenesis of autism is uncertain, it is considered to involve an interaction between multiple genetic and environmental risk factors that are present in the few first years of life (Nair, 2000).

The diagnostic criteria for ASD require that symptoms become apparent in early childhood, typically before age three (Dieme et al., 2015). Autism diagnosis currently relies on scales and professional surveyors using behavioral methods. For instance, the Diagnostic and Statistical Manual of Mental Disorders, Fourth Edition (DSM-4) is the 1994 version of the American Psychiatric Association (APA) that provides a classification and diagnostic tool for ASD. Early identification and early intervention of autistic children are recognized as two of the most crucial factors for improving outcomes for individuals affected by ASD (Dawson et al., 2010, 2012; Warren et al., 2011; Zwaigenbaum et al., 2013; Klin et al., 2015). However, due to the challenges of early ASD diagnosis many older children miss the best intervention period.

Metabolic abnormalities associated with ASD include: phenylketonuria (PKU), disorders in purine metabolism, folate deficiency in brain development, succinic semialdehyde dehydrogenase deficiency, Smith-Lemli-Opitz syndrome (SLOS), organic acidurias (e.g., pyridoxine dependency, 3-methylcrotonyl-CoA carboxylase deficiency, and propionic acidemia), and mitochondrial disorders (Manzi et al., 2008; Zecavati and Spence, 2009; Ghaziuddin and Alowain, 2013). The presence of psychiatric, behavioral, and developmental regression together with metabolic disorders in autism (Wanders et al., 1999; Wang et al., 1999; Cox et al., 2001; Kompare and Rizzo, 2008) requires studies concerning the relationship between these pathological states and whether metabolic products of amino acid and lipid synthesis in urine or blood could be autism biomarkers (Schain and Freedman, 1961; Hanley et al., 1977; Bull et al., 2003; Kałużna-Czaplińska, 2011). After glomerular filtration and tubular condensation, the macromolecular proteins in the blood can be filtered and the urine becomes a concentrated organic acid. The natural physiological role of the kidney makes urine the best specimen for analyzing organic acid metabolism.

Several previous studies focused on organic acid biomarkers in autistic patients. Emond et al. (2013) found that levels of citrate, succinate, and glycolate were significantly increased in the urine sample of ASD children, whereas Mavel et al. (2013) found that β-alanine, glycine, taurine, and succinic acid levels were increased in the urine sample. Another study indicated that around 10 metabolites significantly differed between an autism group and the control group (Kałużna-Czaplińska, 2011). Some organic acids were highlighted by multiple studies, while others were seen only in a specific study. In general, microbial metabolites, niacin metabolism, mitochondria-related metabolites, and amino acid metabolites are the most common perturbations in autistic children. These results illustrates the complexity of metabolic disorders and etiology in autistic patients, leading to the exploration of building models for multivariate analysis. A metabolomics study of urine in 22 ASD children and 24 controls built an orthogonal partial least-squares discriminant analysis (OPLS-DA) model (AUROC = 0.91) (Hu, 2003), another one based on 14 ASD and 10 controls obtained a Principal Component Analysis (PCA) model (AUROC = 0.775) and identified a set of organic acids as potential biomarkers (Kałużna-Czaplińska, 2011). These studies do have some limitations, such as different races, limited regions, single algorithm used, and limited sample size. Similar researches with large sample size on Chinese children have rarely been reported. Moreover, some recently developed machine learning algorithms, such as XGBoost, have shown better performance over traditional algorithms on many tasks beyond biomedical domain. Therefore, we launched this representative study of a Chinese population with a larger sample size and a few more recent algorithms.

The aims of this study were to identify metabolic signatures of ASD and to find potential biomarkers for autism diagnosis and possible etiology. We used gas chromatography-mass spectrometry (GC/MS) to assess major metabolic perturbations in organic acid levels in urine from children with autism versus non-autistic subjects. Considering the complexity of ASD, the rise or fall of different organic acids is insufficient. A model using classification analyses of collected data for multiple organic acids that exhibit significant differences between healthy and autistic individuals should be feasible and may allow autistic patients to be distinguished.

MATERIALS AND METHODS

Participants

This prospective study involved children who had autism (AU) and typically developing children (TD) over the period from December 2014 through May 2018. Children in the autistic group were enrolled from the Beijing Herun Clinic. This study was approved by the Peking Union Medical College Hospital (study #ZS-824), written informed consent was obtained from the parents of the participants. All participants were examined by experienced pediatricians.

Inclusion criteria for Autistic Disorder (AU) were as defined by the Diagnostic and Statistical Manual of Mental Disorders, Fourth Edition (DSM-4) (Hu, 2003). All autistic children were assessed by specialized clinicians.

Exclusion criteria were: (1) presence of other diseases such as diabetes or PKU; (2) presence of certain factors that would interfere with the detection of urine organic acids (e.g., renal failure, hepatic insufficiency, dietary intervention therapy); (3) diagnosis of other neuropsychiatric disorders; (4) parents who could not complete the assessment.

Typically developing children were enrolled from primary schools in Beijing.

Procedures

Several precautions were strictly followed both before and after sampling to ensure specimen quality. The precautions and sampling steps were:

Before sampling:

(1) The subjects could not have used antibiotics (oral or infusion) in the previous month. Since some indicators we detect are associated with the intestinal micro-environment, antibiotic usage could affect the results by altering the distribution of intestinal flora.
(2) Both groups were not allowed to take probiotics within 2 weeks of sample collection. Probiotics can also perturb the intestinal micro-environment and affect the accuracy of urine organic acid testing.

(3) Study participants were not allowed to consume fruits or tomatoes within 24 h of sample collection due to the phenol or acid contents of these foods. For example, apples contain polyphenols such as anthocyanins, flavanols, phenolic acids, and catechins. Grapes are also rich in polyphenols. Such compounds can affect various metabolic pathways, and could affect the consistency of our results.

Sampling Steps

Midstream urine from the first morning void was collected in sterile tubes. The samples were placed on dry ice or in a freezer as soon as possible to avoid bacterial growth.

Measures

Information concerning study population characteristics was obtained from the Peking Union Medical College Hospital electronic medical record system. Follow-up information was collected through regular clinic and telephone communication.

All assessments of the children's behavior and dietary habits were provided by the parents and professional third-party institutions. The forms were produced in strict accordance with relevant standards and were completed following delivery of a detailed introduction and description of the study. Samples were collected either in the home or outpatient environment to ensure that external factors did not affect the samples. The researcher confirmed by phone that study guidelines were being followed.

The urine samples were assayed at the Great Plains Laboratory, Inc. (Lenexa, KS, United States). The GC/MS was performed as described in a previous research (Shaw et al., 1995). Due to the limitation of available data, only concentrations of 76 organic acids were reported from the spectrum analysis. Before analyses, all sample concentrations were normalized with urine creatinine as a way of minimizing variability due to differences in urine concentration.

Data Processing and Modeling

The total processes of data processing and modeling are illustrated in **Figure 1**. Sample data from GC/MS were first standardized by creatinine to eliminate urine concentration variabilities. Then the data were further processed with scaling and centering. To avoid data contamination between model building and model testing processes, we set aside an independent testing set from the entire data set in advance. The independent testing set would be strictly excluded from any model building processes so that overfitting effect in testing stage could be minimized. The splitting between testing set and training set were through a random process, while the ratios of control and ASD samples were kept approximately equal in these two sets.

During the model building process, we first trained our models and adjusted algorithm parameters using the training set with all 76 organic acids by maximizing AURs from leave-one-out cross validations. The modeling algorithms included Partial Least Squares Discriminant Analysis (PLS-DA, R mixOmics package),

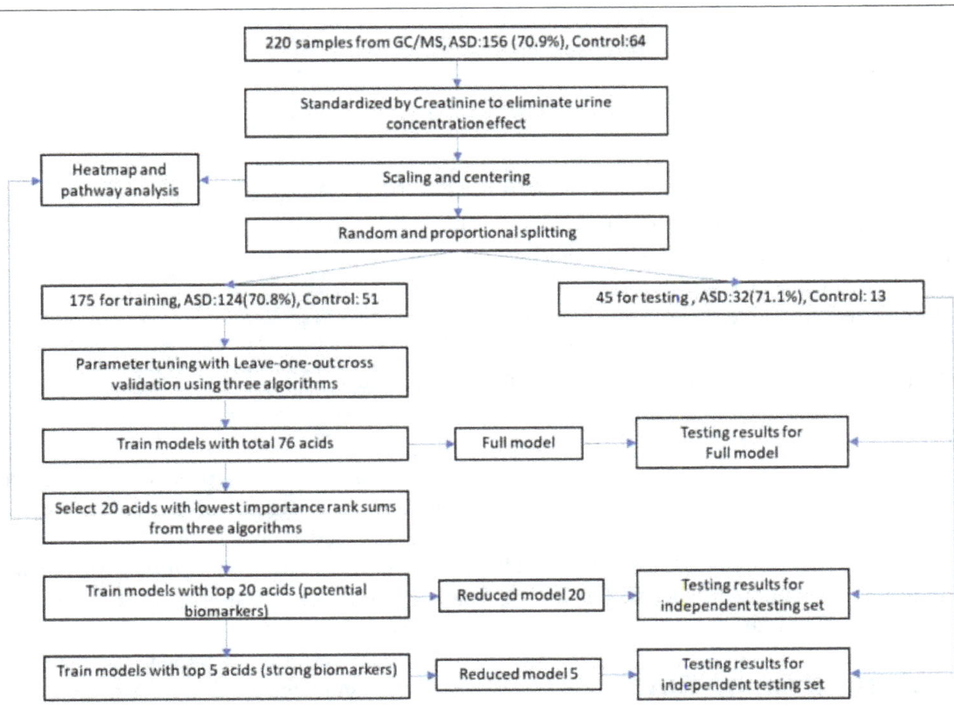

FIGURE 1 | Workflow of data processing and modeling. After standardization, scaling, and centering, sample data were split into training and testing sets, while testing set would be strictly excluded from any model building processes to minimize overfitting. Potential biomarkers were discovered by selecting top N acids from an importance rank sum list generated by three different classification algorithms, while N was determined from testing results of different *N*-values. The discovered biomarkers' potential mechanisms were investigated through heatmap along with associated metabolic pathways.

Support Vector Machine (SVM, R e1071 package), and XGBoost (eXtreme Gradient Boosting, R XGBoost package). The generated models with total 76 acids were designated as full models. Then, full models' classification performance was evaluated using the independent testing set.

To identify potential biomarkers for ASD, we exploited a voting mechanism from all three algorithms to avoid possible biases. First, importance scores of all acids were determined by all the three algorithms using R caret package (Gevrey et al., 2003). Next, each algorithm provided a rank order of all acids according to their importance scores. Then, a list of acids with each acid's sum of importance rank from the three algorithms in descending order was generated. Last, we trained models with only top N acids on the list and tested their classification performance on the testing set to identify the possible biomarkers. The models with top a few acids are referred as reduced models. Biomarkers were determined by observing the testing results of these reduced models on the testing set.

After the detection of biomarkers, to investigate possible mechanism behind them, we produced a heatmap with hierarchical clusters of all sample data and mark these biomarkers on the map after standardization processes. The heatmap was split aligning two dimensions, sample groups, and related metabolic pathways.

Classification algorithms were evaluated using AURs and their confidence intervals were estimated using bootstrapping methods with 2,000 bootstrap steps. Mann–Whitney U-test was used to compare the values for important biomarker acids. Multiple comparisons were adjusted using the false discovery rate (FDR) method (Benjamini and Yekutieli, 2001). Part of evaluations of PLS-DA algorithm was conducted using SIMCA-P Version 11.5 (Umetrics, Umeå, Sweden).

RESULTS

A total of 220 participants were enrolled including 156 autism patients (ASD group) and 64 typically developing children (TD group). The population characteristics of the ASD and TD groups have been summarized in **Table 1**. Among the ASD group, 80.13% were male. In TD group, 73.44% were male. The ASD and TD groups showed no significant differences in gender ($P = 0.285$).

TABLE 1 | Characteristics of ASD group and TD group.

	ASD	TD
	***n* = 156**	***n* = 64**
Age, years	6 (4, 9.75)*	5 (4, 7)*
No. of males (%)	125 (80.13%)	47 (73.44%)
No. of females (%)	31 (19.87%)	17 (26.56%)

*All values are expressed as numbers (percentages) or median value (P25, P75). A total of 220 participants (156 autism patients and 64 typically developing children) were enrolled and divided into the ASD group and TD group. Among the ASD group, 80.13% were male. In TD group, 73.44% were male. The ASD and TD groups showed no significant differences in gender (P = 0.285). *median values (P25, P75).*

TABLE 2 | Potential marker metabolites found in GC/MS of urine samples.

No	Metabolite	Differentiation for autistic samples	*p*-value* after FDR adjustment
1	Phenylactic	↑	0.000
2	3-Hydroxy-3-methylglutaric	↑	0.004
3	Phosphoric	↓	0.001
4	Fumaric	↓	0.003
5	3-Oxoglutaric	↓	0.001
6	Aconitic	↓	0.000
7	*N*-Acetylcysteine (NAC)	↓	0.056
8	Malonic	↓	0.031
9	Tricarballylic	↓	0.052
10	Glycolic	↓	0.140
11	Creatinine	↑	0.010
12	Malic	↓	0.055
13	Oxalic	↑	0.025
14	Tartaric	↓	0.046
15	Pyruvic	↑	0.013
16	4-Cresol	↑	0.030
17	Carboxycitric	↓	0.001
18	3-Hydroxyglutaric	↓	0.071
19	2-Hydroxybutyric	↑	0.330
20	2-Oxoglutaric	↓	0.408

*A voting mechanism from all three algorithms was applied to generate the most important 20 organic acids as potential biomarkers for ASD. We performed U-Mann–Whitney test to determine whether there were significant differences in the levels of these 20 organic acids between ASD and TD children. *p-values were calculated using Mann–Whitney test; ↑, increased level compared with TD; ↓, decreased level compared with TD.*

Data Sets

Two sets, a training set (80%) and a testing set (20%), were randomly separated from the total data set, and each had a similar proportion of ASD children. The training set contained 124 (70.9%) ASD children and 51 TD children, whereas the testing set had 32 (71.1%) ASD and 13 TD children.

Model Building Using Training Set

Using training set, we fine-tuned parameters of the three algorithms. For PLS-DA, the best major parameter, Ncomp, is 2. For SVM, we obtained the best results using linear kernel. For XGBoost, we optimized three major parameters, max_depth, eta, and nrounds with optimal values of 2, 0.15, and 200, respectively.

The model building process employed leave-one-out cross validation as guidance for parameter tuning. The final results of the full models in this process were shown in **Table 2**. The AURs for these three algorithms were 0.864 (PLS-DA), 0.833 (SVM), and 0.931 (XGBoost) in training set with leave-one-out cross validation.

The PCA result on training set with all acids is on **Figure 2A**. From the figure, we see that PCA could not distinguish between ASD and TD groups, since the new components variables generated with maximal variances might not be aligned with the outcome groups. However, it does identify some outliers. To make models more robust, we did not remove these outliers in the following analyses.

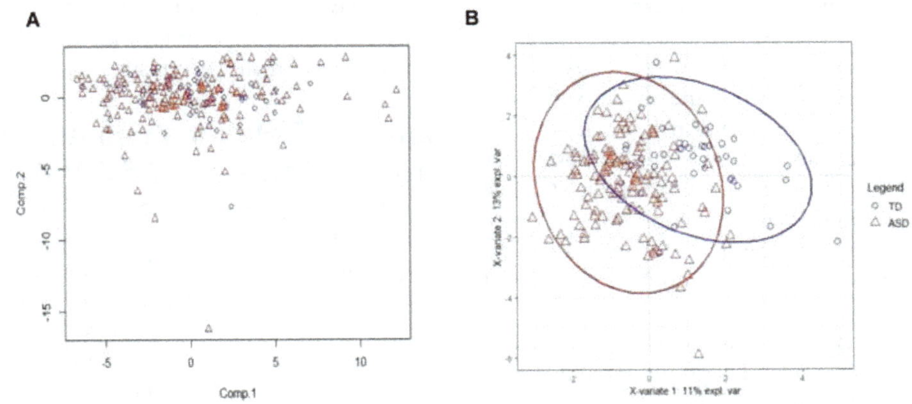

FIGURE 2 | PCA and PLSDA score plots. (A) The Principal Component Analysis (PCA) score plot on training set with all 75 acids. **(B)** The PLS-DA score plot on training set with selected 20 biomarker acids. With first two components, R2X (cum) = 0.26, R2Y (cum) = 0.535, Q2 (cum) = 0.386.

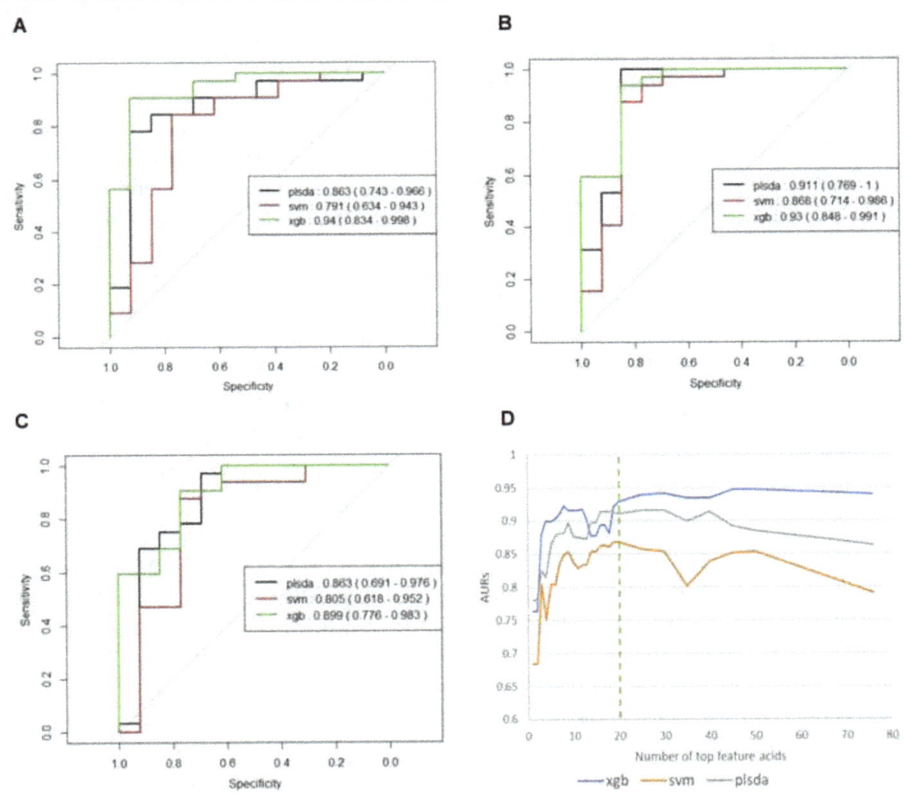

FIGURE 3 | (A) ROCs of final models on independent testing set based on all 76 organic acids. **(B)** ROCs of final models on independent testing set based on top 20 organic acids. **(C)** ROCs of final models on independent testing set based on top five organic acids. **(D)** Curves of AURs against selected top acids. Top 20 acids represent the best collection of possible ASD biomarkers, while adding more will make AURs for SVM and PLS-DA decrease and make AUR for XGB appear platformed.

Model Testing Using Independent Testing Set

To avoid any possible overfitting, we tested the full model on the independent testing set and obtained AURs of 0.863 (PLS-DA), 0.791 (SVM), and 0.94 (XGBoost). These results had shown similar values with those in training stage showing that training stage has generated little overfitting to the training set.

Potential Marker Metabolites

We used the testing resulting of reduced models to identify potential markers. The results of these reduced models are shown in **Supplementary Table S1** and **Figure 3. Figure 3D** the curves of AURs against different N selected top acids on testing set. Clearly, top 20 acids represent the best collection of possible ASD biomarkers, while adding more acids to the model will make AURs for SVM and PLS-DA decrease and make AUR for XGB appear platformed (The ensemble mechanism of XGBoost might make it more robust to irrelevant features). Actually, XGBoost achieved an AUR of 0.93 which was very close to the value of 0.94 in full model, and this suggest that these top 20 acids could capture most of the features of ASD. Even top 5 acids could get an AUR of 0.899.

The 20 identified potential marker metabolites are listed in **Table 2**. Their levels compared with TD group are also shown in **Table 2**. Using these 20 identified marker metabolites, we draw the score plot of PLA-DA of training set on **Figure 2B**. There is a separation between TD and ASD groups with R2X (cum) = 0.26, R2Y (cum) = 0.535, Q2 (cum) = 0.386, *p*-value of CV-anova = 1.26183e-006.

Heatmap Analysis of Metabolic Pathway

We tried to use heatmap with hierarchical clustering to discovery possible related metabolic pathways (**Supplementary Figure S1**). Rows of the heatmap represent different samples from TD and ASD groups, while columns represent different metabolites grouped in different metabolic pathways. The pathway names are listed in the figure legend. The heatmap shows that the identified biomarker metabolite acids are distributed across a wide variety of pathways: Intestinal Microbial Overgrowth, Amino Acid Metabolism, nutritional, Krebs Cycle, Oxalate Metabolism, Glycolytic Cycle, and Mineral Metabolism. This diverse distribution suggests that these organic acids may act on a variety of metabolic pathways and reflects the complexity of metabolic abnormalities in autism.

DISCUSSION

To identify metabolic signatures of ASD and find organic acids in urine that could act as potential biomarkers for diagnosis and disease treatment, three algorithms (PLS-DA, SVM, and XGBoost) were used to analyze GC/MS data for urine samples. The results showed the effectiveness of this method in distinguishing ASD children from TD children. XGBoost model produced the best results (AUROC = 0.94) among the three algorithms. The modeling was performed on the basis of all 76 organic acids, among which the top 20 acids were identified as potential biomarkers with a voting mechanism from all three algorithms. To go a step further, we selected top 5 acids as strong biomarkers. The amount of phenylactic acid was significantly higher in the ASD group, whereas the amounts of aconitic acid, phosphoric acid, 3-oxoglutaric acid, and carboxycitric acid were significantly lower in the ASD group. These organic acids are involved in a variety of metabolic pathways including amino acid metabolism, intestinal flora, energy metabolism (Krebs Cycle), and bone salt metabolism. Although a total of 76 organic acids contributed to modeling, we just involved the top 5 ones in discussion part since they made significant contributions in modeling, which may indicate the major metabolic abnormality of autism.

Complex Relationships Among Urinary Organic Acids and ASD Pathogenesis

The heatmap generated from GC/MS analysis of urinary organic acids showed the complex relationship among these compounds in ASD. Several organic acids were in the same pathway, whereas others are involved in multiple pathways. To date, the metabolites that have been explored as possible ASD biomarkers include: nutritional markers, microbiome metabolites, amino acid metabolites, Krebs cycle metabolites, pyrimidine metabolites, neurotransmitter metabolites, products of ketone, and fatty acid oxidation and mineral metabolism, as well as indicators of detoxification and fluid intake (e.g., creatinine) (Kałużna-Czaplińska, 2011).

These organic acids may affect the function of intestinal flora. In our study, we also collected stool specimens from the study participants. Analysis of stool samples and the intestinal flora is underway, and the abundance of intestinal flora combined with findings for urinary organic acid metabolism should strengthen the diagnostic potential of these compounds.

The organic acids we identified may affect nervous system development and thus we included assessments of neurological symptoms (e.g., unexplained excitability or mania) on the study scales. We will examine whether the severity of these symptoms in ASD and the CARS and ABC scores are relevant in a future study.

The Diagnostic Potential of the Established Model

Calibration and optimization of parameters is a critical step in model building. Three algorithms (PLS-DA, SVM, and XGBoost) were examined to achieve this task. Among them, the first two algorithms, PLS-DA and SVM, were previously described (West et al., 2014; Dieme et al., 2015). To our knowledge, application of the XGBoost algorithm in a model of urine organic acids to distinguish children with ASD from TD children has not been previously reported.

Among the three algorithms, XGBoost had an AOC of 0.94. Use of the XGBoost algorithm is an innovation in autism-related research (Chen and Guestrin, 2016), and the efficiency of this model differs from that described in earlier studies. XGBoost has been proved to have better performance than other more traditional models in many machine learning tasks outside biomedical domains. This is largely due to its built-in ensemble mechanism and its ability to capture non-linear features. In contrast, traditional linear algorithm for metabolite analysis, PLS-DA, is limited in capturing non-linear relations. This has also been observed in this study. In addition, XGBoost also shows more robustness to adding more irrelevant features than SVM and PLA-DA. Conclusively, the establishment of this model increases the possibility of early diagnosis of autism. The examination of organic acids in urine is non-invasive and relatively inexpensive, the requirements for sample collection are not strict and the operability is very high.

Notable Changes in Urinary Organic Acid Levels in ASD Patients

The PLS-DA score plot shows a clear distinction among the distribution of metabolite profiles between TD and ASD children. Our analyses showed that 5 urinary organic acids had significant differences between ASD and TD children and thus could have diagnostic potential as ASD biomarkers.

The ASD group had higher levels of phenylactic acid but decreased amounts of aconitic acid, phosphoric acid, 3-oxoglutaric acid, and carboxycitric acid compared to TD children. These metabolites are associated with multiple biochemical processes (Koulman et al., 2009). Phenylactic acid is a byproduct of amino acid metabolism, and the higher levels seen for ASD children could indicate abnormalities in the function of enzymes involved in amino acid metabolism. Moreover, phenylactic acid can inhibit the growth of Gram-negative and Gram-positive bacteria, as well as some fungi. Thus, elevated phenylactic acid levels could inhibit the normal function of the intestinal microflora and exacerbate metabolic disorders. Intestinal microbes can affect neurotransmitter production in the central nervous system and in turn affect the induction of endogenous sensations, production of bacterial metabolites, and mucosal immune-related activity (Carabotti et al., 2015). Moreover, phenylactic acid is a metabolite of phenethylamine, which acts as a monoaminergic neuromodulator and as a neurotransmitter in the human central nervous system to promote neuron excitation (Sabelli et al., 1976).

Also in the context of intestinal flora, levels of carboxycitric acid and 3-oxoglutarate acid were significantly decreased in the ASD group relative to the TD group. Carboxycitric acid can be a marker of intestinal microbial overgrowth, particularly yeast and fungi. Certain strains of the mold *Aspergillus niger* have efficient citric acid production and can be used for industrial-scale citric acid production (Lotfy et al., 2007). Although to our knowledge, this study is the first to report a significant decrease of carboxycitric acid in urine samples from ASD children, other studies identified intestinal microbe metabolites as potential agents that can affect nervous system function. Meanwhile, carboxycitric acid, a product of the Krebs Cycle, showed decreased levels in our assays and may be indicative of energy metabolism disorders in children with autism. We also found that 3-oxoglutarate, a common metabolite of yeast and fungi (Thomas et al., 2010; MacFabe et al., 2011; Kocovska et al., 2012), was significantly lower in children with autism. The low concentrations of both carboxycitric acid and 3-oxoglutarate that we observed in urine from autistic patients could be due to increased uptake of these compounds across the blood-brain barrier of the brain. Our results are consistent with previous studies that showed anti-fungal treatments for children with autism can effectively reduce the amounts of corresponding organic acid indicators (Cobb and Cobb, 2010), and suggests that gastrointestinal yeast could provide a basis for dietary adjustments such as gluten/casein-free diets that are important for children's nervous system development and could mitigate autism symptoms. 3-oxoglutarate in urine is associated with the presence of harmful gut flora such as *Candida albicans* (Schmidt, 1994). These results support the reliability of the gut-brain axis and suggest new avenues of study for autism.

Aconitic acid is produced from citric acid dehydration that occurs during the Krebs Cycle and is a marker of mitochondrial activity. Mitochondrial disease, either through maternal inheritance or other causes, is present in up to 5% of autistic children (Rossignol and Frye, 2012; Frye et al., 2013). Previous studies reported that *cis*-acotinic acid levels are increased in children with autism (Noto et al., 2014; Mussap et al., 2016). Here, we found that acotinic acid levels were decreased in the ASD group relative to the TD group, which is indicative of energy metabolism deficiencies in energy metabolism of ASD. In the Krebs Cycle, citrate undergoes stereospecific isomerization to isocitrate by the enzyme aconitase hydratase and the intermediate *cis*-aconitate (Mussap et al., 2016). Meanwhile, *trans*-aconitic acid (TAA) acts as an anti-inflammatory agent in plant-based treatments for rheumatoid arthritis used in Brazil, and could be one explanation for the decreased levels of aconitic acid in the ASD group. Similarly, it has been reported that inflammatory mediators may play crucial role in some neuropsychiatric diseases. Dan et al. (2015) found that homocysteine (Hcy) and uric acid (UA) may contribute to the pathogenesis of multiple system atrophy (MSA) and serum Hcy together with UA levels could be a diagnostic tool of MSA (AUROC = 0.736). In addition, another cross-sectional study supported that low serum UA levels may indicate a higher risk of Parkinson's disease (PD) and serum UA level could serve as an indirect biomarker of prediction in PD (Mengqiu et al., 2013).

Phosphoric acid is important for bone metabolism. In our study population we observed decreased amounts of phosphoric acid in ASD children relative to TD children, which could suggest that ASD pathology involves abnormal bone metabolism, although this possibility requires further investigation. Vitamin D regulates bone formation and density by promoting absorption of key intestinal compounds such as calcium and phosphate. Imbalances in phosphoric acid could be related to an imbalance of several other substances. In pregnant women, vitamin D deficiencies can affect regulatory T cell function and in turn immune responses. Such vitamin D deficiencies can impact the developing fetus and could increase the risk for autism. Vitamin D is also critical during development of the fetal nervous system through regulation of the expression of several nerve growth factors as well as transforming factor beta 2 (TGF-b2) and neurotrophin 3 and 4. Previous studies showed that some children with autism have vitamin D deficiency (Pioggia et al., 2014; Uğur and Gürkan, 2014). The amount of serum 25 (OH) D_3 is significantly lower in children with ASD, indicating that lower 25 (OH) D levels could be an independent risk factor for autism, and may be independently associated with disease severity (Gong et al., 2014). Our findings support observations of disorders in bone salt metabolism in children with autism, and are also consistent with clinical symptoms indicating that reduced bone mineral density is common in children with autism.

CONCLUSION

In this study, we used GC/MS to evaluate major metabolic fluctuations in 76 organic acids present in urine from 156 children with ASD and from 64 non-autistic children. Three algorithms, Partial Least Squares-Discriminant Analysis (PLS-DA), Support Vector Machine (SVM), and eXtreme Gradient Boosting (XGBoost), were used to develop models to distinguish ASD from TD children and to detect potential biomarkers. By a voting mechanism, 20 acids have been successfully identified as potential ASD biomarkers and reduced model with top 20 acids achieved 0.93 and represent a good collection of potential ASD biomarkers. These biomarkers were distributed across a wide variety of metabolic pathways, indicating the complicated mechanism behind ASD. XGBoost algorithm has shown better classification performance and more robustness than other traditional algorithms.

In summary, urine organic acids detection with GC/MS combined with XGBoost algorithm could represent a novel, non-invasive and accurate strategy for diagnosis of autism and the discovered potential biomarkers could be valuable for future research on the pathogenesis of autism and possible interventions, and have a range of clinical applications.

ETHICS STATEMENT

This study was carried out in accordance with the recommendations of Chinese Academy of Medical Sciences Peking Union Medical College Hospital Ethics Review Committee The protocol was approved by the Chinese Academy of Medical Sciences Peking Union Medical College Hospital Ethics Review Committee.

AUTHOR CONTRIBUTIONS

QC, YQ, XY, and X-jX contributed to the conception and design of the study. XY and X-jX enrolled the patients and controls, and collected all the clinical data, and urine samples. QC and YQ transferred the data to a database, analyzed the data, and wrote the first draft of the manuscript. YT analyzed the data, set up diagnosis model, and revised the figures. All authors contributed to the manuscript revision, and read, and approved the submitted version of the manuscript.

FUNDING

This study was supported by Peking Union Medical Foundation.

ACKNOWLEDGMENTS

We would like to thank the reviewers for their comments. We were particularly indebted to the families and children involved in this study; the study would not have been possible without their collaboration.

REFERENCES

Benjamini, Y., and Yekutieli, D. (2001). The control of the false discovery rate in multiple testing under dependency. *Ann. Stat.* 29, 1165–1188. doi: 10.1186/1471-2105-9-114

Bull, G., Shattock, P., Whiteley, P., Anderson, R., Groundwater, P. W., Lough, J. W., et al. (2003). Indolyl-3-acryloylglycine (IAG) is a putative diagnostic urinary marker for autism spectrum disorders. *Med. Sci. Monit.* 9:CR422.

Carabotti, M., Scirocco, A., Maselli, M. A., and Severi, C. (2015). The gut-brain axis: interactions between enteric microbiota, central and enteric nervous systems. *Ann. Gastroenterol. Quart. Publ. Hellen. Soc. Gastroenterol.* 28, 203–209.

Chen, T., and Guestrin, C. (2016). "XGBoost: a scalable tree boosting system," in *Proceedings of the 12th ACM SIGKDD International Conference on Knowledge Discovery and Data Mining*, (New York, NY: ACM).

Cobb, M. L., and Cobb, A. (2010). *Treatment of Autism Using Probiotic Composition.* New Zealand: Cobb And Company.

Cox, K. B., Hamm, D. A., Millington, D. S., Matern, D., Vockley, J., Rinaldo, P., et al. (2001). Gestational, pathologic and biochemical differences between very long-chain acyl-CoA dehydrogenase deficiency and long-chain acyl-CoA dehydrogenase deficiency in the mouse. *Hum. Mol. Genet.* 10, 2069–2077. doi: 10.1093/hmg/10.19.2069

Dan, C., Xiaobo, W., Jing, Z., Rui, W., Xu, L., Xiaofeng, X., et al. (2015). Contra-directional expression of serum homocysteine and uric acid as important biomarkers of multiple system atrophy severity: a cross-sectional study. *Front. Cell. Neurosci.* 9:247. doi: 10.3389/fncel.2015.00247

Dawson, G., Jones, E. J., Merkle, K., Venema, K., Lowy, R., Faja, S., et al. (2012). Early behavioral intervention is associated with normalized brain activity in young children with autism. *J. Am. Acad. Child Adolesc. Psychiatry* 51, 1150–1159. doi: 10.1016/j.jaac.2012.08.018

Dawson, G., Rogers, S., Munson, J., Smith, M., Winter, J., Greenson, J., et al. (2010). Randomized, controlled trial of an intervention for toddlers with autism: the early start denver model. *Pediatrics* 125:e17. doi: 10.1542/peds.2009-0958

Dieme, B., Mavel, S., Blasco, H., Tripi, G., Bonnetbrilhault, F., Malvy, J., et al. (2015). Metabolomics study of urine in autism spectrum disorders using a multiplatform analytical methodology. *J. Proteome Res.* 14, 5273–5282. doi: 10.1021/acs.jproteome.5b00699

Emond, P., Mavel, S., Aidoud, N., Nadal-Desbarats, L., Montigny, F., Bonnet-Brilhault, F., et al. (2013). GC-MS-based urine metabolic profiling of autism spectrum disorders. *Anal. Bioanal. Chem.* 405, 5291–5300. doi: 10.1007/s00216-013-6934-x

Frye, R. E., Melnyk, S., and Macfabe, D. F. (2013). Unique acyl-carnitine profiles are potential biomarkers for acquired mitochondrial disease in autism spectrum disorder. *Transl. Psychiatry* 3:e220. doi: 10.1038/tp.2012.143

Gevrey, M., Dimopoulos, I., and Lek, S. (2003). Review and comparison of methods to study the contribution of variables in artificial neural network models. *Ecol. Modell.* 160, 249–264. doi: 10.1016/s0304-3800(02)00257-0

Ghaziuddin, M., and Alowain, M. (2013). Autism spectrum disorders and inborn errors of metabolism: an update. *Pediatr. Neurol.* 49, 232–236. doi: 10.1016/j.pediatrneurol.2013.05.013

Gong, Z. L., Luo, C. M., Wang, L., Shen, L., Wei, F., Tong, R. J., et al. (2014). Serum 25-hydroxyvitamin D levels in Chinese children with autism spectrum disorders. *Neuroreport* 25, 23–27. doi: 10.1097/WNR.0000000000000034

Hanley, H. G., Stahl, S. M., and Freedman, D. X. (1977). Hyperserotonemia and amine metabolites in autistic and retarded children. *Arch. Gen. Psychiatry* 34, 521–531.

Hu, R. J. (2003). Diagnostic and statistical manual of mental disorders (DSM-IV). *Encycl. Neurol. Sci.* 25, 4–8.

Kałużna-Czaplińska, J. (2011). Noninvasive urinary organic acids test to assess biochemical and nutritional individuality in autistic children. *Clin. Biochem.* 44,

686–691. doi: 10.1016/j.clinbiochem.2011.01.015

Keller, F., and Persico, A. M. (2003). The neurobiological context of autism. *Mol. Neurobiol.* 28, 1–22. doi: 10.1385/mn%3A28%3A1%3A1

Klin, A., Klaiman, C., and Jones, W. (2015). Reducing age of autism diagnosis: developmental social neuroscience meets public health challenge. *Rev. Neurol.* 60(Suppl. 1), S3–S11.

Kocovska, E., Fernell, E., Billstedt, E., Minnis, H., and Gillberg, C. (2012). Vitamin D and autism: clinical review. *Res. Dev. Disabil.* 33, 1541–1550. doi: 10.1016/j.ridd.2012.02.015

Kompare, M., and Rizzo, W. B. (2008). Mitochondrial fatty-acid oxidation disorders. *Semin. Pediatr. Neurol.* 15, 140–149. doi: 10.1016/j.spen.2008.05.008

Koulman, A., Lane, G. A., Harrison, S. J., and Volmer, D. A. (2009). From differentiating metabolites to biomarkers. *Anal. Bioanal. Chem.* 394, 663–670. doi: 10.1007/s00216-009-2690-3

Lotfy, W. A., Ghanem, K. M., and El-Helow, E. R. (2007). Citric acid production by a novel *Aspergillus niger* isolate: II. Optimization of process parameters through statistical experimental designs. *Bioresourc. Technol.* 98, 3470–3477. doi: 10.1016/j.biortech.2006.11.032

MacFabe, D. F., Cain, N. E., Boon, F., Ossenkopp, K. P., and Cain, D. P. (2011). Effects of the enteric bacterial metabolic product propionic acid on object-directed behavior, social behavior, cognition, and neuroinflammation in adolescent rats: relevance to autism spectrum disorder. *Behav. Brain Res.* 217, 47–54. doi: 10.1016/j.bbr.2010.10.005

Manzi, B., Loizzo, A. L., Giana, G., and Curatolo, P. (2008). Autism and metabolic diseases. *J. Child Neurol.* 11, 90–90.

Mavel, S., Nadal-Desbarats, L., Blasco, H., Bonnet-Brilhault, F., Barthelemy, C., Montigny, F., et al. (2013). 1H-13C NMR-based urine metabolic profiling in autism spectrum disorders. *Talanta* 114, 95–102. doi: 10.1016/j.talanta.2013.03.064

Mengqiu, P., Huimin, G., Ling, L., Yunqi, X., Mei, L., Jing, Z., et al. (2013). Serum uric acid in patients with Parkinson's disease and vascular parkinsonism: a cross-sectional study. *Neuroimmunomodulation* 20, 19–28. doi: 10.1159/000342483

Mussap, M., Noto, A., and Fanos, V. (2016). Metabolomics of autism spectrum disorders: early insights regarding mammalian-microbial cometabolites. *Expert Rev. Mol. Diagnost.* 16:869. doi: 10.1080/14737159.2016.1202765

Nair, M. K. (2000). Autism spectrum disorders. *Neuron.* 28, 355–363.

Noto, A., Fanos, V., Barberini, L., Grapov, D., Fattuoni, C., Zaffanello, M., et al. (2014). The urinary metabolomics profile of an Italian autistic children population and their unaffected siblings. *J. Matern. Fetal Neonatal Med.* 27((Suppl. 2), 46–52. doi: 10.3109/14767058.2014.954784

Pioggia, G., Tonacci, A., Tartarisco, G., Billeci, L., Muratori, F., Ruta, L., et al. (2014). Autism and lack of D3 vitamin: a systematic review. *Res. Autism Spectr. Disord.* 8, 1685–1698. doi: 10.1016/j.rasd.2014.09.003

Rossignol, D. A., and Frye, R. E. (2012). Mitochondrial dysfunction in autism spectrum disorders: a systematic review and meta-analysis. *Mol. Psychiatry* 17, 290–314. doi: 10.1038/mp.2010.136

Sabelli, H. C., Mosnaim, A. D., Vazquez, A. J., Giardina, W. J., Borison, R. L., and Pedemonte, W. A. (1976). Biochemical plasticity of synaptic transmission: a critical review of Dale's Principle. *Biol. Psychiatry* 11, 481–524.

Schain, R. J., and Freedman, D. X. (1961). Studies on 5-hydroxyindole metabolism in autistic and other mentally retarded children. *J. Pediatr.* 58, 315–320. doi: 10.1016/s0022-3476(61)80261-8

Schmidt, M. A. (1994). *Tired of Being Tired: Overcoming Chronic Fatigue and Low Vitality.* Berkeley, CA: Frog, Ltd.

Shaw, W., Kassen, E., and Chaves, E. (1995). Increased urinary excretion of analogs of Krebs cycle metabolites and arabinose in two brothers with autistic features. *Clin. Chem.* 41, 1094–1104.

Thomas, R. H., Foley, K. A., Mepham, J. R., Tichenoff, L. J., Possmayer, F., and MacFabe, D. F. (2010). Altered brain phospholipid and acylcarnitine profiles in propionic acid infused rodents: further development of a potential model of autism spectrum disorders. *J. Neurochem.* 113, 515–529. doi: 10.1111/j.1471-4159.2010.06614.x

Uğur, Ç, and Gürkan, C. K. (2014). Serum vitamin D and folate levels in children with autism spectrum disorders. *Res. Autism Spectr. Disord.* 8, 1641–1647. doi: 10.1016/j.rasd.2014.09.002

Wanders, R. J., Vreken, P., den, Boer ME, Wijburg, F. A., van, Gennip AH, and IJlst, L. (1999). Disorders of mitochondrial fatty acyl-CoA β-oxidation. *J. Inherit. Metab. Dis.* 22, 442–487.

Wang, S. S., Fernhoff, P. M., Hannon, W. H., and Khoury, M. J. (1999). Medium chain acyl-CoA dehydrogenase deficiency human genome epidemiology review. *Genet. Med.* 1, 332–339. doi: 10.1097/00125817-199911000-00004

Warren, Z., Mcpheeters, M. L., Sathe, N., Foss-Feig, J. H., Glasser, A., and Veenstra-Vanderweele, J. (2011). A systematic review of early intensive intervention for autism spectrum disorders. *Pediatrics* 127:e1303. doi: 10.1542/peds.2011-0426

West, P. R., Amaral, D. G., Bais, P., Smith, A. M., Egnash, L. A., Ross, M. E., et al. (2014). Metabolomics as a tool for discovery of biomarkers of autism spectrum disorder in the blood plasma of children. *PLoS One* 9:e112445. doi: 10.1371/journal.pone.0112445

Zecavati, N., and Spence, S. J. (2009). Neurometabolic disorders and dysfunction in autism spectrum disorders. *Curr. Neurol. Neurosci. Rep.* 9, 129–136. doi: 10.1093/brain/awx054

Zwaigenbaum, L., Bryson, S., and Garon, N. (2013). Early identification of autism spectrum disorders. *Behav. Brain Res.* 251, 133–146. doi: 10.1016/j.bbr.2013.04.004

6

Proteomics Study of Peripheral Blood Mononuclear Cells (PBMCs) in Autistic Children

Liming Shen[1], Chengyun Feng[2†], Kaoyuan Zhang[1†], Youjiao Chen[1,3†], Yan Gao[2], Junyan Ke[1], Xinqian Chen[1], Jing Lin[1], Cuihua Li[1], Javed Iqbal[1], Yuxi Zhao[1] and Weibin Wang[4]*

[1]College of Life Science and Oceanography, Shenzhen University, Shenzhen, China, [2]Maternal and Child Health Hospital of Baoan, Shenzhen, China, [3]Xiang Ya Changde Hospital, Changde, China, [4]School of Art, Shenzhen University, Shenzhen, China

Correspondence:
Liming Shen
slm@szu.edu.cn

†These authors have contributed equally to this work

Autism is one of the most common neurological developmental disorder associated with social isolation and restricted interests in children. The etiology of this disorder is still unknown. There is neither any confirmed laboratory test nor any effective therapeutic strategy to diagnose or cure it. To search for biomarkers for early detection and exploration of the disease mechanisms, here, we investigated the protein expression signatures of peripheral blood mononuclear cells (PBMCs) in autistic children compared with healthy controls by using isobaric tags for relative and absolute quantitation (iTRAQ) proteomics approach. The results showed a total of 41 proteins as differentially expressed in autistic group as compared to control. These proteins are found associated with metabolic pathways, endoplasmic reticulum (ER) stress and protein folding, endocytosis, immune and inflammatory response, plasma lipoprotein particle organization, and cell adhesion. Among these, 17 proteins (13 up-regulated and four down-regulated) are found to be linked with mitochondria. Eight proteins including three already reported proteins in our previous studies were selected to be verified. Five already reported autism associated pro-inflammatory cytokines [interferon-γ (IFN-γ), interleukin-1β (IL-1β), IL-6, IL-12, and tumor necrosis factor-α (TNF-α)] were detected in plasma by enzyme-linked immunosorbent assay (ELISA) analysis. The results were consistent with proteomic results and reports from previous literature. These results proposed that PBMCs from autistic children might be activated, and ER stress, unfolded protein response (UPR), acute-phase response (APR), inflammatory response, and endocytosis may be involved in autism occurrence. These reported proteins may serve as potential biomarkers for early diagnosis of autism. More specifically, simultaneous detection of three proteins [complement C3 (C3), calreticulin (CALR), and SERPINA1] in the plasma and PBMCs could increase the authenticity of detection.

Keywords: autism, biomarkers, iTRAQ, peripheral blood mononuclear cells, proteomics

---

Abbreviations: APR, acute-phase response; ASD, Autism spectrum disorder; ELISA, enzyme-linked immunosorbent assay; ER stress, endoplasmic reticulum; MS, mass spectrometry; iTRAQ, isobaric tags for relative and absolute quantitation; PBMCs, peripheral blood mononuclear cells; TLR, toll-like receptor; UPR, unfolded protein response.

INTRODUCTION

Autism spectrum disorder (ASD) is a group of developmental neurological disorders characterized by various impairments in communication and social interactions as well as restricted interests and repetitive behaviors (Faras et al., 2010). Based on DSM-IV (Fourth Edition of the Diagnostic and Statistical Manual of Mental Disorders), it can be referred as childhood autism, Asperger syndrome, Rett syndrome (RTT), pervasive developmental disorders and other childhood disintegrative disorders. Among these, autism is the most severe and classical disorder (Rangasamy et al., 2013).

Over the past 20 years, the prevalence of ASD has been continuously increasing all over the world. As the etiology and pathogenesis have not yet been completely elucidated, ASD diagnosis remained a behavioral or symptomatic rather than a molecular diagnosis. Due to lack of information regarding molecular mechanisms of the disease, no effective therapeutic approach is currently available. However, the previous studies suggest that early behavioral intervention is associated with normalized patterns of brain activity. Therefore, early diagnosis of this disease is crucial and provides interventions that can significantly influence children's outcomes (Dawson et al., 2012; Dawson, 2013). Thus, intensive research has been made to identify biological markers for disease management and early diagnosis. Meanwhile, the etiology underlying ASD at the molecular, cellular and systems level remained elusive and needs to be further clarified.

The etiology of ASD is commonly described as a genetic predisposition combined with an environmental impact (Chaste and Leboyer, 2012). It is estimated that 400–1,000 genes are likely to be involved in autism (Masi et al., 2017a). However, it is a heterogeneous disorder with complex genetic basis. Only 10%–15% of ASD cases may be etiologically related to known genetic disorders and specific genes still need to be associated with autism (Folstein and Rosen-Sheidley, 2001). No single gene can be considered "causal" for more than 1% of cases of idiopathic autism (Hu, 2013). Interestingly, recent studies demonstrated that the large set of ASD genes converges on a smaller number of key pathways and developmental stages of the brain. For example, many ASD genes are known to regulate brain development and/or synapse function (Krishnan et al., 2016). Thus, it will be quite interesting to study the ASD from the protein perspective.

Genomic research has increased the importance of studying ASD-related differentially expressed genes from peripheral tissues (blood and peripheral blood cells) and postmortem brains of ASD subjects (Baron et al., 2006; Hu et al., 2006; Nishimura et al., 2007; Kuwano et al., 2011). However, for a variety of reasons, ASD related brain studies are very difficult, therefore, performed at a limited level. Interestingly, a moderate correlation of gene expression between peripheral blood cells and brain tissue in humans has been reported, supporting the usefulness of peripheral blood cells in gene expression studies for psychiatric research (Sullivan et al., 2006). In addition, infection and immune responses have already been implicated in ASD. Immunity and inflammation-associated lymphoblastoid cell lines (LCLs) have been used by a number of groups to study gene expression in ASD (Hu, 2014). Besides, monocytes in blood and microglia in the brain have very similar transcriptomes, while abnormalities in microglia have been observed in ASD brains (Vargas et al., 2005; Morgan et al., 2010). Dysfunction in peripheral blood mononuclear cells (PBMCs) could result in long-term immune alterations in ASDs has already been reported (Ashwood et al., 2006; Enstrom et al., 2010), and the alterations of mRNA expressions in PBMCs obtained from ASD subjects has also been determined (Glatt et al., 2012). Therefore, PBMCs may represent a useful tool to investigate systemic neurochemical changes in neurodevelopmental diseases. Keeping in mind the above discussion, there must be some protein changes that can be recorded which might prove as potential biomarkers and can be used in ASD diagnosis. In the present study, we have made an attempt to search for protein based potential biomarkers for the diagnosis of autism and tried to further clarify the molecular mechanisms of this disease by using isobaric tags for relative and absolute quantitation (iTRAQ) quantitative proteomics approach in autistic children.

MATERIALS AND METHODS

Subjects Population

Twenty four male and six female autistic children (2–6 years old) were recruited along with gender and age-matched controls from Populations and Family Planning Hospital of Baoan. The diagnosis of autism was based on the criteria of autistic disorders as defined in the DSM-IV by a child neuropsychiatrist. There were no significant differences in weight, height or body mass index (BMI) between the case and control groups. The experiments were performed with the written consent of the caretakers of the children under observation according to the guidelines of this hospital (Feng et al., 2017; Shen et al., 2018).

Protein Sample Preparation

Blood samples (5 ml) were collected in EDTA-coated plastic tubes in the morning while the subjects were in the fasting state. PBMCs were separated by density gradient centrifugation using Ficoll-Hypaque (Sigma-Aldrich, St. Louis, MO, USA) as previously described (Nilsson et al., 2008). The cells were lysed in lysis buffer (7 M urea, 2 M thiourea, 4% (w/v) CHAPS, 40 mM dithiothreitol (DTT), and 40 mM Tris base), sonicated 10 times for 5 s with 10 s pause interval in an ice-water bath, and centrifuged at $13{,}800\times g$, at 4°C for 60 min (Heraeus Fresco 17 Centrifuge, Thermo Fisher Scientific Inc., Waltham, MA, USA). The supernatant was taken and stored at −80°C until use. The protein concentrations were determined and optimized by Bradford assay. An overview of the workflow used in this study is shown in **Figure 1**.

iTRAQ Labeling and High-pH RPLC Fractionation

The iTRAQ analysis was performed according to the previous study (Sun et al., 2015; Shen et al., 2017; Zhao et al., 2017;

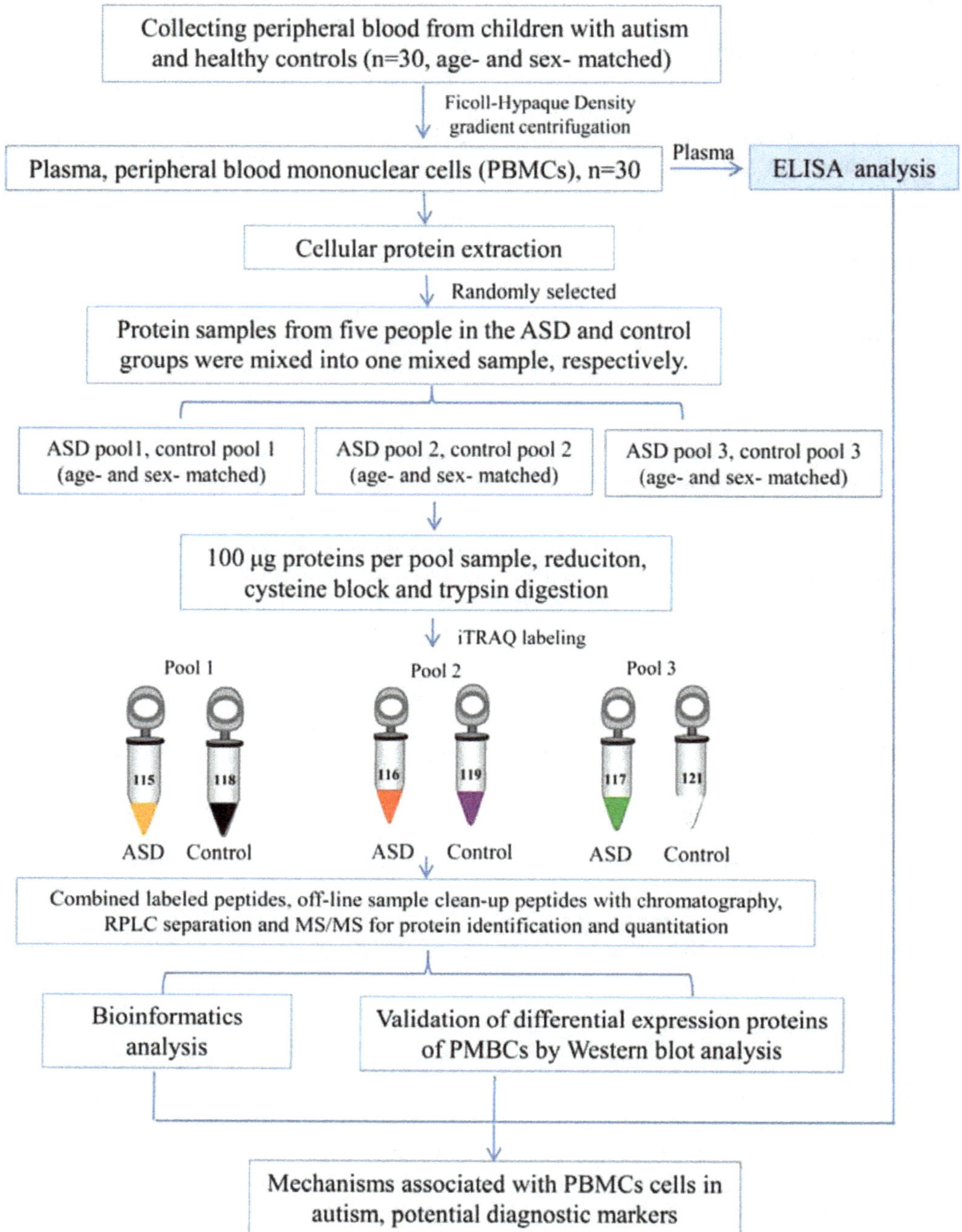

FIGURE 1 | Workflow used in this study.

Iqbal et al., 2018). As shown in **Figure 1**, protein samples were analyzed in three biological replicates. In each repetition, we randomly selected five children with ASD from the total recruitment of autistic children, including one girl and four boys, and then selected age and gender matched healthy controls. Equal amounts of plasma were taken from autistic and control children and mixed to form autistic and control pool samples, respectively. Protein extraction (100 μg) from each sample was reduced, alkylated and digested with trypsin (Promega, Madison, WI, USA) at a ratio of 1:30 at 37°C for overnight, and then labeled with iTRAQ reagents (AB Sciex, Foster City, CA, USA). Three samples from autistic children were labeled with iTRAQ tags 115, 116, 117, and the healthy controls with 118, 119 and 121 tags, respectively. After labeling, these were incubated at room temperature for 1 h, and then mixed and lyophilized. The dried samples were reconstituted in 100 μL of double-distilled water and injected into the Agilent [high-performance liquid chromatography (HPLC); Agilent Technologies, Santa Clara,

CA, USA] with a high pH RP (reverse phase) column (Durashell, C18, 250 mm × 4.6 mm, 5 μm; Bonna-Agela Technologies Inc., Wilmington, DE, USA). Peptides were eluted and combined into 10 groups and lyophilized (Shen et al., 2017; Zhao et al., 2017).

NanoLC-MS/MS (Mass Spectrometry) Analysis

An Ultra 2D Plus nanoflow HPLC (Eksigent Inc., Dublin, CA, USA) coupled with Triple TOF 5600 system (AB Sciex) was used for the analytical separation of peptides (Sun et al., 2015; Shen et al., 2017; Zhao et al., 2017; Iqbal et al., 2018). Labeled peptides were loaded on the column (ChromXP C18, 3 μm, 350 μm × 0.5 mm, Eksigent) with trapping and desalting carried out at 5 μL/min for 5 min using mobile phase A (2% acetonitrile, 0.1% formic acid). Analytical separation was carried out with ChromXP C18 (3 μm, 75 μm × 150 mm, Eksigent) at a flow rate of 350 nL/min. The elution gradient was run using mobile phase A and B (98% acetonitrile, 0.1% formic acid). Gradient of mobile phase and run time are shown in **Supplementary Table S1**. The mass spectrometric data was acquired in positive ion mode, with a 2.4-kV ion spray voltage, 30-psi curtain gas, 5-psi nebulizer gas, and an interface heater temperature of 150°C. The scan scope for TOF-mass spectrometry (MS) is 350–1,500 m/z, and peptides with +2 to +5 charge states were selected for MS/MS analysis (mass range of 100–1,500 m/z). Survey scans were acquired in 0.25 s and a maximum of 30 product ion scans were run with accumulation time of 80 ms for each product ion scan. Smart information-dependent acquisition (IDA) was activated with automatic collision energy and automatic MS/MS accumulation.

Database Search and iTRAQ Quantification

Protein identification and quantification were performed using ProteinPilot v4.5 (AB Sciex) with the Paragon Algorithm against the uniprot "complete proteome" human proteins database. To reduce false-positive identification results, false discovery rate (FDR) less than 1% was required for the identification of proteins (Tambor et al., 2016). The ProteinPilot Descriptive Statistics Template was used for estimation of FDR associated with quantification results (Tambor et al., 2016). Based on a 95% confidence level, at least one unique peptide per protein group was required for identifying proteins, and two quantified peptides were required for quantifying proteins. The cutoff values of 1.5-fold for up-regulated and 0.67-fold for down-regulated proteins, *P*-value <0.05, and consistent change in ratios in all cross comparisons (115:118, 115:119, 115:121; 116:118, 116:119, 116:121; 117:118, 117:119, 117:121), were established for significantly differentially expressed proteins between autistic patients and controls. This significant change was further determined through the conversion of $\log_2$ ratios (include ASD vs. control, control vs. control), followed by data normalization, and statistical *t*-test, and cluster analysis by using OMICSBEAN online tools[1].

Bioinformatics Analysis

The differentially expressed proteins were loaded to DAVID (Database for Annotation, Visualization and Integrated Discovery[2]) database for biological process (BP), cellular component (CC), and Kyoto Encyclopedia of Genes and Genomes (KEGG) pathways analysis. Protein-protein interaction (PPI) networks were analyzed by using OMICSBEAN[1] database. Functional interaction network analysis was performed using ClueGO cytoscape plugin (Bindea et al., 2009). GO (gene ontology) categories and pathways searched include BPs, molecular functions (MFs), Kyoto Encyclopedia of Genes and Genomes (KEGG), REACTOME and Wiki pathways.

Western Blot Analysis

To validate quantitative proteomic results, protein samples were selected randomly from the cases and controls with gender and age-matched (n = 5). The samples were analyzed by Western blotting using specific antibodies. Proteins (20 μg/lane) were separated by SDS-PAGE on 12% polyacrylamide gels, and then transferred to polyvinylidene fluoride (PVDF) membranes (Millipore, Billerica, MA, USA), and blots were blocked with 5% skimmed-dried milk in phosphate-buffered saline (PBS: 137 mM NaCl, 10 mM phosphate buffer, and 2.7 mM KCl, pH 7.4) for 1 h and then washed with PBS containing 0.2% (v/v) tween 20 (PBST) and further incubated for overnight at 4°C using primary antibodies against, alpha-1-antitrypsin (SERPINA1), ATP synthase subunit alpha, mitochondrial (ATP5A1), ATP synthase subunit beta, mitochondrial (ATP5B), calreticulin (CALR), complement C3 (C3), cytochrome b-c1 complex subunit 2, mitochondrial (UQCRC2), malate dehydrogenase, mitochondrial (MDH2), and flotillin-1 (FLOT1), at optimized dilutions with PBST. All primary antibodies were purchased from Abcam Inc (Cambridge, MA, USA). After washing with PBST, the blots were then incubated in 1:5,000-diluted horseradish peroxidase (HRP)-conjugated secondary antibody (Abmart Inc, Shanghai, China) for 2 h at room temperature. The membranes were washed three times each for 5 min in PBST and developed with enhanced chemiluminescence (ECL) kit (Pierce ECL detection kit, Thermo Fisher Scientific Inc, Rockford, USA). Immunoreactive signals were detected with a Kodak Image Station 4000MM imaging system (Carestream Health Inc., Rochester, NY, USA). Quantitative analysis of protein bands was performed using Quantity One analysis software (Bio-Rad, USA).

ELISA Analysis

Plasma from individual autistic patients and controls was used to carry out the quantitative detection of SERPINA1 and CALR using a commercially available enzyme-linked immunosorbent assay (ELISA) kit (Uscn Life Science Inc., Cloud-Clone Corp., USA) as per instructions from the manufacturer. Five pro-inflammatory cytokines i.e., interferon-γ (IFN-γ) interleukin-1β (IL-1β), IL-6, IL-12, and tumor necrosis factor-α (TNF-α) were also measured using ELISA kits (Neobioscience Technology Company, Guangdong, China) following the manufacturer's instructions. The ELISA results were normalized to total protein concentrations.

[1]http://www.omicsbean.cn/

[2]http://david.abcc.ncifcrf.gov/

Statistical Analysis

For Western blot and ELISA analysis, statistically significant difference was determined by *t*-test with GraphPad Prism Software (GraphPad Software, Inc., San Diego, CA, USA). *P* value < 0.05 was considered as statistically significant.

RESULTS

iTRAQ Comparative Proteomics Results

By iTRAQ analysis, a total of 2,816 proteins were successfully identified with quantification of 2,117 proteins (**Supplementary Table S2**). Forty-one proteins were identified as differentially expressed proteins between autistic children and healthy controls (**Table 1**, **Figure 2**, and **Supplementary Table S3**). Among these, 32 proteins were significantly up-regulated and nine down-regulated. Interestingly, three proteins, i.e., C3, CALR, and SERPINA1 were also identified as differentially expressed proteins in the plasma of autistic children in our previous study (Shen et al., 2018). The expression trends of C3 and SERPINA1 found here are consistent with the previous study. However, the level of CALR is significantly up-regulated in this study and down-regulated in the previous study (Shen et al., 2018).

Bioinformatics Analysis of the Differentially Expressed Proteins

The differentially expressed proteins were analyzed by different databases. By using DAVID database, BP analysis showed that these proteins are mainly related to dicarboxylic acid metabolic process, erobic respiration, cellular respiration, organic acid metabolic process, tricarboxylic acid cycle (TCA cycle), carboxylic acid metabolic process, response to endoplasmic reticulum (ER) stress, protein folding, response to unfolded protein, protein folding in ER, ATF6-mediated unfolded protein response (UPR), toll-like receptor (TLR) signaling pathway, exocytosis, receptor-mediated endocytosis, cell adhesion, regulation of response to stress, and regulation of immune system process, et cetera (**Figure 3A**). CC analysis showed that these proteins are integral part of extracellular exosome, extracellular vesicle, extracellular organelle, focal adhesion, myelin sheath, mitochondrion, cell-substrate adherens junction, cell-substrate junction, adherens junction, anchoring junction, et cetera (**Figure 3B**). Pathway analyses indicated that they are involved in the carbon metabolism, citrate cycle (TCA cycle), 2-Oxocarboxylic acid metabolism, glyoxylate and dicarboxylate metabolism, biosynthesis of antibiotics, Parkinson's disease, biosynthesis of amino acids, and Huntington's disease (**Figure 3C**). The BPs and pathways related to these proteins obtained from DAVID database are listed in **Supplementary Table S4**, including the count, percent (%) of associated genes, *P*-values, and gene names related to the different GO categories and pathways. Protein-protein interactions (PPIs) obtained from OMICSBEAN database is shown in **Figure 3D**. Twenty-nine proteins interact with each other in a protein interaction network, similar to pathway analysis by DAVID database. Some metabolic processes and ER related cascades are linked to these proteins. Moreover, complement and coagulation processes are also involved.

The results of Cytoscape analysis are overlapping with DAVID and OMICSBEAN analysis. The BPs and MFs associated with these proteins include cellular respiration, regulation of plasma lipoprotein particle levels, tricarboxylic acid metabolic process, protein folding in ER, acute-phase response (APR), S100 protein binding, IL-12-mediated signaling pathway, et cetera (**Figure 4A**). Pathway analysis showed that these proteins are mainly involved in citrate cycle (TCA cycle), mitochondrial protein import, mitochondrial biogenesis, ATF6 (ATF6-alpha) activates chaperones, apoptotic cleavage of cellular proteins, complement and coagulation cascades, and IL-12 family signaling, et cetera (**Figure 4B**).

The BPs and MFs related to these proteins and obtained from Cytoscape are given in **Supplementary Table S5**, and pathways related to them are presented in **Supplementary Table S6**. GO Term, ontology source, term and group *P*-values, GO Groups, percent (%) of associated genes, gene number, and gene names associated with the differentially expressed proteins are listed in these two tables. Of note, 17 proteins, i.e., ACO2, ATP5A1, ATP5B, DLD, ETFA, GLUD1, GOT2, HSPA5, HSPA9, HSPD1, IDH2, MDH2, ME2, STOM, TUFM, UQCRC2, and VDAC3 belong to mitochondria. Interestingly, except for GPD2, UQCRC2, and VDAC3, all of the other proteins were up-regulated in the autistic children compared to healthy controls. Meanwhile, nine proteins i.e., ACO2, ATP5A1, ATP5B, DLD, GLUD1, GOT2, IDH2, MDH2, and UQCRC2, are found associated with metabolic pathways, while seven proteins i.e., ACO2, DLD, GLUD1, GOT2, IDH2, MDH2, and ME2 in carbon metabolism, four proteins i.e., ACO2, DLD IDH2, and MDH2 in TCA cycle, and five proteins i.e., ACO2, DLD, IDH2, MDH2, and ME2 in pyruvate metabolism (**Figure 5A**). These results suggest that the mitochondrial and metabolic pathways may be involved in pathologic mechanism of PBMCs from autistic children. Some other notable proteins are divided into several groups, including response to ER stress (CALR, P4HB, FLOT1, HSPA5, HSP90B1, HYOU1), protein folding in ER (CALR, HSPA5, HSP90B1), unfolded protein binding (CALR, HSP90B1, HSPA5, HSPA9, HSPD1), ER-nucleus signaling pathway and ATF6 (ATF6-alpha) activates chaperones (ALB, APOA1, CALR, HSP90B1, HSPA5), XBP1s activates chaperone genes (CALR, HSP90B1, HSPA5, HYOU1), CREB3 factors activating genes (ALB, APOA1, CALR, HSP90B1, HSPA5); endocytosis (ALB, ANXA11, APOA1, C3, CALR, FLOT1, LBP, HSP90B1, and HYOU1; **Supplementary Tables S4–S6**). These above mentioned proteins might be associated with ER stress and UPR, APR and inflammatory responses, suggesting that these processes might be involved in the pathophysiology of autism (**Figure 5B**). In addition, there are 11, 13, and 12 proteins which are associated with myelin sheath, focal adhesion, and cell adhesion (**Supplementary Table S4**), respectively.

Validation of Differentially Expressed Proteins by Western Blot Analysis

We have selected eight proteins i.e., C3, CALR, SERPINA1, FLOT1, ATP5A1, ATP5B, MDH2, and UQCRC2 to be validated

TABLE 1 | The differentially expressed proteins identified in peripheral blood mononuclear cells (PBMCs) from children with autism and healthy controls.

No.	Protein name	Accession #	Gene name	Peptides (95%)	% Cov	Fold change[c]	Pval (FDR correction)
1	**60 kDa heat shock protein, mitochondrial** (+)[a,b]	P10809	HSPD1	59	68.9	4.67	0.013902986
2	**78 kDa glucose-regulated protein** (+)	P11021	HSPA5	49	64.8	2.08	2.24E-06
3	**Aconitate hydratase, mitochondrial** (+)	Q99798	ACO2	14	42.3	3.95	9.25E-10
4	Alpha-1-antitrypsin* (+)	P01009	SERPINA1	15	58.1	2.53	0.002748253
5	Annexin A11 (–)	P50995	ANXA11	18	30.5	0.55	2.69E-07
6	Apolipoprotein A-I (+)	P02647	APOA1	15	56.6	3.78	0.000365353
7	**Aspartate aminotransferase, mitochondrial** (+)	P00505	GOT2	7	40	2.38	3.80E-06
8	**ATP synthase subunit alpha, mitochondrial** (+)	P25705	ATP5A1	61	65.6	2.94	0.019869459
9	**ATP synthase subunit beta, mitochondrial** (+)	P06576	ATP5B	67	83.4	4.66	5.11E-05
10	Calreticulin* (+)	P27797	CALR	26	58	2.93	8.09E-06
11	Chromobox protein homolog 3 (+)	Q13185	CBX3	10	50.8	3.31	3.02E-05
12	Complement C3* (+)	P01024	C3	38	43.8	2.69	1.46E-05
13	**Cytochrome b-c1 complex subunit 2, mitochondrial** (–)	P22695	UQCRC2	26	64	0.52	0.002836642
14	Deoxynucleoside triphosphate triphosphohydrolase SAMHD1 (+)	Q9Y3Z3	SAMHD1	14	35.1	2.16	6.94621E-05
15	**Dihydrolipoyl dehydrogenase, mitochondrial** (+)	P09622	DLD	12	48.5	2.17	0.000101238
16	**Electron transfer flavoprotein subunit alpha, mitochondrial** (+)	P13804	ETFA	7	49	2.49	4.02001E-08
17	Endoplasmin (+)	P14625	HSP90B1	31	54.9	1.97	0.01778616
18	**Erythrocyte band 7 integral membrane protein** (–)	P27105	STOM	78	77.4	0.48	2.63E-07
19	Flotillin-1 (–)	O75955	FLOT1	20	61.4	0.45	0.003135849
20	Flotillin-2 (–)	Q14254	FLOT2	17	55.6	0.30	1.13E-04
21	**Glutamate dehydrogenase 1, mitochondrial** (+)	P00367	GLUD1	17	44.6	2.50	5.48E-05
22	**Glycerol-3-phosphate dehydrogenase, mitochondrial** (–)	P43304	GPD2	34	61.1	0.58	0.001016776
23	Heparin cofactor 2 (+)	P05546	SERPIND1	5	18.2	4.42	0.001552831
24	Hypoxia up-regulated protein 1 (+)	Q9Y4L1	HYOU1	28	48.4	1.98	0.001809154
25	Inter-alpha-trypsin inhibitor heavy chain H4 (+)	Q14624	ITIH4	10	26.5	3.90	6.04E-06
26	**Isocitrate dehydrogenase [NADP], mitochondrial** (+)	P48735	IDH2	20	60	2.39	0.001550526
27	Lamin-B1 (+)	P20700	LMNB1	20	54.3	7.74	2.24E-06
28	Lamin-B2 (+)	Q03252	LMNB2	10	49.7	3.77	1.24E-06
29	Lipopolysaccharide-binding protein (+)	P18428	LBP	7	33.9	5.48	0.008200263
30	**Malate dehydrogenase, mitochondrial** (+)	P40926	MDH2	16	55	2.95	0.002301777
31	**NAD-dependent malic enzyme, mitochondrial** (+)	P23368	ME2	20	64	2.34	8.07E-06
32	Neuroblast differentiation-associated protein AHNAK (+)	Q09666	AHNAK	23	32.4	3.08	6.08E-06
33	Plastin-2 (+)	P13796	LCP1	41	55	2.42	1.90E-04
34	Plectin (–)	Q15149	PLEC	65	46.8	0.60	0.006498826
35	Probable ubiquitin carboxyl-terminal hydrolase FAF-X (–)	Q93008	USP9X	11	22	0.51	7.70E-05
36	Protein disulfide-isomerase(+)	P07237	P4HB	36	58.9	1.99	5.08E-06
37	Ras GTPase-activating-like protein IQGAP1 (+)	P46940	IQGAP1	37	46.7	2.80	6.60E-06
38	Serum albumin (+)	P02768	ALB	42	64.5	2.91	0.004346685
39	**Stress-70 protein, mitochondrial** (+)	P38646	HSPA9	19	54.2	1.85	3.42E-05
40	Vimentin (+)	P08670	VIM	28	62	2.07	0.0011167
41	**Voltage-dependent anion-selective channel protein 3** (–)	Q9Y277	VDAC3	36	68.2	0.35	0.000430871

[a](+), proteins increased in abundant; (–), proteins decreased in abundant. [b]The differentially expressed proteins belong to mitochondrial proteins are indicated in bold. [c]Fold change, $P < 0.05$ vs. the control. "" The protein has been identified as differentially expressed protein in the blood of autistic patients in our previous study (Shen et al., 2018).*

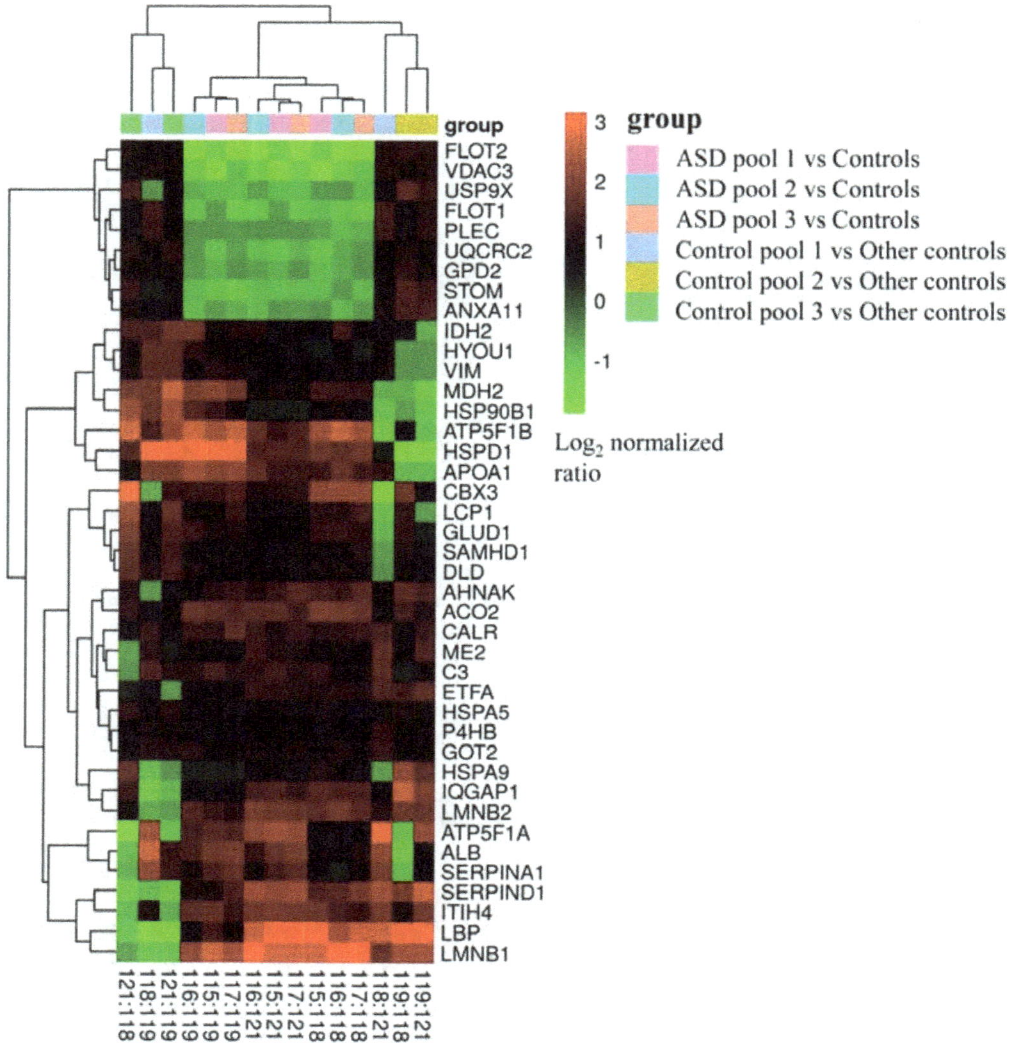

FIGURE 2 | Cluster map the differentially expressed proteins in all cross comparisons. Three mixed samples from autistic children were labeled with isobaric tags for relative and absolute quantitation (iTRAQ) tags 115, 116, 117, and the healthy controls with 118, 119 and 121 tags, respectively.

by Western blot analysis. Of which, three proteins, i.e., C3, CALR, and SERPINA1, have already been identified as differentially expressed proteins in the plasma of autistic children in our previous studies (Shen et al., 2018). These are also associated with important functions and pathways, such as metabolic pathways, ER stress, and endocytosis, etc. Consistent with the iTRAQ results, significant decrease in the expression levels of FLOT1 and UQCRC2 in the autistic patients were detected, whereas the levels of C3, CALR, SERPINA1, ATP5A1, ATP5B, and MDH2 were significantly higher than those in healthy controls (**Figure 6**, $P < 0.05$).

ELISA Analysis

As mentioned above, three proteins (C3, CALR, and SERPINA1) have been identified in our previous study (Shen et al., 2018). Being already validated in our previous study, the expression level of C3 has not been validated here. Instead, we validated the levels of the other two proteins (CALR and SERPINA1) in the plasma by ELISA. As shown in **Figures 7A,B**, the results of ELISA are consistent with iTRAQ analysis. In addition, considering the potential involvement in inflammation, altered levels of pro-inflammatory cytokines have been observed in ASD individuals (Ashwood et al., 2011; Ibrahim et al., 2015; Masi et al., 2015; Xu et al., 2015). In this study, levels of IFN-γ, IL-1β, IL-6, IL-12 and TNF-α were detected in plasma (**Figures 7C–G**). Consistent with the previous studies (Ashwood et al., 2011; Ibrahim et al., 2015; Masi et al., 2015; Xu et al., 2015), these were significantly higher in autistic patients than in healthy controls.

DISCUSSION

In the present study, we have made an attempt to identify proteomic changes in PBMCs from the autistic children. Total

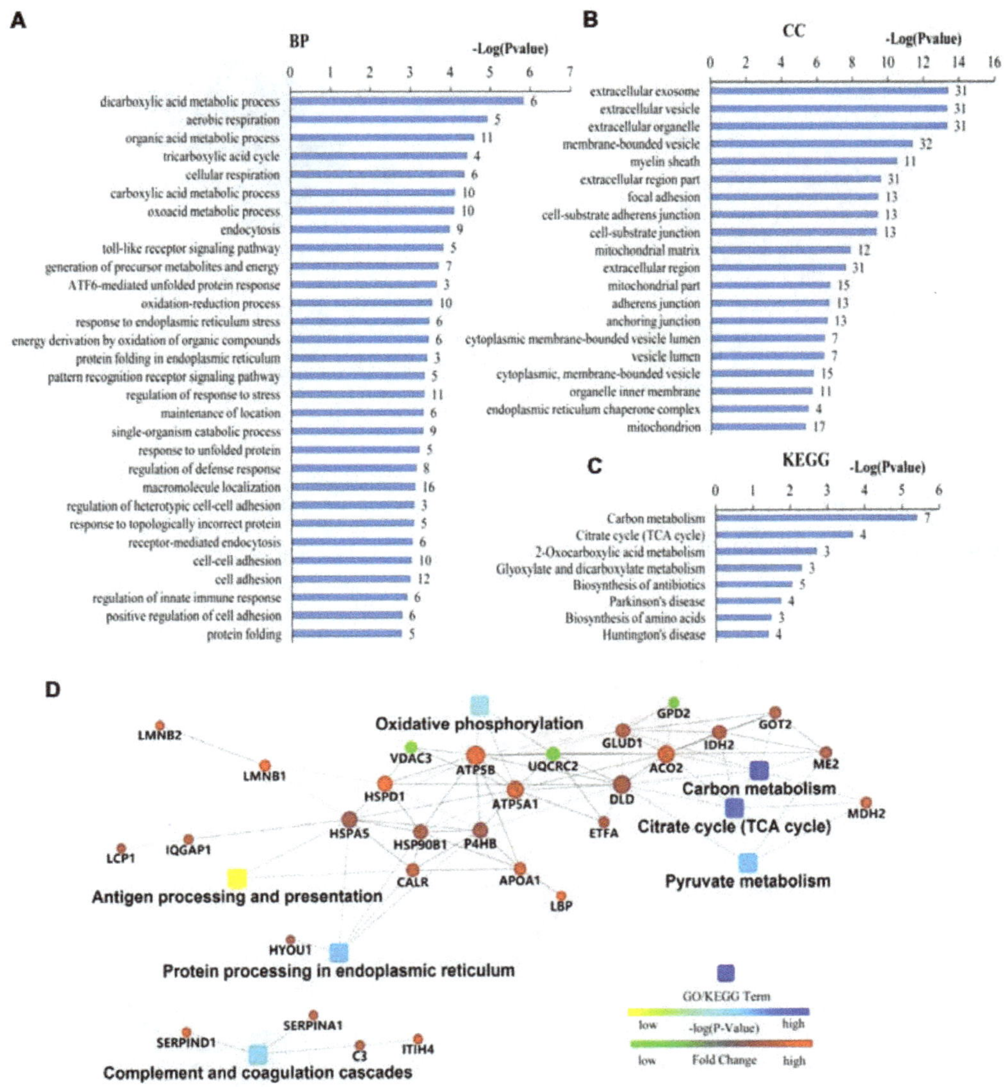

FIGURE 3 | Bioinformatics analysis of 41 differentially expressed proteins in peripheral blood mononuclear cells (PBMCs) from autistic children and healthy subjects. **(A)** The top 30 ranking of biological process (BP) based on gene ontology (GO). **(B)** The top 20 ranking of cellular components (CCs) based on GO. **(C)** By using DAVID analysis, the Kyoto Encyclopedia of Genes and Genomes (KEGG) signal transduction pathways are associated with these proteins. **(D)** Protein-protein interaction (PPI) networks of differentially expressed proteins. The networks analysis was carried out by using OMICSBEAN. **(A–C)** Number of proteins associated with each category and *P*-value for gene-enrichment analysis is shown on the right of each term bar.

of 41 differentially expressed proteins are found in autistic subjects as compared to healthy controls. These proteins are mainly related to mitochondrial and metabolic pathways, ER stress and protein folding, plasma lipoprotein particle levels, endocytosis, immune and inflammatory response, complement and coagulation cascades, focal adhesion, extracellular matrix, and cell-cell adherens, oxidation-reduction process, et cetera suggesting that a variety of mechanisms are associated with PBMCs in autistic children, thereby might be contributing to the development of autism.

Lot of evidence suggests that mitochondrial dysfunction may be associated with ASD. The brain of individuals with ASD may have an abnormality in carbohydrate metabolism and bioenergetics, which in turn influence some clinical symptoms, e.g., the social and cognitive deficits in ASD (Frye and Rossignol, 2011). A recent meta-analysis found that abnormal biochemical markers of mitochondrial function are relatively common in the general population of children with ASD. Moreover, it was found that a relatively high percentage of children with ASD (~5%) have mitochondrial disease (MD; Rossignol and Frye, 2012). Some studies have demonstrated decreased efficiency of electron transport chain (ETC) complex, TCA cycle and pyruvate dehydrogenase enzyme activities, as well as differences in mitochondrial gene expression in the brain tissues of individuals with autism (Rossignol and Frye, 2014). However, in this study, among the 17 differentially expressed mitochondrial proteins,

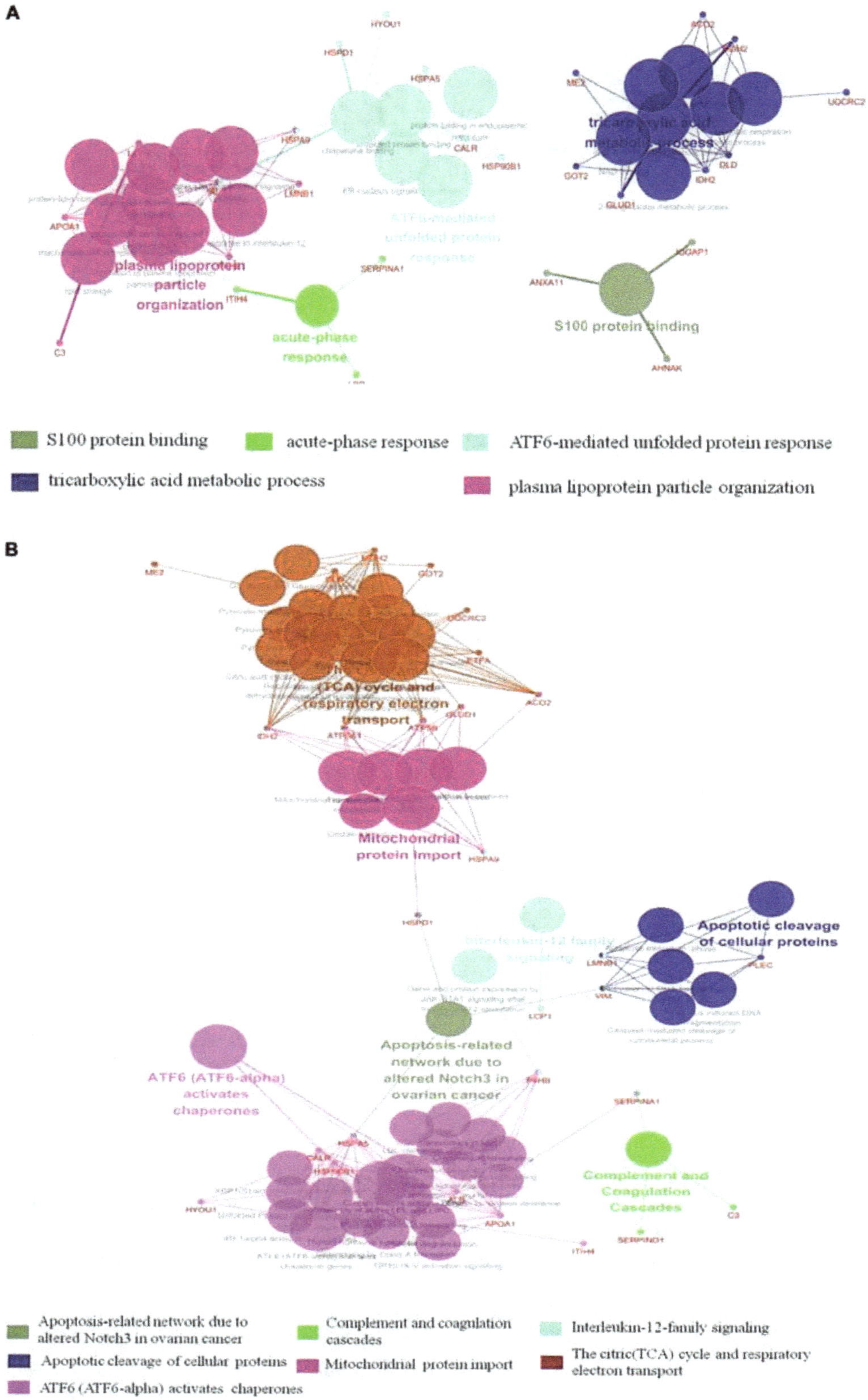

FIGURE 4 | Functional interaction network analysis was performed using ClueGO cytoscape plugin. **(A)** The differentially expressed 41 proteins were mapped to the GO categories (BPs and molecular function, MF). **(B)** The differentially expressed proteins were mapped to KEGG pathway, REACTOME pathway and Wiki pathway. Panels **(A,B)** are separately uploaded in the **Supplementary Figure S1**.

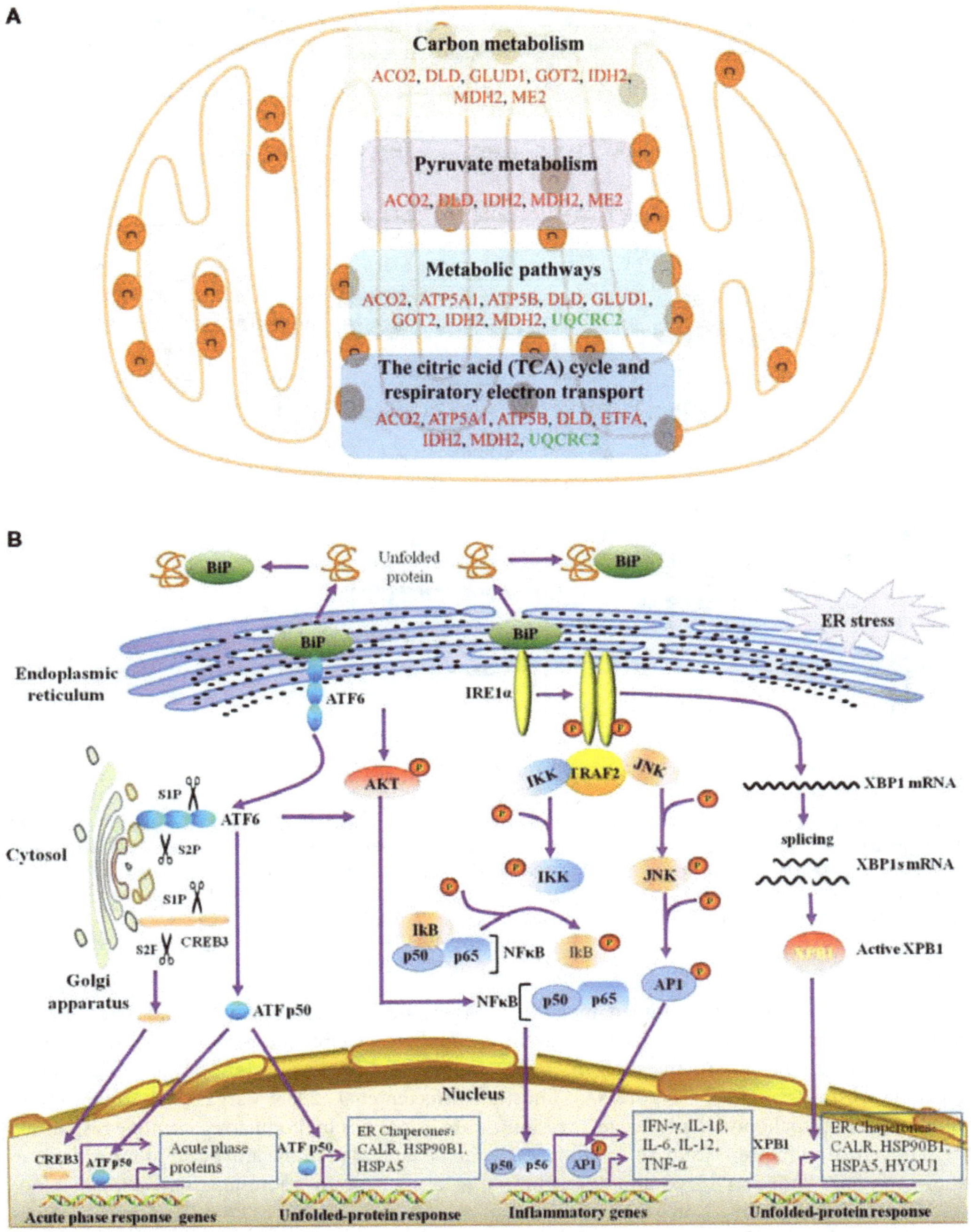

FIGURE 5 | Mitochondrial, endoplasmic reticulum (ER)-stress, unfolded protein response (UPR), inflammatory response and acute phase response pathways are associated with differentially expressed proteins. **(A)** The differentially expressed proteins belonged to mitochondrial proteins are mainly divided into four categories, which are associated with different pathways. **(B)** ER-stress, UPR, acute phase response pathways are shown. ATF6 and IRE1α pathways may be involved in the unfolded-protein response and inflammatory response of PBMCs in autistic children. Upon dissociation from BiP in response to ER stress, ATF6 translocates to the Golgi apparatus, where it is cleaved by the proteases site-1 protease (S1P) and S2P. This process results in the release of a functional (bZIP-containing) fragment of ATF6 into the cytosol. This fragment then migrates to the nucleus and activates transcription. In response to ER stress, IRE1α autophosphorylates, thereby activating its RNase activity and splices XBP1 mRNA to spliced XBP1 mRNA, which codes for a transcription factor XBP1s that translocates to the nucleus and regulates genes involved in UPR and ER-associated degradation (ERAD). In addition, ATF6 can also trigger NFκB-mediated inflammation *via* Akt kinase phosphorylation (pAkt). IRE1α induces the expression of inflammatory genes through the activation of the JNK-AP1 and NF-κB-Iκ-B pathways. Moreover, active ATF6 and CREB3 can induce the transcription of acute phase response genes. CREB3 is cleaved by the Golgi resident proteases S1P and S2P. This protein fragment then transits from the cytosol to the nucleus where it activates transcription of target genes. The differentially expressed proteins associated with ER stress, protein folding in ER, unfolded protein binding, ATF6 activates chaperones, XBP1s activates chaperones, IRE1alpha activates chaperones, CREB3 factors activate genes, and acute inflammatory response, are listed in **Supplementary Tables S4–S6**.

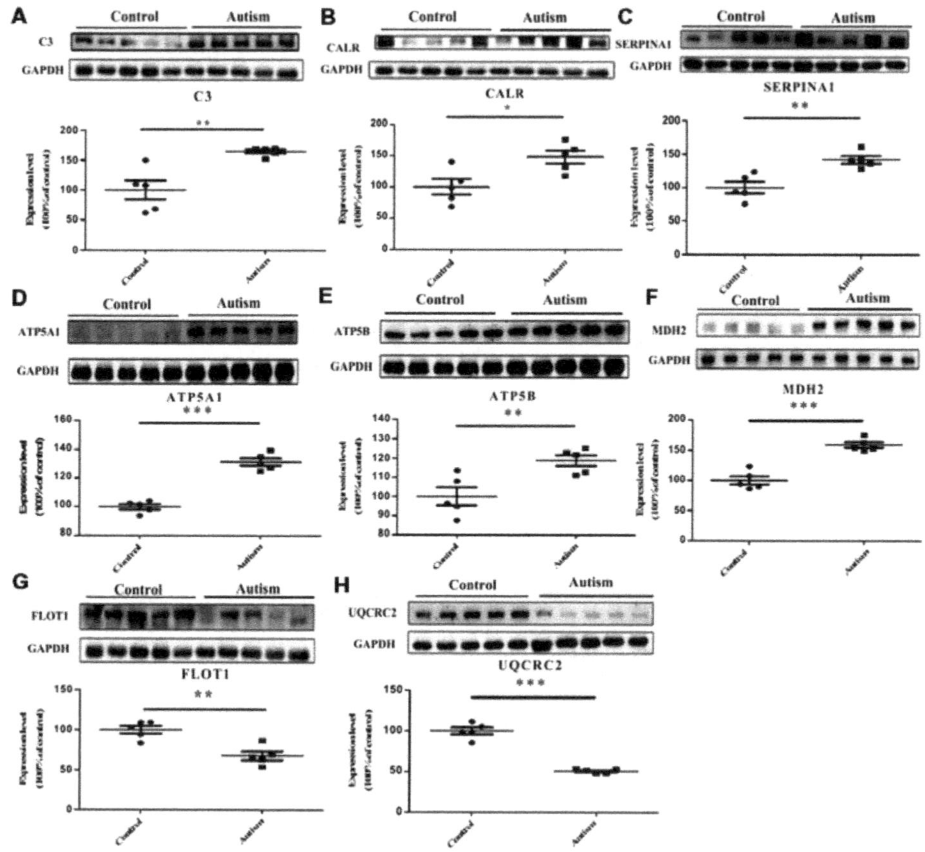

FIGURE 6 | Validation of differentially expressed proteins in PBMCs of children with autism by Western blot analysis. **(A)** Complement C3 (C3). **(B)** Calreticulin (CALR). **(C)** Alpha-1-antitrypsin (SERPINA1). **(D)** ATP synthase subunit alpha, mitochondrial (ATP5A1). **(E)** ATP synthase subunit beta, mitochondrial (ATP5B). **(F)** Malate dehydrogenase, mitochondrial (MDH2). **(G)** Flotillin-1 (FLOT1). **(H)** Cytochrome b-c1 complex subunit 2, mitochondrial (UQCRC2). The level of protein expression is normalized with the mean of the controls (n = 5), with each bar representing the standard deviation (SD; $P < 0.05$). The upper images of Western blot analysis correspond to the lower histograms of semiquantification. *$P < 0.05$, **$P < 0.01$, ***$P < 0.001$.

14 proteins were up-regulated in children with autism, including nine proteins associated with metabolic pathways, seven, four and five proteins involved in carbon metabolism, TCA cycle, and pyruvate metabolism, respectively (**Figure 5A**). Thus, our results showed that the mitochondrial protein expression patterns of PBMCs in autistic children seem to be different than previous studies on mitochondria (Frye and Rossignol, 2011; Rossignol and Frye, 2014). This implicates that the energy metabolism might be increased in the PBMCs of autistic children. Based on these findings, we may hypothesize that the PBMCs may be activated in children with autism. It may be similar to the microglial cells, whose phenotype closely resemble to monocytes/macrophages, has been reported to be activated in the brain of patients with ASD in multiple studies (Morgan et al., 2010; Rodriguez and Kern, 2011; Suzuki et al., 2013). Indeed, monocytes can serve as precursors for a number of tissue specific myeloid lineage cells including macrophages, dendritic cells, and microglia. PBMCs recruited to the central nervous system (CNS) develop into exogenously derived microglial cells or bone marrow derived microglial (BMDM) cells (Jyonouchi et al., 2011). The peripherally-activated monocytes can also enter into the brain parenchyma and release cytokines. Increased numbers of circulating monocytes have been observed in the blood and in postmortem brain tissues from ASD individuals (Sweeten et al., 2003; Vargas et al., 2005). Dendritic cells, which are important in modulating immune responses, were also found to be increased in the amygdala of individuals with ASD (Breece et al., 2013). In addition, monocytes in blood and microglia in the brain have very similar transcriptomes (Vargas et al., 2005; Morgan et al., 2010). A recent transcriptomic analysis of the autistic brain has shown the presence of two modules in the ASD brain: a neuronal module enriched for known autism susceptibility genes, and a module enriched for immune genes and glial markers (Voineagu et al., 2011). The later immune-glial module has less pronounced genetic component and thus is most likely to be either a secondary phenomenon or the result of environmental factors (Voineagu et al., 2011). Another study reported more thickened and irregular arrangement of mitochondrial cristae in PBMCs from autistic patients, implying that an activated status of mitochondria cope with an increased energy requirement in PBMCs (Siniscalco et al., 2012). Taken together, we propose that mitochondrial function may be

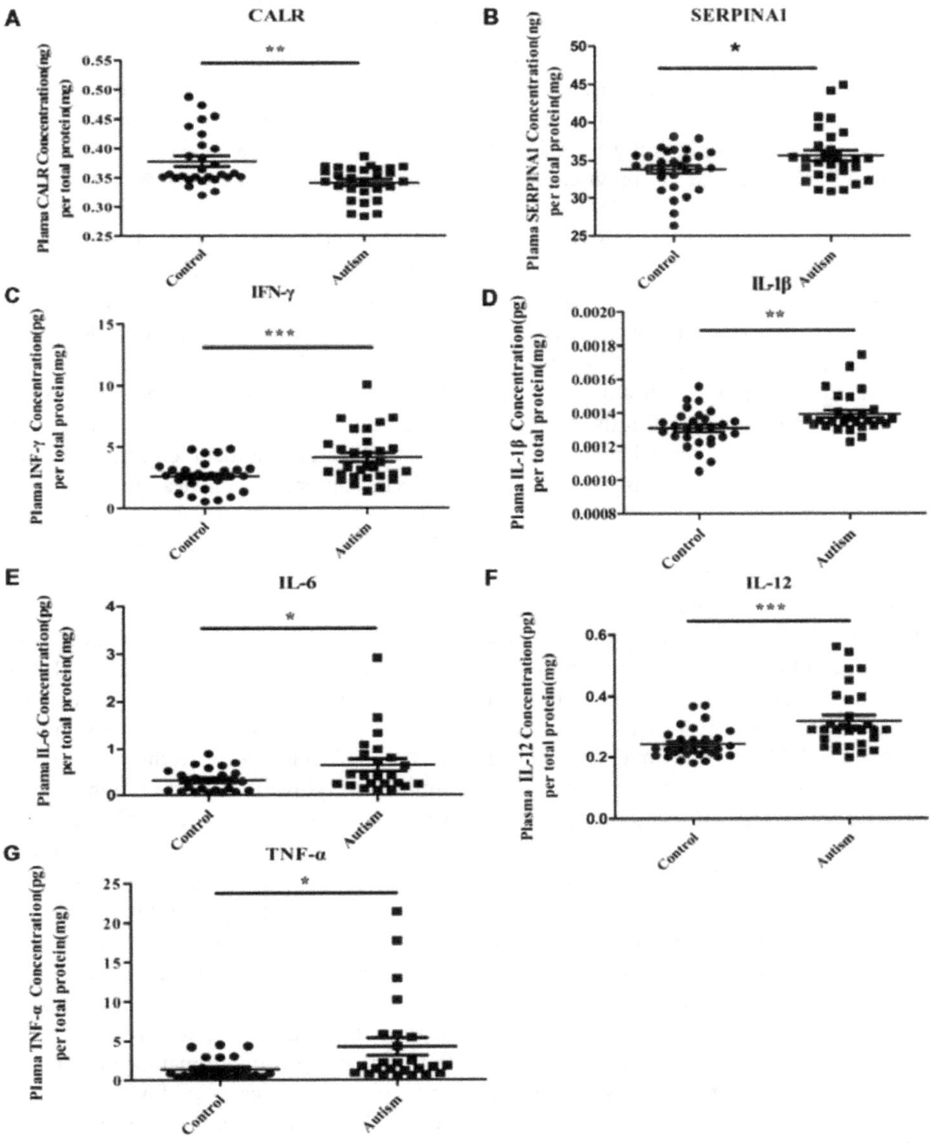

FIGURE 7 | Some of differentially expressed proteins were detected in PBMCs and pro-inflammatory cytokines were detected in plasma of children with autism by enzyme-linked immunosorbent assay (ELISA) analysis. **(A)** Calreticulin (CALR). Autism and control group, $n = 28$. **(B)** Alpha-1-antitrypsin (SERPINA1). Autism and control group, $n = 29$. **(C)** Interferon-γ (IFN-γ). Autism and control group, $n = 30$. **(D)** Interleukin-1β (IL-1β). Autism and control group, $n = 28$. **(E)** Interleukin-6 (IL-6). Autism and control group, $n = 23$. **(F)** IL-12. Autism and control group, $n = 30$. **(G)** Tumor necrosis factor-α (TNF-α). Autism and control group, $n = 25$. The graphical results depict the mean ± SD, $^*P < 0.05$, $^{**}P < 0.01$, $^{***}P < 0.001$. CALR and SERPINA1 were detected in PBMCs and others pro-inflammatory cytokines were detected in plasma.

enhanced in PBMCs and microglial cells of children with autism, whereas it might be a dysfunction in the neurons of the patients.

The mitochondrial "activation" in PBMCs of autistic children may be associated with the inflammatory and immune response. A number of studies have reported evidence of immune dysregulation and/or inflammation in individuals with ASD (Masi et al., 2015; Xu et al., 2015). Abnormal levels of various inflammatory cytokines and chemokines have been found in ASD patients in PBMCs, serum or plasma, brain tissues, and cerebrospinal fluid (CSF; Masi et al., 2015; Xu et al., 2015). For example, a series of studies found that pro-inflammatory cytokines include IFN-γ, IL-1β, IL-6, IL-12, and TNF-α were significantly higher in ASD patients, whereas anti-inflammatory cytokine IL-10 and transforming growth factor beta1 (TGF-β1) was reduced in controls (Ashwood et al., 2011; Ibrahim et al., 2015; Masi et al., 2015; Xu et al., 2015). In the brain, cytokine imbalances in ASDs may contribute directly to ASD neural dysfunction. They may influence the behavior through affecting the neurotransmitter function, neuroendocrine activity, neurogenesis, and alterations to brain circuitry (Masi et al., 2017b). On the other hand, peripheral cytokine signals are believed to access the brain (Goines and Ashwood, 2013), while changes in peripheral cytokine expression have been correlated with ASD, severity of behavioral impairments and associated symptoms (Masi et al., 2017b). In this study, several proteins associated with an acute phase response, immune and inflammatory response and IL-12 family signaling were found to enhance expression in PBMCs. Similar to previous study (Glatt et al., 2012), in transcription analyses of PBMCs, it was revealed that differentially expressed genes in ASD subjects are related to immune response, inflammation, IFN signaling and chemokine pathways. Here, five cytokines (IFN-γ, IL-1β, IL-6, IL-12, and TNF-α) were detected to be increased in plasma of autistic children. Together, these data further support that PBMCs may be activated in children with autism, which play an important role in the pathobiology of autism. Hence, supporting the view that immune system disturbances may be activated and continuously contribute to the onset of ASD in a pro-inflammatory state (Ashwood et al., 2006; Enstrom et al., 2010; Masi et al., 2017b).

It is noteworthy that several differentially expressed proteins found here relate to protein folding and unfolded protein binding. ATF6 and XBP1 activate chaperone genes, CREB3 factors activate genes and ER-nucleus signaling pathways were identified as related to these differentially expressed proteins between the case and control groups in the present study. It suggests that ER stress, UPR and APR may be involved in PBMCs from children of autism and link to the occurrence of autism (**Figure 5B**). The ER is a multifunctional organelle that coordinates protein folding, lipid biosynthesis, and calcium storage and release. Perturbations that disrupt ER homeostasis lead to ER stress and activation of signaling cascades termed as UPR (Chaudhari et al., 2014). The main UPR branches include PERK [PKR (dsRNA-dependent protein kinase)-like ER kinase], inositol-requiring enzyme 1 (IRE-1), and ATF-6. Under basal conditions, these specialized ER membrane-associated sensor proteins are bound by the ER chaperone BiP (also known as Grp78 or HSPA5) and are maintained in an inactive state (Zhang and Kaufman, 2008; Chaudhari et al., 2014). Accumulation of unfolded/misfolded/mutated proteins in the ER lumen activates adaptive UPR mechanisms through release of BiP from the sensor proteins and initiation of specific cellular responses. All these events points towards the restoration of ER homeostasis (Chaudhari et al., 2014). The released ATF6 acts as a transcription factor, which travels to the nucleus and binds to ER-stress response elements (ERSE) and regulates gene expression of proteins involved in ER stress and UPR, along with Grp78, PDIs, and activate transcription of major APR genes. In response to ER stress, IRE1α autophosphorylates, thereby activates its RNase activity. It then splices XBP1 mRNA to splice XBP1 mRNA, which code for a transcription factor XBP1s that translocates to the nucleus and regulates genes involved in UPR and ER-associated degradation (ERAD; Zhang and Kaufman, 2008; Chaudhari et al., 2014). Likewise, CREB3 proteins were also identified to mediate the APR (Fox and Andrew, 2015). Thus, our results suggest that activation of ATF6, XBP1s and CREB3 may be involved in ER stress, UPR, and APR in autistic PBMCs (**Figure 5B**). Interestingly, a recent study showed a significant increase in the mRNA levels of ATF4, ATF6, PERK, XBP1, CHOP, and IRE1 in the middle frontal gyrus of ASD subjects (Crider et al., 2017). Another study showed that the activation of UPR specifically regulated glutamate neurotransmission in the cerebellum of a mouse model of autism (Trobiani et al., 2018). Taken together, these results support that ER stress and UPR may be involved in pathogenesis of ASD.

In addition, ATF6 activation can induce inflammation *via* promoting the transcription of genes for cytokines, chemokines, and other pro-inflammatory molecules by nuclear factor-κB (NF-κB) pathway (Zhang and Kaufman, 2008; Chaudhari et al., 2014). IRE1α can activate the JNK-AP1 and NF-κB pathways and induces the expression of inflammatory genes (Zhang and Kaufman, 2008; Chaudhari et al., 2014). Thus, these may have a correlation between ER stress and inflammatory responses in the PBMCs of autistic children and pathogenesis of autism. Indeed, compared with healthy controls, NF-κB DNA binding activity was found elevated in peripheral blood samples of children with autism (Naik et al., 2011), and increased NF-κB expression levels were also found in post-mortem samples of orbitofrontal cortex from autistic patients, suggesting the activation of NF-κB pathways (Young et al., 2011). Likewise, five proteins i.e., FLOT1, FLOT2, HSP90B1, HSPD1, LBP are related to the TLR signaling pathway in this study, suggesting that it may be associated with inflammatory processes of PBMCs from autistic children. Recent studies have shown that TLR control of immune response is altered in monocyte cultures from children with ASD (Enstrom et al., 2010) and associated microglial cells (Réus et al., 2015). Activation of TLR signaling can trigger NF-κB-mediated inflammatory response. The activation of inflammatory pathways result in the release of pro-inflammatory cytokines such as IL-1β, IL-6, IL-12, and TNF-α, IFN-γ, et cetera, which then amplify the inflammatory reactions (Lawrence, 2009; Enstrom et al., 2010). Hence, it can be proposed that ER stress, UPR and ATF6 pathway, IRE1α pathway, TLR signaling pathway and pro-inflammatory cytokines might be involved in inflammatory processes of PBMCs from autistic children. Besides ASD, ER stress and UPR have been observed in a variety of diseases including metabolic disease, neurodegenerative disease, inflammatory disease, cancer, and autoimmunity (Wang and Kaufman, 2012). The induction of ER stress and activation of the UPR *in vivo* is attributable to both intrinsic and extrinsic factors (Wang and Kaufman, 2016). For autism, autism-associated mutations in several genes have been shown to affect protein folding and lead to activation of the UPR and ER stress (Fujita et al., 2010; Ulbrich et al., 2016). It may also be due to oxidative stress, autoimmune system, and inflammatory factors that need to be further clarified.

Additionally, inflammation is a controlled response of the host to infection or injury that involves various molecular, cellular and physiological changes and is coordinated primarily by specific cell adhesion molecules and chemo-attractants (Ghosh et al., 2014). Circulating monocytes then migrate across the endothelium to gain access to the site of infection or injury (Ghosh et al., 2014). Here, some proteins involved in cell adhesion, focal adhesion, cell-substrate junction, adherens junction, and anchoring junction, may be related to the recruitment and migration of PBMCs from autistic patients, thereby contributing to inflammatory reaction in the cells. In addition, the inflammatory processes are accompanied by phagocytic reactions. Endocytosis plays an important role in inflammation. In this study, nine proteins associated with endocytosis were found to be altered between autistic subjects, implying that they may be enhanced in PBMCs of autistic children.

Furthermore, these proteins may serve as candidate biomarkers for the diagnosis of autism. However, the mechanisms associated with these proteins such as inflammation, protein misfolding and alteration of mitochondrial activity are presumably common responses to many internal and external challenges, thereby affecting their specificity as a diagnostic marker. Nevertheless, very recently, two review studies on autism proteomics and biomarkers highlighted the close relationship between these mechanisms and ASD (Abraham et al., 2019; Shen et al., 2019). They may be interacted with each other, and related to the occurrence and development of these diseases, and may be primary or secondary phenomena (Abraham et al., 2019). Given the complexity of ASD pathogenesis, a panel of proteins rather than a single protein could be a more powerful approach to diagnose this disease. Besides, discovering and detecting parallel change between CNS and peripheral samples is one of the strategies for finding diagnostic markers for ASD (Hayashi-Takagi et al., 2014; Shen et al., 2019). Indeed, various abnormalities in immunological markers or immune functions, including CSF or brain tissue-associated immune abnormalities have been a recurring theme in ASD research (Abraham et al., 2019). In addition, as mentioned above, ER stress has been observed in the brains of autistic children (Crider et al., 2017), and UPR activation has also been observed in the cerebellum of a mouse model of autism (Trobiani et al., 2018). Therefore, these proteins still have the potential to become diagnostic markers. Moreover, here, three proteins, i.e., C3, CALR, and SERPINA1, were simultaneously changed in blood and cells of autistic subjects, suggesting that analyses of their expression levels both in the plasma and PBMCs in case and control groups could increase the specificity of the marker. Interestingly, the expression of CALR is reversed in the current study of PBMCs and plasma from our previous study (Shen et al., 2018). It might reflect differences in the utility of each biological specimen for diagnosis. Complement protein C3 has also been detected to be increased in plasma of children with ASD in a previous study (Corbett et al., 2007). The complement system, a complex protein network initially identified as part of the innate immune system, is an essential regulator of cell and tissue homeostasis. C3 is the central component of the complement system which induces inflammatory, immunomodulatory and metabolic responses. In addition, C5 was detected to be increased in autistic children in our previous study (Shen et al., 2018). Besides, three proteins i.e., A2M, SERPINA1, and SERPIND1 were also associated with complement and coagulation cascades in the present study, indicating that complement system and coagulation cascades may be involved in the pathogenesis of autism.

In conclusion, to the best of our knowledge, this is the first study to investigate PBMCs from children with autism using iTRAQ technique, and 41 differentially expressed proteins were identified between the case and control groups. Of which 17 mitochondrial proteins associated with different metabolic pathways were increased in autistic children. Some of them were verified and five pro-inflammatory cytokines were found to be increased in the plasma of autistic children. The results showed that ER stress and the UPR, APR and inflammatory response were associated with PBMCs from autistic children, and they may be induced by activation of ATF6, XBP1s, and CREB3. ATF6, IRE1α and TLR signals trigger the activation of NF-κB that may be responsible for the inflammatory response in the PBMCs of autistic children. The recruitment, migration, and endocytosis of PBMCs may also be involved in the inflammatory process. Our results suggest that the PBMCs from autistic children might be activated and are linked to the occurrence of autism. These proteins may serve as candidate proteins for the diagnosis of autism and needs to be studied further. Meanwhile, it is necessary to point out that the present study is a preliminary investigation. These differentially expressed proteins need to be further validated by using Western blot analysis and/or ELISA assay, and a large scale validation and a non-mixed sample strategy for proteomics analysis are also required.

ETHICS STATEMENT

The research was approved by Human Research Ethics Committees of Maternal and Child Health Hospital of Baoan and complies with the guidelines of the Helsinki Declaration. Written informed consent for study participation was obtained from parents of children.

AUTHOR CONTRIBUTIONS

LS and CF conceived and designed the experiments, analyzed the data and drafted the manuscript. KZ, YC, JK, XC, JL, CL, JI, and YZ performed the experiments and helped to revise the manuscript. YG carried out the clinical diagnosis. CF, YG, and WW recruited patients, and collected the blood samples and helped to revise the manuscript. All authors read and approved the final manuscript.

FUNDING

This study was financially supported by National Natural Science Foundation of China (Grant No. 31870825), and the Shenzhen Bureau of Science, Technology and Information (Nos. JCYJ20170412110026229, JCYJ20150529164656093, JCYJ20150402100258220), and the humanities and social sciences research project of the Ministry of Education (17YJA760052), and the philosophy and social science project of Guangdong Province (GD16XYS22).

ACKNOWLEDGMENTS

We are grateful to Shuiming Li at instrument analysis center of Shenzhen University (Xili Campus) for their technical assistance.

SUPPLEMENTARY MATERIAL

FIGURE S1 | Figures 4A,B are presented separately.

TABLE S1 | Gradient of mobile phase and run time of nanoLC-MS/MS analysis.

TABLE S2 | List all quantitative proteins in the peripheral blood mononuclear cells (PBMCs) in this study.

TABLE S3 | Differentially expressed proteins identified from the peripheral blood mononuclear cells (PBMCs) of autistic children and healthy controls.

TABLE S4 | Differentially expressed proteins associated with gene ontology (GO) and signal transduction pathways in DAVID analysis.

TABLE S5 | Differentially expressed proteins associated with gene ontology (GO) by using ClueGO analysis.

TABLE S6 | Differentially expressed proteins associated with signal transduction pathways by using ClueGO analysis.

REFERENCES

Abraham, J., Szoko, N., and Natowicz, M. R. (2019). "Proteomic investigations of autism spectrum disorder: past findings, current challenges, and future prospects," in *Reviews on Biomarker Studies in Psychiatric and Neurodegenerative Disorders. Advances in Experimental Medicine and Biology*, ed. P. Guest (Cham: Springer), 235–252.

Ashwood, P., Krakowiak, P., Hertz-Picciotto, I., Hansen, R., Pessah, I., and Van de Water, J. (2011). Elevated plasma cytokines in autism spectrum disorders provide evidence of immune dysfunction and are associated with impaired behavioral outcome. *Brain Behav. Immun.* 25, 40–45. doi: 10.1016/j.bbi.2010.08.003

Ashwood, P., Wills, S., and Van de Water, J. (2006). The immune response in autism: a new frontier for autism research. *J. Leukoc. Biol.* 80, 1–15. doi: 10.1189/jlb.1205707

Baron, C. A., Liu, S. Y., Hicks, C., and Gregg, J. P. (2006). Utilization of lymphoblastoid cell lines as a system for the molecular modeling of autism. *J. Autism Dev. Disord.* 36, 973–982. doi: 10.1007/s10803-006-0134-x

Bindea, G., Mlecnik, B., Hackl, H., Charoentong, P., Tosolini, M., Kirilovsky, A., et al. (2009). ClueGO: a Cytoscape plug-in to decipher functionally grouped gene ontology and pathway annotation networks. *Bioinformatics* 25, 1091–1093. doi: 10.1093/bioinformatics/btp101

Breece, E., Paciotti, B., Nordahl, C. W., Ozonoff, S., Van de Water, J. A., Rogers, S. J., et al. (2013). Myeloid dendritic cells frequencies are increased in children with autism spectrum disorder and associated with amygdala volume and repetitive behaviors. *Brain Behav. Immun.* 31, 69–75. doi: 10.1016/j.bbi.2012.10.006

Chaste, P., and Leboyer, M. (2012). Autism risk factors: genes, environment, and gene-environment interactions. *Dialogues Clin. Neurosci.* 14, 281–292.

Chaudhari, N., Talwar, P., Parimisetty, A., Lefebvre d'Hellencourt, C., and Ravanan, P. (2014). A molecular web: endoplasmic reticulum stress, inflammation, and oxidative stress. *Front. Cell. Neurosci.* 8:213. doi: 10.3389/fncel.2014.00213

Corbett, B. A., Kantor, A. B., Schulman, H., Walker, W. L., Lit, L., Ashwood, P., et al. (2007). A proteomic study of serum from children with autism showing differential expression of apolipoproteins and complement proteins. *Mol. Psychiatry* 12, 292–306. doi: 10.1038/sj.mp.4001943

Crider, A., Ahmed, A. O., and Pillai, A. (2017). Altered expression of endoplasmic reticulum stress-related genes in the middle frontal cortex of subjects with autism spectrum disorder. *Mol. Neuropsychiatry* 3, 85–91. doi: 10.1159/000477212

Dawson, G. (2013). Early intensive behavioral intervention appears beneficial for young children with autism spectrum disorders. *J. Pediatr.* 162, 1080–1081. doi: 10.1016/j.jpeds.2013.02.049

Dawson, G., Jones, E. J., Merkle, K., Venema, K., Lowy, R., Faja, S., et al. (2012). Early behavioral intervention is associated with normalized brain activity in young children with autism. *J. Am. Acad. Child Adolesc. Psychiatry* 51, 1150–1159. doi: 10.1016/j.jaac.2012.08.018

Enstrom, A. M., Onore, C. E., Van de Water, J. A., and Ashwood, P. (2010). Differential monocyte responses to TLR ligands in children with autism spectrum disorders. *Brain Behav. Immun.* 24, 64–71. doi: 10.1016/j.bbi.2009.08.001

Faras, H., Al Ateeqi, N., and Tidmarsh, L. (2010). Autism spectrum disorders. *Ann. Saudi Med.* 30, 295–300. doi: 10.4103/0256-4947.65261

Feng, C., Chen, Y., Pan, J., Yang, A., Niu, L., Min, J., et al. (2017). Redox proteomic identification of carbonylated proteins in autism plasma: insight into oxidative stress and its related biomarkers in autism. *Clin. Proteomics* 14:2. doi: 10.1186/s12014-017-9138-0

Folstein, S. E., and Rosen-Sheidley, B. (2001). Genetics of autism: complex aetiology for a heterogeneous disorder. *Nat. Rev. Genet.* 2, 943–955. doi: 10.1038/35103559

Fox, R. M., and Andrew, D. J. (2015). Transcriptional regulation of secretory capacity by bZip transcription factors. *Front. Biol.* 10, 28–51. doi: 10.1007/s11515-014-1338-7

Frye, R. E., and Rossignol, D. A. (2011). Mitochondrial dysfunction can connect the diverse medical symptoms associated with autism spectrum disorders. *Pediatr. Res.* 69, 41R–71R. doi: 10.1203/pdr.0b013e318212f16b

Fujita, E., Dai, H., Tanabe, Y., Zhiling, Y., Yamagata, T., Miyakawa, T., et al. (2010). Autism spectrum disorder is related to endoplasmic reticulum stress induced by mutations in the synaptic cell adhesion molecule, CADM1. *Cell Death Dis.* 1:e47. doi: 10.1038/cddis.2010.23

Ghosh, M., Gerber, C., Rahman, M. M., Vernier, K. M., Pereira, F. E., Subramani, J., et al. (2014). Molecular mechanisms regulating CD13-mediated adhesion. *Immunology* 142, 636–647. doi: 10.1111/imm.12279

Glatt, S. J., Tsuang, M. T., Winn, M., Chandler, S. D., Collins, M., Lopez, L., et al. (2012). Blood-based gene expression signatures of infants and toddlers with autism. *J. Am. Acad. Child Adolesc. Psychiatry* 51, 934.e2–944.e2. doi: 10.1016/j.jaac.2012.07.007

Goines, P. E., and Ashwood, P. (2013). Cytokine dysregulation in autism spectrum disorders (ASD): possible role of the environment. *Neurotoxicol. Teratol.* 36, 67–81. doi: 10.1016/j.ntt.2012.07.006

Hayashi-Takagi, A., Vawter, M. P., and Iwamoto, K. (2014). Peripheral biomarkers revisited: integrative profiling of peripheral samples for psychiatric research. *Biol. Psychiatry* 75, 920–928. doi: 10.1016/j.biopsych.2013.09.035

Hu, V. W. (2013). The expanding genomic landscape of autism: discovering the 'forest' beyond the 'trees'. *Future Neurol.* 8, 29–42. doi: 10.2217/fnl.12.83

Hu, V. W. (2014). *Frontiers in Autism Research new Horizons for Diagnosis and Treatment.* Hackensack, NJ: World Scientific.

Hu, V. W., Frank, B. C., Heine, S., Lee, N. H., and Quackenbush, J. (2006). Gene expression profiling of lymphoblastoid cell lines from monozygotic twins discordant in severity of autism reveals differential regulation of neurologically relevant genes. *BMC Genomics* 7:118. doi: 10.1186/1471-2164-7-118

Ibrahim, S., El-Waleely, T., Zakaria, N., and Ismail, R. (2015). A study of serum interleukin-12 in a sample of autistic children in Egypt. *Egypt. J. Psychiatry* 36:81. doi: 10.4103/1110-1105.158115

Iqbal, J., Zhang, K., Jin, N., Zhao, Y., Liu, Q., Ni, J., et al. (2018). Effect of sodium selenate on hippocampal proteome of 3×Tg-AD mice-exploring the antioxidant dogma of selenium against Alzheimer's disease. *ACS Chem. Neurosci.* 9, 1637–1651. doi: 10.1021/acschemneuro.8b00034

Jyonouchi, H., Geng, L., Streck, D. L., and Toruner, G. A. (2011). Children with autism spectrum disorders (ASD) who exhibit chronic gastrointestinal (GI) symptoms and marked fluctuation of behavioral symptoms exhibit distinct innate immune abnormalities and transcriptional profiles of peripheral blood (PB) monocytes. *J. Neuroimmunol.* 238, 73–80. doi: 10.1016/j.jneuroim.2011.07.001

Krishnan, A., Zhang, R., Yao, V., Theesfeld, C. L., Wong, A. K., Tadych, A., et al. (2016). Genome-wide prediction and functional characterization of the genetic basis of autism spectrum disorder. *Nat. Neurosci.* 19, 1454–1462. doi: 10.1038/nn.4353

Kuwano, Y., Kamio, Y., Kawai, T., Katsuura, S., Inada, N., Takaki, A., et al. (2011). Autism-associated gene expression in peripheral leucocytes commonly observed between subjects with autism and healthy women having autistic children. *PLoS One* 6:e24723. doi: 10.1371/journal.pone.0024723

Lawrence, T. (2009). The nuclear factor NF-κB pathway in inflammation. *Cold Spring Harb. Perspect. Biol.* 1:a001651. doi: 10.1101/cshperspect.a001651

Masi, A., DeMayo, M. M., Glozier, N., and Guastella, A. J. (2017a). An overview of autism spectrum disorder, heterogeneity and treatment options. *Neurosci. Bull.* 33, 183–193. doi: 10.1007/s12264-017-0100-y

Masi, A., Glozier, N., Dale, R., and Guastella, A. J. (2017b). The immune system, cytokines, and biomarkers in autism spectrum disorder. *Neurosci. Bull.* 33, 194–204. doi: 10.1007/s12264-017-0103-8

Masi, A., Quintana, D. S., Glozier, N., Lloyd, A. R., Hickie, I. B., and Guastella, A. J. (2015). Cytokine aberrations in autism spectrum disorder: a systematic review and meta-analysis. *Mol. Psychiatry* 20, 440–446. doi: 10.1038/mp.2014.59

Morgan, J. T., Chana, G., Pardo, C. A., Achim, C., Semendeferi, K., Buckwalter, J., et al. (2010). Microglial activation and increased microglial density observed in the dorsolateral prefrontal cortex in autism. *Biol. Psychiatry* 68, 368–376. doi: 10.1016/j.biopsych.2010.05.024

Naik, U. S., Gangadharan, C., Abbagani, K., Nagalla, B., Dasari, N., and Manna, S. K. (2011). A study of nuclear transcription factor-kappa B in childhood autism. *PLoS One* 6:e19488. doi: 10.1371/journal.pone.0019488

Nilsson, C., Aboud, S., Karlén, K., Hejdeman, B., Urassa, W., and Biberfeld, G. (2008). Optimal blood mononuclear cell isolation procedures for γ interferonenzyme-linked immunospot testing of healthy Swedish and Tanzanian subjects. *Clin. Vaccine Immunol.* 15, 585–589. doi: 10.1128/cvi.00161-07

Nishimura, Y., Martin, C. L., Vazquez-Lopez, A., Spence, S. J., Alvarez-Retuerto, A. I., Siqman, M., et al. (2007). Genome-wide expression profiling of lymphoblastoid cell lines distinguishes different forms of autism and reveals shared pathways. *Hum. Mol. Genet.* 16, 1682–1698. doi: 10.1093/hmg/ddm116

Rangasamy, S., D'Mello, S. R., and Narayanan, V. (2013). Epigenetics, autism spectrum, and neurodevelopmental disorders. *Neurotherapeutics* 10, 742–756. doi: 10.1007/s13311-013-0227-0

Réus, G. Z., Fries, G. R., Stertz, L., Badawy, M., Passos, I. C., Barichello, T., et al. (2015). The role of inflammation and microglial activation in the pathophysiology of psychiatric disorders. *Neuroscience* 300, 141–154. doi: 10.1016/j.neuroscience.2015.05.018

Rodriguez, J. I., and Kern, J. K. (2011). Evidence of microglial activation in autism and its possible role in brain underconnectivity. *Neuron Glia Biol.* 7, 205–213. doi: 10.1017/s1740925x12000142

Rossignol, D. A., and Frye, R. E. (2012). Mitochondrial dysfunction in autism spectrum disorders: a systematic review and meta-analysis. *Mol. Psychiatry* 17, 290–314. doi: 10.1038/mp.2010.136

Rossignol, D. A., and Frye, R. E. (2014). Evidence linking oxidative stress, mitochondrial dysfunction and inflammation in the brain of individuals with autism. *Front. Physiol.* 5:150. doi: 10.3389/fphys.2014.00150

Shen, L., Liao, L., Chen, C., Guo, Y., Song, D., Wang, Y., et al. (2017). Proteomics analysis of blood serums from Alzheimer's disease patients using iTRAQ labeling technology. *J. Alzheimers Dis.* 56, 361–378. doi: 10.3233/jad-160913

Shen, L., Zhang, K., Feng, C., Chen, Y., Li, S., Iqbal, J., et al. (2018). iTRAQ based proteomic analysis reveals protein profile in plasma from children with autism. *Proteomics Clin. Appl.* 12:e1700085. doi: 10.1002/prca.201700085

Shen, L., Zhao, Y., Zhang, H., Feng, C., Gao, Y., Zhao, D., et al. (2019). "Advances in biomarker studies in autism spectrum disorders," in *Reviews on Biomarker Studies in Psychiatric and Neurodegenerative Disorders*, ed. P. Guest (Cham: Springer), 207–233.

Siniscalco, D., Sapone, A., Giordano, C., Cirillo, A., de Novellis, V., de Magistris, L., et al. (2012). The expression of caspases is enhanced in peripheral blood mononuclear cells of autism spectrum disorder patients. *J. Autism Dev. Disord.* 42, 1403–1410. doi: 10.1007/s10803-011-1373-z

Sullivan, P. F., Fan, C., and Perou, C. M. (2006). Evaluating the comparability of gene expression in blood and brain. *Am. J. Med. Genet. B Neuropsychiatr. Genet.* 141B, 261–268. doi: 10.1002/ajmg.b.30272

Sun, N., Sun, W., Li, S., Yang, J., Yang, L., Quan, G., et al. (2015). Proteomics analysis of cellular proteins co-immunoprecipitated with nucleoprotein of influenza A virus (H7N9). *Int. J. Mol. Sci.* 16, 25982–25998. doi: 10.3390/ijms161125934

Suzuki, K., Sugihara, G., Ouchi, Y., Nakamura, K., Futatsubashi, M., Takebayashi, K., et al. (2013). Microglial activation in young adults with autism spectrum disorder. *JAMA Psychiatry* 70, 49–58. doi: 10.1001/jamapsychiatry.2013.272

Sweeten, T. L., Posey, D. J., and McDougle, C. J. (2003). High blood monocyte counts and neopterin levels in children with autistic disorder. *Am. J. Psychiatry* 160, 1691–1693. doi: 10.1176/appi.ajp.160.9.1691

Tambor, V., Hunter, C., Seymour, S. L., Kacerovsky, M., Stulik, J., and Lenco, J. (2016). Combination of isobaric tagging reagents and cysteinyl peptide enrichment for in-depth quantification. Available online at: https://sciex.com/Documents/tech%20notes/cysteine-targeting_TechNote_4630212.pdf.

Trobiani, L., Favaloro, F. L., Di Castro, M. A., Di Mattia, M., Cariello, M., Miranda, E., et al. (2018). UPR activation specifically modulates glutamate neurotransmission in the cerebellum of a mouse model of autism. *Neurobiol. Dis.* 120, 139–150. doi: 10.1016/j.nbd.2018.08.026

Ulbrich, L., Favaloro, F. L., Trobiani, L., Marchetti, V., Patel, V., Pascucci, T., et al. (2016). Autism-associated R451C mutation in neuroligin3 leads to activation of the unfolded protein response in a PC12 Tet-On inducible system. *Biochem. J.* 473, 423–434. doi: 10.1042/bj20150274

Vargas, D. L., Nascimbene, C., Krishnan, C., Zimmerman, A. W., and Pardo, C. A. (2005). Neuroglial activation and neuroinflammation in the brain of patients with autism. *Ann. Neurol.* 57, 67–81. doi: 10.1002/ana.20315

Voineagu, I., Wang, X., Johnston, P., Lowe, J. K., Tian, Y., Horvath, S., et al. (2011). Transcriptomic analysis of autistic brain reveals convergent molecular pathology. *Nature* 474, 380–384. doi: 10.1038/nature10110

Wang, S., and Kaufman, R. J. (2012). The impact of the unfolded protein response on human disease. *J. Cell Biol.* 197, 857–867. doi: 10.1083/jcb.201110131

Wang, M., and Kaufman, R. J. (2016). Protein misfolding in the endoplasmic reticulum as a conduit to human disease. *Nature* 529, 326–335. doi: 10.1038/nature17041

Xu, N., Li, X., and Zhong, Y. (2015). Inflammatory cytokines: potential biomarkers of immunologic dysfunction in autism spectrum disorders. *Mediators Inflamm.* 2015:531518. doi: 10.1155/2015/531518

Young, A. M., Campbell, E., Lynch, S., Suckling, J., and Powis, S. J. (2011). Aberrant NF-kappaB expression in autism spectrum condition: a mechanism for neuroinflammation. *Front. Psychiatry* 2:27. doi: 10.3389/fpsyt.2011.00027

Zhang, K., and Kaufman, R. J. (2008). From endoplasmic-reticulum stress to the inflammatory response. *Nature* 454, 455–462. doi: 10.1038/nature07203

Zhao, D., Shen, L., Wei, Y., Xie, J., Chen, S., Liang, Y., et al. (2017). Identification of candidate biomarkers for the prediccearly stages of pregnancy using iTRAQ quantitative proteomics. *Proteomics Clin. Appl.* 11, 7–8. doi: 10.1002/prca.201600152

7

IRSp53 Deletion in Glutamatergic and GABAergic Neurons and in Male and Female Mice Leads to Distinct Electrophysiological and Behavioral Phenotypes

Yangsik Kim[1†], Young Woo Noh[2†], Kyungdeok Kim[2], Esther Yang[3], Hyun Kim[3] and Eunjoon Kim[2,4]*

[1]Graduate School of Medical Science and Engineering, Korea Advanced Institute of Science and Technology (KAIST), Daejeon, South Korea, [2]Department of Biological Sciences, Korea Advanced Institute of Science and Technology (KAIST), Daejeon, South Korea, [3]Department of Anatomy, College of Medicine, Korea University, Seoul, South Korea, [4]Center for Synaptic Brain Dysfunctions, Institute for Basic Science (IBS), Daejeon, South Korea

Correspondence:
Eunjoon Kim
kime@kaist.ac.kr

[†]These authors have contributed equally to this work

IRSp53 (also known as BAIAP2) is an abundant excitatory postsynaptic scaffolding protein implicated in autism spectrum disorders (ASD), schizophrenia, and attention-deficit/hyperactivity disorder (ADHD). IRSp53 is expressed in different cell types across different brain regions, although it remains unclear how IRSp53 deletion in different cell types affects brain functions and behaviors in mice. Here, we deleted IRSp53 in excitatory and inhibitory neurons in mice and compared resulting phenotypes in males and females. IRSp53 deletion in excitatory neurons driven by *Emx1* leads to strong social deficits and hyperactivity without affecting anxiety-like behavior, whereas IRSp53 deletion in inhibitory neurons driven by *Viaat* has minimal impacts on these behaviors in male mice. In female mice, excitatory neuronal IRSp53 deletion induces hyperactivity but moderate social deficits. Excitatory neuronal IRSp53 deletion in male mice induces an increased ratio of evoked excitatory and inhibitory synaptic transmission (E/I ratio) in layer V pyramidal neurons in the prelimbic region of the medial prefrontal cortex (mPFC), whereas the same mutation does not alter the E/I ratio in female neurons. These results suggest that IRSp53 deletion in excitatory and inhibitory neurons and in male and female mice has distinct impacts on behaviors and synaptic transmission.

Keywords: autism, synapse, IRSp53, mPFC, social interaction, hyperactivity

INTRODUCTION

IRSp53 (encoded by *Baiap2*) is a multi-domain scaffolding or adaptor protein that is abundantly present in the postsynaptic density of excitatory synapses (Sheng and Kim, 2011; Kang et al., 2016). IRSp53 directly interacts with PSD-95 and Shank, excitatory postsynaptic scaffolding proteins known to regulate synapse assembly and function and implicated in various brain disorders, including autism spectrum disorders (ASD; Sheng and Sala, 2001; Sheng and Hoogenraad, 2007; Jiang and Ehlers, 2013; Sala et al., 2015; Monteiro and Feng, 2017).

Functionally, IRSp53 regulates dendritic spines and synaptic function through its ability to coordinate Rac and Cdc42 small GTPase-dependent modulation of actin filaments (Kang et al., 2016), the main cytoskeleton of dendritic spines (Sala and Segal, 2014).

Global deletion of IRSp53 in mice decreases dendritic spine density in the cortex and induces abnormal behaviors, including social-interaction deficits, hyperactivity, and cognitive impairments (Sawallisch et al., 2009; Chung et al., 2015), in line with the reported implication of IRSp53/BAIAP2 in ASD (Celestino-Soper et al., 2011; Levy et al., 2011; Toma et al., 2011), schizophrenia (Fromer et al., 2014; Purcell et al., 2014), and attention-deficit/hyperactivity disorder (ADHD; Ribasés et al., 2009; Liu et al., 2013). In addition, global IRSp53 deletion in mice abnormally increases the function of N-methyl-D-aspartate receptors (NMDARs) in the hippocampus, and the NMDAR antagonist memantine improves social deficits in IRSp53-mutant mice (Kim et al., 2009; Chung et al., 2015; Bobsin and Kreienkamp, 2016), supporting the growing importance of NMDAR dysfunction in ASD (Lee et al., 2015). A previous study has shown that IRSp53 is expressed in various cell types, including excitatory neurons in the neocortex and GABAergic neurons in the striatum and cerebellum (Burette et al., 2014). However, the impacts of cell type-specific IRSp53 expression on brain functions and behaviors, including social interaction, remain essentially unknown.

Here, we restricted *Irsp53* knockout (KO) in dorsal telencephalic glutamatergic neurons using *Emx1*-Cre mice and GABAergic neurons using *Viaat*-Cre mice, and found that glutamatergic *Irsp53* KO led to social deficits and hyperactivity associated with increased ratio of evoked excitatory and inhibitory synaptic transmission (E/I ratio) in the medial prefrontal cortex (mPFC) of male mice. In female mice, glutamatergic *Irsp53* KO led to moderate social deficits that are associated with an unaltered cortical E/I ratio.

MATERIALS AND METHODS

Animals

Mice were bred and maintained according to the Requirements of Animal Research at KAIST. All procedures were approved and followed by the Committee of Animal Research at KAIST (KA201). We used male mice for behavioral, electrophysiological, and other (biochemical, FISH, and tdTomato expression in Emx1- and Viaat-Cre mice) experiments; female mice were also used for behavioral tests [three-chamber and open-field test (OFT)] and electrophysiology.

Mice were fed *ad libitum*, and 2–4 mice were housed together in a cage under a 12-h light-dark cycle. There were no differences in the body weights of age-matched mouse groups. Mice were identified by polymerase chain reaction (PCR) genotyping using the following PCR primers: IRSp53 flox AGGAGGTGTTTCTGCTCTGG/AATAGCAGTCTGGGGTC TGG; Cre CGTACTGACGGTGGGAGAAT/TGCATGATCT CCGGTATTGA.

Behavioral Assays

All behavioral assays were performed using age-matched C57BL6/J mice (8–16 weeks) generated by Cre/+; *Irsp53*$^{flox/+}$ × *Irsp53*$^{flox/flox}$ mating. All behavioral assays were performed during light-off periods. The light condition for all behavioral assays was ~120 lux. There were at least 1 day-long rest periods between tests. The behavioral assays were performed in the order of the open field test, elevated plus-maze (EPM) test, and three-chamber social interaction test. Behavioral assays were recorded as video files (.avi format) and analyzed by Ethovision XT 10 (Noldus, The Netherlands).

Three-Chamber Social Interaction Test

The three-chambered social-interaction test was performed as described previously (Moy et al., 2004; Silverman et al., 2010). The apparatus had the following dimensions; W 60 × H 40 × D 20 cm for the whole apparatus, and W 20 × H 20 × D 20 cm for each chamber. The side chambers contained an aluminum grid with a curved face to confine the mouse/object. The assay consisted of three sessions. During the first 10-min session, a subject mouse was allowed to freely explore all three chambers for habituation. Then the mouse was confined briefly in the center chamber, while a novel object and a WT stranger mouse, stranger 1, were placed in the side chambers behind the aluminum grid in a random manner to minimize the influences of side bias. The subject mouse was then allowed to freely explore all three chambers for 10 min. Before the last session, the subject mouse was again gently guided to the center chamber while the object was replaced with another WT mouse, stranger 2. The subject mouse was again allowed to freely explore all three chambers for 10 min.

In a modified three-chamber social interaction test performed for five consecutive days to measure social novelty in mice (Bariselli et al., 2018), we used the same apparatus and social interaction scheme. This test used an empty aluminum grid without an object, unlike the conventional three-chamber social interaction test. A subject mouse was exposed to the first stranger for the first 4 days to maximize habituation to the stranger, and the stranger was placed in alternate chambers to suppress the effect of side bias. One day 5, the first stranger was replaced with the second stranger to measure social-novelty recognition.

All stranger mice were age-matched males and were habituated to the side chambers in advance during the previous day for 30 min. The positions of the object and stranger mouse were alternated between tests to minimize the influences of side preference.

Open-Field Test

Mice were placed in the center region of an open-field box (40 × 40 × 40 cm). Open-field locomotor activities were measured for 60 min.

Elevated Plus-Maze Test

An elevated-plus maze was made of gray acryl with four arms, each 30-cm long and 5-cm wide (Walf and Frye, 2007). The height of the maze was elevated 75 cm above the ground. The light condition of closed arms was ~0 lux. A test mouse was placed in the center of the maze at the junction of the four arms in the beginning and was allowed to freely explore the maze for 10 min.

Whole-Cell Recordings

Coronal slices (mPFC) were prepared using a vibratome (VT1200S, Leica, Germany) in ice-cold dissection buffer (in mM: 212 sucrose, 25 $NaHCO_3$, 5 KCl, 1.25 NaH_2PO_4, 10 D-glucose, 2 sodium pyruvate, 1.2 sodium ascorbate, 3.5 $MgCl_2$, 0.5 $CaCl_2$ bubbled with 95% O2/5% CO_2). The slices were recovered at 32 °C in normal artificial cerebrospinal fluid (ACSF; in mM: 125 NaCl, 25 $NaHCO_3$, 2.5 KCl, 1.25 NaH_2PO_4, 10 D-glucose, 1.3 $MgCl_2$, 2.5 $CaCl_2$) and thereafter maintain at room temperature. Cells were visualized using infrared differential interference contrast video microscopy (Olympus, BX50XI). Whole-cell current-clamp recordings were made by using a MultiClamp 700B amplifier (Molecular Devices).

For voltage-clamp recordings, recording pipettes (3–5 MΩ) were filled with a solution containing (in mM) 120 $CsMeSO_4$, 15 CsCl, 10 TEA-Cl, 8 NaCl, 10 HEPES, 0.25 EGTA, 5 QX-314, 4 MgATP, and 0.3 NaGTP, pH 7.25–7.35 (280–300 mOsm; Rothwell et al., 2014). Signals were filtered at 2 kHz and digitized at 10 kHz. Miniature excitatory postsynaptic currents (mEPSCs) were recorded in the presence of AP5 (50 μM) and tetrodotoxin (1 μM) at the holding potential of −70 mV. Miniature inhibitory postsynaptic currents (mIPSCs) were recorded at the holding potential of 0 mV, as described previously (Liang et al., 2015). For voltage-clamp recordings with electrical stimulation (NMDA/AMPA ratio, paired-pulse ratio, and excitatory/inhibitory ratio), a stimulus pipette was located 100 μm toward the pia from the patched cell. Stimulus electrode was soaked in the abovementioned bath solution, and 1/15 Hz stimulation was used to obtain baseline responses (20/8/20 for NMDA/AMPA ratio, paired-pulse ratio, and excitatory/inhibitory ratio, respectively). Stimulus intensity was modified in different experiments (NMDA/AMPA ratio, <10 pA at 50 ms after stimulation; paired-pulse ratio, 60 pA < EPSC1 < 200 pA).

For current-clamp recordings, recording pipettes (3–5 MΩ) were filled with a solution containing (in mM) 120 Kgluconate, 20 HEPES, 0.4 EGTA, 2.8 NaCl, 5 TEA-Cl, 2.5 MgATP, and 0.25 NaGTP, pH 7.25–7.35 (280–300 mOsm). Picrotoxin (100 μM) and NBQX (10 μM) were present throughout the experiments to block inhibitory and excitatory synaptic transmissions, respectively. If the series resistance changed by more than 20%, data were not included in the analysis. Membrane potentials were not corrected for junction potentials (estimated to be 10 mV). To obtain sustained firings, a series of current (1 s duration, 50 pA steps for mPFC) was injected. To measure action potential thresholds, a series of current steps (2 ms duration at 2.5 Hz, 0–2,500 pA range, +10 pA step increments) were injected into patched neurons until an action potential was generated. To measure the input resistance, hyperpolarizing current steps (1 s duration, 0 to −100 pA, −25 pA step increments) were injected into patched neurons. All voltage measures were taken after neurons had reached a stable response (Chen et al., 2013).

Immunoblotting and Immunofluorescence

For immunoblotting experiments, a fresh brain was homogenized with ice-cold lysis buffer containing 320 mM sucrose, 10 mM HEPES pH 7.4, 5 mM EDTA, and protease inhibitors. For immunofluorescence experiments, isoflurane-anesthetized mice were transcardially perfused with 4% paraformaldehyde in phosphate-buffered saline (PFA/PBS), followed by brain removal and incubation in 4% PFA/PBS for 24 h for fixation. Fixed brains were sectioned (100 μm) using a vibratome (VT1200S, Leica, Germany) and subjected to immunofluorescence staining for IRSp53. The following antibodies were purchased commercially: BAIAP2/IRSp53 antibody (1:1,000, Atlas, rabbit, HPA023310), and α-tubulin antibody (1:10,000, Sigma, mouse, T9026). For immunoblotting, secondary antibodies for BAIAP2/IRSp53 and β-tubulin antibodies were donkey anti-rabbit antibody with 800 nm detection (LiCor, 1:10,000) and donkey anti-mouse antibody with HRP (Jackson, 1:10,000), respectively.

Fluorescent *in situ* Hybridization

Frozen sections (14 μm thick) were cut coronally through the hippocampal formation. The sections were thaw-mounted onto Superfrost Plus Microscope Slides (Thermo Fisher Scientific, Waltham, MA, USA; 12-550-15). The sections were fixed in 4% formaldehyde for 10 min, dehydrated in increasing concentrations of ethanol for 5 min, and finally air-dried. Tissues were then pretreated for protease digestion for 10 min at room temperature. For RNA detection, incubations with different amplifier solutions were performed in a HybEZ hybridization oven (ACDBio, Newark, CA, USA) at 40°C. The probes used in this study were three synthetic oligonucleotides complementary to the nucleotide (nt) sequence 2–1,268 of Mm-Baiap2-C1, nt 464–1,415 of Mm-Slc17a7/Vglut1-C2, nt 1986–2,998 of Mm-Slc17a6/Vglut2-C3, nt 62–3,113 of Mm-Gad1-C3, nt 552–1,506 of Mm-Gad2-C2 (ACDBio, Newark, CA, USA). The labeled probes were conjugated to Atto 550 (C1), Alexa Fluor 488 (C2), and Atto 647 (C3). The sections were hybridized at 40°C with labeled probe mixtures (C1 + C2 + C3) per slide for 2 h. Then the non-specifically hybridized probes were removed by washing the sections, three times each in 1× wash buffer at room temperature for 2 min. Amplification steps involved sequential incubations with Amplifier 1-FL for 30 min, Amplifier 2-FL for 15 min, Amplifier 3-FL for 30 min, and Amplifier 4 Alt B-FL at 40°C for 15 min. Each amplifier solution was removed by washing three times with 1× wash buffer for 2 min at room temperature. Fluorescent images were acquired using TCS SP8 Dichroic/CS (Leica), and the ImageJ program (NIH) was used to analyze the images.

Statistics

Statistical data analysis was performed using Prism 6 (GraphPad). Data normality was determined using the Shapiro-Wilk normality test. Data with normal distribution were analyzed using Student's *t*-test and analysis of variance (ANOVA), followed by *post hoc* tests. Data failing the normality test were analyzed using the Mann–Whitney test. ROUT method was used to exclude outliers with a Q coefficient of 1%. Exact

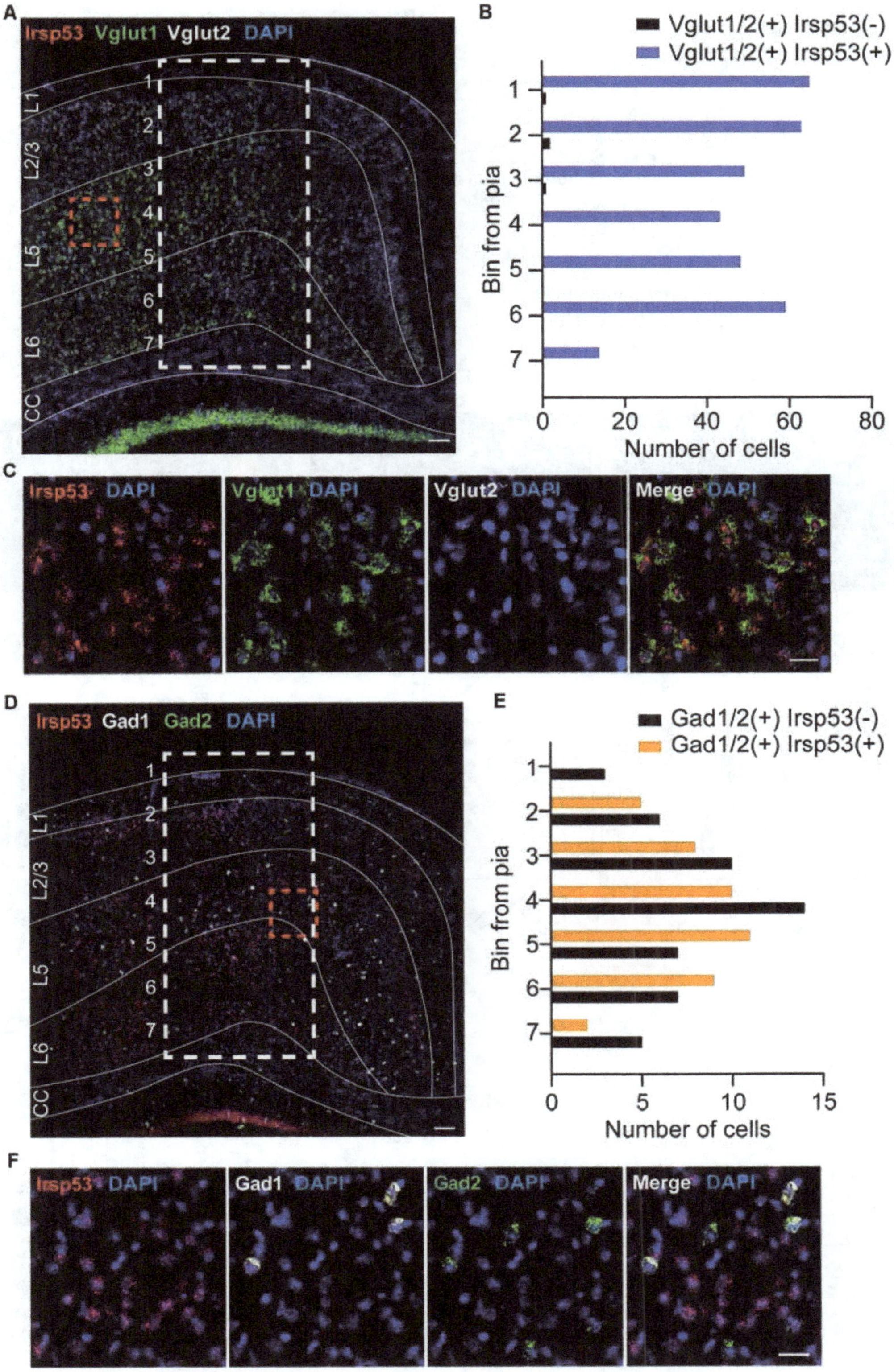

FIGURE 1 | *Irsp53* mRNAs are primarily detected in glutamatergic but minimally in GABAergic neurons in the cortex. **(A–F)** Coronal sections of WT mice (8 weeks) were subjected to fluorescence *in situ* hybridization. Note that *Irsp53/Baiap2* mRNAs are detected in *Vglut1/2*-positive glutamatergic neurons but minimally in *Gad1/2*-positive GABAergic neurons in the motor and somatosensory cortex. DAPI was used for nuclear staining. Red dashed line boxes were enlarged to show the levels of neuronal colabelings, and white dashed line boxes with subdivisions across cortical depth were used to quantify the colabelings. L1, cortical layer 1; CC, corpus callosum. Scale bar, 100 μm **(A,D)** and 25 μm **(C,F)**.

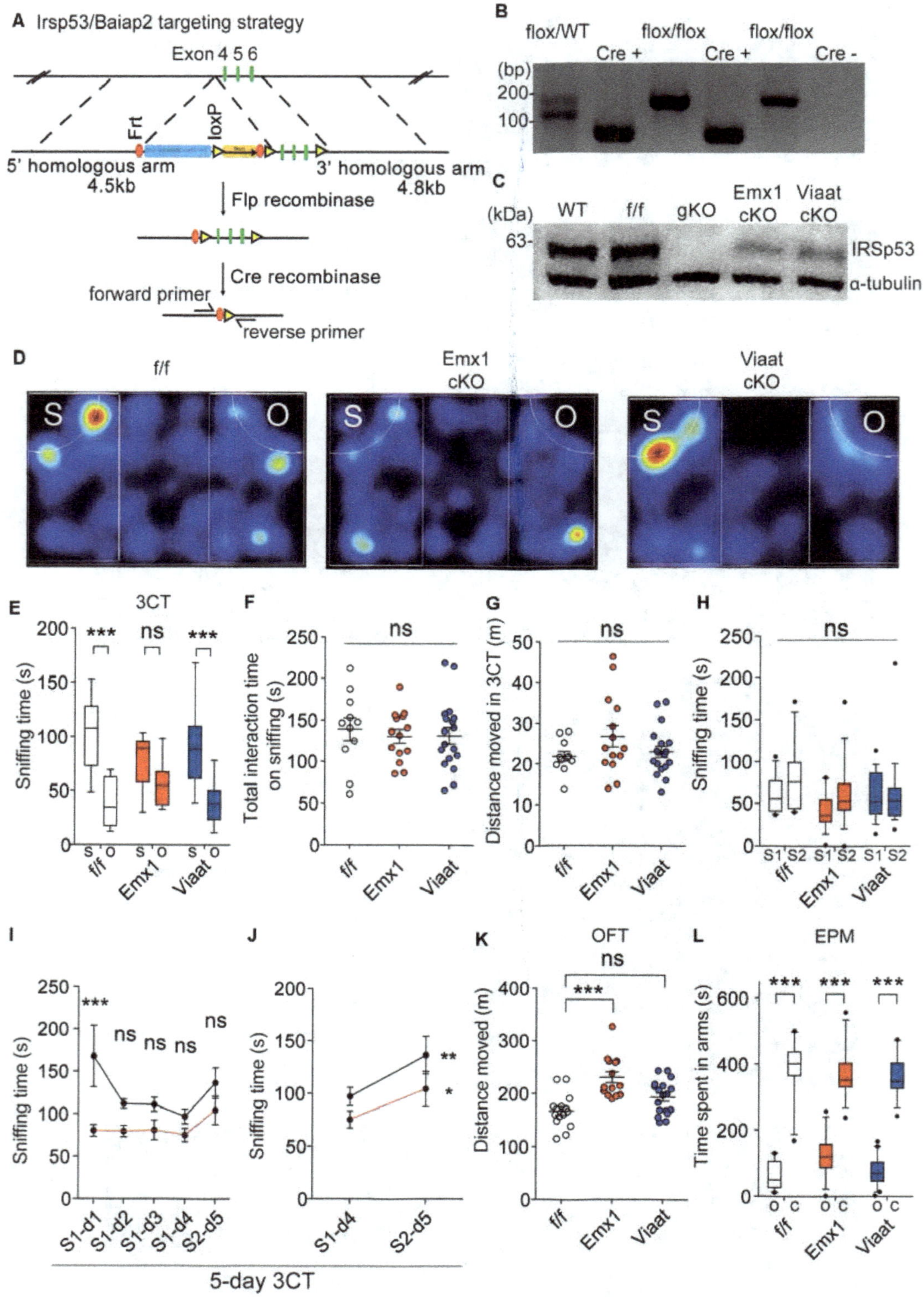

FIGURE 2 | *Irsp53* deletion in glutamatergic but not GABAergic neurons induces social deficits and hyperactivity. **(A)** Schematic for conditional *Irsp53/Baiap2* knockout (KO). **(B)** Polymerase chain reaction (PCR) genotyping of *Irsp53*$^{fl/fl}$ mice and conditional *Irsp53*-KO mice (*Emx1-Cre;Irsp53*$^{fl/fl}$ or *Viaat-Cre;Irsp53*$^{fl/fl}$ mice) using primer sets directed for the Irsp53/Baiap2 allele and Cre recombinase. The two bands in the WT/flox lane represent PCR products from *Irsp53* alleles with and without the Frt + LoxP sites. **(C)** Levels of IRSp53 proteins in global IRSp53-KO (gKO) mice, *Emx1-Cre;Irsp53*$^{fl/fl}$ mice (Emx1 cKO), and *Viaat-Cre;Irsp53*$^{fl/fl}$ mice (Viaat cKO). Whole-brain lysates from mice at P56 were used for immunoblotting. **(D–G)** Suppressed social interaction in *Emx1-Cre;Irsp53*$^{fl/fl}$ but not

(Continued)

FIGURE 2 | Continued
Viaat-Cre;Irsp53$^{fl/fl}$ mice (2 months; males) in the three-chamber social interaction test (3CT), as shown by time spent sniffing social/object target, as compared with control *Irsp53*$^{fl/fl}$ mice. S, social target (stranger mouse); O, object target. Note that total time spent sniffing and distance moved in the 3CT apparatus are normal in the mutant mice. n = 11 mice (*Irsp53*$^{fl/fl}$ or f/f), 14 mice (Emx1-cKO), and 18 mice (Viaat-cKO), ***$P < 0.001$; ns, not significant, two-way analysis of variance (ANOVA) with Bonferroni's test. 3CT, interaction factor/$F_{(2,94)} = 5.317$, chamber $F_{(1,94)} = 67.54$, genotype $F_{(2,94)} = 0.7795$; total time spent sniffing, $F_{(2,40)} = 0.1732$; total distance moved, $F_{(2,40)} = 1.824$. **(H)** Lack of social novelty recognition in *Emx1-Cre;Irsp53*$^{fl/fl}$, *Viaat-Cre;Irsp53*$^{fl/fl}$, and control (*Irsp53*$^{fl/fl}$) mice (2 months; males) in the three-chamber test. S1, old stranger; S2, new stranger. n = 11 mice (*Irsp53*$^{fl/fl}$ or f/f), 14 mice (Emx1-cKO), and 18 mice (Viaat-cKO), ns, not significant, two-way ANOVA with Bonferroni's test, interaction $F_{(2,80)} = 0.8983$, chamber $F_{(1,80)} = 3.370$, genotype $F_{(2,80)} = 1.632$. **(I,J)** Normal social novelty recognition in *Emx1-Cre;Irsp53*$^{fl/fl}$ mice (2 months; males) in the 5-day three-chamber test, as shown by the difference in sniffing time for an old stranger (S1) and a new stranger (S2) on day 4 and 5, respectively. Note that control (*Irsp53*$^{fl/fl}$) mice show normal levels of habituation to S1, as shown by the time sniffing S1 across days 1–4 that becomes insignificant on days 2–4. n = 8 mice (*Irsp53*$^{fl/fl}$ or f/f), eight mice (Emx1-cKO), *$P < 0.05$, **$P < 0.01$, ***$P < 0.001$; ns, not significant, two-way ANOVA with Bonferroni's test and repeated-measures AVOVA with Bonferroni's test. Five-day three-chamber test, day 1–5, interaction $F_{(4,28)} = 1.769$, time $F_{(4,28)} = 3.103$, genotype $F_{(1,7)} = 29.86$; day 4–5, interaction $F_{(1,7)} = 0.9518$, time $F_{(1,7)} = 8.614$, genotype $F_{(1,7)} = 11.62$. **(K)** Increased locomotor activity in *Emx1-Cre;Irsp53*$^{fl/fl}$ but not in *Viaat-Cre;Irsp53*$^{fl/fl}$ mice (2 months; males) in the open-field test (OFT). n = 15 mice (f/f), 14 mice (Emx1-cKO), and 18 mice (Viaat-cKO), ***$P < 0.001$; ns, not significant, one-way ANOVA with Bonferroni's test, $F_{(2,44)} = 12.60$. **(L)** Normal anxiety-like behavior in *Emx1-Cre;Irsp53*$^{fl/fl}$ and *Viaat-Cre;Irsp53*$^{fl/fl}$ mice (2 months; males) in the elevated plus-maze (EPM) test, as shown by time spent in open/closed arms. O, open arm; C, closed arm. n = 15 mice (f/f), 14 mice (Emx1-cKO), and 18 mice (Viaat-cKO), ***$P < 0.001$, two-way ANOVA with Bonferroni's test, interaction $F_{(2,88)} = 3.848$, arm $F_{(1,88)} = 485.2$, genotype $F_{(2,88)} = 1.518$.

numbers of mice used and the statistical details are shown in **Supplementary Table S1**.

RESULTS

Irsp53 mRNA Expression in Glutamatergic and GABAergic Neurons in the Cortex

To explore specific brain cell types that contribute to social deficits and hyperactivity observed in global *Irsp53*-KO mice (Chung et al., 2015), we first determined IRSp53 expression in glutamatergic and GABAergic neurons by *in situ* fluorescence hybridization. *Irsp53* mRNA was readily detected in *Vglut1/2*-positive glutamatergic neurons in the cortex, but it was minimally detectable in *Gad1/2*-positive GABAergic neurons (**Figures 1A–F**). Quantitative analysis indicated that colabelings of *Irsp53* and *Vglut1/2* mRNAs were not different across the depth of cortical layers, whereas colabelings of *Irsp53* and *Gad1/2* mRNAs, although sparse (~13% of the *Irsp53*-*Vglut1/2* colabelings in number), were stronger in middle layers. These results are consistent with the reported expression of IRSp53 protein primarily in glutamatergic but not GABAergic neurons in the cortex and hippocampus, although IRSp53 protein is also detectable in striatal and cerebellar GABAergic neurons (Burette et al., 2014).

Irsp53 Deletion in Dorsal Telencephalic Glutamatergic but Not GABAergic Neurons Induces Social Deficits and Hyperactivity

For conditional *Irsp53* KO in glutamatergic or GABAergic neurons, we generated a novel mouse line in which exons 4–6 of *Irsp53* are floxed (*Irsp53*$^{fl/fl}$ mice) and crossed them with *Emx1-Cre* (Jax005628; dorsal telencephalic glutamatergic; Gorski et al., 2002) and *Viaat-Cre* (Jax017535; Chao et al., 2010) mice, respectively (**Figure 2A**). The resulting conditional *Irsp53*-KO mouse lines, *Emx1-Cre; Irsp53*$^{fl/fl}$ and *Viaat-Cre; Irsp53*$^{fl/fl}$, were verified by PCR genotyping and immunoblot analysis (**Figures 2B,C**). IRSp53 protein levels in *Emx1-Cre; Irsp53*$^{fl/fl}$ and *Viaat-Cre; Irsp53*$^{fl/fl}$ whole brains were $\sim 29 \pm 4\%$ and $\sim 64 \pm 4\%$ of WT values, respectively. Appropriate expression of Cre in the mouse lines used in this study was confirmed by crossing with a reporter mouse line (Ai9 tdTomato line; JAX 007909; Madisen et al., 2010; **Supplementary Figure S1**).

In behavioral experiments performed using male mice, *Emx1-Cre;Irsp53*$^{fl/fl}$ mice displayed impaired social interaction in the three-chamber test compared with control (*Irsp53*$^{fl/fl}$) mice without Cre expression (**Figures 2D,E**). These changes did not accompany altered total social interaction or locomotor activity in the three-chamber apparatus (**Figures 2F,G**).

Changes in social novelty recognition during the three-chamber test could not be determined because control *Irsp53*$^{fl/fl}$ mice did not prefer to explore a novel stranger (**Figure 2H**). However, an additional test for social novelty recognition termed 5-day three-chamber test, where a subject mouse was exposed to the first stranger mouse for four consecutive days for full habituation followed by exposure to the second stranger mouse on day 5 (Bariselli et al., 2018), *Emx1-Cre;Irsp53*$^{fl/fl}$ mice displayed normal social novelty recognition that is comparable to that of control (*Irsp53*$^{fl/fl}$) mice (**Figures 2I,J**).

Emx1-Cre;Irsp53$^{fl/fl}$ mice displayed hyperactivity in the OFT but normal anxiety-like behavior in the EPM test (**Figures 2K,L**). *Viaat-Cre;Irsp53*$^{fl/fl}$ mice showed no detectable changes in social interaction, locomotor activity, or anxiety-like behavior (**Figures 2D,E,L**). Control (*Irsp53*$^{fl/fl}$) mice showed normal social interaction and locomotor activity, compared with WT mice (without *Irsp53*$^{fl/fl}$ and Cre alleles; **Supplementary Figures 2A,B**). In addition, mice expressing Cre alone (*Emx1-Cre* and *Viaat-Cre*) showed normal social interaction, locomotion, or anxiety-like behavior (**Supplementary Figures 2C–E**). Therefore, *Irsp53* KO in dorsal telencephalic glutamatergic, but not GABAergic, neurons leads to social deficits and hyperactivity in mice, similar to those in global *Irsp53*-KO mice (Chung et al., 2015).

Emx1-Cre; Irsp53$^{fl/fl}$ and *Viaat-Cre; Irsp53*$^{fl/fl}$ Mice Show Distinct Changes in Synaptic Transmission and Intrinsic Excitability in mPFC Pyramidal Neurons

To explore mechanisms underlying the social deficits and hyperactivity in *Emx1-Cre; Irsp53*$^{fl/fl}$ mice, we analyzed synaptic and neuronal properties in the mPFC, a brain region that displayed decreased excitatory synapse density in global *Irsp53*-

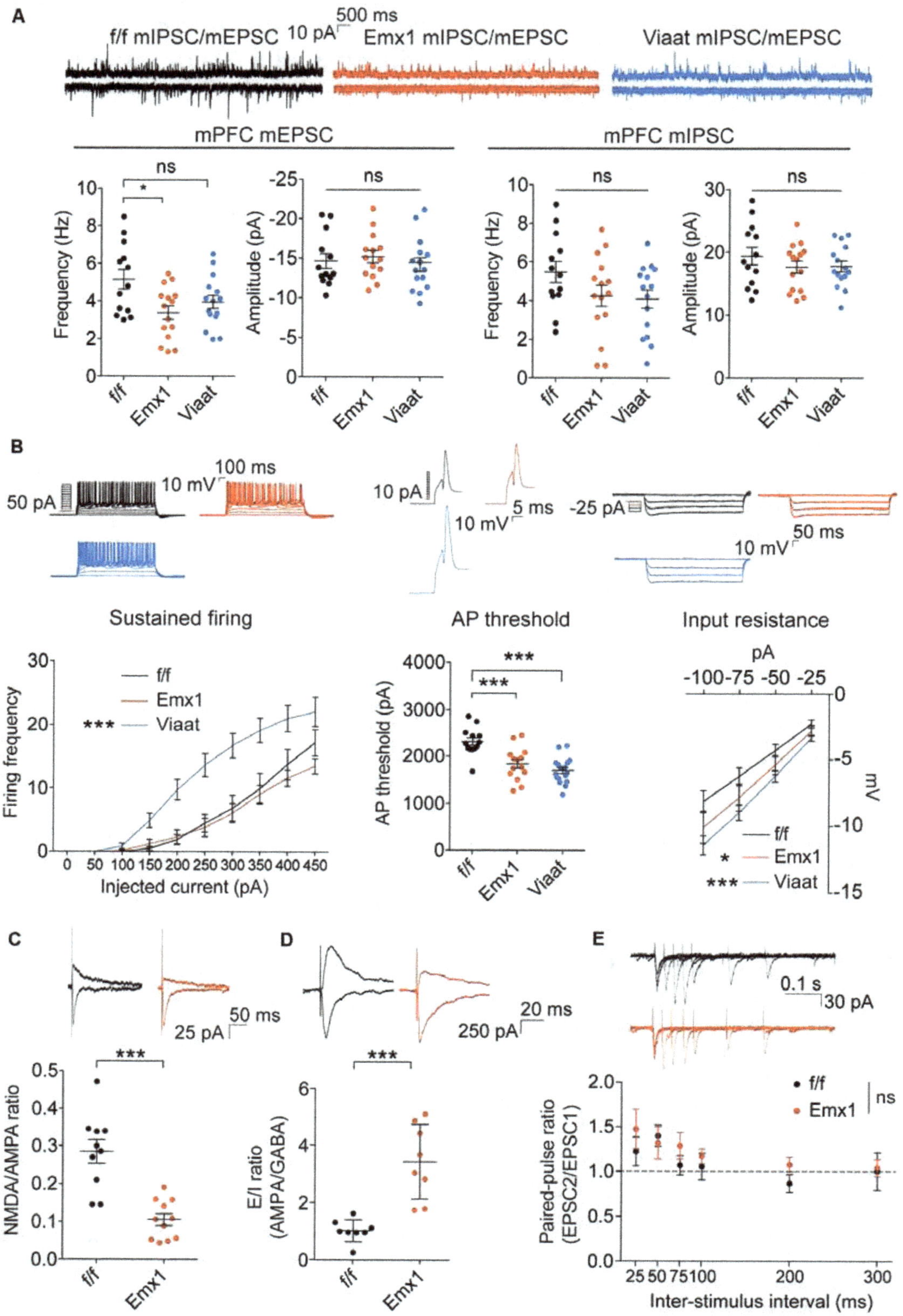

FIGURE 3 | *Emx1-Cre;Irsp53*$^{fl/fl}$ and *Viaat-Cre;Irsp53*$^{fl/fl}$ mice show distinct changes in synaptic transmission and intrinsic excitability in medial prefrontal cortex (mPFC) pyramidal neurons. **(A)** Miniature excitatory postsynaptic currents (mEPSCs) and miniature inhibitory postsynaptic currents (mIPSCs) in layer V pyramidal neurons in the prelimbic region of the mPFC in *Emx1-Cre;Irsp53*$^{fl/fl}$ and *Viaat-Cre;Irsp53*$^{fl/fl}$ mice (3 months; male). Note that the frequency of mEPSCs is significantly decreased in *Emx1-Cre;Irsp53*$^{fl/fl}$ mice. *n* = 13 neurons from three mice for f/f-mEPSC, 14, 3 for Emx1-mEPSC, 15, 3 for Viaat-mEPSC, 13, 3 for f/f-mIPSC, 15, 3 for

(*Continued*)

FIGURE 3 | Continued
Emx1-mIPSC, and 15, 3 for Viaat-mIPSC, $^{*}P < 0.05$, ns, not significant, one-way ANOVA with Bonferroni's test. mEPSC frequency, $F_{(2,39)} = 4.119$; mEPSC amplitude, $F_{(2,39)} = 0.342$; mIPSC frequency, $F_{(2,40)} = 2.012$; mIPSC amplitude, $F_{(2,40)} = 0.7806$. **(B)** Intrinsic excitability in layer V pyramidal neurons in the prelimbic region of the mPFC in *Emx1-Cre;Irsp53*$^{fl/fl}$ and *Viaat-Cre;Irsp53*$^{fl/fl}$ mice (3 weeks; male). Note that intrinsic excitability is increased both in *Emx1-Cre;Irsp53*$^{fl/fl}$ and *Viaat-Cre;Irsp53*$^{fl/fl}$ mice. n = 13, 3 for f/f-firing frequency, 14, 3 for Emx1-firing frequency, 18, 3 for Viaat-firing frequency, 13, 3 for f/f-AP threshold, 14, 3 for Emx1-AP threshold, 18, 3 for Viaat-AP threshold, 13, 3 for f/f-input resistance, 14, 3 for Emx1-input resistance, 18, 3 for Viaat-input resistance, $^{*}P < 0.05$, $^{***}P < 0.001$; ns, not significant, one-way ANOVA with Bonferroni's test for AP threshold, two-way ANOVA with Bonferroni's test for firing frequency and input resistance. Sustained firing, interaction $F_{(18,420)} = 3.165$, current $F_{(9,420)} = 61.89$, genotype $F_{(2,420)} = 56.73$; action potential threshold, $F_{(2,42)} = 16.14$; input resistance, interaction $F_{(6,168)} = 0.5088$, current $F_{(3,168)} = 60.88$, genotype $F_{(2,168)} = 11.33$. **(C)** Decreased ratio of evoked N-methyl-D-aspartate receptors (NMDAR)-EPSCs and AMPA receptor (AMPAR)-EPSCs in *Emx1-Cre;Irsp53*$^{fl/fl}$ layer V pyramidal neurons in the prelimbic region of the mPFC (2 months; male). n = 10 neurons for three mice for f/f, 11, 3 for Emx1, $^{***}P < 0.001$, Student's t-test, $t = 5.250$, $df = 19$. **(D)** Increased ratio of evoked EPSCs and IPSCs in *Emx1-Cre;Irsp53*$^{fl/fl}$ layer V pyramidal neurons in the prelimbic region of the mPFC (2 months; male). n = 8 neurons for three mice for f/f, 8, 3 for Emx1, $^{***}P < 0.001$, Student's t-test, $t = 5.019$, $df = 14$. **(E)** Normal paired-pulse ratio in *Emx1-Cre;Irsp53*$^{fl/fl}$ layer V pyramidal neurons in the prelimbic region of the mPFC (2 months; male). n = 10 neurons for three mice for f/f, 9, 3 for Emx1, ns, not significant, two-way ANOVA with Bonferroni's test, interaction $F_{(5,85)} = 0.6379$, time $F_{(5,85)} = 4.100$, genotype $F_{(1,17)} = 0.7348$.

KO mice (Chung et al., 2015). The frequency but not amplitude of mEPSCs in the *Emx1-Cre; Irsp53*$^{fl/fl}$ mPFC (layer V pyramidal neurons in the prelimbic area) was decreased, whereas mIPSCs were normal (**Figure 3A**), in line with the reported decrease in excitatory synaptic transmission and dendritic spine density in mPFC pyramidal neurons from *Irsp53*-null mice (Chung et al., 2015). In addition, these neurons showed moderately increased intrinsic excitability, as shown by action potential threshold and input resistance (**Figure 3B**), likely to compensate for the decreased excitatory synaptic input. In *Viaat-Cre; Irsp53*$^{fl/fl}$ mice, however, mEPSCs or mIPSCs were normal in layer V mPFC neurons (**Figure 3A**). Intriguingly, the intrinsic excitability was strongly increased, as shown by current-firing curve, action potential threshold, and input resistance (**Figure 3B**).

When evoked synaptic transmission was measured, the ratio of NMDAR-mediated EPSCs and AMPA receptor (AMPAR)-mediated EPSCs was decreased in *Emx1-Cre; Irsp53*$^{fl/fl}$ layer V pyramidal neurons (**Figure 3C**). In addition, the ratio of evoked EPSCs and IPSCs was increased in *Emx1-Cre; Irsp53*$^{fl/fl}$ layer V pyramidal neurons (**Figure 3D**). These changes were not associated with an altered paired-pulse ratio at excitatory synapses (**Figure 3E**). These results collectively suggest that *Irsp53* deletion in glutamatergic neurons leads to reduced spontaneous excitatory but not inhibitory synaptic transmission, decreased ratio of evoked NMDAR-EPSCs/AMPAR-EPSCs, increased ratio of evoked EPSCs/IPSCs, and increased neuronal excitability in layer V mPFC neurons. Distinctly, GABAergic *Irsp53* deletion strongly increases neuronal excitability without affecting spontaneous excitatory or inhibitory synaptic transmission.

Male and Female *Emx1-Cre; Irsp53*$^{fl/fl}$ Mice Show Distinct Changes in Synaptic Transmission and Behaviors

The abovementioned behavioral and electrophysiological results were obtained from male *Emx1-Cre; Irsp53*$^{fl/fl}$ mice. Given that male-female differences could affect these phenotypes, we measured social interaction and locomotor activity in *Emx1-Cre;Irsp53*$^{fl/fl}$ mice. Intriguingly, female *Emx1-Cre;Irsp53*$^{fl/fl}$ mice showed normal three-chamber social interaction in the three-chamber test, although there was a decreasing tendency, as compared with control (*Irsp53*$^{fl/fl}$) mice (**Figure 4A**), indicative of male-female difference in social interaction. In contrast, female *Emx1-Cre;Irsp53*$^{fl/fl}$ mice showed strong hyperactivity in the OFT (**Figure 4B**), similar to male *Emx1-Cre;Irsp53*$^{fl/fl}$ mice.

When excitatory synaptic transmission was measured in layer V pyramidal neurons in the prelimbic area of the mPFC from female *Emx1-Cre;Irsp53*$^{fl/fl}$ mice, there was a decrease in the amplitude, but not frequency, of mEPSCs in female mutant neurons, compared with WT neurons (**Figure 4C**), which contrasts with the decreased frequency but not amplitude of mEPSCs in male mutant neurons (**Figure 3A**). In addition, there were no genotype differences in the ratio of evoked EPSCs/IPSCs or the paired-pulse ratio in layer V pyramidal neurons (**Figures 4D,E**). These results collectively suggest that *Irsp53* deletion induces distinct changes in behaviors and excitatory synaptic transmission in the mPFC.

DISCUSSION

We attempted here to restrict *Irsp53* deletion to Emx1-positive glutamatergic and Viaat-positive GABAergic neurons to investigate the impact of IRSp53 KO in the respective neurons on mouse behaviors and synaptic/neuronal properties. *Irsp53* KO in Emx1-positive dorsal telencephalic glutamatergic neurons leads to both social interaction deficits and hyperactivity, two key behavioral phenotypes observed in global *Irsp53*-KO mice (Chung et al., 2015), whereas *Irsp53* KO in Viaat-positive GABAergic neurons does not affect social interaction or hyperactivity. Therefore, *Irsp53* expression in glutamatergic neurons in the cortex, where Emx1 is strongly expressed, seems to be important for normal social interaction and locomotor activity. This is in line with the well-known importance of the PFC in the regulation of social cognition and interaction, previously reported in studies with human subjects as well as WT and mutant mice carrying ASD- and schizophrenia-related gene mutations (Ernst et al., 1997; Mundy, 2003; Pierce et al., 2004; Carper and Courchesne, 2005; Amodio and Frith, 2006; Gilbert et al., 2008; Rinaldi et al., 2008; Shalom, 2009; Courchesne et al., 2011; Yizhar et al., 2011; Testa-Silva et al., 2012; Liang et al., 2015; Barak and Feng, 2016; Ko, 2017; Selimbeyoglu et al., 2017; Cao et al., 2018; Pirone et al., 2018; Wang et al., 2018, 2019; Guo et al., 2019; Lazaro et al., 2019; Phillips et al., 2019; Yoo et al., 2019).

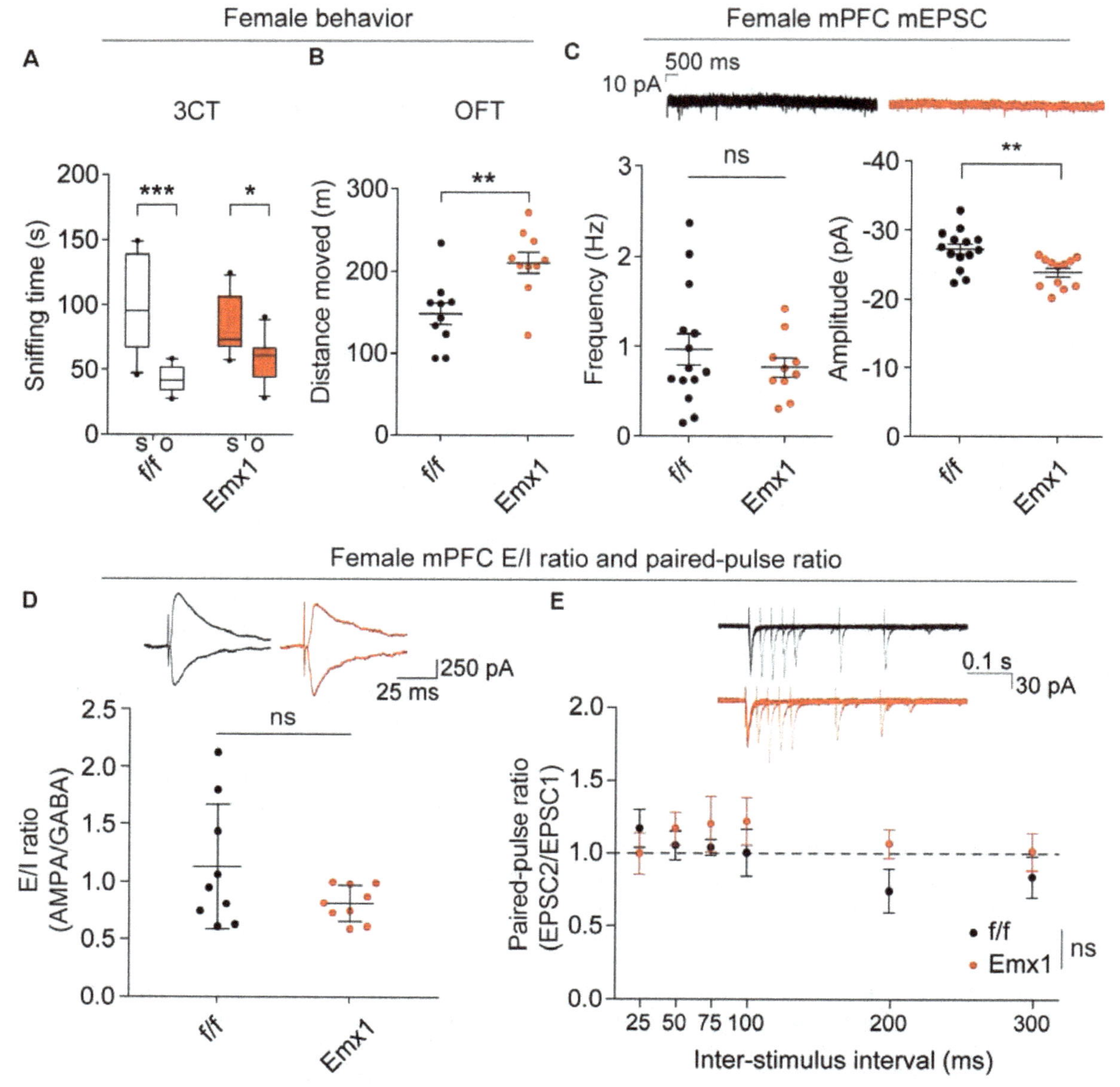

FIGURE 4 | Female *Emx1-Cre;Irsp53*$^{fl/fl}$ mice show distinct changes in synaptic transmission and behaviors. **(A)** Normal social interaction in female *Emx1-Cre;Irsp53*$^{fl/fl}$ mice in the three-chamber test (2 months; females). n = 10 mice (*Irsp53*$^{fl/fl}$ or f/f), 10 mice (Emx1-cKO), $^*P < 0.05$, $^{***}P < 0.001$, two-way ANOVA with Bonferroni's test, interaction $F_{(1,36)} = 4.035$, chamber $F_{(1,36)} = 31.58$, genotype $F_{(1,36)} = 0.0003937$. **(B)** Hyperactivity in female *Emx1-Cre;Irsp53*$^{fl/fl}$ mice in the OFT (2 months; females). n = 10 mice (*Irsp53*$^{fl/fl}$ or f/f), 10 mice (Emx1-cKO), $^{**}P < 0.01$, Student's t-test, $t = 3.434$, $df = 18$. **(C)** Decreased amplitude but normal frequency of mEPSCs in layer V pyramidal neurons in the prelimbic region of the mPFC in *Emx1-Cre;Irsp53*$^{fl/fl}$ (3 months; females). n = 14 neurons from three mice for f/f-mEPSC, 10, 3 for Emx1-mEPSC in mPFC, $^{**}P < 0.01$; ns, not significant, Mann-Whitney test for frequency, Student's t-test for amplitude. mEPSC frequency, Mann-U 62; mEPSC amplitude, $t = 3.278$, $df = 24$. **(D)** Normal ratio of evoked EPSCs and IPSCs in layer V pyramidal neurons in the prelimbic region of the mPFC in female *Emx1-Cre;Irsp53*$^{fl/fl}$ mice (2–3 months; females). n = 9 neurons for three mice for f/f, 9, 3 for Emx1, ns, not significant, Student's t-test, $t = 1.675$, $df = 16$. **(E)** Normal paired-pulse ratio in layer V pyramidal neurons in the prelimbic region of the mPFC in female *Emx1-Cre;Irsp53*$^{fl/fl}$ (2–3 months; females). n = 6 neurons for three mice for f/f, 6, 3 for Emx1, ns, not significant, two-way ANOVA with Bonferroni's test, interaction $F_{(5,90)} = 0.8666$, time $F_{(5,90)} = 0.9748$, genotype $F_{(1,18)} = 0.6927$.

Irsp53 KO restricted to Emx1-positive glutamate neurons induces decreased mEPSC frequency, decreased NMDA/AMPA ratio, and increased E/I ratio in layer V pyramidal neurons in the prelimbic region of the mPFC. These changes are associated with moderately increased neuronal excitability. Whether these changes alter the output function of the mutant layer V pyramidal neurons under basal or social conditions would require additional analyses. However, the mPFC is known to receive afferent projections from various brain regions (Riga et al., 2014; Root et al., 2015; Murugan et al., 2017; Park and Moghaddam, 2017; Knowland and Lim, 2018). In particular, the prelimbic region of the mPFC receives strong afferent projections from limbic regions of the cortex as well as other subcortical areas, including basal forebrain, thalamus, amygdala, hypothalamus, and midbrain (Hoover and Vertes, 2007). In addition, layer V pyramidal neurons in the prelimbic area project to various subcortical regions, including lateral hypothalamus, striatum, and basolateral amygdala (Sesack et al., 1989; Gabbott et al., 2005). Therefore, the altered spontaneous and evoked synaptic transmission and intrinsic excitability of the mutant layer V pyramidal neurons might change their output functions and contribute to social deficits and hyperactivity observed in *Emx1-Cre;Irsp53*$^{fl/fl}$ mice.

Emx1-Cre;Irsp53$^{fl/fl}$ males show strong social deficits whereas females show only modestly suppressed social interaction, while they both show comparable hyperactivity. This suggests that the hyperactivity is not the key confounding factor contributing to the social deficits. Notably, spontaneous excitatory synaptic transmission is distinctly changed in layer V pyramidal neurons in the prelimbic area in male and female *Emx1-Cre;Irsp53*$^{fl/fl}$ mice; decreased mEPSC frequency in male neurons and decreased mEPSC amplitude (not frequency) in female neurons. This difference, although intriguing, is less likely to induce a qualitative difference in the output function of these neurons. Importantly, however, the E/I ratio of evoked synaptic transmission was increased in male, but female, layer V pyramidal neurons. Although further details remain to be determined, these results are in line with the reported association of altered E/I ratio in cortical neurons with social deficits (Yizhar et al., 2011; Nelson and Valakh, 2015; Lee et al., 2017; Selimbeyoglu et al., 2017). In addition, these results add to the emerging notion that non-sex-differential factors such as synaptic transmission and neuronal properties (relative to sex-differential factors such as hormone and X-Y chromosomes) may contribute to the male-female phenotypic differences in animal models of autism (Werling and Geschwind, 2013; Barak and Feng, 2016; Lo et al., 2016; Werling et al., 2016; Jung et al., 2018). Last, our data indicate that GABAergic neuronal deletion of IRSp53 in male mice minimally affects social and locomotor activities. However, this does not exclude the possibility that female mice with the same mutation show some positive electrophysiological and behavioral phenotypes.

In conclusion, our data suggest that *Irsp53* KOs restricted to glutamatergic neurons and GABAergic neurons and in male and female mice lead to distinct behavioral deficits and changes in synaptic and neuronal properties in the mPFC.

ETHICS STATEMENT

The animal study was reviewed and approved by the Committee of Animal Research at Korea Advanced Institute of Science and Technology (KAIST).

AUTHOR CONTRIBUTIONS

YK performed most of the experiments except for FISH experiments. YK, YN, and KK performed the electrophysiological experiments. EY performed the FISH experiments. YK, HK, and EK designed the experiments and wrote the manuscript.

FUNDING

This work was supported by the Institute for Basic Science (IBS-R002-D1 to EK).

REFERENCES

Amodio, D. M., and Frith, C. D. (2006). Meeting of minds: the medial frontal cortex and social cognition. *Nat. Rev. Neurosci.* 7, 268–277. doi: 10.1038/nrn1884

Barak, B., and Feng, G. (2016). Neurobiology of social behavior abnormalities in autism and Williams syndrome. *Nat. Neurosci.* 19, 647–655. doi: 10.1038/nn.4276

Bariselli, S., Hörnberg, H., Prévost-Solié, C., Musardo, S., Hatstatt-Burklé, L., Scheiffele, P., et al. (2018). Role of VTA dopamine neurons and neuroligin 3 in sociability traits related to nonfamiliar conspecific interaction. *Nat. Commun.* 9:3173. doi: 10.1038/s41467-018-05382-3

Bobsin, K., and Kreienkamp, H. J. (2016). Severe learning deficits of IRSp53 mutant mice are caused by altered NMDA receptor dependent signal transduction. *J. Neurochem.* 136, 752–763. doi: 10.1111/jnc.13428

Burette, A. C., Park, H., and Weinberg, R. J. (2014). Postsynaptic distribution of IRSp53 in spiny excitatory and inhibitory neurons. *J. Comp. Neurol.* 522, 2164–2178. doi: 10.1002/cne.23526

Cao, W., Lin, S., Xia, Q. Q., Du, Y. L., Yang, Q., Zhang, M. Y., et al. (2018). Gamma oscillation dysfunction in mPFC leads to social deficits in neuroligin 3 R451C knockin mice. *Neuron* 98:670. doi: 10.1016/j.neuron.2018.04.025

Carper, R. A., and Courchesne, E. (2005). Localized enlargement of the frontal cortex in early autism. *Biol. Psychiatry* 57, 126–133. doi: 10.1016/j.biopsych.2004.11.005

Celestino-Soper, P. B., Shaw, C. A., Sanders, S. J., Li, J., Murtha, M. T., Ercan-Sencicek, A. G., et al. (2011). Use of array CGH to detect exonic copy number variants throughout the genome in autism families detects a novel deletion in TMLHE. *Hum. Mol. Genet.* 20, 4360–4370. doi: 10.1093/hmg/ddr363

Chao, H. T., Chen, H., Samaco, R. C., Xue, M., Chahrour, M., Yoo, J., et al. (2010). Dysfunction in GABA signalling mediates autism-like stereotypies and Rett syndrome phenotypes. *Nature* 468, 263–269. doi: 10.1038/nature09582

Chen, B. T., Yau, H. J., Hatch, C., Kusumoto-Yoshida, I., Cho, S. L., Hopf, F. W., et al. (2013). Rescuing cocaine-induced prefrontal cortex hypoactivity prevents compulsive cocaine seeking. *Nature* 496, 359–362. doi: 10.1038/nature12024

Chung, W., Choi, S. Y., Lee, E., Park, H., Kang, J., Park, H., et al. (2015). Social deficits in IRSp53 mutant mice improved by NMDAR and mGluR5 suppression. *Nat. Neurosci.* 18, 435–443. doi: 10.1038/nn.3927

Courchesne, E., Mouton, P. R., Calhoun, M. E., Semendeferi, K., Ahrens-Barbeau, C., Hallet, M. J., et al. (2011). Neuron number and size in prefrontal cortex of children with autism. *JAMA* 306, 2001–2010. doi: 10.1001/jama.2011.1638

Ernst, M., Zametkin, A. J., Matochik, J. A., Pascualvaca, D., and Cohen, R. M. (1997). Low medial prefrontal dopaminergic activity in autistic children. *Lancet* 350:638. doi: 10.1016/s0140-6736(05)63326-0

Fromer, M., Pocklington, A. J., Kavanagh, D. H., Williams, H. J., Dwyer, S., Gormley, P., et al. (2014). De novo mutations in schizophrenia implicate synaptic networks. *Nature* 506, 179–184. doi: 10.1038/nature12929

Gabbott, P. L., Warner, T. A., Jays, P. R., Salway, P., and Busby, S. J. (2005). Prefrontal cortex in the rat: projections to subcortical autonomic, motor, and limbic centers. *J. Comp. Neurol.* 492, 145–177. doi: 10.1002/cne.20738

Gilbert, S. J., Bird, G., Brindley, R., Frith, C. D., and Burgess, P. W. (2008). Atypical recruitment of medial prefrontal cortex in autism spectrum disorders: an fMRI study of two executive function tasks. *Neuropsychologia* 46, 2281–2291. doi: 10.1016/j.neuropsychologia.2008.03.025

Gorski, J. A., Talley, T., Qiu, M., Puelles, L., Rubenstein, J. L., and Jones, K. R. (2002). Cortical excitatory neurons and glia, but not GABAergic neurons, are produced in the Emx1-expressing lineage. *J. Neurosci.* 22, 6309–6314. doi: 10.1523/JNEUROSCI.22-15-06309.2002

Guo, B., Chen, J., Chen, Q., Ren, K., Feng, D., Mao, H., et al. (2019). Anterior cingulate cortex dysfunction underlies social deficits in Shank3 mutant mice. *Nat. Neurosci.* 22, 1223–1234. doi: 10.1038/s41593-019-0445-9

Hoover, W. B., and Vertes, R. P. (2007). Anatomical analysis of afferent projections to the medial prefrontal cortex in the rat. *Brain Struct. Funct.* 212, 149–179. doi: 10.1007/s00429-007-0150-4

Jiang, Y. H., and Ehlers, M. D. (2013). Modeling autism by SHANK gene mutations in mice. *Neuron* 78, 8–27. doi: 10.1016/j.neuron.2013.03.016

Jung, H., Park, H., Choi, Y., Kang, H., Lee, E., Kweon, H., et al. (2018). Sexually dimorphic behavior, neuronal activity, and gene expression in Chd8-mutant mice. *Nat. Neurosci.* 21, 1218–1228. doi: 10.1038/s41593-018-0208-z

Kang, J., Park, H., and Kim, E. (2016). IRSp53/BAIAP2 in dendritic spine development, NMDA receptor regulation, and psychiatric disorders. *Neuropharmacology* 100, 27–39. doi: 10.1016/j.neuropharm.2015.06.019

Kim, M. H., Choi, J., Yang, J., Chung, W., Kim, J. H., Paik, S. K., et al. (2009). Enhanced NMDA receptor-mediated synaptic transmission, enhanced long-term potentiation, and impaired learning and memory in mice lacking IRSp53. *J. Neurosci.* 29, 1586–1595. doi: 10.1523/JNEUROSCI.4306-08.2009

Knowland, D., and Lim, B. K. (2018). Circuit-based frameworks of depressive behaviors: the role of reward circuitry and beyond. *Pharmacol. Biochem. Behav.* 174, 42–52. doi: 10.1016/j.pbb.2017.12.010

Ko, J. (2017). Neuroanatomical substrates of rodent social behavior: the medial prefrontal cortex and its projection patterns. *Front. Neural Circuits* 11:41. doi: 10.3389/fncir.2017.00041

Lazaro, M. T., Taxidis, J., Shuman, T., Bachmutsky, I., Ikrar, T., Santos, R., et al. (2019). Reduced prefrontal synaptic connectivity and disturbed oscillatory population dynamics in the CNTNAP2 model of autism. *Cell Rep.* 27, 2567.e6–2578.e6. doi: 10.1016/j.celrep.2019.05.006

Lee, E. J., Choi, S. Y., and Kim, E. (2015). NMDA receptor dysfunction in autism spectrum disorders. *Curr. Opin. Pharmacol.* 20C, 8–13. doi: 10.1016/j.coph.2014.10.007

Lee, E., Lee, J., and Kim, E. (2017). Excitation/inhibition imbalance in animal models of autism spectrum disorders. *Biol. Psychiatry* 81, 838–847. doi: 10.1016/j.biopsych.2016.05.011

Levy, D., Ronemus, M., Yamrom, B., Lee, Y. H., Leotta, A., Kendall, J., et al. (2011). Rare de novo and transmitted copy-number variation in autistic spectrum disorders. *Neuron* 70, 886–897. doi: 10.1016/j.neuron.2011.05.015

Liang, J., Xu, W., Hsu, Y. T., Yee, A. X., Chen, L., and Sudhof, T. C. (2015). Conditional neuroligin-2 knockout in adult medial prefrontal cortex links chronic changes in synaptic inhibition to cognitive impairments. *Mol. Psychiatry* 20, 850–859. doi: 10.1038/mp.2015.31

Liu, L., Sun, L., Li, Z. H., Li, H. M., Wei, L. P., Wang, Y. F., et al. (2013). BAIAP2 exhibits association to childhood ADHD especially predominantly inattentive subtype in Chinese Han subjects. *Behav. Brain Funct.* 9:48. doi: 10.1186/1744-9081-9-48

Lo, S. C., Scearce-Levie, K., and Sheng, M. (2016). Characterization of social behaviors in caspase-3 deficient mice. *Sci. Rep.* 6:18335. doi: 10.1038/srep18335

Madisen, L., Zwingman, T. A., Sunkin, S. M., Oh, S. W., Zariwala, H. A., Gu, H., et al. (2010). A robust and high-throughput Cre reporting and characterization system for the whole mouse brain. *Nat. Neurosci.* 13, 133–140. doi: 10.1038/nn.2467

Monteiro, P., and Feng, G. (2017). SHANK proteins: roles at the synapse and in autism spectrum disorder. *Nat. Rev. Neurosci.* 18, 147–157. doi: 10.1038/nrn.2016.183

Moy, S. S., Nadler, J. J., Perez, A., Barbaro, R. P., Johns, J. M., Magnuson, T. R., et al. (2004). Sociability and preference for social novelty in five inbred strains: an approach to assess autistic-like behavior in mice. *Genes Brain Behav.* 3, 287–302. doi: 10.1111/j.1601-1848.2004.00076.x

Mundy, P. (2003). Annotation: the neural basis of social impairments in autism: the role of the dorsal medial-frontal cortex and anterior cingulate system. *J. Child Psychol. Psychiatry* 44, 793–809. doi: 10.1111/1469-7610.00165

Murugan, M., Jang, H. J., Park, M., Miller, E. M., Cox, J., Taliaferro, J. P., et al. (2017). Combined social and spatial coding in a descending projection from the prefrontal cortex. *Cell* 171, 1663.16–1677.16. doi: 10.1016/j.cell.2017.11.002

Nelson, S. B., and Valakh, V. (2015). Excitatory/inhibitory balance and circuit homeostasis in autism spectrum disorders. *Neuron* 87, 684–698. doi: 10.1016/j.neuron.2015.07.033

Park, J., and Moghaddam, B. (2017). Risk of punishment influences discrete and coordinated encoding of reward-guided actions by prefrontal cortex and VTA neurons. *Elife* 6:e30056. doi: 10.7554/elife.30056

Phillips, M. L., Robinson, H. A., and Pozzo-Miller, L. (2019). Ventral hippocampal projections to the medial prefrontal cortex regulate social memory. *Elife* 8:e44182. doi: 10.7554/elife.44182

Pierce, K., Haist, F., Sedaghat, F., and Courchesne, E. (2004). The brain response to personally familiar faces in autism: findings of fusiform activity and beyond. *Brain* 127, 2703–2716. doi: 10.1093/brain/awh289

Pirone, A., Alexander, J. M., Koenig, J. B., Cook-Snyder, D. R., Palnati, M., Wickham, R. J., et al. (2018). Social stimulus causes aberrant activation of the medial prefrontal cortex in a mouse model with autism-like behaviors. *Front. Synaptic Neurosci.* 10:35. doi: 10.3389/fnsyn.2018.00035

Purcell, S. M., Moran, J. L., Fromer, M., Ruderfer, D., Solovieff, N., Roussos, P., et al. (2014). A polygenic burden of rare disruptive mutations in schizophrenia. *Nature* 506, 185–190. doi: 10.1038/nature12975

Ribasés, M., Bosch, R., Hervás, A., Ramos-Quiroga, J. A., Sánchez-Mora, C., Bielsa, A., et al. (2009). Case-control study of six genes asymmetrically expressed in the two cerebral hemispheres: association of BAIAP2 with attention-deficit/hyperactivity disorder. *Biol. Psychiatry* 66, 926–934. doi: 10.1016/j.biopsych.2009.06.024

Riga, D., Matos, M. R., Glas, A., Smit, A. B., Spijker, S., and Van Den Oever, M. C. (2014). Optogenetic dissection of medial prefrontal cortex circuitry. *Front. Syst. Neurosci.* 8:230. doi: 10.3389/fnsys.2014.00230

Rinaldi, T., Perrodin, C., and Markram, H. (2008). Hyper-connectivity and hyper-plasticity in the medial prefrontal cortex in the valproic acid animal model of autism. *Front. Neural Circuits* 2:4. doi: 10.3389/neuro.04.004.2008

Root, D. H., Melendez, R. I., Zaborszky, L., and Napier, T. C. (2015). The ventral pallidum: subregion-specific functional anatomy and roles in motivated behaviors. *Prog. Neurobiol.* 130, 29–70. doi: 10.1016/j.pneurobio.2015.03.005

Rothwell, P. E., Fuccillo, M. V., Maxeiner, S., Hayton, S. J., Gokce, O., Lim, B. K., et al. (2014). Autism-associated neuroligin-3 mutations commonly impair striatal circuits to boost repetitive behaviors. *Cell* 158, 198–212. doi: 10.1016/j.cell.2014.04.045

Sala, C., and Segal, M. (2014). Dendritic spines: the locus of structural and functional plasticity. *Physiol. Rev.* 94, 141–188. doi: 10.1152/physrev.00012.2013

Sala, C., Vicidomini, C., Bigi, I., Mossa, A., and Verpelli, C. (2015). Shank synaptic scaffold proteins: keys to understanding the pathogenesis of autism and other synaptic disorders. *J. Neurochem.* 135, 849–858. doi: 10.1111/jnc.13232

Sawallisch, C., Berhörster, K., Disanza, A., Mantoani, S., Kintscher, M., Stoenica, L., et al. (2009). The insulin receptor substrate of 53 kDa (IRSp53) limits hippocampal synaptic plasticity. *J. Biol. Chem.* 284, 9225–9236. doi: 10.1074/jbc.m808425200

Selimbeyoglu, A., Kim, C. K., Inoue, M., Lee, S. Y., Hong, A. S. O., Kauvar, I., et al. (2017). Modulation of prefrontal cortex excitation/inhibition balance rescues social behavior in CNTNAP2-deficient mice. *Sci. Transl. Med.* 9:eaah6733. doi: 10.1126/scitranslmed.aah6733

Sesack, S. R., Deutch, A. Y., Roth, R. H., and Bunney, B. S. (1989). Topographical organization of the efferent projections of the medial prefrontal cortex in the rat: an anterograde tract-tracing study with *Phaseolus vulgaris leucoagglutinin*. *J. Comp. Neurol.* 290, 213–242. doi: 10.1002/cne.902900205

Shalom, D. B. (2009). The medial prefrontal cortex and integration in autism. *Neuroscientist* 15, 589–598. doi: 10.1177/1073858409336371

Sheng, M., and Hoogenraad, C. C. (2007). The postsynaptic architecture of excitatory synapses: a more quantitative view. *Annu. Rev. Biochem.* 76, 823–847. doi: 10.1146/annurev.biochem.76.060805.160029

Sheng, M., and Kim, E. (2011). The postsynaptic organization of synapses. *Cold Spring Harb. Perspect. Biol.* 3:a005678. doi: 10.1101/cshperspect.a005678

Sheng, M., and Sala, C. (2001). PDZ domains and the organization of supramolecular complexes. *Annu. Rev. Neurosci.* 24, 1–29. doi: 10.1146/annurev.neuro.24.1.1

Silverman, J. L., Yang, M., Lord, C., and Crawley, J. N. (2010). Behavioural phenotyping assays for mouse models of autism. *Nat. Rev. Neurosci.* 11, 490–502. doi: 10.1038/nrn2851

Testa-Silva, G., Loebel, A., Giugliano, M., De Kock, C. P., Mansvelder, H. D., and Meredith, R. M. (2012). Hyperconnectivity and slow synapses during early development of medial prefrontal cortex in a mouse model for mental retardation and autism. *Cereb. Cortex* 22, 1333–1342. doi: 10.1093/cercor/bhr224

Toma, C., Hervás, A., Balmaña, N., Vilella, E., Aguilera, F., Cuscó, I., et al. (2011). Association study of six candidate genes asymmetrically expressed in the two cerebral hemispheres suggests the involvement of BAIAP2 in autism. *J. Psychiatr. Res.* 45, 280–282. doi: 10.1016/j.jpsychires.2010.09.001

Walf, A. A., and Frye, C. A. (2007). The use of the elevated plus maze as an assay of anxiety-related behavior in rodents. *Nat. Protoc.* 2, 322–328. doi: 10.1038/nprot.2007.44

Wang, X., Ma, S., Mao, M., Li, C., Shen, X., Xu, S., et al. (2019). RNA-sequencing and bioinformatics analysis of long noncoding RNAs and mRNAs in the prefrontal cortex of mice following repeated social defeat stress. *Biomed. Res. Int.* 2019:7505260. doi: 10.1155/2019/7505260

Wang, W., Rein, B., Zhang, F., Tan, T., Zhong, P., Qin, L., et al. (2018). Chemogenetic activation of prefrontal cortex rescues synaptic and behavioral deficits in a mouse model of 16p11.2 deletion syndrome. *J. Neurosci.* 38, 5939–5948. doi: 10.1523/JNEUROSCI.0149-18.2018

Werling, D. M., and Geschwind, D. H. (2013). Sex differences in autism spectrum disorders. *Curr. Opin. Neurol.* 26, 146–153. doi: 10.1097/WCO.0b013e32835ee548

Werling, D. M., Parikshak, N. N., and Geschwind, D. H. (2016). Gene expression in human brain implicates sexually dimorphic pathways in autism spectrum disorders. *Nat. Commun.* 7:10717. doi: 10.1038/ncomms10717

Yizhar, O., Fenno, L. E., Prigge, M., Schneider, F., Davidson, T. J., O'Shea, D. J., et al. (2011). Neocortical excitation/inhibition balance in information processing and social dysfunction. *Nature* 477, 171–178. doi: 10.1038/nature10360

Yoo, T., Cho, H., Park, H., Lee, J., and Kim, E. (2019). Shank3 exons 14–16 deletion in glutamatergic neurons leads to social and repetitive behavioral deficits associated with increased cortical layer 2/3 neuronal excitability. *Front. Cell. Neurosci.* 13:458. doi: 10.3389/fncel.2019.00458

8

A Whole-Brain Cell-Type-Specific Sparse Neuron Labeling Method and Its Application in a *Shank3* Autistic Mouse Model

Di Chen[1†], Keke Ren[2†], Haiying Liu[2], Honghui Mao[2], Zongyan Li[1], Huiming Mo[3], Shengjun Xie[1], Yiwu Shi[1], Qian Chen[1] and Wenting Wang[2*]*

[1] Institute of Neuroscience, Department of Neurology, The Second Affiliated Hospital of Guangzhou Medical University, Guangzhou, China, [2] Department of Neurobiology, School of Basic Medicine, Fourth Military Medical University, Xi'an, China, [3] Department of Physiology, Medical College of Yan'an University, Yan'an, China

***Correspondence:**
Qian Chen
chenqian1977@hotmail.com
Wenting Wang
wwt0657@fmmu.edu.cn

† These authors have contributed equally to this work

Single neurons, as the basic unit of the brain, consist of a cell body and processes, including dendrites and axons. Even neurons of the same type show various subtle process characteristics to fit into the diverse neural circuits. Different cell types of neurons form complicated circuits in the brain. Therefore, detailed neuronal morphology is required to understand normal neuronal function and pathological mechanisms, such as those that occur in autism. Here, we developed a strategy to sparsely label the same type of neurons throughout the whole brain and tested its application in an autistic animal model—*Shank3* knockout (KO) mice. To achieve this, we designed an adeno-associated virus (AAV) that expresses Cre recombinase-dependent regular and membrane-targeted enhanced green fluorescent protein (EGFP) under a human synapsin 1 promoter and verified it in several Cre transgenic mice. We could sparsely label the projection neurons in multiple brain areas by retro-ocular injection of the virus into CaMKIIα-Cre mice. Then, we analyzed the morphology of the projection neurons in *Shank3* KO mice with this method. We found differential dendritic complexity and dendritic spine changes in projection neurons in *Shank3* KO mice crossed with CaMKIIα-Cre mice compared with littermate control mice in the striatum, cortex, and hippocampus. By combining this method with various Cre mouse lines crossed with mouse models of disease, we can screen the morphological traits of distinct types of neurons throughout the whole brain that will help us to understand the exact role of the specific cell types of neurons not only in autism spectrum disorder (ASD) mouse models but also in other psychiatric disorder mouse models.

Keywords: sparse neuron labeling, neuronal morphology reconstruction, dendritic spine, autism, CaMKIIα, *Shank3*

INTRODUCTION

Neurons are the basic functional units of the nervous system. Billions of neurons form at least a thousand neuron types and integrate into various anatomical circuits for executing complex behaviors. In general, neurons are composed of cell bodies and processes, including dendrites and axons. These structures, particularly dendrites and dendritic spines, are the main subtle structures receiving inputs from neurons and glia cells, which display dynamic remodeling during development, aging, and diseases. Autism spectrum disorders (ASDs), one type of neurodevelopmental disease, have been found to induce morphological changes in the dendritic processes and spines of neurons in related brain regions (Penzes et al., 2011). Various types of neurons play distinct roles in different brain circuits that conduct normal brain functions. Although morphological changes in neurons have been revealed in ASD animal models (Bourgeron, 2009, 2015), structural deficits in different types of neurons have not been fully disclosed. In recent studies, growing evidence has shown that specific neuronal cell types contribute to the mechanisms of behavioral changes in ASD animal models (Tyzio et al., 2014; Bariselli et al., 2016; Zhang Y. et al., 2016; Wang et al., 2017; Guo et al., 2019). Moreover, a considerable number of studies have suggested an association between ASDs and dendritic spine abnormalities involving different stages, such as spine development, maturation, elimination, and pruning (Tang et al., 2014; Yadav et al., 2017; Yoon et al., 2020). Therefore, it is essential to characterize the morphological changes of distinct cell types in the brain circuits of those animal models of disease, which will greatly help us to understand the etiology of ASD, especially dendritic processes and dendritic spines. In addition, there are always a multitude of similar and different types of neurons that intermingle with each other, even in an anatomical region. Thus, single-cell reconstructions with sparse-labeling techniques are very useful for the scrutinization of the process traits of neurons, which will further help us understand the functional role of these neurons.

Many methods have been used to sparsely label single neurons in animal models. For instance, Peça et al. (2011) used the patch-assisted Lucifer yellow cell filling method to sparsely label neurons in the striatum, and they found that young *Shank3B* knockout (KO) mice, an ASD mouse model (we refer to *Shank3* KO throughout the paper), showed increased dendritic complexity and decreased dendritic spine density of medial spiny neurons (MSNs) compared with wild-type (WT) mice. Though this method can help us visualize the structure of single neurons in the brain, the efficiency is relatively low, and information on cell-type specificity is lacking. Zhang Q. et al. (2016) developed a strategy of exiguous labeling of neurons by using an adeno-associated virus (AAV) to express farnesylated enhanced green fluorescent protein (EGFPf). Recently, we confirmed that dendrite processes and dendritic spines showed clear deficits in the indirect-pathway MSNs of the striatum and pyramidal cells in the anterior cingulate cortex in *Shank3* KO mice by using this strategy (Wang et al., 2017; Guo et al., 2019). However, it is time-consuming to achieve cell-type-specific labeling using this method. We had to combine this method with a transgenic reporter mouse line to distinguish striatonigral MSNs from striatopallidal MSNs. Therefore, a more efficient and simpler way to target a defined type of neurons will be useful for us to study the neuronal morphological changes in ASD models.

In this study, we modified an AAV expressing EGFP and EGFPf (Zhang Q. et al., 2016) into a Cre recombinase-dependent version. We performed retro-orbital injection of this new virus into CaMKIIα-Cre transgenic mice with different titers and successfully achieved single-cell-type-specific labeling in the different brain regions. The expressions of both EGFP and EGFPf enabled us to visualize the detailed structures of each neuron, even the spines. To explore the cell-type-specific neuronal morphological changes of ASD animal models, we applied this new method in *Shank3* KO mice, which were crossed with CaMKIIα-Cre transgenic mice. We compared dendritic complexity and dendritic spines of the labeled neurons between WT and *Shank3* KO mice in different brain regions. Our results showed that dendritic complexity and spine density were reduced to various degrees in the striatum, cortex, and dentate gyrus (DG) of this ASD mouse model. This highly efficient single-cell-type-specific labeling method allowed us to visualize the single-cell morphology not only in normal brains but also in autistic brains.

MATERIALS AND METHODS

Vector Preparation

To make the pAAV-hSyn-DIO-EGFP-P2A-EGFPf construct, EGFP and EGFPf sequences were PCR amplified from a pAAV-hSyn-EGFP-P2A-EGFPf-WPRE-HGHpA construct (Addgene, #74513). The loxP, loxP2272, and P2A sequences were added during the PCR amplification. The primer sequences were as follows: DIO-GFPf-F1: 5′-ATTGTAGCTGCTATT AGCAATATGAAACCTCTTAATAACTTCGTATAGCATACAT TATACGAAGTTATTCAGGAGAGCACACACTTGC-3′, DIO-GFPf-R1: 5′-GAATAACAGTGATAATTTCTGGGTTAAGGCA AATAACTTCGTATAGGATACTTTATACGAAGTTATGCCAC CATGGTGAGCAAGGGCG-3′, DIO-GFPf-F2: 5′-ACCGG CTAGAGGATCCATAACTTCGTATAGGATACTTTATACGAA GTTATGCAGAATGGTAGCTGGATTGTAGCTGCTATTAGC AA-3′, and DIO-GFPf-R2: 5′-GATTATCGATAAGCTTATAAC TTCGTATAGCATACATTATACGAAGTTATTCTTTGCACCA TTCTAAAGAATAACAGTGATAATTTCTGG-3′.

PCR-amplified fragments were ligated with *Bam*HI and *Hind*III linearized pAAV-hSyn-EGFP-P2A-EGFPf-WPRE-HGHpA construct using an Infusion cloning kit (Takara Bio Inc., Japan). The pAAV-hSyn-DIO-EGFP-P2A-EGFPf construct was confirmed with Sanger sequencing.

Mice

All procedures were approved by the Institutional Animal Care and Use Committee of the Fourth Military Medical University (FMMU). Mice were housed in a room maintained at a constant temperature and on a 12-h light/dark cycle (light from 08:00 to 20:00). Water and food were available *ad libitum*. *Shank3B* KO mice were gifts from Guoping Feng's laboratory at MIT. The CaMKIIα-Cre transgenic line was from the Jackson Laboratory (calcium/calmodulin-dependent protein kinase II alpha promoter driving Cre recombinase expression, stock no.: 005359), and *Sst*-IRES-Cre knock-in mice were from the Jackson Laboratory (express Cre recombinase in somatostatin-expressing neurons, stock no.: 013044). *Shank3*$^{+/+}$:CaMKIIα-Cre hemizygotes and *Shank3*$^{-/-}$:CaMKIIα-Cre hemizygotes were obtained from *Shank3*$^{+/-}$:CaMKIIα-Cre hemizygotes crossed with *Shank3*$^{+/-}$ mice. Ten-week-old male and female mice were handled by experimenters who were blinded to the genotypes and groups.

Cell Culture

Primary dissociated cortical neurons were prepared from postnatal day 0 WT mice by using standard protocols, as previously described (Ramamoorthi et al., 2011). Cortical neurons (2×10^5) were plated into one well of a 24-well plate that was precoated with 20 μg ml^{-1} poly-D-lysine (Sigma–Aldrich, United States) and 4 μg ml^{-1} laminin (Life Technologies, United States). The cultures were treated with AraC (1 μg ml^{-1}; Sigma–Aldrich, United States) on day 5 *in vitro* and maintained for up to 18 days after plating. One microliter of $AAV_{PhP.eB}$-hSyn-DIO-EGFP-P2A-EGFPf 1.3E + 12 gc/ml with 1 μl of AAV_8-CaMKIIα-ΔCre-mKate2 (1.0E + 13 gc/ml) or AAV_8-CaMKIIα-Cre-mKate2 (1.0E + 13 gc/ml) was added to one well at DIV10, and neurons were fixed with 4% paraformaldehyde (PFA) for imaging at DIV18. With these viral titers, almost all pyramidal neurons were infected by AAV_8-CaMKIIα-ΔCre-mKate2 or AAV_8-CaMKIIα-Cre-mKate2, which expressed red fluorescence. We observed that ~80% of pyramidal neurons expressed EGFP and red fluorescence when infected with both AAV_8-CaMKIIα-Cre-mKate2 and $AAV_{PhP.eB}$-hSyn-DIO-EGFP-P2A-EGFPf virus.

AAV Production and Purification

The AAV was packaged by PackGene Biotech in China. Triple-plasmid transfection using polyethylenimine (PEI MAX, Cat. 24765; Polysciences, United States) was carried out to produce the recombinant AAV. The plasmids pAAV-hSyn-DIO-EGFP-P2A-EGFPf, pHelper, and pRep2Cap-PhP.eB, which encode the Rep2 and PhP.eB capsid proteins, were cotransfected into HEK293T cells. The cells were cultured in Dulbecco's modified essential medium (DMEM; Invitrogen, United States), containing 10% fetal bovine serum (Gibco, United States) and 1% penicillin–streptomycin, in an incubator at 37°C with 5% CO_2. HEK293T cells were seeded in 150-mm dishes at a density of 1×10^7 cells per dish 24 h prior to transfection. Cells were transfected with 12 μg of pHelper plasmid, 10 μg of AAV pRep2Cap-PhP.eB plasmid, and 6 μg of pAAV-hSyn-DIO-EGFP-P2A-EGFPf plasmid for each plate. At 72 h post transfection, cells were harvested by 4000 *g* centrifugation at 4°C for 30 min. The pellet was collected and resuspended in buffer containing 10 mM Tris-HCl, pH 8.0. The suspension was subjected to four freeze–thaw cycles by dry ice/ethanol and a 37°C water bath. The cell debris was sonicated and then digested with DNase I (200 units in 1.5 ml) for 1 h at 37°C. Following centrifugation at 10,000 *g* for 10 min at 4°C, the supernatant was collected as the AAV crude lysate. The crude lysate was diluted with 10 mM Tris-HCl pH 8.0 to a final volume of 10 ml and then bottom-loaded on a discontinuous gradient of 15, 25, 40, and 60% iodixanol in a 39-ml ultracentrifuge tube (QuickSeal, 342414, Beckman, United States). After ultracentrifugation at 350,000 *g* at 18°C for 1 h, 3-ml fractions in the 40% lower layer and 0.5 ml of the 60% upper layer were collected. The fractions were desalted using a 100-kDa cutoff ultrafiltration tube (15 ml; Millipore, United States), and the buffer was changed to phosphate buffer saline (PBS). The purified AAV was stored at −80°C until use. The AAV genome copy titers were determined by real-time quantitative PCR (qPCR).

Retro-Ocular Injection

Mice were given retro-ocular injection of AAV as previously described (Yardeni et al., 2011; Zhang Q. et al., 2016). Briefly, mice were anesthetized with 3% isoflurane (RWD Life Science, China). Then, 100 μl of $AAV_{PhP.eB}$-DIO-EGFP-P2A-EGFPf with a titer of 1.3E + 12 gc/ml (PackGene Biotech, LLC, China) was injected into the retro-orbital sinus with a 27-G needle and a 1-ml syringe. The mice were then placed in a warm and moist environment to wait for resuscitation. After resuscitation, the mice were put back in the cage and housed for 3 weeks before the next step.

Immunohistochemistry

Mice were anesthetized with sodium pentobarbital (1%, 40 mg/kg body weight, i.p.) and transcardially perfused with 0.01 M PBS followed by 4% PFA in 0.01 M PBS. Brains were dissected out and postfixed in the same fixative at 4°C overnight. After that, brains were sliced in 200-μm-thick coronal sections by using a Vibratome 1000 (Ted Pella Inc., United States). All sections were serially collected into light-protected six-well plates containing 0.01 M PBS and were stored at 4°C for subsequent immunohistochemical staining.

Brain slices were rinsed once with PBS and permeated with 0.5% Triton X-100 (234729, Sigma, United States) in PBS for 2 h at room temperature. Then, the slices were rinsed once with PBS and incubated with 15% normal goat serum, 5% BSA, and 0.2% Triton X-100 (GBT) for 1 h at room temperature. After that, slices were incubated with primary antibody (**Supplementary Table S1**) at 4°C for 48 h. Then, the slices were washed with GBT five times at room temperature, each time for 15 min. Slices were incubated at 4°C for 12 h with the secondary antibody (**Supplementary Table S1**) and then stained with DAPI (1:1000, D8417, Sigma, United States) in PBS for 15 min at room temperature. Slices were washed five times in PBS with 0.1% Tween-20 and one time in PBS at room temperature, each time for 15 min. All of the above operations were performed on a shaking table with stirring (100 rpm/min). Last, brain slices were mounted on slides with a Fluoromount-G mounting medium (0100-01, Southern Biotech, United States).

Neuronal Imaging and Analysis

An Olympus FV1000 confocal microscope and Olympus FLUOVIEW software (ver.1.7a, Olympus, Japan) were used for image acquisition. Images were acquired at a resolution of 1024 pixels in the *X–Y* dimension. *Z* dimensions were variable. To obtain the overall distribution of EGFP-labeled neurons throughout the whole brain, a low-power objective lens (10×, numerical aperture = 0.4) was used to obtain the images, and then XuvStitch software, Ver. 1.8.099 (Emmenlauer et al., 2009), was used to stitch the images. The number of EGFP-labeled neurons in similar brain regions of WT and KO mice was counted manually. For the analysis of dendritic branches, most of the neurons were imaged using a 40× objective lens (numerical aperture = 0.9). Since the pyramidal neurons in layers V–VI of the cortex are larger than those in the other regions, a 20× objective lens (numerical aperture = 0.9) was used for imaging. The *Z*-dimensional increment was 1 μm for *Z*-stack images in both conditions. A 60× objective lens (numerical aperture = 1.42) was used for dendritic spine imaging. The *Z*-dimensional increment was 0.1–0.3 μm for the spine *Z*-stack images.

Neurons selected for analysis were randomly picked from at least 10 brain slices of three WT and three *Shank3* KO mice. The stack images were analyzed using Imaris software (version 7.7.1, serial number: 32mr-rfhf-7hbu-jb58, Bitplane, Switzerland). To eliminate the interference of neighboring neuronal dendrites, the confocal imaging files were converted to Imaris file format with the "Imaris File Converter," and 3D reconstruction of a single neuron was performed using the "volume rendering" function. The pictures shown in this paper were captured using the "snapshot" tools. The total length of dendrites and the volume of the cell body were automatically calculated. For the Sholl analysis, the spheres were constructed continuously from the center of the cell body with the radius increased by 10 μm. The number of intersections between each sphere and dendrites was calculated for comparison. Compared with using 2D images, using 3D images for Sholl analysis can provide statistical results that are closer to the real structure of the neurons, especially when analyzing dendrites with different angles.

To compare the difference in spine density between the WT and KO mice, spines in secondary dendrites with 80-μm length were chosen for the analysis. The spines in the dendrites were detected by Imaris software semiautomatically. The mislabeled spines were deleted manually. Spine shape was defined by the length of the spine and the width of the spine neck and the spine head, which allowed us to classify the spines into four types: stubby, mushroom, long thin, and filopodia. The stubby type had a length < 1 μm; the mushroom type had a length > 3 μm, and the maximum width of the head/the mean of the neck was > 2; the long thin type had a ratio of the mean width of the head/mean width of the neck of ≥ 1; and the rest of the spines were filopodia. Spine measurements were performed using Matlab-XTension Spines Classifier in Imaris. All imaging data were analyzed by a person who was blinded to the experimental groups.

Statistical Analysis

All data were transferred to SPSS 21.0 (IBM, United States) for analysis and to Prism 6.0 (GraphPad Software, Inc., United States) for graphing. All data were subjected to the normality test by the Shapiro–Wilk test and the homogeneity of variance test by Levene's test before further statistical analysis. Data are presented as the mean ± SEM, and the *n* value given for each experiment refers to the number of cells analyzed. All error bars indicate the SEM. Details of the particular statistical methods and results can be found in **Supplementary Tables S2, S3**. The results of two-group comparisons were analyzed by using a two-tailed unpaired *t*-test except as mentioned in the text. The significance levels for all tests were set at $^{*}p < 0.05$, $^{**}p < 0.01$, $^{***}p < 0.001$, and $^{****}p < 0.0001$.

RESULTS

Construction of the AAV-hSyn-DIO-EGFP-P2A-EGFPf Vector

To achieve neuronal cell-type-specific labeling *in vivo*, we chose the double-floxed inversed orientation (DIO) switch system, also known as the flip-excision (FLEX) Cre-switch system, to control EGFP reporter expression with Cre recombinase driven by specific promoters (Atasoy et al., 2008). The FLEX Cre-switch system consists of two pairs of heterotypic loxP-variant recombination sites, namely, loxP, having the WT sequence, and lox2272, having a mutated sequence flanking a pair of open reading frames. Both loxP variants are recognized by Cre recombinase, but only identical pairs of loxP sites can recombine with each other and not with any other variants (**Figure 1A**). A previous study showed that the detailed neuronal structure, including the dendrites and spines, can be visualized with an AAV-expressing EGFP and membrane-targeted EGFPf linked by self-cleaving P2A peptide (EGFP-P2A-EGFPf, hereafter referred to as EGFPf) (Zhang Q. et al., 2016). Encouraged by this, we inserted the inversed EGFPf coding sequence floxed by a pair of loxP and lox2272 sites into an AAV construct with the human *synapsin* promoter, which drives gene expression in neurons. In the absence of Cre recombinase, EGFPf is not expressed due to its antisense orientation. In the presence of Cre recombinase, the loxP and lox2272 sites undergo recombination with the other loxP and lox2272 sites, respectively, resulting in the inversion of EGFPf and the excision of one from each pair of identical recombination sites. Then, EGFPf is expressed in a Cre-dependent manner (**Figure 1A**). To verify whether this strategy works and how stringent it is, we tested this system in primary cultured neurons first. We transfected AAV_8-CaMKIIα-ΔCre-mKate2 and $AAV_{PhP.eB}$-Syn-DIO-EGFP-P2A-EGFPf virus into primary cultured cortical neurons as a negative control. In ΔCre, the catalytic domain of Cre recombinase was deleted. The neurons infected with these two viruses showed only a red color, without the expression of EGFPf, which suggested that the expression of ΔCre-mKate2 was not able to turn on the expression of EGFPf (**Figure 1B**). We infected primary cultured cortical neurons with AAV_8-CaMKIIα-Cre-mKate2 and $AAV_{PhP.eB}$-DIO-EGFP-P2A-EGFPf virus. Strong EGFPf expression was visualized in red AAV_8-CaMKIIα-Cre-mKate2-infected neurons (**Figure 1C**). From these data, we confirmed that the expression of EGFPf in our construct depended on Cre recombinase driven by a specific promoter.

Sparse Labeling of CaMKIIα-Positive Neurons Throughout the Whole Brain

Systematic AAV injection provides an alternative non-invasive method for the broad delivery of genes to the nervous system. To achieve cell-type-specific labeling of neurons throughout the whole brain, we performed retro-orbital injection of $AAV_{PhP.eB}$-hSyn-DIO-EGFP-P2A-EGFPf virus in CaMKIIα-Cre transgenic mice (**Figure 2A**). AAV-PhP.eB is a novel capsid that can transduce the majority of neurons across many regions of the adult mouse brain and spinal cord after intravenous injection

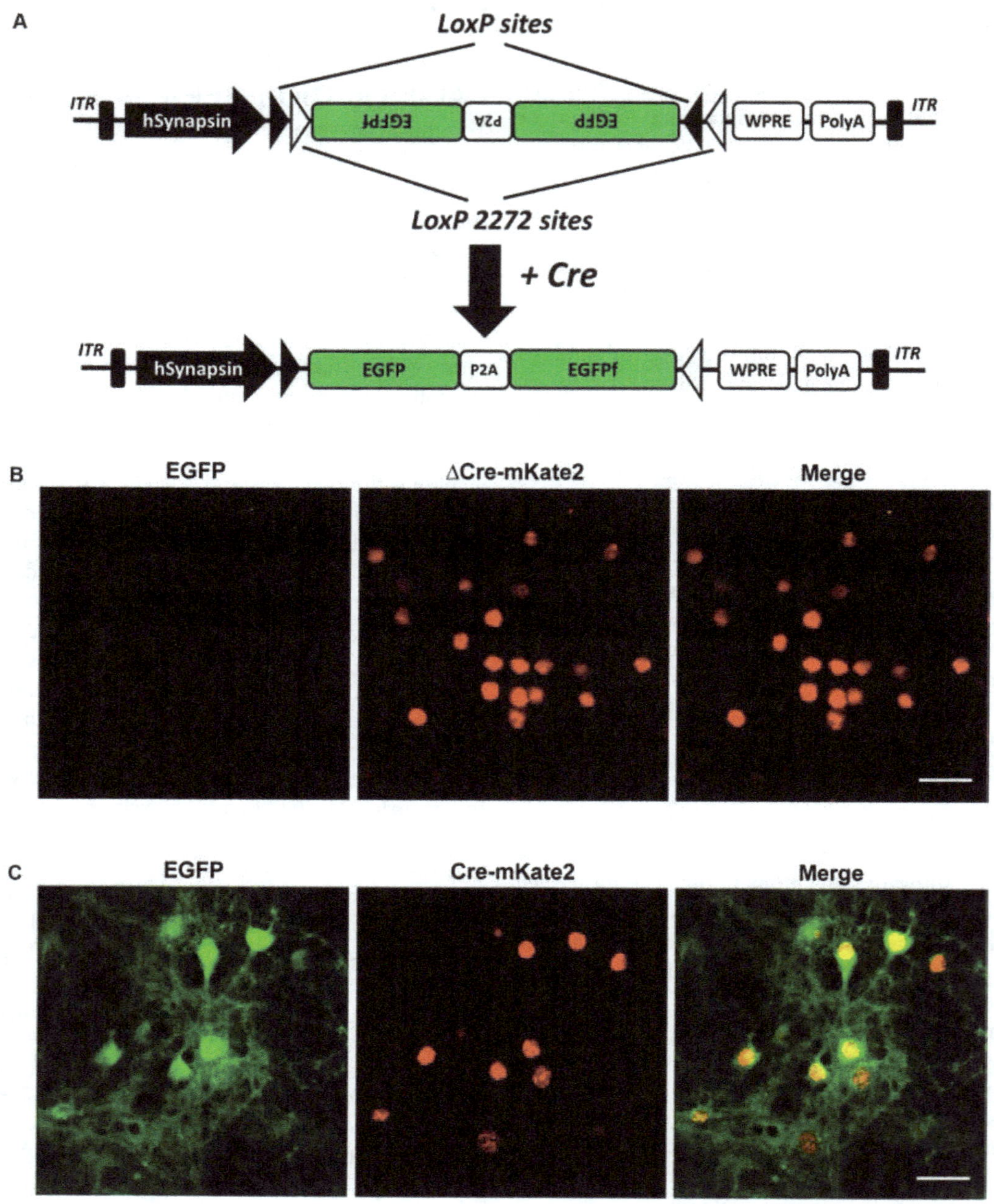

FIGURE 1 | Selective CaMKIIα-Cre virus mediated EGFP expression of AAV-hSyn-DIO-EGFP-P2A-EGFPf in primary cultured cortical neurons. **(A)** Schematic illustration of the AAV-hSyn-DIO-EGFP-P2A-EGFPf construct. Expression of EGFP under the control of the neuron-specific human *synapsin* promoter (hSyn). EGFP and EGFPf are floxed by a pair of loxP (filled triangles) and lox2272 (empty triangles) sites. In the absence of Cre recombinase, the EGFP and EGFPf coding sequences are inverted relative to the hSyn promoter. When expressed, Cre recombinase inverts the EGFP and EGFPf sequences into an active orientation by "flipping" and then "locking" the lox2272 and loxP sites. ITR, inverted terminal repeat; P2A, porcine teschovirus-1 2A; WPRE, Woodchuck hepatitis virus posttranscriptional regulatory element. **(B)** Confocal images of primary cultured cortical neurons infected with AAV_8-CaMKIIα – ΔCre-mKate2 and $AAV_{PhP.eB}$-Syn-DIO-EGFP-P2A-EGFPf virus (negative control). **(C)** Confocal images of primary cultured cortical neurons infected with AAV_8-CaMKIIα-Cre-mKate2 and $AAV_{PhP.eB}$-hSyn-DIO-EGFP-P2A-EGFPf. Images show EGFP (green) and ΔCre/Cre-mKate2 (red) expression. Scale bar: 50 μm.

(Chan et al., 2017). We titrated the injected viral load to achieve sparse labeling of the neurons in the adult mouse brain. To visualize all labeled neurons, we performed immunofluorescence histochemistry with an EGFP antibody to amplify the EGFPf signal. A series of images in **Figure 2B** show a CaMKIIα-Cre mouse brain, from rostral to caudal, in the low-magnification field 3 weeks after viral injection. The morphology of all labeled neurons could be easily identified in those sections.

To assess the specificity of this strategy, we performed immunofluorescent staining with an anti-CaMKIIα antibody to test whether the EGFPf-labeled neurons were CaMKIIα-positive neurons. As expected, EGFPf fluorescence colocalized

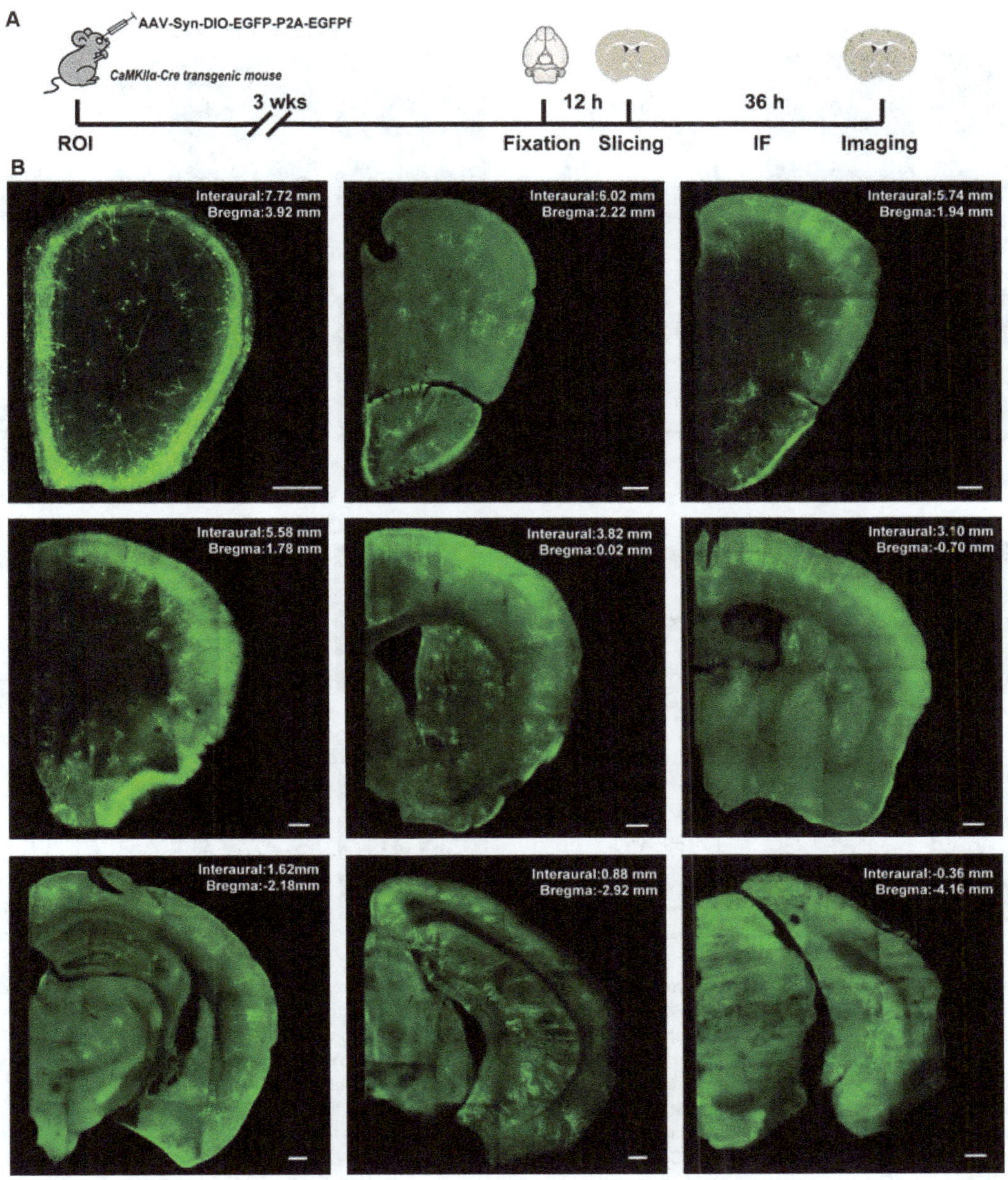

FIGURE 2 | The expression of AAV-hSyn-DIO-EGFP-P2A-EGFPf in the CaMKIIα-Cre transgenic mouse brain. **(A)** Schematic illustration of the experimental workflow. ROI, retro-orbital injection; IF, immunofluorescence staining. **(B)** A series of confocal images shows the distribution of sparsely labeled neurons in different brain regions from a CaMKIIα-Cre transgenic mouse. Scale bar: 300 μm.

with CaMKIIα immunostaining in various regions, including the cortex and striatum, which are the major expression areas of the endogenous CaMKIIα protein (**Supplementary Figure S1**). Interestingly, we found that some EGFPf-labeled neurons were CaMKIIα positive in the hilus region of the DG, in which there are many GABAergic interneurons. Next, we performed 3D reconstructions of EGFPf-labeled neurons in different brain regions and analyzed the complexity of their dendritic trees. In **Figure 3** and **Supplementary Figure S2**, we exhibit some examples of the original images and their 3D reconstructed images of EGFPf-labeled neurons from CaMKIIα-Cre mice. EGFPf-labeled neurons presented a classic pyramidal shape in the frontal association cortex, secondary motor cortex, piriform cortex, and CA1 in the hippocampus. However, the detailed dendritic processes of these neurons were conspicuously divergent. In addition, some EGFPf-labeled neurons also showed different shapes in other areas. For example, in the striatum, the EGFPf labeling depicted the radial dendritic pattern that fits in the projection GABAergic medium-sized spiny neurons (MSNs). In the DG and olfactory bulb, the green fluorescence indicated the granule cell shape. In the agranular insular cortex, some EGFPf even labeled non-pyramidal cell types (**Figure 3** and

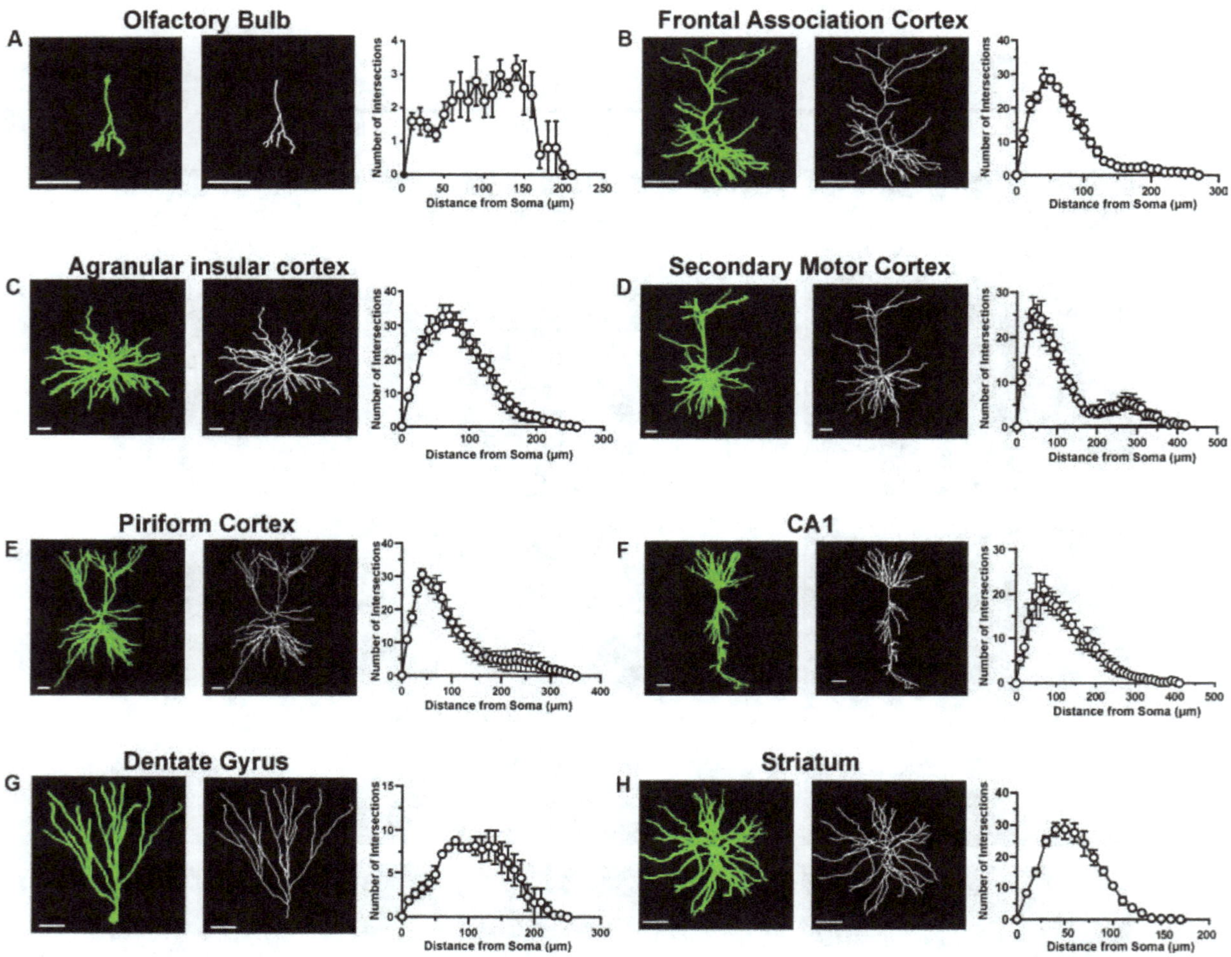

FIGURE 3 | Morphological analysis of single neurons in different brain areas. **(A)** A representative labeled neuron and its reconstructed image (left panel) in the olfactory bulb from a CaMKIIα-Cre transgenic mouse brain; Sholl analysis of labeled neurons in the olfactory bulb (right panel, $n = 5$ neurons from three mice). **(B)** A representative labeled neuron and its reconstructed image (left panel) in the frontal association cortex from a CaMKIIα-Cre transgenic mouse brain; Sholl analysis of labeled neurons in the frontal association cortex (right panel, $n = 5$ neurons from three mice). **(C)** A representative labeled neuron and its reconstructed image (left panel) in the agranular insular cortex from a CaMKIIα-Cre transgenic mouse brain; Sholl analysis of labeled neurons in the agranular insular cortex (right panel, $n = 5$ neurons from three mice). **(D)** A representative labeled neuron and its reconstructed image (left panel) in the secondary motor cortex from a CaMKIIα-Cre transgenic mouse brain; Sholl analysis of labeled neurons in the secondary motor cortex (right panel, $n = 5$ neurons from three mice). **(E)** A representative labeled neuron and its reconstructed image (left panel) in the piriform cortex from a CaMKIIα-Cre transgenic mouse brain; Sholl analysis of labeled neurons in the piriform cortex (right panel, $n = 5$ neurons from three mice). **(F)** A representative labeled neuron and its reconstructed image (left panel) in the CA1 of the hippocampus from a CaMKIIα-Cre transgenic mouse brain; Sholl analysis of labeled neurons in the CA1 of the hippocampus (right panel, $n = 5$ neurons from three mice). **(G)** A representative labeled neuron and its reconstructed image (left panel) in the dentate gyrus from a CaMKIIα-Cre transgenic mouse brain; Sholl analysis of labeled neurons in the dentate gyrus (right panel, $n = 5$ neurons from three mice). **(H)** A representative labeled neuron and its reconstructed image (left panel) in the striatum from a CaMKIIα-Cre transgenic mouse brain; Sholl analysis of labeled neurons in the striatum (right panel, $n = 5$ neurons from three mice). Scale bar: 50 μm.

Supplementary Figure S2). Our results were similar to a previous finding using CaMKIIα-GFP mice (Wang et al., 2013).

To broaden the application of our strategy in other Cre transgenic mouse lines, we tested the labeling effect with a *Somatostatin* Cre transgenic mouse line (SST-Cre) in which Cre is expressed in SST-positive interneurons in the brain. After viral injection, we found that EGFPf-labeled neurons showed morphological traits of interneurons (**Supplementary Figure S3**). The EGFPf-labeled neurons were SST protein-positive interneurons as revealed by SST immunostaining (**Supplementary Figure S3**). These results further confirmed that our strategy was suitable for cell-type-specific labeling and could potentially be applied in other Cre transgenic mouse lines.

Visualization of the Morphological Traits of CaMKIIα-Positive Neurons in *Shank3* KO Mouse Brains

After we confirmed that the FLEX-EGFPf switch system can successfully label single neurons in CaMKIIα-Cre transgenic mice, we wanted to test whether this method could also be used to visualize the morphological traits of single neurons in *Shank3* KO autistic mouse models. We crossed *Shank3* heterozygous mice with CaMKIIα-Cre transgenic mice to obtain *Shank3* KO:CaMKIIα-Cre mice and their littermate controls (WT:CaMKIIα-Cre, **Supplementary Figure S4**). After that, we performed retro-orbital injection of $AAV_{PhP.eB}$-hSyn-DIO-EGFP-P2A-EGFPf virus in these mice and analyzed the labeled neurons in several brain areas. Previous studies have shown that the striatum is the major impaired brain region in *Shank3* KO mice (Peça et al., 2011; Mei et al., 2016; Zhou et al., 2016; Wang et al., 2017). First, we performed 3D reconstruction of MSNs and analyzed the neuronal morphological traits of WT and *Shank3* KO mice in the striatum (**Figures 4A–C**). The results showed that the dendritic complexity in *Shank3* KO mice was reduced compared with that in WT mice (**Figure 4D**, WT: $n = 44$ neurons from three mice; KO: $n = 37$ neurons from three mice, Friedman's M test, $p = 0.005$). And we found reduced intersections in 50 and 60 μm *Shank3* KO mice compared with WT mice (Sholl radius in 50 μm, WT: 24.77 ± 1.19, KO: 21.19 ± 0.94, $p = 0.02$; Sholl radius in 60 μm, WT: 23.3 ± 1.24, KO: 19.78 ± 0.98, $p = 0.03$). There was no difference in dendritic length or volume between *Shank3* KO and WT mice (**Figures 4E,F**, dendritic length, WT: 2,544 ± 135.5 μm, $n = 40$ neurons from three mice, KO: 2,272 ± 99.64 μm, $n = 36$ neurons from three mice, two-tailed unpaired separate variance estimation t-test, $p = 0.11$; dendritic volume, WT: 2,246 ± 217.7 μm^3, $n = 40$ neurons from three mice, KO: 2,356 ± 323.2 μm^3, $n = 37$ neurons from three mice, Mann–Whitney U-test, $p = 0.36$). The total dendritic spine density was reduced in *Shank3* KO mice compared with WT mice (**Figures 4G,H**, total spine density, WT: 15.58 ± 0.63/10 μm, $n = 19$ dendrites from three mice, KO: 13.43 ± 0.62/10 μm, $n = 18$ dendrites from three mice, $p = 0.02$). Among the different spine types, the density of mushroom and long thin spines reduced, but the density of the stubby and filopodia spines did not (**Figures 4G,I** and **Supplementary Figures S6A–C**, mushroom spine density, WT: 2.0 ± 0.15/10 μm, $n = 19$ dendrites from three mice, KO: 1.46 ± 0.16/10 μm, $n = 18$ dendrites from three mice, $p = 0.02$; stubby spine density, WT: 2.37 ± 0.23/10 μm, $n = 19$ dendrites from three mice, KO: 2.65 ± 0.33/10 μm, $n = 18$ dendrites from three mice, $p = 0.49$; long thin spine density, WT: 1.30 ± 0.19/10 μm, $n = 19$ dendrites from three mice, KO: 0.72 ± 0.15/10 μm, $n = 18$ dendrites from three mice, $p = 0.03$; filopodia spine density, WT: 9.91 ± 0.66/10 μm, $n = 19$ dendrites from three mice, KO: 8.59 ± 0.43/10 μm, $n = 18$ dendrites from three mice, two-tailed separate variance estimation, $p = 0.10$).

Our recent work shows that the cortex exhibited neuronal morphological deficits in *Shank3* KO mice (Guo et al., 2019). Thus, we analyzed the dendritic processes and spines of pyramidal neurons in the cortex of WT and *Shank3* KO mice. The Sholl analysis results showed that the dendritic complexity of *Shank3* KO pyramidal neurons was reduced compared with that of WT mice (**Figures 5A–D**, WT: $n = 17$ neurons from three mice, KO: $n = 17$ neurons from three mice, Friedman's M test, $p < 0.0001$). We found a reduction in intersections of 40–90 μm in *Shank3* KO mice compared to WT (Sholl radius in 40 μm, WT: 29.18 ± 1.82, KO: 23.65 ± 1.87, $p = 0.04$; Sholl radius in 50 μm, WT: 29.76 ± 1.93, KO: 24 ± 1.71, $p = 0.03$; Sholl radius in 60 μm, WT: 29.53 ± 2.24, KO: 22.71 ± 1.50, $p = 0.02$; the Sholl radius in 70 μm, WT: 27.35 ± 2.04, KO: 21.06 ± 1.59, $p = 0.02$; Sholl radius in 80 μm, WT: 23.88 ± 1.78, KO: 17.47 ± 1.38, $p = 0.008$; Sholl radius in 90 μm, WT: 19.71 ± 1.73, KO: 53 ± 1.63, $p = 0.04$). There was no significant reduction in the total dendritic length or volume of labeled neurons in *Shank3* KO mice compared with WT mice (**Figures 5E,F**, dendritic length, WT: 3265 ± 343.4 μm, $n = 16$ neurons from three mice, KO: 2831 ± 171.0 μm, $n = 18$ neurons from three mice, two-tailed unpaired separate variance, $p = 0.27$; dendritic volume, WT: 2705 ± 306.1 μm^3, $n = 16$ neurons from three mice, KO: 2269 ± 266.8 μm^3, $n = 18$ neurons from three mice, Mann–Whitney U-test, $p = 0.20$). The total dendritic spine density was reduced significantly in *Shank3* KO mice compared with WT mice (**Figures 5G,H**, WT total spine density: 12.46 ± 1.29/10 μm, $n = 18$ dendrites from three mice, KO total spine density: 7.64 ± 0.53/10 μm, $n = 20$ dendrites from three mice, two-tailed unpaired separate variance estimation t-test, $p = 0.002$). Among the different spine types, the density of mushroom, stubby, and filopodia spines was reduced, but not that of the long thin spines (**Figures 5G,I** and **Supplementary Figures S6D–F**, mushroom spine density, WT: 1.53 ± 0.20/10 μm, $n = 17$ dendrites from three mice, KO: 0.45 ± 0.06/10 μm, $n = 20$ dendrites from three mice, Mann–Whitney U-test, $p < 0.0001$; stubby spine density, WT: 1.81 ± 0.24/10 μm, $n = 18$ dendrites from three mice, KO: 3.91 ± 0.27/10 μm, $n = 20$ dendrites from three mice, $p < 0.0001$; long thin spine density, WT: 1.96 ± 0.57/10 μm, $n = 18$ dendrites from three mice, KO: 1.25 ± 0.18/10 μm, $n = 20$ dendrites from three mice, Mann–Whitney U-test, $p = 0.86$; filopodia spine density, WT: 6.91 ± 1.24/10 μm, $n = 18$ dendrites from three mice, KO: 2.03 ± 0.40/10 μm, $n = 20$ dendrites from three mice, Mann–Whitney U-test, $p = 0.001$). In addition, we also analyzed the basal dendrites from pyramidal cells of cortical layers V–VI, which have a large cell body and long dendritic processes. Interestingly, we found that these neurons of *Shank3* KO mice showed more complicated dendrites than those of WT mice (**Supplementary Figures S5A–C**, WT: $n = 11$ neurons from three mice; KO: $n = 14$ neurons from three mice, Friedman's M test, $p < 0.0001$). Increased intersections were found from 100 to 120 μm in *Shank3* KO mice compared with WT mice (Sholl radius in 100 μm, WT: 11.36 ± 1.94, KO: 17.86 ± 2.05, $p = 0.03$; Sholl radius in 110 μm, WT: 8.91 ± 1.48 KO: 14 ± 1.83, $p < 0.05$; Sholl radius in 120 μm, WT: 6 ± 1.18, KO: 10.71 ± 1.48, $p = 0.03$). However, there were no changes in dendritic length or volume between *Shank3* KO and WT mice (**Supplementary Figures S5D,E**, dendritic length, WT: 3001 ± 308.3 μm, $n = 11$ neurons from three mice, KO: 3081 ± 246.9 μm, $n = 14$ neurons from three mice, $p = 0.84$; dendritic volume, WT: 2826 ± 592.7 μm^3, $n = 11$ neurons from three mice, KO: 5109 ± 1138 μm^3, $n = 14$ neurons from three mice, $p = 0.27$).

In addition to the striatum and cortex, *Shank3* is also expressed in the hippocampus (Peça et al., 2011). Previous work did not find memory-related behavior or neuronal function deficits of the hippocampus in *Shank3* KO mice. Therefore, we investigated the cell structure characteristics of dentate granule cells in WT and *Shank3* KO mice as a negative control (**Figures 6A–C**). We found that dendritic complexity of *Shank3* KO mice was reduced compared with that of WT

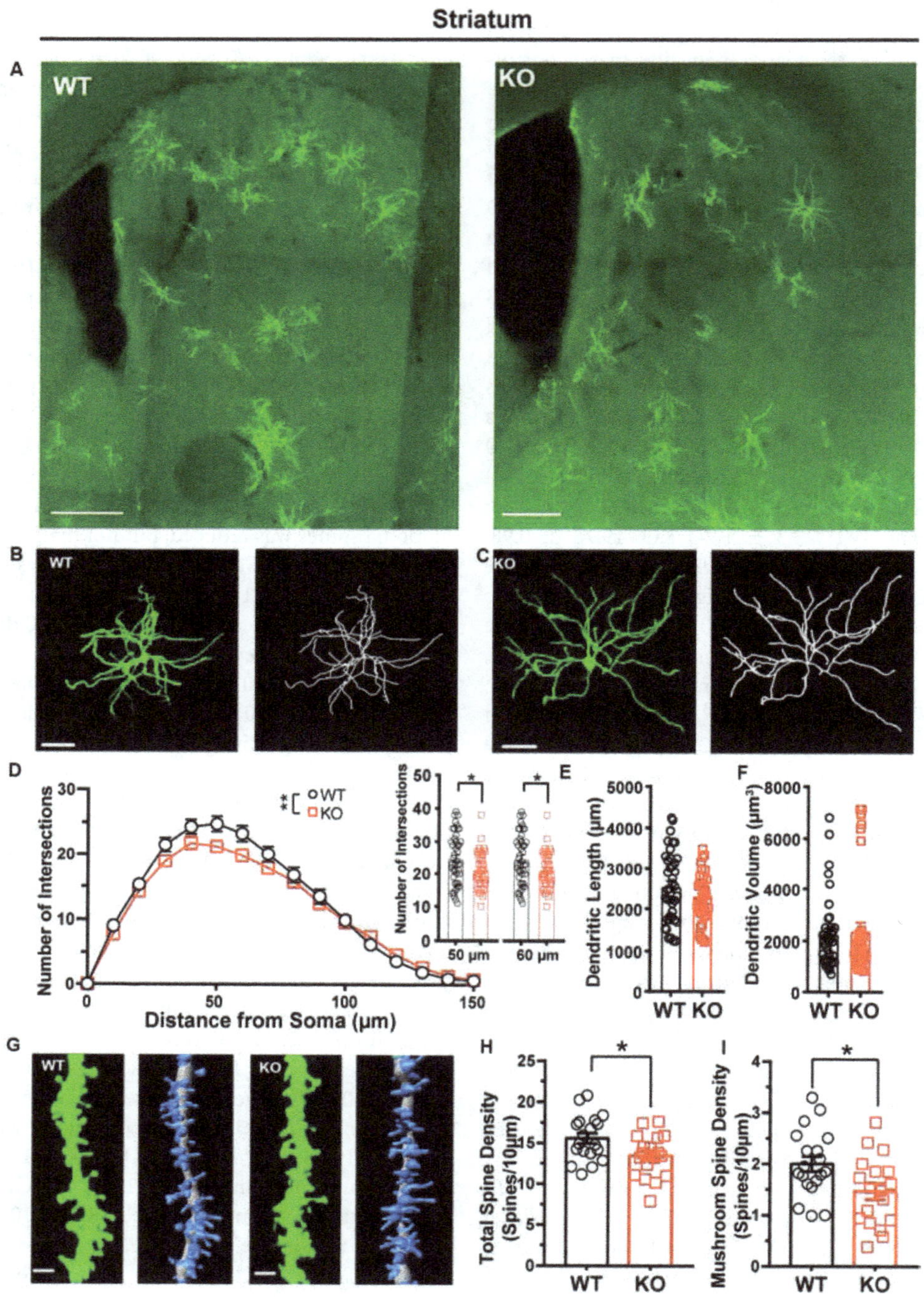

FIGURE 4 | Dendritic complexity and dendritic spine density were reduced in medium-sized spiny neurons (MSNs) from the striatum of *Shank3* KO mice. **(A)** Representative images showing the distribution of labeled neurons in the striatum of WT and KO mice. Scale bar: 200 μm. Representative projection neurons and reconstructed images in the striatum of WT **(B)** and KO mice **(C)**. Scale bar: 50 μm. **(D)** Sholl analysis showed reduced dendritic complexity of MSNs in KO mice compared with WT mice, and specific differences existed between WT and KO mice in Sholl radius (WT: $n = 44$ neurons from three mice; KO: $n = 37$ neurons from three mice, Friedman's M test, $\chi^2 = 7.750$, $df = 1$, $p = 0.005$; Sholl radius in 50 μm, WT: 24.77 ± 1.19, KO: 21.19 ± 0.94, two-tailed unpaired t-test, $t = 2.30$, $df = 79$, $p = 0.02$; Sholl radius in 60 μm, WT: 23.3 ± 1.24, KO: 19.78 ± 0.98, two-tailed unpaired t-test, $t = 2.17$, $df = 79$, $p = 0.03$). **(E)** The dendritic length of MSNs was similar between KO mice and WT mice (WT: 2,544 ± 135.5 μm, $n = 40$ neurons from three mice; KO: 2272 ± 99.64 μm, $n = 36$ neurons from three mice, two-tailed unpaired separate variance estimation t-test, $t = 1.62$, df = 69.84, $p = 0.11$). **(F)** The dendritic volume of MSNs was similar between KO mice and WT mice (WT: 2246 ± 217.7 μm^3, $n = 40$ neurons from three mice; KO: 2356 ± 323.2 μm^3, $n = 37$ neurons from three mice, Mann–Whitney U-test, $Z = -0.91$, $p = 0.36$). **(G)** Representative spine and reconstructed images in the striatum of WT (left panel) and KO mice (right panel). Scale bar: 2 μm. **(H)** The total dendritic spine density was reduced in KO mice compared with WT mice (WT: 15.58 ± 0.63/10 μm, $n = 19$ dendrites from three mice; KO: 13.43 ± 0.62/10 μm, $n = 18$ dendrites from three mice, two-tailed unpaired t-test, $t = 2.44$, $df = 35$, $p = 0.02$). **(I)** The density of mushroom spines was reduced in KO mice compared with WT mice (WT: 2.00 ± 0.15/10 μm, $n = 19$ dendrites from three mice; KO: 1.46 ± 0.16/10 μm, $n = 18$ dendrites from three mice; two-tailed unpaired t-test, $t = 2.47$, $df = 35$, $p = 0.02$). Data are presented as the mean ± SEM. $^*p < 0.05$, $^{**}p < 0.01$. WT, wild-type mice; KO, *Shank3* KO mice.

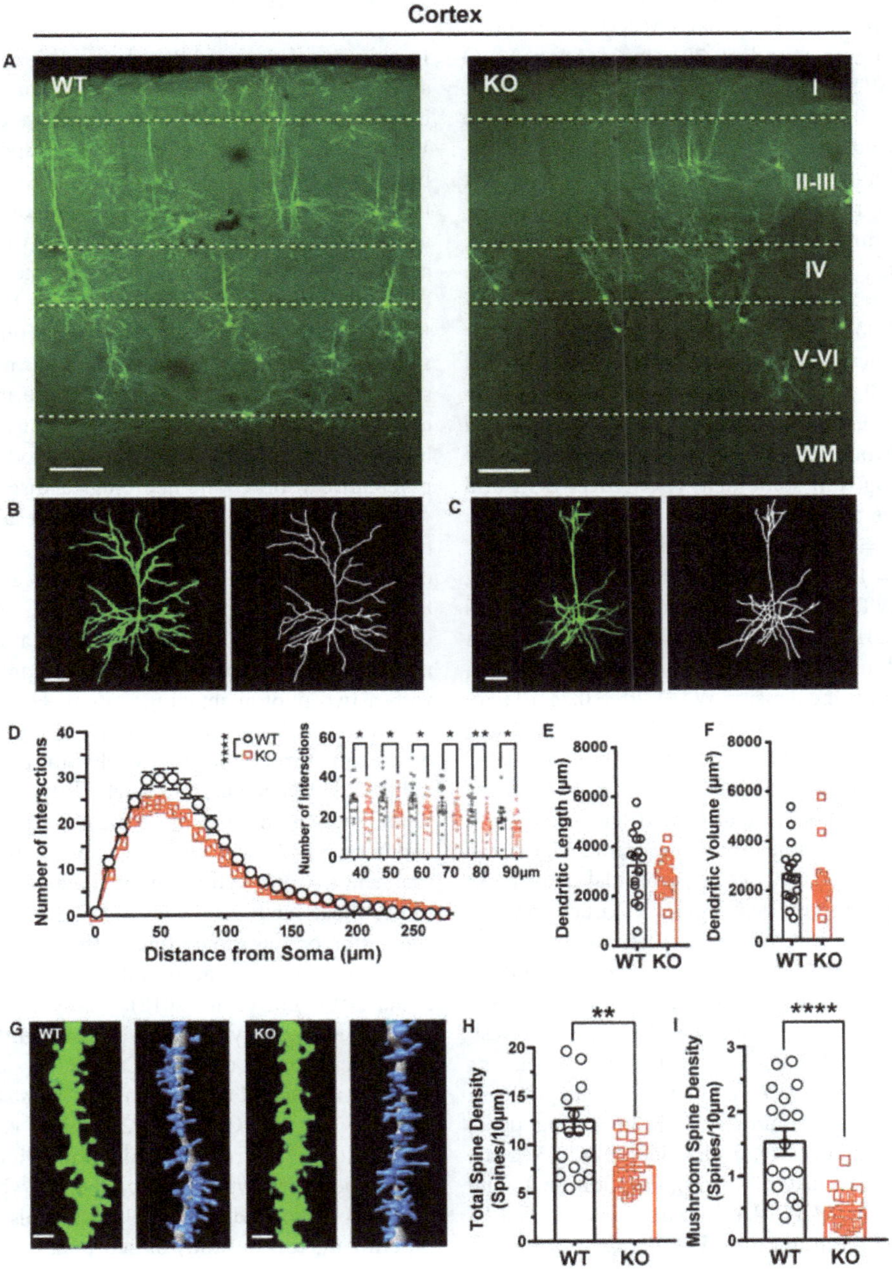

FIGURE 5 | Dendritic complexity and dendritic spine density were reduced in pyramidal neurons from the cortex of *Shank3* KO mice. **(A)** Representative images showing the distribution of labeled neurons in the cortex of WT and KO mice. Scale bar: 200 μm. WM: white matter. Representative projection neurons and reconstructed images in the cortex of WT **(B)** and KO mice **(C)**. Scale bar: 50 μm. **(D)** Sholl analysis showed reduced dendritic complexity of pyramidal neurons in KO mice compared with WT mice, and specific differences existed between WT and KO mice in Sholl radius (WT: $n = 17$ neurons from three mice, KO: $n = 17$ neurons from three mice, Friedman's *M* test, $\chi^2 = 12.63$, $df = 1$, $p < 0.0001$; Sholl radius in 40 μm, WT: 29.18 ± 1.82, KO: 23.65 ± 1.87, two-tailed unpaired *t*-test, $t = 2.12$, $df = 32$, $p = 0.04$; Sholl radius in 50 μm, WT: 29.76 ± 1.93, KO: 24 ± 1.71, two-tailed unpaired *t*-test, $t = 2.24$, $df = 32$, $p = 0.03$; Sholl radius in 60 μm, WT: 29.53 ± 2.24, KO: 22.71 ± 1.50, two-tailed unpaired *t*-test, $t = 2.53$, $df = 32$, $p = 0.02$; Sholl radius in 70 μm, WT: 27.35 ± 2.04, KO: 21.06 ± 1.59, two-tailed unpaired *t*-test, $t = 2.44$, $df = 32$, $p = 0.02$; Sholl radius in 80 μm, WT: 23.88 ± 1.78, KO: 17.47 ± 1.38, two-tailed unpaired *t*-test, $t = 2.84$, $df = 32$, $p = 0.008$; Sholl radius in 90 μm, WT: 19.71 ± 1.73, KO: 14.53 ± 1.63, two-tailed unpaired *t*-test, $t = 2.18$, $df = 32$, $p = 0.04$). **(E)** The dendritic lengths of pyramidal neurons were similar between KO mice and WT mice (WT: 3,265 ± 343.4 μm, $n = 16$ neurons from three mice; KO: 2,831 ± 171 μm, $n = 18$ neurons from three mice, two-tailed unpaired separate variance, $t = 1.13$, $df = 22.16$, $p = 0.27$). **(F)** The dendritic volume of pyramidal neurons was similar between KO mice and WT mice (WT: 2705 ± 306.1 μm^3, $n = 16$ neurons from three mice; KO: 2269 ± 266.8 μm^3, $n = 18$ neurons from three mice. Mann–Whitney *U*-test, $Z = -1.28$, $p = 0.20$). **(G)** Representative spine and reconstructed images in the cortex of WT (left) and KO mice (right). Scale bar: 2 μm. **(H)** The total dendritic spine density was reduced in KO mice compared with WT mice (WT: 12.46 ± 1.29/10 μm, $n = 18$ dendrites from three mice; KO: 7.64 ± 0.53/10 μm, $n = 20$ dendrites from three mice; two-tailed unpaired separate variance estimation *t*-test, $t = 3.46$, $df = 22.71$, $p = 0.002$). **(I)** The density of mushrooms was reduced in KO mice compared with WT mice (WT: 1.5 ± 0.20/10 μm, $n = 17$ dendrites from three mice; KO: 0.45 ± 0.06/10 μm, $n = 20$ dendrites from three mice. Mann–Whitney *U*-test, $Z = -4.09$, $p < 0.0001$). Data are presented as the mean ± SEM. $^*p < 0.05$, $^{**}p < 0.01$, $^{****}p < 0.0001$. WT, wild-type mice; KO, *Shank3* KO mice.

mice (**Figure 6D**, WT: $n = 13$ neurons from three mice, KO: $n = 12$ neurons from three mice, Friedman's M test, $p < 0.0001$). A reduced intersection was found at 70 μm in *Shank3* KO mice compared with WT mice (Sholl radius at 70 μm, WT: 7.69 ± 0.51, KO: 5.75 ± 0.49, $p = 0.01$). There was no difference in dendritic length or volume between *Shank3* KO mice and WT mice (**Figures 6E,F**, dendritic length, WT: 1387 ± 96.76 μm, $n = 12$ neurons from three mice, KO: 1101 ± 112.4 μm, $n = 12$ neurons from three mice, $p = 0.07$; dendritic volume, WT: 1879 ± 541.2 μm^3, $n = 12$ neurons from three mice, KO: 1253 ± 224.3 μm^3, $n = 12$ neurons from three mice, Mann–Whitney U-test, $p = 1.00$). The total spine density was similar between *Shank3* KO mice and WT mice (**Figures 6G,H**, total spine density, WT: 20.40 ± 1.29/10 μm, $n = 19$ dendrites from three mice, KO: 21.49 ± 1.17/10 μm, $n = 18$ dendrites from three mice, $p = 0.54$). Among the different spine types, we found a reduction only in long thin spine density (**Figures 6G,I** and **Supplementary Figures S6G–I**, mushroom spine density, WT: 3.8 ± 0.40/10 μm, $n = 19$ dendrites from three mice, KO: 3.56 ± 0.28/10 μm, $n = 18$ dendrites from three mice, $p = 0.59$; stubby spine density, WT: 2.46 ± 0.46/10 μm, $n = 19$ dendrites from three mice; KO: 2.81 ± 0.34/10 μm, $n = 18$ dendrites from three mice, two-tailed unpaired separate variance estimation t-test, $p = 0.55$; long thin spine density, WT: 1.20 ± 0.24/10 μm, $n = 19$ dendrites from three mice, KO: 0.50 ± 0.16/10 μm, $n = 18$ dendrites from three mice, Mann–Whitney U-test, $p = 0.01$; filopodia spine density, WT: 12.91 ± 0.82/10 μm, $n = 19$ dendrites from three mice, KO: 14.62 ± 1.21/10 μm, $n = 18$ dendrites from three mice, $p = 0.25$). In addition to dentate granular cells, we also compared the dendritic processes of pyramidal neurons in the CA1 of the hippocampus between *Shank3* KO mice and WT mice and did not find significant differences, including the Sholl intersections, dendritic length, and volume (**Supplementary Figures S5F–J**, Sholl intersections WT: $n = 11$ neurons from three mice; KO: $n = 7$ neurons from three mice, Friedman's M test, $p = 0.08$; dendritic length, WT: 5793 ± 1313 μm, $n = 13$ neurons from three mice, KO: 5757 ± 1775 μm, $n = 7$ neurons from three mice, $p = 0.61$; dendritic volume, WT: 2836 ± 226.5 μm^3, $n = 13$ neurons from three mice, KO: 3660 ± 418.5 μm^3, $n = 7$ neurons from three mice, $p = 0.07$). In addition to the morphological changes of EGFPf-labeled neurons in *Shank3* KO mice, we found that the number of EGFPf-labeled neurons was different between *Shank3* KO:CaMKIIα-Cre mice and their littermate controls. We counted the EGFP-labeled neurons in the striatum and cortex in those mice. The number of EGFPf-labeled neurons in the striatum was greater in WT mice than in KO mice (**Supplementary Figure S7A**, WT: 56.5 ± 3.84, $n = 12$ slice dendrites from three mice, KO: 34.17 ± 2.01, $n = 12$ slices from three mice, $p < 0.0001$). The number of EGFPf-labeled neurons in the sensory and motor cortex was higher in WT mice than in KO mice (**Supplementary Figure S7B**, WT: 40.67 ± 2.21, $n = 12$ slice dendrites from three mice, KO: 25.92 ± 0.85, $n = 12$ slices from three mice, $p < 0.0001$).

Overall, we confirmed that the FLEX-EGFPf switch system can successfully label single neurons in Cre transgenic mice, and this method could also be used to visualize the morphological traits of single neurons in autistic mouse models.

DISCUSSION

In this study, we established a FLEX-EGFPf switch system to sparsely label the specific types of neurons throughout the whole brain of Cre transgenic mice using systematic AAV injection. We verified the labeling effect and the specificity of this strategy both *in vitro* and *in vivo*. Furthermore, we applied this method to investigate the dendritic process complexity and dendritic spine density of projection neurons in various brain areas in an autistic mouse model, *Shank3* KO mice. The results suggested that the projection neurons in different brain regions of *Shank3* KO mice showed diverse neuronal morphological deficits in the striatum, cortex, and hippocampus. Our method provided a new straightforward approach to screen the morphological changes of specific types of neurons throughout the whole brain. It can be used not only for ASD mouse models but also for other psychiatric disorder and neurological disease animal models.

There are several strategies for sparse labeling of specific types of neurons in the brain. Filling dye into a certain type of neuron-expressed fluorescent protein is an easy way to implement this requirement (Ren et al., 2017). This method can be used to visualize neuronal morphology after electrophysiological recording. This method can also be applied *in vivo* combined with a two-photon imaging system. However, the efficiency of this method is relatively low, and it cannot label the specific types of neurons throughout the whole brain. Recently, more genetic methods have been used to label cell-type-specific neurons in the brain, such as mosaicism with a repeat frameshift strategy (Lu and Yang, 2017) and stochastic gene activation with a regulated sparseness strategy (Ibrahim et al., 2018). Though it is powerful to use those methods for labeling neurons in mouse brains, the generation of new mouse lines is time-consuming. There are also dual-virus systems to accomplish cell-type-specific labeling (Zhu et al., 2014; Lin et al., 2018). Compared with those methods, our current strategy is simple and straightforward. First, for cell type specificity, we used the Cre-loxP system, which has already been demonstrated to be a mature and straightforward strategy. Our AAV-hSyn-DIO-EGFP-P2A-EGFPf vector could potentially be used for most Cre transgenic mouse lines. This method could also achieve cell-type-specific labeling when combined with a specific promoter-driven Cre virus. This study will streamline experiments for the study of neuronal morphological changes in mouse models of psychiatric disorders and neurological diseases. Second, the labeling of sparseness and stochasticity is simple and controllable through the adjustment of the viral titer in our method. Third, we selected EGFPf as the reporter protein to visualize the neurons to achieve fine process labeling. This fluorescence reporter has been proven to be a good indicator for dendritic spine labeling (Cai et al., 2013; Zhang Q. et al., 2016; Wang et al., 2017; Guo et al., 2019). Fourth, our virus delivery method is uncomplicated and suitable for mice from P0 to adulthood. However, since it takes 3 weeks to obtain good expression of EGFPf in our method, it is hard for the morphological characteristics of the early neurodevelopmental study of ASD models with such long expression times. This is quite important, particularly for neurodevelopmental disorders, such as ASD. To conquer this problem, we will try to use *in utero*

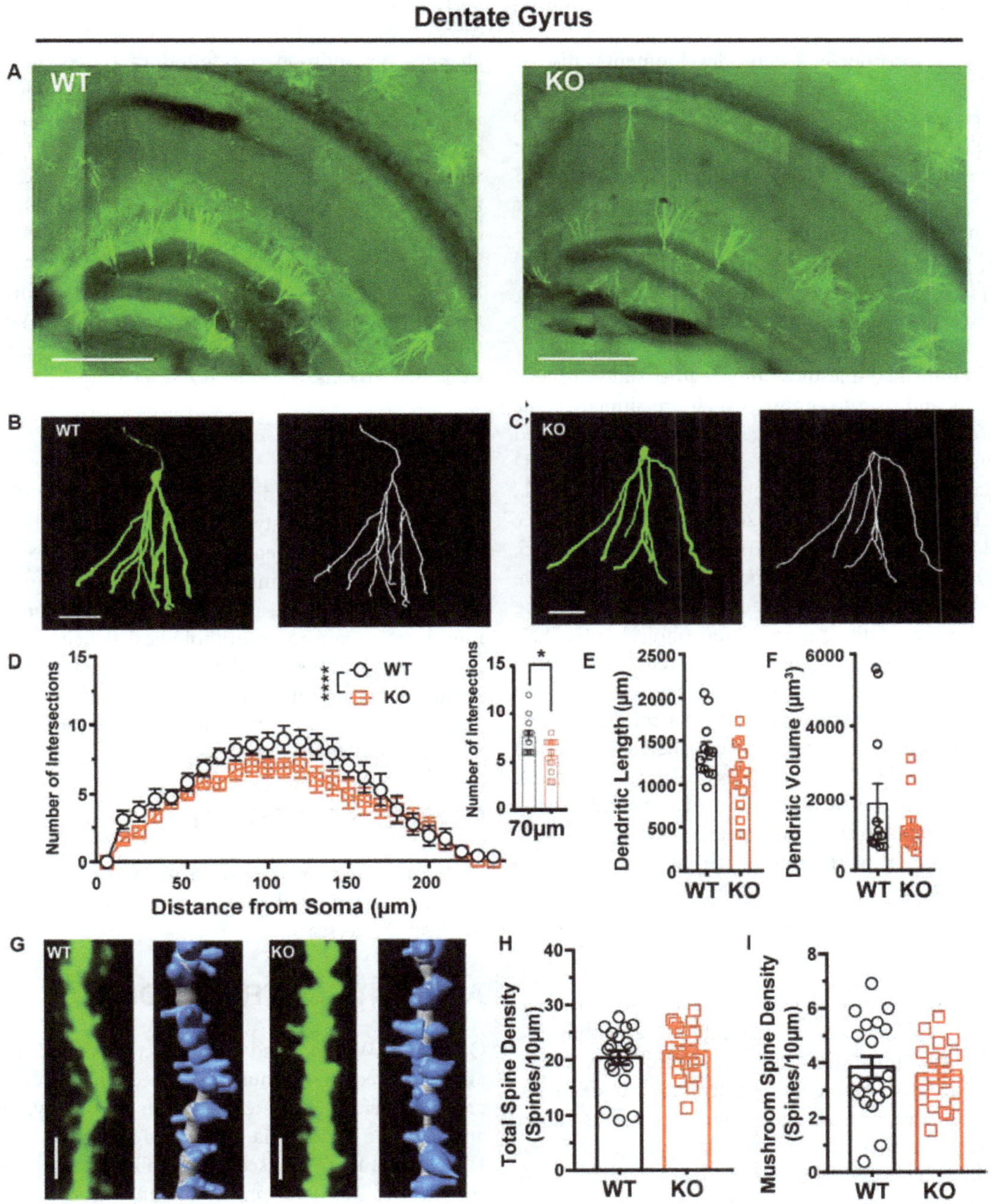

FIGURE 6 | Dendritic complexity was reduced, but dendritic spine density was relatively normal in the dentate granular neurons from the hippocampus of *Shank3* KO mice. **(A)** Representative images showing the distribution of labeled neurons in the dentate gyrus (DG) of WT and KO mice. Scale bar: 500 μm. Representative projection neurons and reconstructed images in the DG of WT **(B)** and KO mice **(C)**. Scale bar: 50 μm. **(D)** Sholl analysis showed that the dendritic complexity of DGs in KO mice was similar to that in WT mice, and specific differences existed between WT and KO mice in Sholl radius (WT: $n = 13$ neurons from three mice, KO: $n = 12$ neurons from three mice, Friedman's *M* test, $\chi^2 = 24.35$, $df = 1$, $p < 0.0001$; Sholl radius in 70 μm, WT: 7.69 ± 0.51, KO: 5.75 ± 0.49, two-tailed unpaired *t*-test, $t = 2.72$, $df = 23$, $p = 0.01$). **(E)** The dendritic lengths of dentate granular neurons were similar between KO mice and WT mice (WT: 1387 ± 96.76 μm, $n = 12$ neurons from three mice; KO: 1101 ± 112.4 μm, $n = 12$ neurons from three mice; two-tailed unpaired *t*-test, $t = 1.94$, $df = 22$, $p = 0.07$). **(F)** The dendritic volume of dentate granular neurons was similar between KO mice and WT mice (WT: 1879 ± 541.2 μm^3, $n = 12$ neurons from three mice; KO: 1253 ± 224.3 μm^3, $n = 12$ neurons from three mice; Mann–Whitney *U*-test, $Z = 0.000$, $p = 1.00$). **(G)** Representative spine and reconstructed images in the hippocampus of WT (left) and KO mice (right). Scale bar: 2 μm. **(H)** The total spine density was similar between *Shank3* KO mice and WT mice (WT: 20.40 ± 1.29/10 μm, $n = 19$ dendrites from three mice; KO: 21.49 ± 1.17/10 μm, $n = 18$ dendrites from three mice; two-tailed unpaired *t*-test, $t = -0.62$, $df = 35$, $p = 0.54$). **(I)** The mushroom spine density was similar between KO mice and WT mice (WT: 3.8 ± 0.40/10 μm, $n = 19$ dendrites from three mice; KO: 3.56 ± 0.28/10 μm, $n = 18$ dendrites from three mice; two-tailed unpaired *t*-test, $t = 0.55$, $df = 35$, $p = 0.59$). Data are presented as the mean ± the SEM. *$p < 0.05$, ****$p < 0.0001$. WT, wild-type mice; KO, *Shank3* KO mice.

viral injection to apply this method in visualizing neurons during the postnatal stages.

Autism spectrum disorder is a neurodevelopmental disease that is characterized by social dysfunction and repetitive behaviors (Willsey and State, 2015). Though the causes of ASD are still unclear, extensive genetic studies have suggested that genetic abnormalities contribute to the etiology of ASD. *Shank3* is an ASD risk gene that has been proven by human genetic studies and animal models (Monteiro and Feng, 2017). SHANK3 is a scaffolding protein that involves a cytoskeleton-associated signaling complex at the postsynaptic density of excitatory synapses in the mammalian brain (Naisbitt et al., 1999; Sheng and Kim, 2000). Several groups generated different *Shank3* KO mouse lines and confirmed that those mouse lines showed social interaction deficits and overgrooming, which are similar to the phenotypes observed in ASD patients. These studies suggested that these mouse lines are promising mouse models for ASD research (Bozdagi et al., 2010; Peça et al., 2011; Wang et al., 2011; Kouser et al., 2013; Lee et al., 2015; Speed et al., 2015; Jaramillo et al., 2016; Mei et al., 2016; Wang et al., 2016; Zhou et al., 2016). Among the *Shank3* KO mouse lines, we chose *Shank3B* KO in our study (Peça et al., 2011). In the initial characterization of the neuronal morphology of MSNs in *Shank3B* KO mice, Peça et al. (2011) found that young (4-week) *Shank3B* KO mice showed an increased dendritic complexity and total dendritic length of MSNs compared with the MSNs in WT mice. Interestingly, we labeled the MSNs in the striatum of *Shank3B* KO:CaMKIIα-Cre mice and found no difference in total dendritic length but decreased dendritic complexity. We speculate that the major reason for these inconsistent results might be the mouse age difference between our study and that of Peça and colleagues. We used older (10-week-old) mice than the younger mice (4-week-old) used in the previous study. A previous clinical study showed that brain size in autistic patients was slightly reduced at birth, dramatically increased within the first year of life, but then plateaued so that the majority of patients were within the normal range by adulthood (Redcay and Courchesne, 2005). The discrepancy in the total dendritic length and dendritic complexity between the previous study and our results might capture the different stages of the MSN dendritic changes in *Shank3B* KO mice. For dendritic spine density, both Peça's results and our results showed a significant reduction in *Shank3B* KO compared with WT animals. Additionally, reports from other laboratories (Bozdagi et al., 2010; Wang et al., 2011; Kouser et al., 2013) showed a similar reduction of dendritic spines in other *Shank3* KO mice. These results suggested that dendritic spine changes might be a key morphological deficit in *Shank3* KO mice. In addition, we also analyzed the dendritic processes and spines of pyramidal neurons in the cortex in *Shank3B* KO:CaMKIIα-Cre mice. The results showed a significant reduction in both dendritic complexity and spine density of layer II–III neurons in *Shank3B* KO mice compared with littermate controls. Interestingly, we found that *Shank3B* KO mice showed even more complicated dendrites in layer V–VI pyramidal neurons than WT mice. This result indicated that *Shank3B* insufficiency caused heterogeneous changes in the cortex. Further study is needed to determine the consequences of changes in animal behavior caused by these heterogeneous changes. In addition, we found that the number of EGFPf-labeled neurons was less in *Shank3* KO:CaMKIIα-Cre mice than in WT:CaMKIIα-Cre mice. One of the possible reasons is the reduction of projection neurons in *Shank3* KO mice compare with those in WT animals. And also, SHANK3 and CaMKIIα are two extremely abundant proteins in the postsynaptic densities of excitatory synapses. A recent study showed that SHANK3 interacts with CaMKIIα through its N-terminal domain. The lack of SHANK3 might cause changes in the function and distribution of CaMKIIα (Perfitt et al., 2020). We speculate that the fewer number of EGFPf-labeled neurons might be caused by these two reasons.

CONCLUSION

In summary, we developed a simple and straightforward strategy to perform sparse cell-type-specific neuronal labeling throughout the whole brain. Moreover, we used this strategy to analyze the dendritic complexity and spine density of the projection neurons in the striatum, cortex, and hippocampus in *Shank3* KO mice. We found heterogeneous morphological deficits of single neurons in this ASD mouse model. Our method has many potential implications for future understanding of the cell-type-specific changes that occur in not only ASD but also other psychiatric disorders and neurological diseases.

ETHICS STATEMENT

The animal study was reviewed and approved by the Institutional Animal Care and Use Committee of the Fourth Military Medical University.

AUTHOR CONTRIBUTIONS

QC and WW conceived the project, designed the experiments, and prepared the manuscript based on the draft by DC. DC and KR performed the experiments and analyzed the data. HL analyzed the data. HMa performed statistical analyses. KR, ZL, HMo, SX, and YS revised it critically for important intellectual content. All authors approved the final version of the manuscript submitted for publication, all persons designated authors qualify for authorship, and all those who qualify for authorship are listed.

FUNDING

This work was supported by the Natural Science Foundation of China (Grant Nos. 81871078 to QC and 81771476 to WW) and the Science and Technology Project of Guangzhou (Grant No. 201904010275 to YS).

ACKNOWLEDGMENTS

We thank Haifeng Zhang (Fourth Military Medical University)

for technical support and suggestions of neuronal 3D reconstruction. We thank American Journal Experts (AJE) for English language editing (certificate verification code: E8F0-FB18-2891-1B46-4549).

REFERENCES

Atasoy, D., Aponte, Y., Su, H. H., and Sternson, S. M. (2008). A FLEX switch targets Channelrhodopsin-2 to multiple cell types for imaging and long-range circuit mapping. *J. Neurosci.* 28, 7025–7030. doi: 10.1523/jneurosci.1954-08.2008

Bariselli, S., Tzanoulinou, S., Glangetas, C., Prevost-Solie, C., Pucci, L., Viguie, J., et al. (2016). SHANK3 controls maturation of social reward circuits in the VTA. *Nat. Neurosci.* 19, 926–934. doi: 10.1038/nn.4319

Bourgeron, T. (2009). A synaptic trek to autism. *Curr. Opin Neurobiol.* 19, 231–234. doi: 10.1016/j.conb.2009.06.003

Bourgeron, T. (2015). From the genetic architecture to synaptic plasticity in autism spectrum disorder. *Nat. Rev. Neurosci.* 16, 551–563. doi: 10.1038/nrn3992

Bozdagi, O., Sakurai, T., Papapetrou, D., Wang, X., Dickstein, D. L., Takahashi, N., et al. (2010). Haploinsufficiency of the autism-associated Shank3 gene leads to deficits in synaptic function, social interaction, and social communication. *Mol. Autism.* 1:15. doi: 10.1186/2040-2392-1-15

Cai, D., Cohen, K. B., Luo, T., Lichtman, J. W., and Sanes, J. R. (2013). Improved tools for the Brainbow toolbox. *Nat. Methods* 10, 540–547. doi: 10.1038/nmeth.2450

Chan, K. Y., Jang, M. J., Yoo, B. B., Greenbaum, A., Ravi, N., Wu, W. L., et al. (2017). Engineered AAVs for efficient noninvasive gene delivery to the central and peripheral nervous systems. *Nat. Neurosci.* 20, 1172–1179. doi: 10.1038/nn.4593

Emmenlauer, M., Ronneberger, O., Ponti, A., Schwarb, P., Griffa, A., Filippi, A., et al. (2009). XuvTools: free, fast and reliable stitching of large 3D datasets. *J. Microsc.* 233, 42–60. doi: 10.1111/j.1365-2818.2008.03094.x

Guo, B., Chen, J., Chen, Q., Ren, K., Feng, D., Mao, H., et al. (2019). Anterior cingulate cortex dysfunction underlies social deficits in Shank3 mutant mice. *Nat. Neurosci.* 22, 1223–1234. doi: 10.1038/s41593-019-0445-9

Ibrahim, L. A., Huang, J. J., Wang, S. Z., Kim, Y. J., Zhang, L. I., and Tao, H. W. (2018). Sparse labeling and neural tracing in brain circuits by STARS strategy: revealing morphological development of type II spiral ganglion neurons. *Cereb. Cortex* 29:1700. doi: 10.1093/cercor/bhy202

Jaramillo, T. C., Speed, H. E., Xuan, Z., Reimers, J. M., Liu, S., and Powell, C. M. (2016). Altered striatal synaptic function and abnormal behaviour in Shank3 Exon4-9 deletion mouse model of autism. *Autism Res.* 9, 350–375. doi: 10.1002/aur.1529

Kouser, M., Speed, H. E., Dewey, C. M., Reimers, J. M., Widman, A. J., Gupta, N., et al. (2013). Loss of predominant Shank3 isoforms results in hippocampus-dependent impairments in behavior and synaptic transmission. *J. Neurosci.* 33, 18448–18468. doi: 10.1523/JNEUROSCI.3017-13.2013

Lee, J., Chung, C., Ha, S., Lee, D., Kim, D. Y., Kim, H., et al. (2015). Shank3-mutant mice lacking exon 9 show altered excitation/inhibition balance, enhanced rearing, and spatial memory deficit. *Front. Cell Neurosci.* 9:94. doi: 10.3389/fncel.2015.00094

Lin, R., Wang, R., Yuan, J., Feng, Q., Zhou, Y., Zeng, S., et al. (2018). Cell-type-specific and projection-specific brain-wide reconstruction of single neurons. *Nat. Methods* 15, 1033–1036. doi: 10.1038/s41592-018-0184-y

Lu, X. H., and Yang, X. W. (2017). Genetically-directed Sparse Neuronal Labeling in BAC Transgenic Mice through Mononucleotide Repeat Frameshift. *Sci. Rep.* 7:43915. doi: 10.1038/srep43915

Mei, Y., Monteiro, P., Zhou, Y., Kim, J. A., Gao, X., Fu, Z., et al. (2016). Adult restoration of Shank3 expression rescues selective autistic-like phenotypes. *Nature* 530, 481–484. doi: 10.1038/nature16971

Monteiro, P., and Feng, G. (2017). SHANK proteins: roles at the synapse and in autism spectrum disorder. *Nat. Rev. Neurosci.* 18, 147–157. doi: 10.1038/nrn.2016.183

Naisbitt, S., Kim, E., Tu, J., Xiao, B., Sala, C., Valtschanoff, J., et al. (1999). Shank, a novel family of postsynaptic density proteins that binds to the NMDA receptor/PSD-95/GKAP complex and cortactin. *Neuron* 23, 569–582. doi: 10.1016/s0896-6273(00)80809-0

Peça, J., Feliciano, C., Ting, J., Wang, W., Wells, M., Venkatraman, T., et al. (2011). Shank3 mutant mice display autistic-like behaviours and striatal dysfunction. *Nature* 472, 437–442. doi: 10.1038/nature09965

Penzes, P., Cahill, M. E., Jones, K. A., Vanleeuwen, J. E., and Woolfrey, K. M. (2011). Dendritic spine pathology in neuropsychiatric disorders. *Nat. Neurosci.* 14, 285–293. doi: 10.1038/nn.2741

Perfitt, T. L., Wang, X., Dickerson, M. T., Stephenson, J. R., Nakagawa, T., Jacobson, D. A., et al. (2020). Neuronal L-Type calcium channel signaling to the nucleus requires a novel CaMKIIα-Shank3 interaction. *J. Neurosci.* 40, 2000–2014. doi: 10.1523/JNEUROSCI.0893-19.2020

Ramamoorthi, K., Fropf, R., Belfort, G. M., Fitzmaurice, H. L., Mckinney, R. M., Neve, R. L., et al. (2011). Npas4 regulates a transcriptional program in CA3 required for contextual memory formation. *Science* 334, 1669–1675. doi: 10.1126/science.1208049

Redcay, E., and Courchesne, E. (2005). When is the brain enlarged in autism? A meta-analysis of all brain size reports. *Biol. Psychiatry* 58, 1–9. doi: 10.1016/j.biopsych.2005.03.026

Ren, K., Guo, B., Dai, C., Yao, H., Sun, T., Liu, X., et al. (2017). Striatal distribution and cytoarchitecture of dopamine receptor subtype 1 and 2: evidence from double-labeling transgenic mice. *Front. Neural Circ.* 11:57. doi: 10.3389/fncir.2017.00057

Sheng, M., and Kim, E. (2000). The Shank family of scaffold proteins. *J. Cell Sci.* 113(Pt 11), 1851–1856.

Speed, H. E., Kouser, M., Xuan, Z., Reimers, J. M., Ochoa, C. F., Gupta, N., et al. (2015). Autism-associated insertion mutation (InsG) of Shank3 Exon 21 Causes impaired synaptic transmission and behavioral deficits. *J. Neurosci.* 35, 9648–9665. doi: 10.1523/JNEUROSCI.3125-14.2015

Tang, G., Gudsnuk, K., Kuo, S. H., Cotrina, M. L., Rosoklija, G., Sosunov, A., et al. (2014). Loss of mTOR-dependent macroautophagy causes autistic-like synaptic pruning deficits. *Neuron* 83, 1131–1143. doi: 10.1016/j.neuron.2014.07.040

Tyzio, R., Nardou, R., Ferrari, D. C., Tsintsadze, T., Shahrokhi, A., Eftekhari, S., et al. (2014). Oxytocin-mediated GABA inhibition during delivery attenuates autism pathogenesis in rodent offspring. *Science* 343, 675–679. doi: 10.1126/science.1247190

Wang, W., Li, C., Chen, Q., Van Der Goes, M. S., Hawrot, J., Yao, A. Y., et al. (2017). Striatopallidal dysfunction underlies repetitive behavior in Shank3-deficient model of autism. *J. Clin. Invest.* 127, 1978–1990. doi: 10.1172/JCI87997

Wang, X., Bey, A. L., Katz, B. M., Badea, A., Kim, N., David, L. K., et al. (2016). Altered mGluR5-Homer scaffolds and corticostriatal connectivity in a Shank3 complete knockout model of autism. *Nat. Commun.* 7:11459. doi: 10.1038/ncomms11459

Wang, X., Mccoy, P. A., Rodriguiz, R. M., Pan, Y., Je, H. S., Roberts, A. C., et al. (2011). Synaptic dysfunction and abnormal behaviors in mice lacking major isoforms of Shank3. *Hum. Mol. Genet.* 20, 3093–3108. doi: 10.1093/hmg/ddr212

Wang, X., Zhang, C., Szabo, G., and Sun, Q. Q. (2013). Distribution of CaMKIIalpha expression in the brain in vivo, studied by CaMKIIalpha-GFP mice. *Brain Res.* 1518, 9–25. doi: 10.1016/j.brainres.2013.04.042

Willsey, A. J., and State, M. W. (2015). Autism spectrum disorders: from genes to neurobiology. *Curr. Opin. Neurobiol.* 30, 92–99. doi: 10.1016/j.conb.2014.10.015

Yadav, S., Oses-Prieto, J. A., Peters, C. J., Zhou, J., Pleasure, S. J., Burlingame, A. L., et al. (2017). TAOK2 Kinase mediates PSD95 stability and dendritic spine maturation through Septin7 Phosphorylation. *Neuron* 93, 379–393. doi: 10.1016/j.neuron.2016.12.006

Yardeni, T., Eckhaus, M., Morris, H. D., Huizing, M., and Hoogstraten-Miller, S. (2011). Retro-orbital injections in mice. *Lab. Anim.* 40, 155–160. doi: 10.1038/laban0511-155

Yoon, S., Parnell, E., Kasherman, M., Forrest, M. P., Myczek, K., Premarathne, S., et al. (2020). Usp9X Controls Ankyrin-repeat domain protein homeostasis during dendritic spine development. *Neuron* 105:506-521.e7. doi: 10.1016/j.neuron.2019.11.003

Zhang, Q., Gao, X., Li, C., Feliciano, C., Wang, D., Zhou, D., et al. (2016). Impaired dendritic development and memory in Sorbs2 knock-out mice. *J. Neurosci.* 36, 2247–2260. doi: 10.1523/JNEUROSCI.2528-15.2016

Zhang, Y., Cao, S. X., Sun, P., He, H. Y., Yang, C. H., Chen, X. J., et al. (2016). Loss of MeCP2 in cholinergic neurons causes part of RTT-like phenotypes via alpha7 receptor in hippocampus. *Cell Res.* 26, 728–742. doi: 10.1038/cr.2016.48

Zhou, Y., Kaiser, T., Monteiro, P., Zhang, X., Van Der Goes, M. S., Wang, D., et al. (2016). Mice with Shank3 mutations associated with ASD and Schizophrenia display both shared and distinct defects. *Neuron* 89, 147–162. doi: 10.1016/j.neuron.2015.11.023

Zhu, Y., Xu, J., Hauswirth, W. W., and Devries, S. H. (2014). Genetically targeted binary labeling of retinal neurons. *J. Neurosci.* 34, 7845–7861. doi: 10.1523/JNEUROSCI.2960-13.2014

9

Decrease of GSK-3β Activity in the Anterior Cingulate Cortex of *Shank3b*$^{-/-}$ Mice Contributes to Synaptic and Social Deficiency

Mengmeng Wang[1†], Xinyan Liu[1†], Yilin Hou[1,2†], Haifeng Zhang[1], Junjun Kang[1], Fei Wang[1], Youyi Zhao[1,3], Jing Chen[4], Xufeng Liu[2], Yazhou Wang[1] and Shengxi Wu[1]**

[1]Department of Neurobiology, Institute of Neurosciences, School of Basic Medicine, Fourth Military Medical University, Xi'an, China, [2]Department of Military Psychology, Fourth Military Medical University, Xi'an, China, [3]State Key Laboratory of Military Stomatology and National Clinical Research Center for Oral Diseases and Shaanxi Engineering Research, Department of Anethesiology, Center for Dental Materials and Advanced Manufacture, School of Stomatology, Fourth Military Medical University, Xi'an, China, [4]Department of Anatomy, School of Basic Medicine, Fourth Military Medical University, Xi'an, China

***Correspondence:**
Shengxi Wu
shengxi@fmmu.edu.cn
Yazhou Wang
yazhouw@fmmu.edu.cn

†These authors have contributed equally to this work

Social deficiency is one of the core syndromes of autism spectrum disorders (ASD), for which the underlying developmental mechanism still remains elusive. Anterior cingulate cortex (ACC) plays a key role in integrating social information and regulating social behavior. Recent studies have indicated that synaptic dysfunction in ACC is essential for ASD social defects. In the present study, we investigated the development of synapses and the roles of glycogen synthase kinase 3β (GSK-3β), which mediates multiple synaptic signaling pathways in ACC by using *Shank3b*$^{-/-}$ mice (a widely used ASD mouse model). Our data revealed that *Shank3b* mutation abolished the social induced c-Fos expression in ACC. From 4 weeks post-birth, neurons in *Shank3b*$^{-/-}$ ACC exhibited an obvious decrease in spine density and stubby spines. The length and thickness of post-synaptic density (PSD), the expression of vesicular glutamate transporter 2 (vGlut2) and glutamate receptor 2 (GluR2), and the frequency of miniature excitatory post-synaptic currents (mEPSCs) were significantly reduced in *Shank3b*$^{-/-}$ACC. Interestingly, the levels of phosphorylated GSK-3β (Ser9), which inhibits the activity of GSK-3β, decreased along the same time course as the levels of GluR2 increased in ACC during development. *Shank3b* mutation leads to a dramatic increase of pGSK-3β (Ser9), and decrease of pPSD95 (a substrate of GSK-3β) and GluR2. Local delivery of AAV expressing constitutively active GSK-3β restored the expression of GluR2, increased the spine density and the number of mature spines. More importantly, active GSK-3β significantly promoted the social activity of *Shank3b*$^{-/-}$ mice. These data, in together, indicate that decrease of GSK-3β activity in ACC may contribute to the synaptic and social defects of *Shank3b*$^{-/-}$ mice. Enhancing GSK-3β activity may be utilized to treat ASD in the future.

Keywords: Shank3b, social behavior, anterior cingulate cortex, synapse, glycogen synthase kinase 3β

INTRODUCTION

Autism spectrum disorders (ASDs) are a group of neural developmental disorders characterized by repetitive stereotype behaviors and social defects (Takumi et al., 2019). Hundreds of related genetic mutations have been identified in human patients (Jacob et al., 2019). Among these candidate genes, Src-homology domain 3 (SH3) and multiple ankyrin repeat domains 3b (*Shank3b*) is one of the few genes which can cause the core syndrome of ASD at single mutation (Peca et al., 2011; Varghese et al., 2017). SHANK3 is a post-synaptic scaffold protein widely expressed by excitatory neurons, and interacts with multiple synaptic proteins (Monteiro and Feng, 2017). Even heterozygous *Shank3b* mice exhibit repetitive grooming and social defects (Dhamne et al., 2017; Qin et al., 2018). Previous studies have revealed that dysfunction of striatum glutamatergic transmission is essential for the repetitive grooming behavior of *Shank3b*$^{-/-}$ mice (Wang et al., 2017). The mechanism underlying the social deficiency of *Shank3b*$^{-/-}$ mice remains largely unknown.

Proper social behavior is essential for mammalian survival and reproduction. Among the brain regions involved in the regulation or generation of social behavior, anterior cingulate cortex (ACC) is regarded as the core region for integrating social information afferents from other brain regions such as the hippocampus, thalamus, and prefrontal cortex (PFC; Apps et al., 2016). Recently, our study demonstrated that the dysfunction of ACC, especially the dysfunction of excitatory synaptic transmission, accounted for the social deficiency in *Shank3b*$^{-/-}$ mice (Guo et al., 2019). Developmental synaptic deficiency has been proposed to be a key pathological change of ASDs (Lima Caldeira et al., 2019). How *Shank3b* mutation leads to synaptic defects in ACC is an interesting topic to be explored.

Glycogen synthase kinase 3β (GSK-3β) is a conserved serine/threonine kinase highly abundant in the brain. It is involved in multiple cellular process and signaling pathways, particularly Wnt signaling and mTOR signaling (Meffre et al., 2014; Hermida et al., 2017). In neurons, the function of GSK-3β is closely related to synaptic development and plasticity (Hur and Zhou, 2010). It can phosphorylate the N-methyl-D-aspartate (NMDA) receptor and post-synaptic density protein 95 (PSD95), thereby modulating the function of glutamic synapses (Peineau et al., 2007; Nelson et al., 2013). Considering that SHANK3B is located mainly in the post-synaptic components of excitatory synapses, we are curious as to whether GSK-3β are involved in the social deficiency of *Shank3b*$^{-/-}$ mouse.

In the present study, we investigated the synaptic defects in the ACC of *Shank3b*$^{-/-}$ mice during development. Our data demonstrated that the decrease of GSK-3β activity in ACC contributed to the synaptic and social deficiency of *Shank3b*$^{-/-}$ mice.

MATERIALS AND METHODS

Animals and Virus Injection

Shank3b$^{-/-}$ mice were a gift from Prof. Guoping Feng as described (Peca et al., 2011). The mice were maintained and housed in the animal facility of the Fourth Military Medical University at an ambient temperature of 25°C, with a 12 h light and 12 h dark cycle and bred by mating heterozygous male with heterozygous female. The mice were given ad libitum access to food and water. All procedures conducted with mice were in compliance with the guidelines for experimental animal care and use by the Committee of the Animal Care and Use Committee of Fourth Military Medical University. The protocol of animal experiments was approved by the Committee of the Animal Care and Use Committee of Fourth Military Medical University.

Recombinant adeno-associated virus (rAAV) expressing constitutive active GSK-3β (converting Ser9 into Ala9, 1×10^{13} PFU) driven by hSyn promoter was obtained from BrainVTA (Wuhan, China). The virus was injected into the bilateral ACC of *Shank3b*$^{-/-}$ mice (4 weeks old) at 0.2 mm right or left to Bregma, 0.75 mm anterior to Bregma with 400 nl per point and 1 mm in depth. AAV expressing luciferase was used as control.

Golgi Staining

Golgi staining was performed as previously described with minor modifications (Zhang et al., 2011). Animals were perfused with 0.9% saline solution or 0.01 M phosphate-buffered saline (PBS; pH 7.4). The brain tissue was removed and immersed in Golgi-cox solution (consisting 5% potassium chromate, 5% potassium dichromate, and 5% mercuric chloride) for further fixation, after which the tissue was maintained in the dark at room temperature for 2–3 days. Then, the brains were transferred to a fresh Golgi-Cox Solution for additional 14 days. After that, the brains were transferred to 25%–30% sucrose for 2 more days. Coronal sections (100–200 μm) were cut serially. For staining, brain sections were washed in deionized water for 1 min, placed in 50% NH_4OH for 30 min, and subsequently in fixing solution (Kodak; Rochester, NY, USA) for an additional 30 min. The sections were then incubated in 5% sodium thiosulfate for 10 min. After rinsing with distilled water, dehydration with gradient ethanol was performed. The sections were finally mounted and observed under the bright field of confocal microscope FV1000, images were taken by z-stack scanning with the excitation wavelength of 405 nm, and then the virtual color was converted into red color.

Western-Blotting

ACC tissues were carefully dissected and lysed by an RIPA buffer at the presence of a proteinase inhibitors cocktail. Protein concentration was determined by BCA assay. Protein samples were separated in 10%–12% acrylamide gels by SDS-PAGE and transferred to PVDF membranes. Membranes were blocked in TBS containing 0.1% (v/v) Tween 20 (TBS-T) and 5% (w/v) nonfat milk before incubation with primary antibodies. The following antibodies were used: rabbit anti-p-GSK-3β (ser9; 1:1,000; 9323s, Cell Signaling Technology), rabbit anti-total GSK- 3β (1:1,000; ab93926, Abcam), rabbit anti-β-catenin (1:1,000; #8480, Cell Signaling Technology), rabbit anti-p70-S6 (Thr421/Ser424; 1:1,000; #9204, Cell Signaling Technology), rabbit anti-mTOR (1:1,000; 2971s, Cell Signaling Technology), rabbit anti-GluR2 (1:1,000; 11994-1-AP, ProteinTech), rabbit anti-pPSD95 (1:1,000; ab172628, Abcam), and rabbit anti-vGlut2

(1:1,000; #71555, CST). After four washes with TBS-T, membranes were incubated with HRP-conjugated anti-mouse secondary antibodies (Cat. CW0102S, CWBIO Company Limited), or HRP-conjugated anti-rabbit secondary antibodies (Cat. EK020; 1:3,000; Zhuangzhi Biotech Company Limited). Bands were visualized by an ECL kit (Thermo). Images were taken by Tanon imaging system, and analyzed by ImageJ. For quantification of blots, the ratios of $\frac{\text{gray scale of target protein}}{\text{gray scale of } \beta\text{-actin}}$ in experimental groups were compared to those of control groups.

Behavior Assay

Three-Chamber Test

The 3-Chamber apparatus was an opaque acrylic box with two pull-out doors and three chambers. Each chamber was identical in size (41 × 20 cm), with the dimensions of the entire box being 63 (length) 43 (width) × 23 cm (height). There was a 10-cm gap between adjacent chambers which could be opened or closed with the removable doors. Before tests, mice were individually habituated in the 3-Chamber apparatus for 10 min. After habituation, a C57 stimulus mouse of same age and same sex was placed in the inverted wired cylinder in the "social chamber." The cylinder in the "non-social chamber" remained empty. The time the tested mice spent in the social vs. non-social chambers during the 10 min test period was measured. Only when all four paws entered the chamber, the mouse was considered to be within a specific chamber. The behaviors of each mouse were video-recorded during the entire test to assess the details of social behavior (rear, contact, sniff, grooming, stretch, withdrawal, and nose-to-nose). The chamber was cleaned by 75% ethanol between each test. The time and traveled distance were analyzed by using SMART3.0 software (Panlab Harvard Apparatus, Spain).

Resident-Juvenile-Intruder Home-Cage Test

Social interaction was examined as described with minor modifications (Felix-Ortiz and Tye, 2014). Briefly, a male adult *Shank3b*$^{-/-}$ mouse was allowed to explore freely for 1 min (habituation) in his home cage. Another novel juvenile (3–4 weeks old) male C57BL/6 mouse was introduced to the cage and allowed to explore freely for 3 min (test session). Juvenile mice were used to avoid mutual aggression. All behaviors were video recorded and analyzed by a researcher blind to the testing condition. The time and frequency of direct contact (pushing the snout or head underneath the juvenile's body and crawling over or under the juvenile's body) were measured.

Immunohistochemistry

Animals were sacrificed and perfused intracardially with 4% cold paraformaldehyde phosphate buffer (pH 7.4). Brain tissue was cryoprotected by 20%–30% sucrose. For each mouse, serial sections (20 μm in thickness for each section) were cut and all the sections were collected onto eight slides. For immunostaining, the sections were blocked by 0.01 M PBS containing 0.3% Triton X-100 and 3% bovine serum albumin (BSA) for 1 h. Primary antibodies were used as following: rabbit anti-c-Fos (1:500; F7799, Sigma), mouse anti-NeuN (1:600; ab104224, Abcam), guinea pig anti-vGluT2 (1:200; 135404, synaptic system), mouse anti-MAP2 (1:400; MAB3418X, Millipore), and rabbit anti-vGlut2 (1:1,000; #71555, CST). After primary antibodies incubation and washing with PBS, sections were incubated with their corresponding secondary antibodies conjugated with Alexa Fluor 594 or Alexa Fluor 488 (Jackson Immunoresearch) for 2–4 h at room temperature protected from light. The nuclei were counterstained by DAPI (1:1,000, Sigma). All immunostained sections were photographed under a confocal microscope (FV1000, Olympus) with the same setting.

Electron Microscopic Study

Animals were perfusion fixed with a mixture of 4% paraformaldehyde containing 1% glutaraldehyde. Tissue sections of 50 μm were prepared with a vibratome and further fixed with 1% osmium tetroxide, dehydrated with graded ethanol, replaced with propylene oxide, and flat-embedded in Epon 812. The sections were trimmed under a stereomicroscope and mounted onto blank resin stubs for ultrathin sectioning. Ultrathin sections (70–90 nm) were prepared on an LKB Nova Ultratome (Bromma). After being counterstained with uranyl acetate and lead citrate, the sections were examined under a JEM-1230 electron microscope (JEM, Tokyo).

Patch-Clamp Recording

Coronal brain slices (300 μm) at the level of the ACC were prepared. Slices were transferred to submerged recovery chamber with oxygenated (95% O_2 and 5% CO_2) artificial CSF containing (in mM) 124 NaCl, 2.5 KCl, 2 $CaCl_2$, 1 $MgSO_4$, 25 $NaHCO_3$, 1 NaH_2PO_4, and 10 glucose at room temperature for at least 1 h. The recording pipettes (3–5Ω) were filled with a solution containing (in mM) 145 K-gluconate, 5 NaCl, 1 $MgCl_2$, 0.2 EGTA, 10 HEPES, 2 Mg-ATP, 0.1 Na_3-GTP, and 10 phosphocreatine disodium (adjusted to pH 7.2 with KOH). The internal solution (in mM) 140 cesium methanesulfonate, 5 NaCl, 0.5 EGTA, 10 HEPES, 2 MgATP, 0.1 Na_3GTP, 0.1 spermine, 2 QX-314 bromide, and 10 phosphocreatine disodium (adjusted to pH 7.2 with CsOH) was used in the experiment. For miniature EPSC miniature excitatory post-synaptic current (mEPSC) recording, 1 μM TTX and 100 μM picrotoxin were added in the perfusion solution. Picrotoxin (100 μM) was present to block GABAA receptor-mediated inhibitory synaptic currents. Data were excluded when the resting membrane potential of neurons was more positive than −60 mV and action potentials did not have overshoot. Data were filtered at 1 kHz, and digitized at 10 kHz. The mEPSCs were detected and analyzed using Mini Analysis (Synaptosoft Inc., Decatur, GA, USA).

Morphological Analysis

All images of Golgi staining and immunofluorescent staining were taken by Olympus FV1000. For sholl analysis, in cases where individual neurons could not be identified, branches of non-target neurons were manually erased so that the target neuron with full processes was clearly left in the field. The branch intersections and length of dendrites were determined by serial circles surrounding cell body every 5 μm until reaching the end of the longest dendrite using ImageJ. For spine analysis, IMARIS 7.5 filament tracer was used to reconstruct each dendrite. Using customized algorithms, spines were classified as filopodia, stubby, long-thin, or mushroom (Berry and Nedivi, 2017). For the fluorescent intensity, images were taken under the same setting (at least five images from each animal) and analyzed by ImageJ as described (Bhat et al., 2017).

Data Analysis

Western-blotting images were analyzed by ImageJ. For immunohistochemistry and Western-blots, at least three biological repeats were performed for each experiment. For behavior study, at least 15 mice were included in each group. The data were presented as means ± standard error of mean (SEM). The normality was assessed by the Shapiro–Wilk test. Data were analyzed by one-way analysis of variance (ANOVA) except for Sholl analysis which was analyzed by two-way ANOVA, followed by Dunnett *post hoc* using SPSS 16.0 (Chicago, IL, USA) or by unpaired, two-tailed Student's *t*-test. *P*-values less than 0.05 were considered as statistically significant.

RESULTS

Compromised Response of ACC Neurons to Social Stimulus in *Shank3b*$^{-/-}$ Mice

We first analyzed the response of ACC neurons to social stimulation. The expression of c-Fos, a quick-response gene widely used to reflect neuronal activation, was examined at 1 h after the 3-chamber test. The testing mice were placed into the "social chamber" for 10 min, and the control mice placed in the "non-social chamber" for 10 min. The average social time was approximately 270 s. Very few or no c-Fos-positive neurons could be observed in the ACC of both WT and *Shank3b*$^{-/-}$ mice under control conditions (**Figure 1A**, left panels; **Figure 1B**). A lot of c-Fos-positive neurons were found in the ACC of social stimulated WT mice, while the number of c-Fos-positive neurons in the ACC of social stimulated *Shank3b*$^{-/-}$ mice remained at a similar level as that in WT control (**Figure 1A**, right panels; **Figure 1B**). Both in WT and *Shank3b*$^{-/-}$ mice, there was no c-Fos expression in striatum, the key region involved in the grooming phenotype of *Shank3b*$^{-/-}$ mice (**Supplementary Figure S1**). These data indicated that ACC, but not striatum, responds to social stimulation, which can be compromised by *Shank3b* mutation.

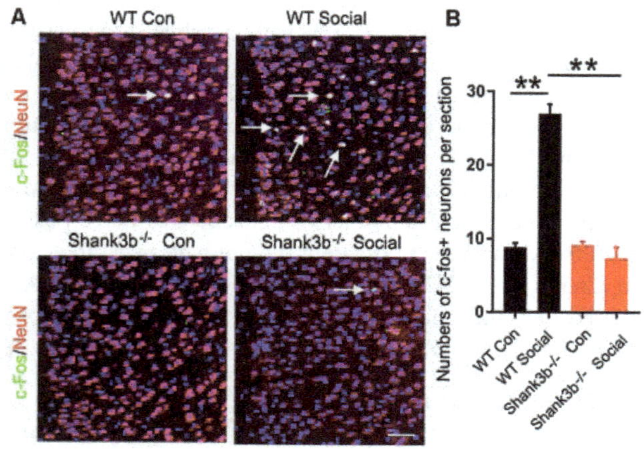

FIGURE 1 | Response of anterior cingulate cortex (ACC) neurons to social stimulation in WT and *Shank3b*$^{-/-}$ mice. **(A)** Double-immunostaining of c-Fos/NeuN in the ACC of WT control (Con) mice, social stimulated WT mice (WT social), *Shank3b*$^{-/-}$ control mice and social stimulated *Shank3b*$^{-/-}$ mice. **(B)** Quantification of c-Fos/NeuN-positive cells. Notice that social behavior elicits c-Fos expression in WT ACC but not in *Shank3b*$^{-/-}$ ACC. Arrows point to double-positive cells. Bar = 120 μm. Values represent mean ± SEM. $^{**}P < 0.01$. $N = 5$ mice per group. One-way analysis of variance (ANOVA).

Abnormal Synaptic Development in the ACC of *Shank3b*$^{-/-}$ Mice

Because SHANK3B is mainly expressed in synaptic sites of excitatory neurons, we focused on the synaptic development of pyramidal neurons in ACC. Golgi staining was conducted at 2, 3, and 4 weeks post-birth. A gradual morphological differentiation was observed. Typical spines along dendrites were not detected until 4 weeks post-birth (**Supplementary Figure S2**). Therefore, in the present study, we mainly analyzed phenotype at 4 weeks post-birth. Sholl analysis showed that there was no difference in the total dendritic length between *Shank3b*$^{-/-}$ ACC neurons and WT ACC neurons. However, significantly less basal dendrite branches and more proximal apical branches were found in *Shank3b*$^{-/-}$ ACC neurons (**Figure 2A**), indicating that *Shank3b* may influence the dendrite development of ACC pyramidal neurons.

We next evaluated the spine development in the ACC neurons of *Shank3b*$^{-/-}$ mice with focus on basal dendrites. Quantification showed that the density of spines along basal dendrites was remarkably reduced in *Shank3b*$^{-/-}$ neurons as compared with that of WT neurons (**Figure 2B**, left and middle panels). Further analysis of the sub-types of spines showed that there was no change of immature filodopia and thin spines. However, the number of stubby spines decreased significantly (**Figure 2B**, right panel), indicating that the maturation of excitatory synapses may be affected by *Shank3b* mutation. In line with this result, immunohistochemistry and Western-blotting showed that the expression of vesicular glutamate transporter 2 (vGlut2) was significantly reduced in the ACC of *Shank3b*$^{-/-}$ mice (**Figure 2C**). Electron microscopic study further revealed that the average length and thickness of PSD were significantly reduced in the ACC of *Shank3b*$^{-/-}$ mice (**Figure 2D**). Further, patch-clamp recording showed that the frequency of mEPSC was significantly reduced in the ACC of *Shank3b*$^{-/-}$ mice (**Figure 2E**). These data indicate that *Shank3b* mutation may impair the formation and function of excitatory synapses in ACC.

Decrease of GSK-3β Activity and GluR2 Expression in the ACC of *Shank3b*$^{-/-}$ Mice

To explore the possible underpin mechanisms, we focused on GSK-3β signaling, a key kinase involved in the dendrites growth and polarization of neurons. GSK-3β interacts with multiple signaling pathways, such as Wnt/β-catenin signaling, mTOR signaling and MAPK signaling (Hur and Zhou, 2010;

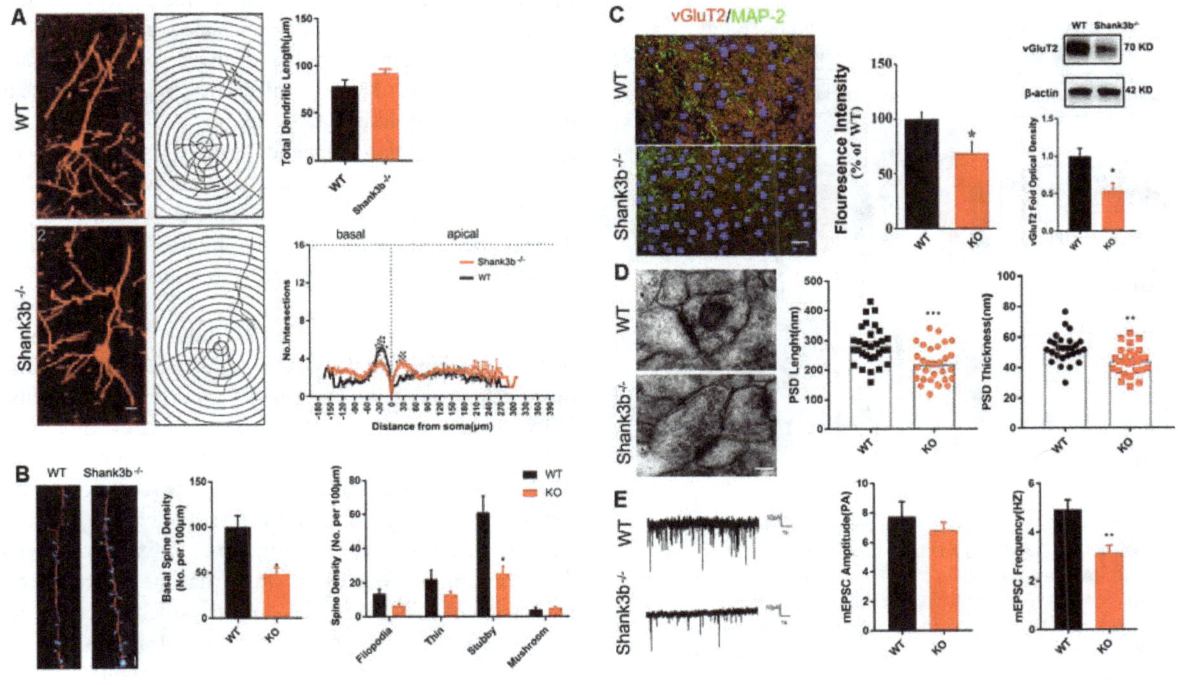

FIGURE 2 | Effects of *Shank3b* mutation on the dendrite and synapse development in ACC. **(A)** Sholl analysis of Golgi images of pyramidal neurons in WT and *Shank3b*$^{-/-}$ ACC 4 weeks post-birth. Notice the fewer branches in the basal dendrites of *Shank3b*$^{-/-}$ mice of 4 weeks old. **(B)** Imaris analysis of spines in basal dendrites of WT and *Shank3b*$^{-/-}$ neurons. Notice the decrease of total spine density and stubby spines. **(C)** Double-immunostaining of vesicular glutamate transporter 2 (vGlut2)/MAP2 and Western-blotting of vGluT2. Notice the weaker expression of vGluT2 in *Shank3b*$^{-/-}$ ACC. **(D)** Electron microscopic study of synaptic ultrastructure in WT and *Shank3b*$^{-/-}$ ACC at 4 weeks post-birth. The average length and thickness of post-synaptic density (PSD) was reduced. **(E)** Patch-clamp recording of miniature excitatory post-synaptic current (mEPSC) in WT and *Shank3b*$^{-/-}$ ACC. Notice the reduction of frequency of mEPSC in *Shank3b*$^{-/-}$ ACC. Bars = 2 μm **(A,B)**, 150 μm **(C)** and 135 nm **(D)**. Values represent mean ± SEM. $^{*}P < 0.05$. $^{**}P < 0.01$. $N = 6$ mice per group in **(A,B)**, 30 neurons per group in **(C)**, five mice per group in **(D)** and six neurons per group **(E)**. Two-way ANOVA **(A)**, One-way ANOVA **(B)** and Student's *t*-test **(C–E)**.

Hermida et al., 2017), and phosphorylates many cytoskeleton proteins (Buttrick and Wakefield, 2008), thereby regulating dendrite development. We first investigated the expression of phosphorylated GSK-3β (p-GSK-3β, Ser 9), an inactive form of GSK-3β, and glutamate receptor 2 (GluR2), a major AMPA receptor which is correlated to synaptic localization of SHANK3 (Grimes and Jope, 2001; Ha et al., 2018). During postnatal development of ACC, the expression of GluR2 increased from 3 weeks, and remained at a high level from then on (**Figure 3A**). Interestingly, the expression of p-GSK-3β (Ser 9) in ACC dramatically decreased from 3 weeks, and stayed at a low level from then on (**Figure 3B**). These data revealed an inverse expression trend of GSK-3β activity and GluR2 protein during development. We then analyzed the expression of GSK-3β and GluR2 in the ACC of *Shank3b*$^{-/-}$ mice at 4 weeks (**Figure 3C**). The expression of GluR2 decreased significantly in *Shank3b*$^{-/-}$ ACC. The levels of p-GSK-3β (Ser 9) were significantly increased in the ACC of *Shank3b*$^{-/-}$ mice, while the levels of total GSK-3β kept unchanged (**Figure 3C**). Since p-GSK-3β (Ser 9) is an inhibitory form of GSK-3β, we next examined the phosphorylation of PSD95, a substrate of GSK-3β. The results showed that p-PSD95 was significantly reduced in *Shank3b*$^{-/-}$ ACC (**Figure 3C**). Further, we assessed the expression of Akt and p70-S6, two key proteins which modulate GSK-3β activity. The phosphorylation of Akt was increased in the ACC of *Shank3b*$^{-/-}$ mice while the expression of total Akt and p70-S6 remained unchanged (**Figure 3C, Supplementary Figure S3A**). The levels of p-GSK-3β in mPFC and striatum of *Shank3b*$^{-/-}$ mice remained at similar levels as those in WT mice (**Supplementary Figure S3B**). These data indicated that GSK-3β activity is lowered in *Shank3b* deficient neurons.

Rescue of Synaptic Development and Social Behavior by ACC Expression of Constitutive Active GSK-3β

To investigate the effects of enhancing GSK-3β activity on synapse development, we injected AAV-expressing constitutive active GSK-3β (aGSK-3β) into the ACC of *Shank3b*$^{-/-}$ mice. Our preliminary experiments showed that it was very hard to precisely inject the virus into ACC at 3 weeks or earlier, possibly due to the small size of ACC (data not shown). We performed virus injection at 4 weeks post-birth and the area of virus diffusion was determined by mixing Hoeschst33342 with virus aliquots (**Figure 4A**). Three weeks later, significant up-regulation of total GSK-3β was confirmed by Western-blotting (**Figure 4B**). Although the total length of dendrites was not significantly affected by aGSK-3β, more dendrite intersections were found in *Shank3b*$^{-/-}$ ACC treated with aGSK-3β than control (**Figure 4C**). Further, Sholl analysis showed that branches along

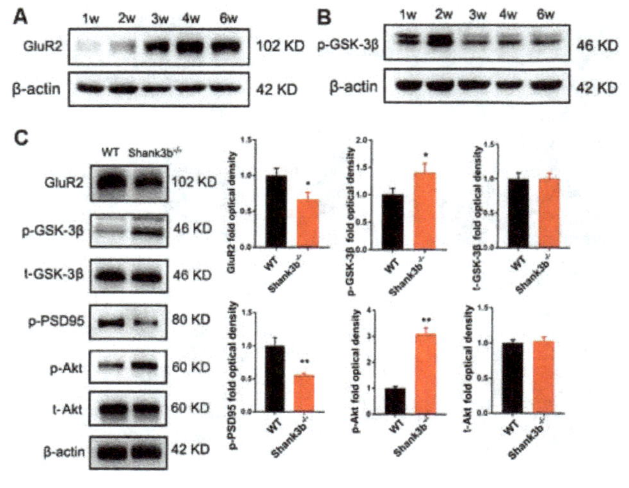

FIGURE 3 | Expression of glutamate receptor 2 (GluR2) and glycogen synthase kinase 3β (GSK-3β) during postnatal development and in *Shank3b*$^{-/-}$ ACC. **(A)** Western-blotting of GluR2 in the ACC of 1, 2, 3, 4 and 6 weeks (w) old mice. **(B)** Western-blotting of p-GSK-3β (S9) in the ACC of 1, 2, 3, 4 and 6 w old mice. Notice the increase of GluR2 and decrease of p-GSK-3β (S9) from 3 w on. **(C)** Western-blotting of GluR2, p-GSK-3β, total GSK-3β (t-GSK-3β), phosphorylated PSD-95 (pPSD-95), phosphorylated Akt (p-Akt), and total Akt (t-Akt) in WT and *Shank3b*$^{-/-}$ ACC. Notice the up-regulation of p-GSK-3β and p-Akt, and down-regulation of GluR2 and pPSD-95 in *Shank3b*$^{-/-}$ ACC. Values represent mean ± SEM. $^{*}P < 0.05$. $^{**}P < 0.01$. $N = 6$ mice per group. Student's *t*-test.

both the basal and apical dendrites were significantly increased in aGSK-3β-treated neurons (**Figure 4C**). More importantly, not only was the spine density increased (**Figure 4D**), but the mature spines (stubby and mushroom spines) were also remarkably increased (**Supplementary Figure S4**). In addition, the expression of GluR2 was significantly up-regulated in the *Shank3b*$^{-/-}$ ACC treated with aGSK-3β (**Figure 4E**). These data indicated that aGSK-3β could rescue the synapse formation in *Shank3b* deficient ACC.

We next tested whether over-expressing aGSK-3β in ACC could affect the social behavior of *Shank3b*$^{-/-}$ mice. In the 3-chamber test which measures social approach and preference for social novelty, control *Shank3b*$^{-/-}$ mice spent similar time exploring the cylinder containing social mice as exploring the empty cylinder (**Figure 5A**). *Shank3b*$^{-/-}$ mice treated with aGSK-3β spent obviously more time in the box containing social mice (**Figure 5A**). In the resident-juvenile-intruder home-cage test which measures social interaction, *Shank3b*$^{-/-}$ mice treated with aGSK-3β showed significantly more direct contact with the juvenile intruder, while *Shank3b*$^{-/-}$ mice treated with control virus showed no obvious interests to the juvenile intruder (**Figure 5B**). These data suggested that over-expressing aGSK-3β in ACC can rescue the social deficiency of *Shank3b*$^{-/-}$ mice.

DISCUSSION

Recently, we reported that ACC is a key region for the social deficit of *Shank3b*$^{-/-}$ mice. In the present study, we further analyzed the effects of *Shank3b* mutation on the morphological development of ACC neurons with focus on synaptogenesis. Our data revealed a defect of excitatory synaptic development and a decrease of GSK-3β activity in the ACC of *Shank3b*$^{-/-}$ mice. Interestingly, the expression of constitutive active GSK-3β in ACC rescued both the synaptic and social deficiency caused by *Shank3b* mutation. Our data further supported a crucial role of ACC in social function. Considering the extensive connection of ACC, it will be interesting to investigate how the interaction between ACC and its connecting regions, such as PFC, affects social behavior.

Of the current hypothesis about the development of ASD, "developmental synaptopathie" has drawn more and more attention in recent years (Ebrahimi-Fakhari and Sahin, 2015), which implies that the disruption of the synaptic excitation and inhibition (E/I) is crucial for the progress of ASD (Howell and Smith, 2019). Shank3 is one of the few genes whose single mutation is sufficient to induce typical autism syndrome. The dysfunction of excitatory synapses in the striatum of *Shank3*$^{-/-}$ mice has been attributed to the reduction of NMDA/AMPA ratio which in turn results in the silence of excitatory synapses (Jaramillo et al., 2016). Our data showed that in the ACC of *Shank3*$^{-/-}$ mice, the density of spines, the length and thickness of PSD, and the expression of GluR2 were significantly reduced. These data demonstrated the abnormal development of excitatory synapses in the ACC of *Shank3b*$^{-/-}$ mice. The reduction of vGluT2 is interesting. Our electrophysiological data are in line with this observation. It is possible that post-synaptic SHANK3B may affect synaptic transmission through neurexin-neuroligin-mediated transsynaptic signaling (Arons et al., 2012). Considering that previous studies have reported presynaptic localization of Shank3 in developing neurons (Halbedl et al., 2016; Wu et al., 2017) and that our data were obtained at 4w post-birth, it may be possible that SHANK3 may play a role in the presynaptic function during development. Because SHANK3B could also be expressed by GABAergic neurons, the possibility that abnormal inhibition may affect the morphology of neurons and regulate the structural and functional plasticity of glutamatergic synapses is interesting, and deserves to be further investigated.

The existence of six protein-protein interaction domains in SHANK3B imparts it with the ability to interact with or affect diverse synaptic proteins. Dozens of Shank3-interacting proteins have been identified, such as Contactin, Homer, and SAPAP (Monteiro and Feng, 2017). Recently, SHANK3B has been reported to directly interact with β-catenin (Qin et al., 2018), a Wnt signaling protein which can modulate synapse formation and stability. As an upstream molecule of β-catenin in Wnt signaling, GSK-3β is mainly distributed in post-synaptic components. Our data showed a significant enhancement of p-GSK-3β (S9) in the ACC of *Shank3b*$^{-/-}$ mice, suggesting that GSK-3β activity was inhibited in *Shank3b*$^{-/-}$ mice, which is consistent with previous reports that Wnt/β-catenin is activated in *Shank3b* deficient PFC (Qin et al., 2018). The inverse expression trend of GSK-3β and GluR2, and the rescue effects of aGSK-3β on GluR2 indicated a relationship

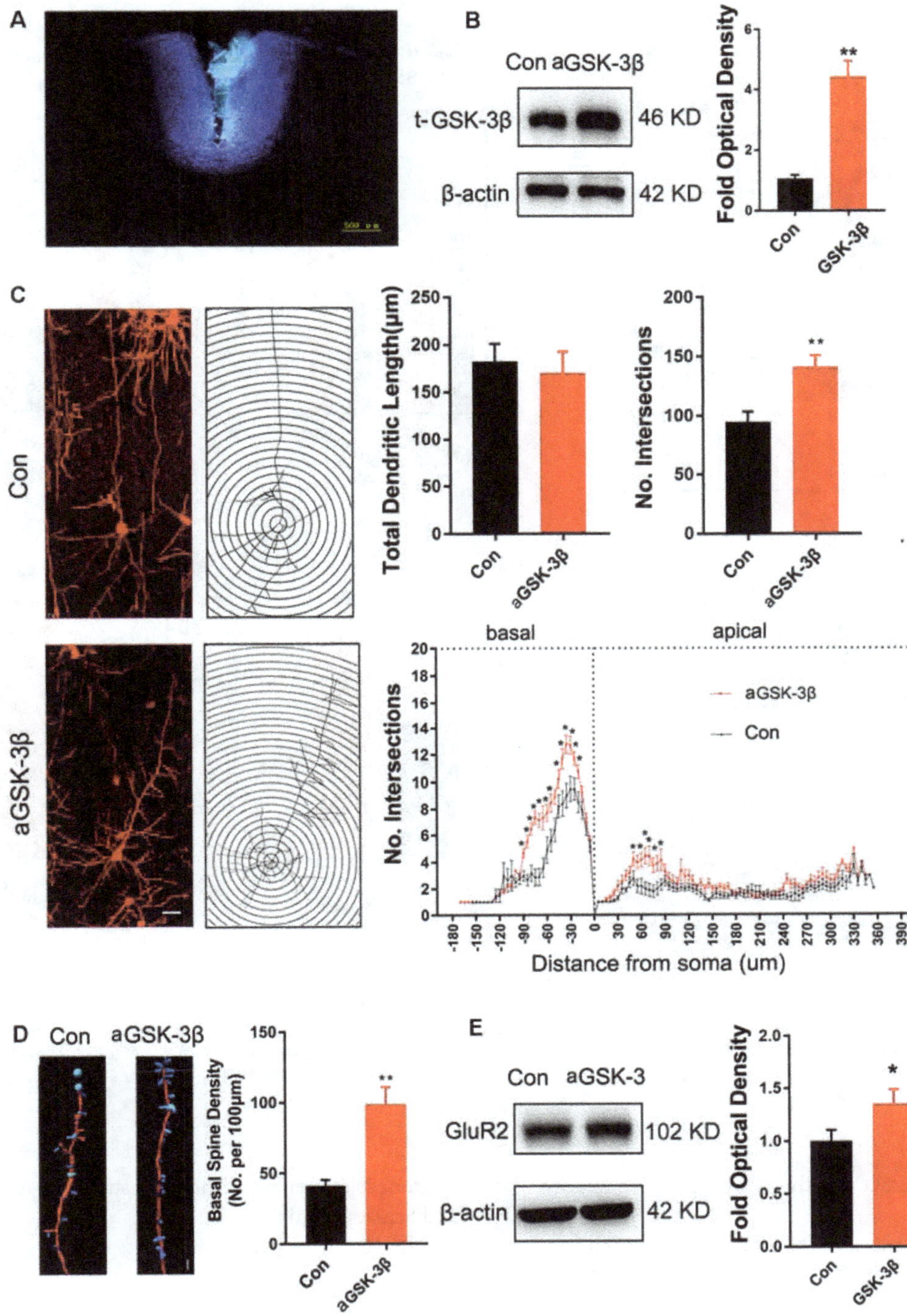

FIGURE 4 | Effects of over-expressing constitutive active GSK-3β (aGSK-3β) in *Shank3b*$^{-/-}$ ACC on the development of dendrites and spines. **(A)** Hoescht33342 staining of injection site at 24 h after virus injection in *Shank3b*$^{-/-}$ mice of 4 weeks old. **(B)** Western-blotting of t-GSK-3β in ACC at 3 weeks after injecting AAV expressing aGSK-3β. **(C)** Sholl analysis of Golgi images of pyramidal neurons in control and aGSK-3β treated *Shank3b*$^{-/-}$ ACC. Notice the increase of dendritic intersections, and particularly basal branches in the aGSK-3β treated *Shank3b*$^{-/-}$ neurons. **(D)** Imaris analysis of spines along basal dendrites of control and aGSK-3β treated *Shank3b*$^{-/-}$ neurons. Notice the increase of spine density by aGSK-3β. Values represent mean ± SEM. $^{*}P < 0.05$. $^{**}P < 0.01$. Bar = 20 μm **(C)** and 2 μm **(D)**. $N = 3$ mice per group **(B)**, and 6 mice per group **(C–E)**. Student's *t*-test **(A,D,E)**. Two-way ANOVA **(B)**.

between the expression of GluR2 and GSK-3β activity. The involvement of GSK-3β in the synapse dysfunction of other ASD models (e.g., FMR1$^{-/-}$ mice) has been documented (Mines et al., 2010; Caracci et al., 2016). Knocking out *GSK-3β* in neurons resulted in fewer spines (Kondratiuk et al., 2017), similar to what we have observed. Whether SHANK3B

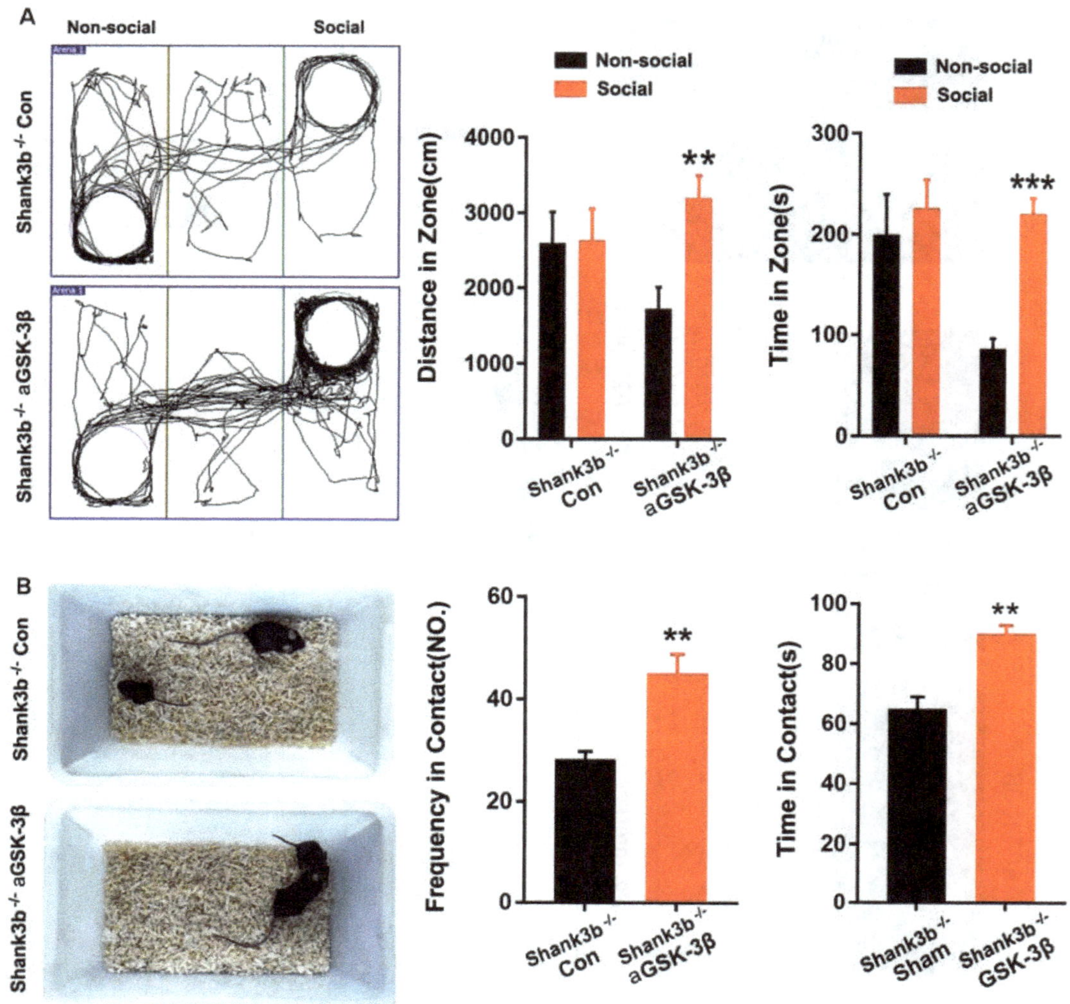

FIGURE 5 | Effects of over-expressing aGSK-3β in *Shank3b*$^{-/-}$ ACC on social behavior. **(A)** Three-chamber tests of control *Shank3b*$^{-/-}$ mice and *Shank3b*$^{-/-}$ mice treated with aGSK-3β at 3 weeks after virus injection. Notice that aGSK-3β treatment significantly rescued the social preference of *Shank3b*$^{-/-}$ mice. **(B)** Resident-juvenile-intruder home-cage test of control *Shank3b*$^{-/-}$ mice and *Shank3b*$^{-/-}$ mice treated with aGSK-3β. Notice that aGSK-3β treatment significantly enhanced social contact of *Shank3b*$^{-/-}$ mice with juvenile intruder. Values represent mean ± SEM. $^{**}P < 0.01$. $^{***}P < 0.001$. $N = 15$ mice per group **(A,B)**. One-way ANOVA **(A)**. Student's *t*-test **(B)**.

could directly interact with GSK-3β is worthy of further exploration.

Importantly, our data showed that expressing constitutive active GSK-3β in *Shank3b*$^{-/-}$ ACC could rescue both synaptic development and social function. The rescue of GluR2 expression may be achieved by its downstream β-catenin signaling. So far, there still lacks effective treatment for the social deficiency in ASD patients. Considering too much activation of GSK-3β by constitutive a GSK-3β may lead to inhibitory effects, pharmacologically enhancing GSK-3β activity might be an alternative for the improving social behavior in ASD patients.

Considering the multiple signaling GSK-3β involved and the wide distribution of GSK-3β, it is possible that this synaptic function of SHANK3B may also be important for the pathology of many other neuropsychiatric and neurodevelopmental disorders, such as Alzheimer's disease and Schizophrenia.

ETHICS STATEMENT

The animal study was reviewed and approved by the Committee of the Animal Care and Use Committee of Fourth Military Medical University. Written informed consent was obtained from the owners for the participation of their animals in this study.

AUTHOR CONTRIBUTIONS

MW, XL and YH conducted most of the experiments, collected and analyzed the data. HZ and YZ contributed to morphological analysis. JK contributed to electron microscropic study. FW contributed to electrophysiology. JC contributed to Golgi staining. XL contributed to behavior analysis. SW and YW conceived the study, provided financial support, analyzed the data, and prepared the manuscript.

FUNDING

This work was supported by the National Natural Science Foundation of China to SW (Grant No. 81730035) and to YW (Grant No. 81571224).

ACKNOWLEDGMENTS

We thank Drs. Li Zhang, Lirong Liang, and Chuchu Qi for their technical help, and Prof. Wenting Wang for helpful discussion.

SUPPLEMENTARY MATERIAL

FIGURE S1 | Double-immunostaining of c-Fos with NeuN in the striatum of WT and *Shank3b*$^{-/-}$ mice after social stimulation. Notice that there are no c-Fos-positive cells in the striatum of WT and *Shank3b*$^{-/-}$ mice after social stimulation.

FIGURE S2 | Images of Golgi staining in ACC at 2w **(A)**, 3w **(C)** and 4w **(E)** post-birth. Images of dendritic spines in pyramidal neurons at 2w **(B)**, 3w **(D)** and 4w **(F)** post-birth 4.

FIGURE S3 | **(A)** Western blotting and quantification of p70-S6 in WT ACC and *Shank3b*$^{-/-}$ ACC. $N = 6$ mice per group. **(B)** Western-blotting and quantification of p-GSK-3βin the mPFC and striatum of WT and *Shank3b*$^{-/-}$ mice. $N = 4$ mice per group.

FIGURE S4 | Densities of different types of basal spines of control and aGSK-3β treated *Shank3b*$^{-/-}$ ACC. Notice the increase of stubby and mushroom spines by aGSK-3β. Values represent mean ± SE. $^{*}P < 0.05$, $^{***}P < 0.001$.

REFERENCES

Apps, M. A., Rushworth, M. F., and Chang, S. W. (2016). The anterior cingulate gyrus and social cognition: tracking the motivation of others. *Neuron* 90, 692–707. doi: 10.1016/j.neuron.2016.04.018

Arons, M. H., Thynne, C. J., Grabrucker, A. M., Li, D., Schoen, M., Cheyne, J. E., et al. (2012). Autism-associated mutations in ProSAP2/Shank3 impair synaptic transmission and neurexin-neuroligin-mediated transsynaptic signaling. *J. Neurosci.* 32, 14966–14978. doi: 10.1523/JNEUROSCI.2215-12.2012

Berry, K. P., and Nedivi, E. (2017). Spine dynamics: are they all the same? *Neuron* 96, 43–55. doi: 10.1016/j.neuron.2017.08.008

Bhat, S. A., Goel, R., Shukla, R., and Hanif, K. (2017). Platelet CD40L induces activation of astrocytes and microglia in hypertension. *Brain Behav. Immun.* 59, 173–189. doi: 10.1016/j.bbi.2016.09.021

Buttrick, G. J., and Wakefield, J. G. (2008). PI3-K and GSK-3: Akt-ing together with microtubules. *Cell Cycle* 7, 2621–2625. doi: 10.4161/cc.7.17.6514

Caracci, M. O., Ávila, M. E., and De Ferrari, G. V. (2016). Synaptic Wnt/GSK3β signaling hub in autism. *Neural Plast.* 2016:9603751. doi: 10.1155/2016/9603751

Dhamne, S. C., Silverman, J. L., Super, C. E., Lammers, S. H. T., Hameed, M. Q., Modi, M. E., et al. (2017). Replicable *in vivo* physiological and behavioral phenotypes of the Shank3B null mutant mouse model of autism. *Mol. Autism* 8:26. doi: 10.1186/s13229-017-0142-z

Ebrahimi-Fakhari, D., and Sahin, M. (2015). Autism and the synapse: emerging mechanisms and mechanism-based therapies. *Curr. Opin. Neurol.* 28, 91–102. doi: 10.1097/wco.0000000000000186

Felix-Ortiz, A. C., and Tye, K. M. (2014). Amygdala inputs to the ventral hippocampus bidirectionally modulate social behavior. *J. Neurosci.* 34, 586–595. doi: 10.1523/JNEUROSCI.4257-13.2014

Grimes, C. A., and Jope, R. S. (2001). The multifaceted roles of glycogen synthase kinase 3β in cellular signaling. *Prog. Neurobiol.* 65, 391–426. doi: 10.1016/s0301-0082(01)00024-7

Guo, B., Chen, J., Chen, Q., Ren, K., Feng, D., Mao, H., et al. (2019). Anterior cingulate cortex dysfunction underlies social deficits in Shank3 mutant mice. *Nat. Neurosci.* 22, 1223–1234. doi: 10.1038/s41593-019-f13780445-9

Ha, H. T. T., Leal-Ortiz, S., Lalwani, K., Kiyonaka, S., Hamachi, I., Mysore, S. P., et al. (2018). Shank and zinc mediate an AMPA receptor subunit switch in developing neurons. *Front. Mol. Neurosci.* 11:405. doi: 10.3389/fnmol.2018.00405

Halbedl, S., Schoen, M., Feiler, M. S., Boeckers, T. M., and Schmeisser, M. J. (2016). Shank3 is localized in axons and presynaptic specializations of developing hippocampal neurons and involved in the modulation of NMDA receptor levels at axon terminals. *J. Neurochem.* 137, 26–32. doi: 10.1111/jnc.13523

Hermida, M. A., Dinesh Kumar, J., and Leslie, N. R. (2017). GSK3 and its interactions with the PI3K/AKT/mTOR signalling network. *Adv. Biol. Regul.* 65, 5–15. doi: 10.1016/j.jbior.2017.06.003

Howell, B. W., and Smith, K. M. (2019). Synaptic structural protein dysfunction leads to altered excitation inhibition ratios in models of autism spectrum disorder. *Pharmacol. Res.* 139, 207–214. doi: 10.1016/j.phrs.2018.11.019

Hur, E. M., and Zhou, F. Q. (2010). GSK3 signalling in neural development. *Nat. Rev. Neurosci.* 11, 539–551. doi: 10.1038/nrn2870

Jacob, S., Wolff, J. J., Steinbach, M. S., Doyle, C. B., Kumar, V., and Elison, J. T. (2019). Neurodevelopmental heterogeneity and computational approaches for understanding autism. *Transl. Psychiatry* 9:63. doi: 10.1038/s41398-019-0390-0

Jaramillo, T. C., Speed, H. E., Xuan, Z., Reimers, J. M., Liu, S., and Powell, C. M. (2016). Altered striatal synaptic function and abnormal behaviour in Shank3 Exon4-9 deletion mouse model of autism. *Autism Res.* 9, 350–375. doi: 10.1002/aur.1529

Kondratiuk, I., Łęski, S., Urbańska, M., Biecek, P., Devijver, H., Lechat, B., et al. (2017). GSK-3β and MMP-9 cooperate in the control of dendritic spine morphology. *Mol. Neurobiol.* 54, 200–211. doi: 10.1007/s12035-015-9625-0

Lima Caldeira, G., Peça, J., and Carvalho, A. L. (2019). New insights on synaptic dysfunction in neuropsychiatric disorders. *Curr. Opin. Neurobiol.* 57, 62–70. doi: 10.1016/j.conb.2019.01.004

Meffre, D., Grenier, J., Bernard, S., Courtin, F., Dudev, T., Shackleford, G., et al. (2014). Wnt and lithium: a common destiny in the therapy of nervous system pathologies? *Cell. Mol. Life Sci.* 71, 1123–1148. doi: 10.1007/s00018-013-1378-1

Mines, M. A., Yuskaitis, C. J., King, M. K., Beurel, E., and Jope, R. S. (2010). GSK3 influences social preference and anxiety-related behaviors during social interaction in a mouse model of fragile X syndrome and autism. *PLoS One* 5:e9706. doi: 10.1371/journal.pone.0009706

Monteiro, P., and Feng, G. (2017). SHANK proteins: roles at the synapse and in autism spectrum disorder. *Nat. Rev. Neurosci.* 18, 147–157. doi: 10.1038/nrn.2016.183

Nelson, C. D., Kim, M. J., Hsin, H., Chen, Y., and Sheng, M. (2013). Phosphorylation of threonine-19 of PSD-95 by GSK-3β is required for PSD-95 mobilization and long-term depression. *J. Neurosci.* 33, 12122–12135. doi: 10.1523/JNEUROSCI.0131-13.2013

Peca, J., Feliciano, C., Ting, J. T., Wang, W., Wells, M. F., Venkatraman, T. N., et al. (2011). Shank3 mutant mice display autistic-like behaviours and striatal dysfunction. *Nature* 472, 437–442. doi: 10.1038/nature09965

Peineau, S., Taghibiglou, C., Bradley, C., Wong, T. P., Liu, L., Lu, J., et al. (2007). LTP inhibits LTD in the hippocampus *via* regulation of GSK3β. *Neuron* 53, 703–717. doi: 10.1016/j.neuron.2007.01.029

Qin, L., Ma, K., Wang, Z. J., Hu, Z., Matas, E., Wei, J., et al. (2018). Social deficits in Shank3-deficient mouse models of autism are rescued by histone deacetylase (HDAC) inhibition. *Nat. Neurosci.* 21, 564–575. doi: 10.1038/s41593-018-0110-8

Takumi, T., Tamada, K., Hatanaka, F., Nakai, N., and Bolton, P. F. (2019). Behavioral neuroscience of autism. *Neurosci. Biobehav. Rev.* doi: 10.1016/j.neubiorev.2019.04.012 [Epub ahead of print].

Varghese, M., Keshav, N., Jacot-Descombes, S., Warda, T., Wicinski, B., Dickstein, D. L., et al. (2017). Autism spectrum disorder: neuropathology and animal models. *Acta Neuropathol.* 134, 537–566. doi: 10.1007/s00401-017-1736-4

Wang, W., Li, C., Chen, Q., van der Goes, M. S., Hawrot, J., Yao, A. Y., et al. (2017). Striatopallidal dysfunction underlies repetitive behavior in Shank3-deficient model of autism. *J. Clin. Invest.* 127, 1978–1990. doi: 10.1172/jci87997

Wu, S., Gan, G., Zhang, Z., Sun, J., Wang, Q., Gao, Z., et al. (2017). A presynaptic function of shank protein in *Drosophila*. *J. Neurosci.* 37, 11592–11604. doi: 10.1523/JNEUROSCI.0893-17.2017

Zhang, B., Li, A., Yang, Z., Wu, J., Luo, Q., and Gong, H. (2011). Modified Golgi-Cox method for micrometer scale sectioning of the whole mouse brain. *J. Neurosci. Methods* 197, 1–5. doi: 10.1016/j.jneumeth.2010.10.001

10

Disc1 Carrier Mice Exhibit Alterations in Neural pIGF-1Rβ and Related Kinase Expression

Razia Sultana, Amita Shrestha, Charles C. Lee and Olalekan M. Ogundele*

Department of Comparative Biomedical Sciences, Louisiana State University School of Veterinary Medicine, Baton Rouge, LA, United States

***Correspondence:**
Olalekan M. Ogundele
ogundele@lsu.edu

Mutation of the *disc1* gene underlies a broad range of developmental neuropsychiatric defects, including schizophrenia, depression, and bipolar disorder. The pathophysiological phenotypes linked with *disc1* mutation are due to the truncation of the DISC1 primary protein structure. This leads to a defective post-synaptic scaffolding and kinase—GSK3β and Erk1/2—signaling. As a result, synaptic function and maintenance are significantly impaired in the *disc1* mutant brain. Among several other pathways, GSK3β and Erk1/2 are involved in insulin-like growth factor 1 receptor (IGF-1Rβ) kinase signaling. Although *disc1* mutation alters these kinases, it is unclear if the mutation impacts IGF-1R expression and activity in the brain. Here, we demonstrate that the expression of active IGF-1Rβ (pIGF-1Rβ) is altered in the hippocampus and prefrontal cortex (PFC) of *disc1* mutant mice and vary with the dose of the mutation (homozygous and heterozygous). The expression of pIGF-1Rβ decreased significantly in 129S (*hom, disc1*$^{-/-}$) brains. In contrast, 129S:B6 (*het, disc1*$^{+/-}$) brains were characterized by an increase in pIGF-1Rβ when compared with the C57BL/6 (*disc1*$^{+/+}$) level. The decrease in pIGF-1Rβ level for the 129S brains was accompanied by the loss of Akt activity (S473 pAkt) and decreased Ser9 phosphorylation of GSK3β (increased basal GSK3β). Additionally, hippocampal and cortical pErk1/2 activity increased in the 129S hippocampus and cortex. Although 129S:B6 recorded alterations in pIGF-1Rβ-pAkt-GSK3β (like 129S), there was no observable change in pErk1/2 activity for the heterozygote (*disc1*$^{+/-}$) mutant. In addition to GSK3β inhibition, we conclude that pIGF-1R, pAkt, and pErk1/2 are potential targets in *disc1*$^{-/-}$ mutant brain. On the other hand, pIGF-1R and pAkt can be further explored in *disc1*$^{+/-}$ brain.

Keywords: *disc1*, disease models, cognition, pIGF-1Rβ, Erk1/2, GSK3β

INTRODUCTION

In humans, *disc1* gene mutation is an associative cause of a broad range of developmental neuropsychiatric disorders (Clapcote and Roder, 2006; Koike et al., 2006; Ross et al., 2006; Kvajo et al., 2008; Brandon et al., 2009; Soares et al., 2011; Wang et al., 2011; Wexler and Geschwind, 2011; Zheng et al., 2011; Gómez-Sintes et al., 2014).

Neuropsychiatric conditions resulting from *disc1* mutation are attributable to the involvement of the gene product, DISC1 protein, in neurodevelopment, synaptogenesis, neurite outgrowth, neurotransmitter signaling, and synaptic plasticity (Koike et al., 2006; Ross et al., 2006; Brandon et al., 2009; Kim et al., 2009; Lee et al., 2011a; Ramsey et al., 2011; Wexler and Geschwind, 2011; Dachtler et al., 2016; Tomoda et al., 2016). DISC1 is a regulatory post-synaptic scaffolding protein that is linked to kinase signaling, cytoskeleton, and excitatory neurotransmitter receptors (Ross et al., 2006; Kvajo et al., 2008; Ramsey et al., 2011). Notably, DISC1 is involved in the scaffolding of post-synaptic N-Methyl-D-Aspartate Receptor 1 through its interaction with the GluN1 and GluN2B subunits. As a result of this interaction, DISC1 directs the translocation of NMDAR to the post-synaptic membrane and controls aspects of plasticity (Malavasi et al., 2018). Mutation of the *disc1* gene leads to a truncation of the DISC1 primary protein structure and is accompanied by an incremental loss of NMDAR function (Ramsey et al., 2011; Wexler and Geschwind, 2011; Snyder and Gao, 2013; Malavasi et al., 2018). This underlies long-term potentiation (LTP) defects that lead to spine dysgenesis and cognitive decline. As such, the neural changes caused by *disc1* mutations produce behavioral phenotypes that are characteristic of neuropsychiatric disorders with associative NMDAR hypofunction (Koike et al., 2006; Kvajo et al., 2008; Lee et al., 2011a,b; Lipina et al., 2011; Namba et al., 2011; Ramsey et al., 2011; Snyder and Gao, 2013; Gómez-Sintes et al., 2014; Tomoda et al., 2016; Shao et al., 2017; Malavasi et al., 2018).

DISC1 protein signaling regulates the synaptic activity of GSK3β (Kvajo et al., 2008; Kim et al., 2009; Lee et al., 2011b; Lipina et al., 2011) and Erk1/2 (Soares et al., 2011). Owing to the role of GSK3β (Clayton et al., 2010; Hur and Zhou, 2010; Lee et al., 2011b; Emamian, 2012; Kitagishi et al., 2012; Dachtler et al., 2016; Swiatkowski et al., 2017; Wang et al., 2017) and Erk1/2 (Xia et al., 1996; Roux and Blenis, 2004; Roskoski, 2012; Xing et al., 2016; Nikolaienko et al., 2017; Ohta et al., 2017; Gao and Zhao, 2018; Iyaswamy et al., 2018; Pucilowska et al., 2018) in the control of neurodevelopment, synaptogenesis, and spine plasticity, *disc1* mutations lead to detrimental changes in synaptic function and behavior. With that said, drugs that modulate GSK3β (Lee et al., 2011b; Emamian, 2012; Bhat et al., 2018) and Erk1/2 (Lu and Dwyer, 2005; Pereira et al., 2014; Tassin et al., 2015; Aringhieri et al., 2017; Hirayama-Kurogi et al., 2017) have shown significant promise in treating synaptic and behavioral defects of schizophrenia, depression, and bipolar disorder.

In the developing nervous system, deficiency in neurotrophic factors (e.g., IGF-1, BDNF, and NGF), and a change in the expression of their associated receptors leads to dendritic spine malformations (Ohta et al., 2017; Reim and Schmeisser, 2017). Specifically, attenuation of insulin-like growth factor 1 receptor (IGF-1Rβ) kinase activity in the developing brain abrogates synaptogenesis and leads to dendritic spine loss (Lee C. C. et al., 2011; Lee et al., 2011b; González Burgos et al., 2012; Nakahata and Yasuda, 2018). This is attributable to the dysregulation of downstream kinases—GSK3β, Erk1/2, Akt/PKB—involved in the control of neuronal migration, differentiation, dendritogenesis, and structural organization within the nervous system (Nieto Guil et al., 2017; Reim and Schmeisser, 2017). Accordingly, genetic knockdown or overexpression of these kinases leads to abnormalities in dendrite morphology, synaptic pruning, and behavior (Wan et al., 2007; Del'Guidice and Beaulieu, 2010; Lee C. C. et al., 2011; Emamian, 2012; Kitagishi et al., 2012; Wang et al., 2017).

Although *disc1 mutation* promulgates erroneous GSK3β and Erk1/2 activity, the impact on pIGF-1Rβ expression and activity is yet to be investigated in the cognitive centers. Erk1/2 and GSK3β are downstream effector molecules of pIGF-1Rβ kinase activity and are involved in the maintenance of the synaptic structure. GSK3β and Erk1/2 activity are also pertinent to the propagation of LTP, and coupling of synaptic function to cellular regulation (Peineau et al., 2007; Dewachter et al., 2009; Vara et al., 2009; Giachello et al., 2010; Shahab et al., 2014). Downstream of pIGF-1Rβ, Erk1/2 (Roux and Blenis, 2004; Roskoski, 2012) and GSK3β (Hur and Zhou, 2010) are involved related pathways that regulates cell proliferation and cell survival. As such, alteration in the activity of these kinases in *disc1* mutation may disrupt signaling cascades that involve pIGF-1Rβ.

The study provides evidence of pIGF-1Rβ dysregulation in the hippocampus and prefrontal cortex (PFC) of mutant *disc1* carrier mice. In addition to changes in neural GSK3β and Erk1/2 expression, heterozygous *129S:B6* ($disc1^{+/-}$) and homozygous *129S* ($disc1^{-/-}$) carriers exhibit a change in neural pIGF-1Rβ expression. Here, we show some of the differences and similarities in the pattern of pIGF-1Rβ dysregulation for the hippocampus and PFC of these *disc1* carrier mice.

MATERIALS AND METHODS

The 129S ($disc1^{-/-}$) mice (RRID:IMSR_JAX:002448) were acquired from the Jackson Lab (Bar Harbor, ME, United States) and have a spontaneous C-terminal truncation mutation in the *disc1* gene (Clapcote and Roder, 2006). The 129S:B6 ($disc1^{+/-}$) line (RRID:IMSR_JAX:101043) is from a cross of the 129S and C57BL/6J mouse lines. For comparison, we used the C57BL/6J (B6) line (RRID:IMSR_JAX:000664) as carriers of the wild-type *disc1* gene ($disc1^{+/+}$). We have previously demonstrated that 129S mice vary behaviorally from all other inbred strains, including the C57BL/6J, and have phenotypes that are similar to other *disc1* knockout strains (Sultana et al., 2019). Animals were housed under standard laboratory conditions of 12 h alternating light and dark cycle with food and water provided *ad libitum*. All animal handling procedures were approved by the Institutional Animal Care and Use Committee (IACUC) of the Louisiana State University School of Veterinary Medicine. Adult mice (PND 90–100) weighing between 22–26 g were used for this study (C57BL/6J: $n = 9$, 129S:B6: $n = 9$; 129S: $n = 10$).

Specimen Preparation

Mice were euthanized in an isoflurane chamber. Subsequently, the animals were transcardially perfused with 10 mM PBS (pH 7.4). The whole brain was harvested and rapidly placed in cold artificial cerebrospinal fluid (aCSF) maintained on ice, and saturated with 95% Oxygen/5%CO_2. A clean razor blade was used to cut the brain—along the sagittal plane—into two (left and right) hemispheres. The left and right hemispheres were microdissected, and the hippocampus was extracted by exposing the space between the cortex and corpus callosum. A surgical blade was used to cut the PFC. The harvested hippocampal and prefrontal cortical tissue was kept in separate tubes and stored at −80°C until further use.

Immunoblotting

Frozen hippocampal and prefrontal cortical tissue were incubated on ice with RIPA lysis cocktail containing protease and phosphatase inhibitors. After 30 min, the incubated tissue was rapidly homogenized to obtain tissue lysate. This was further centrifuged to obtain a supernatant containing cytoplasmic, membrane and synaptic fragments (whole lysate). To enrich synaptosomes, we used a previously established Sucrose-HEPES gradient technique (Kamat et al., 2014; Tenreiro et al., 2017). Ten microliter whole lysate or 4 μl synaptosomal extract containing 10 μg of protein was processed for SDS-PAGE electrophoresis (C57BL/6J: $n = 4$, 129S:B6: $n = 4$; 129S: $n = 5$). After western blotting (wet transfer), Polyvinylidene fluoride membrane (PVDF) was incubated in Tris-buffered saline (with 0.01% Tween 20) for 15 min (i.e., TBST) at room temperature. Afterward, the membrane was blocked in 3% bovine serum albumin (prepared in TBST) for 50 min at room temperature. The protein of interest and house-keeping protein were detected using the following primary antibodies; Rabbit anti-GSK-3β (Cell Signaling #12456S), Rabbit anti-Phospho-GSK-3α/β:Ser21/9 (Cell Signaling #9331S), Rabbit anti-Phospho-Erk1/Erk2:Thr185/Tyr187 (Thermofisher Scientific ABfinity™ Antibody #700012), Rabbit anti Erk1/2 Antibody (Thermofisher Scientific # PA1-4703), Rabbit anti-Phospho-IGF1Rβ:Tyr1161 Antibody (Thermofisher Scientific #PA5-37601), Rabbit anti-Phospho-IGF1R/Insulin Receptor β:Tyr1131/1146 Antibody (Cell Signaling #3021S), Rabbit anti-IGF1-Rβ (Cell Signaling #3027S), Rabbit anti-Akt (Cell Signaling #9272S), and Rabbit anti-Phospho Akt: Ser473 (Cell Signaling #4060S). All primary antibodies were diluted in the blocking solution at 1:1,000. Subsequently, the primary antibodies were detected using Chicken anti-Rabbit-HRP secondary antibody (Thermofisher Scientific #A15987) at a dilution of 1:5,000 or 1:10,000. The reaction was developed using a chemiluminescence substrate (Thermofisher-#34579). To normalize protein expression, the membranes were treated with Restore PLUS Western Blot Stripping Buffer (Thermofisher Scientific #46430) and re-probed with β-Actin (8H10D10) Mouse mAb HRP Conjugate (Cell Signaling #12262S). Protein expression was normalized *per lane* using the corresponding β-Actin expression. At least two repeats were performed for each of the proteins quantified by immunoblotting. Protein expression for the experimental groups was compared using One-Way ANOVA with Tukey *post hoc* test. Significance was also confirmed using the Kruskal-Wallis test (GraphPad Prism version 8.0). Here, we have presented One-Way ANOVA outcomes as bar charts with error bars depicting the mean and standard error of mean, respectively.

Immunofluorescence

After perfusion with 10 mM PBS (pH 7.4), the whole-brain was fixed in 4% phosphate-buffered paraformaldehyde (PB-PFA) overnight, and then transferred to 4% PB-PFA containing 30% sucrose for cryopreservation. Free-floating cryostat sections (20 μm) were obtained and preserved in 48-well plates containing 10 mM PBS at 4°C (C57BL/6J: $n = 5$, 129S:B6: $n = 5$; 129S: $n = 5$). The sections were washed three times (5 min each) in 10 mM PBS (pH 7.4) on a slow orbital shaker. Subsequently, non-specific blocking was performed in either 5% normal goat serum (Vector Labs #S-1000), chicken serum (Abcam #ab7477) or donkey Serum (Abcam #ab7475), prepared in 10 mM PBS + 0.03% Triton-X100, for 1 h at room temperature. The sections were incubated overnight at 4°C in primary antibody diluted in blocking solution (10 mMPBS+0.03% Triton-X 100 and 5% normal goat, chicken or donkey serum). The following primary antibodies were used for this procedure; Rabbit anti-Phospho-GSK-3α/β:Ser21/Ser9 (Cell Signaling #9331S), Rabbit anti-Phospho-IGF-1R beta:Tyr1161 Antibody (Thermofisher Scientific #PA5-37601), and Rabbit anti-NeuN Alexa-488 Conjugate (EMD Millipore #MAB377XMI MI). Subsequently, the sections were washed two times in 10 mM PBS in preparation for secondary antibody incubation. The sections were subsequently incubated in Goat anti-Rabbit Alexa 568 (Thermofisher Scientific #A-11036) secondary antibody for 1 h at room temperature, with gentle shaking (35rpm). Immunolabeled sections were washed and mounted on gelatin-coated slides using ProLong™ Diamond Antifade Mountant containing DAPI (Thermofisher Scientific #P36971).

Quantification

Fluorescence imaging was performed using a Nikon-*NiU* fluorescence upright microscope configured for 3D imaging. Z-stacks were obtained and converted into 2D images through the extended depth focus (EDF) option on Nikon Element software. Normalized fluorescence intensity for immunolabeled proteins in the hippocampus and medial PFC was performed in optical slices for serial section images ($n = 5$ per group). Fluorescence intensity was quantified using Nikon Element AR. Mean cell count and intensity were determined per unit area in several fields of view for consecutive sections. Fluorescence intensity was normalized by applying a uniform exposure time for a fluorophore-labeled protein in the control and test brain slices.

Statistical Analysis

Statistical comparison between C57BL/6J (*disc1*$^{+/+}$), 129S:B6 (*disc1*$^{+/-}$), and *129S* (*disc1*$^{-/-}$), protein expression and fluorescence intensity were determined using one-way ANOVA with Tukey *post hoc* test. Significance was also confirmed using the Kruskal-Wallis test (GraphPad Prism version 8.0). Here, we have presented one-way ANOVA outcomes as bar charts with error bars depicting the mean and standard error of mean, respectively.

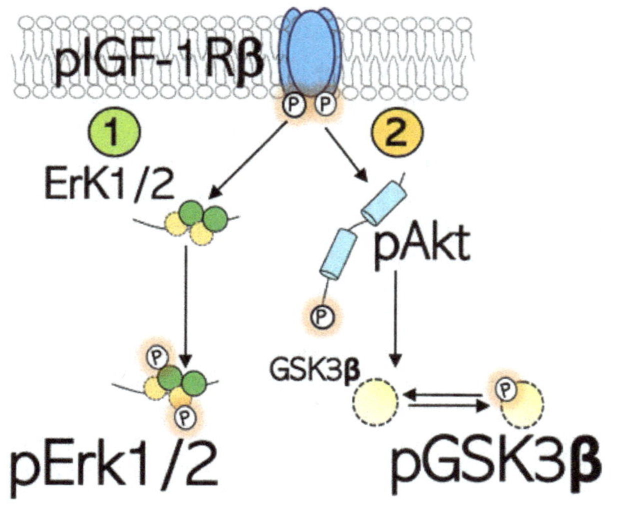

FIGURE 1 | Schematic illustration of the IGF-1R signaling. IGF-1Rβ is activated by phosphorylation of the Tyrosine (Tyr) residue of the kinase domain. (1) pIGF-1Rβ kinase signaling increases Erk1/2 phosphorylation and activity. This signaling pathway directs cell proliferation. (2) pIGF-1Rβ kinase signaling facilitates Ser473 phosphorylation of Akt (pAkt), which in turn phosphorylates (inactivates) GSK3β at Ser9 site (pGSK3β).

RESULTS

Differential dysregulation of neural pIGF-1Rβ activity occurred in the hippocampus and PFC of the 129S:B6 (*disc1*$^{+/-}$) and 129S (*disc*$^{-/-}$) mice. Truncation of the primary structure of synaptic scaffolding protein, DISC1, leads to an increase in GSK3β signaling (Lee et al., 2011b; Lipina et al., 2011) and altered Erkl/2 signaling (Soares et al., 2011). Mechanistically, pIGF-1Rβ kinase signaling increases Akt-PKB phosphorylation (pAkt), which in turn phosphorylates (inactivates) GSK3β (Wan et al., 2007; Del'Guidice and Beaulieu, 2010; Chandarlapaty et al., 2011; Wang et al., 2017). Thus, in the 129S:B6 and 129S brain, we determined whether a change in GSK3β and ErK1/2 activity that is linked to discl mutation also involves alterations in neural pIGF-1Rβ level (**Figure 1**). While the *discl* gene mutation caused a change in neural pIGF-1Rβ activity, the pattern of dysregulation varied with the dose of the mutation. The 129S:B6 hippocampus and PFC recorded an increase in pIGF-1Rβ expression when compared with the C57BL/6J. In contrast, the 129S hippocampus and PFC exhibited a loss of neural pIGF-1Rβ vs. the C57BL/6J and 129S:B6.

Subsequent analysis of Akt, GSK3β, and Erkl/2 expression showed that a decreased pIGF-1Rβ level in the 129S brain may be related to DISC1 loss of function. As such, in the *disc1*$^{-/-}$ brain, a decrease in pIGF-1Rβ was accompanied by a loss of pAkt (Ser473), increased basal GSK3β activity, and a general increase in pErkl/pErk2 activity.

pIGF-1Rβ

pIGF-1Rβ expression was significantly downregulated in 129S hippocampal whole lysates when compared with B6 ($p < 0.05$) and 129S:B6 ($p < 0.001$; **Figures 2A,B**). Interestingly, 129S:B6 hippocampus recorded an increase in pIGF-1Rβ expression when compared with the control ($p < 0.001$). To verify this outcome, we assessed pIGF-1Rβ expression in CA1, CA3 and DG neurons (NeuN) using immunofluorescence quantification method (**Figures 2C–E**). In the 129S:B6 hippocampus, increased pIGF-1Rβ protein level (**Figures 2A,B**) was associated with an increase in pIGF-1Rβ fluorescence for NeuN$^+$ cells in the CA1 and CA3 pyramidal layers (**Figure 2F**; $p < 0.001$). Conversely, decreased pIGF-1Rβ expression in 129S hippocampal lysate (**Figures 2A,B**) was accompanied by a lower pIGF-1Rβ fluorescence in the NeuN$^+$ cells of CA1 ($p < 0.01$), CA3 ($p < 0.05$), and DG ($p < 0.001$) when compared with B6 (**Figure 2F**, see also **Supplementary Figure S1**).

In a subsequent experiment, we performed immunoblotting to detect pIGF-1Rβ and IGF-1Rβ in hippocampal synaptosomal tissue extracts (**Figure 2G**). Our results revealed that basal IGF-1Rβ expression in hippocampal synaptosomal extracts was unaffected by the heterozygote dose of discl mutation (*disc1*$^{+/-}$). When synaptosomal IGF-1Rβ expression was normalized by β-actin, there was no significant difference in comparison with the B6 mice (*disc1*$^{+/+}$). In contrast, homozygote (*disc1*$^{-/-}$) dose of the mutation caused a significant decrease in basal synaptosomal IGF-1Rβ level versus the B6 (*disc1*$^{+/+}$, $p < 0.01$) and 129S:B6 (*disc1*$^{+/-}$, $p < 0.01$; **Figure 2G**). In subsequent analysis, we determined IGF-1R kinase activity by normalizing pIGF-1Rβ with basal IGF-1Rβ expression (**Figure 2I**). Although IGF-1Rβ expression was relatively unchanged in 129S:B6 (*disc1*$^{+/-}$) synaptosomal extracts, there was a significant increase in normalized pIGF-1Rβ which indicates an increased activity vs. the B6 ($p < 0.05$; **Figure 2I**). On the other hand, the observed decline in IGF-1Rβ level in the 129S hippocampal synaptosomal extracts did not translate into a change in pIGF-1Rβ activity. Thus, IGF-1Rβ normalized pIGF-1Rβ activity was unchanged when the 129S hippocampal synaptosomal level was compared when with B6 (*disc1*$^{+/+}$; **Figure 2I**). Together, these outcomes suggest that pIGF-1Rβ activity, and not the expression, is altered in partial loss of discl function (*disc1*$^{+/-}$). On the other hand, decreased IGF-1Rβ expression may be the hallmark of *disc1*$^{-/-}$-related loss of pIGF-1Rβ function.

Similar to the hippocampus, loss of DISC1 function (*disc1*$^{-/-}$) in the PFC is associated with a decrease in cortical pIGF-1Rβ expression (**Figure 3A**, also **Supplementary Figure S2.1**) when compared with 129S:B6 (*disc1*$^{+/-}$, $p < 0.01$) and B6 (*disc1*$^{+/+}$, $p < 0.01$; **Figure 3B**). In support of this outcome, normalized pIGF-1Rβ fluorescence (**Figure 3C**, also **Supplementary Figures S2.2,S2.3**) decreased significantly in the PFC of 129S mice when compared with 129S:B6 ($p < 0.001$) and B6 ($p < 0.01$; **Figure 3D**). To determine the expression of pIGF-1Rβ in cortical neurons, pIGF-1Rβ immunofluorescence was combined with the NeuN labeling of pyramidal neurons (**Figure 3E**). In addition to the reduced cortical pIGF-1Rβ fluorescence, the mean expression of pIGF-1Rβ in neurons (NeuN) decreased significantly in the 129S PFC. When compared with the B6 ($p < 0.01$) and 129S:B6 ($p < 0.001$), neurons in the

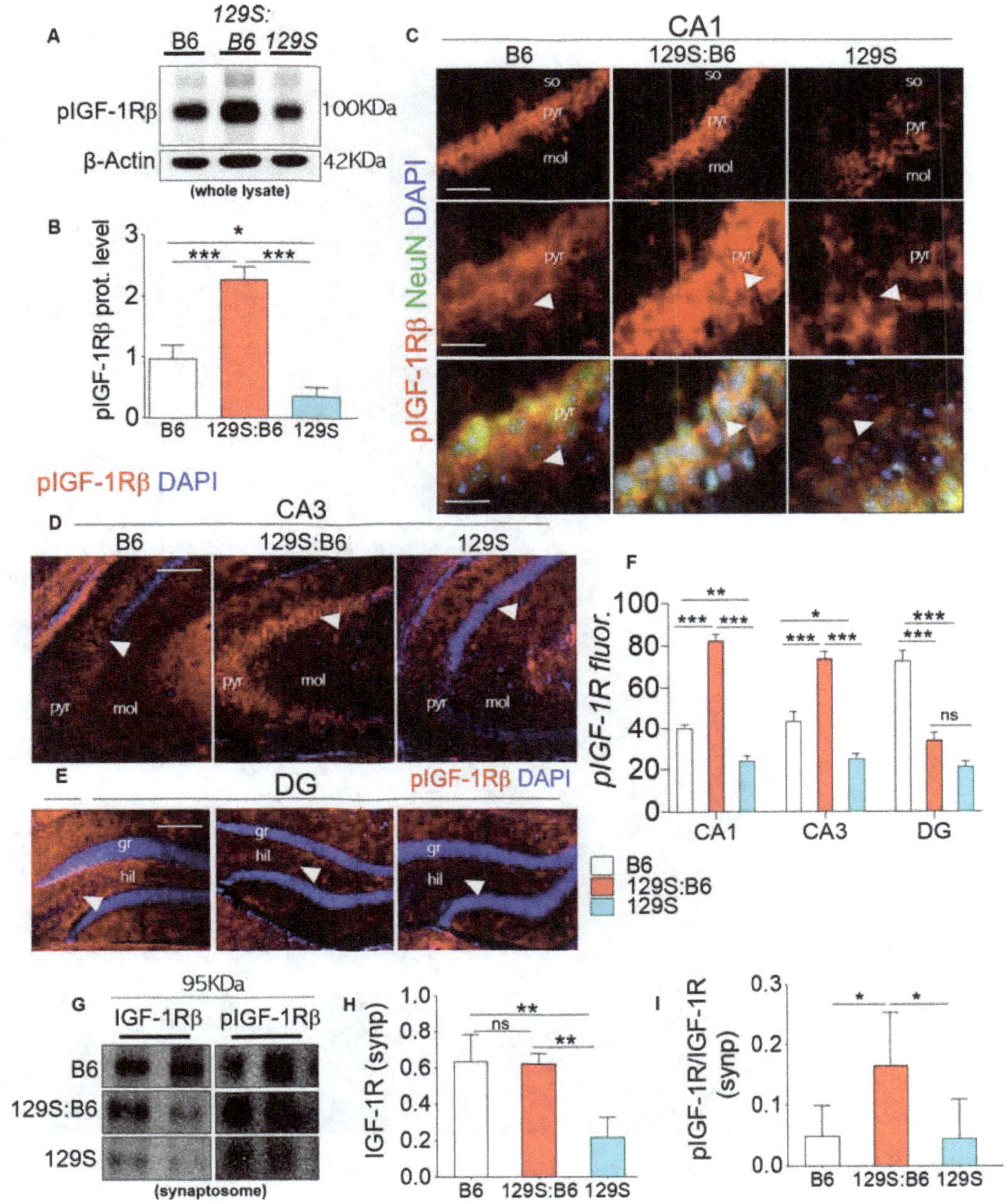

FIGURE 2 | Expression of pIGF-1Rβ in B6 (*disc1*$^{+/+}$), 129S:B6 (*disc1*$^{+/-}$), and 129S (*disc1*$^{-/-}$), hippocampus. **(A)** Representative western blots demonstrating pIGF-1Rβ expression in B6, 129S:B6 and 129S hippocampal whole lysate. **(B)** One-way ANOVA comparison of β-actin normalized pIGF-1Rβ expression. **(C)** Representative immunofluorescence images showing the expression of pIGF-1Rβ in the CA1 (scale bar = 60 μm and 40 μm). **(D,E)** Representative immunofluorescence images showing the expression of pIGF-1Rβ in the CA3, and DG regions of the hippocampus (scale bar = 80 μm; so, stratum oriens; pyr, pyramidal layer; mol, molecular layer; gr, granular layer; and hil: hilus of dentate gyrus). **(F)** Bar graph illustrating statistical comparison for pIGF-1Rβ fluorescence intensity in the CA1, CA3, and DG. **(G)** Representative western blots demonstrating IGF-1Rβ and pIGF-1Rβ expression in B6, 129S:B6 and 129S hippocampal synaptosomal (synp) extracts. **(H,I)** A statistical representation of normalized synaptosomal IGF-1Rβ and pIGF-1Rβ expression [(n = 4 to n = 6 per group; **B,F,H,I**) *$p < 0.05$, **$p < 0.01$, ***$p < 0.001$; ns, no significance].

129S PFC showed a statistical decrease in the pIGF-1Rβ level (**Figure 3F**).

pAkt

The kinase activity of pIGF-1Rβ involves the downstream activation of Akt (PBK) through Thr308 phosphorylation (**Figure 1**). Given that the complete activation of Akt requires Ser473 phosphorylation, here, we evaluated the expression of pAkt (S473) in C57BL/6J, 129S:B6 and 129S brains. Akt expression was determined by normalizing the basal protein level with β-actin. The threshold of Akt activity was determined by normalizing S473 phosphorylated Akt with Akt protein level.

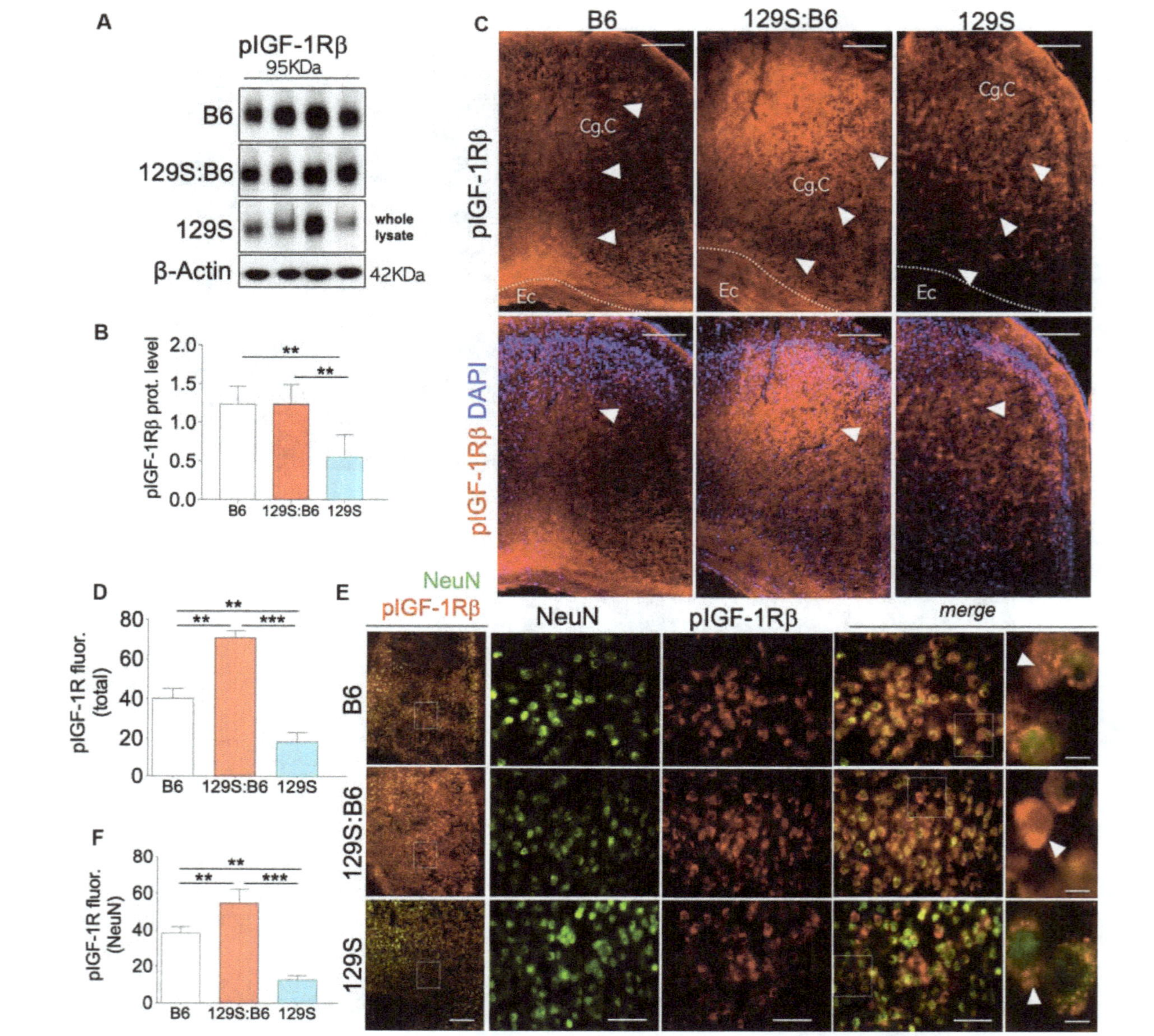

FIGURE 3 | Prefrontal cortex (PFC) expression of pIGF-1Rβ in 129S:B6 and 129S mice. **(A)** Representative western blots for pIGF-1Rβ detection in prefrontal cortical whole tissue lysate. **(B)** One-Way ANOVA comparison of normalized cortical pIGF-1Rβ expression. **(C)** Low magnification immunofluorescence images demonstrating an increase in pIGF-1Rβ expression in the 129S:B6 PFC, and a decrease in the 129S cortex (scale bar = 200 μm; Cg. C: cingulate cortex and Ec: external capsule). **(D)** Bar graph comparing pIGF-1Rβ fluorescence intensity in the PFC. **(E)** Double fluorescence immunolabeling for NeuN/pIGF-1Rβ co-localization in the PFC (scale bar = 200 μm, 60 μm, and 10 μm). **(F)** Quantification of pIGF-1Rβ fluorescence intensity in NeuN-labeled PFC neurons [(n = 4 to n = 6 per group; **B,D,F**); $^{**}p < 0.01$ and $^{***}p < 0.001$].

Partial (*disc1*$^{+/-}$) and total (*disc1*$^{-/-}$) ablation of DISC1 function did not alter the basal Akt level in the 129S hippocampus (**Figure 4A**). As a result, no significant change was recorded for Akt expression when 129S was compared with 129S:B6 and B6. Similarly, Akt expression in the 129S:B6 hippocampus did not change significantly vs. the B6 levels (**Figure 4B**). Although the disc1 ablation did not impact Akt expression, subsequent analysis of Akt activity level revealed otherwise (**Figure 4C**). The loss of DISC1 function in the 129S hippocampus significantly reduced S473 phosphorylation of Akt when compared with the control (B6; $p < 0.01$). Although the 129S:B6 did not record a decline in pIGF-1R activity or Akt expression, the *disc1*$^{+/-}$ phenotype was also characterized by a reduction of S473 pAkt; compared with B6 level ($p < 0.05$). As such, there was no significant difference in normalized hippocampal S473 pAkt when 129S was compared with 129S:B6 level. Furthermore, both mutant phenotypes (*disc1*$^{+/-}$ and *disc1*$^{-/-}$) recorded a significant loss of S473 pAkt when compared with the B6 (*disc1*$^{+/+}$). Based on these outcomes, loss of S473 pAkt activity in the 129S (*disc1*$^{-/-}$) hippocampus may be directly linked to the decline in hippocampal pIGF-1Rβ activity. However, since the pIGF-1Rβ activity did not reduce in the 129S:B6 hippocampus, loss of S473 pAkt activity might have occurred as a result of other changes directly linked to a defective DISC1 signaling.

Similar to the hippocampus, there was no significant change in basal Akt expression for the *disc1*$^{-/-}$ (129S) and *disc1*$^{+/-}$ (129S:B6) PFC when compared with the B6 group (*disc1*$^{+/+}$; **Figures 4D,E**). Likewise, the normalized S473 pAkt level decreased significantly in the 129S PFC when compared with the B6 (**Figure 4F**; $p < 0.05$). An empirical decrease in S473 pAkt was also recorded in the 129S:B6 PFC (**Figure 4F**). Based on previously established pIGF-1Rβ kinase signaling mechanism (**Figure 1**), suppression of S473 pAkt in the 129S PFC (**Figures 4D–F**; $p < 0.05$) agrees with the loss of pIGF-1Rβ activity (**Figure 3**). Together, these results indicate that pAkt attenuation in the 129S PFC, and not 129S:B6, may be linked to a decrease in pIGF-1Rβ activity.

GSK3β

GSK3β is involved in several cellular processes that occur downstream of IGF-1Rβ and other tyrosine kinase receptors (Rtks). Unlike IGF-1Rβ and Akt, GSK3β is basally active and does not require phosphorylation to be activated (Dewachter et al., 2009; Hur and Zhou, 2010; Emamian, 2012; Bhat et al., 2018). Mechanistically, phosphorylation of GSK3β (pGSK3β) at the Ser9 site by S473 pAkt attenuates basal GSK3β activity. Here, we used western blotting to detect basal GSK3β expression, and the threshold of Ser9 GSK3β phosphorylation in the hippocampus and PFC. To determine basal GSK3β level, GSK3β was normalized with β-actin. Likewise, the threshold of Ser9 GSK3β phosphorylation was determined by normalizing Ser9 pGSK3β with basal GSK3β.

Based on the previously established pIGF-1Rβ kinase signaling mechanism (Dyer et al., 2016), our results revealed that the threshold of Ser9 GSK3β phosphorylation agrees with the S473 pAkt level in the 129S:B6 and 129S hippocampus. Loss of S473 pAkt (**Figures 4A–C**) in the hippocampus was accompanied by a decrease in Ser9 pGSK3β in the 129S:B6 ($p < 0.001$) and 129S ($p < 0.001$) hippocampus (**Figures 5A,B**); compared with C57BL/6J. Since GSK3β is basally active, a decrease in the threshold of Ser9 GSK3β phosphorylation indicates an upregulation of GSK3β activity in the 129S:B6 and 129S hippocampus. Accordingly, a decrease in Ser9 GSK3β phosphorylation was accompanied by an upregulation of basal GSK3β level in the 129S:B6 ($p < 0.001$) and 129S ($p < 0.001$) hippocampus when compared with the control (**Figures 5A,B**). Although there was no significant difference in basal GSK3β level when 129S was compared with 129S:B6 hippocampus, the 129S hippocampus showed a significant decrease in normalized Ser9 pGSK3β vs. 129S:B6 ($p < 0.05$; **Figure 5B**). The result suggests that the *disc1*$^{-/-}$ phenotype (129S) underlie a higher level of GSK3β activity when compared with *disc1*$^{+/-}$ (129S:B6). The result is further supported by immunofluorescence labeling of pGSK3α/β in the hippocampus (**Figure 5C**). Fluorescence intensity for immunolabeled pGSK3α/β decreased significantly for the

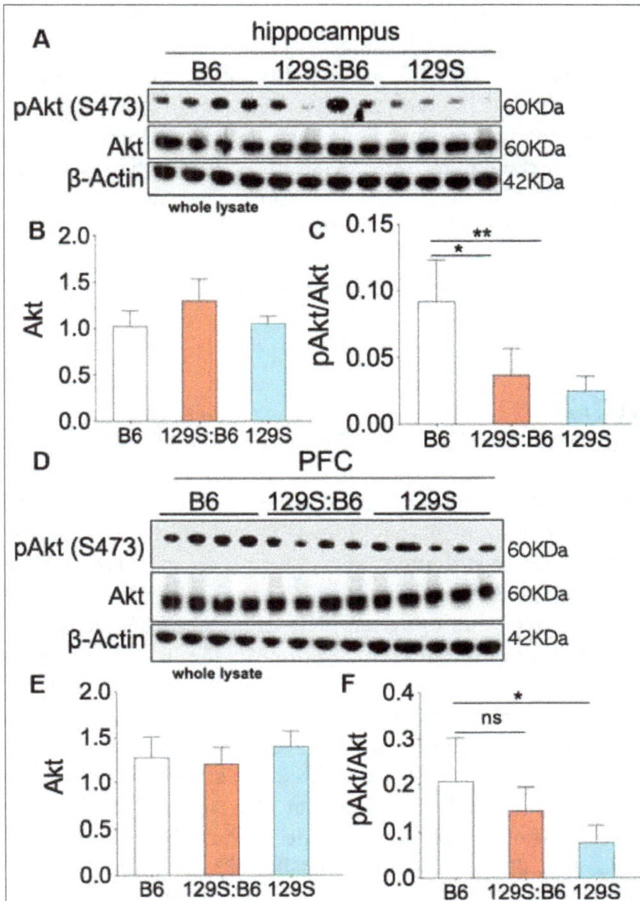

FIGURE 4 | Akt phosphorylation (Ser473) in the 129S:B6 and 129S hippocampus and PFC. **(A)** Western blots demonstrating Akt and *Ser473*-pAkt expression in hippocampal whole lysate. **(B,C)** Bar graphs (One-Way ANOVA) illustrating β-actin normalized Akt expression, and Akt normalized *Ser473*-pAkt expression in hippocampal whole lysate. **(D)** Representative western blots demonstrating normalized Akt and *Ser473*-pAkt expression in prefrontal cortical whole tissue lysate. **(E,F)** Bar graphs representing the relative expressions of Akt and *Ser473*-pAkt in B6 and 129S mutants PFC [($n = 4$ to $n = 6$ per group; **B,C,E,F**); ns: no significance, $^{*}p < 0.05$ and $^{**}p < 0.01$].

129S:B6 ($p < 0.001$) and 129S ($p < 0.001$) CA1 when compared with B6 (**Figure 5D**).

Given that Ser9 pGSK3β is pertinent to synaptic plasticity (Peineau et al., 2007; Clayton et al., 2010; Hur and Zhou, 2010; Lee et al., 2011b), we further compared GSK3β activity in 129S:B6 and 129S hippocampal synaptosomal extracts. Similar to whole lysate immunoblot outcomes, there is a significant loss of Ser9 pGSK3β in the 129S:B6 ($p < 0.001$) and 129S ($p < 0.001$) hippocampal synaptosomal extracts (**Figures 5E,F**; vs. B6). Based on these results, we determined that basal GSK3β activity is significantly upregulated at the cellular and synaptic levels as a result of *disc1*$^{+/-}$ (129S:B6) and *disc1*$^{-/-}$ (129S) mutation (**Figure 5G**).

Immunoblot analysis of the prefrontal cortical whole lysate revealed a significant increase in basal GSK3β activity for the 129S:B6 ($p < 0.05$) and 129S ($p < 0.05$) brain (**Figures 5H,I**).

Contrary to the hippocampus, the 129S:B6 cortex showed an increase in normalized Ser9 pGSK3β level ($p < 0.01$; **Figure 5I**) vs. the C57BL/6J. This indicates a decreased GSK3β activity in the 129S:B6 PFC compared with the control (B6). Interestingly, for the 129S PFC, there was no significant change in Ser9 pGSK3β level vs. the C57BL/6J (**Figures 5G–I**). From these outcomes, we determine that an increase in prefrontal cortical basal GSK3β activity is a shared attribute of 129S:B6 and 129S PFC. However, the pattern of cortical dysregulation of Ser9 pGSK3β may be dose-specific.

Erk1/2

Downstream of pIGF-1Rβ, phosphorylation of Erk1/2 (p42, p44) promotes cell proliferation (Roux and Blenis, 2004; Roskoski, 2012; Xing et al., 2016). This is particularly important in brain development as pIGF-1Rβ and pErk1/2 signaling regulates the distribution of neurons per unit area (Xing et al., 2016; Lin et al., 2017; Nieto Guil et al., 2017). However, given that upstream pIGF-1Rβ/pAkt/GS3β activity is dysregulated in the $disc1^{+/-}$ and $disc1^{-/-}$ brain, we compared the expression of pErk1/2 in the PFC and hippocampus of these mice strains. The expression of Erk1/2 was normalized with β-actin. To determine Erk1/2 activity (phosphorylation), pErk1 and pErk2 were normalized with the corresponding Erk1 or Erk2 levels. Immunoblot detection of pErk1 and pErk2 in whole hippocampal lysate (**Figure 6A**) showed that DISC1 loss of function did not alter the overall activity of these proteins. As such, there was no significant difference in pErK1 and pErK2 level when 129S ($disc1^{-/-}$) was compared to 129S:B6 level ($disc1^{+/-}$). Similarly, the 129S:B6 levels were not significantly different when compared with B6 ($disc1^{+/+}$; **Figures 6B,C**).

In subsequent analysis, we determined the synaptic activity of Erk by detecting pErk1/Erk1 and pErk2/Erk2 in hippocampal synaptosomal extracts (**Figure 6D**). Although total Erk activity was unchanged in the 129S hippocampus (**Figures 6A–C**), there was a significant increase in synaptic pErk1/pErk2 activity. When compared with the 129S:B6 ($disc1^{+/-}$) and B6 ($disc1^{+/+}$), the 129S group recorded an increase in normalized pErk1, pErk2, and pErk1/2 levels (**Figures 6E–G**; $p < 0.01$). It is important to note that the total synaptic Erk1/2 and pErK1/2 protein levels were downregulated by several folds in the 129S mutants, compared with 129S:B6 and B6 hippocampus (**Figure 6D**).

Immunoblot analysis of whole PFC lysate showed a significant increase in basal Erk1/2 protein level for the 129S:B6 ($p < 0.05$) and 129S ($p < 0.05$) PFC (**Figures 6H,I**). Analysis of pErk1 and pErk2 activity in the cortex showed some variations when compared with the hippocampus. Similar to the hippocampus, there was no significant change in total pErk1 activity for the 129S PFC; compared with the B6 and 129S:B6 (**Figure 6J**). Interestingly, the 129S PFC recorded a significant increase in pErk2 activity when compared with B6 and 129S:B6 ($p < 0.01$; **Figure 6K**). These outcomes suggest that $disc1^{-/-}$ mutation impacts pErK2 function in the PFC and not pErk1.

Our results also showed that the heterozygote disc1 mutation (129S:B6) did not impact pErk1/2 activity in the hippocampus and PFC. As such, there was no significant difference in normalized pErk1 and pErk2 levels when we compared 129S:B6 to B6 hippocampus (**Figures 6A,B**). This was also the case for the synaptic activity of pErk1 and pErk2 (**Figures 6D–G**). Similarly, prefrontal cortical expression of pErk1 and pErk2 were not significantly different when the 129S:B6 ($disc1^{+/-}$) was compared to B6 ($disc1^{+/+}$; **Figures 6H,K,L**).

DISCUSSION

Disc1 mutation is an associative cause of human neuropsychiatric disorders linked with schizophrenia, bipolar depression, and some cases of autism (Brandon et al., 2009; Wexler and Geschwind, 2011; Zheng et al., 2011; Gómez-Sintes et al., 2014; St Clair and Johnstone, 2018). *Disc1* mutation alters the activity of GSK3β, Erk1/2, and Akt in the nervous system (Kim et al., 2009; Soares et al., 2011; Aringhieri et al., 2017; Hirayama-Kurogi et al., 2017; Malavasi et al., 2018). Owing to the role of Erk1/2 and GSK3β in the control of cortical organization, synaptic development, and LTP, *disc1* mutation underlies a broad range of synaptic and neuropsychiatric defects. 129S mice show prominent anatomical brain changes, with observable neuropsychiatric phenotypes in postnatal development (Soares et al., 2011; Sultana et al., 2019). Similarly, disruption of neurotrophic cues involving DISC1, Erk1/2 or GSK3β signaling in the C57BL/6J brain disrupts cell migration and cortical lamination patterns (Koike et al., 2006; Ross et al., 2006; Kvajo et al., 2008; Kim et al., 2009; Lee et al., 2011a,b; Namba et al., 2011; Xing et al., 2016; Nieto Guil et al., 2017).

Erroneous regulation of Erk1/2 signaling promulgates cell proliferation abnormalities in the developing cortical circuit. Experimental hyperactivation of Erk1/2 in the cortex caused a significant increase in neuron count, and morphological defects (Morales-Garcia et al., 2014; Xing et al., 2016). To this effect, pharmacological inhibition of Erk1/2 signaling rescued some of the synaptic and behavioral phenotypes associated with developmental neuropsychiatric defects in mice (Lu and Dwyer, 2005; Soares et al., 2011; Pereira et al., 2014; Tassin et al., 2015; Aringhieri et al., 2017; Hirayama-Kurogi et al., 2017; Pucilowska et al., 2018). Similarly, there is evidence that pharmacological inhibition or genetic ablation of neural GSK3β activity rescued dendritic spine and behavioral abnormalities linked to *disc1* mutation, and other forms of schizophrenia (Lee et al., 2011b; Lipina et al., 2011).

In addition to their role in DISC1 signaling, GSK3β and Erk1/2 are controlled by upstream pIGF-1Rβ activity. An important question yet to be addressed is whether a change in expression of these kinases in the *disc1* mutant brain impacts pIGF-1Rβ activity. Based on previously established mechanisms for pIGF-1Rβ signaling (Dyer et al., 2016), we considered the possible link between IGF-1Rβ, Akt, Erk1/2, GSK3β in the *disc1* mutant brain. In addition to a change in the activity of GSK3β and Erk1/2,

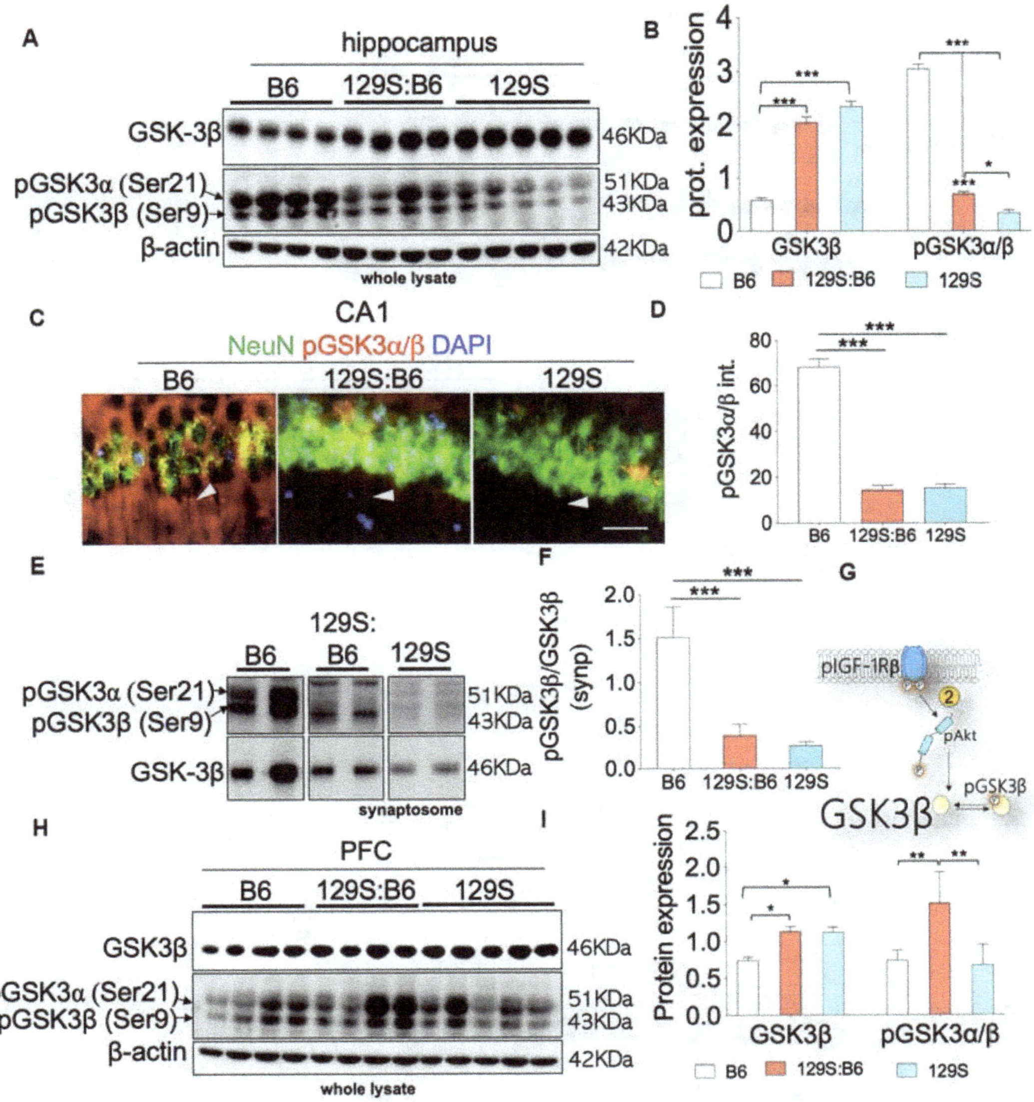

FIGURE 5 | GSK3β activity in the B6, 129S:B6 and 129S brain. **(A)** Representative western blots illustrating the expression of GSK3β and pGSK3β in the hippocampus of B6, 129S:B6 and 129S strains. **(B)** Bar graph illustrating the statistical difference in β-actin normalized GSK3β expression, GSK3β normalized pGSK3β expression in the hippocampus. **(C)** Fluorescence images depicting the loss of pGSK3α(Ser21)/β(Ser9) expression in the 129S:B6 and 129S hippocampal neurons (CA1; scale bar = 60 μm). **(D)** Bar graph illustrating the statistical comparison of pGSK3β fluorescence intensity in the CA1. **(E,F)** Western blots and bar graph illustrating normalized pGSK3β expression in the hippocampal synaptosomal extract. **(G)** Schematic illustration of the pIGF-1Rβ signaling and downstream modulation of GSK3β by Ser473-pAkt. 129S:B6 and 129S hippocampus showed Ser473-pAkt loss and increased basal activity of GSK3β. **(H,I)** Representative western blots and bar graphs illustrating the expression of GSK3β and pGSK3β in the prefrontal cortical whole lysate [(n = 4 to n = 6 samples per group; **B,D,F,I**); $^{*}p < 0.05$, $^{**}p < 0.01$ and $^{***}p < 0.001$].

neural pIGF-1R expression changed in the *disc1* mutant hippocampus and PFC. Analysis of pIGF-1Rβ-GSK3β signaling showed that the decrease in neural pIGF-1Rβ in the 129S hippocampus was accompanied by the suppression of S473 pAkt. Likewise, the loss of S473 pAkt may be linked to a decrease in Ser9 phosphorylation (inactivation) of pGSK3β (Wan et al., 2007; Kitagishi et al., 2012; Levenga et al., 2017). From these outcomes, we deduced that the dysregulation of DISC1-associated proteins (GSK3β/Erk1/2) impacts pIGF-1Rβ activity in the *disc1* mutant brain (**Figure 1**).

Our results revealed that an increase in basal GSK3β activity, in the hippocampus of mutant *disc1* carrier mice, is associated with the dysregulation of DISC1-GSK3β interaction, and pAkt-mediated regulation of GSK3β. Thus, in both $disc1^{+/-}$ and $disc1^{-/-}$ brain, there was a decrease in Ser473 pAkt and a reduction in Ser 9 phosphorylation of GSK3β. This indicates an increase in basal GSK3β activity. A similar increase in GSK3β activity was also observed at the synaptic level. Accordingly, 129S:B6 and 129S synaptosomal extracts recorded a decrease in normalized Ser9 pGSK3β level when compared with the control (B6; **Figures 5E,F**). Like the hippocampus, the PFC of mutant

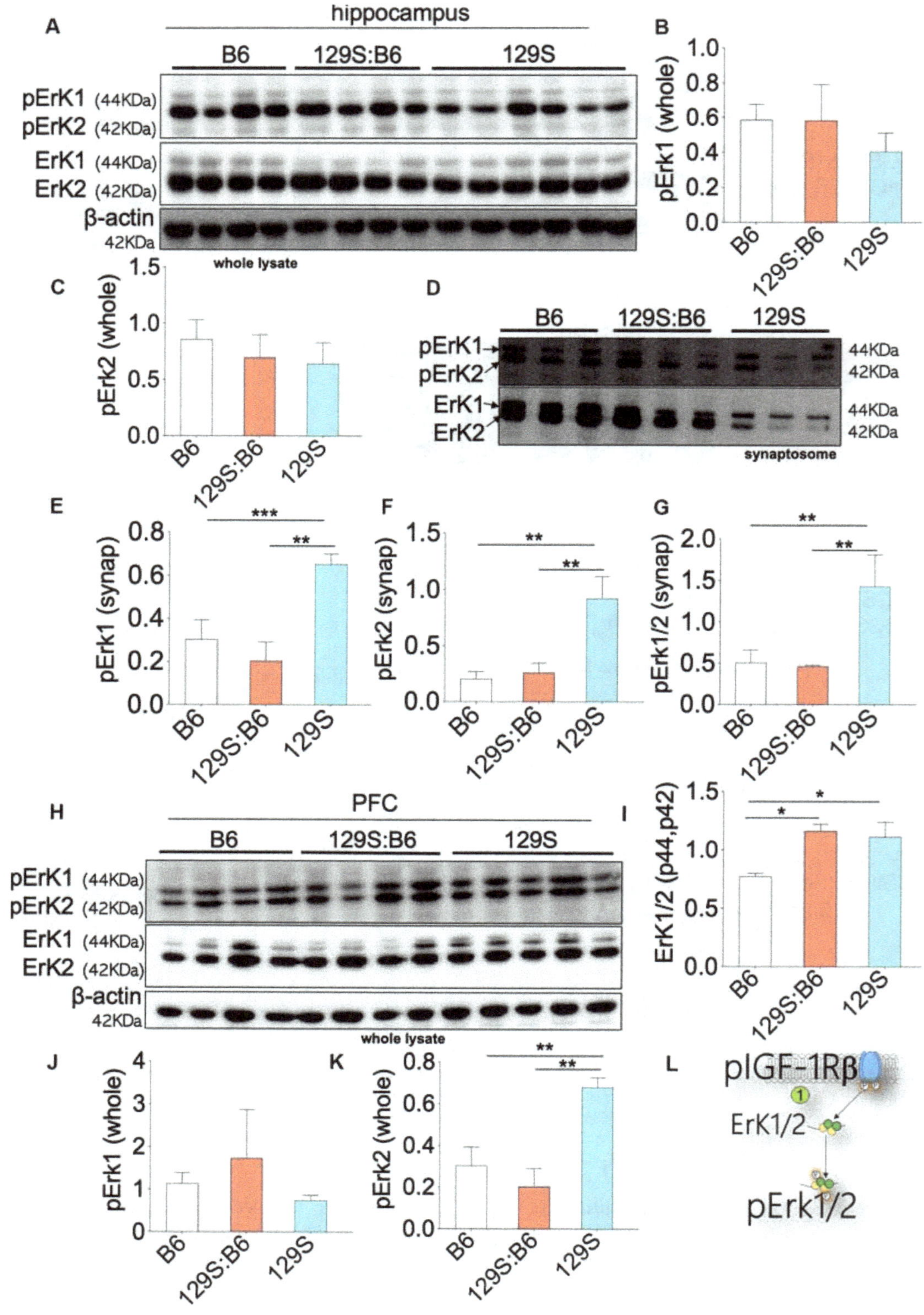

FIGURE 6 | Erk1/2 expression in the B6, 129S:B6 and 129S brain. **(A)** Immunoblots demonstrating the expression of Erk1/2 and pErk1/2 in the hippocampus. **(B,C)** Bar graph illustrating Erk (1 and 2) normalized pErk1 and pErk2 expression in the whole hippocampal lysate. **(D)** Representative western blots illustrating the expression of pErk1 and pErk2 in hippocampal synaptosomal extracts. **(E–G)** Bar graphs representing Erk normalized pErk1, pErk2, and total pErk1/2 expression in hippocampal synaptosomal extracts. **(H)** Immunoblots illustrating prefrontal total cortical Erk1/2 expression. **(I)** Bar graph demonstrating a significant increase in total PFC Erk1/2 expression for the 129S:B6 and 129S mice. **(J,K)** Bar graph representing the expression of Erk normalized pErk1 and pErk2 expression in cortical whole lysate. **(L)** Schematic illustration demonstrating an increase in cortical Erk1/2 expression. [**(E–G,I,K)**; *p < 0.05, **p < 0.01, and ***p < 0.001].

disc1 carriers also exhibits a significant increase in basal GSK3β expression when compared with the control (B6; **Figure 5I**). However, the pattern of GSK3β activity was different when the hippocampus was compared with the cortex. While the 129S:B6 (*disc1*$^{+/-}$) showed an increase in normalized Ser9 pGSK3β, the 129S (*disc1*$^{-/-}$) PFC recorded no significant change vs. the control.

The observed prefrontal cortical GSK3β activity may be related to the dysregulation of pIGF-1Rβ-pAkt in the mutant cortex. As shown previously, the *disc1*$^{+/-}$ (129S:B6) brain was characterized by an increase in pIGF-1Rβ expression (**Figures 3D–F**). When compared with the control (B6), the level of normalized S473 pAkt was also unchanged for the 129S:B6 cortex (**Figure 4F**). Thus, there is a possibility that an increase in pIGF-1Rβ expression promulgates a higher level of Ser9 pGSK3β in the 129S:B6 cortex, compared with the 129S. Interestingly, the loss of pIGF-1Rβ in the *disc1*$^{-/-}$ (129S) cortex (**Figure 3D–F**), coupled with a decrease in S473 pAkt (**Figure 4F**) did not affect the Ser9 pGSK3β threshold. These results suggest that change in Ser9 pGSK3β in the 129S (*disc1*$^{-/-}$) PFC may not be directly linked to pIGF-1Rβ dysregulation.

In addition to a defective pIGF-1Rβ-pAkt-GSK3β, Erk1/2 activity is also dysregulated in the hippocampus and PFC of 129S (*disc1*$^{-/-}$) mutant mice. Specifically, there was an increase in pErk1/2 activity in the hippocampus and pErk2 activity in the PFC of 129S mice. Interestingly, increased ErK activity appeared to phenotype-specific. While the 129S (*disc1*$^{-/-}$) recorded an increased synaptic pErk level, there was no significant change in pErk activity for the 129S:B6 (*disc1*$^{+/-}$) brain when compared with the control (B6; **Figure 6**). Given that a pIGF-1Rβ decreased in 129S hippocampal whole lysate and synaptosomal extracts, it is likely that pErk increase may be associated with other changes linked to disc1 mutation and post-synaptic DISC1 activity. Similarly, increased pErk2 levels in the 129S PFC demonstrate that a change in Erk activity may not be dependent on pIGF-1Rβ. The limitation of the current study is that loss or gain of function experiments have not been performed for Erk, GSK3β, and Akt. Thus, the results are still preliminary and descriptive.

Taken together, these outcomes suggest that the hippocampus and PFC show distinct patterns of kinase dysregulation in *disc1* mutation. Also, the pattern of dysregulation may vary with the mutation dose. While the 129S:B6 showed mostly GSK3β dysregulation, the 129S brain recorded significant changes in GSK3β and Erk1/2.

FUTURE DIRECTIONS

Although Erk1/2 and GSK3β inhibitors are now being explored as therapeutic agents in developmental neuropsychiatric disorders, our results suggest that a broader target involving pIGF-1Rβ may be required for effective control of the pathway. The outcome of this study also revealed a general decrease in neural pIGF-1Rβ as a result of *disc1* mutations (**Figures 1**, **2**). This is in agreement with previous studies that explored IGF-1 therapy to attenuate schizophrenia pathophysiology (Venkatasubramanian et al., 2010; Bou Khalil, 2011; Demirel et al., 2014). On the other hand, an increase in pIGF-1Rβ in the 129S:B6 brain suggests that IGF-1Rβ blockers could be explored as therapeutic targets for some *disc1* carriers. In addition to an increase in GSK3β activity, pErk1/2 is also upregulated in the 129S brain. Thus, a combination of GSK3β and Erk1/2 inhibitors could be further explored.

SUMMARY

In summary, our results show that neural pIGF-1Rβ expression is altered in 129S:B6 and 129S mice compared with C57BL/6J animals. Furthermore, both strains were characterized by a significant change in GSK3β and Erk1/2 expression patterns in the hippocampus and PFC (**Supplementary Table S1**). We deduce that some of these changes may be directly related to pIGF-1Rβ expression. Thus, targeting IGF-1Rβ in addition to the kinases (GSK3β and Erk1/2) may reduce the phenotypic burden of some developmental neuropsychiatric disorders.

DATA AVAILABILITY STATEMENT

The raw data supporting the conclusions of this article will be made available by the authors, without undue reservation, to any qualified researcher.

ETHICS STATEMENT

The animal study was reviewed and approved by Louisiana State University School of Veterinary Medicine IACUC Committee.

AUTHOR CONTRIBUTIONS

OO and CL designed the experiments. OO, AS and RS conducted the experiments and analyzed the results. OO and CL prepared the manuscript. OO, CL, RS and AS checked the manuscript.

FUNDING

This study was supported by School of Veterinary Medicine, Louisiana State University (LSU-SVM) COPR Grant awarded to OO. Also, National Institute of Mental Health (NIH) Grant R03 MH 104851 awarded to CL.

SUPPLEMENTARY MATERIAL

FIGURE S1 | Low magnification merged fluorescence images for **Figures 2D,E**.

FIGURE S2 | S2.1: Immunoblots showing the expression of pIGF-1Rβ in the PFC (as presented in **Figure 3A**) S2.2: pIGF-1Rβ immunofluorescence in the B6, 129S:B6 and 129S mPFC (see also **Figure 3C**). S2.3: pIGF-1Rβ and NeuN immunofluorescence in the B6, 129S:B6 and 129S mPFC (also **Figure 3E**; low magnification image).

TABLE S1 | Summary of results.

REFERENCES

Aringhieri, S., Kolachalam, S., Gerace, C., Carli, M., Verdesca, V., Brunacci, M. G., et al. (2017). Clozapine as the most efficacious antipsychotic for activating ERK 1/2 kinases: role of 5-HT_{2A} receptor agonism. *Eur. Neuropsychopharmacol.* 27, 383–398. doi: 10.1016/j.euroneuro.2017.02.005

Bhat, R. V., Andersson, U., Andersson, S., Knerr, L., Bauer, U., and Sundgren-Andersson, A. K. (2018). The conundrum of GSK3 inhibitors: is it the dawn of a new beginning? *J. Alzheimers Dis.* 64, S547–S554. doi: 10.3233/jad-179934

Bou Khalil, R. (2011). Recombinant human IGF-1 for patients with schizophrenia. *Med. Hypotheses* 77, 427–429. doi: 10.1016/j.mehy.2011.06.001

Brandon, N. J., Millar, J. K., Korth, C., Sive, H., Singh, K. K., and Sawa, A. (2009). Understanding the role of DISC1 in psychiatric disease and during normal development. *J. Neurosci.* 29, 12768–12775. doi: 10.1523/jneurosci.3355-09.2009

Chandarlapaty, S., Sawai, A., Scaltriti, M., Rodrik-Outmezguine, V., Grbovic-Huezo, O., Serra, V., et al. (2011). AKT inhibition relieves feedback suppression of receptor tyrosine kinase expression and activity. *Cancer Cell* 19, 58–71. doi: 10.1016/j.ccr.2010.10.031

Clapcote, S. J., and Roder, J. C. (2006). Deletion polymorphism of Disc1 is common to all 129 mouse substrains: implications for gene-targeting studies of brain function. *Genetics* 173, 2407–2410. doi: 10.1534/genetics.106.060749

Clayton, E. L., Sue, N., Smillie, K. J., O'Leary, T., Bache, N., Cheung, G., et al. (2010). Dynamin I phosphorylation by GSK3 controls activity-dependent bulk endocytosis of synaptic vesicles. *Nat. Neurosci.* 13, 845–851. doi: 10.1038/nn.2571

Dachtler, J., Elliott, C., Rodgers, R. J., Baillie, G. S., and Clapcote, S. J. (2016). Missense mutation in DISC1 C-terminal coiled-coil has GSK3β signaling and sex-dependent behavioral effects in mice. *Sci. Rep.* 6:18748. doi: 10.1038/srep18748

Del'Guidice, T., and Beaulieu, J. M. (2010). [Psychotropic drugs and the involvement of the Akt/GSK3 signalling pathway in mental illnesses]. *Med. Sci.* 26, 647–651. doi: 10.1051/medsci/2010266-7647

Demirel, A., Demirel, O. F., Emul, M., Duran, A., and Ugur, M. (2014). Relationships between IGF-1, schizophrenia, and treatment of metabolic syndrome. *Compr. Psychiatry* 55, 1391–1397. doi: 10.1016/j.comppsych.2014.04.008

Dewachter, I., Ris, L., Jaworski, T., Seymour, C. M., Kremer, A., Borghgraef, P., et al. (2009). GSK3β, a centre-staged kinase in neuropsychiatric disorders, modulates long term memory by inhibitory phosphorylation at serine-9. *Neurobiol. Dis.* 35, 193–200. doi: 10.1016/j.nbd.2009.04.003

Dyer, A. H., Vahdatpour, C., Sanfeliu, A., and Tropea, D. (2016). The role of insulin-like growth factor 1 (IGF-1) in brain development, maturation and neuroplasticity. *Neuroscience* 325, 89–99. doi: 10.1016/j.neuroscience. 2016.03.056

Emamian, E. S. (2012). AKT/GSK3 signaling pathway and schizophrenia. *Front. Mol. Neurosci.* 5:33. doi: 10.3389/fnmol.2012.00033

Gao, M., and Zhao, L. R. (2018). Turning death to growth: hematopoietic growth factors promote neurite outgrowth through MEK/ERK/p53 pathway. *Mol. Neurobiol.* 55, 5913–5925. doi: 10.1007/s12035-017-0814-x

Giachello, C. N., Fiumara, F., Giacomini, C., Corradi, A., Milanese, C., Ghirardi, M., et al. (2010). MAPK/Erk-dependent phosphorylation of synapsin mediates formation of functional synapses and short-term homosynaptic plasticity. *J. Cell Sci.* 123, 881–893. doi: 10.1242/jcs.056846

Gómez-Sintes, R., Kvajo, M., Gogos, J. A., and Lucas, J. J. (2014). Mice with a naturally occurring DISC1 mutation display a broad spectrum of behaviors associated to psychiatric disorders. *Front. Behav. Neurosci.* 8:253. doi: 10.3389/fnbeh.2014.00253

González Burgos, I., Nikonenko, I., and Korz, V. (2012). Dendritic spine plasticity and cognition. *Neural Plast.* 2012:875156. doi: 10.1155/2012/875156

Hirayama-Kurogi, M., Takizawa, Y., Kunii, Y., Matsumoto, J., Wada, A., Hino, M., et al. (2017). Downregulation of GNA13-ERK network in prefrontal cortex of schizophrenia brain identified by combined focused and targeted quantitative proteomics. *J. Proteomics* 158, 31–42. doi: 10.1016/j.jprot.2017.02.009

Hur, E. M., and Zhou, F. Q. (2010). GSK3 signalling in neural development. *Nat. Rev. Neurosci.* 11, 539–551. doi: 10.1038/nrn2870

Iyaswamy, A., Kammella, A. K., Thavasimuthu, C., Wankupar, W., Dapkupar, W., Shanmugam, S., et al. (2018). Oxidative stress evoked damages leading to attenuated memory and inhibition of NMDAR-CaMKII-ERK/CREB signalling on consumption of aspartame in rat model. *J. Food Drug Anal.* 26, 903–916. doi: 10.1016/j.jfda.2017.11.001

Kamat, P. K., Kalani, A., and Tyagi, N. (2014). Method and validation of synaptosomal preparation for isolation of synaptic membrane proteins from rat brain. *MethodsX* 1, 102–107. doi: 10.1016/j.mex.2014.08.002

Kim, J. Y., Duan, X., Liu, C. Y., Jang, M. H., Guo, J. U., Pow-anpongkul, N., et al. (2009). DISC1 regulates new neuron development in the adult brain via modulation of AKT-mTOR signaling through KIAA1212. *Neuron* 63, 761–773. doi: 10.1016/j.neuron.2009.08.008

Kitagishi, Y., Kobayashi, M., Kikuta, K., and Matsuda, S. (2012). Roles of PI3K/AKT/GSK3/mTOR pathway in cell signaling of mental illnesses. *Depress. Res. Treat.* 2012:752563. doi: 10.1155/2012/752563

Koike, H., Arguello, P. A., Kvajo, M., Karayiorgou, M., and Gogos, J. A. (2006). Disc1 is mutated in the 129S6/SvEv strain and modulates working memory in mice. *Proc. Natl. Acad. Sci. U S A* 103, 3693–3697. doi: 10.1073/pnas.0511189103

Kvajo, M., McKellar, H., Arguello, P. A., Drew, L. J., Moore, H., MacDermott, A. B., et al. (2008). A mutation in mouse Disc1 that models a schizophrenia risk allele leads to specific alterations in neuronal architecture and cognition. *Proc. Natl. Acad. Sci. U S A* 105, 7076–7081. doi: 10.1073/pnas.0802615105

Lee, F. H., Fadel, M. P., Preston-Maher, K., Cordes, S. P., Clapcote, S. J., Price, D. J., et al. (2011a). Disc1 point mutations in mice affect development of the cerebral cortex. *J. Neurosci.* 31, 3197–3206. doi: 10.1523/jneurosci.4219-10.2011

Lee, F. H., Kaidanovich-Beilin, O., Roder, J. C., Woodgett, J. R., and Wong, A. H. (2011b). Genetic inactivation of GSK3alpha rescues spine deficits in Disc1-L100P mutant mice. *Schizophr. Res.* 129, 74–79. doi: 10.1016/j.schres.2011.03.032

Lee, C. C., Huang, C. C., and Hsu, K. S. (2011). Insulin promotes dendritic spine and synapse formation by the PI3K/Akt/mTOR and Rac1 signaling pathways. *Neuropharmacology* 61, 867–879. doi: 10.1016/j.neuropharm.2011.06.003

Levenga, J., Wong, H., Milstead, R. A., Keller, B. N., LaPlante, L. E., and Hoeffer, C. A. (2017). AKT isoforms have distinct hippocampal expression and roles in synaptic plasticity. *Elife* 6:e30640. doi: 10.7554/elife.30640

Lin, Y., Liu, H., Waraky, A., Haglund, F., Agarwal, P., Jernberg-Wiklund, H., et al. (2017). SUMO-modified insulin-like growth factor 1 receptor (IGF-1R) increases cell cycle progression and cell proliferation. *J. Cell. Physiol.* 232, 2722–2730. doi: 10.1002/jcp.25818

Lipina, T. V., Kaidanovich-Beilin, O., Patel, S., Wang, M., Clapcote, S. J., Liu, F., et al. (2011). Genetic and pharmacological evidence for schizophrenia-related Disc1 interaction with GSK-3. *Synapse* 65, 234–248. doi: 10.1002/syn.20839

Lu, X. H., and Dwyer, D. S. (2005). Second-generation antipsychotic drugs, olanzapine, quetiapine and clozapine enhance neurite outgrowth in PC12 cells *via* PI3K/AKT, ERK and pertussis toxin-sensitive pathways. *J. Mol. Neurosci.* 27, 43–64. doi: 10.1385/jmn:27:1:043

Malavasi, E. L. V., Economides, K. D., Grunewald, E., Makedonopoulou, P., Gautier, P., Mackie, S., et al. (2018). DISC1 regulates N-methyl-D-aspartate receptor dynamics: abnormalities induced by a Disc1 mutation modelling a translocation linked to major mental illness. *Transl. Psychiatry* 8:184. doi: 10.1038/s41398-018-0228-1

Morales-Garcia, J. A., Palomo, V., Redondo, M., Alonso-Gil, S., Gil, C., Martinez, A., et al. (2014). Crosstalk between phosphodiesterase 7 and glycogen synthase kinase-3: two relevant therapeutic targets for neurological disorders. *ACS Chem. Neurosci.* 5, 194–204. doi: 10.1021/cn400166d

Nakahata, Y., and Yasuda, R. (2018). Plasticity of spine structure: local signaling, translation and cytoskeletal reorganization. *Front. Synaptic Neurosci.* 10:29. doi: 10.3389/fnsyn.2018.00029

Namba, T., Ming, G. L., Song, H., Waga, C., Enomoto, A., Kaibuchi, K., et al. (2011). NMDA receptor regulates migration of newly generated neurons in the adult hippocampus *via* disrupted-in-schizophrenia 1 (DISC1). *J. Neurochem.* 118, 34–44. doi: 10.1111/j.1471-4159.2011.07282.x

Nieto Guil, A. F., Oksdath, M., Weiss, L. A., Grassi, D. J., Sosa, L. J., Nieto, M., et al. (2017). IGF-1 receptor regulates dynamic changes in neuronal polarity during cerebral cortical migration. *Sci. Rep.* 7:7703. doi: 10.1038/s41598-017-08140-5

Nikolaienko, O., Eriksen, M. S., Patil, S., Bito, H., and Bramham, C. R. (2017). Stimulus-evoked ERK-dependent phosphorylation of activity-regulated cytoskeleton-associated protein (Arc) regulates its neuronal subcellular localization. *Neuroscience* 360, 68–80. doi: 10.1016/j.neuroscience.2017.07.026

Ohta, K. I., Suzuki, S., Warita, K., Kaji, T., Kusaka, T., and Miki, T. (2017). Prolonged maternal separation attenuates BDNF-ERK signaling correlated with spine formation in the hippocampus during early brain development. *J. Neurochem.* 141, 179–194. doi: 10.1111/jnc.13977

Peineau, S., Taghibiglou, C., Bradley, C., Wong, T. P., Liu, L., Lu, J., et al. (2007). LTP inhibits LTD in the hippocampus *via* regulation of GSK3beta. *Neuron* 53, 703–717. doi: 10.1016/j.neuron.2007.01.029

Pereira, A., Zhang, B., Malcolm, P., Sugiharto-Winarno, A., and Sundram, S. (2014). Quetiapine and aripiprazole signal differently to ERK, p90RSK and c-Fos in mouse frontal cortex and striatum: role of the EGF receptor. *BMC Neurosci.* 15:30. doi: 10.1186/1471-2202-15-30

Pucilowska, J., Vithayathil, J., Pagani, M., Kelly, C., Karlo, J. C., Robol, C., et al. (2018). Pharmacological inhibition of ERK signaling rescues pathophysiology and behavioral phenotype associated with 16p11.2 chromosomal deletion in mice. *J. Neurosci.* 38, 6640–6652. doi: 10.1523/jneurosci.0515-17.2018

Ramsey, A. J., Milenkovic, M., Oliveira, A. F., Escobedo-Lozoya, Y., Seshadri, S., Salahpour, A., et al. (2011). Impaired NMDA receptor transmission alters striatal synapses and DISC1 protein in an age-dependent manner. *Proc. Natl. Acad. Sci. U S A* 108, 5795–5800. doi: 10.1073/pnas.1012621108

Reim, D., and Schmeisser, M. J. (2017). Neurotrophic factors in mouse models of autism spectrum disorder: focus on BDNF and IGF-1. *Adv. Anat. Embryol. Cell Biol.* 224, 121–134. doi: 10.1007/978-3-319-52498-6_7

Roskoski, R. Jr. (2012). ERK1/2 MAP kinases: structure, function, and regulation. *Pharmacol. Res.* 66, 105–143. doi: 10.1016/j.phrs.2012.04.005

Ross, C. A., Margolis, R. L., Reading, S. A., Pletnikov, M., and Coyle, J. T. (2006). Neurobiology of schizophrenia. *Neuron* 52, 139–153. doi: 10.1016/j.neuron.2006.09.015

Roux, P. P., and Blenis, J. (2004). ERK and p38 MAPK-activated protein kinases: a family of protein kinases with diverse biological functions. *Microbiol. Mol. Biol. Rev.* 68, 320–344. doi: 10.1128/mmbr.68.2.320-344.2004

Shahab, L., Plattner, F., Irvine, E. E., Cummings, D. M., and Edwards, F. A. (2014). Dynamic range of GSK3α not GSK3β is essential for bidirectional synaptic plasticity at hippocampal CA3-CA1 synapses. *Hippocampus* 24, 1413–1416. doi: 10.1002/hipo.22362

Shao, L., Lu, B., Wen, Z., Teng, S., Wang, L., Zhao, Y., et al. (2017). Disrupted-in-Schizophrenia-1 (DISC1) protein disturbs neural function in multiple disease-risk pathways. *Hum. Mol. Genet.* 26, 2634–2648. doi: 10.1093/hmg/ddx147

Snyder, M. A., and Gao, W. J. (2013). NMDA hypofunction as a convergence point for progression and symptoms of schizophrenia. *Front. Cell. Neurosci.* 7:31. doi: 10.3389/fncel.2013.00031

Soares, D. C., Carlyle, B. C., Bradshaw, N. J., and Porteous, D. J. (2011). DISC1: structure, function and therapeutic potential for major mental illness. *ACS Chem. Neurosci.* 2, 609–632. doi: 10.1021/cn200062k

St Clair, D., and Johnstone, M. (2018). Using mouse transgenic and human stem cell technologies to model genetic mutations associated with schizophrenia and autism. *Philos. Trans. R. Soc. Lond. B Biol. Sci.* 373:20170037. doi: 10.1098/rstb.2017.0037

Sultana, R., Ogundele, O. M., and Lee, C. C. (2019). Contrasting characteristic behaviours among common laboratory mouse strains. *R. Soc. Open Sci.* 6:190574. doi: 10.1098/rsos.190574

Swiatkowski, P., Nikolaeva, I., Kumar, G., Zucco, A., Akum, B. F., Patel, M. V., et al. (2017). Role of Akt-independent mTORC1 and GSK3β signaling in sublethal NMDA-induced injury and the recovery of neuronal electrophysiology and survival. *Sci. Rep.* 7:1539. doi: 10.1038/s41598-017-01826-w

Tassin, T. C., Benavides, D. R., Plattner, F., Nishi, A., and Bibb, J. A. (2015). Regulation of ERK kinase by MEK1 kinase inhibition in the brain. *J. Biol. Chem.* 290, 16319–16329. doi: 10.1074/jbc.M115.654897

Tenreiro, P., Rebelo, S., Martins, F., Santos, M., Coelho, E. D., Almeida, M., et al. (2017). Comparison of simple sucrose and percoll based methodologies for synaptosome enrichment. *Anal. Biochem.* 517, 1–8. doi: 10.1016/j.ab.2016.10.015

Tomoda, T., Sumitomo, A., Jaaro-Peled, H., and Sawa, A. (2016). Utility and validity of DISC1 mouse models in biological psychiatry. *Neuroscience* 321, 99–107. doi: 10.1016/j.neuroscience.2015.12.061

Vara, H., Onofri, F., Benfenati, F., Sassoe-Pognetto, M., and Giustetto, M. (2009). ERK activation in axonal varicosities modulates presynaptic plasticity in the CA3 region of the hippocampus through synapsin I. *Proc. Natl. Acad. Sci. U S A* 106, 9872–9877. doi: 10.1073/pnas.0900077106

Venkatasubramanian, G., Chittiprol, S., Neelakantachar, N., Shetty, T., and Gangadhar, B. N. (2010). Effect of antipsychotic treatment on insulin-like growth factor-1 and cortisol in schizophrenia: a longitudinal study. *Schizophr. Res.* 119, 131–137. doi: 10.1016/j.schres.2010.01.033

Wan, X., Harkavy, B., Shen, N., Grohar, P., and Helman, L. J. (2007). Rapamycin induces feedback activation of Akt signaling through an IGF-1R-dependent mechanism. *Oncogene* 26, 1932–1940. doi: 10.1038/sj.onc.1209990

Wang, Q., Charych, E. I., Pulito, V. L., Lee, J. B., Graziane, N. M., Crozier, R. A., et al. (2011). The psychiatric disease risk factors DISC1 and TNIK interact to regulate synapse composition and function. *Mol. Psychiatry* 16, 1006–1023. doi: 10.1038/mp.2010.87

Wang, Y., Sawyer, T. W., Tse, Y. C., Fan, C., Hennes, G., Barnes, J., et al. (2017). Primary blast-induced changes in Akt and GSK3β phosphorylation in rat hippocampus. *Front. Neurol.* 8:413. doi: 10.3389/fneur.2017.00413

Wexler, E. M., and Geschwind, D. H. (2011). DISC1: a schizophrenia gene with multiple personalities. *Neuron* 72, 501–503. doi: 10.1016/j.neuron.2011.10.023

Xia, Z., Dudek, H., Miranti, C. K., and Greenberg, M. E. (1996). Calcium influx *via* the NMDA receptor induces immediate early gene transcription by a MAP kinase/ERK-dependent mechanism. *J. Neurosci.* 16, 5425–5436. doi: 10.1523/jneurosci.16-17-05425.1996

Xing, L., Larsen, R. S., Bjorklund, G. R., Li, X., Wu, Y., Philpot, B. D., et al. (2016). Layer specific and general requirements for ERK/MAPK signaling in the developing neocortex. *Elife* 5:e11123. doi: 10.7554/elife.11123

Zheng, F., Wang, L., Jia, M., Yue, W., Ruan, Y., Lu, T., et al. (2011). Evidence for association between Disrupted-in-Schizophrenia 1 (DISC1) gene polymorphisms and autism in Chinese Han population: a family-based association study. *Behav. Brain Funct.* 7:14. doi: 10.1186/1744-9081-7-14

11

Reward-Related Behavioral, Neurochemical and Electrophysiological Changes in a Rat Model of Autism Based on Prenatal Exposure to Valproic Acid

Sara Schiavi[1†], Daniela Iezzi[2†], Antonia Manduca[1], Stefano Leone[1], Francesca Melancia[1], Carmen Carbone[2], Michele Petrella[3], Guido Mannaioni[2], Alessio Masi[2,3†] and Viviana Trezza[1*†]*

[1]Department of Science, Section of Biomedical Sciences and Technologies, University "Roma Tre", Rome, Italy, [2]Department of Neuroscience, Psychology, Drug Research and Child Health -NEUROFARBA-, Section of Pharmacology and Toxicology, School of Psychology, University of Florence, Florence, Italy, [3]School of Pharmacy, University of Camerino, Camerino, Italy

***Correspondence:**
Alessio Masi
alessio.masi@unifi.it
Viviana Trezza
viviana.trezza@uniroma3.it

[†]These authors have contributed equally to this work

Prenatal exposure to the antiepileptic drug valproic acid (VPA) induces autism spectrum disorder (ASD) in humans and autistic-like behaviors in rodents, which makes it a good model to study the neural underpinnings of ASD. Rats prenatally exposed to VPA show profound deficits in the social domain. The altered social behavior displayed by VPA-exposed rats may be due to either a deficit in social reward processing or to a more general inability to properly understand and respond to social signals. To address this issue, we performed behavioral, electrophysiological and neurochemical experiments and tested the involvement of the brain reward system in the social dysfunctions displayed by rats prenatally exposed to VPA (500 mg/kg). We found that, compared to control animals, VPA-exposed rats showed reduced play responsiveness together with impaired sociability in the three-chamber test and altered social discrimination abilities. In addition, VPA-exposed rats showed altered expression of dopamine receptors together with inherent hyperexcitability of medium spiny neurons (MSNs) in the nucleus accumbens (NAc). However, when tested for socially-induced conditioned place preference, locomotor response to amphetamine and sucrose preference, control and VPA-exposed rats performed similarly, indicating normal responses to social, drug and food rewards. On the basis of the results obtained, we hypothesize that social dysfunctions displayed by VPA-exposed rats are more likely caused by alterations in cognitive aspects of the social interaction, such as the interpretation and reciprocation of social stimuli and/or the ability to adjust the social behavior of the individual to the changing circumstances in the social and physical environment, rather than to inability to enjoy the pleasurable aspects of the social interaction. The observed neurochemical and electrophysiological alterations in the NAc may contribute to the inability of VPA-exposed rats to process and respond to social cues, or, alternatively, represent a compensatory mechanism towards VPA-induced neurodevelopmental insults.

Keywords: autism, valproate, social play behavior, dopamine, electrophysiology

INTRODUCTION

Although the precise causes of autism spectrum disorder (ASD) are still the subject of significant debate, a number of factors (rare gene mutations, gene variations and adverse environmental events) have been identified that, interacting in complex ways, affect early brain development contributing to the risk of ASD. Among the environmental factors involved in the pathogenesis of ASD, it has been well documented that prenatal exposure to the antiepileptic drug valproic acid (VPA) is associated with increased risk of neurodevelopmental delay and autistic symptoms in the offspring. Indeed, when given during gestation, VPA not only increases the risk for various congenital malformations (Kozma, 2001; Kini et al., 2006), but also induces core autistic symptoms in the offspring, i.e., impaired communication, reduced sociability and stereotyped behaviors (Williams and Hersh, 1997; Williams et al., 2001). Based on this clinical evidence, prenatal exposure to VPA in rodents has been validated as a drug-induced preclinical model of ASD (Roullet et al., 2013; Nicolini and Fahnestock, 2018; Tartaglione et al., 2019). In agreement with the clinical data, rodents exposed to VPA during pregnancy show marked behavioral impairments resembling the core and secondary signs of ASD (Rodier et al., 1996; Narita et al., 2002; Miyazaki et al., 2005; Schneider and Przewłocki, 2005; Servadio et al., 2016; Melancia et al., 2018). Since impaired social interaction is a key feature of ASD, a valid animal model is expected to exhibit deficits in this behavioral domain. Rodents are highly social species that engage in complex patterns of social behavior such as parental care and social play behavior (Panksepp et al., 1984; Ricceri et al., 2007). Rats prenatally exposed to VPA show a wide range of deficits in the social domain. At infancy, they show deficits in social communication and social discrimination, i.e., they are unable to properly communicate with their mother and siblings when removed from the nest and cannot discriminate between a neutral scent and their own nest odor (Schneider and Przewłocki, 2005; Dufour-Rainfray et al., 2010; Favre et al., 2013; Servadio et al., 2016; Bronzuoli et al., 2018; Cartocci et al., 2018; Melancia et al., 2018). At adolescence, VPA-exposed rats display atypical patterns of social play behavior, that is the most characteristic and rewarding social activity displayed by young mammals: indeed, compared to control animals, rats prenatally exposed to VPA respond to play solicitation mainly by partial rotation and evasion, rather than reciprocating the playful interaction (Servadio et al., 2016; Melancia et al., 2018). The social deficits displayed by VPA-exposed rats are long lasting, since they also persist at adulthood (Schneider and Przewłocki, 2005; Schneider et al., 2006, 2008; Markram et al., 2008; Kim et al., 2011, 2014; Servadio et al., 2016, 2018; Hirsch et al., 2018; Melancia et al., 2018; Fontes-Dutra et al., 2019) and are evocative of the social disturbances displayed by autistic patients over the course of development.

The pervasive social deficits found in autistic patients have been initially explained in terms of cognitive impairments and inability to infer others' mental states. More recently, they have been related to blunted social reward processing, i.e., inability to enjoy and prolong reciprocal social interactions, which has been hypothesized to be the consequence of abnormal activity of the brain reward circuit in social contexts (Chevallier et al., 2012; Pellissier et al., 2018). Along this line, the social dysfunctions displayed by VPA-exposed rats may be caused by either their inability to properly understand and respond to social signals by the social partner or by a failure of their reward system to assign a positive value to the social experience. The aim of the present study was to address this issue by performing behavioral, neurochemical and electrophysiological experiments in rats prenatally exposed to VPA. In particular, we determined whether the social deficits displayed by VPA-exposed rats are associated with changes in more specific reward-related behaviors, including social, drug and food rewards. Furthermore, given the important role of corticolimbic dopamine in (social) reward processes (Gunaydin et al., 2014; Vanderschuren et al., 2016), we measured the expression of D1 and D2 dopamine receptors in the prefrontal cortex (PFC), dorsal striatum (DS), nucleus accumbens (NAc) and hippocampus (HIPP) of VPA-exposed rats, since these brain areas play an important role in the modulation of social behavior. Last, since activation of dopaminergic terminals in the NAc of rats during bouts of interaction with novel conspecifics has been reported (Robinson et al., 2002; Gunaydin et al., 2014) and given the important role of NAc dopamine in rewarding forms of social interaction such as social play (Manduca et al., 2016), we addressed the role of the NAc in the social impairment displayed by VPA-exposed rats by performing electrophysiological experiments in this brain area.

MATERIALS AND METHODS

Animals

Female Wistar rats (Charles River, Italy), weighing 250 ± 15 g, were mated overnight. The morning when spermatozoa were found was designated as gestational day 1. Pregnant rats were singly housed in Macrolon cages [40 (length) × 26 (width) × 20 (height) cm], under controlled conditions (temperature 20–21°C, 55%–65% relative humidity and 12/12 h light cycle with lights on at 07:00 h). Food and water were available *ad libitum*. On gestational day 12.5, females received a single intraperitoneal injection of either VPA or saline (SAL). Newborn litters found up to 17:00 h were considered to be born on that day [postnatal day (PND) 0]. On PND 1, the litters were culled to eight animals (six males and two females), to reduce the litter size-induced variability in the growth and development of pups during the postnatal period. On PND 21, the pups were weaned and housed in groups of three. The experiments were carried out on the male offspring during adolescence (PNDs 35–40) and adulthood (PNDs 90–95). One male pup per litter from different litters per treatment group was used in each experiment. For the flow cytometric experiments, we used brain samples from the VPA- and SAL-exposed rats tested in the social play behavior, the three-chamber and the social discrimination tests. Other cohorts of VPA- and SAL-exposed rats were used for the electrophysiology experiments and to investigate amphetamine-induced hyperlocomotion, sucrose preference and socially-induced Conditioned Place Preference (sCPP). The exact sample size (n) for each experimental group/condition is indicated in the figure legends. The sample size was based on our previous experiments and power analysis performed with the software G power.

The experiments were approved by the Italian Ministry of Health (Rome, Italy) and performed in agreement with the Animals in Research: Reporting *in vivo* Experiments (ARRIVE) guidelines (Kilkenny et al., 2010), with the guidelines released by the Italian Ministry of Health (D.L. 26/14) and the European Community Directive 2010/63/EU. In particular, the experimental protocol was approved by the Animal Care Committees of both Roma Tre and Florence Universities and by the Italian Ministry of Health (authorization numbers: 31-2019-PR and 955/2015-PR).

Drugs

VPA (Cayman Chemical, Ann Arbor, MI, USA) was dissolved in saline at a concentration of 250 mg/ml and administered at a dose (500 mg/kg) and time (gestational day 12.5) that have been shown to induce autistic-like behavioral changes in the offspring (Servadio et al., 2016; Melancia et al., 2018). Amphetamine (AMPH, Research Biochemicals International) was dissolved in saline and administrated at the dose of 0.5 mg/kg 30 min before the open field test to both VPA- and SAL-exposed offspring. We used a dose of AMPH that is known to affect locomotor activity without inducing stereotyped behaviors (Fowler et al., 2003; Manduca et al., 2014).

Behavioral Tests

Social Play Test

The test was performed in a sound-attenuated chamber under dim light conditions, as previously described (Trezza and Vanderschuren, 2008, 2009). At PNDs 35–40, rats were individually habituated to the test cage for 10 min on the 2 days before testing. On the test day, the animals were isolated for 3 h before testing. The test consisted of placing each experimental rat together with an untreated animal for 15 min in the testing chamber. In rats, a bout of social play behavior starts with one rat soliciting ("pouncing") another animal, by attempting to nose or rub the nape of its neck. The animal that is pounced upon can respond in different ways: if the animal fully rotates to its dorsal surface, "pinning" is the result (one animal lying with its dorsal surface on the floor with the other animal standing over it), which is considered the most characteristic posture of social play behavior in rats. The following parameters were scored for each animal of a pair using the Observer 3.0 software (Noldus, The Netherlands): (1) number of pinning events; (2) number of pouncing events; (3) evasion (the animal that is pounced upon does not prolong the playful interaction but rather runs away); and (4) play responsiveness [the percentage of response to play solicitation, as the probability of an animal of being pinned in response to pouncing by the stimulus partner (Servadio et al., 2016)]. Time spent in social exploration (the total amount of time spent in non-playful forms of social interaction, like sniffing any part of the body of the test partner, including the anogenital area, or grooming any part of the partner body).

Three-Chambers Test

The test was performed as previously described (Servadio et al., 2016). The apparatus was a rectangular three-chamber box, with two lateral chambers (30 × 35 × 35 cm; l × w × h) connected to a central chamber (15 × 35 × 35 cm; l × w × h). Each lateral chamber contained a small Plexiglas cylindrical cage. At PND 90, each experimental rat was individually allowed to explore the three-chamber apparatus for 10 min and then confined in the central compartment. An unfamiliar stimulus animal was confined in a cage located in one chamber of the apparatus, while the cage in the other chamber was left empty. Both doors to the side chambers were then opened, allowing the experimental animal to explore the apparatus for 10 min. The discrimination index was scored using the Observer 3.0 software (Noldus, The Netherlands) and was calculated as the difference in time spent sniffing the stimulus animal and the time spent exploring the empty chamber, expressed as the percentage ratio of the total time spent exploring both the stimulus animal and the empty chamber.

Social Discrimination Test

The test was performed as previously described (Melancia et al., 2018). Briefly, animals were isolated for 7 days before testing. The test consisted of a learning trial and a retrieval trial, which were separated by a 30 min intertrial interval. During the learning trial, a juvenile (30 days old) unfamiliar rat was introduced into the home cage of the experimental rat for 5 min. The time spent by the experimental rat investigating (sniffing, allogrooming and following) the juvenile was measured. Thirty-minutes after, the juvenile used in the learning trial was returned to the same adult's cage together with a novel juvenile. The time spent by the adult exploring the novel and the familiar juveniles was monitored for 5 min. The discrimination index was calculated as the difference in time exploring the novel and the familiar animal, expressed as the percentage ratio of the total time spent exploring both animals (Campolongo et al., 2007).

Open Field Test

To assess whether adolescent and adult VPA- and SAL-exposed rats similarly responded to AMPH-induced hyperlocomotion, animals from both experimental groups were tested for horizontal locomotor activity in a squared box [40 (length) × 40 (width) × 60 (height) cm]. Each animal was placed in the central zone of the apparatus and allowed to explore for 30 min. Total locomotor activity (expressed as the frequency of crossings in the arena) was analyzed during the 30-min test session. After each session, the apparatus was cleaned with ethanol 70%.

Sucrose Preference Test

At both adolescence and adulthood, rats were tested for preference of a 2% sucrose solution, using a two-bottle choice procedure (Monteggia et al., 2007) with slight modifications. Subjects were housed singly for the 3 days of test. Rats were given two bottles, one of sucrose (2%) and one of tap water.

Every 24 h the amount of sucrose and water consumed was evaluated. To prevent potential location preference of drinking, the position of the bottles was changed every 24 h. The preference for the sucrose solution was calculated as the percentage of sucrose solution ingested relative to the total amount of liquid consumed.

Socially-Induced Conditioned Place Preference

The sCPP test was performed at adolescence and adulthood as previously described (Wei et al., 2015). Briefly, rats were placed in an acrylic box [75 (length) × 35 (width) × 35 (height) cm], divided into two chambers by a clear acrylic wall with a small opening. Each chamber contained different types of autoclaved, novel bedding (Sanyx Bio Ultra litter and Padovan Sandy Litter), which differed in texture and shade (white vs. dark-brown). A 30-min preconditioning test was used to establish any baseline preference for either of the two types of novel bedding. Individual rats with strong preference for either type of bedding were excluded (typically, those that spent more than 1.5× time on one bedding over the other). The next day, each experimental animal was assigned to a social cage with cage-mates to be conditioned to one type of novel bedding for 24 h (CS+). Then, the experimental rat was moved to an isolated cage with the other type of bedding for 24 h (CS−). Bedding assignments were counterbalanced for an unbiased design. Animals were then tested alone for 30 min in the two-chambered box and the time spent in each chamber was calculated to determine post-conditioning preference for either type of bedding. Fresh bedding was used at each step and chambers were thoroughly cleaned between sessions with ethanol 70% to avoid olfactory confounders.

Brain Samples Collection

Rats were rapidly decapitated, and their brains were removed and cut into coronal slices on a cold plate. The PFC, DS, NAc and hippocampus (HIPP) were dissected by hand under microscopic control within 2 min as previously described (Hill et al., 2010; Trezza et al., 2012; Gray et al., 2015).

Flow Cytometric Experiments

Brain samples for each brain area were transferred with PBS into 1.5 ml tube. After centrifugation, the pellet was digested with Trypsin (0.1%) for 30 min at 37°C on slight agitation. Cell suspensions were filtered with CellTrics (100 μm) and washed with 5 ml of PBS. A little sample of suspension was analyzed for forward and side scatter parameter for neuron population quality control (Cruz et al., 2013). Each sample was fixed with PFA (1%), permeabilized with ice-cold ethanol (70%) and incubated for at least 2 h at −20°C. Next, cells were centrifuged, rehydrated with 1 ml PBS/BSA (1%)/Triton (0.1%), aliquoted in 96 well tissue culture plates with conical bottom. Samples were incubated for 1 h RT with primary antibody anti-D1 (1:100 diluted, Novusbio AB81296) and D2 dopamine receptors (1:100 diluted, Santa Cruz SC-7523). The cells were washed and incubated with secondary antibody anti-rabbit and anti-goat Alexa 488 conjugated. All samples were counterstained with propidium iodide/RNase buffer for nuclei identification (with G0 cell cycle phase DNA content) and for singlet/doublets discrimination. Mean fluorescence intensity of 20,000 useful cellular events for each sample, was calculated.

Whole-Cell Patch Clamp Recordings in Acute Brain Slices

Preparation of acute brain slices was performed with established procedures (Carbone et al., 2017). In brief, 1-month old male Wistar rats were anesthetized with isoflurane and decapitated. The brain was quickly removed and glued to the bottom of a vibroslicer slicing chamber (Leica VT 1000S, Leica Microsystem, Wetzlar, Germany). Coronal brain slices (250 μm) containing the NAc were cut in a slicing solution composed of (in mM): N-methyl-D-glucamine (92), 4-(2-hydroxyethyl)-1-piperazine-1-ethanesulfonic acid (20), glucose (25), $NaHCO_3$ (30), NaH_2PO_4 (1.25), KCl (2.5), $MgSO_4$ (10), $CaCl_2$ (0.5). During slicing, the solution was kept cold and infused with a 95% O_2 + 5% CO_2 gas mixture. Slices were transferred to a warm (34–35°C), carbo-oxygenated recovery bath containing artificial Cerebral Spinal Fluid (aCSF) of the following composition (in mM): NaCl (130), KCl (3.5), NaH_2PO_4 (1.25), $NaHCO_3$ (25), glucose (10), $CaCl_2$ (2) and $MgSO_4$ (1). Slices were allowed to recover for at least 30 min prior to experiments. During recordings, a single slice was kept in a flow chamber positioned under the microscope objective and continuously perfused with warm (34–35°C), carbo-oxygenated aCSF. Whole-cell pipettes were pulled from thin-walled borosilicate capillaries (Harvard Apparatus, London, UK) with a vertical puller (Narishige PP830, Narishige International Limited, London, UK) and back-filled with an intracellular solution containing (in mM): K+ methanesulfonate (120), KCl (15), HEPES (10), EGTA (0.1), $MgCl_2$ (2), Na_2Phosphocreatine (5), Na_2GTP (0.3) and MgATP (2), resulting in a bath resistance of 3–5 MΩ. Unless otherwise specified, all drugs were purchased from Sigma-Aldrich (St. Louis, MO, USA) and bath-applied. Access resistance was monitored during voltage clamp recordings with 100-ms, −10-mV steps, throughout the experiment. Recordings undergoing a drift in access resistance ≥ 10% were discarded. No whole-cell compensations were used. Signals were sampled at 10 kHz and low-pass filtered at 3 kHz with an Axon Multiclamp 700B (Molecular Devices, Sunnyvale, CA, USA). NAc-MSNs were identified by their morphological and electrophysiological properties (Cepeda et al., 2008). To examine the effects of VPA prenatal exposure on medium spiny neuron (MSN) excitability, current clamp input-output curves were obtained by injecting 800 ms-current steps with amplitude ranging from −50 to +550 pA with 50 pA increments. Inwardly rectifying potassium currents (IKir) were obtained by imposing 500 ms-voltage steps with amplitude ranging from −150 to −60 mV with 10 mV increments. Potassium currents were recorded in the presence of tetrodotoxin (TTX, 1 μM, Tocris, Biosciences, Bristol, UK), a blocker of voltage-dependent sodium channels. IKir was isolated as the 1 mM CsCl-sensitive component. IKir current density was obtained by normalizing current amplitudes for membrane capacitance (derived from the area underlying current peaks elicited by −10 mV steps) and expressed as pA/pF.

Statistical Analysis

Behavioral and neurochemical data are expressed as mean ± SEM. To assess the effects of the prenatal treatment (VPA or SAL) on the parameters measured, data were analyzed with Student's t-tests. Two-way analysis of variance (ANOVA) was used to assess the effects of prenatal and postnatal treatments in the open field test, using prenatal (VPA or SAL) and postnatal (AMPH or vehicle) treatments as between-subjects factor. Two-way ANOVA was followed by Student's–Newman–Keuls *post hoc* test where appropriate. All behavioral tests were scored by a trained observer who was unaware of treatment condition to reduce performance bias. Random allocation of animals to treatment groups and to behavioral tasks and blinding of investigators assessing outcomes were adopted to reduce selection and detection bias. All behavioral data were tested for normality.

For electrophysiological experiments, data are presented as mean ± SEM of n cells obtained from N animals. Statistical significance was assessed with student's t-test for unpaired samples (Microcal Origin 9.1; Northampton, MA, USA). Significance at the $P < 0.05$, 0.01 and 0.001 level is indicated with *, ** and ***, respectively, in figures. Graphs and representative traces were generated with Microcal Origin 9.1. Example traces represent typical observations.

RESULTS

Social Play Test

VPA-exposed rats showed reduced play responsiveness compared with SAL-exposed animals (t = 3.67, p = 0.002, df = 16; **Figure 1A**). Indeed, while no differences were found between SAL- and VPA-exposed animals in the number of pinning (t = 0.81, p = n.s., df = 16; data not shown) and pouncing (t = −0.86, p = n.s., df = 16; data not shown), VPA-exposed rats displayed a higher frequency of partial rotation (t = −2.81, p = 0.013, df = 16; **Figure 1B**) compared to SAL-exposed animals. No differences in the total time spent in general social exploration were found between SAL- and VPA-exposed animals (t = 1.43, p = n.s., df = 16, data not shown).

Three-Chambers Test

VPA-exposed rats showed decreased sociability in the three-chamber test, as they spent less time sniffing the stimulus animal compared to SAL-exposed rats, showing a lower discrimination index (t = 2.27, p = 0.039, df = 14; **Figure 1C**).

Social Discrimination Test

VPA-exposed animals showed impaired social discriminative abilities as they showed a lower discrimination index in the social discrimination test compared with SAL-exposed animals (t = 2.27, p = 0.044, df = 14; **Figure 1D**).

Amphetamine-Induced Hyperlocomotion

AMPH increased locomotor activity of SAL- and VPA-exposed rats both at adolescence and adulthood. A two-way ANOVA analysis performed on the frequency of crossing after treatment with AMPH or its vehicle gave the following results: PNDs 35–40 ($F_{(\text{prenatal treat.})1,28}$ = 1.56, p = n.s.; $F_{(\text{treat.})1,28}$ = 10.97, $p < 0.01$; $F_{(\text{prenatal treat.} \times \text{treat.})1,28}$ = 0.1; p = n.s.); PNDs 90–95 ($F_{(\text{prenatal treat.})1,27}$ = 1.40, p = n.s.; $F_{(\text{treat.})1,27}$ = 33.05, $p < 0.001$; $F_{(\text{prenatal treat.} \times \text{treat.})1,27}$ = 0.76; p = n.s.). *Post hoc* analysis revealed that AMPH increased the frequency of crossing both in SAL- (PNDs 35–40: $p < 0.05$; PNDs 90–95: $p < 0.001$) and VPA-exposed rats (PNDs 35–40: $p < 0.05$; PNDs 90–95: p = 0.002; **Figures 2A–D**).

Sucrose Preference Test

Both SAL- and VPA-exposed rats preferred the sucrose over the water solution the in the sucrose preference test, at both PNDs 35–40 and 90–95 (PNDs 35–40: SAL: t = −10.53, $p < 0.001$, df = 16; VPA: t = −17.65, $p < 0.001$, df = 12, **Figure 2B**; PNDs 90–95: SAL: t = −10.43, $p < 0.001$, df = 18; VPA: t = −11.76, $p < 0.001$, df = 18; **Figure 2E**).

Socially-Induced Conditioned Place Preference

Both at adolescence and adulthood, VPA-exposed rats did not show deficits in the sCPP test. Indeed, during the test session animals of both experimental groups spent more time in the chamber containing the bedding used for the social conditioning (CS+; PNDs 35–40: Saline group: t = −2.63, $p < 0.05$, df = 22; VPA group: t = −3.31, $p < 0.01$, df = 22; **Figure 2C**; PNDs 90–95: Saline group: t = −2.19, $p < 0.05$, df = 14; VPA group: t = −2.55, $p < 0.05$, df = 20; **Figure 2F**).

Flow Cytometric Analysis of Dopamine Receptors

At adolescence, VPA-exposed rats shows a significative increase in D2 dopamine receptor expression in the NAc (SAL-exposed animals: MFI = 2,891; VPA-exposed animals: MFI = 5,272, $p < 0.05$; **Figures 3A,B**).

At adulthood, VPA-exposed rats showed a significative increase in D1 dopamine receptor expression in the NAc (SAL-exposed animals: MFI = 4,789; VPA-exposed animals: MFI = 6,690, p = 0.025; **Figure 3C**) and HIPP (SAL-exposed animals: MFI = 3,987; VPA group: MFI = 5,299, p = 0.008; **Figure 3C**), whereas D2 dopamine receptors were significative increased only in the NAc (SAL-exposed animals: MFI = 1,697; VPA-exposed animals: MFI = 2,152, p = 0.022; **Figure 3D**).

Electrophysiological Recordings of NAc MSNs in Acute Brain slices

Whole cell patch clamp recordings were obtained from NAc MSNs in acute coronal slices prepared from SAL- and VPA-exposed rats at PNDs 30–35 (N = 9 and 7, respectively, **Figures 4A,B**). While we found no differences in passive membrane properties between MSNs from SAL-exposed rats (SAL MSNs) and VPA-exposed rats (VPA MSNs; input resistance: SAL MSNs = 111.4 ± 8.81 MΩ, n = 22; VPA MSNs = 139.2 ± 12.78 MΩ, n = 23; membrane capacitance: SAL MSNs = 45.73 ± 3.07 pF, n = 23; VPA MSNs = 47.36 ± 4.49 pF n = 26; threshold: SAL MSNs = −39.43 ± 1.3 mV, n = 35; VPA MSNs = −39.96 ± 0.93 mV, n = 33; p = n.s.; all; **Figure 4C**), the latter group showed a significant depolarization

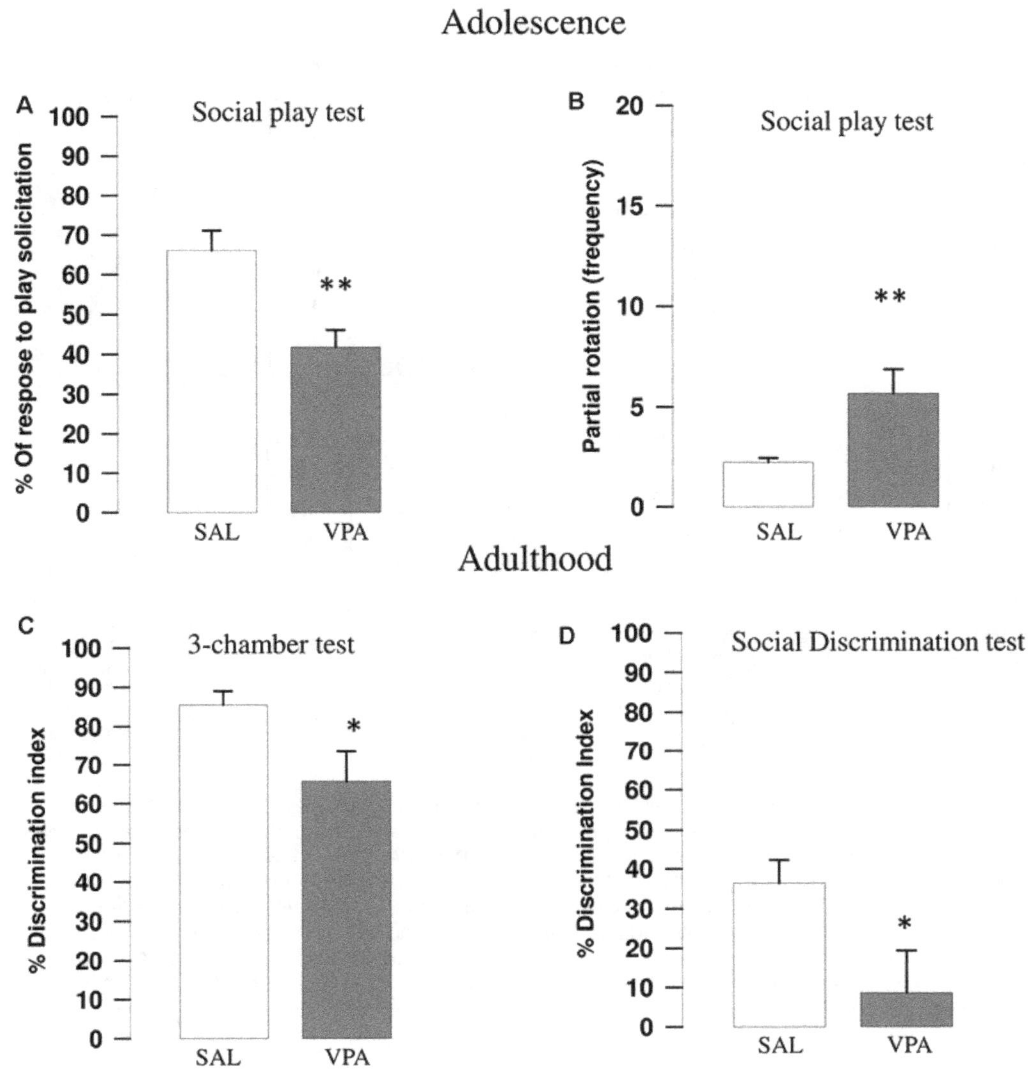

FIGURE 1 | Valproic acid (VPA)-exposed rats showed altered social play behavior, impaired sociability in the three-chamber test and reduced social discrimination abilities. VPA-exposed rats showed reduced response to play solicitation **(A)** and increased frequency of partial rotation (**B**; n = SAL 9, n = VPA 9). VPA-exposed rats also showed reduced sociability in the three-chamber test **(C)**, since they showed a lower discrimination index indicating (i.e., they spent less time sniffing the stimulus animal compared to SAL-exposed rats; n = SAL 8, n = VPA 8). VPA-exposed rats also showed impaired social discrimination as they displayed a lower discrimination index compared to SAL-exposed animals in the social discrimination task (**D**; n = SAL 8, n = VPA 8). Data represent mean values ± SEM; $^*p < 0.05$, $^{**}p < 0.01$, vs. SAL group (Student's t-test).

of the resting membrane potential as compared to SAL MSNs (SAL MSNs = −77.59 ± 0.83 mV, n = 35; VPA MSNs = −71.72 ± 0.98 mV, n = 37; p = 0.0008; **Figure 4C**). We then determined the intrinsic excitability of MSNs in acute slices containing the NAc by measuring the number of action potentials elicited by depolarizing current steps of increasing amplitude. **Figure 5A** shows a direct comparison of representative voltage responses obtained at each value of imposed current from SAL and VPA MSNs. The minimal value of current amplitude required to elicit an action potential in VPA MSNs was significantly lower compared to SAL MSNs (100 pA vs. 200 pA). However, as the amplitude of the depolarizing current increased (≥250 pA), while the number of APs fired by SAL MSNs increased linearly, VPA MSNs progressively lost the ability to fire action potentials. The plot in **Figure 5B** reports the mean number of APs ± SEM fired by SAL (black) and VPA (green) MSNs vs. imposed current (SAL MSNs, n = 35, vs. VPA MSNs n = 37; 150 pA; p = 0.01; 200 pA; p = 0.03; 350 pA; p = 0.02; ≥ 400 pA; p < 0.0001). Depolarized resting potential and altered AP discharge pattern are consistent with a change in the density of whole-cell K^+ currents. Based on the reported relevance of the inward-rectifying K^+ current (IKir) in setting resting potential in MSNs (Kreitzer, 2009), we measured whole-cell currents elicited at hyperpolarizing potentials in control aCSF and in the presence of 1 mM Cs^+, a IKir blocker (Cazorla et al., 2012).

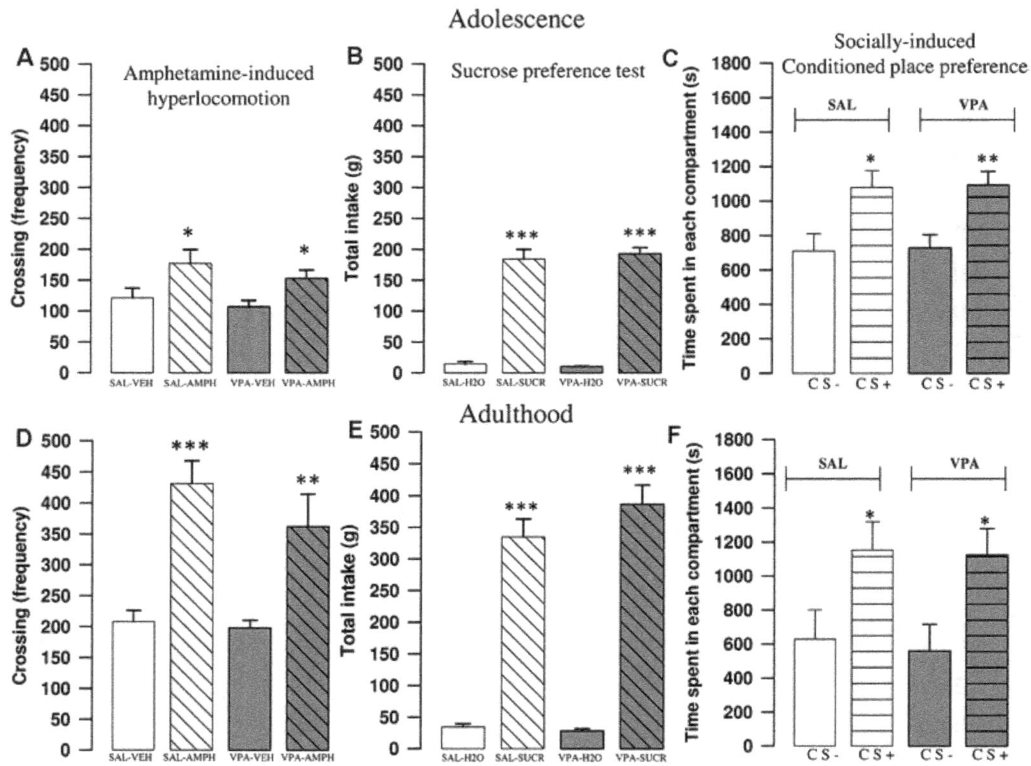

FIGURE 2 | VPA-exposed rats did not differ from control rats in AMPH-induced hyperlocomotion, sucrose preference and socially-induced Conditioned Place Preference (sCPP). In the open field test, AMPH increased the frequency of crossing both in SAL- and VPA-exposed rats at postnatal days (PNDs) 30–35 (**A**; n = SAL-VEH 7, n = SAL-AMPH 7, n = VPA-VEH 9, n = VPA-AMPH 9) and PNDs 90–95 (**D**; n = SAL-VEH 8, n = SAL-AMPH 7, n = VPA-VEH 8, n = VPA-AMPH 8). Data represent mean values ± SEM; *$p < 0.05$, **$p < 0.01$, ***$p < 0.001$ vs. SAL-VEH group (Student-Newman-Keuls *post hoc* test). No differences were found between SAL- and VPA-exposed rats in the sucrose preference test, both at PNDs 30–35 (**B**; n = SAL 10, n = VPA 10) and PNDs 90–95 (**E**; n = SAL 10, n = VPA 10). Data represent mean values ± SEM; *** $p < 0.001$ vs. SAL-H_2O and vs. VPA-H_2O groups (student's t-test). In the sCPP test, both SAL- and VPA-exposed rats spent more time in the chamber containing the bedding where social interaction previously occurred (CS+), both at PNDs 30–35 (**C**; n = SAL 12, n = VPA 12) and PNDs 90–95 (**F**; n = SAL 8, n = VPA 11). Data represent mean values ± SEM; *$p < 0.05$, **$p < 0.01$, vs. SAL-CS- and VPA-CS- groups (Student's t-test).

Figure 6A shows representative inward currents obtained in control solution (I_{aCSF}) and 1 mM Cs^+ (I_{Cs}). IKir is obtained by subtracting I_{Cs} from I_{aCSF}. Current-voltage relationship reveals a significant reduction of IKir current density in VPA MSNs (SAL MSNs, $n = 7$, VPA MSNs, $n = 5$; $p < 0.05$ where indicated; **Figure 6B**).

DISCUSSION

Clinical studies have repeatedly reported that maternal use of VPA during pregnancy can induce a wide range of abnormalities in the exposed children, ranging from structural malformations to more subtle autistic-like behaviors. For this reason, prenatal VPA exposure is nowadays considered an environmental risk factor involved in the pathogenesis of ASD (Christensen et al., 2013; Nicolini and Fahnestock, 2018). Based on the robust clinical evidence, prenatal exposure to VPA in rodents has been validated as a drug-induced preclinical model of ASD (Roullet et al., 2013; Ranger and Ellenbroek, 2016; Tartaglione et al., 2019).

In the present study, we show that prenatal exposure to VPA causes selective deficits in the social domain in the rat offspring at different developmental periods, together with changes in D1 and D2 dopamine receptor expression in the NAc and hyperexcitability in this same brain area, but without inducing changes in social and non-social reward-related behaviors.

According to the DSM-5 diagnostic criteria, persistent deficits in social communication and social interaction are key features of ASD. Social play behavior has a crucial role in the identification and diagnosis of ASD (Jordan, 2003; Jarrold et al., 2013) Social play is the first form of non-mother directed social behavior displayed by most mammals at young age (Panksepp et al., 1984; Vanderschuren et al., 1997, 2016). In ASD, play patterns are characterized not only by deficient cognitive complexity but also by a typical asocial dimension. Since the opportunity to engage in social play is crucial to acquire proper social and cognitive skills (Vanderschuren et al., 2016; Nijhof et al., 2018), the lack of social play in children with ASD has deleterious effects on their development, leading to long lasting deficits in self-awareness, social competence, problem solving and behavioral flexibility. In line with the social deficits reported in previous

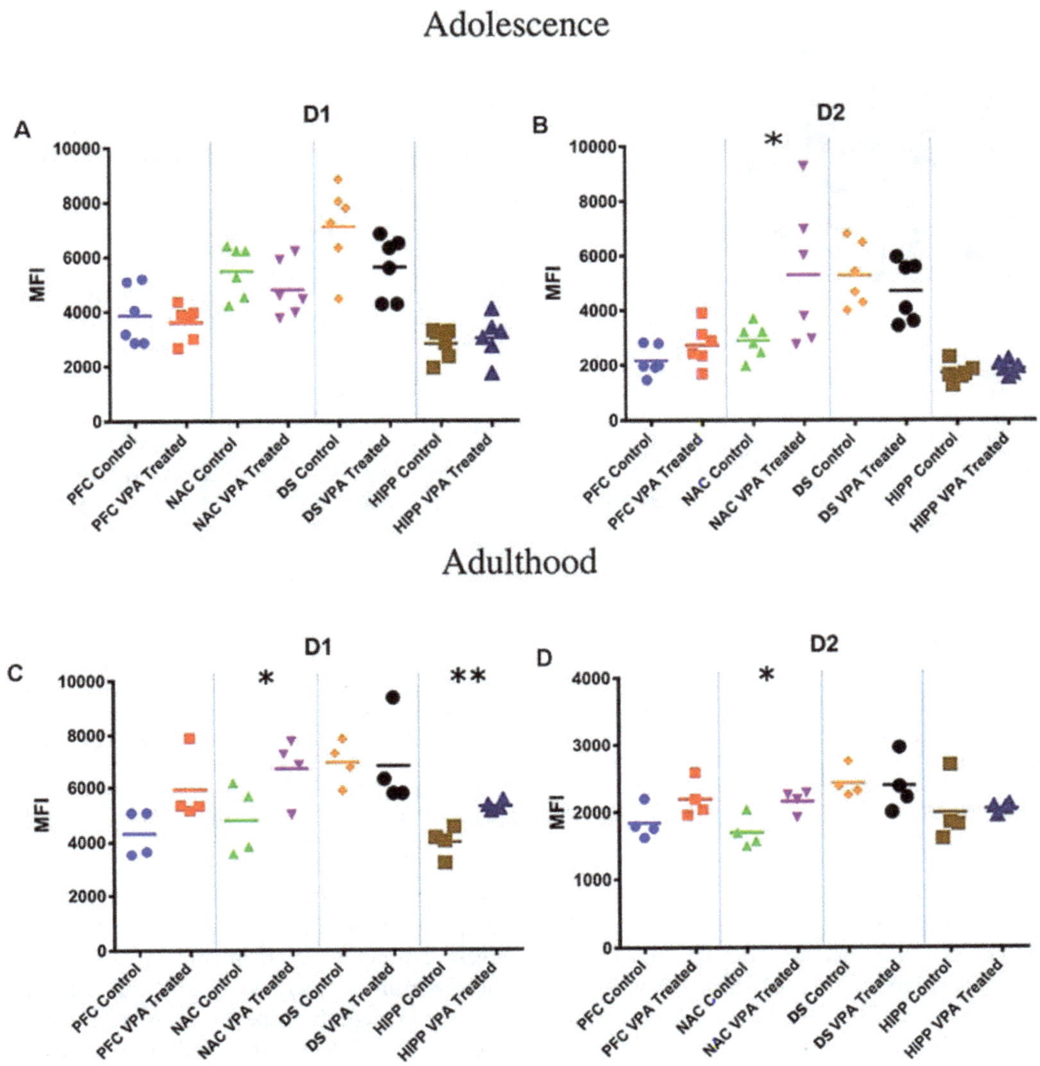

FIGURE 3 | Flow cytometric analysis of dopamine receptors. No differences between VPA-exposed and SAL-exposed rats were found in D1 dopamine receptor expression in prefrontal cortex, nucleus accumbens, dorsal striatum and hippocampus **(A)**. At PNDs 30–35, VPA-exposed rats showed a significant increase in D2 dopamine receptor expression in the nucleus accumbens (NAc) **(B)** compared to SAL-exposed rats (n = SAL 6, n = VPA 6). At PNDs 90–95, VPA-exposed rats showed increased expression of D1 dopamine receptor expression in NAc and hippocampus **(C)**, while D2 receptor expression was increased only in the NAc (**D**; n = SAL 5, n = VPA 5). Data represent mean values ± SEM; $^{*}p < 0.05$, $^{**}p < 0.01$ vs. SAL group (Student's t-test).

studies (Schneider and Przewłocki, 2005; Schneider et al., 2006; Felix-Ortiz and Febo, 2012; Servadio et al., 2016; Melancia et al., 2018), we confirm here that adolescent rats prenatally exposed to VPA show decreased responsiveness to play solicitation, since they respond to play solicitation mainly by partial rotation than reciprocating the playful interaction. Notably, these social deficits were long lasting. Indeed, VPA exposed rats showed social deficits also when tested at adulthood in the three-chamber and social discrimination tests. These data corroborate our previous findings showing that prenatal VPA exposure induces in the rat offspring a wide range of social impairments in the course of development, ranging from social play deficits to altered sociability and social discrimination (Servadio et al., 2016, 2018; Melancia et al., 2018) and are in line with clinical observation that children, adolescents and adults with ASD demonstrate marked socio-communicative deficits (Lai et al., 2011; Dworzynski et al., 2012; Head et al., 2014).

As it has been hypothesized for autistic patients (Chevallier et al., 2012), the wide range of social dysfunctions displayed by VPA-exposed rats may be due to either their inability to properly percept, understand and respond to socially relevant cues, or to a failure of their brain reward system to assign a positive value to the social experience (Pellissier et al., 2018). To address this issue, we performed neurochemical and electrophysiological experiments focusing on brain areas involved in reward processing, and performed additional behavioral experiments to investigate if VPA-exposed rats differ from control animals in responding to social and other (non-social) rewarding stimuli.

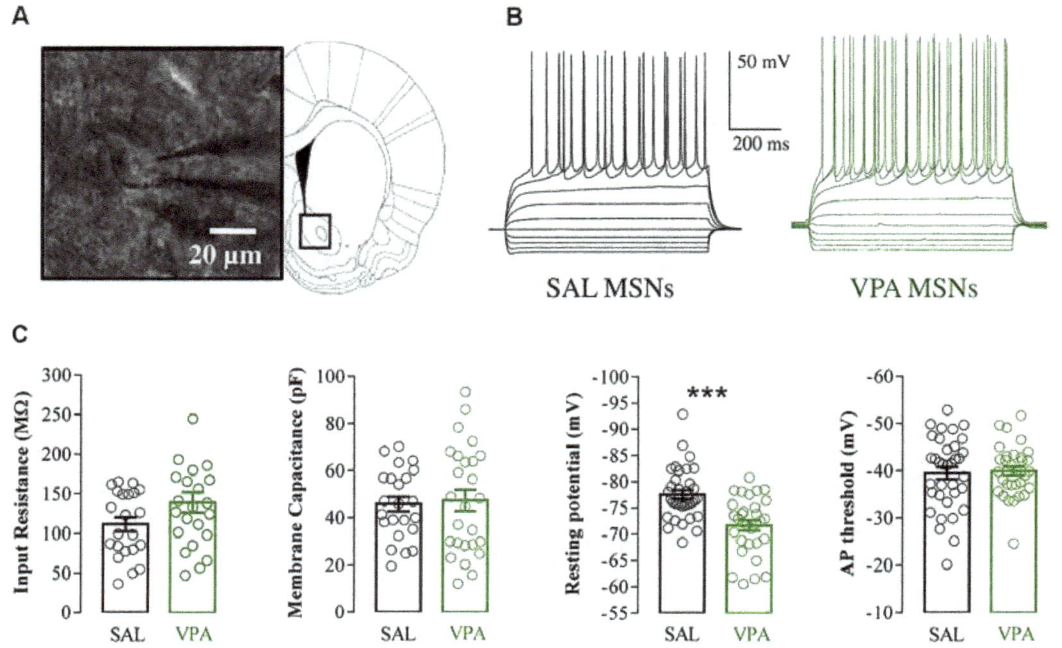

FIGURE 4 | Electrophysiological properties of SAL medium spiny neurons (MSNs) and VPA MSNs. **(A)** NAc-MSN visualized with infrared video microscopy (*left*) and schematic representation of a coronal brain slice at the level of the NAc (*right*). **(B)** Representative voltage traces of SAL MSNs and VPA MSNs evoked by injection of hyperpolarizing and depolarizing current pulses (800 ms from −200 pA to 250 pA in 50 pA steps). **(C)** Passive membrane properties of SAL MSNs and VPA MSNs; input resistance (SAL MSNs 111.4 ± 8.81 MΩ, $n = 22$; VPA MSNs 139.2 ± 12.78 MΩ, $n = 23$), membrane capacitance (SAL MSNs 45.73 ± 3.07 pF $n = 23$; VPA MSNs 47.36 ± 4.49 pF, $n = 26$); resting membrane potential (SAL MSNs −77.59 ± 0.83 mV, $n = 35$; VPA MSNs −71.72 ± 0.98 mV, $n = 37$) and AP threshold (SAL MSNs −39.43 ± 1.3 mV, $n = 35$; VPA MSNs −39.96 ± 0.93 mV, $n = 33$). Data represent mean values ± SEM; ***$p < 0.001$ vs. SAL group (Student's *t*-test).

Brain regions involved in the control of social behavior include corticolimbic structures and their altered functionality may represent one neural substrate contributing to the social impairments characteristic of ASD (Scott-Van Zeeland et al., 2010; Chevallier et al., 2012; Ameis and Catani, 2015; Supekar et al., 2018). Notably, these regions are subjected to modulation by dopaminergic neurons and it has been suggested that a dysfunction of dopaminergic neurotransmission in the mesocorticolimbic circuit leads to the social deficits observed in ASD (Paval et al., 2017): thus, it has been demonstrated that striatal MSNs show enriched expression of genes associated with ASD (Chang et al., 2015) and that ASD-associated mutations affect specific MSN subtypes (Portmann et al., 2014; Rothwell et al., 2014; for a review, see Rothwell, 2016).

In autistic subjects, dopamine imbalances, manifested as either hyperactivity or hypoactivity of midbrain dopaminergic pathways, have been detected, highlighting the heterogeneity of the disease (Paval et al., 2017).

Dopamine activation of D1 and D2 receptors in corticolimbic regions is also important for the expression of social behavior in rodents (Robinson et al., 2002; Gunaydin et al., 2014; Manduca et al., 2016; Kopec et al., 2018). Therefore, although the social impairments observed in VPA-exposed animals likely cannot be ascribed to the alteration of a single neurotransmitter system, we focused the biochemical and electrophysiological analyses on dopaminergic neurotransmission in corticolimbic brain areas. We measured the expression of D1 and D2 dopamine receptors in the PFC, DS, NAc and HIPP since these brain areas play not only an important role in the modulation of the rewarding properties of social interactions but have also a key role in cognitive aspects of the social repertoire (e.g., social cognition). While the DS and NAc have a well-recognized role in the modulation of several aspects of reward-related behaviors (for a review, see Bhanji and Delgado, 2014), the PFC and HIPP have also been found to be deeply involved in cognitive aspects of social behavior (Vanderschuren et al., 2016; Montagrin et al., 2018).

We found that, compared to control animals, adolescent rats prenatally exposed to VPA showed increased expression of D2 dopamine receptors in the NAc. At adulthood, they showed increased expression of D1 dopamine receptors in the NAc and hippocampus and of D2 receptors in the NAc. These results suggest that the social deficits displayed by VPA-exposed rats in the course of development may arise from dopaminergic dysfunctions in both these brain regions.

In line with our results, changes in hippocampal dopamine and D1 receptor levels associated with social deficits have been demonstrated in a genetic mouse model exhibiting autism-relevant behavioral abnormalities (Liu et al., 2017). Furthermore, mice knockout for genes strongly associated with ASD, such as Cntnap4 (Karayannis et al., 2014) and neuroligin-3 (Rothwell et al., 2014) mutant mice, show changes in NAc dopaminergic neurotransmission together

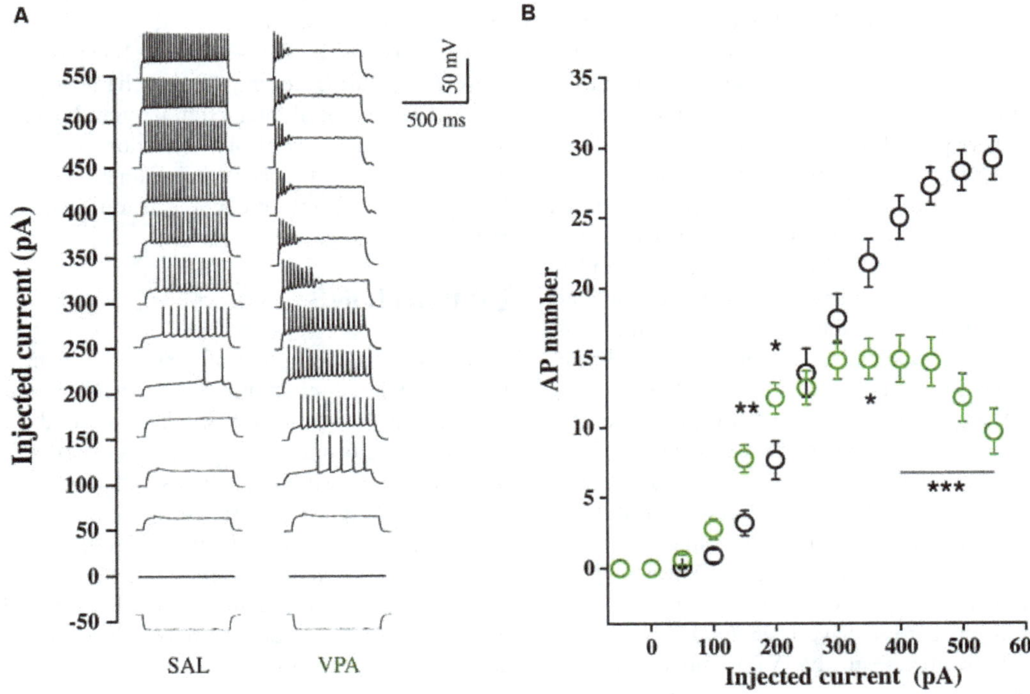

FIGURE 5 | Intrinsic excitability of SAL MSNs and VPA MSNs. **(A)** Representative voltage traces obtained in response to–50 to 550 pA current steps (800 ms duration, 50 pA amplitude) from resting potential, recorded from SAL and VPA MSNs. **(B)** Number of APs fired plotted against current steps of increasing value (SAL MSNs, $n = 35$; VPA MSNs, $n = 37$). Data represent mean values ± SEM; *$p < 0.05$, **$p < 0.01$, ***$p < 0.001$ vs. SAL group (Student's t-test).

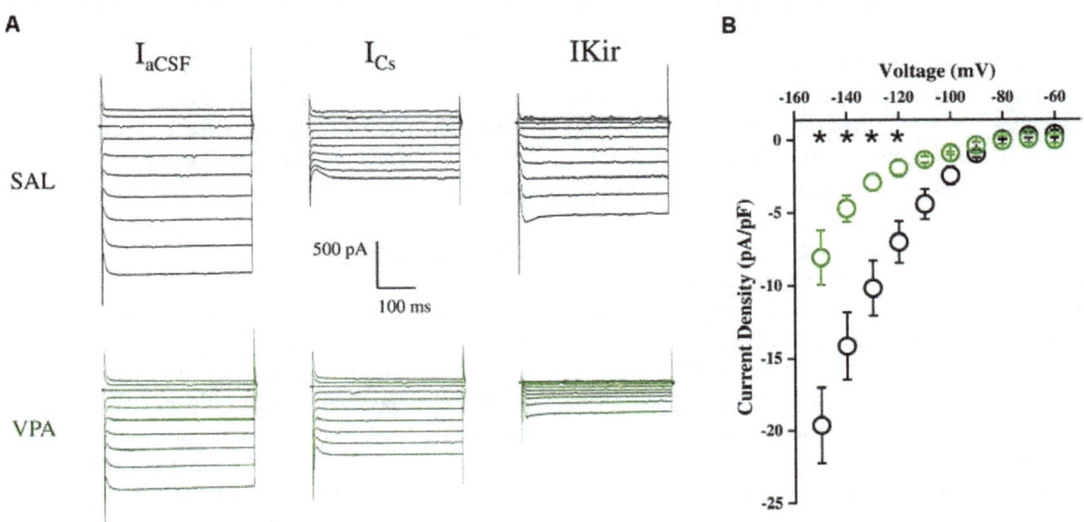

FIGURE 6 | Inwardly rectifying potassium current (IKir) density in SAL MSNs and VPA MSNs. **(A)** Representative IKir traces obtained at hyperpolarized membrane potentials (−60 to −150 mV in 10 mV steps) obtained from SAL and VPA MSNs. IKir is obtained by subtracting I_{Cs} from I_{aCSF}. Current-voltage relationship of IKir current density in SAL and VPA MSNs. **(B)** Current-voltage relationship of IKir current density in SAL and VPA MSNs (SAL MSNs, $n = 7$; VPA MSNs $n = 5$). Data represent mean values ± SEM; *$p < 0.05$ vs. SAL group (Student's t-test).

with deficits in the core ASD behavioral domains. Recently, it has also been demonstrated that altered VTA dopamine neuron function represents a key mechanism by which insufficiency of SHANK3, encoding the synapse scaffolding protein SHANK3, generates impaired social preference in mice (Bariselli et al., 2016).

Building on this evidence, we studied the basic electrophysiological properties of NAc MSNs in acute striatal brain slices of VPA- and SAL-exposed offspring. We found that NAc MSNs of VPA-exposed animals show a significant depolarization of the resting membrane potential and increased excitability in the lower part of the excitability curve, indicating higher firing probability in conditions of normal synaptic excitation. These changes are likely caused by altered Kir current density, known to determine the hyperpolarized value of membrane potential in normal MSNs (~ -85 mV) and to affect their AP discharge pattern (Kreitzer, 2009; Cazorla et al., 2012). The NAc is a major node of the mesolimbic dopaminergic system and the overall impact of NAc output on behavior depends on the relative activity of D1- vs. D2-expressing MSNs. Increased excitability of MSNs of VPA-exposed animals, combined with increased expression of D2R-expressing neurons, is consistent with an imbalance in the direct and indirect pathway activity, in favor of the latter. Proper activation of these pathways underlies proper motor learning as well as the acquisition of reward-related behaviors (Yawata et al., 2012; Shin et al., 2018). Furthermore, extensive alterations in normal gene expression pattern have been found in multiple striatal neuronal populations in the VPA model of ASD (Lauber et al., 2016).

Based on the evidence of neurochemical and electrophysiological changes in the brain reward system of VPA-exposed rats, we tested their behavioral response to different (i.e., social and non-social) rewarding stimuli. First, we tested whether VPA- and SAL-exposed rats differently responded to a dose of amphetamine known to induce hyperlocomotion (Bolanos et al., 1998), a proxy for the ability of the dopaminergic system to respond to pharmacological activation. We found a robust amphetamine-induced increase in motor activity in the open field test in both adolescent and adult VPA- and SAL-exposed animals, showing a same susceptibility to amphetamine-induced hyperlocomotion in both experimental groups.

To examine whether the social impairment displayed by VPA-exposed rats was accompanied by a generalized anhedonic behavior, that is, a reduction in the interest for natural reward, we performed a sucrose preference test. In line with previous studies performed with other preclinical models of ASD (Jamain et al., 2008; Radyushkin et al., 2009) and with clinical studies reporting intact hedonic responses to sweet taste in autistic patients (Damiano et al., 2014), we found that both VPA-exposed and control animals showed preference for the sucrose over the water solution, either at adolescence or adulthood.

To assess whether the social deficits displayed by VPA-exposed animals may be due to aberrant social reward processing, we tested VPA- and SAL-exposed rats in a socially-induced place-conditioning task (sCPP), which involves the association between a social stimulus and a distinct set of contextual cues (Trezza and Vanderschuren, 2009; Dölen et al., 2013; Wei et al., 2015). Attenuated sCPP has been demonstrated in genetic models of ASD such as in fmr1 mutant mice, a model for Fragile X syndrome (Pacey et al., 2011), and BTBR T+tf/J (BTBR) mice (Pearson et al., 2012). However, we here failed to find any difference in sCPP: thus, both VPA- and SAL-exposed animals spent more time during testing in the chamber associated with a bedding where social interaction previously occurred. Thus, the altered pattern of social play behavior, the reduced sociability and the impaired social discrimination abilities displayed by VPA-exposed rats are not accompanied by altered social reward processing.

LIMITATIONS

From the behavioral point of view, the present study has some methodological limitations. Indeed, while we here found that VPA- and SAL-exposed rats similarly respond to amphetamine-induced hyperlocomotion, it still needs to be determined whether VPA- and SAL-exposed animals differ in behavioral set-ups specifically designed to assess drug intake and drug addiction. Similarly, we cannot exclude that VPA-exposed animals would show altered sucrose preference if different concentrations of sucrose solution were used, as found in the SHANK3 mouse model of ASD, where Shank3 mice preferred a sucrose solution at high but not at low concentrations (Bariselli et al., 2016). Last, it is still possible that VPA-exposed rats would show altered social motivation when tested in socially-driven operant conditioning paradigms (Achterberg et al., 2016). Concerning the electrophysiological experiments, the potential limitations in the validity of the information obtained with brain slice recordings is related to the nature of the methodology, which allows for in-depth, reliable interrogation of cell-autonomous electrical properties, but inevitably involves profound alteration of network connectivity, even within the area under examination. Aware of the intrinsic advantages and limitations of this approach, here we focused on neuronal properties that are better preserved in the acute brain slice preparation, such as intrinsic neuronal excitability.

CONCLUSION

Although more levels of analysis are needed to shed light on the mechanisms underlying the aberrant behavior found in VPA-exposed rats, on the basis of the results obtained here we suggest that the reduced play responsiveness, the impaired sociability in the three-chamber test and the reduced discrimination abilities in the social discrimination tasks displayed by VPA-exposed animals reported in the present and in previous studies (Kim et al., 2011, 2013, 2014; Servadio et al., 2016; Melancia et al., 2018) are more likely due to changes in the cognitive functions required for proper social interaction, such as to understand and predict the behaviors of other conspecifics or to adapt the social behaviors of the animal to the changing circumstances in its social and physical environment, or may be due to impairments in aspects of reward processing that could not be detected with the behavioral tasks used in the present work. In this picture, the alteration in the expression of striatal dopamine receptors and in the electrical properties of MSNs in the NAc may be interpreted as a homeostatic mechanism deployed by reward-related brain areas to compensate for VPA-induced neurodevelopmental perturbations. Further behavioral, neurochemical and electrophysiological investigations are required to support this interpretation.

ETHICS STATEMENT

The experiments were approved by the Italian Ministry of Health (Rome, Italy) and performed in agreement with the ARRIVE (Animals in Research: Reporting *in vivo* Experiments; Kilkenny et al., 2010) guidelines, with the guidelines released by the Italian Ministry of Health (D.L. 26/14) and the European Community Directive 2010/63/EU. In particular, the experimental protocol was approved by the Animal Care Committees of both Roma Tre and Florence Universities and by the Italian Ministry of Health (authorization numbers: 31-2019-PR and 955/2015-PR).

AUTHOR CONTRIBUTIONS

SS and FM performed, analyzed and contributed to the design of the behavioral experiments. SL performed, analyzed and designed the flow cytometric experiments. DI, CC and MP performed, analyzed and contributed to the design of the electrophysiology experiments. AMan and GM contributed to the design of the experiments and edited the manuscript. SS and DI wrote the manuscript. VT and AMas supervised the project, designed the experiments and wrote the manuscript.

FUNDING

This work was supported by Marie Curie Career Reintegration Grant PCIG09-GA-2011-293589 (VT), by Jerome Lejeune Foundation (Fondation Jérôme Lejeune) Research grant #1674 (VT) and by Excellence Departments, Ministero dell'Istruzione, dell'Università e della Ricerca (MIUR)-Italy, Grant/Award Numbers: ARTICOLO 1, COMMI 314- 337 LEGGE 232/2016, ARTICOLO 1.

ACKNOWLEDGMENTS

We thank and gratefully acknowledge Mrs. Claudia Sereni, Patricia Jiménez Peinado and Giulia Polese for technical help during the experiments.

REFERENCES

Achterberg, E. J., Van Kerkhof, L. W., Servadio, M., Van Swieten, M. M., Houwing, D. J., Aalderink, M., et al. (2016). Contrasting roles of dopamine and noradrenaline in the motivational properties of social play behavior in rats. *Neuropsychopharmacology* 41, 858–868. doi: 10.1038/npp.2015.212

Ameis, S. H., and Catani, M. (2015). Altered white matter connectivity as a neural substrate for social impairment in autism spectrum disorder. *Cortex* 62, 158–181. doi: 10.1016/j.cortex.2014.10.014

Bariselli, S., Tzanoulinou, S., Glangetas, C., Prevost-Solie, C., Pucci, L., Viguie, J., et al. (2016). SHANK3 controls maturation of social reward circuits in the VTA. *Nat. Neurosci.* 19, 926–934. doi: 10.1038/nn.4319

Bhanji, J. P., and Delgado, M. R. (2014). The social brain and reward: social information processing in the human striatum. *Wiley Interdiscip. Rev. Cogn. Sci.* 5, 61–73. doi: 10.1002/wcs.1266

Bolanos, C. A., Glatt, S. J., and Jackson, D. (1998). Subsensitivity to dopaminergic drugs in periadolescent rats: a behavioral and neurochemical analysis. *Dev. Brain Res.* 111, 25–33. doi: 10.1016/s0165-3806(98)00116-3

Bronzuoli, M. R., Facchinetti, R., Ingrassia, D., Sarvadio, M., Schiavi, S., Steardo, L., et al. (2018). Neuroglia in the autistic brain: evidence from a preclinical model. *Mol. Autism* 9:66. doi: 10.1186/s13229-018-0254-0

Campolongo, P., Trezza, V., Cassano, T., Gaetani, S., Morgese, M. G., Ubaldi, M., et al. (2007). Perinatal exposure to delta-9-tetrahydrocannabinol causes enduring cognitive deficits associated with alteration of cortical gene expression and neurotransmission in rats. *Addict. Biol.* 12, 485–495. doi: 10.1111/j.1369-1600.2007.00074.x

Carbone, C., Costa, A., Provensi, G., Mannaioni, G., and Masi, A. (2017). The hyperpolarization-activated current determines synaptic excitability, calcium activity and specific viability of substantia nigra dopaminergic neurons. *Front. Cell. Neurosci.* 11:187. doi: 10.3389/fncel.2017.00187

Cartocci, V., Catallo, M., Tempestilli, M., Segatto, M., Pfrieger, F. W., Bronzuoli, M. R., et al. (2018). Altered brain cholesterol/isoprenoid metabolism in a rat model of autism spectrum disorders. *Neuroscience* 372, 27–37. doi: 10.1016/j.neuroscience.2017.12.053

Cazorla, M., Shegda, M., Ramesh, B., Harrison, N. L., and Kellendonk, C. (2012). Striatal D2 receptors regulate dendritic morphology of medium spiny neurons *via* Kir2 channels. *J. Neurosci.* 32, 2398–2409. doi: 10.1523/JNEUROSCI.6056-11.2012

Cepeda, C., André, V. M., Yamazaki, I., Wu, N., Kleiman-Weiner, M., and Levine, M. S. (2008). Differential electrophysiological properties of dopamine D1 and D2 receptor-containing striatal medium-sized spiny neurons. *Eur. J. Neurosci.* 27, 671–682. doi: 10.1111/j.1460-9568.2008.06038.x

Chang, J., Gilman, S. R., Chiang, A. H., Sanders, S. J., and Vitkup, D. (2015). Genotype to phenotype relationships in autism spectrum disorders. *Nat. Neurosci.* 18, 191–198. doi: 10.1038/nn.3907

Chevallier, C., Kohls, G., Troiani, V., Brodkin, E. S., and Schultz, R. T. (2012). The social motivation theory of autism. *Trends Cogn. Sci.* 16, 231–239. doi: 10.1016/j.tics.2012.02.007

Christensen, J., Grønborg, T. K., Sørensen, M. J., Schendel, D., Parner, E. T., Pedersen, L. H., et al. (2013). Prenatal valproate exposure and risk of autism spectrum disorders and childhood autism. *JAMA* 309, 1696–1703. doi: 10.1001/jama.2013.2270

Cruz, F. C., Koya, E., Guez-Barber, D. H., Bossert, J. M., Lupica, C. R., Shaham, Y., et al. (2013). New technologies for examining the role of neuronal ensembles in drug addiction and fear. *Nat. reviews. Neurosci.* 14, 743–754. doi: 10.1038/nrn3597

Damiano, C. R., Aloi, J., Burrus, C., Garbutt, J. C., Kampov-Polevoy, A. B., and Dichter, G. S. (2014). Intact hedonic responses to sweet tastes in autism spectrum disorder. *Res. Autism Spectr. Disord.* 8, 230–236. doi: 10.1016/j.rasd.2013.12.003

Dölen, G., Darvishzadeh, A., Huang, K. W., and Malenka, R. C. (2013). Social reward requires coordinated activity of nucleus accumbens oxytocin and serotonin. *Nature* 501, 179–184. doi: 10.1038/nature12518

Dufour-Rainfray, D., Vourc'h, P., Le Guisquet, A. M., Garreau, L., Ternant, D., Bodard, S., et al. (2010). Behavior and serotonergic disorders in rats exposed prenatally to valproate: a model for autism. *Neurosci. Lett.* 470, 55–59. doi: 10.1016/j.neulet.2009.12.054

Dworzynski, K., Ronald, A., Bolton, P., and Happe, F. (2012). How different are girls and boys above and below the diagnostic threshold for autism spectrum disorders? *J. Am. Acad. Child Adolesc. Psychiatry* 51, 788–797. doi: 10.1016/j.jaac.2012.05.018

Favre, M. R., Barkat, T. R., Lamendola, D., Khazen, G., Markram, H., and Markram, K. (2013). General developmental health in the VPA-rat model of autism. *Front. Behav. Neurosci.* 7:88. doi: 10.3389/fnbeh.2013.00088

Felix-Ortiz, A. C., and Febo, M. (2012). Gestational valproate alters BOLD activation in response to complex social and primary sensory stimuli. *PLoS One* 7:e37313. doi: 10.1371/journal.pone.0037313

Fontes-Dutra, M., Della-Flora Nunes, G., Santos-Terra, J., Souza-Nunes, W., Bauer-Negrini, G., Hirsch, M. M., et al. (2019). Abnormal empathy-like pro-social behaviour in the valproic acid model of autism spectrum disorder. *Behav. Brain Res.* 364, 11–18. doi: 10.1016/j.bbr.2019.01.034

Fowler, S. C., Birkestrand, B., Chen, R., Vorontsova, E., and Zarcone, T. (2003). Behavioral sensitization to amphetamine in rats: changes in the rhythm of head movements during focused stereotypies. *Psychopharmacology* 170, 167–177. doi: 10.1007/s00213-003-1528-5

Gray, J. M., Vecchiarelli, H. A., Morena, M., Lee, T. T., Hermanson, D. J., Kim, A. B., et al. (2015). Corticotropin-releasing hormone drives anandamide hydrolysis in the amygdala to promote anxiety. *J. Neurosci.* 35, 3879–3892. doi: 10.1523/JNEUROSCI.2737-14.2015

Gunaydin, L. A., Grosenick, L., Finkelstein, J. C., Kauvar, I. V., Fenno, L. E., Adhikari, A., et al. (2014). Natural neural projection dynamics underlying social behavior. *Cell* 157, 1535–1551. doi: 10.1016/j.cell.2014.05.017

Head, A. M., McGillivray, J. A., and Stokes, M. A. (2014). Gender differences in emotionality and sociability in children with autism spectrum disorders. *Mol. Autism* 5:19. doi: 10.1186/2040-2392-5-19

Hill, M. N., Karatsoreos, I. N., Hillard, C. J., and Mcewen, B. S. (2010). Rapid elevations in limbic endocannabinoid content by glucocorticoid hormones *in vivo*. *Psychoneuroendocrinology* 35, 1333–1338. doi: 10.1016/j.psyneuen.2010.03.005

Hirsch, M. M., Deckmann, I., Fontes-Dutra, M., Bauer-Negrini, G., Della-Flora Nunes, G., Nunes, W., et al. (2018). Behavioral alterations in autism model induced by valproic acid and translational analysis of circulating microRNA. *Food Chem. Toxicol.* 115, 336–343. doi: 10.1016/j.fct.2018.02.061

Jamain, S., Radyushkin, K., Hammerschmidt, K., Granon, S., Boretius, S., Varoqueaux, F., et al. (2008). Reduced social interaction and ultrasonic communication in a mouse model of monogenic heritable autism. *Proc. Natl. Acad. Sci. U S A* 105, 1710–1715. doi: 10.1073/pnas.0711555105

Jarrold, W., Mundy, P., Gwaltney, M., Bailenson, J., Hatt, N., Mcintyre, N., et al. (2013). Social attention in a virtual public speaking task in higher functioning children with autism. *Autism Res.* 6, 393–410. doi: 10.1002/aur.1302

Jordan, R. (2003). Social play and autistic spectrum disorders: a perspective on theory, implications and educational approaches. *Autism* 7, 347–360. doi: 10.1177/1362361303007004002

Karayannis, T., Au, E., Patel, J. C., Kruglikov, I., Markx, S., Delorme, R., et al. (2014). Cntnap4 differentially contributes to GABAergic and dopaminergic synaptic transmission. *Nature* 511, 236–240. doi: 10.1038/nature13248

Kilkenny, C., Browne, W. J., Cuthill, I. C., Emerson, M., and Altman, D. G. (2010). Improving bioscience research reporting: the ARRIVE guidelines for reporting animal research. *J. Pharmacol. Pharmacother.* 1, 94–99. doi: 10.4103/0976-500X.72351

Kim, K. C., Kim, P., Go, H. S., Choi, C. S., Park, J. H., Kim, H. J., et al. (2013). Male-specific alteration in excitatory post-synaptic development and social interaction in pre-natal valproic acid exposure model of autism spectrum disorder. *J. Neurochem.* 124, 832–843. doi: 10.1111/jnc.12147

Kim, K. C., Kim, P., Go, H. S., Choi, C. S., Yang, S. I., Cheong, J. H., et al. (2011). The critical period of valproate exposure to induce autistic symptoms in Sprague–Dawley rats. *Toxicol. Lett.* 201, 137–142. doi: 10.1016/j.toxlet.2010.12.018

Kim, K. C., Lee, D. K., Go, H. S., Kim, P., Choi, C. S., Kim, J. W., et al. (2014). Pax6-dependent cortical glutamatergic neuronal differentiation regulates autism-like behavior in prenatally valproic acid-exposed rat offspring. *Mol. Neurobiol.* 49, 512–528. doi: 10.1007/s12035-013-8535-2

Kini, U., Adab, N., Vinten, J., Fryer, A., and Clayton-Smith, J. (2006). Dysmorphic features: an important clue to the diagnosis and severity of fetal anticonvulsant syndromes. *Arch. Dis. Child Fetal Neonatal. Ed.* 91, F90–F95. doi: 10.1136/adc.2004.067421

Kopec, A. M., Smith, C. J., Ayre, N. R., Sweat, S. C., and Bilbo, S. D. (2018). Microglial dopamine receptor elimination defines sex-specific nucleus accumbens development and social behavior in adolescent rats. *Nat. Commun.* 9:3769. doi: 10.1038/s41467-018-06118-z

Kozma, C. (2001). Valproic acid embryopathy: report of two siblings with further expansion of the phenotypic abnormalities and a review of the literature. *Am. J. Med. Genet.* 98, 168–175. doi: 10.1002/1096-8628(20010115)98:2%3C168::AID-AJMG1026%3E3.0.CO;2-O

Kreitzer, A. C. (2009). Physiology and pharmacology of striatal neurons. *Annu. Rev. Neurosci.* 32, 127–147. doi: 10.1146/annurev.neuro.051508.135422

Lai, M. C., Lombardo, M. V., Pasco, G., Ruigrok, A. N., Wheelwright, S. J., Sadek, S. A., et al. (2011). A behavioral comparison of male and female adults with high functioning autism spectrum conditions. *PLoS One* 6:e20835. doi: 10.1371/journal.pone.0020835

Lauber, E., Filice, F., and Schwaller, B. (2016). Prenatal valproate exposure differentially affects parvalbumin-expressing neurons and related circuits in the cortex and striatum of mice. *Front. Mol. Neurosci.* 9:150. doi: 10.3389/fnmol.2016.00150

Liu, Q., Shi, J., Lin, R., and Wen, T. (2017). Dopamine and dopamine receptor D1 associated with decreased social interaction. *Behav. Brain Res.* 324, 51–57. doi: 10.1016/j.bbr.2017.01.045

Manduca, A., Lassalle, O., Sepers, M., Campolongo, P., Cuomo, V., Marsicano, G., et al. (2016). Interacting cannabinoid and opioid receptors in the nucleus accumbens core control adolescent social play. *Front. Behav. Neurosci.* 10:211. doi: 10.3389/fnbeh.2016.00211

Manduca, A., Servadio, M., Campolongo, P., Palmery, M., Trabace, L., Vanderschuren, L. J., et al. (2014). Strain- and context-dependent effects of the anandamide hydrolysis inhibitor URB597 on social behavior in rats. *Eur. Neuropsychopharmacol.* 24, 1337–1348. doi: 10.1016/j.euroneuro.2014.05.009

Markram, K., Rinaldi, T., La Mendola, D., Sandi, C., and Markram, H. (2008). Abnormal fear conditioning and amygdala processing in an animal model of autism. *Neuropsychopharmacology* 33, 901–912. doi: 10.1038/sj.npp.1301453

Melancia, F., Schiavi, S., Servadio, M., Cartocci, V., Campolongo, P., Palmery, M., et al. (2018). Sex-specific autistic endophenotypes induced by prenatal exposure to valproic acid involve anandamide signalling. *Br. J. Pharmacol.* 175, 3699–3712. doi: 10.1111/bph.14435

Miyazaki, K., Narita, N., and Narita, M. (2005). Maternal administration of thalidomide or valproic acid causes abnormal serotonergic neurons in the offspring: implication for pathogenesis of autism. *Int. J. Dev. Neurosci.* 23, 287–297. doi: 10.1016/j.ijdevneu.2004.05.004

Montagrin, A., Saiote, C., and Schiller, D. (2018). The social hippocampus. *Hippocampus* 28, 672–679. doi: 10.1002/hipo.22797

Monteggia, L. M., Luikart, B., Barrot, M., Theobold, D., Malkovska, I., Nef, S., et al. (2007). Brain-derived neurotrophic factor conditional knockouts show gender differences in depression-related behaviors. *Biol. Psychiatry* 61, 187–197. doi: 10.1016/j.biopsych.2006.03.021

Narita, N., Kato, M., Tazoe, M., Miyazaki, K., Narita, M., and Okado, N. (2002). Increased monoamine concentration in the brain and blood of fetal thalidomide- and valproic acid-exposed rat: putative animal models for autism. *Pediatr. Res.* 52, 576–579. doi: 10.1203/00006450-200210000-00018

Nicolini, C., and Fahnestock, M. (2018). The valproic acid-induced rodent model of autism. *Exp. Neurol.* 299, 217–227. doi: 10.1016/j.expneurol.2017.04.017

Nijhof, S. L., Vinkers, C. H., Van Geelen, S. M., Duijff, S. N., Achterberg, E. J. M., Van Der Net, J., et al. (2018). Healthy play, better coping: the importance of play for the development of children in health and disease. *Neurosci. Biobehav. Rev.* 95, 421–429. doi: 10.1016/j.neubiorev.2018.09.024

Pacey, L. K., Doss, L., Cifelli, C., Van Der Kooy, D., Heximer, S. P., and Hampson, D. R. (2011). Genetic deletion of regulator of G-protein signaling 4 (RGS4) rescues a subset of fragile X related phenotypes in the FMR1 knockout mouse. *Mol. Cell. Neurosci.* 46, 563–572. doi: 10.1016/j.mcn.2010.12.005

Panksepp, J., Siviy, S., and Normansell, L. (1984). The psychobiology of play: theoretical and methodological perspectives. *Neurosci. Biobehav. Rev.* 8, 465–492. doi: 10.1016/0149-7634(84)90005-8

Paval, D., Rad, F., Rusu, R., Niculae, A. S., Colosi, H. A., Dobrescu, I., et al. (2017). Low Retinal Dehydrogenase 1 (RALDH1) level in prepubertal boys with autism spectrum disorder: a possible link to dopamine dysfunction? *Clin. Psychopharmacol. Neurosci.* 15, 229–236. doi: 10.9758/cpn.2017.15.3.229

Pearson, B. L., Bettis, J. K., Meyza, K. Z., Yamamoto, L. Y., Blanchard, D. C., and Blanchard, R. J. (2012). Absence of social conditioned place preference in BTBR T+tf/J mice: relevance for social motivation testing in rodent models of autism. *Behav. Brain Res.* 233, 99–104. doi: 10.1016/j.bbr.2012.04.040

Pellissier, L. P., Gandia, J., Laboute, T., Becker, J. A. J., and Le Merrer, J. (2018). μ-opioid receptor, social behaviour and autism spectrum disorder: reward matters. *Br. J. Pharmacol.* 175, 2750–2769. doi: 10.1111/bph.13808

Portmann, T., Yang, M., Mao, R., Panagiotakos, G., Ellegood, J., Dolen, G., et al. (2014). Behavioral abnormalities and circuit defects in the basal ganglia of a mouse model of 16p11.2 deletion syndrome. *Cell Rep.* 7, 1077–1092. doi: 10.1016/j.celrep.2014.03.036

Radyushkin, K., Hammerschmidt, K., Boretius, S., Varoqueaux, F., El-Kordi, A., Ronnenberg, A., et al. (2009). Neuroligin-3-deficient mice: model of a monogenic heritable form of autism with an olfactory deficit. *Genes Brain Behav.* 8, 416–425. doi: 10.1111/j.1601-183X.2009.00487.X

Ranger, P., and Ellenbroek, B. A. (2016). Perinatal influences of valproate on brain and behaviour: an animal model for autism. *Curr. Top. Behav. Neurosci.* 29, 363–386. doi: 10.1007/7854_2015_404

Ricceri, L., Moles, A., and Crawley, J. (2007). Behavioral phenotyping of mouse models of neurodevelopmental disorders: relevant social behavior patterns across the life span. *Behav. Brain Res.* 176, 40–52. doi: 10.1016/j.bbr.2006.08.024

Robinson, D. L., Heien, M. L., and Wightman, R. M. (2002). Frequency of dopamine concentration transients increases in dorsal and ventral striatum of male rats during introduction of conspecifics. *J. Neurosci.* 22, 10477–10486. doi: 10.1523/jneurosci.22-23-10477.2002

Rodier, P. M., Ingram, J. L., Tisdale, B., Nelson, S., and Romano, J. (1996). Embryological origin for autism: developmental anomalies of the cranial nerve motor nuclei. *J. Comp. Neurol.* 370, 247–261. doi: 10.1002/(sici)1096-9861(19960624)370:2<247::aid-cne8>3.0.co;2-2

Rothwell, P. E. (2016). Autism spectrum disorders and drug addiction: common pathways, common molecules, distinct disorders? *Front. Neurosci.* 10:20. doi: 10.3389/fnins.2016.00020

Rothwell, P. E., Fuccillo, M. V., Maxeiner, S., Hayton, S. J., Gokce, O., Lim, B. K., et al. (2014). Autism-associated neuroligin-3 mutations commonly impair striatal circuits to boost repetitive behaviors. *Cell* 158, 198–212. doi: 10.1016/j.cell.2014.04.045

Roullet, F. I., Lai, J. K., and Foster, J. A. (2013). *In utero* exposure to valproic acid and autism-a current review of clinical and animal studies. *Neurotoxicol. Teratol.* 36, 47–56. doi: 10.1016/j.ntt.2013.01.004

Schneider, T., and Przewłocki, R. (2005). Behavioral alterations in rats prenatally exposed to valproic acid: animal model of autism. *Neuropsychopharmacology* 30, 80–89. doi: 10.1038/sj.npp.1300518

Schneider, T., Roman, A., Basta-Kaim, A., Kubera, M., Budziszewska, B., Schneider, K., et al. (2008). Gender-specific behavioral and immunological alterations in an animal model of autism induced by prenatal exposure to valproic acid. *Psychoneuroendocrinology* 33, 728–740. doi: 10.1016/j.psyneuen.2008.02.011

Schneider, T., Turczak, J., and Przewłocki, R. (2006). Environmental enrichment reverses behavioral alterations in rats prenatally exposed to valproic acid: issues for a therapeutic approach in autism. *Neuropsychopharmacology* 31, 36–46. doi: 10.1038/sj.npp.1300767

Scott-Van Zeeland, A. A., Dapretto, M., Ghahremani, D. G., Poldrack, R. A., and Bookheimer, S. Y. (2010). Reward processing in autism. *Autism Res.* 3, 53–67. doi: 10.1002/aur.122

Servadio, M., Manduca, A., Melancia, F., Leboffe, L., Schiavi, S., Campolongo, P., et al. (2018). Impaired repair of DNA damage is associated with autistic-like traits in rats prenatally exposed to valproic acid. *Eur. Neuropsychopharmacol.* 28, 85–96. doi: 10.1016/j.euroneuro.2017.11.014

Servadio, M., Melancia, F., Manduca, A., Di Masi, A., Schiavi, S., Cartocci, V., et al. (2016). Targeting anandamide metabolism rescues core and associated autistic-like symptoms in rats prenatally exposed to valproic acid. *Transl. Psychiatry* 6:e902. doi: 10.1038/tp.2016.182

Shin, J. H., Kim, D., and Jung, M. W. (2018). Differential coding of reward and movement information in the dorsomedial striatal direct and indirect pathways. *Nat. Commun.* 9:404. doi: 10.1038/s41467-017-02817-1

Supekar, K., Kochalka, J., Schaer, M., Wakeman, H., Qin, S., Padmanabhan, A., et al. (2018). Deficits in mesolimbic reward pathway underlie social interaction impairments in children with autism. *Brain* 141, 2795–2805. doi: 10.1093/brain/awy191

Tartaglione, A. M., Schiavi, S., Calamandrei, G., and Trezza, V. (2019). Prenatal valproate in rodents as a tool to understand the neural underpinnings of social dysfunctions in autism spectrum disorder. *Neuropharmacology.* doi: 10.1016/j.neuropharm.2018.12.024 [Epub ahead of print].

Trezza, V., and Vanderschuren, L. J. (2008). Bidirectional cannabinoid modulation of social behavior in adolescent rats. *Psychopharmacology* 197, 217–227. doi: 10.1007/s00213-007-1025-3

Trezza, V., and Vanderschuren, L. J. (2009). Divergent effects of anandamide transporter inhibitors with different target selectivity on social play behavior in adolescent rats. *J. Pharmacol. Exp. Ther.* 328, 343–350. doi: 10.1124/jpet.108.141069

Trezza, V., Damsteegt, R., Manduca, A., Petrosino, S., Van Kerkhof, L. W., Pasterkamp, R. J., et al. (2012). Endocannabinoids in amygdala and nucleus accumbens mediate social play reward in adolescent rats. *J. Neurosci.* 32, 14899–14908. doi: 10.1523/JNEUROSCI.0114-12.2012

Vanderschuren, L. J., Achterberg, E. J., and Trezza, V. (2016). The neurobiology of social play and its rewarding value in rats. *Neurosci. Biobehav. Rev.* 70, 86–105. doi: 10.1016/j.neubiorev.2016.07.025

Vanderschuren, L. J., Niesink, R. J., and Van Ree, J. M. (1997). The neurobiology of social play behavior in rats. *Neurosci. Biobehav. Rev.* 21, 309–326. doi: 10.1016/s0149-7634(96)00020-6

Wei, D., Lee, D., Cox, C. D., Karsten, C. A., Penagarikano, O., Geschwind, D. H., et al. (2015). Endocannabinoid signaling mediates oxytocin-driven social reward. *Proc. Natl. Acad. Sci. U S A* 112, 14084–14089. doi: 10.1073/pnas.1509795112

Williams, G., King, J., Cunningham, M., Stephan, M., Kerr, B., and Hersh, J. H. (2001). Fetal valproate syndrome and autism: additional evidence of an association. *Dev. Med. Child Neurol.* 43, 202–206. doi: 10.1017/s001216220100038x

Williams, P. G., and Hersh, J. H. (1997). A male with fetal valproate syndrome and autism. *Dev. Med. Child Neurol.* 39, 632–634. doi: 10.1111/j.1469-8749.1997.tb07500.x

Yawata, S., Yamaguchi, T., Danjo, T., Hikida, T., and Nakanishi, S. (2012). Pathway-specific control of reward learning and its flexibility via selective dopamine receptors in the nucleus accumbens. *Proc. Natl. Acad. Sci. U S A* 109, 12764–12769. doi: 10.1073/pnas.1210797109

12

The Liver X Receptor Agonist TO901317 Ameliorates Behavioral Deficits in Two Mouse Models of Autism

*Yulong Cai†, Hongyu Zhong†, Xin Li, Rui Xiao, Lian Wang and Xiaotang Fan**

Department of Developmental Neuropsychology, School of Psychology, Third Military Medical University, Chongqing, China

Correspondence:
Xiaotang Fan
fanxiaotang2005@163.com

† These authors have contributed equally to this work

Autism spectrum disorder (ASD) is a developmental disability characterized by social deficits and repetitive stereotyped behaviors. There are currently no drugs available for the treatment of the core symptoms of ASD, suggesting an urgent need for new therapeutic strategies. The neurobiology of autism is complex, but emerging research indicates that defects in hippocampal neurogenesis are associated with ASD in both humans and mouse models of ASD, leading to the suggestion that restoring neurogenesis may be a novel therapeutic approach for ASD. Here, we found that postnatal treatment with TO901317 (TO), a potent liver X receptor (LXR) agonist, typically activated LXRβ and its target genes in the hippocampus, and alleviated the social deficits and stereotypical behaviors in BTBR T+ tf/J (BTBR) and valproic acid (VPA)-induced mouse models. In addition, we further confirmed that TO postnatal treatment also rescued the inhibition of adult hippocampal neurogenesis in these two models. In summary, our study suggests that LXR agonist targeting hippocampal neurogenesis may represent a novel potential therapy for ASD.

Keywords: autism, neurogenesis, sociability, TO901317, repetitive behavior

INTRODUCTION

Autism spectrum disorder (ASD) is a neurodevelopmental disability characterized by impaired sociability, as well as restricted, repetitive patterns of interests and behaviors (Rubenstein and Merzenich, 2003; Currais et al., 2016; Chao et al., 2018). Over the past decades, the incidence of ASD has increased dramatically, reaching 1 in 59 children (Baio et al., 2018). Existing data have revealed that families with autistic children are faced with high levels of economic pressures without any effective therapy (Chan et al., 2018). Thus, there is an urgent need to determine the etiology of ASD and search for an effective treatment. Despite a growing body of ASD studies, the mechanism underlying this disorder still remains poorly understood. At present, no consensus has been reached regarding the neurobiological mechanisms of ASD, and many factors have been shown to be involved in the pathogenesis of ASD, such as synapse dysfunctions, neuroimmunity, oxidative stress, and neurogenesis (Pardo and Eberhart, 2007; Jyonouchi et al., 2008; Carpita et al., 2018).

Abbreviations: ASD, Autism spectrum disorder; B6, C57BL/6J; BrdU, bromodeoxyuridine; BTBR, BTBR T+ tf/J; DCX, doublecortin; DG, dentate gyrus; DMSO, dimethyl sulfoxide; LXR, liver X receptor; PD, postnatal day; SGZ, subgranular zone; TO, TO901317; VPA, valproic acid.

The hippocampus is a brain region with a high level of plasticity throughout the lifespan, generating new neurons within the subgranular zone (SGZ) of the dentate gyrus (DG) (Xiao et al., 2016; Nam et al., 2017). It demonstrates that new neurons produced in the hippocampus play a critical role in mediating emotion and cognition (Juliandi et al., 2015). Recently, amount of evidences have indicated that deficits in hippocampal neurogenesis are associated with ASD both in humans and in mouse models of ASD (Escamilla et al., 2017; Abookasis et al., 2018). Studies highlight that hippocampal plasticity contributes to social behavior. It seemed that hippocampal neurogenesis triggering plasticity could restore normal behavioral phenotype.

The liver X receptor (LXR), LXRα, and LXRβ, belong to the large family of ligand-activated transcription factors (Mohan and Heyman, 2003; Houck et al., 2004). It has been demonstrated that LXRβ is ubiquitously expressed, and especially abundant in the central nervous system (CNS) and endocrine system, while LXRα expression is restricted to tissues rich in lipid metabolism such as intestine, kidney, liver, and spleen (Peet et al., 1998; Repa and Mangelsdorf, 2000; Whitney et al., 2002). Our previous study confirmed LXRβ was strongly expressed in the hippocampus and involved in the DG formation and neurogenesis. Deletion LXRβ in mice showed decreased neurogenesis in the postnatal and adult hippocampus, as well as autistic-like behaviors, including impaired sociability and increased repetitive self-grooming (Cai et al., 2018). These suggest that LXRβ activation may alleviate autistic-like behaviors by improving neurogenesis.

With the increasing number of animal models, we have a powerful tool to discover the mechanism and treatments of diseases under well-controlled conditions. In recent years, considerable efforts have been made to establish a reliable rodent model that can represent the abnormal behaviors observed in ASD. Among the many models available, the inbred BTBR T+ Itpr3tf/J (BTBR) mouse strain is a very well-built mouse model of autism, which displays increased repetitive self-grooming and marble burying, increased cognitive rigidity, impaired sociability, and abnormal vocalizations (Silverman et al., 2010; Stephenson et al., 2011; Currais et al., 2016). Exposure of mice to valproic acid (VPA) is an another valid ASD model used in preclinical experiments. A single prenatal (embryonic day 13) or neonatal (postnatal day 14) injection of VPA can induce autistic behaviors, including repetitive/stereotypic-like activity, impaired sociability, decreased nociceptive reactivity, and abnormal communication, in mice or rats (Yochum et al., 2008). A growing body of data has identified reduced hippocampal neurogenesis in the adult brain of VPA-exposed and BTBR mice (Yochum et al., 2008; Stephenson et al., 2011; Juliandi et al., 2015). Several studies demonstrated that treatments promoting neurogenesis could improve sociability and decrease repetitive behaviors in these ASD models (Currais et al., 2016; Gobshtis et al., 2017).

In the present study, the role of LXR agonist TO in alleviating autistic behavior in the two ASD mouse models was investigated. Early postnatal mice received TO intraperitoneal injection, the behavior and hippocampal neurogenesis were analyzed. The results showed that TO treatment could increase hippocampal precursor proliferation and alleviate the social deficits in the BTBR and VPA-induced mouse models of ASD, which have shown decreased DG neurogenesis. Our finding indicates that drug development targeting neurogenesis may be an effective method for ASD treatment.

MATERIALS AND METHODS

Animals

All mice were maintained in the Animal Facility of the Third Military Medical University with controlled temperature, standard 12 h light/dark cycle and mouse chow and water provided *ad libitum*. The C57BL/6J (B6) and BTBR mice breeding pairs were provided by the Third Military Medical University and the Model Animal Research Center of Nanjing University (Nanjing, China), respectively. Only the male pups of the B6 and BTBR mice were used in our experiment. All experimental procedures were approved by the Third Military Medical University and were also performed in accordance with the Guidelines for Animal Care and Use. Every effort was made to restrict the use of animals to as few as possible in our experiment.

Drug Treatment

TO Treatment in BTBR Mice

The day of birth was designated as postnatal day 0 (PD 0). B6 male mice were used as the normal controls. On PD 5, male pups were randomly divided into the following four groups: (1) 2% dimethyl sulfoxide (DMSO) (B6), (2) TO (B6+TO), (3) 2% DMSO (BTBR), or (4) TO (BTBR+TO). TO was dissolved in 100% DMSO and diluted with PBS to a final concentration of 2% before intraperitoneal (i.p.) injection to the pups (50 mg/kg) on PD 5, PD 7, PD 9, PD 11, and PD 13 every 2 days (**Figure 1A**). Behavior tests were conducted at the age of 8 weeks.

TO Treatment in VPA-Exposed Mice

The day of birth was designated as PD 0. On PD 13, B6 male mice were randomly divided into the following four groups: (1) 2% DMSO and normal saline (0.9% NaCl) (B6), (2) TO and normal saline (0.9% NaCl) (TO), (3) 2% DMSO and 400 mg/kg VPA (Sigma) (VPA), or (4) pretreatment of TO followed by VPA (VPA+TO). TO was dissolved in 100% DMSO and diluted with PBS to a final concentration of 2% before intraperitoneal (i.p.) injection to the pups (50 mg/kg) on PD 13 and PD 14, once per day. The control groups received an equivalent dose of the vehicle DMSO. On PD 14, the VPA and VPA+TO (2 h after TO injection) received 400 mg/kg VPA intraperitoneally (Yochum et al., 2008). The controls were given the same volume of sterile saline (**Figure 1B**). Behavior tests were conducted at the age of 8 weeks.

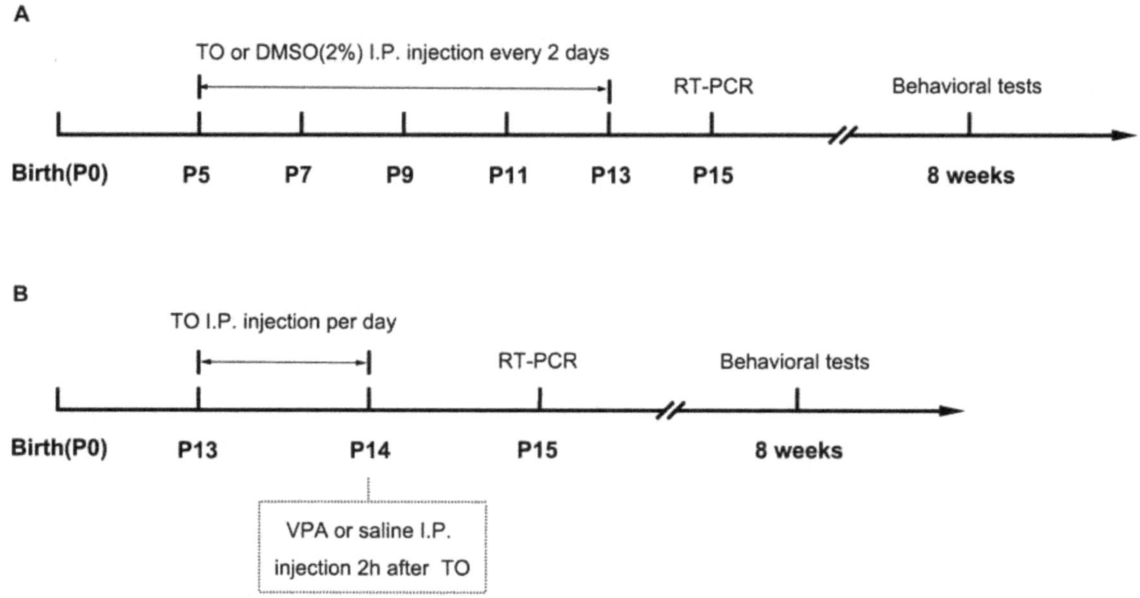

FIGURE 1 | Schematic diagram of the experimental procedures. **(A)** Neonatal male mice (B6 or BTBR) were injected with TO (50 mg/kg) or 2% DMSO from PD 7 to PD 13 every 2 days. The RT-PCR was conducted on PD 15. The behavioral tests were conducted at the age of 8 weeks. **(B)** Neonatal male mice (B6) were injected with TO (50 mg/kg) or 2% DMSO on PD 13 and PD 14, once per day, and then injected with VPA (400 mg/kg) or 0.9% NaCl 2 h after TO injection on PD 14. The RT-PCR was conducted on PD 15. The behavioral tests were conducted at the age of 8 weeks.

Behavioral Tests

Both the three chambered social approaches and self-grooming tests were conducted with B6 and BTBR male mice at the age of 8 weeks during daytime of the circadian cycle. Mice were placed into the experimental room for at least 30 min prior to each test to adjust to the environment. Eight mice per group were utilized for analysis.

Three-Chambered Social Approach

The three-chambered social approach test was performed in a rectangular apparatus (40 cm × 60 cm × 22 cm, divided into three equal parts) based on a previous protocol (Yang et al., 2011). The test consisted of a habituation phase and two testing phases, including sociability and social novelty recognition. During the first 10-min session, the subject mouse was habituated in the center chamber and had free access to the three-chambered box. During the sociability session, the subject mouse was allowed to explore the entire box for another 10 min with a novel male mouse (S1) and a novel object (O) introduced to the side chambers. After that, a third 10-min session was performed to assess the preference of social novelty, in which the object was replaced by an unfamiliar male mouse (S2) at the previous position. Seventy percent of ethanol and water was used to clean the whole arena between tests. The total time in each chamber for each phase was detected by using Ethovision XT 11.5. The preference index, which indicates the numerical time difference between chambers (S1 vs. O or S2 vs. S1) divided by total time in side chambers.

Self-Grooming

Mice were individually and gently placed into a standard mouse cage. The tests consisted of a 10-min habituation phase and a 10-min test phase with a video camera 15 cm away from the cage. The total time of self-grooming and the number of rearings in the test phase were counted with the researcher blinded to the treatment. Seventy percent of ethanol and water was used to clean the whole arena between tests (Silverman et al., 2015).

BrdU Labeling

To assess cell proliferation in the hippocampus, the mice were injected with bromodeoxyuridine (BrdU, 100 mg/kg; Sigma-Aldrich) intraperitoneally every 12 h for 3 times before anesthesia.

Immunohistochemistry and Immunofluorescence

Based on our previous experiment (Liu et al., 2016), the mice were perfused transcardially with 0.9% saline followed by 4% paraformaldehyde (PFA) after deep anesthesia with pentobarbital. The brain was collected and dehydrated completely in 30% sucrose solution with 4% paraformaldehyde at 4°C. Brains were sliced coronally (30 μm thick) and stored at −20°C in cryoprotectant solution. Immunostaining was performed according to our previous method. In short, the brain sections were incubated with a rabbit anti-doublecortin (DCX) (1:1000, Cell Signaling) primary antibody in 1% bovine serum albumin (BSA) (12 h, 4°C).

For BrdU staining, the sections were pretreated with 2 N HCl for 30 min at 37°C and then incubated with mouse anti-BrdU (1:500, BD Biosciences). After that, the sections were incubated with biotin-conjugated secondary antibody (1:200, goat anti-rabbit; Invitrogen) or Cy3 (1:500; donkey anti-mouse; Jackson ImmunoResearch) (2 h, 37°C), then treated with avidin-biotin peroxidase complex (Dako) for immunohistochemistry or 4′, 6-diamidino-2-phenylindole (DAPI, Beyotime, China) for immunofluorescence. The BrdU- or DCX-labeled cells were observed and photographed with a Zeiss (Oberkochen, Germany) Axivert microscope equipped with a Zeiss AxioCam digital color camera connected to the Zeiss AxioVision 3.0 system.

Cell Counting and Unbiased Stereology

According to our previous method (Liu et al., 2016), every 10th section (30 μm thick) through the rostrocaudal extent of the DG was selected to evaluate the number of $BrdU^+$ or DCX^+ cells in the granule cell layer (GCL) plus SGZ. Stereological cell quantification was used as described previously to calculate the total number of the two kinds of cells in the DG. Three mice per group were utilized for analysis.

Real-Time PCR

The brains were isolated on PD 15 and then used for RT-PCR as our previous method (He et al., 2017). Briefly, total RNA was extracted by an RNeasy kit (CWBIO, Cat.CW05815, China) based upon the instructions from the manufacturer. Then, total RNA (approximately 1–2 μg per 20 μl reaction) was reverse transcribed to cDNA using the PrimeScript RT Reagent Kit (Takara) after the concentration was detected qualified by a spectrophotometric instrument (NanoDrop). The CFX96 Real-Time PCR system (Bio-Rad) was used to conduct the RT-PCR analysis. The primer sequences of ABCA1, ABCG1, LXRß, and GAPDH were designed as follows: mouse LXRα, forward: 5′-TCCATCAACCACCCCCACGAC-3′ reverse: 5′-CAGCCAGAAAACACCCAACCT-3′; mouse LXRß, forward: 5′-TCGCCATCAACATCTTCTCAG-3′, reverse: 5′-GTGTGGTAGGCTGAGGTGTAA-3′; mouse ABCA1, forward: 5′-GGGTGAACGAGTTTCGGTATG-3′, reverse: 5′-CTGAAGATGCTTGGCTTTGCT-3′; mouse ABCG1, forward: 5′-AGAAAGGATGAAGGCAGACGG-3′ reverse: 5′-TGCTGGGTTGTGGTAGGTAGGG-3′; and mouse GAPDH, forward: 5′-AGGTCGGTGTGAACGGATTTG-3′, and reverse: 5′-TGTAGACCATGTAGTTGAGGTCA-3′. The relative expression levels were normalized to GAPDH and analyzed using the $2^{-\Delta\Delta Ct}$ method.

Statistical Analyses

The data are presented as the mean ± SEM. The results of self-grooming, real-time PCR and immunostaining were analyzed using two-way ANOVA. The data of the three-chambered social approach task were analyzed with two-way ANOVA, repeated measures ANOVA and paired *t*-test (Silverman et al., 2015; Zhang et al., 2018). Significant effects were evaluated with a least significant difference (LSD) *post hoc* test. The statistical significance was set at $p < 0.05$.

RESULTS

TO Upregulated the Expression of LXRß and Its Target Genes, ABCA1, and ABCG1, in the Hippocampus

It has been verified that LXRß is of great importance in DG neurogenesis and hippocampus-related functions (Cai et al., 2018; Sun et al., 2018). In our further experiment, after the intraperitoneal injection of TO, the relative mRNA level of LXRß in the hippocampus was markedly increased in the B6 and BTBR mice compared with that in the same strains treated with saline (**Figure 2B**). ABCA1 and ABCG1, the target genes of LXRß, were changed similarly to LXRß in the four groups (**Figures 2C,D**).

Similarly, the relative mRNA level of LXRß in the hippocampus was also upregulated in B6 and VPA-exposed mice compared with that in mice treated with saline (**Figure 2F**). In accordance with the upregulation of the LXRβ level, the expression of the downstream genes, ABCA1 and ABCG1, was significantly increased (**Figures 2G,H**). Nevertheless, there was little LXRα expression in the hippocampus of the mice, and TO did not alter the expression of LXRα in any of these mice (**Figures 2A,E**).

Early Postnatal TO Treatment Ameliorated the Social Deficits of BTBR Mice in the 3-Chambered Social Approach Task

In the three-chambered social approach test, sociability was regarded as spending more time in the chamber with a novel mouse than in the chamber with a novel object; the time spent in the chamber with the novel mouse or the novel object was measured in each group (**Figure 3A**). B6 mice are extensively social, which is consistent with the observations of B6 mice in our experiment (**Figure 3B**). There was no clear difference between the saline-treated B6 mice and the TO-treated B6 mice in the sociability test (**Figure 3B**). However, the TO-treated BTBR mice did show a preference toward the side chamber with the novel mouse compared with the saline-treated BTBR mice that were found to have no bias to the chamber with the novel mouse or the novel object (**Figure 3B**). In addition, in the habituation session, all mice from the four groups did not show bias toward any of the three chambers. Furthermore, the social preference index was calculated to evaluate the effect of TO pretreatment on sociability deficits. It was suggested that early postnatal TO administration rescued the social deficits in BTBR mice due to the higher social preference index of TO-treated BTBR mice (**Figure 3C**).

TO Pretreatment in the Early Postnatal Stage Improved the Social Behavior of VPA-Exposed Mice in the 3-Chambered Social Approach Task

We measured the time spent in side chambers in each group (**Figures 4A,D**). As stated above, in the sociability test, the B6 mice spent more time in the chamber with the novel mouse than in the chamber with the novel

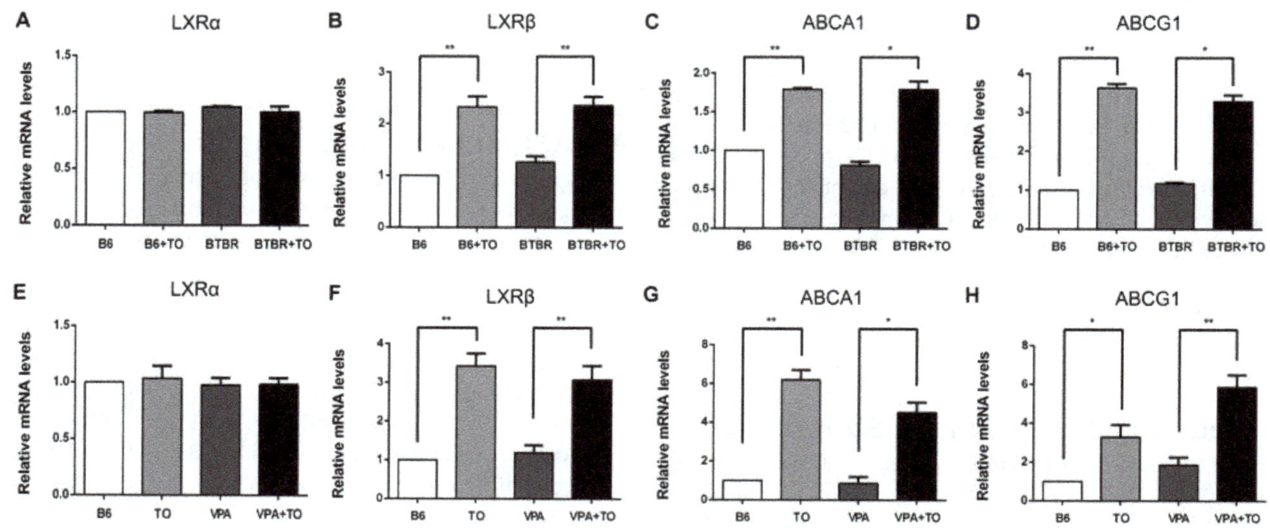

FIGURE 2 | TO treatment upregulated the relative mRNA levels of LXRβ and its target genes, ABCA1 and ABCG1, in the hippocampus. **(A,E)** TO treatment did not influence the expression of LXRα among the mice. **(B–D)** TO treatment increased the expression of LXRβ [two-way ANOVA: drug effect: $F(1,8) = 69.296$, $p < 0.01$; genotype effect: $F(1,8) = 0.997$, $p > 0.05$; drug × genotype effect: $F(1,8) = 0.618$, $p > 0.05$, followed by LSD *post hoc* test] and its target genes, ABCA1 [two-way ANOVA: drug effect: $F(1,8) = 234.636$, $p < 0.01$; genotype effect: $F(1,8) = 2.705$, $p > 0.05$; drug × genotype effect: $F(1,8) = 2.706$, $p > 0.05$, followed by LSD *post hoc* test] and ABCG1 [two-way ANOVA: drug effect: $F(1,8) = 566.361$, $p < 0.01$; genotype effect: $F(1,8) = 0.758$, $p > 0.05$; drug × genotype effect: $F(1,8) = 6.819$, $p < 0.05$, followed by LSD *post hoc* test] in B6 and BTBR mice. **(F–H)** TO treatment upregulated the expression of LXRβ [two-way ANOVA: TO effect: $F(1,8) = 67.092$, $p < 0.01$; VPA effect: $F(1,8) = 0.097$, $p > 0.05$; TO × VPA effect: $F(1,8) = 1.047$, $p > 0.05$, followed by LSD *post hoc* test] and its target genes, ABCA1 [two-way ANOVA: TO effect: $F(1,8) = 87.464$, $p < 0.01$; VPA effect: $F(1,8) = 12.967$, $p < 0.01$; TO × VPA effect: $F(1,8) = 1.428$, $p > 0.05$, followed by LSD *post hoc* test] and ABCG1 [two-way ANOVA: TO effect: $F(1,8) = 53.395$, $p < 0.01$; VPA effect: $F(1,8) = 9.152$, $p < 0.05$; TO × VPA effect: $F(1,8) = 1.010$, $p > 0.05$, followed by LSD *post hoc* test] in the B6 and VPA-exposed mice. Data are presented as the mean ± SEM. $n = 3$. *$p < 0.05$, **$p < 0.01$.

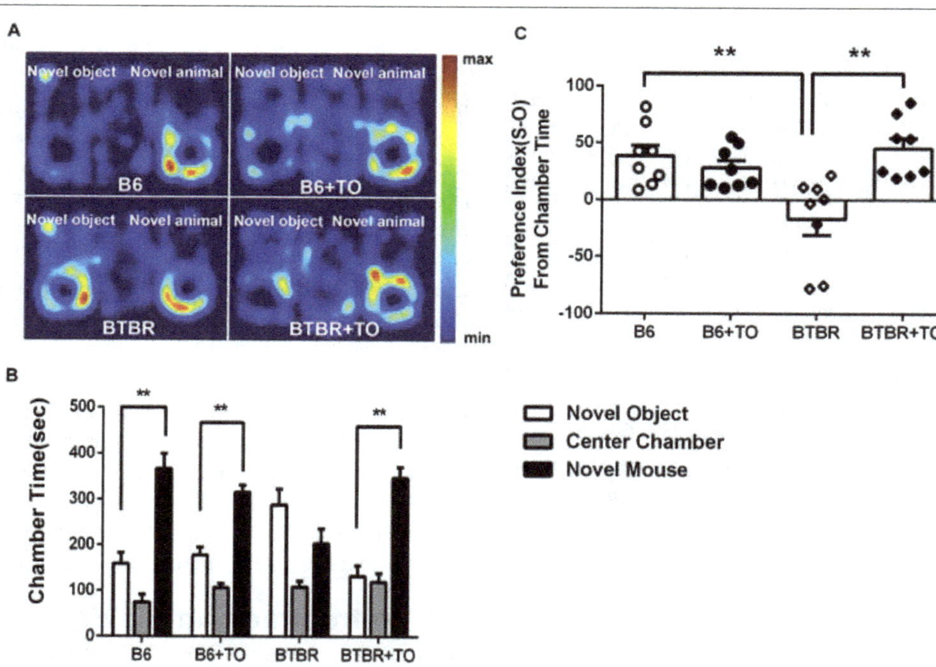

FIGURE 3 | Early postnatal intervention of TO rescued the sociability of BTBR mice. **(A)** Representative heat maps indicate the time distribution of the experimental mice in the sociability test. Warmer colors (red) represent longer stay. **(B)** Saline-treated and TO-treated B6 mice spent more time in the chamber with a novel mouse than with a novel object (paired *t*-test: $p < 0.01$). BTBR mice displayed impaired sociability and showed a preference toward the novel mouse compared with the novel object. Nevertheless, TO pretreatment reversed the preference significantly (paired *t*-test: $p < 0.01$). **(C)** BTBR mice displayed a lower social preference index (S-O/total) than B6 mice, which could be rescued with TO treatment [two-way ANOVA: drug effect: $F(1,28) = 6.616$, $p < 0.05$; genotype effect: $F(1,28) = 3.551$, $p = 0.070$; drug x genotype effect: $F(1,28) = 12.998$, $p < 0.01$, followed by LSD *post hoc* test]. Data are presented as the mean ± SEM. $n = 8$. **$p < 0.01$.

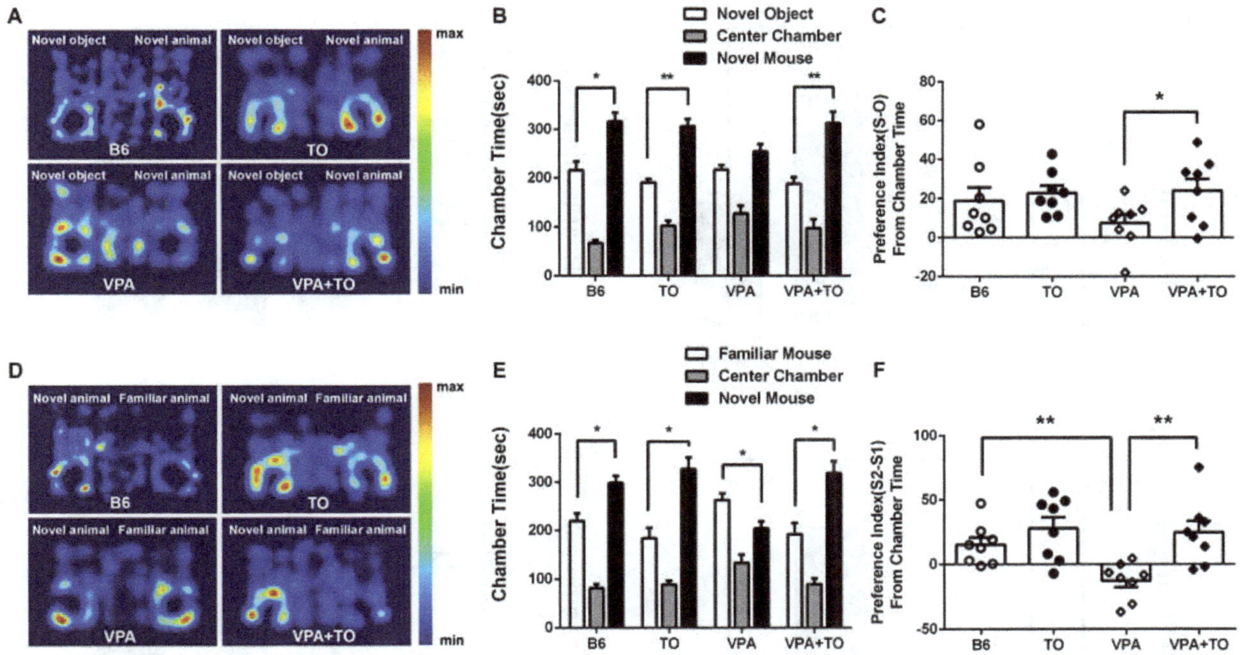

FIGURE 4 | TO pretreatment improved sociability and novel recognition of VPA-exposed mice. **(A)** Representative heat maps indicate the time distribution of the experimental mice in the sociability test. Warmer colors (red) represent longer stay. **(B)** VPA-exposed mice had less interest in the chamber with a novel mouse than did the B6 mice. TO pretreatment greatly alleviated the social deficits of the VPA-exposed mice (paired *t*-test: $p < 0.01$). **(C)** VPA-exposed mice showed a relatively lower preference index (S-O/total) than the B6 mice. TO pretreatment had a clear effect on the improvement of social deficits [two-way ANOVA: TO effect: $F(1,28) = 3.579$, $p = 0.069$; VPA effect: $F(1,28) = 0.888$, $p > 0.05$; TO × VPA effect: $F(1,28) = 1.347$, $p > 0.05$, followed by LSD *post hoc* test]. **(D)** Representative heat maps indicate the time distribution of the experimental mice in the novel recognition test. **(E)** VPA-exposed mice spent more time in the chamber with the familiar mouse (S2) than with the novel mouse (S1) (paired *t*-test: $p < 0.05$). Similarly, TO pretreatment reversed the effect of the VPA exposure (paired *t*-test: $p < 0.05$). **(F)** VPA-exposed mice displayed a significantly lower preference index (S2-S1/total) than the controls; however, TO markedly improved it [two-way ANOVA: TO effect: $F(1,28) = 11.978$, $p < 0.01$; VPA effect: $F(1,28) = 4.690$, $p < 0.05$; TO × VPA effect: $F(1,28) = 2.963$, $p = 0.096$, followed by LSD *post hoc* test]. Data are presented as the mean ± SEM. $n = 8$. $^{*}p < 0.05$, $^{**}p < 0.01$.

object (**Figure 4B**). It has been indicated that VPA exposure during early postnatal development could model ASD in mice. Meeting the description of social deficit in this model extensively, the VPA-induced ASD model mice showed more interest in the side chamber with a novel object than the side chamber with a novel mouse (**Figure 4B**). Nevertheless, following TO treatment, the VPA-exposed mice displayed social behavior comparable to that of controls in the social approach (**Figure 4B**).

In the social novelty recognition test, the B6 mice spent more time in the chamber with the novel mouse (S2) than in the chamber with the familiar mouse (S1) (**Figure 4E**), whereas the VPA-exposed mice exhibited the opposite preference to the side chambers, which also indicated that the social recognition of those mice was impaired (**Figure 4E**). However, TO treatment had a significant effect on the social recognition deficit. As a result, the time VPA-exposed mice spent in side chambers was reversed (**Figure 4E**).

Taken together, the results showed that the social preference index was influenced by VPA exposure and TO pretreatment. During the second 10-min session, the B6 mice displayed higher sociability, with no significant preference between the chambers with a novel mouse or a novel object, than the VPA-exposed mice (**Figure 4C**). However, pretreatment with TO increased the social preference index of VPA-exposed mice (**Figure 4C**), implying that TO markedly improved social deficits in those mice. The conclusions are the same as the social novelty recognition session. There was a significant difference in the social preference index between the saline-treated and VPA-treated mice (**Figure 4F**). TO pretreatment markedly reversed this effect (**Figure 4F**).

Early Postnatal TO Treatment Rescued Spontaneous Behaviors in BTBR Mice and VPA-Exposed Mice

The primary symptoms of BTBR mice are thought to include elevated repetitive self-grooming behavior, similar to the VPA-induced ASD model mice. As reported, the BTBR and VPA-exposed mice did display a markedly elevated frequency of self-grooming compared to the saline-treated B6 mice (**Figures 5A,C**). However, there was a definite drug effect on the self-grooming behavior of the BTBR mice, which was consistent with that of the VPA-exposed mice. Apparently, TO pretreatment lowered the high frequency of self-grooming in the BTBR and VPA-exposed mice (**Figures 5A,C**). Regarding the number of rearings, there was no definite difference among the four groups

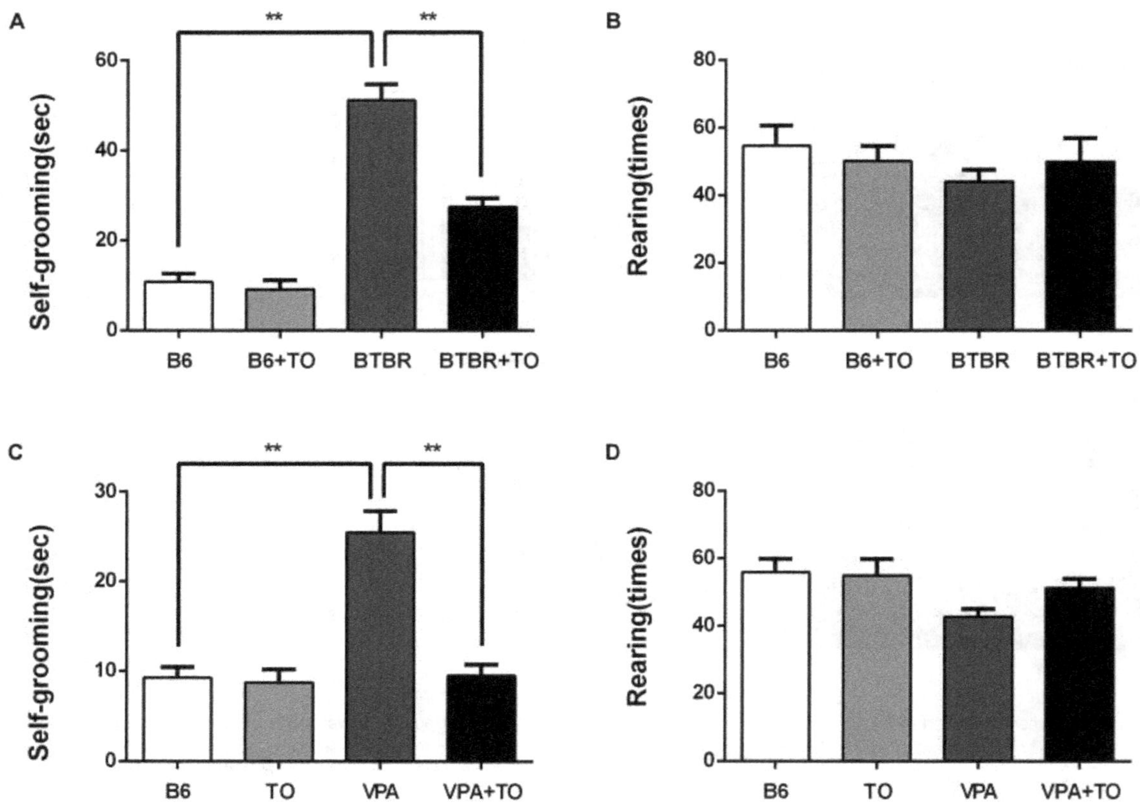

FIGURE 5 | Early postnatal TO treatment rescued spontaneous behaviors in two ASD mouse models (i.e., BTBR and VPA-exposed mice). **(A)** BTBR mice showed high levels of self-grooming compared with B6 mice, and TO alleviated the severe repetitive behavior [two-way ANOVA: drug effect: $F(1,28) = 26.514$, $p < 0.01$; genotype effect: $F(1,28) = 142.912$, $p < 0.01$; drug x genotype effect: $F(1,28) = 20.111$, $p < 0.01$, followed by LSD *post hoc* test]. **(B)** There was no significant difference in the number of rearings among the four groups. **(C)** VPA-exposed mice also displayed high levels of self-grooming compared with the B6 mice, which was also reversed by TO pretreatment [two-way ANOVA: TO effect: $F(1,28) = 24.583$, $p < 0.01$; VPA effect: $F(1,28) = 26.066$, $p < 0.01$; TO × VPA effect: $F(1,28) = 21.419$, $p < 0.01$, followed by LSD *post hoc* test]. **(D)** VPA did not alter the number of rearings. Data are presented as the mean ± SEM. $n = 8$. $^{**}p < 0.01$.

in the two kinds of ASD models (**Figures 5B,D**). In summary, TO pretreatment could effectively improve the self-grooming behavior of the BTBR and B6 mice exposed to VPA in the early postnatal stage.

Early Postnatal TO Treatment Rescued the Declined Hippocampal Neurogenesis in the DG of BTBR Mice

Cell proliferation was evaluated with BrdU incorporated into the DNA in adult DG neurogenesis and was detected in B6 and BTBR mice with or without early postnatal TO treatment (**Figures 6A–D**). Specifically, the number of BrdU-labeled cells was significantly decreased in the SGZ of BTBR mice compared with that in B6 mice (**Figure 6M**). The quantity of these cells in the SGZ of BTBR mice was greatly rescued following TO treatment (**Figure 6M**), indicating that the inhibition of hippocampal precursor proliferation in the BTBR mice could be improved with early postnatal TO treatment.

In addition, DCX immunostaining is the gold standard for assessing immature neurons (**Figures 6E–L**). There was a significant reduction of DCX-marked cells in the SGZ of the BTBR mice compared with that of the B6 mice (**Figure 6N**). However, TO pretreatment could greatly reverse the difference (**Figure 6N**). In addition, TO pretreatment markedly increased DCX-positive cells in the SGZ of B6 mice (**Figure 6N**). Taken together, the results showed that early postnatal TO treatment prevented the suppression of hippocampal neurogenesis in the DG of BTBR mice.

Early Postnatal TO Treatment Rescued VPA-Induced Hippocampal Neurogenesis in the DG of B6 Mice

Currently, VPA exposure during early postnatal development can model ASD, and it is thought to cause a consistent effect on the number of cells incorporated with BrdU or expressing DCX in the DG of VPA-exposed mice (**Figures 7A–L**). We found that the VPA-exposed mice exhibited impaired hippocampal neurogenesis, characterized by significantly decreased BrdU-labeled cells and DCX-positive immature cells in the SGZ, compared with the B6 mice (**Figures 7M,N**). The numerical difference in $BrdU^{+}$ and DCX^{+} cells was markedly reversed with TO pretreatment (**Figures 7M,N**). These results suggested that

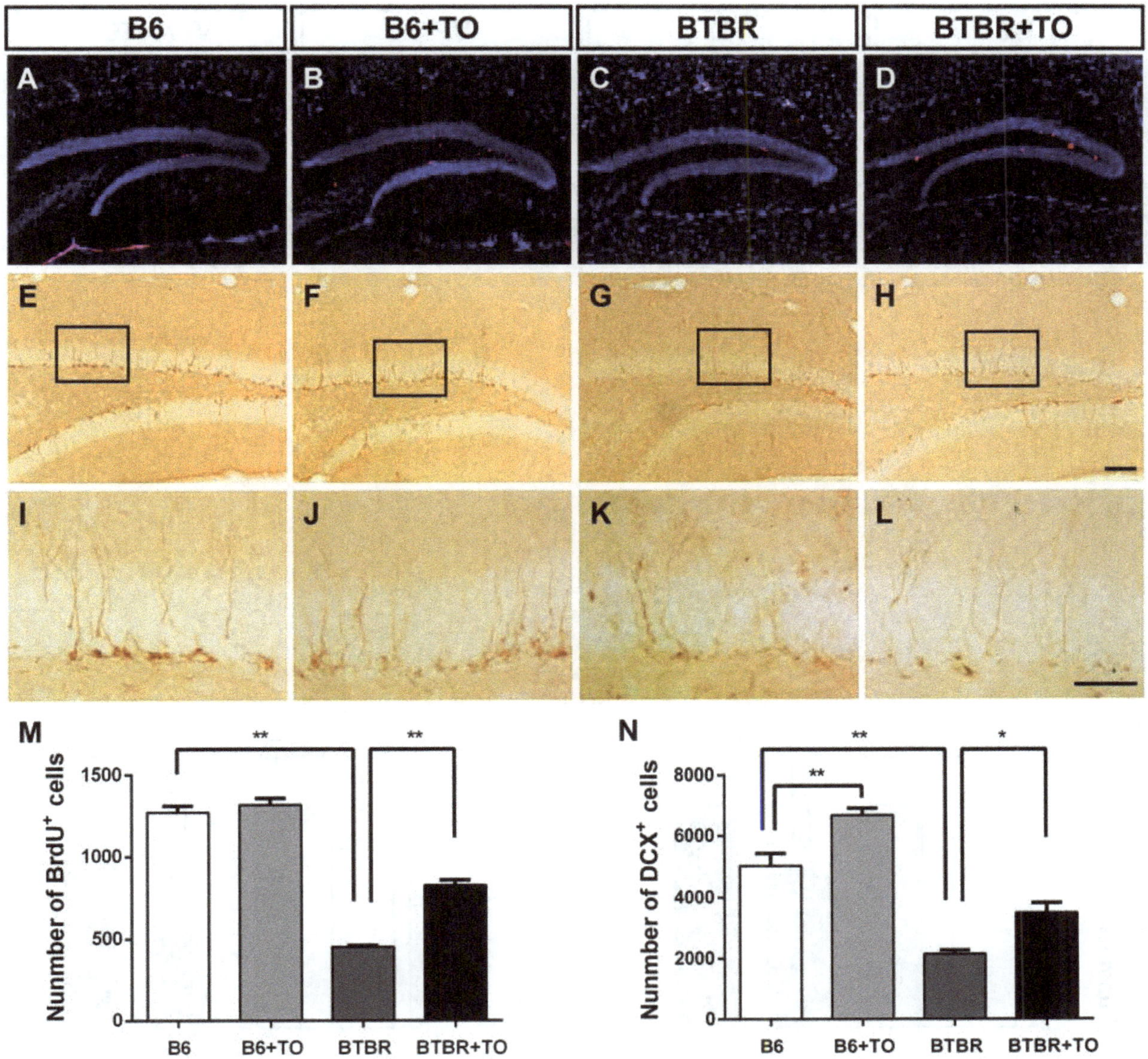

FIGURE 6 | Early postnatal TO treatment promoted an increase in BrdU-labeled cells and DCX-positive cells in the hippocampus. **(A–L)** Representative images of BrdU and DCX immunostaining in the hippocampus of each of the four groups. **(M,N)** As determined with stereological cell quantification of $BrdU^+$ [two-way ANOVA: drug effect: $F(1,8) = 40.833$, $p < 0.01$; genotype effect: $F(1,8) = 391.010$, $p < 0.01$; drug × genotype effect: $F(1,8) = 24.813$, $p < 0.01$, followed by LSD *post hoc* test] and DCX^+ cells [two-way ANOVA: drug effect: $F(1,8) = 26.544$, $p < 0.01$; genotype effect: $F(1,8) = 109.886$, $p < 0.01$; drug × genotype effect: $F(1,8) = 0.262$, $p > 0.05$, followed by LSD *post hoc* test] in the SGZ, BTBR mice had significantly decreased numbers of $BrdU^+$ and DCX^+ cells in the SGZ compared with the SGZ of B6 mice, and TO promoted proliferation of these cells. Data are presented as the mean ± SEM. $n = 3$. Scale bar in **(H)** = 100 μm and applies to **(A–H)**. The scale bar in **(L)** = 50 μm and applies to **(I–L)**. $^*p < 0.05$, $^{**}p < 0.01$.

TO pretreatment ameliorated the VPA-induced impairment of hippocampal neurogenesis.

DISCUSSION

In the current study, we found that early postnatal TO treatment could significantly improve sociability and reduce repetitive behaviors in two ASD mouse models (i.e., BTBR- and VPA-exposed mice). In addition, the results also showed that the deficits in the hippocampus of these two models could be rescued, as indicated by BrdU and DCX staining. The present study shows that abnormal neurogenesis in the brain may play a critical role in the causes of ASD.

To determine whether TO could activate its target genes, we validated their mRNA levels by means of RT-PCR. TO is a non-selective agonist able to activate both LXRα and LXRβ. However, the data showed that there was little LXRα expression in the cortex and hippocampus of the mice (Whitney et al., 2002). Hippocampus is a classic brain region to study neurogenesis

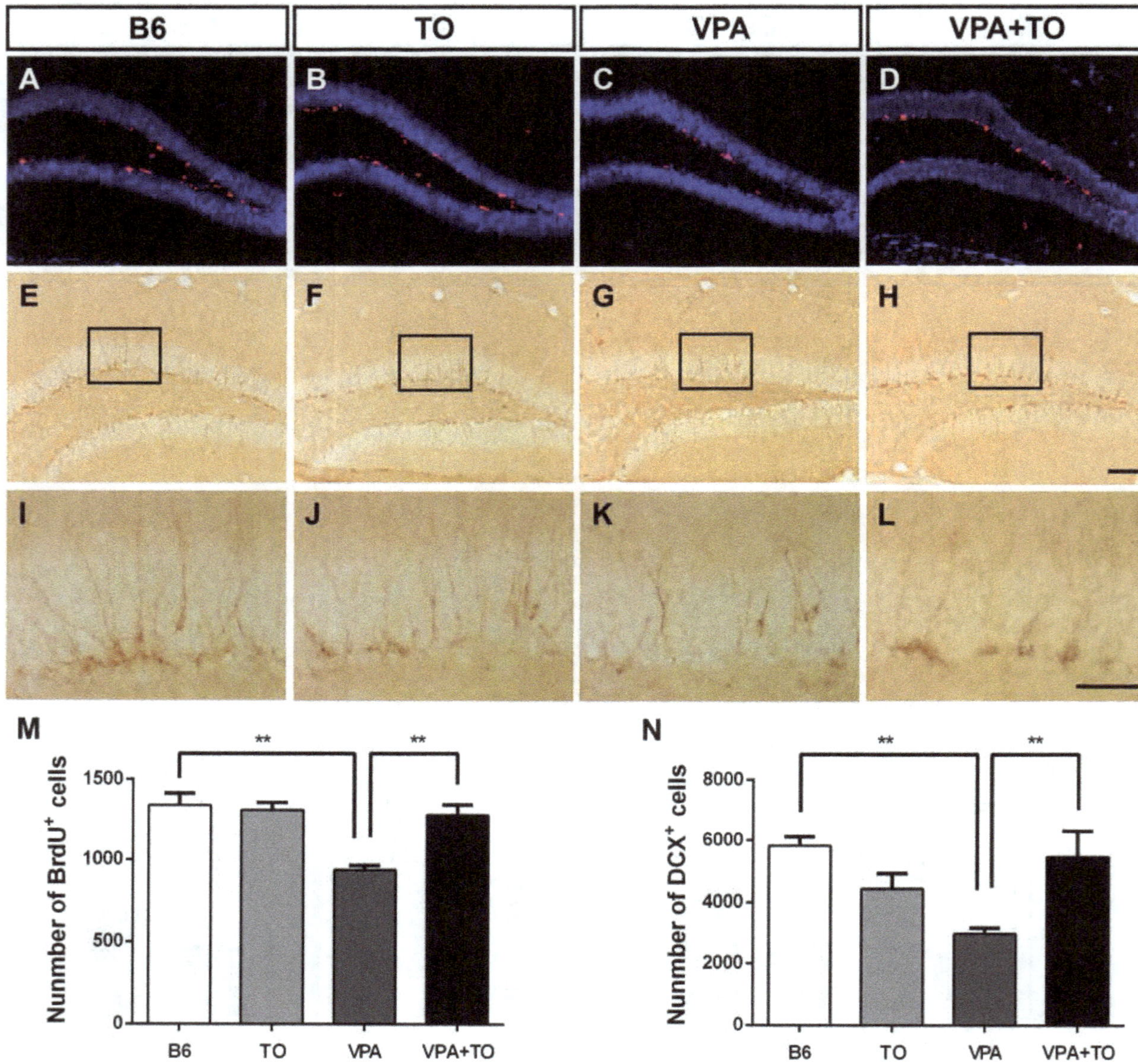

FIGURE 7 | Early postnatal TO treatment prevented the VPA-induced reduction of $BrdU^+$ and DCX^+ cells in the hippocampus. **(A–L)** Representative images of BrdU and DCX immunostaining in the hippocampus of each of the four groups. **(M,N)** As determined with the stereological cell quantification of $BrdU^+$ [two-way ANOVA: TO effect: $F(1,8) = 7.311$, $p < 0.05$; VPA effect: $F(1,8) = 14.067$, $p < 0.01$; TO × VPA effect: $F(1,8) = 10.415$, $p < 0.05$, followed by LSD *post hoc* test] and DCX^+ cells [two-way ANOVA: TO effect: $F(1,8) = 1.056$, $p > 0.05$; VPA effect: $F(1,8) = 2.977$, $p > 0.05$; TO × VPA effect: $F(1,8) = 13.584$, $p < 0.01$, followed by LSD *post hoc* test] in the SGZ, VPA exposure induced a significant reduction of $BrdU^+$ and DCX^+ cells in the SGZ of B6 mice compared with the SGZ of controls, and TO increased the proliferation of these cells. Data are presented as the mean ± SEM. $n = 3$. Scale bar in **(H)** = 100 μm and applies to **(A–H)**. The scale bar in **(L)** = 50 μm and applies to **(I–L)**. $^{**}p < 0.01$.

because of its high level of plasticity throughout the lifespan (Xiao et al., 2016; Nam et al., 2017). In addition, BTBR strain, an idiopathic mouse model of autism, and VPA-induced autism model both have impaired hippocampal neurogenesis. Thus, it's of great value to examine the effect of TO pretreatment on the activation of LXRβ and its target genes, ABCA1 and ABCG1. Our results indicated that the expression of LXRα did not alter after TO administration, but TO could effectively activate LXRβ and its target genes ABCA1 and ABCG1 in the hippocampus of these two mouse models.

The BTBR inbred strain is a common mouse model used in preclinical studies, which shows abnormal social interaction, high levels of repetitive behaviors and reduced ultrasonic vocalizations. To test the impaired sociability of this model, the three-chambered social experiment was applied to our experiment. We found that early postnatal TO administration could significantly alleviate the deficits in the sociability of BTBR mice. In addition, the repetitive self-grooming behavior was also effectively reduced by TO injection. Additionally, we adopted another autistic mouse model, VPA-exposed mice, to validate the therapeutic potential of early postnatal TO treatment and found that TO also contributed to improving the social deficits and repetitive self-grooming behavior of these mice.

Although the exact underlying mechanism of ASD remains unknown, defects in neurogenesis have been shown to be related to this disease both in human and animal models (Wegiel et al., 2010; Bostrom et al., 2016; Gilbert and Man, 2017). Throughout life, active neurogenesis is mainly found in the subventricular zone (SVZ) and SGZ in mammalian brains (Apple et al., 2017). Defects in these regions may have a significant influence on brain functions. MRI evidence showed that there was a significant anatomical abnormality between autistic patients and healthy controls (aged 29 months to 49 years) in the area dentata (AD; DG+CA4) (Saitoh et al., 2001). To date, there is no consensus regarding hippocampal volume. Another clinical study found that the enlargement of the amygdala and hippocampus existed in autistic adolescents (aged 12 to 18 years) compared to the healthy controls (Groen et al., 2010). In addition, an autopsy study revealed multiregional abnormalities in neurogenesis (including DG), neuronal migration and maturation in the ASD brain, which may result in the heterogeneity of the patients' symptoms (Wegiel et al., 2010).

Recently, several autistic mouse models have shown that there are significant changes in the neurogenesis of the hippocampus. MECP2 transgenic mice display reduced maturation of developing neurons and abnormalities in the adult hippocampus (Chen et al., 2017). A drastic decrease was found in adult neurogenesis in the ventral DG in both Shank3+/ΔC and Cntnap2−/− transgenic mice (Cope et al., 2016). Moreover, evidence also showed that there was reduced neurogenesis in the adult hippocampus of the BTBR and VPA-exposed mouse models (Yochum et al., 2008; Stephenson et al., 2011; Juliandi et al., 2015). These findings suggest that neurogenesis in the hippocampus may be related to behavioral deficits in ASD patients and animal models. Impaired adult hippocampal neurogenesis contributed to not only abnormal sociability but increased stereotyped motor behaviors (Wu et al., 2014; Rusznak et al., 2018). Consistent with previous evidence, our study confirmed that the adult BTBR and VPA-exposed mice displayed a significant decrease in the number of BrdU- and DCX-labeled cells in the hippocampus. However, early postnatal TO treatment could markedly rescue the neurogenesis deficits in these autistic mouse models. It is noteworthy that TO pretreatment increased the DCX- but not BrdU- cells in the SGZ of B6 mice that matched with BTBR mice instead of VPA-induced B6 mice, indicating that different administration methods may lead to not exactly the same effect on hippocampal neurogenesis in two mouse models sharing different pathogenesis of autism. Furthermore, $BrdU^{+}$ cells refer to different kinds of proliferating neurons incorporated with BrdU, which indicates an instantaneous state. However, DCX immunostaining is a gold standard to assess neurogenesis. In view of the heterogeneity of autism, the effects of TO pretreament on social behaviors in two mouse models were also not all the same. These results may indicate that TO can improve the behavioral deficits of the BTBR and VPA-exposed mice by promoting hippocampal neurogenesis.

To date, most preclinical studies on ASD have only tested acute drug treatment effects in adult autistic animal models. Regrettably, there is still little evidence that early intervention is a promising therapy for ASD. It has been identified that deficits in adult behaviors and spine morphology could be rescued by early social enrichment in the Fragile X Syndrome mouse model (Oddi et al., 2015). Another preclinical study indicated that vitamin D treatment could prevent autistic behaviors in the maternal immune activation ASD mouse model during pregnancy (Vuillermot et al., 2017). Our recent study demonstrated that early metformin administration during P7-P14 could rescue the behavioral abnormalities of adult BTBR mice (Wang et al., 2018). Early intervention was also applied to our current study; TO treatment was administered before P14, which approximates the period from the last trimester of pregnancy to the first few postnatal years in humans (Olney et al., 2002). It has been uncovered that our strategy of early intervention did contribute to improvements in the impaired behaviors and the suppressed hippocampal neurogenesis in these two models, which might remind us to pay more attention to early treatment of ASD.

In conclusion, the present study shows that behavioral abnormalities in the above two ASD mouse models can be improved by early postnatal TO injection. The possible mechanism may lie in the effect of TO on restoring suppressed hippocampal neurogenesis, which offers a potential approach for early ASD treatment.

ETHICS STATEMENT

All experimental procedures were approved by the Third Military Medical University and were also performed in accordance with the Guidelines for Animal Care and Use. Every effort was made to restrict the use of animals to as few as possible in our experiments.

AUTHOR CONTRIBUTIONS

YC and HZ conducted the experiments, collected and analyzed the data, and drafted the manuscript. XL, RX, and LW contributed to acquisition and analysis of the data. XF designed the experiments, supervised the project, and revised the manuscript.

FUNDING

This study was supported by the National Nature Science Foundation of China (No. 31571069), National Key R&D Program of China (2017YFE0103700).

REFERENCES

Abookasis, D., Lerman, D., Roth, H., Tfilin, M., and Turgeman, G. (2018). Optically derived metabolic and hemodynamic parameters predict hippocampal neurogenesis in the BTBR mouse model of autism. *J. Biophotonics* 11:e201600322. doi: 10.1002/jbio.201600322

Apple, D. M., Solano-Fonseca, R., and Kokovay, E. (2017). Neurogenesis in the aging brain. *Biochem. Pharmacol.* 141, 77–85. doi: 10.1016/j.bcp.2017.06.116

Baio, J., Wiggins, L., Christensen, D. L., Maenner, M. J., Daniels, J., Warren, Z., et al. (2018). Prevalence of autism spectrum disorder among children aged 8 years - autism and developmental disabilities monitoring network, 11 sites, United States, 2014. *MMWR Surveill. Summ.* 67, 1–23. doi: 10.15585/mmwr.ss6706a1

Bostrom, C., Yau, S. Y., Majaess, N., Vetrici, M., Gil-Mohapel, J., and Christie, B. R. (2016). Hippocampal dysfunction and cognitive impairment in fragile-X syndrome. *Neurosci. Biobehav. Rev.* 68, 563–574. doi: 10.1016/j.neubiorev.2016.06.033

Cai, Y., Tang, X., Chen, X., Li, X., Wang, Y., Bao, X., et al. (2018). Liver X receptor beta regulates the development of the dentate gyrus and autistic-like behavior in the mouse. *Proc. Natl. Acad. Sci. U.S.A.* 115, E2725–E2733. doi: 10.1073/pnas.1800184115

Carpita, B., Muti, D., and Dell'Osso, L. (2018). Oxidative stress, maternal diabetes, and autism spectrum disorders. *Oxid. Med. Cell. Longev.* 2018:3717215. doi: 10.1155/2018/3717215

Chan, K. K. S., Lam, C. B., Law, N. C. W., and Cheung, R. Y. M. (2018). From child autistic symptoms to parental affective symptoms: a family process model. *Res. Dev. Disabil.* 75, 22–31. doi: 10.1016/j.ridd.2018.02.005

Chao, O. Y., Yunger, R., and Yang, Y. M. (2018). Behavioral assessments of BTBR T+Itpr3tf/J mice by tests of object attention and elevated open platform: implications for an animal model of psychiatric comorbidity in autism. *Behav. Brain Res.* 347, 140–147. doi: 10.1016/j.bbr.2018.03.014

Chen, Z., Li, X., Zhou, J., Yuan, B., Yu, B., Tong, D., et al. (2017). Accumulated quiescent neural stem cells in adult hippocampus of the mouse model for the MECP2 duplication syndrome. *Sci. Rep.* 7:41701. doi: 10.1038/srep41701

Cope, E. C., Briones, B. A., Brockett, A. T., Martinez, S., Vigneron, P. A., Opendak, M., et al. (2016). Immature neurons and radial glia, but not astrocytes or microglia, are altered in adult cntnap2 and shank3 mice, models of autism. *eNeuro* 3:ENEURO.0196-16.2016. doi: 10.1523/ENEURO.0196-16.2016

Currais, A., Farrokhi, C., Dargusch, R., Goujon-Svrzic, M., and Maher, P. (2016). Dietary glycemic index modulates the behavioral and biochemical abnormalities associated with autism spectrum disorder. *Mol. Psychiatry* 21, 426–436. doi: 10.1038/mp.2015.64

Escamilla, C. O., Filonova, I., Walker, A. K., Xuan, Z. X., Holehonnur, R., Espinosa, F., et al. (2017). Kctd13 deletion reduces synaptic transmission via increased RhoA. *Nature* 551, 227–231. doi: 10.1038/nature24470

Gilbert, J., and Man, H. Y. (2017). Fundamental elements in autism: from neurogenesis and neurite growth to synaptic plasticity. *Front. Cell. Neurosci.* 11:359. doi: 10.3389/fncel.2017.00359

Gobshtis, N., Tfilin, M., Wolfson, M., Fraifeld, V. E., and Turgeman, G. (2017). Transplantation of mesenchymal stem cells reverses behavioural deficits and impaired neurogenesis caused by prenatal exposure to valproic acid. *Oncotarget* 8, 17443–17452. doi: 10.18632/oncotarget.15245

Groen, W., Teluij, M., Buitelaar, J., and Tendolkar, I. (2010). Amygdala and hippocampus enlargement during adolescence in autism. *J. Am. Acad. Child Adolesc. Psychiatry* 49, 552–560. doi: 10.1016/j.jaac.2009.12.023

He, X., Sun, D., Chen, S., and Xu, H. (2017). Activation of liver X receptor delayed the retinal degeneration of rd1 mice through modulation of the immunological function of glia. *Oncotarget* 8, 32068–32082. doi: 10.18632/oncotarget.16643

Houck, K. A., Borchert, K. M., Hepler, C. D., Thomas, J. S., Bramlett, K. S., Michael, L. F., et al. (2004). T0901317 is a dual LXR/FXR agonist. *Mol. Genet. Metab.* 83, 184–187. doi: 10.1016/j.ymgme.2004.07.007

Juliandi, B., Tanemura, K., Igarashi, K., Tominaga, T., Furukawa, Y., Otsuka, M., et al. (2015). Reduced adult hippocampal neurogenesis and cognitive impairments following prenatal treatment of the antiepileptic drug valproic acid. *Stem Cell Rep.* 5, 996–1009. doi: 10.1016/j.stemcr.2015.10.012

Jyonouchi, H., Geng, L., Cushing-Ruby, A., and Quraishi, H. (2008). Impact of innate immunity in a subset of children with autism spectrum disorders: a case control study. *J. Neuroinflammation* 5:52. doi: 10.1186/1742-2094-5-52

Liu, L., Zhang, Q., Cai, Y., Sun, D., He, X., Wang, L., et al. (2016). Resveratrol counteracts lipopolysaccharide-induced depressive-like behaviors via enhanced hippocampal neurogenesis. *Oncotarget* 7, 56045–56059. doi: 10.18632/oncotarget.11178

Mohan, R., and Heyman, R. A. (2003). Orphan nuclear receptor modulators. *Curr. Top. Med. Chem.* 3, 1637–1647. doi: 10.2174/1568026033451709

Nam, S. M., Kim, J. W., Kwon, H. J., Yoo, D. Y., Jung, H. Y., Kim, D. W., et al. (2017). Differential effects of low- and high-dose zinc supplementation on synaptic plasticity and neurogenesis in the hippocampus of control and high-fat diet-fed mice. *Neurochem. Res.* 42, 3149–3159. doi: 10.1007/s11064-017-2353-2352

Oddi, D., Subashi, E., Middei, S., Bellocchio, L., Lemaire-Mayo, V., Guzman, M., et al. (2015). Early social enrichment rescues adult behavioral and brain abnormalities in a mouse model of fragile X syndrome. *Neuropsychopharmacology* 40, 1113–1122. doi: 10.1038/npp.2014.291

Olney, J. W., Tenkova, T., Dikranian, K., Qin, Y. Q., Labruyere, J., and Ikonomidou, C. (2002). Ethanol-induced apoptotic neurodegeneration in the developing C57BL/6 mouse brain. *Brain Res. Dev. Brain Res.* 133, 115–126. doi: 10.1016/s0165-3806(02)00279-1

Pardo, C. A., and Eberhart, C. G. (2007). The neurobiology of autism. *Brain Pathol.* 17, 434–447. doi: 10.1111/j.1750-3639.2007.00102.x

Peet, D. J., Janowski, B. A., and Mangelsdorf, D. J. (1998). The LXRs: a new class of oxysterol receptors. *Curr. Opin. Genet. Dev.* 8, 571–575. doi: 10.1016/s0959-437x(98)80013-0

Repa, J. J., and Mangelsdorf, D. J. (2000). The role of orphan nuclear receptors in the regulation of cholesterol homeostasis. *Annu. Rev. Cell Dev. Biol.* 16, 459–481. doi: 10.1146/annurev.cellbio.16.1.459

Rubenstein, J. L., and Merzenich, M. M. (2003). Model of autism: increased ratio of excitation/inhibition in key neural systems. *Genes Brain Behav.* 2, 255–267. doi: 10.1034/j.1601-183x.2003.00037.x

Rusznak, K., Cseko, K., Varga, Z., Csabai, D., Bona, A., Mayer, M., et al. (2018). Long-term stress and concomitant marijuana smoke exposure affect physiology, behavior and adult hippocampal neurogenesis. *Front. Pharmacol.* 9:786. doi: 10.3389/fphar.2018.00786

Saitoh, O., Karns, C. M., and Courchesne, E. (2001). Development of the hippocampal formation from 2 to 42 years: MRI evidence of smaller area dentata in autism. *Brain* 124(Pt 7), 1317–1324. doi: 10.1093/brain/124.7.1317

Silverman, J. L., Pride, M. C., Hayes, J. E., Puhger, K. R., Butler-Struben, H. M., Baker, S., et al. (2015). GABAB receptor agonist r-baclofen reverses social deficits and reduces repetitive behavior in two mouse models of autism. *Neuropsychopharmacology* 40, 2228–2239. doi: 10.1038/npp.2015.66

Silverman, J. L., Tolu, S. S., Barkan, C. L., and Crawley, J. N. (2010). Repetitive self-grooming behavior in the BTBR mouse model of autism is blocked by the mGluR5 antagonist MPEP. *Neuropsychopharmacology* 35, 976–989. doi: 10.1038/npp.2009.201

Stephenson, D. T., O'Neill, S. M., Narayan, S., Tiwari, A., Arnold, E., Samaroo, H. D., et al. (2011). Histopathologic characterization of the BTBR mouse model of autistic-like behavior reveals selective changes in neurodevelopmental proteins and adult hippocampal neurogenesis. *Mol. Autism* 2:7. doi: 10.1186/2040-2392-2-7

Sun, T., Li, Y. J., Tian, Q. Q., Wu, Q., Feng, D., Xue, Z., et al. (2018). Activation of liver X receptor beta-enhancing neurogenesis ameliorates cognitive impairment induced by chronic cerebral hypoperfusion. *Exp. Neurol.* 304, 21–29. doi: 10.1016/j.expneurol.2018.02.006

Vuillermot, S., Luan, W., Meyer, U., and Eyles, D. (2017). Vitamin D treatment during pregnancy prevents autism-related phenotypes in a mouse model of maternal immune activation. *Mol. Autism* 8:9. doi: 10.1186/s13229-017-0125-120

Wang, L., Cai, Y., and Fan, X. (2018). Metformin administration during early postnatal life rescues autistic-like behaviors in the BTBR T+ Itpr3tf/J Mouse model of autism. *Front. Behav. Neurosci.* 12:290. doi: 10.3389/fnbeh.2018.00290

Wegiel, J., Kuchna, I., Nowicki, K., Imaki, H., Wegiel, J., Marchi, E., et al. (2010). The neuropathology of autism: defects of neurogenesis and neuronal migration, and dysplastic changes. *Acta Neuropathol.* 119, 755–770. doi: 10.1007/s00401-010-0655-654

Whitney, K. D., Watson, M. A., Collins, J. L., Benson, W. G., Stone, T. M., Numerick, M. J., et al. (2002). Regulation of cholesterol homeostasis by the liver X receptors in the central nervous system. *Mol. Endocrinol.* 16, 1378–1385. doi: 10.1210/mend.16.6.0835

Wu, X., Bai, Y., Tan, T., Li, H., Xia, S., Chang, X., et al. (2014). Lithium ameliorates autistic-like behaviors induced by neonatal isolation in rats. *Front. Behav. Neurosci.* 8:234. doi: 10.3389/fnbeh.2014.00234

Xiao, H., Liu, B., Chen, Y., and Zhang, J. (2016). Learning, memory and synaptic plasticity in hippocampus in rats exposed to sevoflurane. *Int. J. Dev. Neurosci.* 48, 38–49. doi: 10.1016/j.ijdevneu.2015.11.001

Yang, M., Silverman, J. L., and Crawley, J. N. (2011). Automated three-chambered social approach task for mice. *Curr. Protoc. Neurosci.* 8:26. doi: 10.1002/0471142301.ns0826s56

Yochum, C. L., Dowling, P., Reuhl, K. R., Wagner, G. C., and Ming, X. (2008). VPA-induced apoptosis and behavioral deficits in neonatal mice. *Brain Res.* 1203, 126–132. doi: 10.1016/j.brainres.2008.01.055

Zhang, Q., Yang, C., Liu, T., Liu, L., Li, F., Cai, Y., et al. (2018). Citalopram restores short-term memory deficit and non-cognitive behaviors in APP/PS1 mice while halting the advance of Alzheimer's disease-like pathology. *Neuropharmacology* 131, 475–486. doi: 10.1016/j.neuropharm.2017.12.021

13

Neuroligin 3 Regulates Dendritic Outgrowth by Modulating Akt/mTOR Signaling

Jing Xu[1,2], Yong-lan Du[1,2], Jing-wei Xu[1,2], Xiao-ge Hu[3], Lin-fan Gu[4], Xiu-mao Li[5], Ping-hong Hu[1,2], Tai-lin Liao[1,2], Qiang-qiang Xia[1,2], Qi Sun[2], Lei Shi[6], Jian-hong Luo[2], Jun Xia[7,8,9], Ziyi Wang[7] and Junyu Xu[1,2]**

[1] Department of Rehabilitation of the Children's Hospital, Zhejiang University School of Medicine, National Clinical Research Center for Child Health, Hangzhou, China, [2] Department of Neurobiology, NHC and CAMS Key Laboratory of Medical Neurobiology, Zhejiang University School of Medicine, Hangzhou, China, [3] Key Laboratory of Tumor Molecular Diagnosis and Individualized Medicine of Zhejiang Province, Zhejiang Provincial People's Hospital, People's Hospital of Hangzhou Medical College, Hangzhou, China, [4] Zhejiang University-University of Edinburgh Institute, Jiaxing, China, [5] Department of Orthopaedics, The Second Affiliated Hospital, School of Medicine, Zhejiang University, Hangzhou, China, [6] JNU-HKUST Joint Laboratory for Neuroscience and Innovative Drug Research, Jinan University, Guangzhou, China, [7] Division of Life Science, The Hong Kong University of Science and Technology, Clear Water Bay, Hong Kong, [8] Division of Biomedical Engineering, The Hong Kong University of Science and Technology, Clear Water Bay, Hong Kong, [9] State Key Laboratory of Molecular Neuroscience, The Hong Kong University of Science and Technology, Clear Water Bay, Hong Kong

***Correspondence:**
Ziyi Wang
mtray@qq.com
Junyu Xu
junyu@zju.edu.cn

Neuroligins (NLs) are a group of postsynaptic cell adhesion molecules that function in synaptogenesis and synaptic transmission. Genetic defects in neuroligin 3 (NL3), a member of the NL protein family, are associated with autism. Studies in rodents have revealed that mutations of NL3 gene lead to increased growth and complexity in dendrites in the central nervous system. However, the detailed mechanism is still unclear. In our study, we found that deficiency of NL3 led to morphological changes of the pyramidal neurons in layer II/III somatosensory cortex in mice, including enlarged somata, elongated dendritic length, and increased dendritic complexity. Knockdown of NL3 in cultured rat neurons upregulated Akt/mTOR signaling, resulting in both increased protein synthesis and dendritic growth. Treating neurons with either rapamycin to inhibit the mTOR or LY294002 to inhibit the PI3K/Akt activity rescued the morphological abnormalities resulting from either NL3 knockdown or knockout (KO). In addition, we found that the hyperactivated Akt/mTOR signaling associated with NL3 defects was mediated by a reduction in phosphatase and tensin (PTEN) expression, and that MAGI-2, a scaffold protein, interacted with both NL3 and PTEN and could be a linker between NL3 and Akt/mTOR signaling pathway. In conclusion, our results suggest that NL3 regulates neuronal morphology, especially dendritic outgrowth, by modulating the PTEN/Akt/mTOR signaling pathway, probably *via* MAGI-2. Thereby, this study provides a new link between NL3 and neuronal morphology.

Keywords: neuroligin 3, Akt/mTOR, dendritic outgrowth, PTEN, MAGI-2

INTRODUCTION

Neuroligins (NLs) are a group of postsynaptic cell adhesion molecules that play a crucial role in synaptogenesis and synaptic transmission (Scheiffele et al., 2000; Dean et al., 2003; Chih et al., 2005). Numerous studies have linked genetic deficits of NLs, especially neuroligin 3 (NL3), to autism spectrum disorders (ASDs) (Jamain et al., 2003; Pardo and Eberhart, 2007). The mice incorporated with NL3 R451C mutation, which is associated with human mental retardation and autism, exhibits impaired social interactions but enhanced spatial learning abilities (Tabuchi et al., 2007). Moreover, NL3 knockout (KO) mice or rats exhibit a series of symptoms of ASD, including increase in motor activity, a lack of social novelty preference, perseverative behaviors, and deficit of olfaction (Radyushkin et al., 2009; Hamilton et al., 2014; Rothwell et al., 2014). However, the detailed cellular signaling pathways underlying the defects caused by malfunction of NL3 are still unclear.

Early neurodevelopment including outgrowth of dendrites and axons is important to maintain the normal function of brains. Dendritic arborization defines the degree of information integration and induction of synaptic plasticity (Hausser et al., 2000). Developmental abnormalities of neuronal dendrites, either over- or under-development, were verified to contribute to multiple mental disorders, including ASD (Kwan et al., 2016; Montani et al., 2017; Dang et al., 2018). Different molecular mechanisms have been indicated to regulate the dendritic outgrowth in the past few decades, including neurotrophic factors (McAllister et al., 1995, 1997) and neurotrophic factor stimulated signaling pathways, such as the mammalian target of rapamycin (mTOR) pathway (Jaworski et al., 2005; Kumar et al., 2005; Urbanska et al., 2012) and extracellular signal-regulated kinases (ERK) pathway (Alonso, 2004; Zhang et al., 2014). Notably, substantial papers have demonstrated that imbalanced mTOR signaling pathway and protein expression would give rise to various autism-like behaviors. The *Tsc1* ± and *Tsc2* ± mice, with decreased suppression of mTOR signaling, i.e., increased mTOR signaling, present aberrant social behaviors which could be reversed by rapamycin treatment (Goorden et al., 2007; Ehninger et al., 2008; Sato et al., 2012). Mouse models with deletion of *Pten* in forebrain neurons, leading to overactive Akt/mTOR signaling, exhibit macrocephalus, seizures, and abnormal social interaction (Kwon et al., 2006). Besides, alternations of downstream components of mTOR pathway, such as KO of *4E-BP2* and overexpression of eIF4E, factors involved in protein translation, also result in social disorder and repetitive behaviors (Gkogkas et al., 2013; Santini et al., 2013). Collectively, the studies of these monogenic mutated mouse models seemed to indicate a tight connection between autism and mTOR signaling pathway, naturally raising a question that whether NL3-related autism model is also associated with this pathway. On the other hand, interestingly, abnormal dendritic growth has been recently reported in neurons with NL3 malfunction: there were a significantly greater number of dendritic branch points in pyramidal neurons of the stratum radiatum of the hippocampus of NL3 R451C knockin mice (Etherton et al., 2011). In addition, an increased axonal growth in climbing fibers of NL3 cerebellar-conditioned KO mice has been observed, which led to an invasion of synaptic terminals into the distal molecular layer and increased climbing fiber synaptic transmission (Baudouin et al., 2012). However, whether abnormal dendritic growth also occurs in NL3-deficient mice and whether NL3 is involved in the molecular pathways regulating dendritic outgrowth, such as mTOR pathway, are still unknown.

In the present study, we employed a lentivirus-based NL3 shRNA and the ASD mouse model with NL3 KO, to examine the relationship between NL3 and mTOR signaling pathway and their roles in the neuronal morphology. We show that NL3 regulates the outgrowth of neuronal dendrites by modulating Akt/mTOR signaling pathway, and the association between NL3 and Akt/mTOR signaling pathway is mediated by phosphatase and tensin (PTEN), probably *via* MAGI-2,a membrane associated guanylate kinase previously known to bind with NL1 (Hirao et al., 1998) and NL2 (Sumita et al., 2007).

MATERIALS AND METHODS

Animals

All procedures were performed in accordance with the National Institutes of Health Guidelines for the Care and Use of Laboratory Animals and approved by the Animal Advisory Committee at Zhejiang University. NL3 KO mice were purchased from the Jackson Laboratory (008394) and housed at the Animal Facility of Zhejiang University under a 12-h light/dark cycle and had access to sufficient food and water. Embryonic day 17 (E17) mice, born by female heterozygous parent, were used for primary cortical neuron cultures after genotyping analysis. Embryonic day 18 (E18) Sprague–Dawley rats were purchased from Shanghai SLAC Laboratory Animal Co., Ltd. and used for primary hippocampal neuron cultures.

Plasmids

Neuroligin 3 shRNA constructs were generated by inserting shRNA double-strand DNAs into the pSuper vector (a gift from Dr. Ip, Hong Kong University of Science and Technology) and then subcloned into the modified pFUGW vector for virus generation. The HIV-1 packing vector Δ8.9 and the VSVg envelope glycoprotein plasmid were gifts from Dr. C. Lois (Massachusetts Institute of Technology). The annealing primers for NL3 shRNA were the following: 5′-GATCTCC*GTAGCCTGGTCCAAATACA*TTCAAGAGA*TGTATTTGGACCAGGCTAC*TTTTTGGAAC-3′ and 5′-TCGAGTTCCAAAAA*GTAGCCTGGTCCAAATACA*TCTCTTGAA*TGTATTTGGACCAGGCTAC*GGA-3′, as used in the previous study (Xia et al., 2019). HA-tagged NL3 constructs were generated by inserting HA tag into the pRK5-NL3 plasmid. pClneoMyc rat S-SCAM alpha was a gift from Yutaka Hata and Yoshimi Takai (Addgene plasmid #40213) (Hirao et al., 1998). PDZ1/2 (amino acids 1273-2046) was cloned into pRK5-myc vector by PCR from the cDNA of a C57BL/6 mouse brain. GFP-PTEN was obtained by PCR amplification from human cDNA library and subcloning into pEGFP-C3 vector by *Sal*I and *Not*I.

Lentivirus Generation and Infection

As previously described (Xu et al., 2016), lentiviral pFUGW constructs, the HIV-1 packing vector Δ8.9, and VSVg envelope glycoprotein plasmid were co-transfected into HEK293T cells in a 2:1.5:1 ratio by calcium phosphate DNA co-precipitation. Fresh culture medium that replaced the transfection medium at 8 h after transfection was collected at 36 h after transfection to harvest the released viral particles. Harvested medium was centrifuged at 1000 r/min at 4°C for 5 min to remove cell debris, filtered through a 0.45-μm filter, and then aliquoted and stored at −80°C. For neuron infection, the viruses were added directly into the culture media according to the titer determined for each batch of viruses.

Cell Cultures and Transfection

Cultured hippocampal neurons were prepared from embryonic day 18 rats (Sprague–Dawley). The pregnant rats were euthanized following deeply anesthetization and the fetuses were removed from their uterus. The hippocampus were dissected out from the fetal brains and then trypsinized and triturated to single-cell suspension. Dissociated hippocampal neurons were cultured in Neurobasal Medium (Life Technologies) containing the B27 supplement (Life Technologies), 2 mM Glutamax (Life Technologies), and penicillin/streptomycin (Life Technologies). The same method was used for culturing cortical neurons from the newborn NL3 KO mice. HEK293T cells were cultured in MEM media (Life Technologies) containing 10% fetal bovine serum (Life Technologies) and penicillin/streptomycin (Life Technologies). HEK293T cells were transfected using the calcium phosphate co-precipitation method, and the medium was completely changed after 8 h.

Antibodies and Chemical Inhibitors

The following primary antibodies were used: NL3 (self-made, generated against the amino-acids 706–825 fragment of NL3, 1:1000 for western blot, 1:100 for immunocytochemistry), MAP2 (Abcam, ab11267, 1:500 for immunocytochemistry), phospho-S6S235/236 (CST, 4858, 1:2000 for western blot), S6 (CST, 2217, 1:2000), phospho-AktT308 (CST, 2965, 1:1000 for western blot, 1:100 for immunocytochemistry), phospho-AktS473 (CST, 4060, 1:1000 for western blot, 1:100 for immunocytochemistry), Akt (CST, 9272, 1:1000), phospho-mTOR-S2448 (CST, 5536, 1:1000), mTOR (CST, 2983, 1:1000), PTEN (HuaBio, ET1606-43, 1:2000 for western blot, 1:200 for immunocytochemistry), puromycin (Millipore, MABE343, 1:10,000), β-actin (HuaBio, EM21002, 1:5000), GAPDH (Beyotime, A7016, 1:10,000), HA-tag (Cell Signaling Technology, 3724, 1:2000 for western blot, 1:500 for immunocytochemistry), and myc-tag (Sigma-Aldrich, 11667149001, 1:2000 for western blot, 1:500 for immunocytochemistry). HRP- and fluorophore-conjugated secondary antibodies were purchased from Jackson ImmunoResearch Laboratories and used 1:500 for immunocytochemistry or 1:10,000 for western blots. Rapamycin (CST, 9904) and LY294002 (CST, 9901) were prepared as 2000 × stock solutions in DMSO and used at working concentrations of 10 nM and 10 μM, respectively.

Immunocytochemistry

Cells cultured on coverslips were fixed with 4% paraformaldehyde in phosphate-buffered saline (PBS) containing 4% sucrose for 15 min, permeabilized with 0.2% Triton X-100 for 10 min, and blocked with 10% normal donkey serum (NDS) for 1 h at room temperature. Thereafter, cells were incubated with primary antibodies in 3% NDS at 4°C overnight and fluorescent secondary antibodies at room temperature for 1 h after washing three times with PBS. Following incubation, washed coverslips were mounted using Mowiol mounting medium (w/v 24% glycerol, 9.6% Mowiol 4-88, 2.5% DABCO; v/v 36% ddH2O, 48% 0.2 M Tris pH 8.5), and imaged under an Olympus FV1000 confocal laser scanning microscope. The intensity of phospho-Akt and PTEN was measured by MetaMorph software. Neuronal morphology was analyzed by extracting and measuring MAP2-positive dendrites. We quantified soma size of the neurons by MetaMorph software. To estimate the dendritic morphology, NeuronJ, an ImageJ plugin, was used for tracing the neurites and quantifying dendritic length and arborization.

SUnSET

Five days after infection of shNL3 lentivirus, puromycin (Sigma) at working concentration (1 μM) was added into the neuronal culture medium and incubated for 30 min. Subsequently, the treated neurons were washed twice with cold PBS and harvested for immunoblotting analysis using the 12D10 monoclonal antibody against puromycin.

Golgi Staining

Golgi stainings were performed using an FD Rapid GolgiStain^{TM} Kit (PK401; FD Neurotechnologies, Inc.) according to the manufacturer's instructions (Shen et al., 2016); 3-month old mice were euthanized using cervical dislocation following deeply anesthetization. Whole brains were isolated quickly from each animal, rinsed once in Milli-Q water, and sequentially immersed in impregnation solution (mixed by Solutions A and B) and Solution C. Tissues were then serially cut into sections of 120-μm thickness with a vibratome (Microm, 920120), stained with silver nitrate solution (Solutions D and E), dehydrated through descending alcohol series, and mounted with Permount lastly (Thermo Fisher Scientific). Images were acquired with a microscope (BX61; Olympus). We reconstructed the neurons by Neuronstudio and measured soma area of somatosensory cortex in the MetaMorph software by filtering puncta with area > 95 μm^2 and length < 40 μm to define a cell body. Dendritic length and arborization were analyzed by NeuronJ and Sholl analysis, respectively, in ImageJ software.

Co-immunoprecipitation

HEK293T cells transfected with different plasmid combinations were lyzed with 1% Triton X-100 in PBS and phosphatase inhibitor cocktail (Sigma-Aldrich) at 36 h after transfection. After centrifugation at 14,000 r/min for 25 min, the supernatant was collected and incubated with antibodies for 2 h at 4°C. Protein A beads (GE Healthcare, 17-0780-01) were then added and incubated for 2 h. The samples were eluted with 1 × SDS sample buffer after washing once with cold PBS (1% TritonX-100), twice with lysis buffer and twice again with PBS buffer, and then analyzed by SDS-PAGE and subjected to western blot analysis.

Statistics

For each quantification, we used more than three independent experimental repeats (*n* represents experimental repeats), and 15–25 neurons were analyzed in each immunostaining experiment. The statistical analyses were conducted with IBM SPSS statistics. Band intensities of western blots were compared with one-sample *t*-test following normalized by setting each control as one. Signal intensities of immunostaining and morphological quantifications for two groups were compared with two-tailed Student's *t*-test. Multiple pairwise comparisons were carried out by one-way ANOVA or two-way ANOVA followed by *post hoc* test. GraphPad Prism 6 was used for data display. Significance is reported as $P < 0.05$, and data were presented as mean ± standard error of the mean (SEM).

RESULTS

Pyramidal Neurons of NL3 KO Mice Exhibit Morphological Changes

To examine if there were any morphological changes in neurons with NL3 deficiency *in vivo*, we conducted Golgi staining to evaluate the growth of neuronal somata and dendrites in NL3 KO mice. As a result, structural changes were observed in the somatosensory cortex from 3-month-old KO mice. The V/VI cortical layers, containing the largest percentage of pyramidal neurons in the mouse cortex, showed larger soma size compared to WT mice (**Figures 1A,C**). In order to reconstruct well-defined single neurons to assess the dendritic structures, we selected pyramidal neurons from layer II/III cortex instead of densely arranged neurons from layer V/VI to be outlined (**Figure 1B**). The length of the dendrites from KO mice, measured by Neuron J, was significantly greater than that of WT mice (**Figure 1D**). Sholl analysis on the tracings showed that the number of dendritic intersections was increased in the KO mice, indicating a higher dendritic complexity (**Figure 1E**). Taken together, the NL3 KO mice exhibited abnormal morphological changes including somatic enlargement and excessive dendritic outgrowth.

NL3 Knockdown Activates mTOR Signaling Pathway and Affects Dendritic Outgrowth

Previous studies have suggested that dysfunction of mTOR signaling pathway, especially its hyperactivity, exists in several mouse models of ASD (Crino et al., 2006; Sharma et al., 2010; Zhou and Parada, 2012). mTOR-dependent activation of the translation machinery is essential for the upregulation of local protein synthesis in neuronal dendrites (Takei et al., 2004). Such regulation in mRNA translation was mainly conducted *via* the substrates of mTOR complex 1 (mTORC1), including both the p70 ribosomal S6 protein kinases 1 and 2 (S6K1/2) and the eukaryotic initiation factor 4E-binding proteins (4E-bps) (Burnett et al., 1998; Gingras et al., 1999; Takei et al., 2004). We wondered whether NL3 deficiency also affects the activity of mTOR signaling pathway, especially the S6K activity. To verify this hypothesis, we conducted RNAi-based downregulation of NL3 expression in cultured rat hippocampal neurons and then examined the activity of mTOR signaling pathway. Immunoblotting analysis confirmed the expression level of endogenous NL3 in shNL3-expressing viruses infected neurons had reduced to 23.8% of the control level (**Figures 2A,B**). Immunostaining against NL3 also showed an apparent decreased expression of endogenous NL3 in the infected neurons (**Figure 2C**). Thereafter, NL3 knockdown was conducted in cultured rat hippocampal neurons at days *in vitro* 5 (DIV5), and the activity of mTOR signaling pathway was determined 5 days later by analyzing the phosphorylation level of S6 ribosomal protein (Ser235/236), the catalytic substrate of S6K (Jeno et al., 1988). Results from western blot assays showed that the phosphorylation level of S6 was significantly increased in neurons with NL3 knockdown (**Figures 2D,E**), indicating that reduction of NL3 protein enhances the activity of mTOR signaling pathway in cultured hippocampal neurons.

Since the phosphorylation of ribosomal protein S6 regulates the translation process in protein synthesis, we next examined whether the reduction of NL3 expression also affected protein synthesis in neurons by performing the surface sensing of translation (SUnSET) assay (Schmidt et al., 2009), in which puromycin, an analog of the aminoacylated tRNA, was incorporated into the nascent polypeptide chain and detected by puromycin antibody to reflect the rate of mRNA translation. Our results showed that the puromycin level of NL3 knockdown group was 27.8% higher than that of the control group (**Figures 2F,G**), suggesting that downregulation of NL3 accelerated basal level of protein synthesis.

Since the disturbance of both mTOR signaling activity and novel protein synthesis occurred in NL3 knockdown neurons, we wondered whether NL3 insufficiency would also result in any morphological changes in neurons. Rat hippocampal neurons infected by knockdown-related lentivirus at DIV1 were immunostained against MAP2 at DIV6, and then examined under confocal microscope for morphological analysis (**Figure 2H**). A 20% of increase in total dendritic length was observed in the neurons infected by shNL3-containing lentivirus, although we detected no significant differences in soma size and dendrite numbers between NL3 knockdown and control groups (**Figure 2I**). Taken together, our results showed that NL3 knockdown could lead to the upregulation of mTOR signaling and increased dendritic growth in neurons.

NL3 Deficiency-Induced Activation of mTOR Pathway Is Mediated by Increased Akt Activity

The mTOR pathway is regulated by several upstream signaling pathways, and one of the most notable pathways is phosphoinositide-3 kinase (PI3K)/Akt. Akt activation was

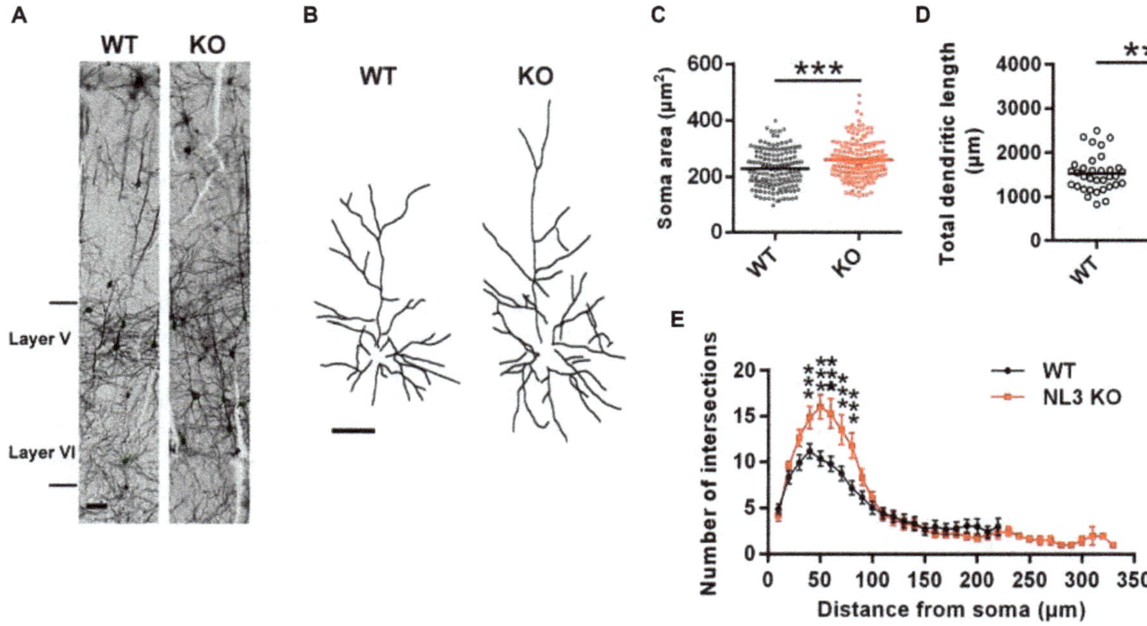

FIGURE 1 | Changes in dendritic outgrowth in NL3 KO somatosensory cortex. **(A)** Golgi staining of somatosensory cortex in NL3 KO (right) and WT (left) littermates at 3 months of age. Layer V and VI were indicated. Scale bar, 50 μm. **(B)** Representative tracings of Golgi-stained pyramidal neurons in layer II/III somatosensory cortex. Left, wild type; right, NL3 KO. Scale bar, 50 μm. Quantifications of the soma area **(C)**, total dendritic length **(D)**, and sholl-analysis for dendritic arborization **(E)** of the pyramidal neurons from layer V/VI somatosensory cortex. Values represent mean ± SEM (for **C**, $n = 147$ and 170 neurons, respectively, and for **D** and **E**, $n = 25$ and 18 pyramidal neurons, respectively, from three pairs of brains; $^{***}p < 0.001$, $^{**}p < 0.01$, unpaired two-tailed Student's *t*-test).

maximized by PI3K/PDK1-mediated phosphorylation at Thr308 site and mTOR complex 2 (mTORC2)-mediated phosphorylation at Ser473 site (Alessi et al., 1996; Sarbassov et al., 2005; Manning and Toker, 2017). We therefore examined whether Akt activity was the key factor mediating the upregulated mTOR signaling by NL3 knockdown. Phospho-specific antibodies against the Thr308 and Ser473 sites of Akt were used for both immunoblotting and immunocytochemistry assays to detect the endogenous phosphorylation level of Akt after NL3 knockdown (**Figures 3A,C,E**). In line with elevated p-S6 level, the phosphorylation levels of both Thr308 and Ser473 sites of Akt were significantly increased in neurons with NL3 knockdown, through either immunoblotting or immunocytochemistry assay (**Figures 3B,D,F**), suggesting that activation of Akt signaling is involved in NL3 knockdown-induced hyperactivated mTOR signaling.

To further determine whether NL3 KO also resembles the effects of NL3 RNAi on Akt signaling and neuronal morphology, as well to exclude the off-target effect of NL3 RNAi, *in vitro* culture of cortical neurons from newborn wild-type (WT) and NL3 KO male mice was performed. Cultured neurons at DIV6 were either blotted or stained with phospho-specific antibodies of Akt (**Figures 4A,C,D**). Compared with the WT group, the phosphorylation level of Akt Thr308 of the NL3 KO group was significantly increased, whereas no significant change of Ser473 phosphorylation was detected either by western blot or confocal microscopy (**Figures 4B,E,F**). These results suggested that NL3 modulates Akt activity primarily *via* its Thr308 site.

Furthermore, we also conducted MAP2 immunostaining of cultured NL3 KO cortical neurons at DIV6 to see whether there were similar abnormalities as in NL3 knockdown neurons (**Figure 4G**). Statistic results showed that, compared with WT neurons, the soma size, the total dendritic length, and the number of dendritic tips of KO neurons were increased by 20, 40, and 27.6%, respectively (**Figure 4H**), which resembled the same morphometrical changes observed from the brain slices (**Figures 1C–E**). On the other hand, no significant difference in number of primary dendrites between WT and NL3 KO neurons was observed.

Pharmacological Inhibition of Akt/mTOR Rescues Structural Abnormalities of Neurons With NL3 Deficiency

Rapamycin and LY294002 are two pharmacological inhibitors of PI3K/Akt/mTOR pathway that are widely used in testing the function of this signaling pathway, which directly inhibit activities of mTORC1 (Kunz et al., 1993; Brown et al., 1994) and PI3K (Vlahos et al., 1994), respectively. To further test if downregulated Akt/mTOR signaling could effectively rescue the molecular as well as the morphometrical abnormalities in neurons caused by NL3 knockdown, rapamycin and LY294002 were added into the cultured neurons separately. Before evaluating the morphological changes of neurons, we first examined the activities of Akt/mTOR pathway after drug treatment to confirm the effectiveness of the drugs (**Figure 5A**). Immunoblotting analysis of cultured rat hippocampal neurons

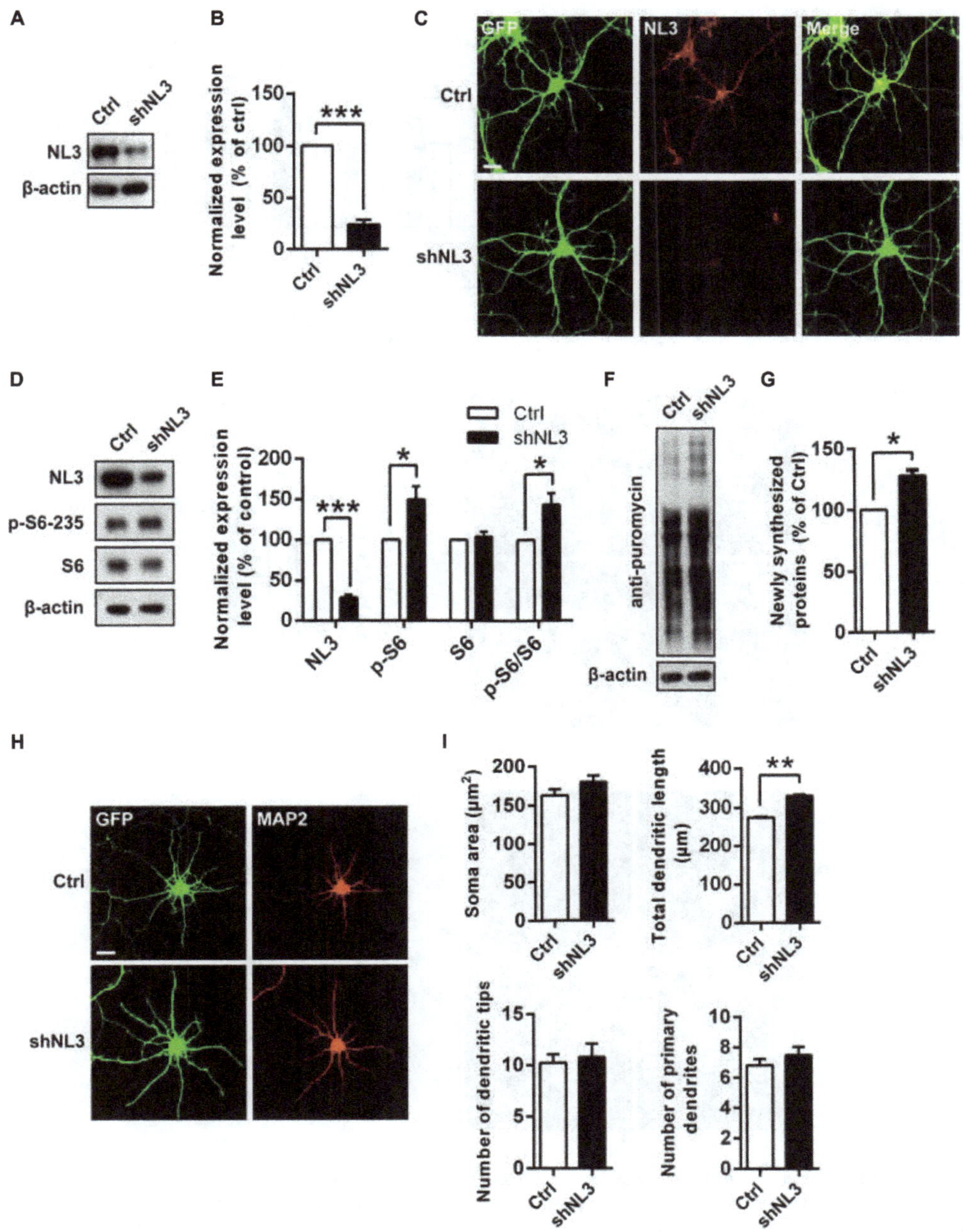

FIGURE 2 | Overactivation of mTOR signaling and abnormal dendritic outgrowth in neurons with NL3 knockdown. **(A)** Western blots of cultured rat hippocampal neurons infected by shNL3-expressing lentivirus or the control lentivirus at DIV5, and harvested at DIV10. Ctrl, control; shNL3, NL3-shRNA. **(B)** Quantification of the NL3 expression as in **A**. NL3 expression of shNL3 infected neurons was reduced by 76% compared with control. Values represent mean ± SEM normalized to control (n = 6 independent experiments; ***p < 0.001, one-sample t-test). **(C)** Immunostaining showed that the NL3 expression was enormously reduced in neurons infected by shNL3 lentivirus. Cultured rat hippocampal neurons infected with related lentivirus at DIV5 were immunostained at DIV10 using NL3-specific antibodies. Scale bar, 20 μm. **(D)** NL3 knockdown leads to hyperphosphorylation of S6. Immunoblots of cultured rat hippocampal neurons infected by shNL3-expressing lentivirus or the control lentivirus at DIV5, and harvested at DIV10. Ctrl, control; shNL3, NL3-shRNA. **(E)** Quantifications of the levels of NL3 and S6 phosphorylation as in **D**. The phosphorylated S6 protein level of the NL3 knockdown group was higher than that of the control group. Values represent mean ± SEM, normalized to control (n = 5 independent experiments; ***p < 0.001, *p < 0.05, one-sample t-test). **(F)** NL3 knockdown promotes protein synthesis in neurons. Immunoblots of cultured rat hippocampal neurons infected with shNL3-expressing or control lentivirus at DIV5, incubated with puromycin at DIV10, and examined for newly synthesized proteins using anti-puromycin antibody. **(G)** Quantification of blots as in **F**. The expression level of puromycin-labeled proteins from neurons with NL3 knockdown was higher than that from control neurons. Values represent mean ± SEM, normalized to control (n = 3 independent experiments; *p < 0.05, one-sample t-test). **(H)** NL3 knockdown affects the outgrowth of dendrites. Photomicrographs of cultured rat hippocampal neurons at DIV6 which were infected with lentivirus co-expressing GFP and shNL3, or vector control at DIV1. GFP signal indicates successful viral infection. Green, GFP; red, MAP2. Scale bar, 20 μm. **(I)** Quantifications of soma size, total dendritic length, and numbers of dendritic terminals and primary dendrites based on MAP2 signals. The neurons in the NL3 knockdown group showed significantly longer dendrites. Values represent mean ± SEM (n = 3 independent experiments; **p < 0.01, paired two-tailed Student's t-test).

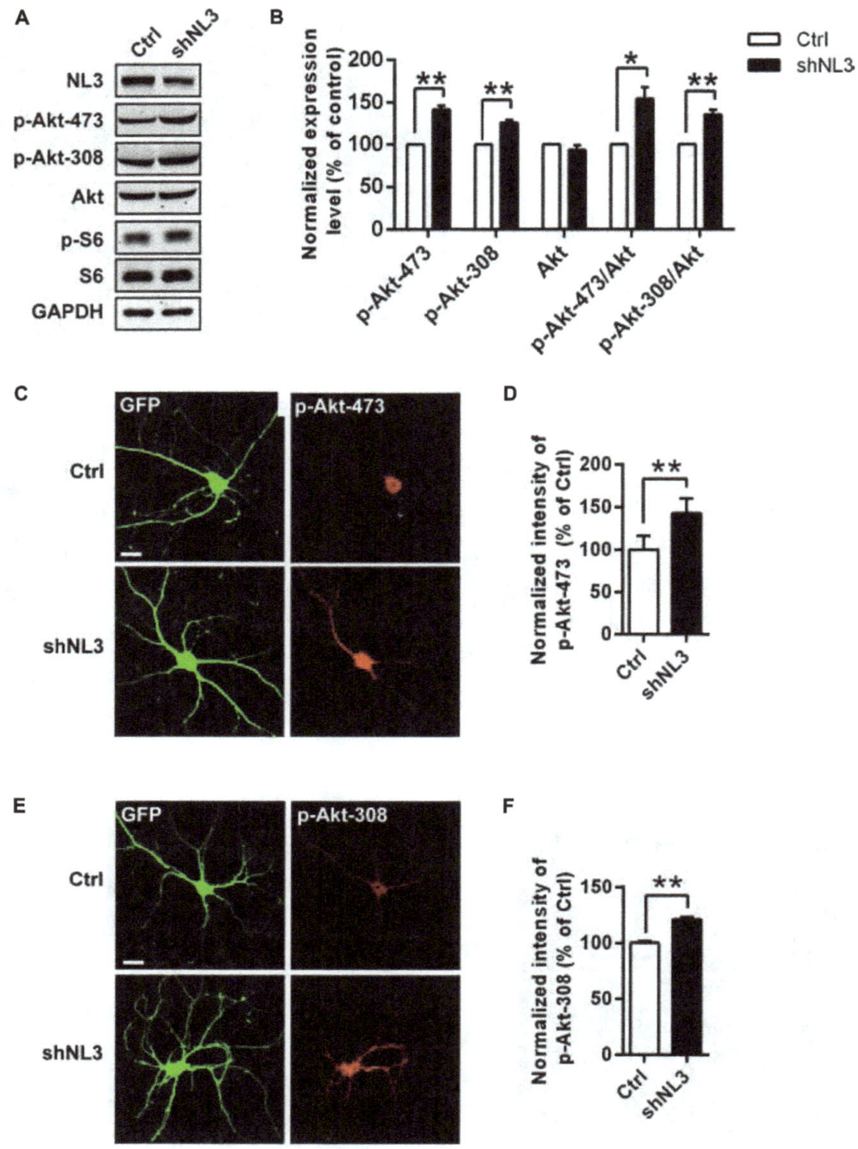

FIGURE 3 | Upregulation of Akt activity in neurons with NL3 knockdown. **(A)** NL3 knockdown increased Akt phosphorylation level. Cultured rat hippocampal neurons were infected by shNL3 or control lentivirus at DIV5, and harvested for western blot analysis at DIV10. p-Akt-473, phosphorylation of Akt Ser473 residue; p-Akt-308, phosphorylation of Akt Thr308 residue. **(B)** Quantifications of the levels of NL3 and Akt Thr308/Ser473 phosphorylation as in **A**. The phosphorylation levels of both Thr308 site and Ser473 site of Akt were significantly increased in neurons with NL3 knockdown. Values represent mean ± SEM, normalized to control ($n = 5$ independent experiments; $^{**}p < 0.01$, $^{*}p < 0.05$, one-sample t-test). **(C,E)** NL3 knockdown increased the phosphorylation levels of both Thr308 and Ser473 sites of Akt. Cultured rat hippocampal neurons infected with related lentivirus at DIV5 were immunostained at DIV10 using phospho-specific antibodies as indicated. Scale bar, 20 μm. Quantifications of the intensities of phosphorylated Akt Ser473 **(D)** and Thr308 **(F)** as in **C** and **E**, respectively. The signal intensities of both phosphorylated Akt Ser473 **(D)** and Thr308 **(F)** were higher in the NL3 knockdown neurons than in their controls. Values represent mean ± SEM normalized to control ($n = 3$ independent experiments; $^{**}p < 0.01$, paired two-tailed Student's t-test).

showed that the activity of Akt at the Ser473 site in the NL3 knockdown group was inhibited by both rapamycin (10 nM, 24 h) and LY294002 (10 μM, 24 h) to the same level as the control group. The decrease in phosphorylation of Akt Ser473 site, which is catalyzed by mTORC2, is consistent with the point that prolonged treatment with rapamycin inhibits mTORC2 assembly and Akt Ser473 phosphorylation (Sarbassov et al., 2006). The phosphorylation of Akt Thr308 site, meanwhile, was greatly reduced in LY294002 treated neurons due to the blocked PI3K. mTOR phosphorylation was potently inhibited by rapamycin but slightly inhibited by LY294002. Finally, the overactivation of S6, the most downstream substrate of mTOR signaling, caused by NL3 knockdown, was reversed by either rapamycin or LY294002 (**Figure 5B**).

We next examined the effects of rapamycin and LY294002 on the morphology of cultured neurons. Neurons infected with shNL3 at DIV1 were treated with vehicle, rapamycin, or LY294002 at DIV5 for 24 h, and then immunostained against

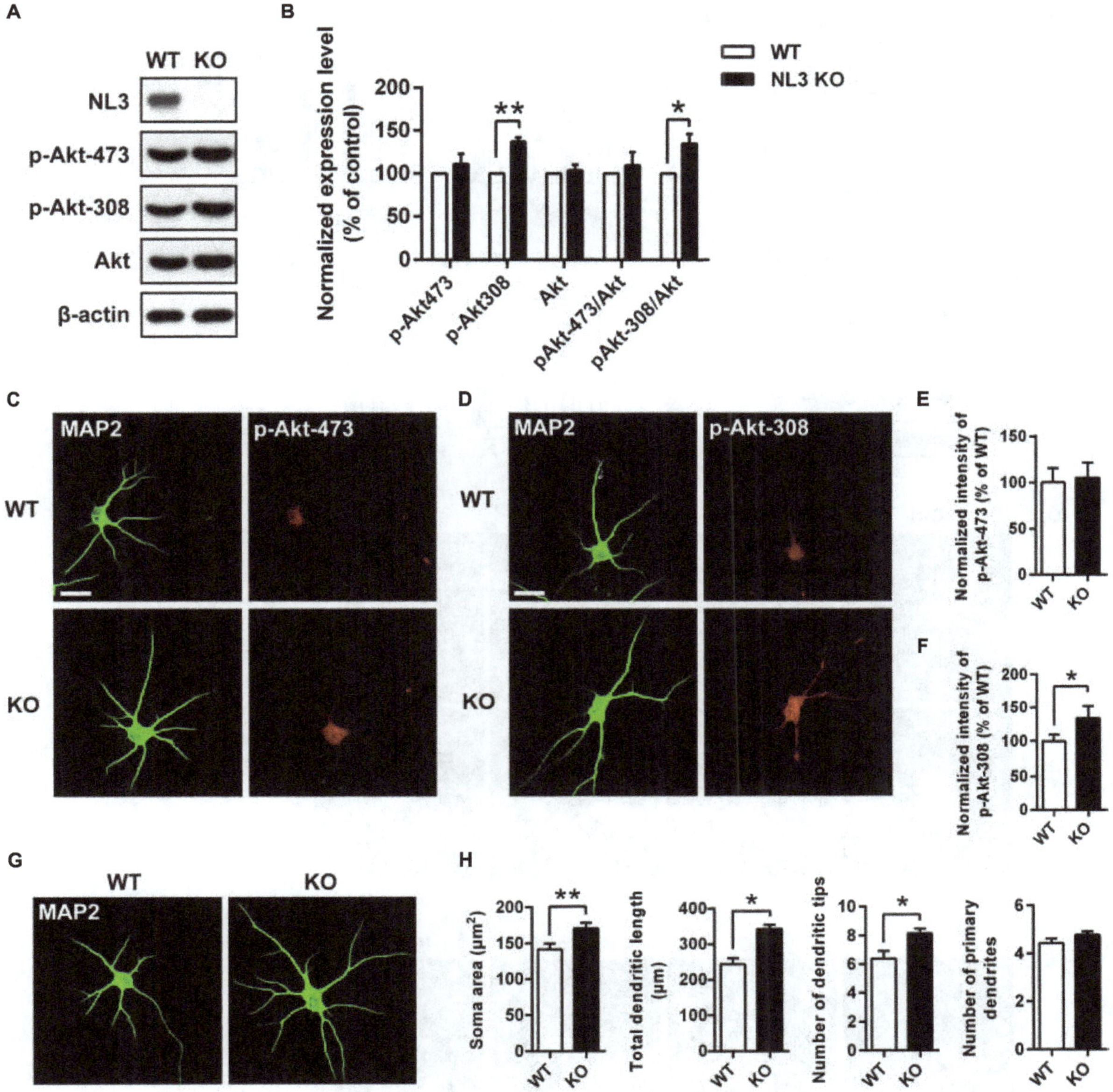

FIGURE 4 | Upregulation of Akt activity and morphological changes in cultured NL3 knockout cortical neurons. **(A)** Western blot showed that Akt phosphorylation at Thr308 was increased in NL3 knockout cortical neurons. The neurons were cultured from NL3 KO newborn mice or WT littermates at P0 and harvested to be immunoblotted at DIV6. WT, wild type; KO, NL3 knockout. **(B)** Quantifications of blots as in **A**. The phosphorylation level of Akt at Thr308 sites was significantly increased in NL3 knockout neurons. Values represent mean ± SEM normalized to control ($n = 5$ independent experiments; $^{**}p < 0.01$, $^{*}p < 0.05$, one-sample *t*-test). **(C,D)** NL3 knockout cortical neurons were processed for immunocytochemistry assay at DIV6 using anti-MAP2 antibody and anti-phospho-specific antibody of Ser473 or Thr308. Scale bar, 20 μm. **(E)** Quantifications of the intensity of phosphorylated Akt at Ser473 site as in **C**. NL3 knockout neurons showed similar intensity of the phosphorylated Akt at Ser473 site with WT neurons. Values represent mean ± SEM normalized to control ($n = 3$ independent experiments; $^{*}p < 0.05$, paired two-tailed Student's *t*-test). **(F)** Quantifications of the intensity of phosphorylated Akt at Thr308 as in **D**. The intensity of the phosphorylated Akt at Thr308 was higher in NL3 knockout neurons than in WT neurons. Values represent mean ± SEM normalized to control ($n = 3$ independent experiments; $^{*}p < 0.05$, paired two-tailed Student's *t*-test). **(G)** Abnormal morphological changes in NL3 KO cortical neurons. Photomicrographs of cortical neurons cultured from NL3 knockout mice were processed for immunostaining using MAP2 antibody to label dendrites at DIV6. Scale bar, 20 μm. **(H)** Quantifications of soma size, total dendritic length, and numbers of dendritic terminals and primary dendrites. Compared with WT neurons, NL3 KO neurons showed larger soma size, longer dendritic length, and increased number of dendritic tips. Values represent mean ± SEM ($n = 4$ independent experiments; $^{**}p < 0.01$, $^{*}p < 0.05$, paired two-tailed Student's *t*-test).

MAP2 as the indicator of neuronal morphology (**Figure 5C**). Statistic results revealed that both rapamycin and LY294002 successfully eliminated the increase of total dendritic length caused by NL3 knockdown (**Figure 5D**).

Moreover, rapamycin and LY294002 were also added, respectively, to NL3 KO neurons at DIV5 before immunostaining (**Figure 5E**) to examine their effects in rescuing the morphological abnormalities after NL3 KO. Compared with WT

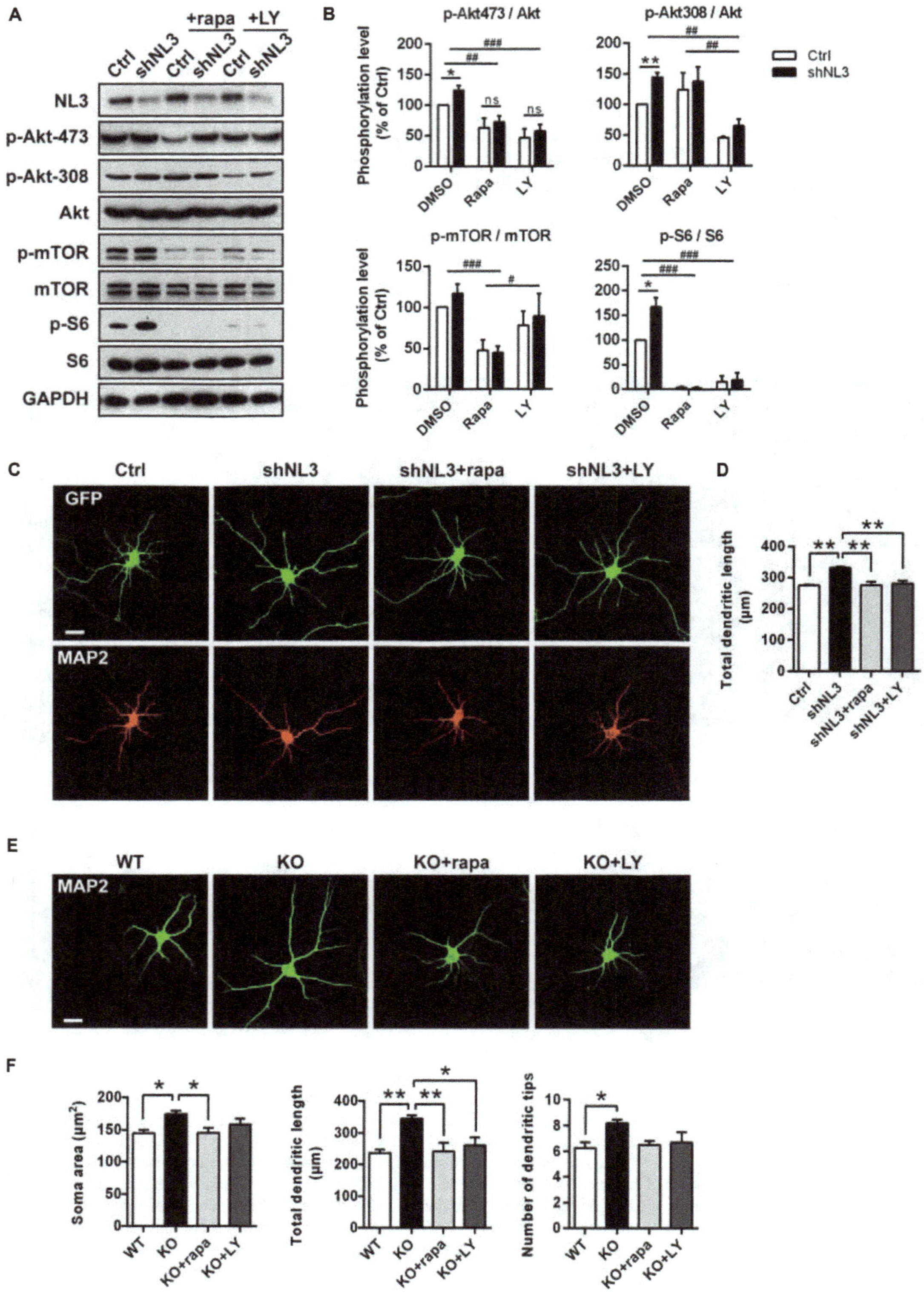

FIGURE 5 | Pharmacological inhibition of mTOR signaling rescued the morphological abnormalities of neurons with NL3 deficiency. **(A)** NL3 knockdown-induced hyperactivation of Akt/mTOR signaling was inhibited by rapamycin and LY294002. Cultured rat hippocampal neurons were infected by shNL3 or control lentivirus at DIV1, incubated with DMSO, rapamycin (10 nM), or LY294002 (10 μM) for 24 h at DIV5, and then harvested and processed for western blot analysis using phospho-specific antibodies of Akt, mTOR, and S6. rapa, rapamycin; LY, LY294002. **(B)** Quantifications of the phosphorylation levels of the proteins involved in Akt/mTOR signaling pathway as in **A**. Values represent mean ± SEM, normalized to control ($n = 5$ independent experiments; $^{**}p < 0.05$, $^{*}p < 0.05$, one-sample

(Continued)

FIGURE 5 | Continued
t-test; $^{###}p < 0.001$, $^{##}p < 0.01$, $^{#}p < 0.05$, two-way ANOVA with *post hoc* Bonferroni test). **(C)** Rapamycin and LY294002 rescued the neuronal morphological abnormalities induced by NL3 knockdown. Neurons with lentiviral infection at DIV1 were treated with rapamycin (10 nM), or LY294002 (10 μM) for 24 h at DIV5, and then processed for immunostaining using anti-MAP2 antibody to label dendrites. Scale bar, 20 μm. **(D)** Quantifications of the total dendritic length of the cultured neurons as in **C**. The neuronal dendrites of the NL3 knockdown group were longer than that of the control group. This increase was eliminated after either rapamycin or LY294002 treatment. Values represent mean ± SEM ($n = 3$ independent experiments; $^{**}p < 0.01$, one-way ANOVA with Tukey's *post hoc* test). **(E)** The abnormal structural changes in NL3 KO cortical neurons were reversed by rapamycin or LY294002. Cortical neurons cultured from NL3 KO mice were incubated with rapamycin (10 nM), or LY294002 (10 μM) for 24 h at DIV5, and processed for immunostaining using anti-MAP2 antibody to label dendrites. Scale bar, 20 μm. **(F)** Quantifications of the soma size, the total dendritic length, and the number of dendritic tips of the neurons as in **E**. The enlarged soma size, elongated dendritic length, and increased number of dendritic tips in NL3 KO neurons were eliminated by rapamycin treatment for NL3 knockout neurons, while LY294002 treatment rescued the enlarged soma size and elongated dendritic length in the knockout neurons. Values represent mean ± SEM ($n = 4$ independent experiments; $^{**}p < 0.01$, $^{*}p < 0.05$, one-way ANOVA with Tukey's *post hoc* test).

neurons, the neurons with NL3 deletion showed larger soma size, longer dendritic length, and increased number of dendritic tips. Moreover, all these three differences were eliminated by rapamycin treatment for NL3 KO neurons, whereas only the former two were rescued by LY294002 treatment (**Figure 5F**). Together, these results indicate that inhibition of Akt/mTOR signaling pathway could effectively rescue the morphological abnormalities caused by NL3 deficiency.

PTEN Mediates the Hyperactivation of Akt/mTOR Signaling Induced by NL3 Knockdown

The results above showed that the Thr308 site but not the Ser473 site of Akt exhibited a significantly increased phosphorylation level in NL3 KO neurons. It raised the possibility that the hyperactive Akt signaling was caused by PDK1 but not mTORC2. Based on these findings, we propose that NL3 may be associated with the upstream kinases which modulate the phosphorylation of the Thr308 site. As well known, PI3K phosphorylates PtdIns(4,5)P2 into PtdIns(3,4,5)P3 which prompts PDK1 to phosphorylate the Thr308 site of Akt. Conversely, the PTEN homolog inhibits the Akt activity by dephosphorylating PtdIns(3,4,5)P3 (Vander Haar et al., 2007). PTEN is found to be associated with ASD accompanying macrocephaly in both patients and murine (Butler et al., 2005; Kwon et al., 2006; Buxbaum et al., 2007; Herman et al., 2007; Orrico et al., 2009). We therefore examined the expression of PTEN in rat neurons with NL3 knockdown (**Figure 6A**). Western blot showed that its expression level was significantly reduced in the NL3 knockdown neurons (**Figure 6B**). We further examined the PTEN expression by immunocytochemical approach (**Figure 6C**). Result also showed a significant reduction of PTEN signal in knockdown group compared to control (**Figure 6D**). In order to rule out the possibility that RNAi itself had an effect on the PTEN/Akt/mTOR activity, we used a lentivirus expressing shRNA specifically targeting NL2 to test its effects on the signaling cascades by western blot (**Supplementary Figure S1A**). The results demonstrated that NL2 knockdown did not overactivate Akt/mTOR pathway, but also reduced the phosphorylation of Akt at Thr308 site, which indicated that the upregulation of Akt/mTOR in NL3 knockdown neurons was not induced by RNAi itself. As well, PTEN expression did not be affected by the shNL2-expressing lentivirus (**Supplementary Figure S1B**). These results indicate that NL3 does regulate PTEN/Akt/mTOR signaling pathway. The insufficient expression of PTEN could be a critical mediator of NL3-related hyperactivation of Akt/mTOR signaling in neurons.

MAGI-2 Is a Potential Scaffold Protein Tethering PTEN to NL3

The decline of both NL3 and PTEN expression levels in cultured rat neurons implied a relationship between these two proteins, yet the underlying mechanism is still unknown. Notably, both NL3 and PTEN contain a C-terminal PDZ-binding motif, which raises a possibility that their interaction may be mediated by a PDZ domain or multi-PDZ domain-containing protein(s).

Membrane associated guanylate kinase, WW, and PDZ domain containing 2 (MAGI-2, also called synaptic scaffolding molecule, S-SCAM) has been reported to interact with NL1 (Hirao et al., 1998) and NL2 (Sumita et al., 2007) *via* its PDZ1 domain at the excitatory and inhibitory synapses, respectively; the interaction between MAGI-2 and NL3 has not been verified yet. In addition, MAGI-2 is found in tumor studies to interact with PTEN *via* its PDZ2 domain and thereby stabilizes the structure of PTEN, increases its membrane trafficking, and enhances its inhibitory effect on Akt signaling and tumor pathogenesis (Wu et al., 2000; Tolkacheva et al., 2001; Nagashima et al., 2015). We hypothesized that MAGI-2 might mediate the NL3-regulated PTEN expression and membrane trafficking by simultaneously interacting with NL3 and PTEN. Hence, we first examined the interaction between NL3 and MAGI-2. Bidirectional Co-IP assays were conducted by overexpressing HA-NL3 and myc-MAGI-2 in HEK293T cells to examine the potential interaction between NL3 and MAGI-2. As expected, myc-MAGI-2 was successfully pulled down by HA-NL3, so was HA-NL3 by myc-MAGI-2 (**Figures 7A,B**). As well, immunostaining revealed that myc-MAGI-2 is co-localized with HA-NL3 on plasma membrane of HEK293T, whereas MAGI-2 alone was distributed diffusely in cytoplasm (**Figure 7C**). These results indicated that NL3 regulates the translocation of MAGI-2 to the plasma membrane through their binding. The interaction between GFP-PTEN and myc-MAGI-2, which was demonstrated in several studies (Wu et al., 2000; Jurado et al., 2010), was also confirmed through the co-IP experiment by us (**Figure 7D**).

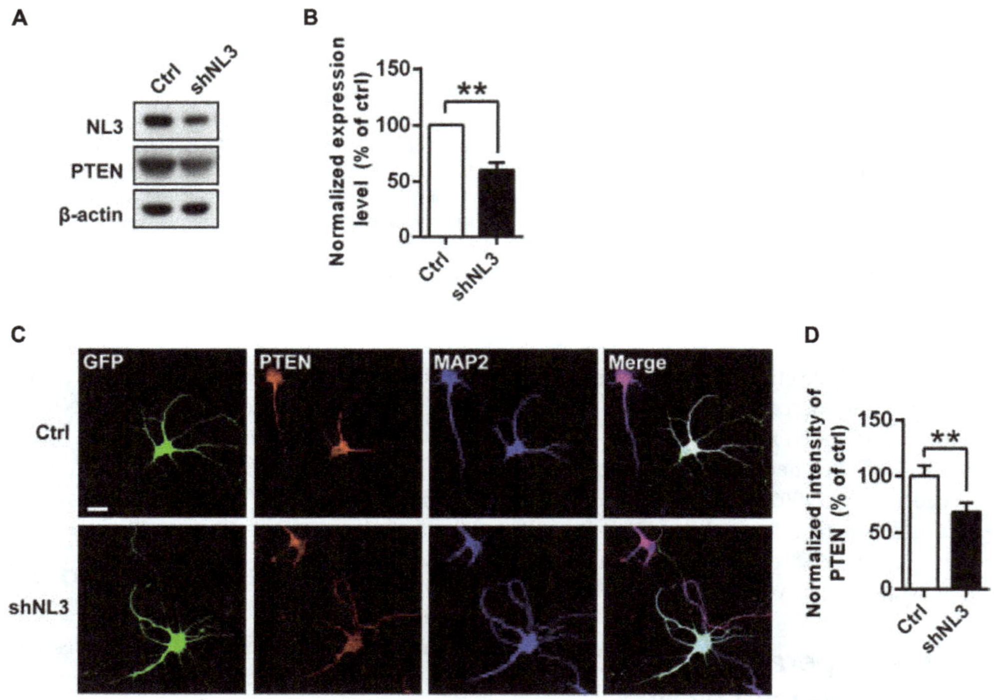

FIGURE 6 | PTEN expression level is down-regulated by NL3 knockdown. **(A)** Western blot showed that NL3 knockdown reduced the protein level of PTEN. Cultured rat hippocampal neurons were infected by shNL3 or control lentivirus at DIV5, and harvested and immunoblotted at DIV10 using antibody against PTEN as indicated. **(B)** Quantification of blots as in **A**. The expression level of PTEN was significantly reduced after NL3 knockdown. Values represent mean ± SEM normalized to control ($n = 5$ independent experiments; $^{**}p < 0.01$, one-sample t-test). **(C)** Immunostaining showed that NL3 knockdown resulted in reduced PTEN expression. Cultured rat hippocampal neurons were infected by shNL3 or control lentivirus at DIV1, and immunoreactived to PTEN (red) and to MAP2 (blue) at DIV6. Scale bar, 20 μm. **(D)** Quantification of PTEN expression level as in **C**. The PTEN expression of the NL3 knockdown group was significantly lower than control. Values represent mean ± SEM normalized to control ($n = 3$ independent experiments; $^{**}p < 0.01$, paired two-tailed Student's t-test).

We next examined whether NL3, MAGI-2, and PTEN can form a complex through the Co-IP assay. Immunoblotting result showed that, without MAGI-2 overexpression, NL3 did not show up in the immunopellet of GFP-PTEN, while in the presence of MAGI-2, NL3 could successfully co-immunoprecipitated with GFP-PTEN (**Figure 7E**), indicating that NL3 is able to form a complex with PTEN in presence of MAGI-2.

Together, these findings indicate that NL3 is able to recruit MAGI-2 to plasma membrane, and then regulate PTEN expression which was stabilized by binding to MAGI-2. Since PTEN works as an inhibitor of Akt/mTOR activity, we think that NL3 modulates Akt/mTOR signaling pathway through interaction with MAGI-2 and PTEN (**Figure 8**). Reduction or absence of NL3 expression leads to decreased trafficking of MAGI-2 to the plasma membrane, which results in unstable conformation and reduced function of PTEN. As a consequence, Akt/mTOR signaling pathway is hyperactivated in response to the reduced inhibitory effects of PTEN.

DISCUSSION

In summary, we have found that the defect of NL3 expression induces hyperactive Akt/mTOR signaling, which results in increased dendritic length and complexity. This aberrant outgrowth of dendrites could be reversed by both rapamycin and LY294002. Furthermore, we demonstrated that NL3 regulates Akt/mTOR signaling *via* PTEN, and MAGI-2 could function as a linker between NL3 and PTEN. Our study not only provides a detailed signaling mechanism in NL3-regulated dendritic outgrowth, but also provides a potential novel link between NL3 and the Akt/mTOR signaling pathway.

In most of our *in vitro* knockdown studies, we used dissociated hippocampal neuron culture as a neuron model because they have much uniformed cell types in culture system and therefore would be much better to elucidate the underlying mechanism of the mTOR signal transducing. However, the results we see in the KO neurons were much significant than that in the cultured knockdown hippocampal neurons as the neurons exerted greater abnormalities in soma size and dendrite extension and branching. It is probably due to the fact that KO has an immediate effect, whereas knockdown is slowly achieved (after at least 96 h). Moreover, there might be residual NL3 protein after NL3 knockdown due to the incompleteness of knockdown efficiency. In addition, the NL3-mediated regulation of neuronal morphology shows certain brain region specificities as we could observe enlarged soma and increased dendritic outgrowth in somatosensory cortex (**Figure 1**) but not in hippocampus (data not shown). Actually, differed function of NL3 in brain regions had been also reported in either NL3 KO or NL3 R451C knockin

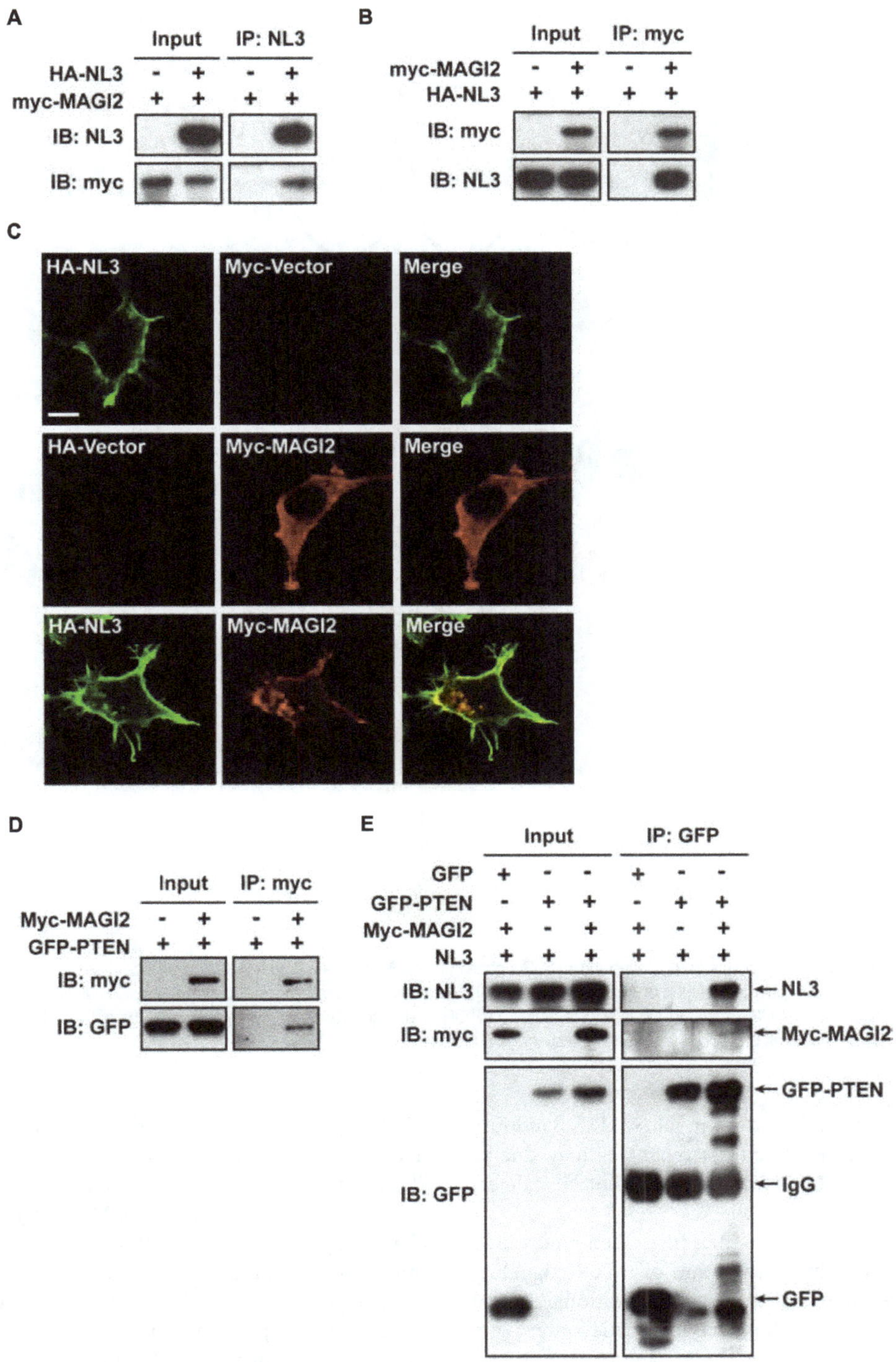

FIGURE 7 | NL3 and PTEN formed a complex via MAGI-2. **(A,B)** Co-immunoprecipitation assays confirmed the interaction between NL3 and MAGI-2. HEK293T cells co-transfected with HA-NL3 and Myc-MAGI-2 plasmids or control plasmids were processed for co-IP assays using either NL3 antibody or myc antibody. Myc-MAGI-2 was pulled down together with HA-NL3 **(A)**, so was HA-NL3 by Myc-MAGI-2 **(B)**. **(C)** Myc-MAGI-2 was co-localized with HA-NL3. Photomicrographs showed that HA antibody immunostained HA-NL3 (green) is localized specifically at plasma membrane, while myc antibody immunostained myc-MAGI-2 (red) was diffusely distributed in cytoplasm in HEK293T. When myc-MAGI-2 was co-transfected with HA-NL3, it was transported to plasma membrane and co-localized with HA-NL3. Scale bar, 10 μm. **(D)** Co-immunoprecipitation assays verified the interaction between MAGI-2 and PTEN. HEK293T cells co-transfected with myc-MAGI-2 and GFP-PTEN plasmids or control plasmids were processed for co-IP assays using myc antibody. GFP-PTEN was pulled down together with myc-MAGI-2. **(E)** Co-immunoprecipitation assays in HEK293T detected that NL3 and PTEN formed a complex via MAGI-2. HEK293T cells co-transfected with NL3, GFP-PTEN, and myc-MAGI-2 or control plasmids were processed for co-IP assays using GFP antibody. NL3 and myc-MAGI-2 were pulled down together with GFP-PTEN.

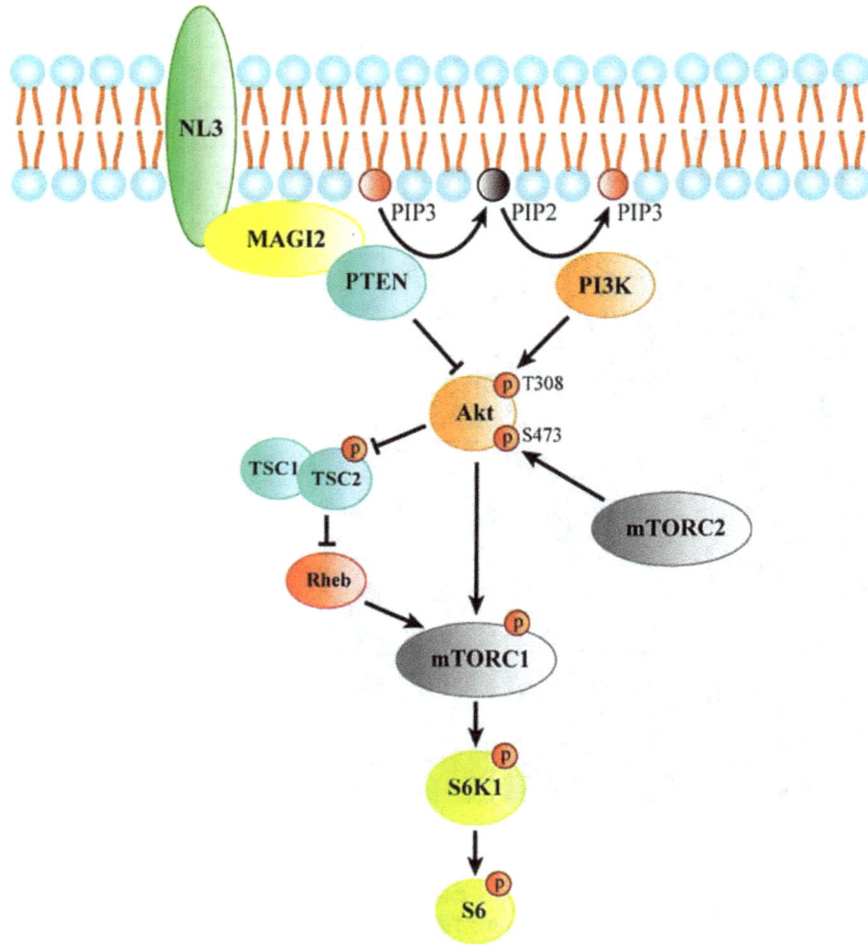

FIGURE 8 | The schematic model of the process of regulating Akt/mTOR signaling by NL3. NL3 recruiting MAGI-2 to plasma membrane which could bind and stabilize PTEN to suppress the Thr308 phosphorylation of Akt catalyzed by PI3K. Akt activation is required not only the phosphorylation of Thr308 site, but also the phosphorylation of Ser473 site by mTORC2. Activated Akt is able to activate mTORC1 directly or via TSC/Rheb pathway. The activated mTORC1 phosphorylates its downstream kinase S6K1 which regulates protein synthesis by activating the substrate S6.

mice (Tabuchi et al., 2007; Etherton et al., 2011; Baudouin et al., 2012; Cao et al., 2018). Such discrepancies may due to the differed expression of NL3 or compensations of NL3 defect across brain regions.

Neuronal morphological abnormalities have been reported in several mouse models with hyperactivation of mTOR signaling pathway. For instance, mouse strains with conditional KO of PTEN showed thickened and elongated dendritic outgrowth, mossy fiber tract enlargement, and soma hypertrophy (Kwon et al., 2006). In disrupted-in-schizophrenia 1 (DISC1) KO adult mice, increase in phosphorylation level of S6 ribosomal protein, soma size, and number of primary dendrites was observed in newborn neurons (Kim et al., 2009). Here, we have demonstrated that the NL3 KO mice, as a monogenic model for ASD, had neuronal morphological abnormalities similar to these mouse models, which add to the evidence that the imbalanced PTEN/Akt/mTOR pathway leads to aberrant neuronal dendritic outgrowth in NL3-related autism model. Furthermore, in addition to the genetic defect in *Tsc1/2* and *Pten*, the lack of FMR1 expression, which leads to fragile X syndrome (FXS), an autism-associated disorder, also demonstrated hyperactive mTOR signaling both in KO mice and in FXS patients (Sharma et al., 2010; Hoeffer et al., 2012). Moreover, multiple autism-like behavioral phenotypes of *Fmr1* KO mice are able to be rescued by removal of S6K1, a downstream kinase of mTOR (Bhattacharya et al., 2012). Taken together with our findings, these studies indicated that hyperactivated mTOR signaling pathway is likely a common mechanism in different ASD models.

However, a study demonstrated that secreted NL3 promotes the growth of malignant glioma through inducing PI3K/mTOR signaling pathway (Venkatesh et al., 2015). Moreover, their recent study showed that when pediatric or adult gliomas are transplanted into NL3 KO mice, the neoplasms are unable to grow (Venkatesh et al., 2017). These studies seemed to be contrary to our findings which suggested that the reduction of NL3 expression in neurons facilitated the activation of Akt/mTOR signaling. We think that there might be three possibilities to explain this discrepancy. First, the upstream regulatory mechanism of the Akt/mTOR pathway in neurons and in glia may be different. We have observed different Akt response to NL3 deletion in neurons and glia, both of which were cultured from P0 littermate mice simultaneously (data not shown). Second, PTEN mutations that weaken its inhibitory effect on Akt/mTOR signaling are frequently found in many tumors including glioblastoma (Ohgaki et al., 2004; Parsa et al., 2007; Zheng et al., 2008; Koul, 2014), which causes more complicated modulation of Akt/mTOR pathway in glioblastoma, compared with normal neurons. Third, the function of soluble (the secreted form) NL3 could be different with its full-length protein, for example, their intra- and extra-cellular binding partners could be varied.

PTEN is a lipid phosphatase, whose substrates are mainly located on the plasma membrane. MAGI-2, a scaffold protein that anchors on the plasma membrane, in previous studies, was demonstrated to interact with the C-terminal PDZ binding motif of PTEN, and recruits PTEN to the membrane. Besides, the binding of MAGI-2 to PTEN not only stabilizes the structure of PTEN but also reduces its degradation, enhancing its inhibitory effect on Akt activity (Wu et al., 2000; Tolkacheva et al., 2001; Valiente et al., 2005). Here, we demonstrated an interaction between MAGI-2 and NL3, similar to the first report of an interaction between NL1 and MAGI-2 by Hirao et al. (1998). Our results suggested that the reduction of NL3 protein level and NL3-MAGI-2 interaction could impair the membrane trafficking and stabilization of PTEN, thus leading to the decreased amount of PTEN which hyperactivated Akt in NL3 knockdown neurons. However, the interaction between endogenous proteins under physiological conditions should be verified further, and substantial studies are required to fully elucidate this mechanism.

In clinical practice, rapamycin, also known as sirolimus, has been used as an immunosuppressive agent to prevent organ transplant rejection (Webster et al., 2006a,b). It was also used for the treatment of patients with lymphangioleiomyomatosis (LAM), a rare, cystic lung disease resulting from inappropriate activation of mTOR (McCormack et al., 2011). What is more, the application of rapamycin in the treatment for tuberous sclerosis, a multisystem genetic disease that features autistic manifestations in approximately 50% patients, has undergone phase III clinical trials (Kingswood et al., 2014; Franz et al., 2018). Our attempt of using rapamycin for treating cultured NL3 deficient neurons showed that it was well able to rescue the abnormalities of neuronal morphology. In view of the results here, we expect that rapamycin could be potentially a common targeting therapeutic agent for ASDs caused by various pathogenic genes. In addition, other proteins upstream or downstream in the mTOR signaling cascade could be potential drug targets for ASD treatment, for example, inhibition of PI3K subunit p110beta activity has been shown to improve the social activity in *Fmr1* KO mice (Gross et al., 2015), and administration of 4EGI-1, a blocker of eIF4E/eIF4G interaction, could effectively reverse the ASD-like behaviors in eIF4E transgenic mice and *4E-BP2*-KO mice (Gkogkas et al., 2013; Santini et al., 2013) and improve the context discrimination in *Fmr1* KO mice (Santini et al., 2017).

ETHICS STATEMENT

The animal study was reviewed and approved by the Zhejiang University.

AUTHOR CONTRIBUTIONS

JunyuX and ZW conceived and directed the project. JingX conducted the experiments involved in this manuscript. Y-LD, J-WX, T-LL, X-GH, P-HH, and QS participated in some of the experiments. LS participated in the SUnSET assay. JingX and X-ML analyzed the data. JunX, X-ML, Q-QX, LS, J-HL, ZW, and JunyuX discussed the data. JingX, X-ML, ZW, and JunyuX wrote the manuscript.

FUNDING

This work was supported by grants from the National Natural Science Foundation of China (31571049 and 31970902 to JunyuX and 81561168022 to J-HL), the Ministry of Science and Technology of China (2015CB910801 to JunyuX), the Zhejiang Provincial Natural Science Foundation of China (LR19H090001 to JunyuX), and the Key Realm R&D Program of Guangdong Province (2019B030335001 to JunyuX).

ACKNOWLEDGMENTS

We are grateful to the Core Facilities of Zhejiang University School of Medicine and Core Facilities of Zhejiang University Center for Neuroscience for technical assistance.

SUPPLEMENTARY MATERIAL

FIGURE S1 | PTEN/Akt/mTOR signaling activity in neurons with NL2 knockdown. **(A)** NL2 knockdown downregulated the phosphorylation of Akt at Thr308 site, but did not affect S6 activity and PTEN expression. Cultured rat hippocampal neurons were infected by shNL2 or control lentivirus at DIV5 and harvested for western blot analysis at DIV10. **(B)** Quantifications of NL2 and PTEN expression, and Akt and S6 phosphorylation as in panel **(A)**. The phosphorylation of Akt Thr308 was significantly decreased in neurons with NL2 knockdown, but that of Akt Ser473 and S6 was not changed. The expression level of PTEN was similar with control group. Values represent mean ± SEM, normalized to control ($n = 4$ independent experiments; $^{***}p < 0.001$, $^{*}p < 0.05$, one-sample t-test).

REFERENCES

Alessi, D. R., Andjelkovic, M., Caudwell, B., Cron, P., Morrice, N., Cohen, P., et al. (1996). Mechanism of activation of protein kinase B by insulin and IGF-1. *EMBO J.* 15, 6541–6551. doi: 10.1002/j.1460-2075.1996.tb01045.x

Alonso, M. (2004). ERK1/2 activation is necessary for BDNF to increase dendritic spine density in hippocampal CA1 pyramidal neurons. *Learn. Mem.* 11, 172–178. doi: 10.1101/lm.67804

Baudouin, S. J., Gaudias, J., Gerharz, S., Hatstatt, L., Zhou, K., Punnakkal, P., et al. (2012). Shared synaptic pathophysiology in syndromic and nonsyndromic rodent models of autism. *Science* 338, 128–132. doi: 10.1126/science.1224159

Bhattacharya, A., Kaphzan, H., Alvarez-Dieppa, A. C., Murphy, J. P., Pierre, P., and Klann, E. (2012). Genetic removal of p70 S6 kinase 1 corrects molecular, synaptic, and behavioral phenotypes in fragile X syndrome mice. *Neuron* 76, 325–337. doi: 10.1016/j.neuron.2012.07.022

Brown, E. J., Albers, M. W., Shin, T. B., Ichikawa, K., Keith, C. T., Lane, W. S., et al. (1994). A mammalian protein targeted by G1-arresting rapamycin-receptor complex. *Nature* 369, 756–758. doi: 10.1038/369756a0

Burnett, P. E., Barrow, R. K., Cohen, N. A., Snyder, S. H., and Sabatini, D. M. (1998). RAFT1 phosphorylation of the translational regulators p70 S6 kinase and 4E-BP1. *Proc. Natl. Acad. Sci. U.S.A.* 95, 1432–1437. doi: 10.1073/pnas.95.4.1432

Butler, M. G., Dasouki, M. J., Zhou, X. P., Talebizadeh, Z., Brown, M., Takahashi, T. N., et al. (2005). Subset of individuals with autism spectrum disorders and extreme macrocephaly associated with germline PTEN tumour suppressor gene mutations. *J. Med. Genet.* 42, 318–321. doi: 10.1136/jmg.2004.024646

Buxbaum, J. D., Cai, G., Chaste, P., Nygren, G., Goldsmith, J., Reichert, J., et al. (2007). Mutation screening of the PTEN gene in patients with autism spectrum disorders and macrocephaly. *Am. J. Med. Genet. Part B* 144b, 484–491. doi: 10.1002/ajmg.b.30493

Cao, W., Lin, S., Xia, Q. Q., Du, Y. L., Yang, Q., Zhang, M. Y., et al. (2018). Gamma Oscillation dysfunction in mPFC leads to social deficits in neuroligin 3 R451C knockin mice. *Neuron* 97, 1253–1260. doi: 10.1016/j.neuron.2018.02.001

Chih, B., Engelman, H., and Scheiffele, P. (2005). Control of excitatory and inhibitory synapse formation by neuroligins. *Science* 307, 1324–1328. doi: 10.1126/science.1107470

Crino, P. B., Nathanson, K. L., and Henske, E. P. (2006). The tuberous sclerosis complex. *N. Engl. J. Med.* 355, 1345–1356.

Dang, T., Duan, W. Y., Yu, B., Tong, D. L., Cheng, C., Zhang, Y. F., et al. (2018). Autism-associated Dyrk1a truncation mutants impair neuronal dendritic and spine growth and interfere with postnatal cortical development. *Mol. Psychiatr.* 23, 747–758. doi: 10.1038/mp.2016.253

Dean, C., Scholl, F. G., Choih, J., DeMaria, S., Berger, J., Isacoff, E., et al. (2003). Neurexin mediates the assembly of presynaptic terminals. *Nat. Neurosci.* 6, 708–716. doi: 10.1038/nn1074

Ehninger, D., Han, S., Shilyansky, C., Zhou, Y., Li, W., Kwiatkowski, D. J., et al. (2008). Reversal of learning deficits in a Tsc2+/- mouse model of tuberous sclerosis. *Nat. Med.* 14, 843–848. doi: 10.1038/nm1788

Etherton, M., Foldy, C., Sharma, M., Tabuchi, K., Liu, X., Shamloo, M., et al. (2011). Autism-linked neuroligin-3 R451C mutation differentially alters hippocampal and cortical synaptic function. *Proc. Natl. Acad. Sci. U.S.A.* 108, 13764–13769. doi: 10.1073/pnas.1111093108

Franz, D. N., Budde, K., Kingswood, J. C., Belousova, E., Sparagana, S., de Vries, P. J., et al. (2018). Effect of everolimus on skin lesions in patients treated for subependymal giant cell astrocytoma and renal angiomyolipoma: final 4-year results from the randomized EXIST-1 and EXIST-2 studies. *J. Eur. Acad. Dermatol. Venereol.* 32, 1796–1803. doi: 10.1111/jdv.14964

Gingras, A. C., Raught, B., and Sonenberg, N. (1999). eIF4 initiation factors: effectors of mRNA recruitment to ribosomes and regulators of translation. *Annu. Rev. Biochem.* 68, 913–963. doi: 10.1146/annurev.biochem.68.1.913

Gkogkas, C. G., Khoutorsky, A., Ran, I., Rampakakis, E., Nevarko, T., Weatherill, D. B., et al. (2013). Autism-related deficits via dysregulated eIF4E-dependent translational control. *Nature* 493, 371–377. doi: 10.1038/nature11628

Goorden, S. M., van Woerden, G. M., van der Weerd, L., Cheadle, J. P., and Elgersma, Y. (2007). Cognitive deficits in Tsc1+/- mice in the absence of cerebral lesions and seizures. *Ann. Neurol.* 62, 648–655. doi: 10.1002/ana.21317

Gross, C., Raj, N., Molinaro, G., Allen, A. G., Whyte, A. J., Gibson, J. R., et al. (2015). Selective role of the catalytic PI3K subunit p110beta in impaired higher order cognition in fragile X syndrome. *Cell Rep.* 11, 681–688. doi: 10.1016/j.celrep.2015.03.065

Hamilton, S. M., Green, J. R., Veeraragavan, S., Yuva, L., McCoy, A., Wu, Y., et al. (2014). Fmr1 and Nlgn3 knockout rats: novel tools for investigating autism spectrum disorders. *Behav. Neurosci.* 128, 103–109. doi: 10.1037/a0035988

Hausser, M., Spruston, N., and Stuart, G. J. (2000). Diversity and dynamics of dendritic signaling. *Science* 290, 739–744. doi: 10.1126/science.290.5492.739

Herman, G. E., Butter, E., Enrile, B., Pastore, M., Prior, T. W., and Sommer, A. (2007). Increasing knowledge of PTEN germline mutations: two additional patients with autism and macrocephaly. *Am. J. Med. Genet. Part A* 143, 589–593. doi: 10.1002/ajmg.a.31619

Hirao, K., Hata, Y., Ide, N., Takeuchi, M., Irie, M., Yao, I., et al. (1998). A novel multiple PDZ domain-containing molecule interacting with N-methyl-D-aspartate receptors and neuronal cell adhesion proteins. *J. Biol. Chem.* 273, 21105–21110. doi: 10.1074/jbc.273.33.21105

Hoeffer, C. A., Sanchez, E., Hagerman, R. J., Mu, Y., Nguyen, D. V., Wong, H., et al. (2012). Altered mTOR signaling and enhanced CYFIP2 expression levels in subjects with fragile X syndrome. *Genes Brain Behav.* 11, 332–341. doi: 10.1111/j.1601-183X.2012.00768.x

Jamain, S., Quach, H., Betancur, C., Rastam, M., Colineaux, C., Gillberg, I. C., et al. (2003). Mutations of the X-linked genes encoding neuroligins NLGN3 and NLGN4 are associated with autism. *Nat. Genet.* 34, 27–29. doi: 10.1038/ng1136

Jaworski, J., Spangler, S., Seeburg, D. P., Hoogenraad, C. C., and Sheng, M. (2005). Control of dendritic arborization by the phosphoinositide-3'-kinase-Akt-mammalian target of rapamycin pathway. *J. Neurosci.* 25, 11300–11312. doi: 10.1523/jneurosci.2270-05.2005

Jeno, P., Ballou, L. M., Novak-Hofer, I., and Thomas, G. (1988). Identification and characterization of a mitogen-activated S6 kinase. *Proc. Natl. Acad. Sci. U.S.A.* 85, 406–410.

Jurado, S., Benoist, M., Lario, A., Knafo, S., Petrok, C. N., and Esteban, J. A. (2010). PTEN is recruited to the postsynaptic terminal for NMDA receptor-dependent long-term depression. *EMBO J.* 29, 2827–2840. doi: 10.1038/emboj.2010.160

Kim, J. Y., Duan, X., Liu, C. Y., Jang, M. H., Guo, J. U., Pow-anpongkul, N., et al. (2009). DISC1 regulates new neuron development in the adult brain via modulation of AKT-mTOR signaling through KIAA1212. *Neuron* 63, 761–773. doi: 10.1016/j.neuron.2009.08.008

Kingswood, J. C., Jozwiak, S., Belousova, E. D., Frost, M. D., Kuperman, R. A., Bebin, E. M., et al. (2014). The effect of everolimus on renal angiomyolipoma in patients with tuberous sclerosis complex being treated for subependymal giant cell astrocytoma: subgroup results from the randomized, placebo-controlled, Phase 3 trial EXIST-1. *Nephrol. Dial. Transplant.* 29, 1203–1210. doi: 10.1093/ndt/gfu013

Koul, D. (2014). PTEN Signaling pathways in glioblastoma. *Cancer Biol. Ther.* 7, 1321–1325. doi: 10.4161/cbt.7.9.6954

Kumar, V., Zhang, M. X., Swank, M. W., Kunz, J., and Wu, G. Y. (2005). Regulation of dendritic morphogenesis by Ras-PI3K-Akt-mTOR and Ras-MAPK signaling pathways. *J. Neurosci.* 25, 11288–11299. doi: 10.1523/jneurosci.2284-05.2005

Kunz, J., Henriquez, R., Schneider, U., Deuter-Reinhard, M., Movva, N. R., and Hall, M. N. (1993). Target of rapamycin in yeast, TOR2, is an essential phosphatidylinositol kinase homolog required for G1 progression. *Cell* 73, 585–596. doi: 10.1016/0092-8674(93)90144-f

Kwan, V., Meka, D. P., White, S. H., Hung, C. L., Holzapfel, N. T., Walker, S., et al. (2016). DIXDC1 phosphorylation and control of dendritic morphology are impaired by rare genetic variants. *Cell Rep.* 17, 1892–1904. doi: 10.1016/j.celrep.2016.10.047

Kwon, C. H., Luikart, B. W., Powell, C. M., Zhou, J., Matheny, S. A., Zhang, W., et al. (2006). Pten regulates neuronal arborization and social interaction in mice. *Neuron* 50, 377–388. doi: 10.1016/j.neuron.2006.03.023

Manning, B. D., and Toker, A. (2017). AKT/PKB signaling: navigating the network. *Cell* 169, 381–405. doi: 10.1016/j.cell.2017.04.001

McAllister, A. K., Katz, L. C., and Lo, D. C. (1997). Opposing roles for endogenous BDNF and NT-3 in regulating cortical dendritic growth. *Neuron* 18, 767–778. doi: 10.1016/s0896-6273(00)80316-5

McAllister, A. K., Lo, D. C., and Katz, L. C. (1995). Neurotrophins regulate dendritic growth in developing visual cortex. *Neuron* 15, 791–803. doi: 10.1016/0896-6273(95)90171-x

McCormack, F. X., Inoue, Y., Moss, J., Singer, L. G., Strange, C., Nakata, K., et al. (2011). Efficacy and safety of sirolimus in lymphangioleiomyomatosis. *N. Engl. J. Med.* 364, 1595–1606. doi: 10.1056/NEJMoa1100391

Montani, C., Ramos-Brossier, M., Ponzoni, L., Gritti, L., Cwetsch, A. W., Braida, D., et al. (2017). The X-linked intellectual disability protein IL1RAPL1 regulates dendrite complexity. *J. Neurosci.* 37, 6606–6627. doi: 10.1523/JNEUROSCI.3775-16.2017

Nagashima, S., Kodaka, M., Iwasa, H., and Hata, Y. (2015). MAGI2/S-SCAM outside brain. *J. Biochem.* 157, 177–184. doi: 10.1093/jb/mvv009

Ohgaki, H., Dessen, P., Jourde, B., Horstmann, S., Nishikawa, T., Di Patre, P. L., et al. (2004). Genetic pathways to glioblastoma: a population-based study. *Cancer Res.* 64, 6892–6899. doi: 10.1158/0008-5472.can-04-1337

Orrico, A., Galli, L., Buoni, S., Orsi, A., Vonella, G., and Sorrentino, V. (2009). Novel PTEN mutations in neurodevelopmental disorders and macrocephaly. *Clin. Genet.* 75, 195–198. doi: 10.1111/j.1399-0004.2008.01074.x

Pardo, C. A., and Eberhart, C. G. (2007). The neurobiology of autism. *Brain Pathol.* 17, 434–447.

Parsa, A. T., Waldron, J. S., Panner, A., Crane, C. A., Parney, I. F., Barry, J. J., et al. (2007). Loss of tumor suppressor PTEN function increases B7-H1 expression and immunoresistance in glioma. *Nat. Med.* 13, 84–88. doi: 10.1038/nm1517

Radyushkin, K., Hammerschmidt, K., Boretius, S., Varoqueaux, F., El-Kordi, A., Ronnenberg, A., et al. (2009). Neuroligin-3-deficient mice: model of a monogenic heritable form of autism with an olfactory deficit. *Genes Brain Behav.* 8, 416–425. doi: 10.1111/j.1601-183X.2009.00487.x

Rothwell, P. E., Fuccillo, M. V., Maxeiner, S., Hayton, S. J., Gokce, O., Lim, B. K., et al. (2014). Autism-associated neuroligin-3 mutations commonly impair striatal circuits to boost repetitive behaviors. *Cell* 158, 198–212. doi: 10.1016/j.cell.2014.04.045

Santini, E., Huynh, T. N., Longo, F., Koo, S. Y., Mojica, E., D'Andrea, L., et al. (2017). Reducing eIF4E-eIF4G interactions restores the balance between protein synthesis and actin dynamics in fragile X syndrome model mice. *Sci. Signal.* 10:eaan0665. doi: 10.1126/scisignal.aan0665

Santini, E., Huynh, T. N., MacAskill, A. F., Carter, A. G., Pierre, P., Ruggero, D., et al. (2013). Exaggerated translation causes synaptic and behavioural aberrations associated with autism. *Nature* 493, 411–415. doi: 10.1038/nature11782

Sarbassov, D. D., Ali, S. M., Sengupta, S., Sheen, J. H., Hsu, P. P., Bagley, A. F., et al. (2006). Prolonged rapamycin treatment inhibits mTORC2 assembly and Akt/PKB. *Mol. Cell.* 22, 159–168. doi: 10.1016/j.molcel.2006.03.029

Sarbassov, D. D., Guertin, D. A., Ali, S. M., and Sabatini, D. M. (2005). Phosphorylation and regulation of Akt/PKB by the rictor-mTOR complex. *Science* 307, 1098–1101. doi: 10.1126/science.1106148

Sato, A., Kasai, S., Kobayashi, T., Takamatsu, Y., Hino, O., Ikeda, K., et al. (2012). Rapamycin reverses impaired social interaction in mouse models of tuberous sclerosis complex. *Nat. Commun.* 3:1292. doi: 10.1038/ncomms2295

Scheiffele, P., Fan, J., Choih, J., Fetter, R., and Serafini, T. (2000). Neuroligin expressed in nonneuronal cells triggers presynaptic development in contacting axons. *Cell* 101, 657–669. doi: 10.1016/s0092-8674(00)80877-6

Schmidt, E. K., Clavarino, G., Ceppi, M., and Pierre, P. (2009). SUnSET, a nonradioactive method to monitor protein synthesis. *Nat. Methods* 6, 275–277. doi: 10.1038/nmeth.1314

Sharma, A., Hoeffer, C. A., Takayasu, Y., Miyawaki, T., McBride, S. M., Klann, E., et al. (2010). Dysregulation of mTOR signaling in fragile X syndrome. *J. Neurosci.* 30, 694–702. doi: 10.1523/JNEUROSCI.3696-09.2010

Shen, Y., Qin, H., Chen, J., Mou, L., He, Y., Yan, Y., et al. (2016). Postnatal activation of TLR4 in astrocytes promotes excitatory synaptogenesis in hippocampal neurons. *J. Cell Biol.* 215, 719–734. doi: 10.1083/jcb.201605046

Sumita, K., Sato, Y., Iida, J., Kawata, A., Hamano, M., Hirabayashi, S., et al. (2007). Synaptic scaffolding molecule (S-SCAM) membrane-associated guanylate kinase with inverted organization (MAGI)-2 is associated with cell adhesion molecules at inhibitory synapses in rat hippocampal neurons. *J. Neurochem.* 100, 154–166. doi: 10.1111/j.1471-4159.2006.04170.x

Tabuchi, K., Blundell, J., Etherton, M. R., Hammer, R. E., Liu, X., Powell, C. M., et al. (2007). A neuroligin-3 mutation implicated in autism increases inhibitory synaptic transmission in mice. *Science* 318, 71–76. doi: 10.1126/science.1146221

Takei, N., Inamura, N., Kawamura, M., Namba, H., Hara, K., Yonezawa, K., et al. (2004). Brain-derived neurotrophic factor induces mammalian target of rapamycin-dependent local activation of translation machinery and protein synthesis in neuronal dendrites. *J. Neurosci.* 24, 9760–9769. doi: 10.1523/jneurosci.1427-04.2004

Tolkacheva, T., Boddapati, M., Sanfiz, A., Tsuchida, K., Kimmelman, A. C., and Chan, A. M. (2001). Regulation of PTEN binding to MAGI-2 by two putative phosphorylation sites at threonine 382 and 383. *Cancer Res.* 61, 4985–4989.

Urbanska, M., Gozdz, A., Swiech, L. J., and Jaworski, J. (2012). Mammalian target of rapamycin complex 1 (mTORC1) and 2 (mTORC2) control the dendritic arbor morphology of hippocampal neurons. *J. Biol. Chem.* 287, 30240–30256. doi: 10.1074/jbc.M112.374405

Valiente, M., Andres-Pons, A., Gomar, B., Torres, J., Gil, A., Tapparel, C., et al. (2005). Binding of PTEN to specific PDZ domains contributes to PTEN protein stability and phosphorylation by microtubule-associated serine/threonine kinases. *J. Biol. Chem.* 280, 28936–28943. doi: 10.1074/jbc.m504761200

Vander Haar, E., Lee, S. I., Bandhakavi, S., Griffin, T. J., and Kim, D. H. (2007). Insulin signalling to mTOR mediated by the Akt/PKB substrate PRAS40. *Nat. Cell Biol.* 9, 316–323. doi: 10.1038/ncb1547

Venkatesh, H. S., Johung, T. B., Caretti, V., Noll, A., Tang, Y., Nagaraja, S., et al. (2015). Neuronal activity promotes glioma growth through neuroligin-3 secretion. *Cell* 161, 803–816. doi: 10.1016/j.cell.2015.04.012

Venkatesh, H. S., Tam, L. T., Woo, P. J., Lennon, J., Nagaraja, S., Gillespie, S. M., et al. (2017). Targeting neuronal activity-regulated neuroligin-3 dependency in high-grade glioma. *Nature* 549, 533–537. doi: 10.1038/nature24014

Vlahos, C. J., Matter, W. F., Hui, K. Y., and Brown, R. F. (1994). A specific inhibitor of phosphatidylinositol 3-kinase, 2-(4-morpholinyl)-8-phenyl-4H-1-benzopyran-4-one (LY294002). *J. Biol. Chem.* 269, 5241–5248.

Webster, A. C., Lee, V. W., Chapman, J. R., and Craig, J. C. (2006a). Target of rapamycin inhibitors (sirolimus and everolimus) for primary immunosuppression of kidney transplant recipients: a systematic review and meta-analysis of randomized trials. *Transplantation* 81, 1234–1248. doi: 10.1097/01.tp.0000219703.39149.85

Webster, A. C., Lee, V. W., Chapman, J. R., and Craig, J. C. (2006b). Target of rapamycin inhibitors (TOR-I; sirolimus and everolimus) for primary immunosuppression in kidney transplant recipients. *Cochrane Database Syst. Rev.* 19:Cd004290.

Wu, X., Hepner, K., Castelino-Prabhu, S., Do, D., Kaye, M. B., Yuan, X. J., et al. (2000). Evidence for regulation of the PTEN tumor suppressor by a membrane-localized multi-PDZ domain containing scaffold protein MAGI-2. *Proc. Natl. Acad. Sci. U.S.A.* 97, 4233–4238. doi: 10.1073/pnas.97.8.4233

Xia, Q. Q., Xu, J., Liao, T. L., Yu, J., Shi, L., Xia, J., et al. (2019). Neuroligins differentially mediate subtype-specific synapse formation in pyramidal neurons and interneurons. *Neurosci. Bull.* 35, 497–506. doi: 10.1007/s12264-019-00347-y

Xu, J., Wang, N., Luo, J. H., and Xia, J. (2016). Syntabulin regulates the trafficking of PICK1-containing vesicles in neurons. *Sci. Rep.* 6:20924. doi: 10.1038/srep20924

Zhang, L., Bartley, C. M., Gong, X., Hsieh, L. S., Lin, T. V., Feliciano, D. M., et al. (2014). MEK-ERK1/2-dependent FLNA overexpression promotes abnormal dendritic patterning in tuberous sclerosis independent of mTOR. *Neuron* 84, 78–91. doi: 10.1016/j.neuron.2014.09.009

Zheng, H., Ying, H., Yan, H., Kimmelman, A. C., Hiller, D. J., Chen, A. J., et al. (2008). p53 and Pten control neural and glioma stem/progenitor cell renewal and differentiation. *Nature* 455, 1129–1133. doi: 10.1038/nature07443

Zhou, J., and Parada, L. F. (2012). PTEN signaling in autism spectrum disorders. *Curr. Opin. Neurobiol.* 22, 873–879. doi: 10.1016/j.conb.2012.05.004

14

mTOR Suppresses Macroautophagy During Striatal Postnatal Development and is Hyperactive in Mouse Models of Autism Spectrum Disorders

*Ori J. Lieberman[1,2], Veronica Cartocci[3], Irena Pigulevskiy[2], Maya Molinari[3], Josep Carbonell[3], Miguel Bellés Broseta[3], Michael R. Post[1], David Sulzer[1], Anders Borgkvist[3] and Emanuela Santini[2,3]**

[1] *Division of Molecular Therapeutics, Department of Psychiatry, Columbia University Vagelos College of Physicians and Surgeons, New York, NY, United States,* [2] *Division of Movement Disorders, Department of Neurology, Columbia University Vagelos College of Physicians and Surgeons, New York, NY, United States,* [3] *Department of Neuroscience, Karolinska Institute, Stockholm, Sweden*

***Correspondence:**
Emanuela Santini
emanuela.santini@ki.se

Macroautophagy (hereafter referred to as autophagy) plays a critical role in neuronal function related to development and degeneration. Here, we investigated whether autophagy is developmentally regulated in the striatum, a brain region implicated in neurodevelopmental disease. We demonstrate that autophagic flux is suppressed during striatal postnatal development, reaching adult levels around postnatal day 28 (P28). We also find that mTOR signaling, a key regulator of autophagy, increases during the same developmental period. We further show that mTOR signaling is responsible for suppressing autophagy, via regulation of Beclin-1 and VPS34 activity. Finally, we discover that autophagy is downregulated during late striatal postnatal development (P28) in mice with *in utero* exposure to valproic acid (VPA), an established mouse model of autism spectrum disorder (ASD). VPA-exposed mice also display deficits in striatal neurotransmission and social behavior. Correction of hyperactive mTOR signaling in VPA-exposed mice restores social behavior. These results demonstrate that neurons coopt metabolic signaling cascades to developmentally regulate autophagy and provide additional evidence that mTOR-dependent signaling pathways represent pathogenic signaling cascades in ASD mouse models that are active during specific postnatal windows.

Keywords: striatum, development, autophagy, mTOR, autism, valproic acid

INTRODUCTION

Best characterized in studies of brewer's yeast, macroautophagy (hereafter referred to as autophagy) is a degradative process for long-lived proteins and damaged organelles (Ohsumi, 2014). In neurons, autophagy is considered to play both protective and pathogenic roles, as it contributes not only to proteostasis and cell survival (Hara et al., 2006; Komatsu et al., 2006; Yamamoto et al., 2006; Yamamoto and Simonsen, 2011), but also to autophagic cell death in neurodegenerative diseases (González-Polo et al., 2005; Wang et al., 2006; Chakrabarti et al., 2009; Yang et al., 2011; Yamamoto and Yue, 2014). Recently, autophagy has been recognized as an important cellular process during neuronal development (Shen and Ganetzky, 2009; Tang et al., 2014; Dragich et al., 2016; Stavoe et al., 2016; Kim et al., 2017; Lieberman et al., 2019a). Autophagic dysfunction is observed in humans with neurodevelopmental disorders (Lee et al., 2013; Poultney et al., 2013; Byrne et al., 2016; Hor and Tang, 2018), and mouse models with reduced autophagy display phenotypes implicated in autism spectrum disorders (ASD) (Tang et al., 2014; Kim et al., 2017; Yan et al., 2018). Importantly, autophagic dysfunction is found in both genetic and environmental animal models of ASD, suggesting its impairment may be a general feature of ASD pathophysiology (Tang et al., 2014; Qin et al., 2016; Zhang et al., 2016, 2019; Wu et al., 2018; Yan et al., 2018). Notably, rodents prenatally exposed to valproic acid (VPA) show a reduction in brain autophagy accompanied by a series of morphological alterations and behavioral impairments consistent with the ASD symptomatology described in patients (Qin et al., 2016; Zhang et al., 2016; Wu et al., 2018; Zhang et al., 2019). Yet, little is known about the developmental regulation of neuronal autophagy and the possible implications for ASD.

Recently, the striatum, which is the main input nucleus of the basal ganglia, a brain circuit controlling action selection and reward processing, has been implicated in the pathophysiology of multiple neurodevelopmental diseases including ASD (Gerfen and Surmeier, 2011; Fuccillo, 2016). Moreover, the principal neurons of the striatum, the spiny projection neurons (SPNs), although they migrate to the striatum during the embryonic period (Song and Harlan, 1994), undergo a significant maturation during the first four postnatal weeks. SPNs receive excitatory inputs from the cortex and thalamus during the second and third postnatal weeks (Tepper et al., 1998). Dopaminergic axons innervate the striatum at birth but their ability to release neurotransmitter increases during the first 2 weeks (Voorn et al., 1988; Lieberman et al., 2018). Finally, the intrinsic excitability of SPNs matures from weeks two through four (Tepper et al., 1998; Peixoto et al., 2016). Notably, autophagy has been proposed to contribute to synaptic maturation and plasticity and dopamine release (Hernandez et al., 2012; Tang et al., 2014; Nikoletopoulou et al., 2017). Thus, establishing whether autophagy is differentially regulated during postnatal development of the striatum and determining whether this temporal regulation is impaired in ASD would provide insights into its role in neurodevelopmental disorders.

Autophagy is a tightly regulated multi-step process (Bento et al., 2016) that, in dividing cells is controlled by energy balance (i.e., nutrient status) and metabolic kinases, including the mammalian target of rapamycin (mTOR). mTOR regulates autophagy via several mechanisms (He and Klionsky, 2009), including by phosphorylating and negatively regulating Unc-51-like autophagy-activating kinase 1 (ULK1) at Ser757 (Jung et al., 2009; Kim et al., 2011). This step prevents ULK1-mediated phosphorylation of Beclin-1 at Ser14, and the subsequent increase of PI3K activity of Vps34 (Russell et al., 2013). These molecular events initiate the formation of preautophagic structures that are subsequently expanded by a molecular cascade resulting in the modification of LC3, one of the mammalian homologs of the yeast Atg8 (Shpilka et al., 2011). Processing of LC3 leads to phagophore expansion and sealing and is used as a biochemical readout of autophagosome formation (Kabeya et al., 2000; Klionsky et al., 2016). The enclosed, mature autophagosome then traffics to the lysosome where the autophagic cargo and cargo adaptors, such as p62, are degraded (Tanida et al., 2005).

Whether similar signaling regulates autophagy in neurons remains controversial. It has been proposed that autophagy may act as a constitutive process for cellular homeostasis, thus circumventing the control of metabolic kinases such as mTOR (Yamamoto and Yue, 2014). The links between nutrient status and autophagy in neurons moreover remain elusive, with reports suggesting a regional and age-specific autophagic response to nutrient deprivation in neurons (Kaushik et al., 2011; Nikoletopoulou et al., 2017) and studies indicating the contrary (Mizushima et al., 2004). Moreover, direct regulation of autophagy by mTOR, independent of nutrient status, has been reported by some (Hernandez et al., 2012; Tang et al., 2014) but not others (Tsvetkov et al., 2010; Maday and Holzbaur, 2016). These contrasting results raise important questions concerning the control of autophagic activity in brain regions implicated in neurodevelopmental diseases, the molecular changes associated with pathologic conditions and the nature of signaling pathways that regulate autophagy in neurons (i.e., signaling operating during nutrient deprivation-induced autophagy in non-neuronal cells).

Using biochemical, pharmacological and histological approaches, we first demonstrate that in SPNs autophagy is dynamically downregulated during postnatal development, following the upregulation of mTOR activity. Then we employ the VPA model of ASD which has construct, face and predictive validity (Chomiak et al., 2013; Roullet et al., 2013; Nicolini and Fahnestock, 2018) to show that in the striatum of ASD model mice, autophagy is specifically reduced during a discrete developmental window (P28). At the same postnatal age, we also observe changes in excitatory synaptic transmission. Finally, we find that mice exposed to VPA *in utero* display a social deficit and that systemic treatment with rapamycin, an inhibitor of mTOR, normalizes it. Our results suggest that autophagy may play temporally-specific roles in brain postnatal development and that it may be one of the pathogenic signaling pathways implicated in neurodevelopmental disorders and ASD.

RESULTS

Markers of Autophagic Activity Decrease During Striatal Postnatal Development

To identify changes in autophagic activity during postnatal striatal development, we collected striata from mice at postnatal days 10, 14, 18, 28 and in adults (postnatal day 120; Tepper et al., 1998; Peixoto et al., 2016; Lieberman et al., 2018). These postnatal ages represent critical timepoints for striatal development. Briefly, synaptic dopamine release has begun and interneurons have begun to mature in the striatum at postnatal day 10 (Plotkin et al., 2005; Ferrari et al., 2012; Lieberman et al., 2018).

By postnatal day 14, excitatory inputs from the cortex and thalamus arrive and eye opening has occurred, providing higher levels of sensory input. P18 represents the end of synaptogenesis and an age immediately before weaning. At age P28, the period of postnatal refinement has ended (Tepper et al., 1998). We compared tissue from these ages to mice in early adulthood at postnatal day 120.

We first measured the levels of DARPP32, a classic SPN marker, and actin as a loading control across postnatal development and found no differences (**Figure 1A**). We then measured the level of total and processed form of the Atg8 family member, LC3B (Tanida et al., 2005; Klionsky et al., 2016). We found a significant effect of age on the levels of processed LC3B (LC3B-ii) relative to actin and unprocessed LC3B (LC3B-i) (**Figures 1A–C**). The level of the autophagic adapter protein, p62, whose steady-state levels are determined by its own autophagic degradation, increased over the postnatal period (**Figure 1D**). These data suggest that overall autophagic activity decreases during the first four postnatal weeks.

LC3 + Puncta Decrease in Striatal Spiny Projection Neurons During Postnatal Development

Western blot analysis of total striatal lysates includes proteins from all cell types present in the striatum, including neurons, glia, and vascular cells. To define the cell type in which the developmental changes in autophagy occur, we utilized a transgenic mouse ubiquitously expressing LC3 fused to both green (GFP) and red fluorescent proteins (RFPs) (**Supplementary Figure S1A**; tandem fluorescent-tagged LC3 or tfLC3) (Li et al., 2014). After processing, LC3 transitions from the cytosol to become membrane-bound on the autophagosome (LC3B-ii). Visualizing the distribution of fluorophore-tagged LC3 (LC3 puncta) provides a well-established assay for monitoring autophagic activity within a cell (Klionsky et al., 2016). Furthermore, as the fluorescence of the GFP component is quenched by the low pH of the lysosome, tfLC3 permits analysis of the total number of autophagosomes and autolysosomes (RFP + puncta) and non-acidified autophagosomes (GFP + RFP + puncta).

We first used 2-photon microscopy to simultaneously image GFP and RFP signals in acute brain slices tfLC3 mice at age P10 and P28 (**Supplementary Figures S1B,C**). At both ages, GFP fluorescence was diffuse in the cytosol and processes of striatal cells and RFP + puncta were present in the soma. The density of the striatal neuropil prevented analysis of tfLC3 + puncta in axons or dendrites (**Supplementary Figures S1B,C**). Because the level of GFP fluorescence was too strong in the soma to discern individual puncta, we used the number of RFP puncta as a proxy for autophagosomes, with the caveat that we were unable to determine whether these puncta were also fused with lysosomes.

To identify the number of RFP + puncta in specific cell types, we perfused mice at age P10 and P28 and co-labeled with cell-type specific markers of striatal neurons. Spiny projection neurons can be identified by immunostaining with antibodies against DARPP-32. We observed a significant decrease in RFP + puncta in DARPP32 + cells between P10 and P28 (**Figures 1E–G**), indicating that the reduction in autophagic activity occurs in SPNs. To determine whether autophagy is similarly regulated in other striatal cells, we quantified the number of RFP + puncta in DARPP32- cells. We did not find a significant difference in the number of RPF + puncta in DARRP32- cells between P10 and P28 (P10 = 15 ± 3.14 and P28 = 22.43 ± 4.12; Unpaired, two-tailed t-test, ns; N = 3 mice/age). These results suggest that the reduction in autophagic activity we measured using biochemical assays of striatal lysates occurs specifically in SPNs.

Autophagosome Biosynthesis Is Suppressed During Postnatal Development

Changes in the level of LC3B-ii, or the number of LC3 puncta, can arise from increases in autophagosome biosynthesis or decreases in the efficiency of autophagosome maturation and lysosomal degradation. To dissect the changes in autophagy during the postnatal period, we developed an *ex vivo* system to test the effects of drugs that do not cross the blood-brain barrier (**Figure 2A**). We generated acute brain slices from P10 or P28 mice and removed non-striatal tissue. We found that neither the slice procedure nor the incubation affected the age-dependent reduction in autophagy markers observed *in vivo* (**Figures 2A,B** compared to **Figure 1**). This confirms that the mechanisms underlying changes in autophagic markers during postnatal development can be defined using this *ex vivo* system.

We incubated slices from mice at age P10 and P28 with bafilomycin A1 (BafA1, 100 nM), a specific inhibitor of the vacuolar proton pump, or vehicle (DMSO, 0.1%) for 3 h, an incubation time similar to that used in cultured cells (Klionsky et al., 2016), to prevent lysosomal acidification and block autophagosome-lysosome fusion. As treatment with BafA1 prevents LC3B-ii degradation, changes in LC3B-ii levels following BafA1 treatment are interpreted as the rate of autophagosome biosynthesis. BafA1 treatment increased LC3B-ii in slices from P10 mice but, had no significant effect in slices from P28 mice (**Figures 2C,D**). BafA1 treatment had no effect on DARPP32 levels at either age (**Figure 2C**). Slices from either age treated with BafA1 for 1 h showed no change in LC3B-ii levels (data not shown). This suggests that the higher baseline level of LC3B-ii at P10 arises from increased autophagosome biosynthesis.

mTOR Signaling Is Upregulated During the Postnatal Development

mTOR signaling is a key negative regulator of autophagic activity. We therefore hypothesized that mTOR activity in the striatum increases during postnatal development and suppresses autophagy.

mTOR kinase activity can be monitored by measuring the state of phosphorylation of its downstream targets. The level of phosphorylation at serine 757 of ULK1, which is phosphorylated by mTOR and inhibits ULK1 kinase activity (Kim et al., 2011), increased during the postnatal period in the striatum (**Figures 3A–C**). We then confirmed that ULK1

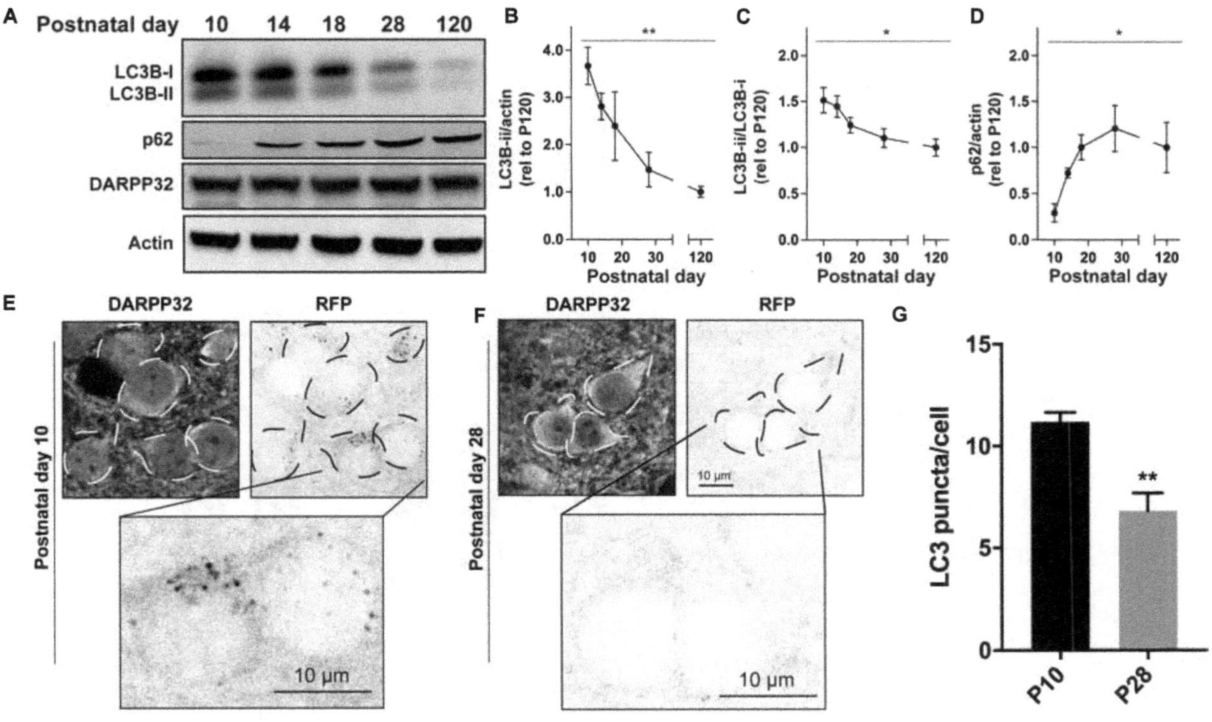

FIGURE 1 | Autophagy decreases during striatal development. **(A)** Representative Western blot images for LC3B, p62, DARPP32, and actin. Quantification of **(B)** LC3B-ii relative to actin, **(C)** LC3B-ii relative to LC3B-i, **(D)** p62 relative to actin normalized to P120 values. Data analyzed with one-way ANOVA; **(B)** Age: $F_{(4,21)} = 6.526$, $p = 0.0014$; **(C)** Age: $F_{(4,22)} = 3.797$, $p = 0.0171$; **(D)** Age: $F_{(4,15)} = 3.762$, $p = 0.0260$. $^{*}p < 0.05$, $^{**}p < 0.01$, n = 4–6 mice/age. **(E,F)** Representative images of DARPP32 stained striatal neurons and RFP fluorescence from mice aged P10 and P28. Dashed lines indicate cell body outlines. **(G)** Quantification of number of LC3 puncta/cell. Unpaired, two-tailed t-test, $t_4 = 4.392$, $p = 0.0118$. N = 3 mice/age, 20–50 cells were analyzed per mouse.

kinase activity is inhibited by monitoring the phosphorylation state of Beclin-1, a ULK1 target. Phosphorylation of Beclin-1 at serine 14 decreased during postnatal development (**Figures 3A–C**). mTOR activity also leads to the indirect phosphorylation of the ribosomal protein S6 (rpS6) on serine 240 and serine 244, via activation of the S6 kinase 1 [S6K1; **Figure 3A** (Magnuson et al., 2012)]. We observed a sharp increase in rpS6 Ser240/244 at P18 before decreasing into adulthood (**Figures 3B,D**). Overall these data indicate an increase in mTOR activity during striatal postnatal development. Interestingly, we did not observe a significant effect of age on phosphorylation of ERK1/2 (**Figures 3B,D**) suggesting that increased mTOR activity during the postnatal period is not associated with a global change in molecular signaling.

mTOR and vps34 Regulate LC3B-ii Levels During Striatal Postnatal Development

mTOR negatively regulates autophagosome biosynthesis by inhibiting ULK1 activity (Jung et al., 2009; Kim et al., 2011). When ULK1 is active, it promotes autophagosome formation by phosphorylating Beclin-1, which increases the PI3K activity of its partner, Vps34 (Russell et al., 2013). To address whether elevated autophagy at P10 was a result of enhanced Vps34 activity, we incubated acute striatal slices with the Vps34 inhibitor, SAR405 (1 μM) or vehicle (DMSO, 0.1%) for 3 h (Ronan et al., 2014). SAR405 significantly reduced the level of LC3B-ii in slices from mice at age P10 but had no effect on slices from P28 mice (**Figures 4A–C**). This demonstrates that elevated autophagic activity in the striatum of early postnatal mice is Vps34-dependent. The lack of effect of SAR405 on autophagic activity at P28 indicates that reduced Vps34 activity, possibly via increased mTOR signaling (**Figure 3**), is responsible for the lower levels of autophagic flux at P28. As predicted SAR405 does not change the levels of phosphorylated Beclin-1 at P10 (veh: 100 ± 9.433 and SAR405: 103.2 ± 6.982; Unpaired, two-tailed t-test, ns. n = 4 slices/3 mice) and P28 (veh: 100 ± 11.89 and SAR405: 85.29 ± 6.813; Unpaired, two-tailed t-test, ns. n = 5 slices/3 mice), indicating that there are no regulatory loops altering the activation of Beclin-1 in response to inhibition of Vsp34 activity.

Having shown that Vps34 drives elevated autophagy at P10, we explored whether enhanced mTOR activity inhibits autophagy at P28. mTOR activity can be pharmacologically inhibited by direct active site inhibitors, such as Torin-1 (Thoreen et al., 2009). We incubated striatal slices from mice at P28 with Torin-1 (5 μM) or vehicle (DMSO, 0.1%) for 3 h and measured LC3B-ii levels. Torin-1 treatment increased LC3B-ii levels and the phosphorylation of Beclin-1 at the ULK1 site (Ser14), suggesting that mTOR inhibition activates autophagy in a ULK1/Beclin-1 dependent manner (**Figures 4D–F**).

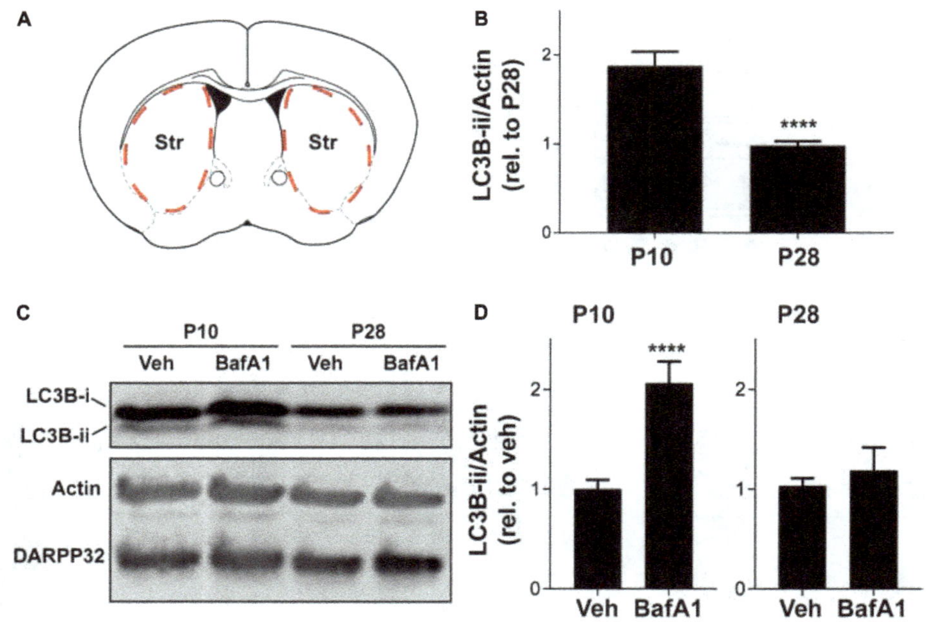

FIGURE 2 | Striatal autophagic flux decreases from P10 to P28. **(A)** Schematic of coronal brain section showing dissection boundaries for *ex vivo* experiments. **(B)** Quantification of LC3B-ii relative to actin for every vehicle-only slice showed in **Figures 4**, **5**. Unpaired, two-tailed *t*-test, $t_{52} = 5.824$, ****$p < 0.0001$. **(C)** Representative Western blot images of actin, DARPP32 and LC3B in slices obtained from P10 or P28 mice, incubated with BafA1 (100 nM, 3 h) or vehicle (Veh; DMSO, 0.1%). **(D)** LC3B-ii relative to actin, normalized to vehicle condition at each age. P10: unpaired, two-tailed *t*-test, $t_{25} = 5.113$, ****$p < 0.0001$; P28: unpaired, two-tailed *t*-test, $t_{10} = 0.6228$, $p = 0.5473$. P10: Veh: $n = 16$ slices, BafA1 $n = 11$ slices from 4 to 6 mice. P28: Veh: $n = 6$ slices, BafA1 $n = 6$ slices from three mice.

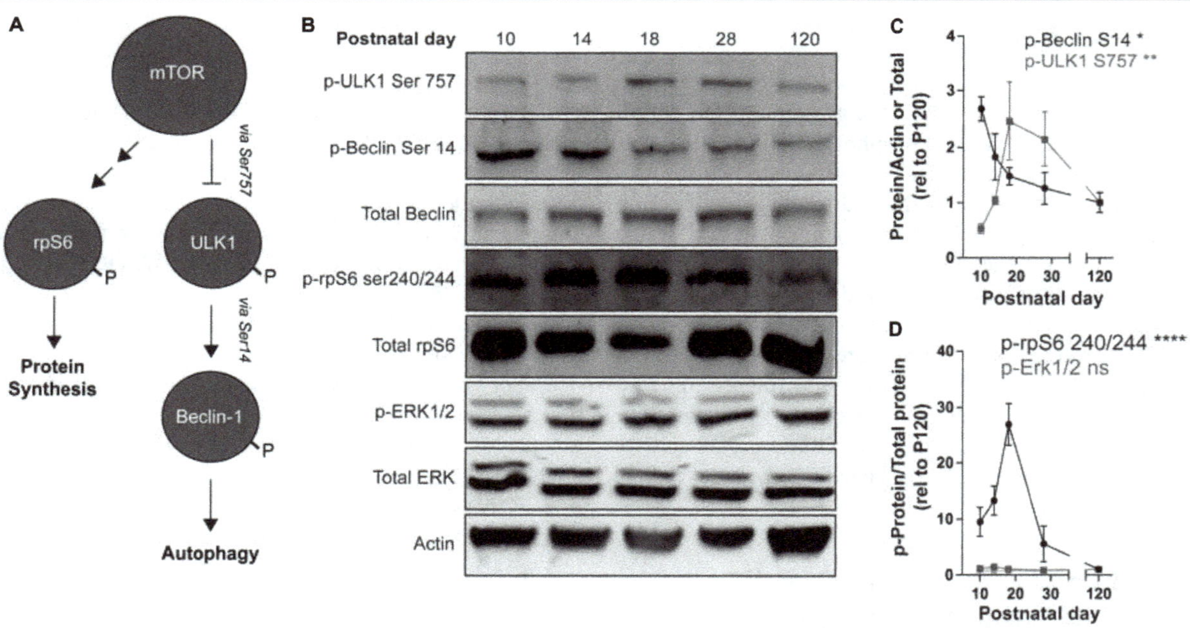

FIGURE 3 | mTOR signaling increases during striatal development. **(A)** Schematic representation of mTOR targets. mTOR inhibits ULK1 activity by phosphorylating Ser757. P-ULK1 activates Vps34 activity (not shown) by phosphorylating Beclin-1 on Ser14. mTOR promotes protein synthesis by activation of S6K-1 (not shown), which phosphorylates rpS6 on Ser240/244. The single and double arrows indicate direct (i.e., ULK1, Beclin-1) and indirect (i.e., rpS6) downstream targets, respectively. **(B)** Representative Western blot images quantified in **(C,D)**. **(C)** Quantification of pULK1 S757 relative to actin (gray squares) and p-Beclin S14 relative to total Beclin-1 (black dots). Data analyzed with one-way ANOVA; p-ULK1 S757/actin: age: $F_{(4,13)} = 6.093$, $p = 0.0055$; p-Beclin-1S14/total Beclin-1: age: $F_{(4,14)} = 4.945$, $p = 0.0107$. **(D)** Quantification of p-rpS6 S240/244 and p-Erk1/2 relative to total rpS6 and total Erk1/2, respectively. Data analyzed with one-way ANOVA; p-rpS6 240/244: age: $F_{(4,20)} = 12.69$, $p < 0.0001$. p-Erk1: age: $F_{(4,17)} = 2.625$, $p = 0.0712$. p-Erk2: age: $F_{(4,17)} = 0.3561$, $p = 0.8362$. $N = 3$–6 mice/age. *$p < 0.05$, **$p < 0.01$, ****$p < 0.0001$.

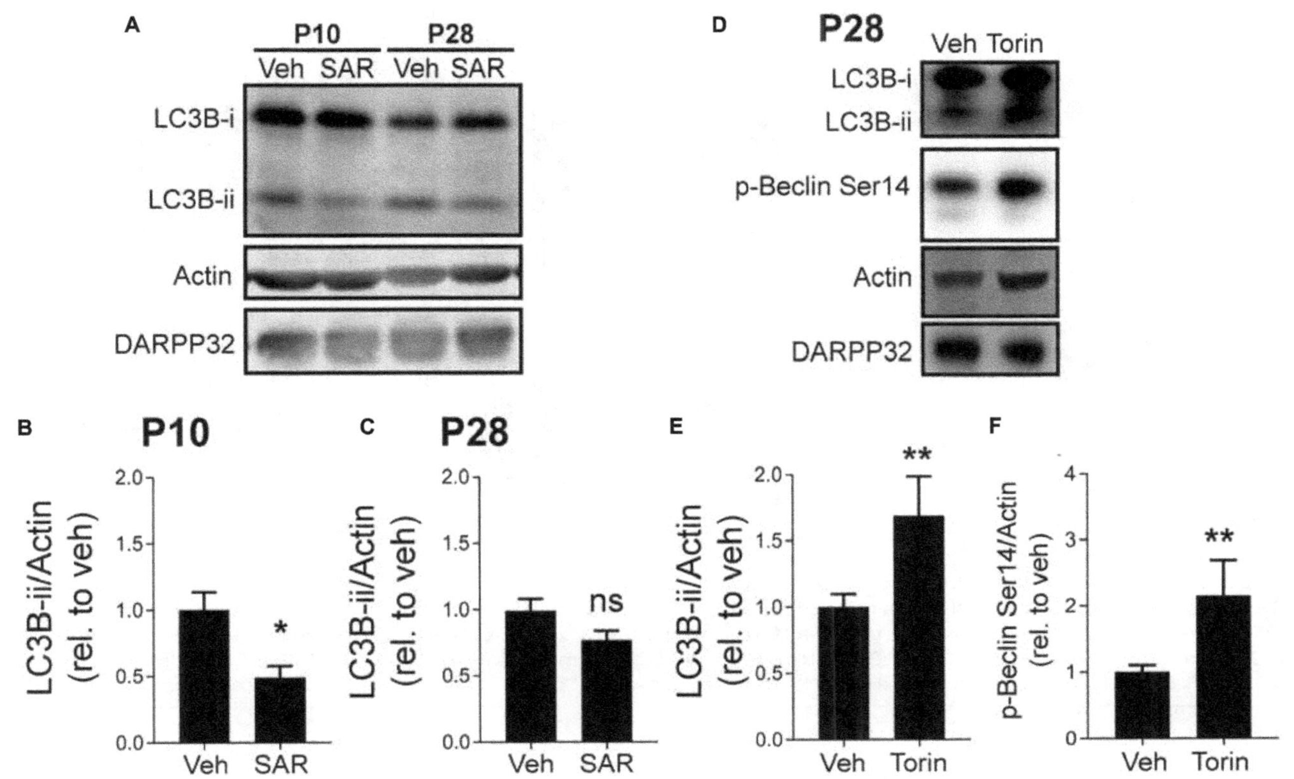

FIGURE 4 | Vps34 activity is required for maintaining LC3B-ii levels at P10 and mTOR inhibition increases p-Beclin-1 and LC3B-ii levels at P28. **(A)** Representative Western blot images for actin, DARPP32 and LC3B-i and -ii in striatal slices obtained from P10 or P28 mice, treated with SAR405 (1 μM) or vehicle (Veh; DMSO, 0.1%). **(B,C)** Quantification of LC3B-ii relative to actin, normalized to vehicle condition at each age. **(B)** P10: unpaired, two-tailed *t*-test, $t_{11} = 2.985$, $p = 0.0124$; P28: unpaired, two-tailed *t*-test, $t_{24} = 1.807$, $p = 0.0922$. P10: Veh: $n = 6$ slices, SAR405 $n = 7$ slices from 3 to 4 mice/age. **(C)** P28: Veh: $n = 9$ slices, Baf $n = 7$ slices from 3 to 4 mice/age. $^*p < 0.05$. **(D)** Representative Western blot images for actin, DARPP32, p-Beclin-1 Ser14 and LC3B-i and -ii in striatal slices from P28 mice, treated with Torin-1 (5 μM) or vehicle (Veh; DMSO, 0.1%). Quantification of **(E)** LC3B-ii and **(F)** p-Beclin S14 relative to actin, normalized to vehicle. Data analyzed with unpaired, two-tailed *t*-test; **(E)** LC3B-ii/actin, $t_{24} = 2.853$, $p = 0.0088$. Veh: $n = 19$ slices, Baf $n = 7$ slices from 5 to 7 mice. $^*p < 0.05$. **(F)** p-Beclin S14/actin, $t_{22} = 3.337$, $p = 0.0030$. $^{**}p < 0.01$, Veh: $n = 18$ slices, Torin-1 $n = 6$ slices from 3 to 5 mice.

Prenatal VPA Exposure Determine a Decrease in Autophagy During the Late Postnatal Period

To gain insights into the involvement of autophagy in neurodevelopmental disorders and ASD, we asked whether autophagic markers are dysregulated during the postnatal striatal development in the VPA mouse model of ASD.

We examined the effects of prenatal VPA exposure [600 mg/kg administered subcutaneously to pregnant mothers at gestational day 12 (Roullet et al., 2013)] on autophagy by collecting the striata of vehicle (Veh) or VPA-treated (VPA) mice at P10 and P28 (**Figure 5A**). Interestingly, we found a significant elevation in phosphorylation of rpS6 at Ser240/244 at P28 but not at P10 in VPA-treated mice compared to vehicle (**Figures 5B–D**), suggesting that mTOR signaling was increased following *in utero* VPA exposure. In agreement, we observed a significant decrease in LC3B-ii and an increase of p62 at P28 but not at P10 in VPA-treated mice compared to vehicle (**Figures 5B,E–H**). We verified that we enriched for striatal tissue in all groups by probing for DARPP-32 (**Figures 5B,I,J**). Overall, these data suggest that prenatal VPA exposure affects mTOR signaling and autophagy only during the late striatal postnatal development (P28).

Prenatal VPA Exposure Induces Impairments in SPNs Synaptic Transmission

Because autophagy is important for synaptic function (Hernandez et al., 2012; Tang et al., 2014; Nikoletopoulou et al., 2017) and prenatal VPA exposure affects synaptic transmission in the hippocampus and cortex (Roullet et al., 2013), we determined whether the reduction in autophagy induced by VPA at P28 was also accompanied by a functional change in striatal synaptic transmission.

To this end we prepared acute brain slices from P28 veh- and VPA-treated mice and recorded excitatory and inhibitory synaptic transmission in SPNs. In VPA-treated mice, we discovered a decrease in the frequency and increase in the amplitude of mEPSCs compared to vehicle treated mice (**Figures 6A–C**). In contrast, prenatal exposure to VPA did not affect mIPSC frequency or amplitude at P28 (**Figures 6D–F**). This data suggest that impaired excitatory

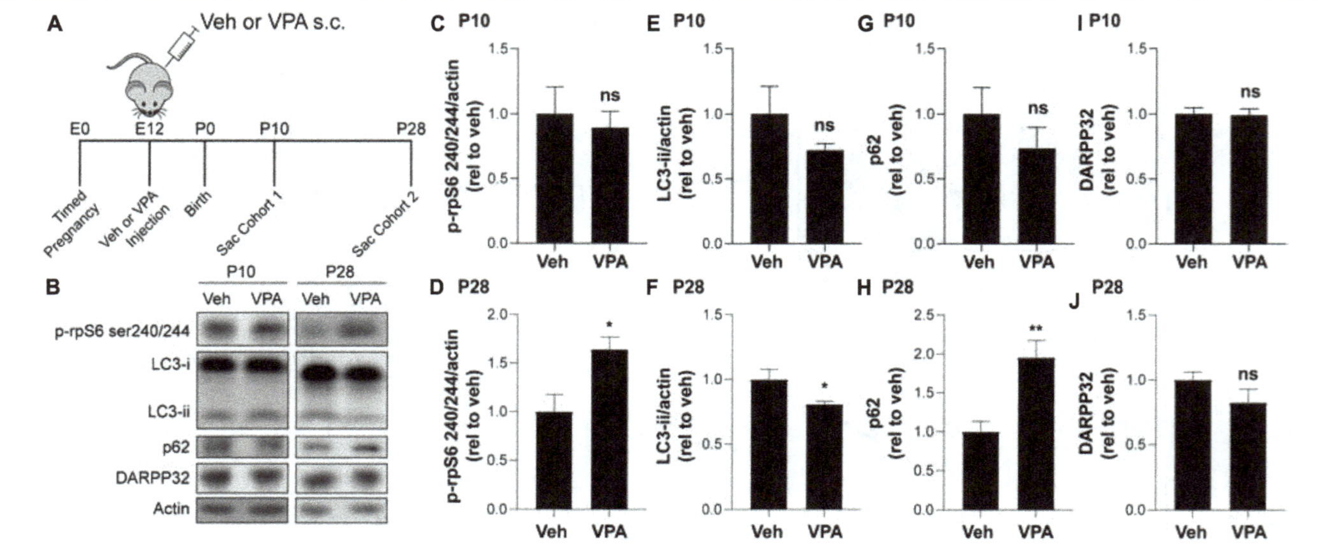

FIGURE 5 | VPA reduces autophagy at P28. **(A)** Schematic of VPA administration. **(B)** Representative Western blot images for LC3B, p62, p-rpS6 S240/244, DARPP32, and actin. **(B–G)** Quantification of **(B–D)** p-rpS6 S240/244 relative to actin, **(B,E,F)** LC3B-ii relative to actin **(B,G,H)** p62 and **(B,I,J)** DARPP32 normalized to VPA untreated (veh, vehicle) mice at P10 and P28, respectively. Data analyzed with unpaired, two-tailed *t*-test; **(C)** p-rpS6 S240/244/actin at P10, ns; **(D)** p-rpS6 S240/244/actin at P28, $t_{11} = 2.882$, $p = 0.0149$ **(E)** LC3B-ii/actin at P10, ns; **(F)** LC3B-ii/actin at P28, $t_{10} = 2.231$, $p = 0.047$; **(G)** p62 at P10, ns; **(H)** p62 at P28, $t_{10} = 3.752$, $p = 0.0038$; **(I)** DARPP32 at P10, ns, and **(J)** DARPP32 at P10, ns, $^{*}p < 0.05$, $^{**}p < 0.01$, ns not significant, $n = 4$–7 mice/treatment.

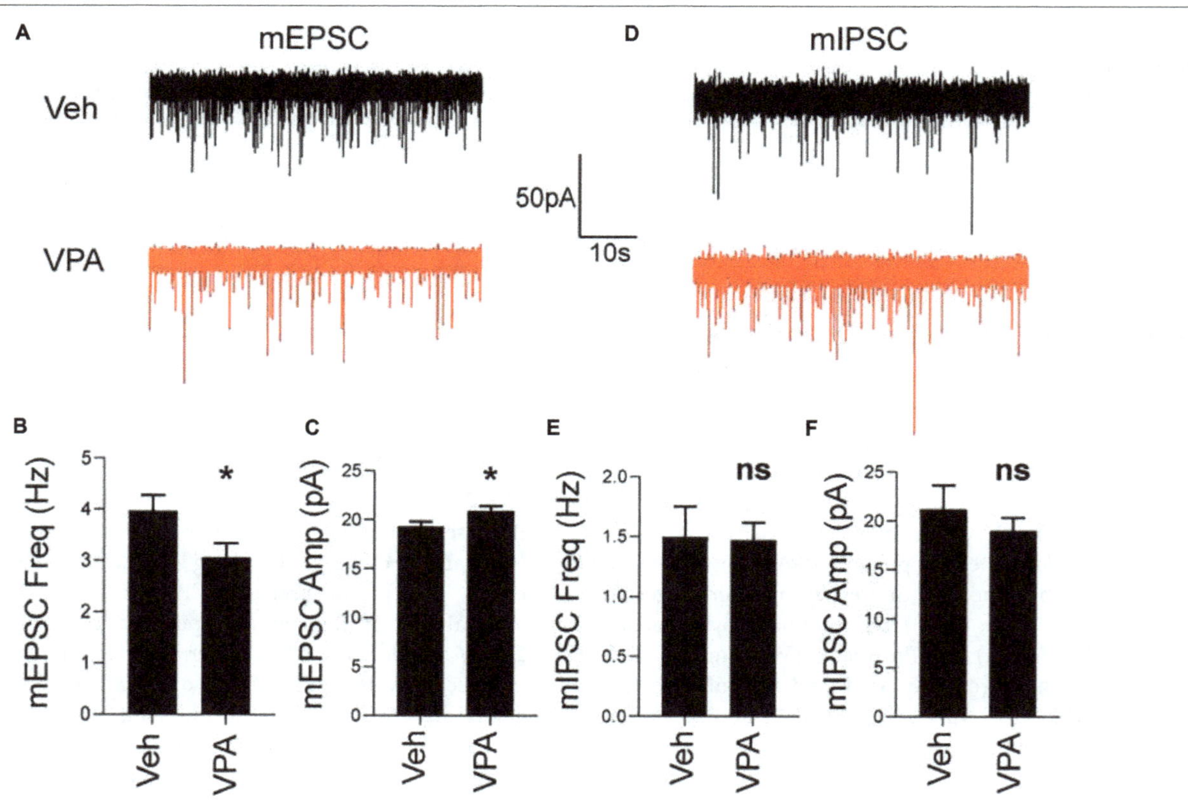

FIGURE 6 | *In utero* VPA exposure impairs striatal excitatory synaptic transmission at P28. **(A)** Representative voltage-clamp recordings of mEPSCs from SPNs in Veh or VPA treated mice. **(B)** Reduction in mEPSC frequency in VPA-treated mice. Veh: $N = 19$ cells, VPA: $N = 21$ cells. $t_{38} = 2.246$, $p = 0.0306$. **(C)** Increased in mEPSC amplitude in VPA-treated mice. Veh: $N = 19$ cells, VPA: $N = 21$ cells. $t_{38} = 2.113$, $p = 0.0412$. **(D)** Representative voltage-clamp recordings of mIPSCs from SPNs in Veh or VPA-treated mice. No difference in mIPSC **(E)** frequency or **(F)** amplitude. Veh: $N = 10$ cells, VPA: $N = 19$ cells. $^{*}p < 0.05$, ns not significant.

transmission occurs in SPNs of mice prenatally exposed to VPA.

Prenatal VPA Exposure Induces Alteration in Social Behavior That Is Normalized by Treatment With Rapamycin

Since repetitive behaviors and social impairments are required for ASD diagnosis [Diagnostic and Statistical Manual of Mental Disorders [DSM-5®], 2013] and are present in genetic models of ASD (Kwon et al., 2006; Ehninger et al., 2008; Zhou et al., 2009; Tsai et al., 2012, 2018; Gkogkas et al., 2013; Santini et al., 2013; Huynh et al., 2015) and VPA-treated rats (Cartocci et al., 2018), we asked whether prenatal exposure to VPA could result in altered repetitive and social behaviors.

We utilized the marble burying test to determine the presence of repetitive behaviors in VPA-exposed or control mice (Thomas et al., 2009, 2012; Henderson et al., 2012; Silverman et al., 2012; Huynh et al., 2014). In this test, the mice are free to explore a cage with 20 marbles arranged in a grid on the surface of the bedding. After 20 min of exploration, we counted the marbles that were buried by the mice. We did not find a significant difference in the number of marbles buried by control and VPA-exposed mice (vehicle-treated mice = 12.86 ± 1.1, VPA-treated mice = 12.57 ± 1.288. Unpaired, two-tailed t-test, ns. $N = 7$ mice/treatment). This result suggests that the onset of the repetitive behaviors occurs later than P28 for VPA-exposed mice.

We utilized the three chamber social arena to assess social behavior in VPA-exposed or control mice (Moy et al., 2008). After a period of habituation (10 min) to the arena, the mice are free to interact for another 10 min with another conspecific mouse (stranger) or with an object confined inside wire cups in the right and left chambers of the arena (**Figure 7A**). We found that VPA exposed mice spent significantly less time interacting with the social cue as compared to vehicle exposed mice (**Figure 7B**).

Since we found that VPA-exposed mice displayed an impairment in social behavior, We also investigated whether inhibiting mTOR activity with rapamycin would result in a normalization of the social abnormalities as described in genetic models of ASD (Zhou et al., 2009; Tsai et al., 2012, 2018; Tang et al., 2014). Rapamycin crosses the blood brain barrier, it has been extensively used *in vivo* to inhibit the activity of mTOR in the multiprotein complex 1 (mTORC1) and, rescue ASD-like behaviors (Zhou et al., 2009; Tsai et al., 2012, 2018; Tang et al., 2014). We treated VPA-exposed and control mice with rapamycin (5 mg/kg; injected intraperitoneally (i.p.) once a day) for 4 days, a treatment that was previously showed to be effective in blocking mTOR in the brain (Ehninger et al., 2008; Santini et al., 2009; Huynh et al., 2014). On the fifth day, 1 h after the rapamycin injection, we subjected the mice to the three chamber arena test. Rapamycin normalized the behavior of VPA-exposed mice. Thus, after rapamycin treatment, the interaction time displayed by vehicle and VPA-treated mice is similar (**Figure 7C**).

Finally, one possible explanation for the social behavior displayed by VPA-exposed mice (at baseline and following rapamycin treatment) is a change in total locomotor activity. We quantified the total locomotor activity of the mice in the three chamber arena and we found no difference between groups (**Figures 7D,E**), suggesting that the changes in the interaction time with the social cue are not caused by alteration in exploratory behavior.

DISCUSSION

Neuronal autophagy has been proposed to play a key role in neurodevelopment and autophagic dysfunction may lead to neurodevelopmental disorders and ASD (Tang et al., 2014; Dragich et al., 2016; Kim et al., 2017; Yan et al., 2018; Lieberman et al., 2019b). In this study we address whether autophagic activity is developmentally controlled in the principal neurons of the striatum, a brain region implicated in neurodevelopmental disorders (Fuccillo, 2016). We found that autophagy is dynamically regulated in SPNs during postnatal development, reaching adult levels around P28. These findings provide mechanistic insight into the regulation of autophagy during striatal postnatal development and establish the basis for a further evaluation of its role in physiological and pathological conditions.

The involvement of the striatum in ASD pathophysiology have been suggested by clinical and experimental observations (Fuccillo, 2016). Magnetic resonance imaging (MRI) and functional-MRI studies indicate anatomical and task-specific alterations in the striatum of ASD patients (Sears et al., 1999; Langen et al., 2007, 2009; Shafritz et al., 2008; Delmonte et al., 2012). Moreover, environmental and genetic animal models of ASD have contributed to conclusively demonstrate a causal relationship between striatal functions and pathophysiological alterations ASD-like (Arndt et al., 2005; Centonze et al., 2008; Shafritz et al., 2008; Shmelkov et al., 2010; Peça et al., 2011; Peñagarikano et al., 2011; Dölen et al., 2013; Santini et al., 2013). Interestingly, we have recently discovered that autophagy is differentially involved in the control of the synaptic functions and excitability of the two subtypes of SPNs (i.e., direct and indirect SPNs; Lieberman et al., 2020). Moreover, mice with specific genetic deletion of atg7, a protein required for autophagy, either in direct or indirect SPNs display hyperactivity, stereotypes and behavioral abnormalities consistent with ASD (Lieberman et al., 2020). Given the dynamic regulations of autophagy occurring in the SPNs during postnatal development and the ASD-like phenotypes displayed by mice with genetic ablation of autophagy in SPNs, the regulation of autophagy during early postnatal development of SPNs may be one of the cellular process disrupted in ASD.

By analyzing key endogenous biochemical markers (such as LC3B-ii, p62, p-Ser757-ULK1, and p-Ser14-Beclin-1), we discovered that autophagy decreases progressively during the postnatal development of SPNs. The autophagy markers were measured in bulk lysates containing neurons, glia and endothelial cells (among others). To identify the cell types that feature changes during postnatal development, we utilized tfLC3 mice (Li et al., 2014). Given the challenges in assaying endogenous autophagic proteins using immunofluorescence, tfLC3 mice

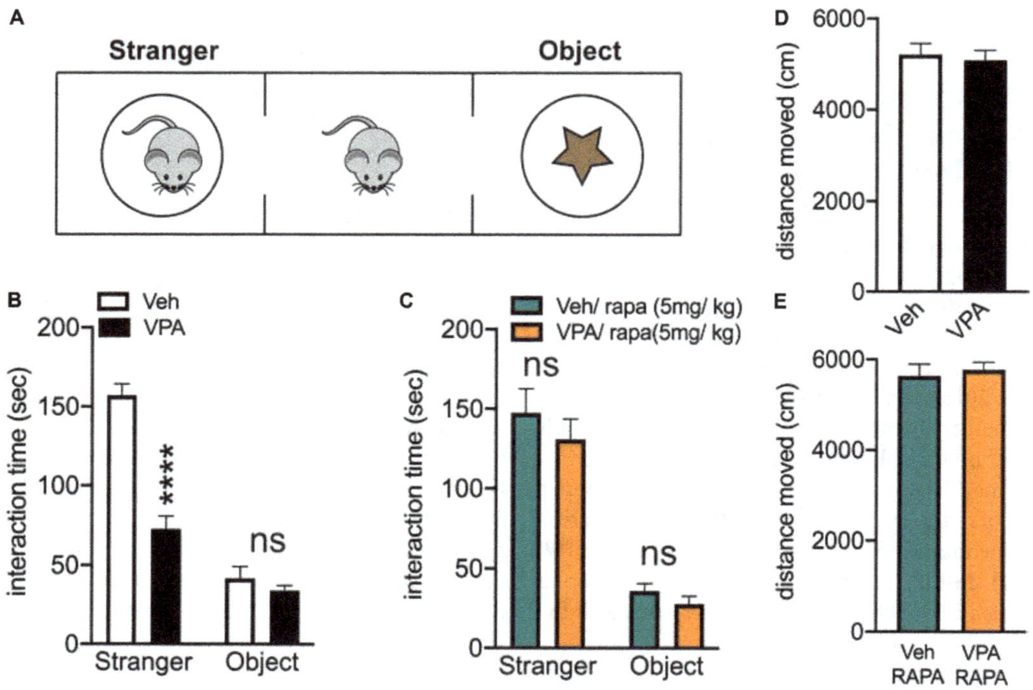

FIGURE 7 | *In utero* exposure to VPA reduces social approach behavior which is rescued by mTOR inhibition. **(A)** Schematic of three chamber arena. Subjects are placed in the center chamber and allowed to explore for 10 min. After this, a conspecific mouse (stranger) is placed in one side chamber and an object is placed in the other side chamber. The subject is allowed to explore the entire arena for 10 min and time spent interacting with either the conspecific (stranger) or the object is recorded. **(B)** The interaction time with stranger and object for control (Veh) and VPA-exposed mice (VPA). Two-way repeated measures ANOVA: treatment x chamber $F_{(1,12)} = 30.48$, $^{****}p < 0.0001$. **(C)** Rapamycin treated Veh and VPA exposed mice show no difference in interaction time with the stranger. Two-way repeated measures ANOVA: treatment x chamber $F_{(1,12)} = 0.1397$, $p = 0.7151$. Treatment: $F_{(1,12)} = 1.584$, $p = 0.2321$. Chamber: $F_{(1,12)} = 89.93$, $p < 0.0001$. **(D,E)** No difference in locomotor activity between Veh and VPA-exposed mice at baseline or following rapamycin treatment. **(D)** unpaired, two-tailed *t*-test, $t_{12} = 0.3940$, $p = 0.7005$. **(E)** Unpaired, two-tailed *t*-test, $t_{12} = 0.4253$, $p = 0.6781$.

provide a unique resource, as overexpressed LC3 is fused to fluorescent proteins that permit morphological characterization of autophagic structure. While the high levels of expression prevented the identification of individual autophagic puncta in both live imaging (**Supplementary Figure S1**) and fixed tissue (not shown), the level of autophagolysosomes represented by RFP-LC3 + puncta was higher in SPN somata at P10 than at P28, in agreement with our biochemical analysis (**Figure 1**).

Autophagic flux is determined by the kinetics of autophagosome biosynthesis, autophagosome maturation and autophagic cargo degradation by lysosomal proteases. Steady-state measurement of LC3B-ii levels provide a useful proxy for the measurement of autophagic activity. An elevated level of LC3B-ii could indicate either increased or decreased autophagic flux, as both increased autophagosome biosynthesis *and* decreased lysosomal degradation of autophagic proteins can increase LC3B-ii (Kabeya et al., 2000; Klionsky et al., 2016). To functionally measure autophagic flux in striatal tissue, we developed an *ex vivo* acute brain slice system and found that steady state increases in LC3B-ii levels at P10 were further elevated by acute blockade of lysosomal degradation with BafA1 compared to LC3B-ii levels at P28. This suggests that increased autophagic flux is responsible for the higher steady-state LC3B-ii levels, as inhibition of lysosomal degradation would not have an effect on LC3B-ii levels if lysosomal degradation were already compromised. These results indicate that the postnatal suppression of autophagy results from changes in autophagosome biosynthesis or maturation.

In line with changes in autophagosome biosynthesis/ maturation during striatal development, we found that mTOR-dependent signaling increases over the course of postnatal development, thereby suppressing autophagosome synthesis via inhibition of ULK1 and Beclin-1 activity. These include downstream targets involved in protein synthesis, such as rpS6, and autophagy, such as ULK1. In this regard, it is interesting to note that the phosphorylation state of rpS6 follows a slightly different pattern than ULK-1 during postnatal development. One of the reasons of this discrepancy may be the different phosphorylation kinetic of activated mTOR on the rpS6, which is an indirect target regulated via S6K-1 (Magnuson et al., 2012), and on ULK-1, which is a direct target (Kim et al., 2011). Alternatively, a reduction in phosphorylated rpS6 may be the result of the enhanced activity of protein phosphatase 1 (PP1), which dephosphorylates rpS6 (Belandia et al., 1994). It has been showed that the phosphorylation of rpS6 in SPNs is determined by the suppression of dephosphorylation via PKA/DARPP-32-mediated inhibition of PP1 (Bonito-Oliva et al., 2013). Thus, it is possible that a reduction in PKA/DARPP-32 results in an increased PP1 activity which, in turn dephosphorylates rpS6. Finally, a reduction of phosphorylated rpS6 may also be achieved by increased activity of PP2A-like phosphatases, which dephosphorylate and reduce the activation of S6K-1 (Magnuson et al., 2012).

mTOR specifically phosphorylates ULK1 at Ser757 and inhibits its kinase activity (Kim et al., 2011). Consistently, we also observed a decrease in the level of phosphorylation on the ULK1 site in Beclin-1, a key component of the class III-PI3K complex required for autophagosome biosynthesis (Itakura et al., 2008; Russell et al., 2013). These results provide a functional readout for increased mTOR activity on autophagy-specific downstream targets and demonstrate a direct link between mTOR signaling and a regulation of autophagy activity observed during the postnatal development. Inhibition of mTOR activity at P28, when mTOR activity is elevated, induces autophagy and increases the phosphorylation of Beclin-1 at Ser14 and LC3B-ii levels. Further work will also focus on whether additional kinases which integrate metabolic status in the periphery, such as AMPK (He and Klionsky, 2009), control developmental changes in neuronal autophagy.

These findings may help to resolve conflicting results present in the literature. Several groups have found that mTOR inhibition fails to increase autophagic activity in primary neuronal culture (Tsvetkov et al., 2010; Maday and Holzbaur, 2016) or *in vivo* (Fox et al., 2010). In contrast, others report that pharmacological (Hernandez et al., 2012; Tang et al., 2014) or genetic inhibition of mTOR drives autophagy (Yan et al., 2018) as well as hyperactivation of mTOR signaling inhibits autophagy in the CNS (McMahon et al., 2012; Tang et al., 2014; Ebrahimi-Fakhari et al., 2016). This discrepancy may arise from model system used (i.e., cell culture vs. *in vivo*), developmental stage, or treatment paradigm. Defining the substrates that mTOR acts on during brain development is critically important given recent approvals of mTOR inhibitors in neurodevelopmental disease (French et al., 2016; Curatolo et al., 2018). Our findings suggest that mTOR signaling is important for the regulation of autophagy during critical developmental windows in neurons in a manner unrelated to nutrient status. mTOR signaling is under the control of several neural-specific signals such as patterned neuronal activity and specific neurotransmitters or neuromodulators (Yin et al., 2006; Santini et al., 2009; Auerbach et al., 2011; Bockaert and Marin, 2015; Sutton and Caron, 2015), suggesting possible mechanisms through which mTOR activity is regulated within developing neural circuits. There is a broad range of significant changes in neurotransmitter content, neuronal firing patterns and synaptic plasticity that occurs during this period, providing a plethora of candidates that could dynamically regulate mTOR signaling and autophagy during the course of postnatal development. Autophagy is also known to regulate surface levels of neurotransmitter receptors, axon pathfinding, synaptic maturation and plasticity, suggesting that autophagy acts dynamically during early postnatal developmental to entrain adult-like neuronal activity that subsequently suppresses autophagy by activating mTOR signaling (Rowland et al., 2006; Hernandez et al., 2012; Shehata et al., 2012; Tang et al., 2014; Dragich et al., 2016; Nikoletopoulou et al., 2017). Such a feedback process may provide a temporal and mechanistic framework for future studies that address the role of autophagy, and its regulation by mTOR, in neuronal development.

The VPA animal model of ASD, a non-genetic model extensively used to study the neurobiology of ASD and to test for novel behavioral and pharmacological treatments thank to its face, construct and predictive validity (Chomiak et al., 2013; Roullet et al., 2013; Nicolini and Fahnestock, 2018). Prenatal exposure to VPA in humans is associated with neural tube defects and other congenital malformations (Jentink et al., 2010; Werler et al., 2011), neurocognitive impairments, including low IQ (Meador et al., 2013) and high risk of ASD (Bromley et al., 2013; Christensen et al., 2013). Similarly, in rodents, VPA induces a robust range of ASD-like behavioral and morphological alterations (reviewed in Chomiak et al., 2013; Roullet et al., 2013; Nicolini and Fahnestock, 2018). Adult rodents exposed to VPA display a reduction of brain autophagy in associations with the behavioral and morphological alterations (Qin et al., 2016; Zhang et al., 2016, 2019; Wu et al., 2018). In line with these results, we found altered autophagic markers, such as decreased LC3B-ii and increased p62, in the striatum of P28 mice prenatally exposed to VPA. Moreover, we discover that at P10 the VPA does not significantly change autophagy. Thus, it seems that prenatal exposure to VPA determines a detectable reduction of striatal autophagy only during the late postnatal development (P28) that it is maintained in the adulthood (Qin et al., 2016; Zhang et al., 2016, 2019; Wu et al., 2018). The lack of detectable change in autophagy at P10 may be the result of the high autophagic flux that masks the impairment in autophagy. Alternatively, it may be due to an ongoing accumulation of autophagic markers that are under detectable threshold at those early time points.

Consistent with our data demonstrating a direct link between dynamic change in mTOR activity and autophagy during postnatal development of SPNs, we found an increased phosphorylation of rpS6 in VPA treated animals at P28. This result suggests that autophagy and protein synthesis are concomitantly dysregulated through aberrant mTOR activity.

Impaired protein synthesis and autophagy have also been described in genetic ASD animal models (Bagni and Zukin, 2019) and the presence of similar changes also in the non-genetic VPA model may indicate that these represent pathogenic signaling pathways underlying ASD. This molecular characterization may be of importance for early detection and therapeutic treatment of ASD.

We also discovered that reduction of autophagy in VPA-treated mice is accompanied by changes in synaptic transmission at P28. We found a decrease in frequency and increase in amplitude of mEPSCs, which may indicate a reduction in the number of spines and an increase in the strength of the synaptic connection in the striatum of mice prenatally exposed to VPA. This synaptic phenotype is in line with a previous publication reporting a reduction of corticostriatal synapses in the rostral striatum of VPA treated mice (Kuo and Liu, 2017). Moreover, decreased mEPSCs frequency in VPA treated mice is also present in the cerebellar cortex (Wang et al., 2018). Reduction in excitatory striatal inputs is also observed in genetic mouse models of ASD (Fuccillo, 2016).

Finally, we found that mice exposed prenatally to VPA display altered social interaction in the three chamber arena test. This is similar to what is observed in rats treated with VPA (Cartocci et al., 2018). Systemic treatment with rapamycin (5 mg/kg/day, injected i.p. for 5 days) normalizes the social impairments of VPA treated mice. We are aware of the fact that rapamycin will likely affect all the molecular pathways regulated by mTOR, including protein synthesis which is an important signaling cascade involved in ASD (Huynh et al., 2014). Moreover, the systemic administration of rapamycin leads to an inhibition of mTOR not only in the striatum but also in other brain regions regulating social behaviors. Further studies with more specific autophagy inhibitors administered locally or with genetic manipulation of autophagic regulators restricted to the striatum are needed to conclusively demonstrate the involvement of striatal autophagy in the generation of social deficits in the VPA animal model.

In summary, we find that the postnatal development of SPNs is correlated with a change in autophagy and this is determined by mTOR signaling status. We also find that in ASD model mice, mTOR-dependent autophagy is downregulated in SPNs and it is accompanied by impairments in synaptic transmission and social behavior in the late postnatal development.

MATERIALS AND METHODS

Animals

Breeder pairs of C57/BL6J were obtained from Jackson Laboratories (Bar Harbor, ME, United States). Mice were checked every day or every other day for pregnancy and new litters. TfLC3 mice were obtained from Jackson Laboratories [C57BL/6-Tg(CAG-RFP/EGFP/Map1lc3b)1Hill/J; Strain No. 027139]. Breeder pairs were housed on a 12-h light/dark cycle with water and food available *ad libitum*. Offspring were weaned between postnatal day 18 and 20 and split into same sex groups of 2–5. Mice of both sexes were utilized for experiments in **Figures 1–4** and data were combined as no effect of gender was observed.

For the VPA experiments, pregnant female breeders received a single subcutaneous injection of VPA at the dose of 600 mg/kg during gestational day 12 (Lauber et al., 2016; Kuo and Liu, 2017; Wang et al., 2018). Control pregnant females received an equivalent dose of vehicle at gestational day 12. Only male mice of the offspring were utilized for these experiments (in **Figures 5–7**) (Lauber et al., 2016; Kuo and Liu, 2017; Wang et al., 2018).

All experimental procedures were approved by the Columbia University Institutional Animal Care and Use Committee and was conducted in accordance with animal care guidelines of National Institute of Health.

In vivo Sample Preparation

Striatal sample preparation was performed as previously described (Santini et al., 2007). Mice at specified ages were rapidly decapitated and their head was briefly placed in liquid nitrogen. The brain was subsequently removed and a single striatum was dissected and flash frozen in liquid nitrogen. Samples were stored at −80°C until the full cohort was collected. Samples were then homogenized in 1% SDS by a brief sonication. Protein content was determined by the BCA assay (Thermo Fisher). No significant effect of age was found on total protein (data not shown). Samples were then boiled in sample buffer and frozen until western blot analysis.

Acute Brain Slice

Acute brain slices were prepared essentially as described (Lieberman et al., 2018). Briefly, mice underwent cervical dislocation and the brain was removed and placed in ice-cold high sucrose cutting solution (in mM): 10 NaCl, 2.5 KCl, 25 $NaHCO_3$, 0.5 $CaCl_2$, 7 $MgCl_2$, 1.25 NaH_2PO_4, 180 sucrose, 10 glucose bubbled with 95% O_2/5% CO_2 to pH 7.4. Brains were mounted on a VT1200 vibratome (Leica Biosystems) and coronal sections (250 μm) including the striatum were collected. For the biochemistry experiments, slices were then transferred to a basin contained ice-cold cutting solution and the striatum was manually dissected. Slices were moved to scintillation vials containing 7 mL of ACSF (in mM): 125 NaCl, 2.5 KCl, 25 $NaHCO_3$, 2 $CaCl_2$, 1 $MgCl_2$, 1.25 NaH_2PO_4, and 10 glucose bubbled with 95% O_2/5% CO_2 to pH 7.4 at 34°C. Slices from two mice at the same age were combined in individual experiments and split into four conditions. Slices were allowed to rest for 1 h followed by addition of vehicle or drug. Following incubation with drug at 34°C for the specified time, slices were removed and flash frozen in liquid nitrogen. After slices were collected from a complete experiment (i.e., slices from 4 to 6 mice per age, at P10 and P28), slices were homogenized by sonication in 1% SDS and prepared as described above for Western blot analysis.

Patch-Clamp Electrophysiology

Recording pipettes were fabricated from borosilicate glass microcapillaries and had resistances of 4–6 MΩ when filled with internal solution (see below). Putative SPNs were visualized in corticostriatal slices with a SliceScope (Scientifica, United Kingdom) equipped with a 40 × 0.8 NA water-immersion objective (LUMPlanFLN, Olympus, United States) and Dodt contrast tube optics. Data were recorded with a MultiClamp 700B amplifier (Molecular Devices, United States), low-pass filtered at 5 kHz and digitized at 10 kHz with a digidata 1550b to a personal computer running pClamp 11 (Molecular Devices). Cell capacitance and series resistance (<25 MOhm) were left uncompensated but were monitored by applying a hyperpolarizing voltage-command (5 mV) at regular intervals. Recordings where series resistance increased above 25 MOhm were discarded.

Whole cell patch-clamp recordings of miniature excitatory and inhibitory synaptic currents (mEPSCs, mIPSCs, "minis") were performed at −70 mV holding potential, in the presence of tetrodotoxin (TTX, 0.5 μM) and picrotoxin (100 μM, mEPSCs) or kynurenic acid (1 mM, mIPSCs). For mEPSCs the recording pipette contained (in mM): K-gluconate, 120; KCl, 20; EGTA, 0.1; HEPES, 10; Na_2-phosphocreatine, 5; Na_2ATP, 4; Na_2GTP, 0.3, adjusted to pH 7.25 with KOH (300 mOsm/l), and for mIPSCs the pipettes contained (in mM): KCl, 140; HEPES, 10; EGTA, 1;

Na_2ATP, 2; Na_2GTP 0.2; pH 7.25. Recordings were performed at 32–34°C (TC324C, Warner Instruments, United States).

The cells were filled with recording solution for at least 10 min and data was collected during 3 min. The amplitude and frequency of the minis were analyzed off-line using Clampfit 10.7. Traces were filtered at 1 kHz and synaptic events were detected using the event detection function and template search. The amplitude and frequency from each recording were averaged and group comparisons were performed between slices using unpaired t-test assuming equal variances. The number of mice were > 4 per group.

Western Blot

Equivalent amount of protein per sample (5–25 μg/well) were loaded into 10, 12, or 4–12% gradient polyacrylamide gels as described (Santini et al., 2007). Protein was transferred from the gel to an Immobilon FL PVDF membrane (pore size 0.2 μm). Blots were blocked in TBS with 0.1% Tween-20 (TBST) and 5% fat-free, dry milk for 1 h at room temperature. Blots were then incubated with primary antibody (see **Table 1** for detailed information regarding antibodies) diluted in TBST with 5% BSA as specified (see **Table 1** for dilution and antibody sources) overnight at 4°C. Blots were then washed with TBST and incubated in secondary antibody for 1 h at room temperature. Blots were developed using either the Odyssey imaging system (LICOR) or an enhanced chemiluminescence (ECL) system (Amersham) and imaged using an Azure Biosystems C600 system. Western blots developed using the Odyssey system were analyzed in Image Studio Lite (LICOR). Western blots developed with the ECL system were analyzed using standard routines in ImageJ. All samples were probed for beta-actin and DARPP32 as loading and dissection controls, respectively.

Drugs and Chemicals

Sodium valproate (VPA) was purchased from ACROS Organics, dissolved in saline solution and administered subcutaneously to pregnant females at the dose of 600 mg/kg. BafA1 and Torin-1 were purchased from Tocris. SAR 405 was purchased from Cayman Chemicals. Unless otherwise stated, all drugs were dissolved in DMSO and slices were incubated in ACSF containing the drugs or equivalent volume of vehicles for 3 h at 34°C. DMSO did not exceed a final concentration of 0.1%. All other chemicals were purchased from Fisher Scientific.

Bafilomycin A1 was used at a concentration of 100 nM, a concentration that effectively blocks autophagolysosome fusion in primary neuronal culture and in transformed cell lines (Yamamoto et al., 1998; Maday and Holzbaur, 2016; Redmann et al., 2017). SAR405 was used at 1 μM in acute brain slice experiments. This concentration showed both maximal efficacy in inhibiting autophagy and no off target effects in cell culture experiments (Ronan et al., 2014). Torin-1 was used at 5 μM. Rapamycin, another mTOR inhibitor is generally used at concentrations between 1 and 5 μM in both cell culture and in acute brain slice; however, Torin-1 has an IC50 of mTORC1 activity about 5X greater than the IC50 of rapamycin (Thoreen et al., 2009). Therefore, we used 5 μM and confirmed that this inhibited rpS6 phosphorylation and mTOR activity in the acute brain slice.

Rapamycin (LC Laboratories) was dissolved in 1% DMSO and 5% Tween-80 in saline and injected i.p. at the dose of 5 mg/kg (vehicle treated mice received an equivalent dose of vehicle). Rapamycin (5 mg/kg) was injected i.p. once a day for 5 days. On the last day of the treatment, the mice were subjected to the three chamber sociability test (see below) 1 h after the injection. This regimen was chosen because it generates brain rapamycin concentrations in a range previously established to inhibit mTOR and normalize ASD-like behaviors and behaviors dependent on mTOR activation (Ehninger et al., 2008; Zhou et al., 2009; Huynh et al., 2014; Tsai et al., 2018).

2p-Microscopy

Two-photon images were acquired on a Prairie Ultima microscope system (Middleton, WI, United States) using PrairieView 4.3 software. Acute brain slices were transferred into a chamber and perfused with oxygenated ACSF at room temperature. Samples were excited with a Coherent (Santa Clara, CA, United States) Chameleon Ultra two-photon laser at 980 nm, and images were simultaneously collected through

TABLE 1 | Antibodies.

Antibody	Company (Catalog No.)	Dilution	Detection method	Notes
Rabbit anti LC3B	Novus Biologicals (NB600-1384)	1:1000	Odyssey	12% SDS-PAGE gel required
Rabbit anti p62	MBL (PM045)	1:1000	Odyssey	Atg7KO validated (data not shown)
Rabbit anti Darpp32	Cell Signaling Technology (2306)	1:2500–5000	Odyssey	
Mouse anti β-Actin	Novus Biologicals (NB600-501)	1:5000–10000	Odyssey	
Rabbit anti p-ULK1 (Ser757)	Cell Signaling Technology (6888)	1:500	Odyssey	
Rabbit anti Beclin	Cell Signaling Technology (3495)	1:1000	ECL	
Rabbit anti p-Beclin-1 (Ser14)	Cell Signaling Technology (84966)	1:1000	ECL	
Rabbit anti S6 ribosomal protein	Cell Signaling Technology (2217)	1:1000–2000	ECL	
Rabbit anti p-S6 ribosomal protein (Ser240/244)	Cell Signaling Technology (2215)	1:1000–2000	ECL	
Rabbit anti p44/42 MAPK (Erk1/2)	Cell Signaling Technology (4695)	1:1000	Odyssey	
Rabbit anti p-p44/42 MAPK (Erk1/2; Thr202/Tyr204)	Cell Signaling Technology (4370)	1:1000	Odyssey	

two photomultiplier tube channels with corresponding 585–630 and 490–560 nm emission windows. The objective used was a 60X, 0.9 NA water immersion lens, and images were 1024 × 1024 pixels in size.

Immunohistochemistry

Mice were deeply anesthestized and transcardially perfused with 0.9% NaCl followed by 4% paraformaldehyde (PFA) in 0.1M phosphate buffer (PB). Brains were removed and post-fixed overnight in 4% PFA in 0.1M PB. Brains were then washed three times in 1X phosphate buffered saline and cut into 40 μm sections using a VT1200 vibratome (Leica Biosystems) and stored in cryoprotectant (0.1M PB, 30% glycerol, 30% ethylene glycol) at −20°C. For immunofluorescence analysis, sections were washed in TBS three times and then blocked and permeabilized for 1 h at room temperature with 10% normal donkey serum (Jackson Immunoresearch) and 0.1% Triton-X in TBS. Sections were then incubated overnight at 4°C with primary antibodies in 2% normal donkey serum, 0.1% Triton-X in TBS. Primary antibodies included: Rabbit anti-DARPP32 (Cell Signaling), and Chicken anti-Green Fluorescent Protein (Abcam). Secondary antibodies with the appropriate conjugated fluorphores were purchased from Invitrogen. The endogenous fluorescence of RFP was imaged. Sections were then washed in TBS and mounted. Images were obtained using a Leica SP5 confocal system with argon, DPSS He/Ne lasers. Images were obtained with a 63X oil immersion objective with a 2X digital zoom at 2048 × 2048 resolution (∼120 nm resolution). All images were taken with the same laser intensity and detector settings with non-saturating pixel intensities.

Image analysis was conducted in ImageJ. Cell bodies were segmented using DARPP32 stained (DARPP32+) and not stained (DARPP32−) cells. RFP + puncta within each segment was counted manually. 10–20 cells were counted per section, 2–4 sections were counted per animal. Average number of puncta per cell was determined from $n = 3$ animals per age. All images were collected, and all analyses were conducted blind to condition.

Marble Burying Test

Marble burying was measured as previously described (Arndt et al., 2005; Centonze et al., 2008; Shafritz et al., 2008; Shmelkov et al., 2010; Peça et al., 2011; Peñagarikano et al., 2011; Dölen et al., 2013; Santini et al., 2013). Briefly, 20 glass marbles (around 15 mm in diameter) were arranged in a symmetrical (4 × 5) grid on the surface of 2–3 cm deep bedding in clean, standard mouse cages with transparent wall extensions (20 cm) to avoid climbing or jumping of mice. Each mouse was placed in the center of the cage for a 20-min exploration period, after which the number of marbles buried was tallied by investigators blind to the treatment. 'Buried' was defined as > 50% covered by bedding according to Thomas et al. (2009). Testing was performed under dim light (∼15 lux) and recorded with a videocamera.

Three Chamber Sociability Test

Social behavior was measured using a 3-chambered social arena as described previously (Moy et al., 2008). Briefly, mice received a 10 min habituation session to the arena in the presence of two wire cages, one in each side of the chamber. A 10 min social preference test followed in which the mice were allowed to explore the arena containing a wired cage with a conspecific mouse (stranger mouse) or a wire cage with an inanimate object in the two lateral chambers. The placement of social and non-social targets was counterbalanced between animals. The measured parameters of social interaction and locomotor activity were the interaction time (sec) with each target (during the social preference test session) and the total distance (cm) moved (during habituation and social preference test sessions) respectively, calculated by Ethovision XT video tracking software (Noldus).

Statistical Analysis

All analysis was conducted blind to condition. For statistical analysis between two groups, unpaired, two-tailed t-tests were used. For analysis between three or more groups, one-way ANOVA was used. Sociability test was analyzed with two-way repeated measure ANOVA (within factors: treatment and social cue), followed by multiple comparisons using Bonferroni's test. Normality was not formally tested. Sample size was not based on a formal power analysis but was based on past work from our groups and similar experiments from the literature. Statistical analysis was conducted in GraphPad Prism 7 (La Jolla, CA, United States). All bar graphs show the mean ± SEM.

ETHICS STATEMENT

The animal study was reviewed and approved by Columbia University Institutional Animal Care and Use Committee.

AUTHOR CONTRIBUTIONS

OL and ES: conception. OL, MP, AB, and ES: methodology. OL, IP, VC, MM, MB, MP, JC, AB, and ES: investigation. OL: writing – original draft and visualization. OL, IP, MP, DS, AB, and ES: writing – review and editing. ES: supervision. DS and ES: funding acquisition.

FUNDING

OL was supported by NIH T32 GM007367 and NIH F30 MH114390, VC by The Foundation Blanceflor Boncompagni Ludovisi, née Bildt, MP by NIH 5T32MH020004, DS by NIH R01 DA007418 and the Simons and JPB Foundations, AB by Swedish Research Council (2016-03129), Magnus Bergvall Foundation, Åhlens Stiftelse, The Karolinska Institute Strategic Research Program in Neuroscience (StratNeuro) and ES by NIH R00 NS087112, Swedish Research Council (2016-02758), The Knut and Alice Wallenberg Academy Fellowship, The Olle Engkvist Byggmästare Foundation, The Karolinska Institute StratNeuro and The Karolinska Institute Internal Fund.

ACKNOWLEDGMENTS

We thank Ai Yamamoto for insightful discussions about the manuscript; Dritan Agalliu for generously sharing the LICOR Odyssey system; and Gilberto Fisone for critical reading of the manuscript. This manuscript has been released as a Pre-Print at bioRxiv.

REFERENCES

Arndt, T. L., Stodgell, C. J., and Rodier, P. M. (2005). The teratology of autism. *Int. J. Dev. Neurosci.* 23, 189–199. doi: 10.1016/j.ijdevneu.2004.11.001

Auerbach, B. D., Osterweil, E. K., and Bear, M. F. (2011). Mutations causing syndromic autism define an axis of synaptic pathophysiology. *Nature* 480, 63–68. doi: 10.1038/nature10658

Bagni, C., and Zukin, R. S. (2019). A synaptic perspective of fragile X syndrome and autism spectrum disorders. *Neuron* 101, 1070–1088. doi: 10.1016/j.neuron.2019.02.041

Belandia, B., Brautigan, D., and Martín-Pérez, J. (1994). Attenuation of ribosomal protein S6 phosphatase activity in chicken embryo fibroblasts transformed by Rous sarcoma virus. *Mol. Cell. Biol.* 14, 200–206. doi: 10.1128/mcb.14.1.200

Bento, C. F., Renna, M., Ghislat, G., Puri, C., Ashkenazi, A., Vicinanza, M., et al. (2016). Mammalian autophagy: how does it work? *Annu. Rev. Biochem.* 85, 685–713. doi: 10.1146/annurev-biochem-060815-14556

Bockaert, J., and Marin, P. (2015). mTOR in brain physiology and pathologies. *Physiol. Rev.* 95, 1157–1187. doi: 10.1152/physrev.00038.2014

Bonito-Oliva, A., Pallottino, S., Bertran-Gonzalez, J., Girault, J.-A., Valjent, E., and Fisone, G. (2013). Haloperidol promotes mTORC1-dependent phosphorylation of ribosomal protein S6 via dopamine- and cAMP-regulated phosphoprotein of 32 kDa and inhibition of protein phosphatase-1. *Neuropharmacology* 72, 197–203. doi: 10.1016/j.neuropharm.2013.04.043

Bromley, R. L., Mawer, G. E., Briggs, M., Cheyne, C., Clayton-Smith, J., García-Fiñana, M., et al. (2013). The prevalence of neurodevelopmental disorders in children prenatally exposed to antiepileptic drugs. *J. Neurol. Neurosurg. Psychiatry* 84, 637–643. doi: 10.1136/jnnp-2012-304270

Byrne, S., Jansen, L., U-King-Im, J.-M., Siddiqui, A., Lidov, H. G. W., Bodi, I., et al. (2016). EPG5-related Vici syndrome: a paradigm of neurodevelopmental disorders with defective autophagy. *Brain* 139, 765–781. doi: 10.1093/brain/awv393

Cartocci, V., Catallo, M., Tempestilli, M., Segatto, M., Pfrieger, F. W., Bronzuoli, M. R., et al. (2018). Altered brain cholesterol/isoprenoid metabolism in a rat model of autism spectrum disorders. *Neuroscience* 372, 27–37. doi: 10.1016/j.neuroscience.2017.12.053

Centonze, D., Rossi, S., Mercaldo, V., Napoli, I., Ciotti, M. T., De Chiara, V., et al. (2008). Abnormal striatal GABA transmission in the mouse model for the fragile X syndrome. *Biol. Psychiatry* 63, 963–973. doi: 10.1016/j.biopsych.2007.09.008

Chakrabarti, L., Eng, J., Ivanov, N., Garden, G. A., and La Spada, A. R. (2009). Autophagy activation and enhanced mitophagy characterize the Purkinje cells of pcd mice prior to neuronal death. *Mol. Brain* 2:24. doi: 10.1186/1756-6606-2-24

Chomiak, T., Turner, N., and Hu, B. (2013). What we have learned about autism spectrum disorder from valproic acid. *Patholog. Res. Int.* 2013:712758. doi: 10.1155/2013/712758

Christensen, J., Grønborg, T. K., Sørensen, M. J., Schendel, D., Parner, E. T., Pedersen, L. H., et al. (2013). Prenatal valproate exposure and risk of autism spectrum disorders and childhood autism. *JAMA* 309, 1696–1703. doi: 10.1001/jama.2013.2270

Curatolo, P., Franz, D. N., Lawson, J. A., Yapici, Z., Ikeda, H., Polster, T., et al. (2018). Adjunctive everolimus for children and adolescents with treatment-refractory seizures associated with tuberous sclerosis complex: post-hoc analysis of the phase 3 EXIST-3 trial. *Lancet Child Adolesc. Health* 2, 495–504. doi: 10.1016/S2352-4642(18)30099-30093

Delmonte, S., Balsters, J. H., McGrath, J., Fitzgerald, J., Brennan, S., Fagan, A. J., et al. (2012). Social and monetary reward processing in autism spectrum disorders. *Mol. Autism* 3:7. doi: 10.1186/2040-2392-3-7

Diagnostic and Statistical Manual of Mental Disorders DSM-5® (2013). Available online at: https://www.appi.org/Diagnostic_and_Statistical_Manual_of_Mental_Disorders_DSM-5_Fifth_Edition (Accessed July 25, 2019).

Dölen, G., Darvishzadeh, A., Huang, K. W., and Malenka, R. C. (2013). Social reward requires coordinated activity of nucleus accumbens oxytocin and serotonin. *Nature* 501, 179–184. doi: 10.1038/nature12518

Dragich, J. M., Kuwajima, T., Hirose-Ikeda, M., Yoon, M. S., Eenjes, E., Bosco, J. R., et al. (2016). Autophagy linked FYVE (Alfy/WDFY3) is required for establishing neuronal connectivity in the mammalian brain. *eLife* 5:e14810. doi: 10.7554/eLife.14810

Ebrahimi-Fakhari, D., Saffari, A., Wahlster, L., Di Nardo, A., Turner, D., Lewis, T. L., et al. (2016). Impaired mitochondrial dynamics and mitophagy in neuronal models of tuberous sclerosis complex. *Cell Rep.* 17, 1053–1070. doi: 10.1016/j.celrep.2016.09.054

Ehninger, D., Han, S., Shilyansky, C., Zhou, Y., Li, W., Kwiatkowski, D. J., et al. (2008). Reversal of learning deficits in a Tsc2± mouse model of tuberous sclerosis. *Nat. Med.* 14, 843–848. doi: 10.1038/nm1788

Ferrari, D. C., Mdzomba, B. J., Dehorter, N., Lopez, C., Michel, F. J., Libersat, F., et al. (2012). Midbrain dopaminergic neurons generate calcium and sodium currents and release dopamine in the striatum of pups. *Front. Cell Neurosci.* 6:7. doi: 10.3389/fncel.2012.00007

Fox, J. H., Connor, T., Chopra, V., Dorsey, K., Kama, J. A., Bleckmann, D., et al. (2010). The mTOR kinase inhibitor Everolimus decreases S6 kinase phosphorylation but fails to reduce mutant huntingtin levels in brain and is not neuroprotective in the R6/2 mouse model of Huntington's disease. *Mol. Neurodegener.* 5:26. doi: 10.1186/1750-1326-5-26

French, J. A., Lawson, J. A., Yapici, Z., Ikeda, H., Polster, T., Nabbout, R., et al. (2016). Adjunctive everolimus therapy for treatment-resistant focal-onset seizures associated with tuberous sclerosis (EXIST-3): a phase 3, randomised, double-blind, placebo-controlled study. *Lancet* 388, 2153–2163. doi: 10.1016/S0140-6736(16)31419-31412

Fuccillo, M. V. (2016). Striatal circuits as a common node for autism pathophysiology. *Front. Neurosci.* 10:27. doi: 10.3389/fnins.2016.00027

Gerfen, C. R., and Surmeier, D. J. (2011). Modulation of striatal projection systems by dopamine. *Annu. Rev. Neurosci.* 34, 441–466. doi: 10.1146/annurev-neuro-061010-113641

Gkogkas, C. G., Khoutorsky, A., Ran, I., Rampakakis, E., Nevarko, T., Weatherill, D. B., et al. (2013). Autism-related deficits via dysregulated eIF4E-dependent translational control. *Nature* 493, 371–377. doi: 10.1038/nature11628

González-Polo, R.-A., Boya, P., Pauleau, A.-L., Jalil, A., Larochette, N., Souquère, S., et al. (2005). The apoptosis/autophagy paradox: autophagic vacuolization before apoptotic death. *J. Cell Sci.* 118, 3091–3102. doi: 10.1242/jcs.02447

Hara, T., Nakamura, K., Matsui, M., Yamamoto, A., Nakahara, Y., Suzuki-Migishima, R., et al. (2006). Suppression of basal autophagy in neural cells causes neurodegenerative disease in mice. *Nature* 441, 885–889. doi: 10.1038/nature04724

He, C., and Klionsky, D. J. (2009). Regulation mechanisms and signaling pathways of autophagy. *Annu. Rev. Genet.* 43, 67–93. doi: 10.1146/annurev-genet-102808-114910

Henderson, C., Wijetunge, L., Kinoshita, M. N., Shumway, M., Hammond, R. S., Postma, F. R., et al. (2012). Reversal of disease-related pathologies in the fragile X mouse model by selective activation of GABAB receptors with arbaclofen. *Sci. Transl. Med.* 4:152ra128. doi: 10.1126/scitranslmed.3004218

Hernandez, D., Torres, C. A., Setlik, W., Cebrián, C., Mosharov, E. V., Tang, G., et al. (2012). Regulation of presynaptic neurotransmission by macroautophagy. *Neuron* 74, 277–284. doi: 10.1016/j.neuron.2012.02.020

Hor, C. H. H., and Tang, B. L. (2018). Beta-propeller protein-associated neurodegeneration (BPAN) as a genetically simple model of multifaceted neuropathology resulting from defects in autophagy. *Rev. Neurosci.* 30, 261–277. doi: 10.1515/revneuro-2018-2045

Huynh, T. N., Santini, E., and Klann, E. (2014). Requirement of Mammalian target of rapamycin complex 1 downstream effectors in cued fear memory reconsolidation and its persistence. *J. Neurosci.* 34, 9034–9039. doi: 10.1523/JNEUROSCI.0878-14.2014

Huynh, T. N., Shah, M., Koo, S. Y., Faraud, K. S., Santini, E., and Klann, E. (2015). eIF4E/Fmr1 double mutant mice display cognitive impairment in addition to ASD-like behaviors. *Neurobiol. Dis.* 83, 67–74. doi: 10.1016/j.nbd.2015.08.016

Itakura, E., Kishi, C., Inoue, K., and Mizushima, N. (2008). Beclin 1 forms two distinct phosphatidylinositol 3-kinase complexes with mammalian Atg14 and UVRAG. *Mol. Biol. Cell* 19, 5360–5372. doi: 10.1091/mbc.E08-01-0080

Jentink, J., Loane, M. A., Dolk, H., Barisic, I., Garne, E., Morris, J. K., et al. (2010). Valproic acid monotherapy in pregnancy and major congenital malformations. *N. Engl. J. Med.* 362, 2185–2193. doi: 10.1056/NEJMoa0907328

Jung, C. H., Jun, C. B., Ro, S.-H., Kim, Y.-M., Otto, N. M., Cao, J., et al. (2009). ULK-Atg13-FIP200 complexes mediate mTOR signaling to the autophagy machinery. *Mol. Biol. Cell* 20, 1992–2003. doi: 10.1091/mbc.E08-12-1249

Kabeya, Y., Mizushima, N., Ueno, T., Yamamoto, A., Kirisako, T., Noda, T., et al. (2000). LC3, a mammalian homologue of yeast Apg8p, is localized in autophagosome membranes after processing. *EMBO J.* 19, 5720–5728. doi: 10.1093/emboj/19.21.5720

Kaushik, S., Rodriguez-Navarro, J. A., Arias, E., Kiffin, R., Sahu, S., Schwartz, G. J., et al. (2011). Autophagy in hypothalamic AgRP neurons regulates food intake and energy balance. *Cell Metab.* 14, 173–183. doi: 10.1016/j.cmet.2011.06.008

Kim, H. J., Cho, M. H., Shim, W. H., Kim, J. K., Jeon, E. Y., Kim, D. H., et al. (2017). Deficient autophagy in microglia impairs synaptic pruning and causes social behavioral defects. *Mol. Psychiatry* 22, 1576–1584. doi: 10.1038/mp.2016.103

Kim, J., Kundu, M., Viollet, B., and Guan, K.-L. (2011). AMPK and mTOR regulate autophagy through direct phosphorylation of Ulk1. *Nat. Cell Biol.* 13, 132–141. doi: 10.1038/ncb2152

Klionsky, D. J., Abdelmohsen, K., Abe, A., Abedin, M. J., Abeliovich, H., Acevedo Arozena, A., et al. (2016). Guidelines for the use and interpretation of assays for monitoring autophagy (3rd edition). *Autophagy* 12, 1–222. doi: 10.1080/15548627.2015.1100356

Komatsu, M., Waguri, S., Chiba, T., Murata, S., Iwata, J., Tanida, I., et al. (2006). Loss of autophagy in the central nervous system causes neurodegeneration in mice. *Nature* 441, 880–884. doi: 10.1038/nature04723

Kuo, H.-Y., and Liu, F.-C. (2017). Valproic acid induces aberrant development of striatal compartments and corticostriatal pathways in a mouse model of autism spectrum disorder. *FASEB J.* 31, 4458–4471. doi: 10.1096/fj.201700054R

Kwon, C.-H., Luikart, B. W., Powell, C. M., Zhou, J., Matheny, S. A., Zhang, W., et al. (2006). Pten regulates neuronal arborization and social interaction in mice. *Neuron* 50, 377–388. doi: 10.1016/j.neuron.2006.03.023

Langen, M., Durston, S., Staal, W. G., Palmen, S. J. M. C., and van Engeland, H. (2007). Caudate nucleus is enlarged in high-functioning medication-naive subjects with autism. *Biol. Psychiatry* 62, 262–266. doi: 10.1016/j.biopsych.2006.09.040

Langen, M., Schnack, H. G., Nederveen, H., Bos, D., Lahuis, B. E., de Jonge, M. V., et al. (2009). Changes in the developmental trajectories of striatum in autism. *Biol. Psychiatry* 66, 327–333. doi: 10.1016/j.biopsych.2009.03.017

Lauber, E., Filice, F., and Schwaller, B. (2016). Prenatal valproate exposure differentially affects parvalbumin-expressing neurons and related circuits in the cortex and striatum of mice. *Front. Mol. Neurosci.* 9:150. doi: 10.3389/fnmol.2016.00150

Lee, K.-M., Hwang, S.-K., and Lee, J.-A. (2013). Neuronal autophagy and neurodevelopmental disorders. *Exp. Neurobiol.* 22, 133–142. doi: 10.5607/en.2013.22.3.133

Li, L., Wang, Z. V., Hill, J. A., and Lin, F. (2014). New autophagy reporter mice reveal dynamics of proximal tubular autophagy. *J. Am. Soc. Nephrol.* 25, 305–315. doi: 10.1681/ASN.2013040374

Lieberman, O. J., Frier, M. D., McGuirt, A. F., Griffey, C. J., Rafikian, E., Yang, M., et al. (2020). Cell-type-specific regulation of neuronal intrinsic excitability by macroautophagy. *eLife* 9:e50843. doi: 10.7554/eLife.50843

Lieberman, O. J., McGuirt, A. F., Mosharov, E. V., Pigulevskiy, I., Hobson, B. D., Choi, S., et al. (2018). Dopamine triggers the maturation of striatal spiny projection neuron excitability during a critical period. *Neuron* 99, 540.e4–554.e4. doi: 10.1016/j.neuron.2018.06.044

Lieberman, O. J., McGuirt, A. F., Tang, G., and Sulzer, D. (2019a). Roles for neuronal and glial autophagy in synaptic pruning during development. *Neurobiol. Dis.* 122, 49–63. doi: 10.1016/j.nbd.2018.04.017

Lieberman, O. J., Pigulevskiy, I., Post, M. R., Sulzer, D., and Santini, E. (2019b). mTOR suppresses macroautophagy during postnatal development of the striatum. *bioRxiv* [Preprint]. doi: 10.1101/536680

Maday, S., and Holzbaur, E. L. F. (2016). Compartment-Specific Regulation of Autophagy in Primary Neurons. *J. Neurosci.* 36, 5933–5945. doi: 10.1523/JNEUROSCI.4401-15.2016

Magnuson, B., Ekim, B., and Fingar, D. C. (2012). Regulation and function of ribosomal protein S6 kinase (S6K) within mTOR signalling networks. *Biochem. J.* 441, 1–21. doi: 10.1042/BJ20110892

McMahon, J., Huang, X., Yang, J., Komatsu, M., Yue, Z., Qian, J., et al. (2012). Impaired autophagy in neurons after disinhibition of mammalian target of rapamycin and its contribution to epileptogenesis. *J. Neurosci.* 32, 15704–15714. doi: 10.1523/JNEUROSCI.2392-12.2012

Meador, K. J., Baker, G. A., Browning, N., Cohen, M. J., Bromley, R. L., Clayton-Smith, J., et al. (2013). Fetal antiepileptic drug exposure and cognitive outcomes at age 6 years (NEAD study): a prospective observational study. *Lancet Neurol.* 12, 244–252. doi: 10.1016/S1474-4422(12)70323-X

Mizushima, N., Yamamoto, A., Matsui, M., Yoshimori, T., and Ohsumi, Y. (2004). In vivo analysis of autophagy in response to nutrient starvation using transgenic mice expressing a fluorescent autophagosome marker. *Mol. Biol. Cell* 15, 1101–1111. doi: 10.1091/mbc.e03-09-0704

Moy, S. S., Nadler, J. J., Poe, M. D., Nonneman, R. J., Young, N. B., Koller, B. H., et al. (2008). Development of a mouse test for repetitive, restricted behaviors: relevance to autism. *Behav. Brain Res.* 188, 178–194. doi: 10.1016/j.bbr.2007.10.029

Nicolini, C., and Fahnestock, M. (2018). The valproic acid-induced rodent model of autism. *Exp. Neurol.* 299, 217–227. doi: 10.1016/j.expneurol.2017.04.017

Nikoletopoulou, V., Sidiropoulou, K., Kallergi, E., Dalezios, Y., and Tavernarakis, N. (2017). Modulation of autophagy by BDNF underlies synaptic plasticity. *Cell Metab.* 26, 230.e5–242.e5. doi: 10.1016/j.cmet.2017.06.005

Ohsumi, Y. (2014). Historical landmarks of autophagy research. *Cell Res.* 24, 9–23. doi: 10.1038/cr.2013.169

Peça, J., Feliciano, C., Ting, J. T., Wang, W., Wells, M. F., Venkatraman, T. N., et al. (2011). Shank3 mutant mice display autistic-like behaviours and striatal dysfunction. *Nature* 472, 437–442. doi: 10.1038/nature09965

Peixoto, R. T., Wang, W., Croney, D. M., Kozorovitskiy, Y., and Sabatini, B. L. (2016). Early hyperactivity and precocious maturation of corticostriatal circuits in Shank3B(-/-) mice. *Nat. Neurosci.* 19, 716–724. doi: 10.1038/nn.4260

Peñagarikano, O., Abrahams, B. S., Herman, E. I., Winden, K. D., Gdalyahu, A., Dong, H., et al. (2011). Absence of CNTNAP2 leads to epilepsy, neuronal migration abnormalities, and core autism-related deficits. *Cell* 147, 235–246. doi: 10.1016/j.cell.2011.08.040

Plotkin, J. L., Wu, N., Chesselet, M.-F., and Levine, M. S. (2005). Functional and molecular development of striatal fast-spiking GABAergic interneurons and their cortical inputs. *Eur. J. Neurosci.* 22, 1097–1108. doi: 10.1111/j.1460-9568.2005.04303.x

Poultney, C. S., Goldberg, A. P., Drapeau, E., Kou, Y., Harony-Nicolas, H., Kajiwara, Y., et al. (2013). Identification of small exonic CNV from whole-exome sequence data and application to autism spectrum disorder. *Am. J. Hum. Genet.* 93, 607–619. doi: 10.1016/j.ajhg.2013.09.001

Qin, L., Dai, X., and Yin, Y. (2016). Valproic acid exposure sequentially activates Wnt and mTOR pathways in rats. *Mol. Cell. Neurosci.* 75, 27–35. doi: 10.1016/j.mcn.2016.06.004

Redmann, M., Benavides, G. A., Berryhill, T. F., Wani, W. Y., Ouyang, X., Johnson, M. S., et al. (2017). Inhibition of autophagy with bafilomycin and chloroquine decreases mitochondrial quality and bioenergetic function in primary neurons. *Redox Biol.* 11, 73–81. doi: 10.1016/j.redox.2016.11.004

Ronan, B., Flamand, O., Vescovi, L., Dureuil, C., Durand, L., Fassy, F., et al. (2014). A highly potent and selective Vps34 inhibitor alters vesicle trafficking and autophagy. *Nat. Chem. Biol.* 10, 1013–1019. doi: 10.1038/nchembio.1681

Roullet, F. I., Lai, J. K. Y., and Foster, J. A. (2013). In utero exposure to valproic acid and autism–a current review of clinical and animal studies. *Neurotoxicol. Teratol.* 36, 47–56. doi: 10.1016/j.ntt.2013.01.004

Rowland, A. M., Richmond, J. E., Olsen, J. G., Hall, D. H., and Bamber, B. A. (2006). Presynaptic terminals independently regulate synaptic clustering and autophagy of GABAA receptors in *Caenorhabditis elegans*. *J. Neurosci.* 26, 1711–1720. doi: 10.1523/JNEUROSCI.2279-05.2006

Russell, R. C., Tian, Y., Yuan, H., Park, H. W., Chang, Y.-Y., Kim, J., et al. (2013). ULK1 induces autophagy by phosphorylating Beclin-1 and activating VPS34 lipid kinase. *Nat. Cell Biol.* 15, 741–750. doi: 10.1038/ncb2757

Santini, E., Heiman, M., Greengard, P., Valjent, E., and Fisone, G. (2009). Inhibition of mTOR signaling in Parkinson's disease prevents L-DOPA-induced dyskinesia. *Sci. Signal.* 2:ra36. doi: 10.1126/scisignal.2000308

Santini, E., Huynh, T. N., MacAskill, A. F., Carter, A. G., Pierre, P., Ruggero, D., et al. (2013). Exaggerated translation causes synaptic and behavioural aberrations associated with autism. *Nature* 493, 411–415. doi: 10.1038/nature11782

Santini, E., Valjent, E., Usiello, A., Carta, M., Borgkvist, A., Girault, J.-A., et al. (2007). Critical involvement of cAMP/DARPP-32 and extracellular signal-regulated protein kinase signaling in L-DOPA-induced dyskinesia. *J. Neurosci.* 27, 6995–7005. doi: 10.1523/JNEUROSCI.0852-07.2007

Sears, L. L., Vest, C., Mohamed, S., Bailey, J., Ranson, B. J., and Piven, J. (1999). An MRI study of the basal ganglia in autism. *Prog. Neuropsychopharmacol. Biol. Psychiatry* 23, 613–624. doi: 10.1016/S0278-5846(99)00020-22

Shafritz, K. M., Dichter, G. S., Baranek, G. T., and Belger, A. (2008). The neural circuitry mediating shifts in behavioral response and cognitive set in autism. *Biol. Psychiatry* 63, 974–980. doi: 10.1016/j.biopsych.2007.06.028

Shehata, M., Matsumura, H., Okubo-Suzuki, R., Ohkawa, N., and Inokuchi, K. (2012). Neuronal stimulation induces autophagy in hippocampal neurons that is involved in AMPA receptor degradation after chemical long-term depression. *J. Neurosci.* 32, 10413–10422. doi: 10.1523/JNEUROSCI.4533-11.2012

Shen, W., and Ganetzky, B. (2009). Autophagy promotes synapse development in *Drosophila*. *J. Cell Biol.* 187, 71–79. doi: 10.1083/jcb.200907109

Shmelkov, S. V., Hormigo, A., Jing, D., Proenca, C. C., Bath, K. G., Milde, T., et al. (2010). Slitrk5 deficiency impairs corticostriatal circuitry and leads to obsessive-compulsive-like behaviors in mice. *Nat. Med.* 16, 598–602. doi: 10.1038/nm.2125

Shpilka, T., Weidberg, H., Pietrokovski, S., and Elazar, Z. (2011). Atg8: an autophagy-related ubiquitin-like protein family. *Genome Biol.* 12:226. doi: 10.1186/gb-2011-12-7-226

Silverman, J. L., Smith, D. G., Rizzo, S. J. S., Karras, M. N., Turner, S. M., Tolu, S. S., et al. (2012). Negative allosteric modulation of the mGluR5 receptor reduces repetitive behaviors and rescues social deficits in mouse models of autism. *Sci. Transl. Med.* 4:131ra51. doi: 10.1126/scitranslmed.3003501

Song, D. D., and Harlan, R. E. (1994). Genesis and migration patterns of neurons forming the patch and matrix compartments of the rat striatum. *Brain Res. Dev. Brain Res.* 83, 233–245. doi: 10.1016/0165-3806(94)00144-148

Stavoe, A. K. H., Hill, S. E., Hall, D. H., and Colón-Ramos, D. A. (2016). KIF1A/UNC-104 transports atg-9 to regulate neurodevelopment and autophagy at synapses. *Dev. Cell* 38, 171–185. doi: 10.1016/j.devcel.2016.06.012

Sutton, L. P., and Caron, M. G. (2015). Essential role of D1R in the regulation of mTOR complex1 signaling induced by cocaine. *Neuropharmacology* 99, 610–619. doi: 10.1016/j.neuropharm.2015.08.024

Tang, G., Gudsnuk, K., Kuo, S.-H., Cotrina, M. L., Rosoklija, G., Sosunov, A., et al. (2014). Loss of mTOR-dependent macroautophagy causes autistic-like synaptic pruning deficits. *Neuron* 83, 1131–1143. doi: 10.1016/j.neuron.2014.07.040

Tanida, I., Minematsu-Ikeguchi, N., Ueno, T., and Kominami, E. (2005). Lysosomal turnover, but not a cellular level, of endogenous LC3 is a marker for autophagy. *Autophagy* 1, 84–91. doi: 10.4161/auto.1.2.1697

Tepper, J. M., Sharpe, N. A., Koós, T. Z., and Trent, F. (1998). Postnatal development of the rat neostriatum: electrophysiological, light- and electron-microscopic studies. *Dev. Neurosci.* 20, 125–145. doi: 10.1159/000017308

Thomas, A., Burant, A., Bui, N., Graham, D., Yuva-Paylor, L. A., and Paylor, R. (2009). Marble burying reflects a repetitive and perseverative behavior more than novelty-induced anxiety. *Psychopharmacology* 204, 361–373. doi: 10.1007/s00213-009-1466-y

Thomas, A. M., Bui, N., Perkins, J. R., Yuva-Paylor, L. A., and Paylor, R. (2012). Group I metabotropic glutamate receptor antagonists alter select behaviors in a mouse model for fragile X syndrome. *Psychopharmacology* 219, 47–58. doi: 10.1007/s00213-011-2375-2374

Thoreen, C. C., Kang, S. A., Chang, J. W., Liu, Q., Zhang, J., Gao, Y., et al. (2009). An ATP-competitive mammalian target of rapamycin inhibitor reveals rapamycin-resistant functions of mTORC1. *J. Biol. Chem.* 284, 8023–8032. doi: 10.1074/jbc.M900301200

Tsai, P. T., Hull, C., Chu, Y., Greene-Colozzi, E., Sadowski, A. R., Leech, J. M., et al. (2012). Autistic-like behaviour and cerebellar dysfunction in Purkinje cell Tsc1 mutant mice. *Nature* 488, 647–651. doi: 10.1038/nature11310

Tsai, P. T., Rudolph, S., Guo, C., Ellegood, J., Gibson, J. M., Schaeffer, S. M., et al. (2018). Sensitive periods for cerebellar-mediated autistic-like behaviors. *Cell Rep.* 25, 357.e4–367.e4. doi: 10.1016/j.celrep.2018.09.039

Tsvetkov, A. S., Miller, J., Arrasate, M., Wong, J. S., Pleiss, M. A., and Finkbeiner, S. (2010). A small-molecule scaffold induces autophagy in primary neurons and protects against toxicity in a Huntington disease model. *Proc. Natl. Acad. Sci. U.S.A.* 107, 16982–16987. doi: 10.1073/pnas.1004498107

Voorn, P., Kalsbeek, A., Jorritsma-Byham, B., and Groenewegen, H. J. (1988). The pre- and postnatal development of the dopaminergic cell groups in the ventral mesencephalon and the dopaminergic innervation of the striatum of the rat. *Neuroscience* 25, 857–887. doi: 10.1016/0306-4522(88)90041-90043

Wang, Q. J., Ding, Y., Kohtz, D. S., Mizushima, N., Cristea, I. M., Rout, M. P., et al. (2006). Induction of autophagy in axonal dystrophy and degeneration. *J. Neurosci.* 26, 8057–8068. doi: 10.1523/JNEUROSCI.2261-06.2006

Wang, R., Tan, J., Guo, J., Zheng, Y., Han, Q., So, K.-F., et al. (2018). Aberrant development and synaptic transmission of cerebellar cortex in a VPA induced mouse autism model. *Front. Cell Neurosci.* 12:500. doi: 10.3389/fncel.2018.00500

Werler, M. M., Ahrens, K. A., Bosco, J. L. F., Mitchell, A. A., Anderka, M. T., Gilboa, S. M., et al. (2011). Use of antiepileptic medications in pregnancy in relation to risks of birth defects. *Ann. Epidemiol.* 21, 842–850. doi: 10.1016/j.annepidem.2011.08.002

Wu, H., Zhang, Q., Gao, J., Sun, C., Wang, J., Xia, W., et al. (2018). Modulation of sphingosine 1-phosphate (S1P) attenuates spatial learning and memory impairments in the valproic acid rat model of autism. *Psychopharmacology* 235, 873–886. doi: 10.1007/s00213-017-4805-4804

Yamamoto, A., Cremona, M. L., and Rothman, J. E. (2006). Autophagy-mediated clearance of huntingtin aggregates triggered by the insulin-signaling pathway. *J. Cell Biol.* 172, 719–731. doi: 10.1083/jcb.200510065

Yamamoto, A., and Simonsen, A. (2011). The elimination of accumulated and aggregated proteins: a role for aggrephagy in neurodegeneration. *Neurobiol. Dis.* 43, 17–28. doi: 10.1016/j.nbd.2010.08.015

Yamamoto, A., Tagawa, Y., Yoshimori, T., Moriyama, Y., Masaki, R., and Tashiro, Y. (1998). Bafilomycin A1 prevents maturation of autophagic vacuoles by inhibiting fusion between autophagosomes and lysosomes in rat hepatoma cell line, H-4-II-E cells. *Cell Struct. Funct.* 23, 33–42. doi: 10.1247/csf.23.33

Yamamoto, A., and Yue, Z. (2014). Autophagy and its normal and pathogenic states in the brain. *Annu. Rev. Neurosci.* 37, 55–78. doi: 10.1146/annurev-neuro-071013-14149

Yan, J., Porch, M. W., Court-Vazquez, B., Bennett, M. V. L., and Zukin, R. S. (2018). Activation of autophagy rescues synaptic and cognitive deficits in fragile X mice. *Proc. Natl. Acad. Sci. U.S.A.* 115, E9707–E9716. doi: 10.1073/pnas.1808247115

Yang, D.-S., Stavrides, P., Mohan, P. S., Kaushik, S., Kumar, A., Ohno, M., et al. (2011). Reversal of autophagy dysfunction in the TgCRND8 mouse model of Alzheimer's disease ameliorates amyloid pathologies and memory deficits. *Brain* 134, 258–277. doi: 10.1093/brain/awq341

Yin, H. H., Davis, M. I., Ronesi, J. A., and Lovinger, D. M. (2006). The role of protein synthesis in striatal long-term depression. *J. Neurosci.* 26, 11811–11820. doi: 10.1523/JNEUROSCI.3196-06.2006

Zhang, J., Zhang, J.-X., and Zhang, Q.-L. (2016). PI3K/AKT/mTOR-mediated autophagy in the development of autism spectrum disorder. *Brain Res. Bull.* 125, 152–158. doi: 10.1016/j.brainresbull.2016.06.007

Zhang, Y., Xiang, Z., Jia, Y., He, X., Wang, L., and Cui, W. (2019). The Notch signaling pathway inhibitor Dapt alleviates autism-like behavior, autophagy and dendritic spine density abnormalities in a valproic acid-induced animal model of autism. *Prog. Neuropsychopharmacol. Biol. Psychiatry* 94:109644. doi: 10.1016/j.pnpbp.2019.109644

Zhou, J., Blundell, J., Ogawa, S., Kwon, C.-H., Zhang, W., Sinton, C., et al. (2009). Pharmacological inhibition of mTORC1 suppresses anatomical, cellular, and behavioral abnormalities in neural-specific Pten knock-out mice. *J. Neurosci.* 29, 1773–1783. doi: 10.1523/JNEUROSCI.5685-08.2009

15

Two Autism/Dyslexia Linked Variations of *DOCK4* Disrupt the Gene Function on Rac1/Rap1 Activation, Neurite Outgrowth and Synapse Development

Miaoqi Huang[1†], Chunmei Liang[1†‡], Shengnan Li[1†‡], Jifeng Zhang[2], Daji Guo[1], Bo Zhao[2], Yuyang Liu[3], Yinghui Peng[1], Junyu Xu[4], Wei Liu[3], Guoqing Guo[2] and Lei Shi[1]*

[1] JNU-HKUST Joint Laboratory for Neuroscience and Innovative Drug Research, College of Pharmacy, Jinan University, Guangzhou, China, [2] Department of Anatomy, Medical College of Jinan University, Guangzhou, China, [3] Shenzhen Key Laboratory for Neuronal Structural Biology, Biomedical Research Institute, Shenzhen Peking University – The Hong Kong University of Science and Technology Medical Center, Shenzhen, China, [4] Department of Neurobiology, Key Laboratory of Medical Neurobiology of the Ministry of Health of China, Collaborative Innovation Center for Brain Science, Zhejiang University School of Medicine, Hangzhou, China

Correspondence:
Lei Shi
t_shilei@jnu.edu.cn;
sophielshi80@gmail.com

[†] These authors have contributed equally to this work

Autism spectrum disorder (ASD) and dyslexia are both neurodevelopmental disorders with high prevalence in children. Both disorders have strong genetic basis, and share similar social communication deficits co-occurring with impairments of reading or language. However, whether these two disorders share common genetic risks remain elusive. *DOCK4* (dedicator for cytokinesis 4), a guanine nucleotide exchange factor (GEF) for the small GTPase Rac1, is one of few genes that are associated with both ASD and dyslexia. Dock4 is important for neuronal development and social behaviors. Two *DOCK4* variations, Exon27-52 deletion (protein product: Dock4-945VS) and a missense mutation at rs2074130 (protein product: Dock4-R853H), are associated with dyslexia and/or ASD with reading difficulties. The present study explores the molecular and cellular functions of these two *DOCK4* variants on neuronal development, by comparing them with the wild-type Dock4 protein. Notably, it is revealed that both mutants of Dock4 showed decreased ability to activate not only Rac1, but also another small GTPase Rap1. Consistently, both mutants were dysfunctional for regulation of cell morphology and cytoskeleton. Using Neuro-2a cells and hippocampus neurons as models, we found that both mutants had compromised function in promoting neurite outgrowth and dendritic spine formation. Electrophysiological recordings further showed that R853H partially lost the ability to promote excitatory synaptic transmission, whereas 945VS totally lost the ability. Together, we identified R853 as a previously uncharacterized site for the regulation of the integrity of Dock4 function, and provides insights in understanding the common molecular pathophysiology of ASD and dyslexia.

Keywords: autism, dendritic spine, Dock4, dyslexia, neuron, neurite, Rac1, Rap1

INTRODUCTION

Dock (dedicator of cytokinesis) protein family, a subtype of atypical guanine nucleotide exchange factors (GEFs) for promoting the activity of Rac1/Cdc42, has been implicated in regulating various processes of brain development and is linked with neurological diseases (Shi, 2013). Among them, Dock4 has attracted recent attention as emerging evidence suggests *DOCK4* as a candidate gene for several neuropsychiatric diseases, including autism spectrum disorder (ASD), dyslexia and schizophrenia (Maestrini et al., 2010; Pagnamenta et al., 2010; Poelmans et al., 2011; Alkelai et al., 2012; Iossifov et al., 2014; Liang et al., 2014; Toma et al., 2014; Warrier et al., 2015; Shao et al., 2016; Lim et al., 2017; Akahoshi and Yamamoto, 2018; Kushima et al., 2018). Our previous study using *Dock4* knockout mice have revealed that Dock4 deficiency *in vivo* leads to autism-like behaviors, including defects in social novelty preference and communication (Guo et al., 2019). In particular, impairment of Dock4-dependent excitatory synapse transmission in hippocampal CA1 pyramidal neurons is a main cause for the social deficits (Guo et al., 2019). Moreover, Dock4 is suggested to play important roles in neuronal development such as axon guidance, dendrite development and dendritic spine morphogenesis (Ueda et al., 2008, 2013; Xiao et al., 2013; Makihara et al., 2018). Dock4 possesses an N-terminal SH3 (Src-homology 3) domain, a DHR1 (Dock homology region 1) domain, and a DHR2 domain which is well-studied as a Rac1-specific GEF domain. Indeed, Rac1 was demonstrated to be a key molecule that mediates Dock4's function in the above studies. Interestingly, evidence from other system suggests that Dock4 is also capable of activating Rap1 (Yajnik et al., 2003), another small G protein involved in cell adhesion and growth. This Rap1-activating function seems to be unique for Dock4, which has been the only Dock reported to possess this ability. However, whether Dock4 regulates Rap1 in the nervous system has not been studied.

It has been found that ASD and dyslexia share similar communication deficits originated from impairments of reading or language. Indeed, difficulties of reading comprehension is a common symptoms in ASD children (prevalence ranging from 6 to 30%) (Hendren et al., 2018). Emerging evidence has suggested that both ASD and dyslexia have strong genetic components in their etiologies that involve multigene interaction (Raskind et al., 2012; Bourgeron, 2015). Notably, *DOCK4* is one of few shared candidate genes for both ASD and dyslexia. Two *DOCK4* variations have been identified in individuals with dyslexia and/or in autism subjects with poor reading abilities (Pagnamenta et al., 2010; Shao et al., 2016) (**Table 1** and **Figure 1A**). The first variation, identified in individuals from a European family with autism and/or reading/spelling difficulties, is a microdeletion at the junction of *DOCK4* and its neighboring gene *IMMP2L* (deletion at chr7:110663978-111257682, GRCh37) (Pagnamenta et al., 2010). This variant leads to the deletion of the DHR2-containing C-terminal coding sequence of *DOCK4* (Exons 27-52), which causes a frameshift of Dock4 protein coding after 945 aa; two missense amino acids, namely Valine (Val) and Serine (Ser), is translated after 945 aa, followed by a premature stop codon (Pagnamenta et al., 2010). The second variation, identified in Chinese dyslexic children, occurs at rs20741307 and causes missense mutation of Dock4 protein, leading to a substitution of Arginine (Arg) at residue 853 with Histidine (His) (Shao et al., 2016). Previously, we showed that the protein product of the *IMMP2L_DOCK4* fusion transcript is unable to exert normal function on Rac1 activation and neurite outgrowth (Xiao et al., 2013). However, whether rs20741307 variation affects these Dock4 abilities has not been explored. Moreover, whether these two variations influence the synaptic regulation function of Dock4 is unclear.

To understand the function of the two dyslexia/autism-linked *DOCK4* variations, we studied the mutant generated by the *IMMP2L_DOCK4* fusion transcript, Dock4-945VS (1–945 aa of Dock4 + Val + Ser), and the missense mutant of rs20741307 variation, Dock4-R853H (Arg^{853}His), by examining their molecular and cellular functions through several assays. Both mutants had abrogated activities on Rac1 and Rap1 activation, and showed compromised function on promoting neurite outgrowth, synapse morphogenesis and transmission. This study provides insights in understanding the common molecular pathophysiology of autism and dyslexia by investigating their shared gene *DOCK4*.

MATERIALS AND METHODS

Constructs, Antibodies, and Reagents

Plasmids of human Dock4 cDNA and its mutants, Dock4 945VS (amino acids 1–945 + Val + Ser), ΔSH3 (amino acids 81–1966), ΔC (amino acids 1–1592), SH3-F (amino acids 1–161), Dock shRNA, and ELMO2 were described previously (Xiao et al., 2013). cDNA of Dock4 R853H was generated by mutagenesis using the following primers, CATGTGTGCACATATCCTTAGCAACGTATT and TGCTAAGGATATGTGCACACATGATCAGGT (Sequence from 5′ to 3′). cDNA of Dock4 AAA (M1475A, S1476A, P1477A) mutant, which is deficient of GEF activity, was constructed by mutagenesis. All cDNAs with a C-terminal Flag tag were subcloned into the pCAGIG vector, which contains a GFP coding sequence separated by an internal ribosome entry site (Ip et al., 2012).

The following primary antibodies were used: Dock4, ELMO2 and GAPDH were purchased from Abcam (Cambridge, United Kingdom); α-tubulin and β-tubulin III were from Sigma; Tau1 and Rap1 were from Millipore (Darmstadt, Germany); Rac1 was from BD Biosciences; Flag was from Sigma. Retinoic acid (RA) was purchased from Sigma, and Rhodamine-phalloidin was from Invitrogen.

Ethics Statement

All experimental procedures involving the use of animals were approved by the Ethics Committee on Animal Experiments at Jinan University, and were strictly performed according to the National Institutes of Health guidelines of the Care and Use of Laboratory Animals. All efforts were made to minimize the suffering and the number of animals used.

TABLE 1 | *DOCK4* variations associated with autism spectrum disorder and Dyslexia.

***DOCK4* variation**[1]	**SNP ID**	**Variant type**	**Allele change**	**Protein change**	**Protein mutant**	**Phenotype**	**Identified Population**	**References**
Deletion at 7:110663978-111257682		CNV	Exon 27-52 deleted	Frame shift after 945a.a., stop at 947a.a.	Dock4-945VS[2]	Autism and/or reading/ spelling difficulties	European	Pagnamenta et al., 2010
7:111487098 (C > T)	rs2074130	Missense	c.2558G > A	p.R853H	Dock-R853H[3]	Developmental dyslexia	Chinese	Shao et al., 2016

[1]Chromosome positions are indicated according to Assembly GRCh37. [2]Dock4-945VS = 1–945 a.a. of Dock4 + Valine + Serine, which are two missense amino acids translated due to codon frame shift. [3]Dock4-R853H = Dock4-Arg^{853}His, in which Arginine at codon 853 is replaced by Histidine due to missense mutation at rs2074130.

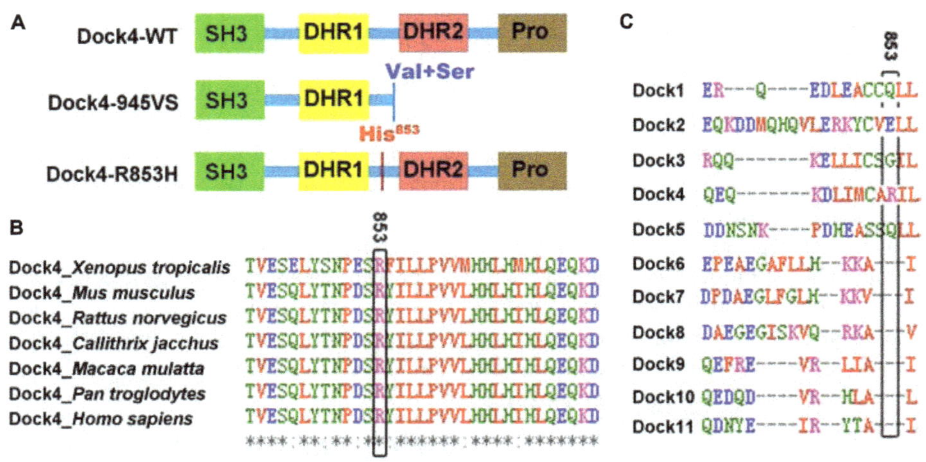

FIGURE 1 | Arg^{853} is a unique site of Dock4 among all Dock family members and is highly conserved during evolution. **(A)** Domain illustrations of Dock4 mutants associated with autism spectrum disorder and dyslexia. **(B)** The 853th Arginine residue of Dock4 is highly conserved in different species during evolution. **(C)** The 853th Arginine residue of Dock4 is not conserved in other Dock family members.

Dock4 KO Mice

Dock4 KO mice (C57BL/6 background) were generated using a standard strategy of Cre-LoxP recombination as previously described (Guo et al., 2019).

Cell Culture and Transfection

Neuro-2a cells and HEK293T cells were cultured as described previously (Xiao et al., 2013). COS7 cells were cultured in RPMI 1640 (Gibco) supplemented with 10% FBS. Transfection of plasmids was using Lipofectamine LTX (Invitrogen). To study neurite outgrowth, the culture medium of Neuro-2a cells was switched into differentiation medium (MEM supplemented with 0.5% FBS) in the presence of 15 μM RA for 48 h (Xiao et al., 2013; Liao et al., 2018).

Primary cultures of rat hippocampal neurons were prepared from E18 Sprague Dawley rat embryos as described previously (Xiao et al., 2013; Tang et al., 2015). Briefly, after dissection the tissue was incubated with trypsin-ETDA (0.5%, Life Technologies) in Ca^{2+} and Mg^{2+} free Hank's balanced salt solution (HBSS with 0.06% D-Glucose, 1 mM Sodium pyruvate and 10 mM HEPES, Life Technologies) for 15 min at 37°C. Cells were washed once with plating medium (MEM supplemented with 10% horse serum, 0.6% glucose and 1 mM pyruvic acid), and suspended through trituration (Life Technologies). Cells were then plated in plating medium onto poly-D-lysine (1 mg/ml, Sigma) coated 18-mm coverslips in 12-well culture plates, at a final density of 4 × 10^4 cells/coverslips. The plating medium was replaced with culture medium (Neurobasal medium supplemented with 2%B27 and 2 mM L-glutamine, Life Technologies) at 3 h after plating. The culture medium was half-changed every 3 days.

For analysis of hippocampal neuronal extension, plasmids were transfected into dissociated neuron suspension in Opti-MEM (Life Technologies) using Lipofectamine 2000 (Life Technologies) as previously described (Xiao et al., 2013), and neuronal morphology was analyzed at 3 days *in vitro* (DIV). For analysis of dendritic spine morphology, transfection of plasmids was performed using Calcium Phosphate precipitation at 9 DIV, and Neuronal morphology was analyzed at 16 DIV (Xiao et al., 2013).

Immunocytochemistry

To study cell morphology and cytoskeleton in COS7 cells, cells were cultured on coverslips, transfected with indicated plasmids, and fixed in 4% paraformaldehyde (Sigma). The cells were permeabilized with a solution of 0.1% Triton X-100 in PBS for 3–5 min, and were then incubated with rhodamine-phalloidin (Invitrogen) for 20 min at room temperature. Cell morphology was photographed using a Zeiss LSM 800 confocal microscope under a 63X objective. To visualize neurites in differentiated Neuro-2a cells, cells were fixed in 4% paraformaldehyde for

20–30 min at room temperature. The cells were blocked with 1% BSA and immunostained with mouse anti-β-tubulin III antibody, followed by incubation with Alexa Fluor 546 goat anti-mouse IgG antibody (Invitrogen). Cell morphology was photographed with a Zeiss Axio Imager A2 microscope (Carl Zeiss AG, Oberkochen, Germany). Quantifications of the neurites and protrusions were made using ImageJ software (National Institutes of Health, Bethesda, MD, United States). To analyze hippocampal neuronal extension, 3 DIV neurons were fixed with 4% paraformaldehyde and subjected to immunostaining with Tau1 antibodies. Neuron morphology was photographed using a Zeiss LSM 800 confocal microscope under a 20X objective (Carl Zeiss AG). Neurite length was measured using ImageJ software. To determine dendritic spine development, 16 DIV neurons were fixed with 4% paraformaldehyde. Dendrites were photographed using a Zeiss LSM 800 confocal microscope under a 63X objective. Spine density was measured using ImageJ software.

Electrophysiology

Whole-cell patch-clamp recordings of miniature excitatory postsynaptic currents (mEPSC) were obtained from transfected cultured hippocampal neurons at 15 DIV (Zhang et al., 2017). Briefly, cells were bathed in an external solution with a pH of 7.3 (128 mM NaCl, 5 mM KCl, 2 mM $CaCl_2$, 1 mM $MgCl_2$, 15 mM glucose, 20 mM HEPES, 1 mM tetrodotoxin, and 100 μM picrotoxin). Recording pipettes were filled with the intracellular solution containing (in mM): 147 KCl, 5 Na_2-phosphocreatine, 2 EGTA, 10 HEPES, 2 MgATP, and 0.3 Na_2GTP. Recordings were performed at room temperature in voltage clamp mode, at a holding potential of −70 mV, using a Multiclamp 700 B amplifier (Molecular Devices, Sunnyvale, CA, United States) and Clampex 10.5 software (Axon Instruments, Union City, CA, United States). The series resistance was below 30 MΩ, and data were acquired at 10 kHz and filtered at 1 kHz. mEPSCs were analyzed using MiniAnalysis software (Synaptosoft, Inc., Decatur, GA, United States).

Rac1/Rap1 Activity Assay

Rac1/Rap1 activity was measured as previously described (Shi et al., 2007; Bai et al., 2018). Briefly, 1 day after transfection, HEK293T cells were lysed on ice in lysis buffer (25 mM Tris-HCl (pH 7.4), 1% Nonidet P-40, 2.5mM $MgCl_2$, 500 mM NaCl, 10% glycerol, 10 μg/ml aprotinin and leupeptin, 1 mM PMSF). Lysates were incubated with glutathione agarose beads coupled to the p21 Rac/Cdc42 binding domain fused to GST (GST-PBD) for Rac1 activity assay, or glutathione agarose beads coupled to GST-RalGDS for Rap1 activity assay, at 4°C for 60 min with rotation. The beads were washed three times with lysis buffer and resuspended with sample buffer. Samples were subjected to Western blot analysis. Signal intensity was quantified by densitometry using ImageJ software.

Statistical Analysis

Data are represented as means ± SEM and were analyzed with Prism 7.0 (GraphPad Software). Comparisons between two experimental groups were performed with unpaired Student's *t*-test. Comparisons among three or more groups were performed with one-way ANOVA. Differences were considered significant if $P < 0.05$.

RESULTS

Arg^{853} Is a Unique Site of Dock4 Among All Dock Families and Is Highly Conserved During Evolution

Arg^{853} of human Dock4 is located in the linker region between DHR1 and DHR2 domains (**Figure 1A**), a region that has no known molecular function yet. We searched the UniProtKB Protein knowledgebase[1] and compared the sequence of amino acid sequences of Dock4 among different species, including frog (*Xenopus tropicalis*), mouse (*Mus musculus*), rat (*Rattus norvegicus*), marmoset (*Callithrix jacchus*), rhesus macaque (*Macaca mulatta*), chimpanzee (*Pan troglodytes*), and human (*Homo sapiens*). By using the Multiple Sequence Alignment analysis tool of Clustal Omega[2], we found that the Arg^{853} and its flanking sequences are highly conserved during evolution (**Figure 1B**). However, this region is not conserved in other Dock family members (**Figure 1C**), suggesting that this region is unique in Dock4.

Both Dock4-R853H and 945VS Lose the GEF Activities to Activate Rac1 and Rap1 GTPases

To study whether the autism/dyslexia-linked variations of *DOCK4* have influences on its Rac1 GEF activity, we compared the abilities of Rac1 activation by Dock4-945VS and R853H with that of the wild-type (WT) protein when exogenously expressed in cells. As previously reported (Xiao et al., 2013), 945VS totally lost the Rac1-activation ability (**Figures 2A,B**). R853H also decreased activated-Rac1 levels when compared to WT, although the reduction was not as robust as that caused by 945VS (**Figures 2A,B**). Besides the ability to activating Rac1, Dock4 is also known to have Rap1 GEF activity in tumor cells (Yajnik et al., 2003). We showed here that Rap1 activation was significantly compromised in *Dock4* KO hippocampus (**Figures 2C,D**), suggesting that Dock4 is capable of activating Rap1 in nervous system. We then examined the abilities of exogenously expressed Dock4-945VS and R853H toward Rap1 activation. Notably, while Dock4-WT remarkably increased activated-Rap1 levels, both mutants lacked this ability (**Figures 2E,F**). Hence, the two autism/dyslexia-linked mutants of Dock4 showed impaired abilities on activation of both Rac1 and Rap1.

The SH3 Domain and DHR2 Domain Are Important for Dock4-Regulated Rap1 Activation

Previously, we found that both the SH3 domain and the DHR2 domain, but not the C terminus, are required for Dock4 GEF

[1] http://www.uniprot.org/

[2] http://www.ebi.ac.uk/Tools/msa/clustalo/

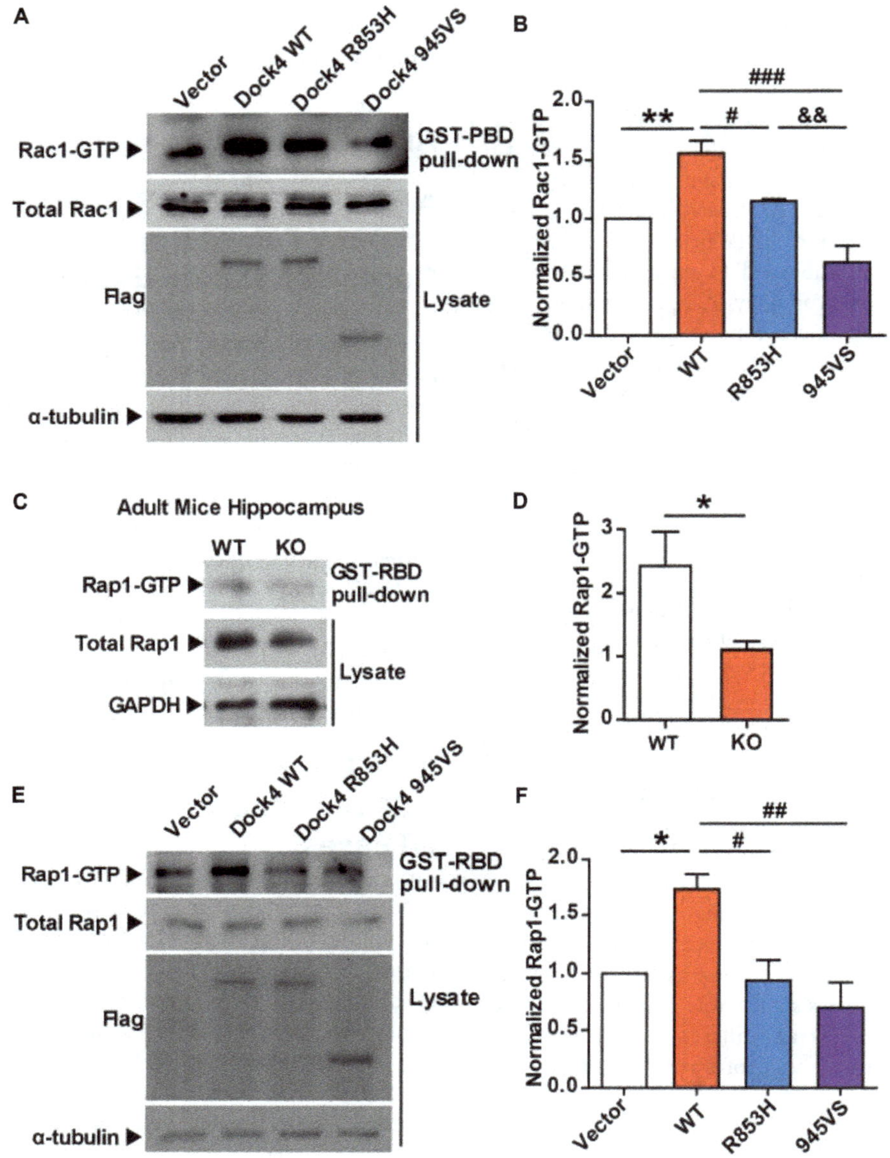

FIGURE 2 | Both 945VS and R853H mutants of Dock4 lose the GEF activities to activate Rac1 and Rap1 GTPases. **(A)** Rac1 activation by Dock4 mutants was abrogated. cDNAs of Dock4-R853H, Dock4-945VS, Dock4-WT (wild-type), or vector were expressed in HEK293T cells, and the levels of activated Rac1 (Rac1-GTP) were measured. **(B)** Rac1-GTP levels were quantified and normalized to total Rac1 levels. Data are shown as mean ± SEM from three independent experiments. $^{**}P < 0.01$, $\#P < 0.05$, $\#\#\#P < 0.001$, $\&\&P < 0.01$, one-way ANOVA. **(C)** Rap1-GTP level was reduced in hippocampus of *Dock4* knockout mice. Adult WT and *Dock4* knockout hippocampus protein was lysed, and the levels of Rap1-GTP were analyzed. **(D)** Rap1-GTP levels were quantified and normalized. Data are shown as mean ± SEM from three independent experiments. $^{*}P < 0.05$, unpaired *t*-test. **(E)** Dock4 mutants failed to activate Rap1. Dock4-R853H, Dock4-R853H or Dock4-WT were expressed in HEK293T cells, and the levels of Rap1-GTP were analyzed. **(F)** Rap1-GTP levels were quantified and normalized. Data are shown as mean ± SEM from three independent experiments. $^{*}P < 0.05$, $\#P < 0.05$, $\#\#P < 0.01$, one-way ANOVA.

activity toward Rac1 (Xiao et al., 2013). We went on to study whether these domains are important for activation of Rap1. Similarly, we observed that the SH3-lacking Dock4 (ΔSH3) could not activate Rap1, whereas the C-terminus-lacking Dock4 (ΔC) had intact Rap1-activation ability (**Figures 3A–C**). As 945VS, which lacks both DHR2 and the C-terminus, lost the Rap1-activating ability, it suggests that the DHR2 is responsible for not only Rac1, but also Rap1 activation. It has been shown that the Dock4 SH3 domain interacts with ELMO2 (Engulfment and cell motility 2), which acts as a co-factor of Dock4 toward Rac1-activation (Patel et al., 2011; Xiao et al., 2013; Laurin and Cote, 2014). To study whether ELMO2 is also important for Rap1 activation, we expressed ELMO2 together with Dock4 full length (FL) or ΔSH3 protein. Notably, ELMO2, without altering Rap1 levels by itself, appeared to further substantiate the effect of Dock4-FL on Rap1 activation (**Figures 3D,E**). In contrast, ELMO2 did not have any effect on Rap1 in Dock4-ΔSH3-expressing cells (**Figures 3D,E**). We further used a fragment

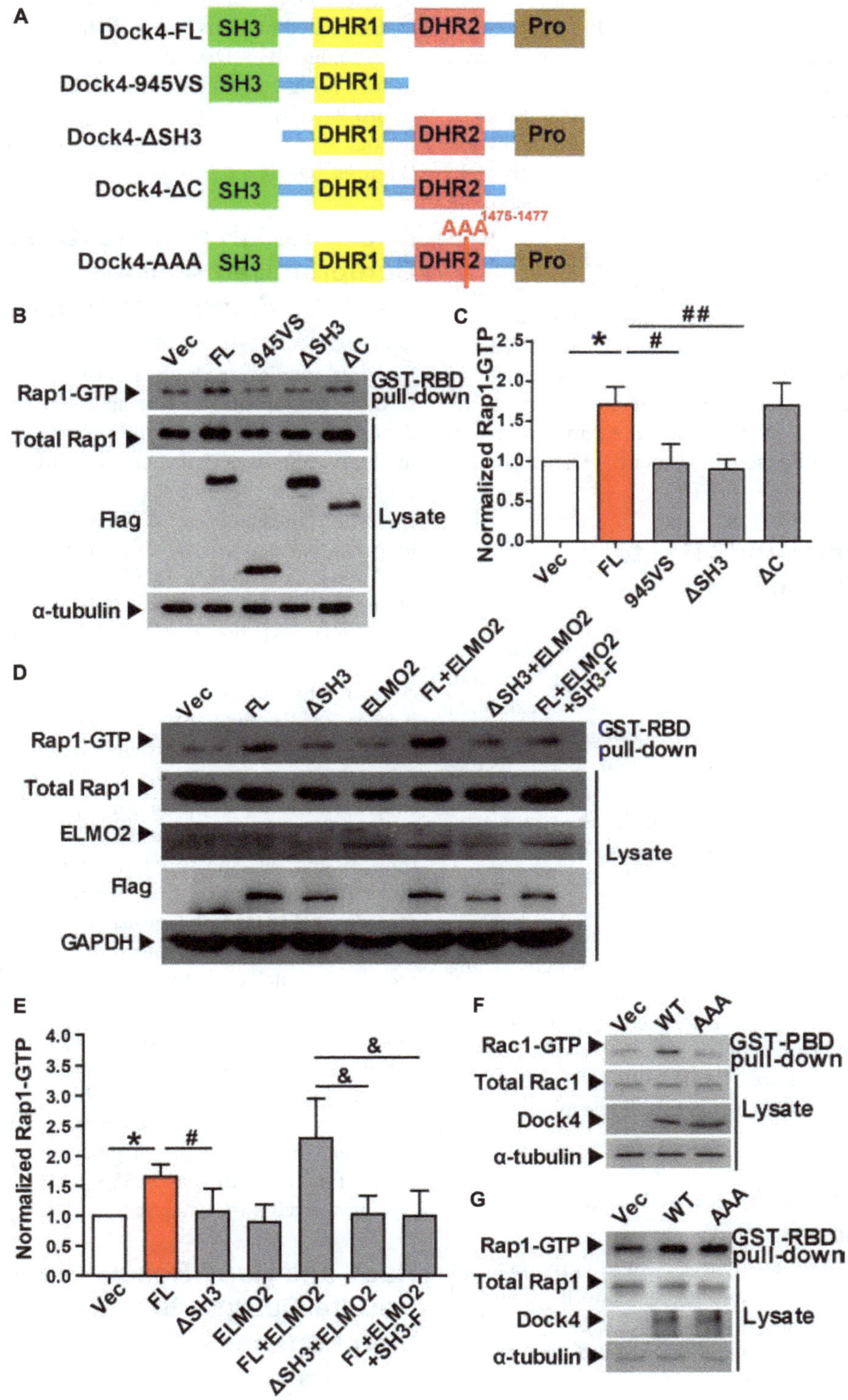

FIGURE 3 | The SH3 domain and DHR2 domain are important for Dock4-regulated Rap1 activation. **(A)** Domain illustrations of Dock4 and its mutants. **(B)** Rap1 activation was analyzed after Dock4-FL and various deletion mutants were transfected in HEK293T cells. **(C)** Rap1-GTP levels were quantified and normalized to total Rap1 expression. Data are shown as mean ± SEM from three independent experiments. *$P < 0.05$, #$P < 0.05$, ##$P < 0.01$, one-way ANOVA. **(D)** Dock4 activates Rap1 through SH3 domain coupling with ELMO2. ELMO2 and Flag-tagged Dock4-FL, ΔSH3 or SH3-F were co-transfected into HEK293T cells as indicated, and the levels of Rap1-GTP were analyzed. **(E)** Rap1-GTP levels were quantified and normalized. Data are shown as mean ± SEM from three independent experiments. *$P < 0.05$, #$P < 0.05$, &$P < 0.05$, one-way ANOVA. **(F,G)** The GEF-dead Dock4-AAA mutant lost Rac1-activating ability, but had intact Rap1-activating ability. Dock4-FL and its AAA mutant were transfected in HEK293T cells. Rac1-GTP **(F)** or Rap1-GTP **(G)** levels were examined.

of N-terminal Dock4 containing the SH3 domain (SH3-F) to compete the ELMO2 binding with Dock4-FL (Xiao et al., 2013). Consistently, when SH3-F was added to the Dock4-FL and ELMO2 complex, the Rap1 activation was completely abolished (**Figures 3D,E**). These results suggest that ELMO2, through forming a complex with Dock4, promotes the function of Dock4's DHR2 domain on both Rac1 and Rap1 activation. As the DHR2 of Dock4 is known as a RacGEF domain, we asked whether its RacGEF catalytic activity is responsible for Rap1 activation. To this end, a RacGEF-dead mutant of Dock4 (in which M1475, S1476, and P1477 in the DHR2 domain are all mutated to alanine), the AAA mutant, was examined (**Figure 3A**). Interestingly, the AAA mutant did lose the ability to activate Rac1, but its Rap1-activating ability was unaltered (**Figures 3F,G**). Therefore, Dock4 does not activate Rap1 the same way as it activates Rac1, and alternate mechanisms besides RacGEF activity may underlie the requirement of DHR2 domain for Rap1 activation.

Dock4-R853H and 945VS Fail to Influence Cell Morphology

We have shown that Dock4-R853H and 945VS exhibit decreased activities toward both Rac1 and Rap1, which regulate cell morphology by influencing cytoskeleton and cell adhesion. Indeed, HEK293T cells overexpressed with Dock4-WT exhibited a spread, elongated morphology with enlargement of both cytosolic and nuclear regions when compared to the vector-expressed cells (**Figures 4A–C**). The cellular location of Dock4-R853H and 945VS was mainly enriched in the cytoplasm, which was similar to that of Dock4-WT (**Figure 4A**). However, Dock4-R853H and 945VS failed to influence the overall cell morphology, as the cellular size was not changed by either mutant (**Figures 4A–C**). We then examined the cytoskeleton in cells expressing different Dock4 forms. Interestingly, strong staining of F-actin was observed in the cytoplasm and at the membrane of cells expressed with Dock4-WT (**Figure 4C**). In contrast, much weaker F-actin staining was observed in R853H- or 945VS-expressed cells (**Figure 4D**). Therefore, Dock4-R853H and 945VS are dysfunctional to regulate cell morphology and cytoskeleton properly.

Dock4-R853H and 945VS Lack Neurite Outgrowth Abilities

Previous evidence has revealed that Dock4 is important for neurite outgrowth and synapse morphogenesis during neuronal development (Ueda et al., 2008, 2013; Xiao et al., 2013). We first examined the ability of Dock4 mutants on promoting neurite outgrowth in Neuro-2a cells, a neuron-like cell line widely used for studying neuronal differentiation and neurite extension. When transfected into Neuro-2a cells, Dock4 substantially promoted neurite elongation upon retinoic acid (RA) stimulation (**Figures 5A–C**). However, neither Dock4-R853H nor Dock4-945VS was able to influence neurite outgrowth, as the neurite length of cells expressed with either mutant was comparable to that of the vector-expressed cells (**Figures 5A–C**). We further studied the neurite regulating roles of the two Dock4 mutants in cultured hippocampal neurons. We transfected either mutant in dissociated neurons before plating, and examined the neurite morphology at 3 DIV, by which time extensive neurites are formed with one differentiated into the axon. As observed in Neuro-2a cells, both mutants lost the ability to promote axon or total neurite elongation when compared to the WT protein (**Figures 5D–F**).

Dock4-R853H and 945VS Have Compromised Abilities to Promote Dendritic Spine Morphogenesis and Synaptic Transmission

Previous studies in both *Dock4* KO mice and in Dock4-shRNA knockdown neurons have shown that Dock4 promotes dendritic spine formation and excitatory synaptic transmission in hippocampus (Ueda et al., 2013; Guo et al., 2019). To investigate the abilities of Dock4-R853H and 945VS on spine morphogenesis, we delivered each plasmid into cultured hippocampal neurons by calcium phosphate transfection at 9 DIV, and the co-expressed GFP was used to indicate morphology of the transfected neurons. The spine number was examined at 16 DIV. As reported before, we observed a remarkable increase of spine density in Dock4-WT expressed neurons as compared to vector expressed neurons (**Figures 6A,B**). However, neither R853H nor 945VS was able to influence spine density (**Figures 6A,B**). By quantifying different types of spines, we found that Dock4 mainly promoted the mushroom-shaped spine, which is believed as the mature spines, whereas both mutants lacked this ability (**Figure 6B**). To further examine synaptic transmission, we measured miniature excitatory postsynaptic current (mEPSC) in these neurons by electrophysiological recordings (**Figure 6C**). Consistently, Dock4-WT increased both amplitude and frequency of mEPSC, suggesting that there were more functional excitatory synapses in Dock4 WT expressed neurons than in vector expressed neurons (**Figures 6C–E**). Interestingly, Dock4-R853H also increased mEPSC amplitude and frequency, but the effect was significantly weaker than that of Dock4-WT (**Figures 6C–E**). By contrast, Dock4-945VS completely lost the ability to promote mEPSC (**Figures 6C–E**). Together, these findings suggest that Dock4-R853H retains partial function, whereas 945VS loses the whole function on regulating excitatory synaptic transmission.

Rac1 and Rap1 Rescue the Defects of Neurite Outgrowth and Spine Morphogenesis in Dock4 Knockdown Neurons

To investigate whether Rac1 and Rap1 differentially participate in Dock4 function, we overexpressed either Rac1 or Rap1 in Dock4 knockdown hippocampal neurons. We studied the rescue effect of Rac1 or Rap1 in two stages of neuronal development. First, transfection of Dock4 shRNA together with either Rac1 or Rap1 was performed before neuronal cell plating, and neurite morphology was examined at 3 DIV (**Figure 7A**). Whereas Dock4 shRNA decreased neurite length significantly, co-expression of

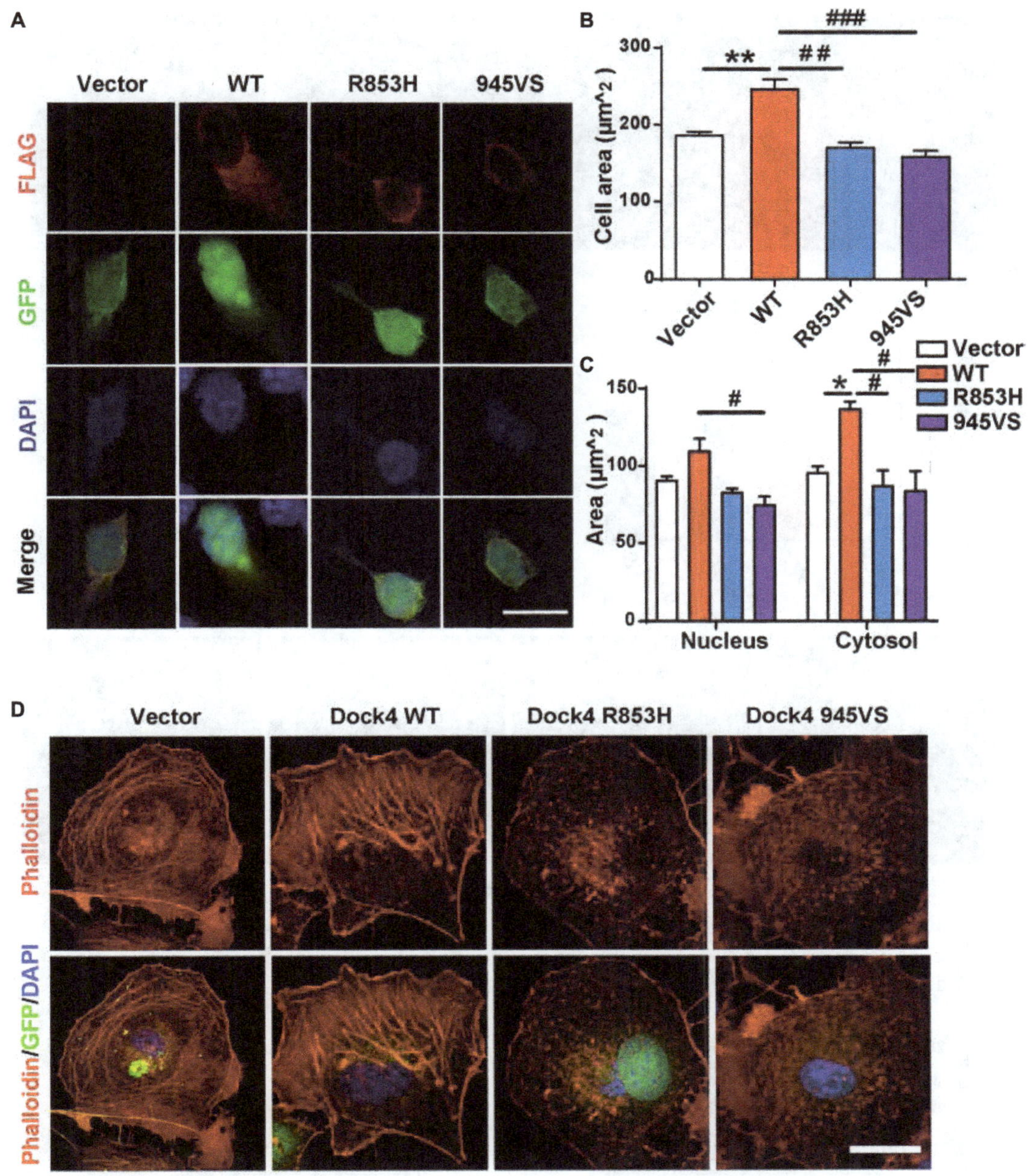

FIGURE 4 | Dock4-R853H and 945VS fail to influence cell morphology. **(A)** Dock4-R853H, Dock4-945VS, Dock4-WT or vector have different morphology in HEK293T. We transfected HEK293T cells with Vector, Flag-tagged Dock4-WT, Dock4-R853H, Dock4-945VS plasmids. Cells were immunostained using Flag antibody. Scale bar, 20 μm. **(B,C)** Total cell area, cytoplasmic area, and nuclear area were measured. Data are shown as mean ± SEM from three independent experiments. $^*P < 0.05$, $^{**}P < 0.01$, $\#P < 0.05$, $\#\#P < 0.01$, $\#\#\#P < 0.001$, one-way ANOVA. At least 20 cells/group were analyzed in each experiment. **(D)** Dock4 R853H and 945VS disrupt actin cytoskeleton in COS7 cells. Cells were immunostained using Phalloidin for visualization of actin cytoskeleton. Scale bar, 50 μm.

either Rac1 or Rap1 was able to rescue this impaired neurite outgrowth (**Figures 7B,C**). Notably, the effect of Rac1 appeared to be stronger than Rap1 (**Figures 7B,C**). Second, transfection of Dock4 shRNA together with either Rac1 or Rap1 was performed at 9 DIV, and spine morphology was examined at 16 DIV (**Figure 7D**). As reported before (Ueda et al., 2013), knockdown of Dock4 resulted in dramatic decrease of spine density, especially the density of the mushroom-shaped mature spines (**Figures 7D,E**). Importantly, overexpression of Rac1 specifically restored the density of these mature spines in Dock4-knockdown neurons (**Figures 7D,E**). Overexpression of Rap1, on the other hand, only promoted growth of filopodia/thin type of spines which are believed as the dynamic immature spines, but could not reverse the decrease of mature spines in Dock4-knockdown neurons (**Figures 7D,E**). These observations are consistent with the current knowledge on Rac1 and Rap1, which are important for spine enlargement and dynamics, respectively (Woolfrey and Srivastava, 2016). Together, the rescue experiments at different

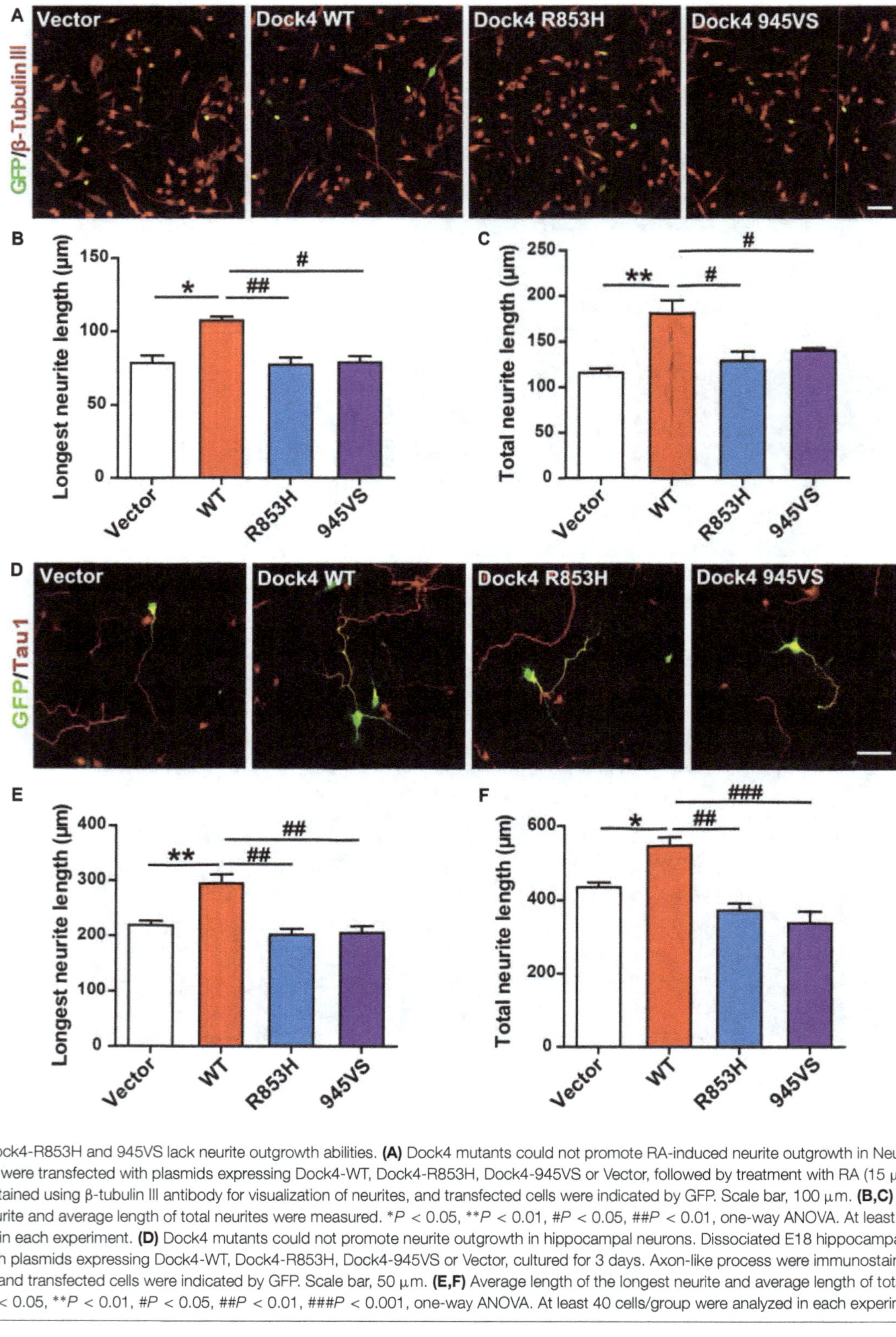

FIGURE 5 | Dock4-R853H and 945VS lack neurite outgrowth abilities. **(A)** Dock4 mutants could not promote RA-induced neurite outgrowth in Neuro-2a cells. Neuro-2a cells were transfected with plasmids expressing Dock4-WT, Dock4-R853H, Dock4-945VS or Vector, followed by treatment with RA (15 μM) for 48 h. Cells were immunostained using β-tubulin III antibody for visualization of neurites, and transfected cells were indicated by GFP. Scale bar, 100 μm. **(B,C)** Average length of the longest neurite and average length of total neurites were measured. *$P < 0.05$, **$P < 0.01$, #$P < 0.05$, ##$P < 0.01$, one-way ANOVA. At least 40 cells/group were analyzed in each experiment. **(D)** Dock4 mutants could not promote neurite outgrowth in hippocampal neurons. Dissociated E18 hippocampal neurons were transfected with plasmids expressing Dock4-WT, Dock4-R853H, Dock4-945VS or Vector, cultured for 3 days. Axon-like process were immunostained with Tau1 (red) antibody, and transfected cells were indicated by GFP. Scale bar, 50 μm. **(E,F)** Average length of the longest neurite and average length of total neurites were measured. *$P < 0.05$, **$P < 0.01$, #$P < 0.05$, ##$P < 0.01$, ###$P < 0.001$, one-way ANOVA. At least 40 cells/group were analyzed in each experiment.

neuronal developmental stages suggest that Rac1 and Rap1 may corporately participate in Dock4-mediated neurite outgrowth, and Rac1 is specifically required for Dock4-mediated formation of mature spines.

DISCUSSION

ASD and dyslexia are both neurodevelopmental disorders with high prevalence in children. As there are not many comorbidity

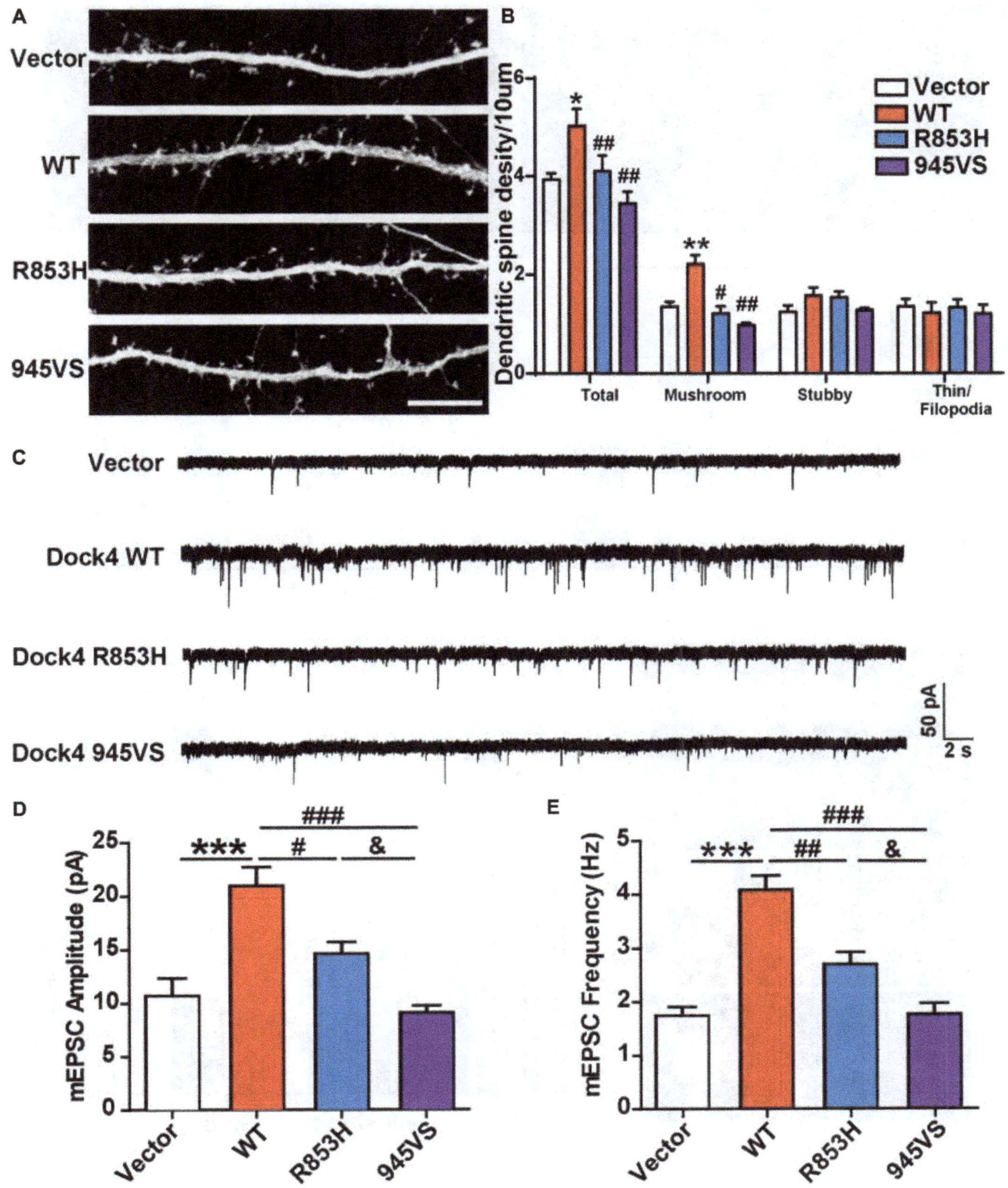

FIGURE 6 | Dock4-R853H and 945VS have compromised abilities to promote dendritic spine morphogenesis and synaptic transmission. **(A)** Dock4 mutants could not promote dendritic spine formation in hippocampal neurons. 9 DIV hippocampal neurons were transfected with plasmids expressing Dock4-WT, Dock4-R853H, Dock4-945VS or Vector and analyzed at 16 DIV. Scale bar, 10 μm. **(B)** Density of total spines and different types of spines were measured. Data are shown as mean ± SEM from three independent experiments. *$P < 0.05$, **$P < 0.01$, #$P < 0.05$, ##$P < 0.01$, one-way ANOVA. At least 30 cells/group were analyzed in each experiment. **(C)** Miniature excitatory postsynaptic currents (mEPSCs) of hippocampal neurons expressed with Dock4-WT, Dock4-R853H, Dock4-945VS or Vector. Amplitude **(D)** and frequency **(E)** were quantified. ***$P < 0.001$, #$P < 0.05$, ##$P < 0.01$, ###$P < 0.001$, &$P < 0.05$, one-way ANOVA. At least 10 cells/group were analyzed in each experiment.

studies of ASD and dyslexia, it is arguable whether the co-occurring reading difficulties in ASD are the same as in dyslexia, which is mainly characterized by phonological deficits (Hendren et al., 2018). Nonetheless, both diseases are well-documented comorbid diseases of language impairment (LI) with similar language traits, suggesting that ASD may share etiologies of language and verbal communication deficits with dyslexia and LI (Eicher and Gruen, 2015). Despite heterogeneous origins, emerging genetic and pathological findings point to a conclusion that ASD is a disease with impaired neuronal connectivity (Bourgeron, 2015). A large amount of high risk ASD genes play important roles at the synapse, in particular, at

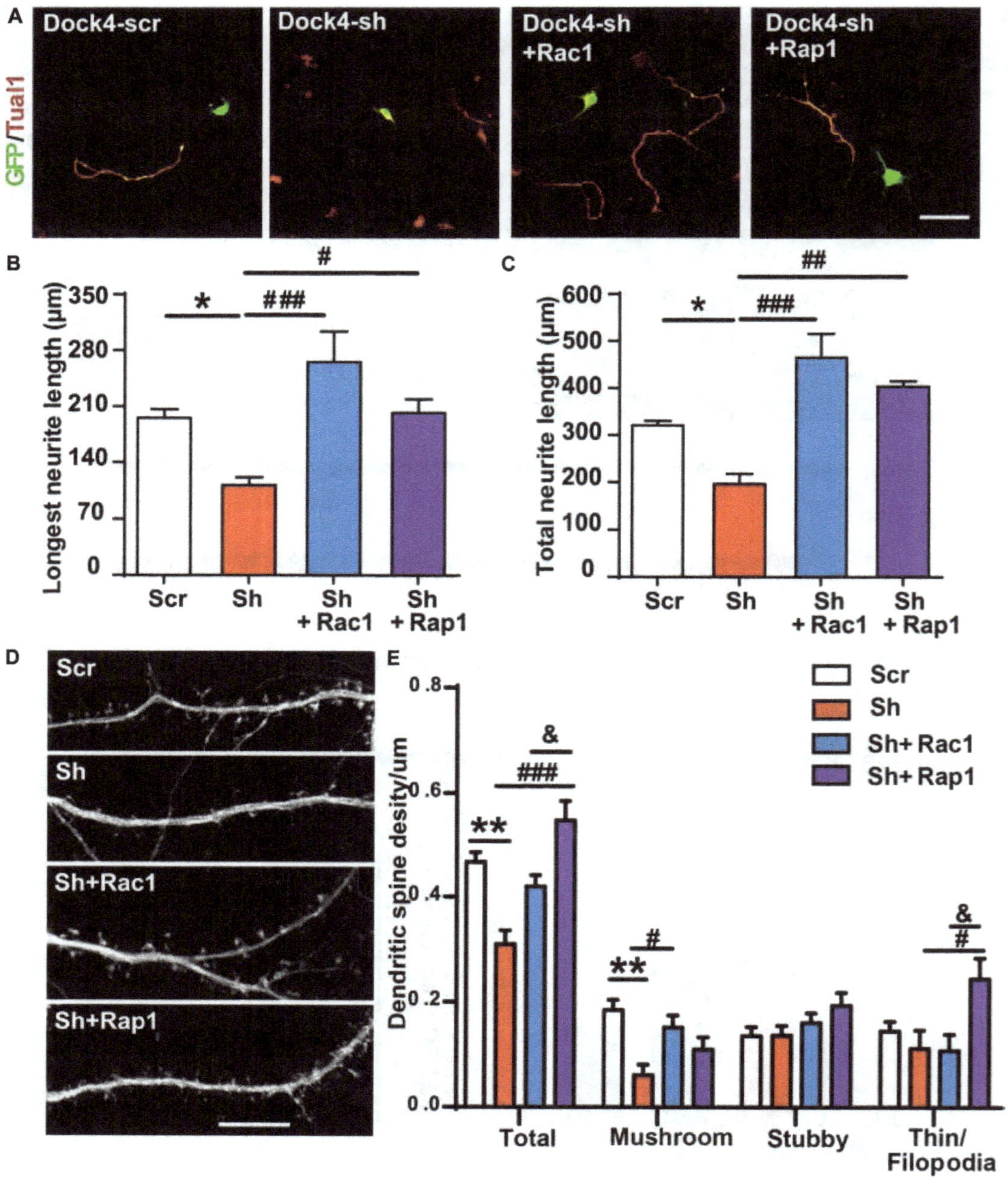

FIGURE 7 | Rac1 and Rap1 rescue the defects of neurite outgrowth and spine morphogenesis in Dock4 knockdown neurons. **(A)** Rac1 and Rap1 rescue neurite outgrowth defects in Dock4-knockdown hippocampal neurons. Dissociated E18 hippocampal neurons were transfected with plasmids expressing Dock4-scramble shRNA (Scr), Dock4-shRNA (sh), sh + Rac1, or sh + Rap1, and cultured for 3 days. Axon-like processes were immunostained with Tau1 (red) antibody, and transfected cells were indicated by GFP. Scale bar, 50 μm. Average length of the longest neurite **(B)** and total neurites **(C)** was measured. $*P < 0.05$, $\#P < 0.05$, $\#\#P < 0.01$, $\#\#\#P < 0.001$, one-way ANOVA. At least 40 cells/group were analyzed in each experiment. **(D)** 9 DIV hippocampal neurons were transfected with plasmids expressing Scr, sh, sh + Rac1, or sh + Rap1. Spine morphology was analyzed at 16 DIV. Scale bar, 10 μm. **(E)** Densities of total spines and different types of spines were measured. Data are shown as mean ± SEM from three independent experiments. $**P < 0.01$, $\#P < 0.05$, $\#\#\#P < 0.001$, $\&P < 0.05$, one-way ANOVA. At least 20 cells/group were analyzed in each experiment.

the postsynaptic sites of the excitatory synapses. These include synaptic receptors, adhesion molecules, scaffolding proteins and cytoskeletal regulators. The molecular pathophysiology of dyslexia is less understood, but lines of evidence suggest that disruptions of neuronal migration and neurite outgrowth contribute importantly to the pathogenesis of the disease (Poelmans et al., 2011; Shao et al., 2016; Guidi et al., 2018). So far, very few shared risk genes have been identified in both ASD and dyslexia. As a candidate gene for both disorders, *DOCK4* draws attention for understanding their common etiology.

The current study focuses on two *DOCK4* variants, Exon27-52 deletion (protein product: Dock4-945VS and rs2074130 variation (protein product: Dock4-R853H), which are associated with dyslexia and/or ASD with reading difficulties. Among them, the molecular function of Dock4-R853H is uncharacterized before. In the initial biochemical assays, we found that the RacGEF activities of both mutants are compromised. The loss of RacGEF activity is expected for Dock4-945VS because this mutant lacks the entire GEF domain, i.e., DHR2 domain. Interestingly, R853H also showed moderate decrease in RacGEF activity. The current study further confirms that Rap1 is another small GTPase besides Rac1 that can be activated by Dock4 in brain. Both Dock4-945VS and R853H totally lost the ability to activate Rap1. Domain mapping analysis suggests that similar to Rac1 activation (Xiao et al., 2013), DHR2 domain as well as binding to ELMO2 via SH3 domain are necessary for Rap1 activation. However, the RacGEF catalytic activity of DHR2 is not necessary for Rap1 activation, suggesting Dock4 uses different mechanism to activate Rac1 and Rap1 respectively. Further studies will be required to investigate whether DHR2 directly activates Rap1 or via binding to other Rap1-regulating proteins. Nonetheless, these studies suggest that R853 is probably a critical residue for the regulation of the DHR2 domain function. R853 and its flanking regions are unique sequence in Dock4 among Dock family members, it may represent a special site of regulation only in Dock4 but not in other Docks. Further analysis will be necessary to understand whether this residue is important for directly maintaining the structural integrity of the protein, or for recruiting other critical regulators that in turn control the function of the protein.

Cellular assays in this study reveal that both Dock4-R853H and 945VS lack the abilities to influence cell morphology, promote neurite outgrowth, and induce spine morphogenesis. By using electrophysiological approaches, we further demonstrate that Dock4-R853H is still able to promote excitatory synaptic transmission, although this ability is weaker than the WT protein. Dock4-945VS, on the other hand, completely fails to regulate synaptic transmission. This difference could be due to the fact that Dock4-R853 still retains some level of Rac1-activating ability, whereas 945VS lost both Rac1- and Rap1-activating abilities. Indeed, we showed that Rac1 is mainly required for the formation of mature spines regulated by Dock4, suggesting that Rac1 may be the primary small GTPases downstream of Dock4 for functional synapse formation and transmission.

Findings in this study are consistent with the neurodevelopment impairment hypothesis of ASD and dyslexia, in which *DOCK4* contributes to a shared genetic factor for both disorders. Using *Dock4* knockout mice, we have shown that deficiency of *Dock4 in vivo* leads to social and communication deficits (Guo et al., 2019). Findings of the current study provide further molecular and cellular evidence that Dock4-dependent regulation of neuronal development may underlie the neurobiology basis of social communication and language development. Therefore, investigating the mechanism by which Dock4 and its downstream molecules regulate neuronal function and behavior provides more evidence for understanding the pathogenesis of the co-occurring symptoms of ASD and dyslexia.

ETHICS STATEMENT

The animal study was reviewed and approved by the Jinan University.

AUTHOR CONTRIBUTIONS

MH, CL, SL, JZ, DG, BZ, and YP performed the experiments. YL and WL purified the Rac1- and Rap1-binding protein domains for Rac1 and Rap1 assays. MH, CL, SL, YP, GG, and LS analyzed the data. MH, CL, SL, JX, and LS did data interpretation and figure organization. MH and LS wrote the manuscript.

FUNDING

This work was supported by the Academy of Medical Sciences Newton Advanced Fellowship in partnership with the Royal Society and the National Natural Science Foundation of China (United Kingdom/China Grant Numbers: AOMS-NAF0051003/81761130084), Key Realm R&D Program of Guangdong Province (2019B030335001), Local Innovative and Research Teams Project of Guangdong Pearl River Talents Program (2017BT01Y036), and Shenzhen Basic Research Grants (JCYJ20170411090807530).

ACKNOWLEDGMENTS

We thank colleagues and students in Shi Group of JNU-HKUST Joint Lab for Neuroscience and Innovative Drug Research for constructive discussions on this study.

REFERENCES

Akahoshi, K., and Yamamoto, T. (2018). Interstitial deletion within 7q31.1q31.3 in a woman with mild intellectual disability and schizophrenia. *Neuropsychiatr. Dis. Treat.* 14, 1773–1778. doi: 10.2147/NDT.S168469

Alkelai, A., Lupoli, S., Greenbaum, L., Kohn, Y., Kanyas-Sarner, K., Ben-Asher, E., et al. (2012). DOCK4 and CEACAM21 as novel schizophrenia candidate genes in the Jewish population. *Int. J. Neuropsychopharmacol.* 15, 459–469. doi: 10.1017/S1461145711000903

Bai, Y., Guo, D., Sun, X., Tang, G., Liao, T., Peng, Y., et al. (2018). Balanced Rac1 activity controls formation and maintenance of neuromuscular acetylcholine receptor clusters. *J. Cell Sci.* 131:jcs215251. doi: 10.1242/jcs.215251

Bourgeron, T. (2015). From the genetic architecture to synaptic plasticity in autism spectrum disorder. *Nat. Rev. Neurosci.* 16, 551–563. doi: 10.1038/nrn3992

Eicher, J. D., and Gruen, J. R. (2015). Language impairment and dyslexia genes influence language skills in children with autism spectrum disorders. *Autism. Res.* 8, 229–234. doi: 10.1002/aur.1436

Guidi, L. G., Velayos-Baeza, A., Martinez-Garay, I., Monaco, A. P., Paracchini, S., Bishop, D. V. M., et al. (2018). The neuronal migration hypothesis of dyslexia: a critical evaluation 30 years on. *Eur. J. Neurosci.* 48, 3212–3233. doi: 10.1111/ejn.14149

Guo, D., Peng, Y., Wang, L., Sun, X., Wang, X., and Liang, C. (2019). Autism-like social deficit generated by Dock4 deficiency is rescued by restoration of Rac1 activity and NMDA receptor function. *Mol. Psychiatry* doi: 10.1038/s41380-019-0472-7 [Epub ahead of print].

Hendren, R. L., Haft, S. L., Black, J. M., White, N. C., and Hoeft, F. (2018). Recognizing psychiatric comorbidity with reading disorders. *Front. Psychiatry* 9:101. doi: 10.3389/fpsyt.2018.00101

Iossifov, I., O'roak, B. J., Sanders, S. J., Ronemus, M., Krumm, N., and Levy, D. (2014). The contribution of de novo coding mutations to autism spectrum disorder. *Nature* 515, 216–221. doi: 10.1038/nature13908

Ip, J. P., Shi, L., Chen, Y., Itoh, Y., Fu, W. Y., Betz, A., et al. (2012). Alpha2-chimaerin controls neuronal migration and functioning of the cerebral cortex through CRMP-2. *Nat. Neurosci.* 15, 39–47. doi: 10.1038/nn.2972

Kushima, I., Aleksic, B., Nakatochi, M., Shimamura, T., Okada, T., and Uno, Y. (2018). Comparative analyses of copy-number variation in autism spectrum disorder and schizophrenia reveal etiological overlap and biological insights. *Cell Rep.* 24, 2838–2856. doi: 10.1016/j.celrep.2018.08.022

Laurin, M., and Cote, J. F. (2014). Insights into the biological functions of Dock family guanine nucleotide exchange factors. *Genes Dev.* 28, 533–547. doi: 10.1101/gad.236349.113

Liang, S., Wang, X. L., Zou, M. Y., Wang, H., Zhou, X., and Sun, C. H. (2014). Family-based association study of ZNF533, DOCK4 and IMMP2L gene polymorphisms linked to autism in a northeastern Chinese Han population. *J. Zhejiang Univ. Sci. B* 15, 264–271. doi: 10.1631/jzus.B1300133

Liao, Y., Zhuang, X., Huang, X., Peng, Y., Ma, X., Huang, Z. X., et al. (2018). A Bivalent securinine compound SN3-L6 induces neuronal differentiation via translational upregulation of neurogenic transcription factors. *Front. Pharmacol* 9:290. doi: 10.3389/fphar.2018.00290

Lim, E. T., Uddin, M., De Rubeis, S., Chan, Y., Kamumbu, A. S., and Zhang, X. (2017). Rates, distribution and implications of postzygotic mosaic mutations in autism spectrum disorder. *Nat. Neurosci.* 20, 1217–1224. doi: 10.1038/nn.4598

Maestrini, E., Pagnamenta, A. T., Lamb, J. A., Bacchelli, E., Sykes, N. H., and Sousa, I. (2010). High-density SNP association study and copy number variation analysis of the AUTS1 and AUTS5 loci implicate the IMMP2L-DOCK4 gene region in autism susceptibility. *Mol. Psychiatry* 15, 954–968. doi: 10.1038/mp.2009.34

Makihara, S., Morin, S., Ferent, J., Cote, J. F., Yam, P. T., and Charron, F. (2018). Polarized Dock Activity Drives Shh-Mediated Axon Guidance. *Dev. Cell* 46, e417. doi: 10.1016/j.devcel.2018.07.007

Pagnamenta, A. T., Bacchelli, E., De Jonge, M. V., Mirza, G., Scerri, T. S., and Minopoli, F. (2010). Characterization of a family with rare deletions in CNTNAP5 and DOCK4 suggests novel risk loci for autism and dyslexia. *Biol Psychiatry* 68, 320–328. doi: 10.1016/j.biopsych.2010.02.002

Patel, M., Pelletier, A., and Cote, J. F. (2011). Opening up on ELMO regulation: new insights into the control of Rac signaling by the DOCK180/ELMO complex. *Small GTPases* 2, 268–275. doi: 10.4161/sgtp.2.5.17716

Poelmans, G., Buitelaar, J. K., Pauls, D. L., and Franke, B. (2011). A theoretical molecular network for dyslexia: integrating available genetic findings. *Mol. Psychiatry* 16, 365–382. doi: 10.1038/mp.2010.105

Raskind, W. H., Peter, B., Richards, T., Eckert, M. M., and Berninger, V. W. (2012). The genetics of reading disabilities: from phenotypes to candidate genes. *Front. Psychol.* 3:601. doi: 10.3389/fpsyg.2012.00601

Shao, S., Kong, R., Zou, L., Zhong, R., Lou, J., and Zhou, J. (2016). The roles of genes in the neuronal migration and neurite outgrowth network in developmental dyslexia: single- and multiple-risk genetic variants. *Mol. Neurobiol.* 53, 3967–3975. doi: 10.1007/s12035-015-9334-8

Shi, L. (2013). Dock protein family in brain development and neurological disease. *Commun. Integr. Biol.* 6:e26839. doi: 10.4161/cib.26839

Shi, L., Fu, W. Y., Hung, K. W., Porchetta, C., Hall, C., Fu, A. K., et al. (2007). Alpha2-chimaerin interacts with EphA4 and regulates EphA4-dependent growth cone collapse. *Proc. Natl. Acad. Sci. U.S.A* 104, 16347–16352. doi: 10.1073/pnas.0706626104

Tang, G., Dong, X., Huang, X., Huang, X. J., Liu, H., Wang, Y., et al. (2015). A natural diarylheptanoid promotes neuronal differentiation via activating ERK and PI3K-Akt dependent pathways. *Neuroscience* 303, 389–401. doi: 10.1016/j.neuroscience.2015.07.019

Toma, C., Torrico, B., Hervas, A., Valdes-Mas, R., Tristan-Noguero, A., Padillo, V., et al. (2014). Exome sequencing in multiplex autism families suggests a major role for heterozygous truncating mutations. *Mol. Psychiatry* 19, 784–790. doi: 10.1038/mp.2013.106

Ueda, S., Fujimoto, S., Hiramoto, K., Negishi, M., and Katoh, H. (2008). Dock4 regulates dendritic development in hippocampal neurons. *J. Neurosci. Res.* 86, 3052–3061. doi: 10.1002/jnr.21763

Ueda, S., Negishi, M., and Katoh, H. (2013). Rac GEF Dock4 interacts with cortactin to regulate dendritic spine formation. *Mol. Biol. Cell* 24, 1602–1613. doi: 10.1091/mbc.E12-11-0782

Warrier, V., Chakrabarti, B., Murphy, L., Chan, A., Craig, I., Mallya, U., et al. (2015). A pooled genome-wide association study of asperger syndrome. *PLoS One* 10:e0131202. doi: 10.1371/journal.pone.0131202

Woolfrey, K. M., and Srivastava, D. P. (2016). Control of dendritic spine morphological and functional plasticity by small GTPases. *Neural. Plast.* 2016:3025948. doi: 10.1155/2016/3025948

Xiao, Y., Peng, Y., Wan, J., Tang, G., Chen, Y., Tang, J., et al. (2013). The atypical guanine nucleotide exchange factor Dock4 regulates neurite differentiation through modulation of Rac1 GTPase and actin dynamics. *J. Biol. Chem.* 288, 20034–20045. doi: 10.1074/jbc.M113.458612

Yajnik, V., Paulding, C., Sordella, R., Mcclatchey, A. I., Saito, M., Wahrer, D. C. R., et al. (2003). DOCK4, a GTPase activator, is disrupted during tumorigenesis. *Cell* 112, 673–684. doi: 10.1016/s0092-8674(03)00155-7

Zhang, J., Yin, Y., Ji, Z., Cai, Z., Zhao, B., Li, J., et al. (2017). Endophilin2 interacts with GluA1 to Mediate AMPA receptor endocytosis induced by oligomeric amyloid-beta. *Neural. Plast.* 2017:8197085. doi: 10.1155/2017/8197085

16

Cell Type-Specific Gene Network-Based Analysis Depicts the Heterogeneity of Autism Spectrum Disorder

Jinting Guan [1,2]*, *Yiping Lin* [1] *and Guoli Ji* [1,2,3]

[1] *Department of Automation, Xiamen University, Xiamen, China,* [2] *National Institute for Data Science in Health and Medicine, Xiamen University, Xiamen, China,* [3] *Innovation Center for Cell Signaling Network, Xiamen University, Xiamen, China*

Correspondence:
Jinting Guan
jtguan@xmu.edu.cn

Autism spectrum disorder (ASD) is a complex neuropsychiatric disorder characterized by substantial heterogeneity. To identify the convergence of disease pathology on common pathways, it is essential to understand the correlations among ASD candidate genes and study shared molecular pathways between them. Investigating functional interactions between ASD candidate genes in different cell types of normal human brains may shed new light on the genetic heterogeneity of ASD. Here we apply cell type-specific gene network-based analysis to analyze human brain nucleus gene expression data and identify cell type-specific ASD-associated gene modules. ASD-associated modules specific to different cell types are relevant to different gene functions, for instance, the astrocytes-specific module is involved in functions of axon and neuron projection guidance, GABAergic interneuron-specific modules are involved in functions of postsynaptic membrane, extracellular matrix structural constituent, and ion transmembrane transporter activity. Our findings can promote the study of cell type heterogeneity of ASD, providing new insights into the pathogenesis of ASD. Our method has been shown to be effective in discovering cell type-specific disease-associated gene expression patterns and can be applied to other complex diseases.

Keywords: cell type-specific, gene network, cell type heterogeneity, autism, gene function

INTRODUCTION

Autism spectrum disorder (ASD) is a complex neuropsychiatric disorder with substantial phenotypic and genetic heterogeneity, characterized by impairments in social interaction and communication, and repetitive and restricted behaviors. Until now, about a thousand genes, each with different functions, have been linked to ASD, while it remains unclear how disruptions in these genes can lead to a common clinical phenotype. For identifying potential converged molecular pathways, it is essential to study the correlations among ASD candidate genes. Since ASD is believed to result from functional aberrations within brains, it was hypothesized that investigating functional relationships between ASD candidate genes in normal human brains may provide convergent mechanistic insight into the genetic heterogeneity of ASD (Mahfouz et al., 2015). With this hypothesis, several studies constructed a gene co-expression network based on bulk transcriptomic data of normal human brains and mapped ASD candidate genes or/and cell type markers to the gene modules, whose functions were analyzed for identifying the pathways and cell types which may be dysregulated in ASD (Ben-David and Shifman, 2012; Parikshak et al., 2013; Willsey et al., 2013; Mahfouz et al., 2015).

The human brain is a highly heterogeneous organ with different sets of cell types that are highly interconnected. Genes may demonstrate diverse functions across different brain cell types. Although bulk transcriptomic studies revealed convergence of disease pathology on common pathways (Voineagu et al., 2011; Gupta et al., 2014), the human brain cell type-specific molecular pathology of ASD is still needed to study. Here we hypothesize further that different gene functions in different human brain cell types may be dysregulated in ASD; investigating functional interactions between ASD candidate genes in different cell types of normal human brains may provide new insight into the genetic heterogeneity of ASD. Therefore, it is essential to construct gene networks in a cell type-specific way for identifying the vulnerable cell types and converged pathways among ASD candidate genes in different cells.

In this paper, we apply cell type-specific gene network-based analysis to analyze human brain nucleus gene expression data. To study the heterogeneity of ASD in aberrant gene expression between cell types, we identify cell type-specific ASD-associated gene modules and analyze dysregulated functions in ASD specific to cell types. Compared with other studies, our method has been shown to be effective in discovering cell type-specific disease-associated gene expression patterns.

MATERIALS AND METHODS

Gene Expression Data

We used the gene expression data of 15,928 human brain nuclei from middle temporal gyrus of human cortex (Hodge et al., 2019). These nuclei were from eight human donor brains, of which 15,206 were from postmortem donors with no known neuropsychiatric or neurological conditions and 722 were from distal and normal tissues of neurosurgical donors. We downloaded the data from Allen Institute for Brain Science and preprocessed it with R package of scran (Lun et al., 2016), including the quality control of nuclei and genes, removing a minority of nuclei assigned to different cell cycle phases and normalizing the data. We used ComBat to regress out the technical factor (seq_batch) which contributed to the heterogeneity of gene expression. Nuclear and mitochondrial genes downloaded from Human MitoCarta2.0 (Calvo et al., 2016) were excluded and protein-coding genes were retained. Then we obtained the expression level of 17,120 protein-coding genes in 12,506 nuclei, including 8,994, 2,762, 227, 3, 15, 112, 133, and 260 nuclei from glutamatergic neuron, GABAergic interneuron, astrocytes, endothelial, microglia, oligodendrocytes, oligodendrocyte precursor cell (OPC), and unclassified cell class (denoted by "No"), respectively. The classified nuclei were also defined into 75 distinct cell clusters, including 24, 45, 2, 1, 1, 1, and 1 cell clusters from glutamatergic neuron, GABAergic interneuron, astrocytes, endothelial, microglia, oligodendrocytes, and OPC. Then we used scran to obtain 7,011 highly variable protein-coding genes across all nuclei for performing subsequent analyses, which were genes with biological components that are significantly greater than zero at a false discovery rate (FDR) of 0.1.

Construction of Cell Type-Related Gene Network

For each cell type, we extracted the gene expression data of nuclei from the cell type and constructed a gene co-expression network using WGCNA (weighted gene co-expression network analysis) (Langfelder and Horvath, 2008). The unsigned gene network was built using function of *blockwiseModules* with parameters of *corType* = "pearson," *TOMType* = "signed," *minModuleSize* = 30, *minKMEtoStay* = 0.2, and *mergeCutHeight* = 0.2. To assess the preservation between gene modules built from each cell type and from other cell types, the function of *modulePreservation* (Langfelder et al., 2011) in WGCNA was applied to calculate module preservation statistics. The median of Zsummary values was used to further evaluate if a candidate gene module is cell type-specific. We calculated the correlation of module eigengene (the first principal component) and each gene, defined as module membership. For the genes with top 50 module membership, we applied Cytoscape (Shannon et al., 2003) to plot the correlation network based on the topology overlap matrix (TOM) from WGCNA.

Curated ASD Candidate Gene Set

A total of 822 ASD candidate genes were downloaded from the gene scoring module in Simons Foundation Autism Research Initiative (SFARI), which include the genes from categories of S (syndromic), 1 (high confidence), 2 (strong candidate), 3 (suggestive evidence), and 4 (minimal evidence).

Calculation of Cell Type Specificity of Genes

To identify cell type-specific gene modules, we first calculated cell type specificity of genes using a method similar to that in the study of (McKenzie et al., 2018), where specificity was defined as the minimum fold change in expression between the cell type of interest and each of the other cell types. For this, we calculated the counts per million (CPM) using the R package of edgeR (Robinson et al., 2010). The specificity of gene g in the interested cell type indexed by c was calculated as:

$$specificity_{g,c} = \min_{r\in\{1,2,\ldots,k\}\setminus c} \frac{\sum_{i=1}^{N_c} \exp(i,g,c)/N_c}{\sum_{j=1}^{N_r} \exp(j,g,r)/N_r}$$

where each of k cell types was denoted by a numerical index from the set$\{1,2....,k\}$, r denoted one cell type from the reference cell set, N_c and N_r were the numbers of nuclei classified into cell types of c and r respectively, $\exp(i,g,c)$ denotes the expression of gene g in nucleus i from cell type of c. The genes with top 500 specificity values were used as cell type-specific genes to assess the cell type enrichment for each considered gene module. The gene modules built from a cell type significantly enriched with the specific genes of the cell type but not enriched with other kinds of cell type-specific genes are considered as candidate cell type-specific gene modules.

Gene Set Enrichment and Functional Annotation Analyses

For a considered gene module, we used hypergeometric tests to assess the significance of enrichment of cell type-specific genes or ASD candidate genes. The correction for multiple testing was performed by controlling FDR with the Benjamini–Hochberg method. Gene ontology analysis was performed using the R package of clusterProfiler (Yu et al., 2012), with background genes set as the genes in the analyzed expression matrix. The GO term whose FDR-adjusted P-value < 0.1 and the number of genes in the term is not less than five was reported. The function of *simplify* was used to remove redundant significant GO terms with default parameters.

RESULTS

Overview of Analysis Workflow

To study the dysregulated functions in ASD specific to cell types, we applied cell type-specific gene network-based analysis to identify cell type-specific ASD-associated gene modules. The analysis workflow can be seen in **Figure 1**. After pre-processing the data matrix (see Materials and Methods), we first used the broad definition of cell type, the classification of cell classes, to identify cell class-specific ASD-associated gene modules. Specifically, for each cell class, we constructed a gene co-expression network (**Supplementary Table 1**). Then SFARI ASD candidate genes were used to identify ASD-associated gene modules. The gene modules significantly enriched with ASD candidate genes (FDR-corrected P-value < 0.1) are considered as ASD-associated gene modules. Next, we calculated cell class specificity of genes (see Materials and Methods), and cell class-specific genes (**Supplementary Table 2**) were used to assess the cell class enrichment for each ASD-associated module. The ASD-associated gene modules built from a cell class significantly enriched with the specific genes of the cell class (FDR-corrected P-value < 0.1) but not enriched with other kinds of cell class-specific genes are considered as candidate cell class-specific ASD-associated gene modules. Then the function of *modulePreservation* in WGCNA was applied to calculate module preservation statistics between gene modules build from each cell class and from other cell classes (**Supplementary Table 1**).

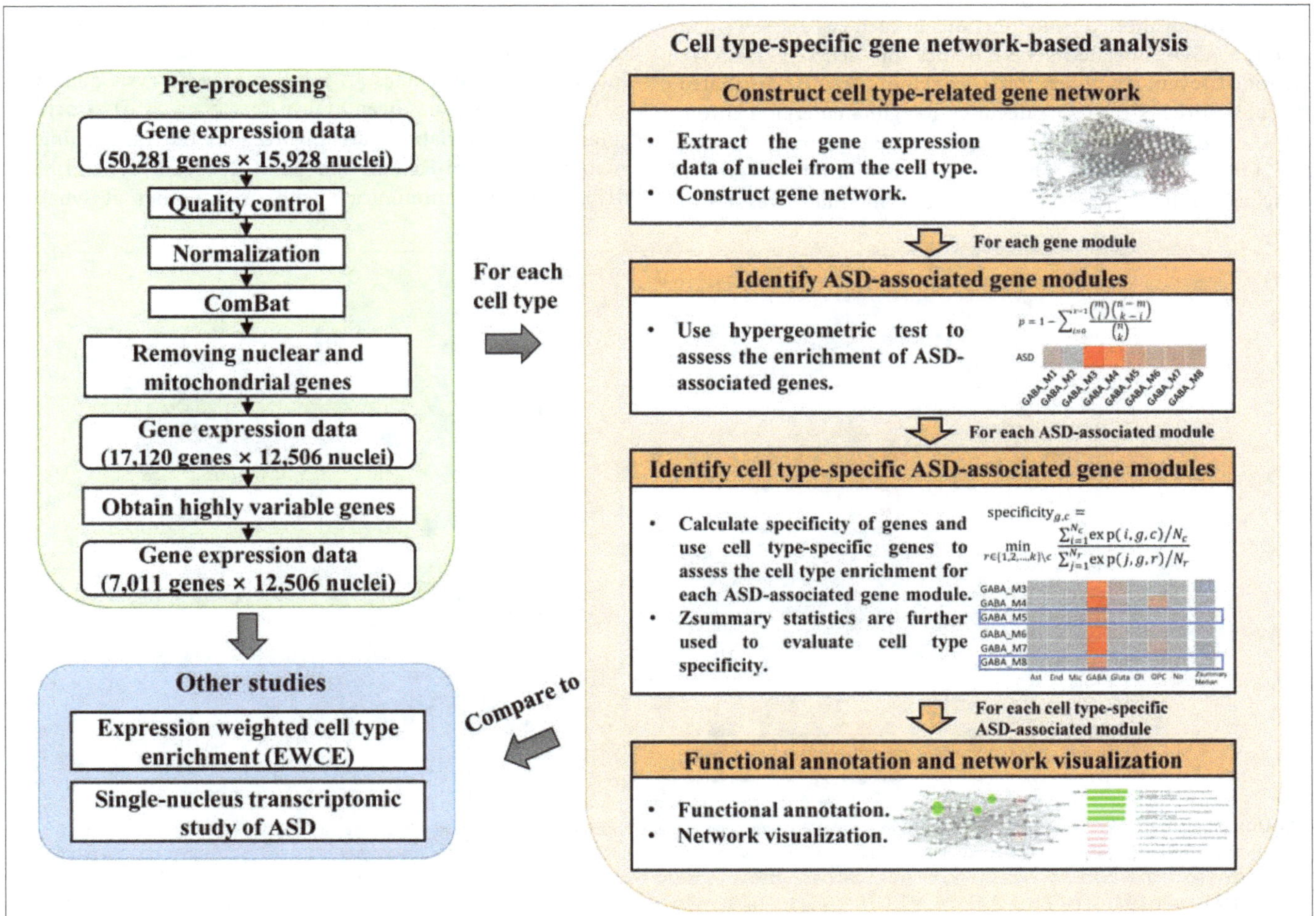

FIGURE 1 | The analysis workflow which includes pre-processing of gene expression data, cell type-specific gene network-based analysis, and comparison to other studies.

As Zsummary < 2 implies no evidence for module preservation (Langfelder et al., 2011), we reported the candidate cell class-specific ASD-associated gene modules whose medians of Zsummary are smaller than two as cell class-specific ASD-associated gene modules. These gene modules are not preserved from the considered cell class to other cell classes, which implies they are cell type-specific. In addition, we also adopted the classification of cell clusters and identified cell cluster-specific ASD-associated gene modules. The classification of cell clusters and the calculated cell cluster specificity of genes can be seen in **Supplementary Table 3.** By applying functional annotation analysis for cell type-specific ASD-associated gene modules, we study the probably affected functions by ASD specific to cell types. Network visualization was performed to prioritize genes that may be used as therapeutic targets of ASD. Lastly, we applied expression weighted cell type enrichment (EWCE) (Skene and Grant, 2016) and also analyzed the single-nucleus gene expression data of cortical tissue samples from ASD patients and healthy controls reported in (Velmeshev et al., 2019) to validate our results.

Cell Type-Specific Gene Network-Based Analysis

To analyze the affected gene functions in each cell class, we first detected ASD-associated gene modules for each cell class. We identified seven, six, three, three, one and one ASD-associated modules enriched in GO categories for glutamatergic neuron, GABAergic interneuron, astrocytes, microglia, oligodendrocytes, and OPC (**Figure 2A**). The top five significant GO terms enriched in these ASD-associated gene modules are shown as **Supplementary Figure 1**. To further study the dysregulated functions specific to cell classes, we identified six candidate cell class-specific ASD-associated gene modules, which are Ast_M2, GABA_M5, GABA_M8, Gluta_M1, Gluta_M3, and OPC_M10. Combining the Zsummary statistics calculated by WGCNA (**Supplementary Table 1**), modules of Ast_M2, GABA_M5, GABA_M8, and Gluta_M1 were retained, which are considered as cell class-specific ASD-associated gene modules. To identify the functions specific to each cell class-specific ASD-associated gene module, we report the GO terms only enriched in one module. The top specific GO terms enriched in cell class-specific ASD-associated gene modules can be seen in **Table 1**.

For astrocytes, the cell class-specific ASD-associated gene module is relevant to the functions of axon and neuron projection guidance, and sprouting angiogenesis. Astrocytes perform a variety of tasks from axon guidance and synaptic support to the control of the blood brain barrier and blood flow (Blackburn et al., 2009). The dysfunctions of astrocytes in modulating the development of synapse and interplay with neurons have already been shown to be implicated with ASD (Allen and Eroglu, 2017; Russo et al., 2017). For GABAergic interneuron, the functions of cell class-specific ASD-associated gene modules are related to postsynaptic membrane, extracellular matrix structural constituent, and ion transmembrane transporter activity. As to glutamatergic neuron, functions of phosphatase binding and protein kinase A binding may be dysregulated in ASD. Until now, it has been known that many ASD-associated mutations and variations are involved in the functioning of synapses (Ebrahimi-Fakhari and Sahin, 2015; Gilbert and Man, 2017). Neurons communicate with one another at synapses

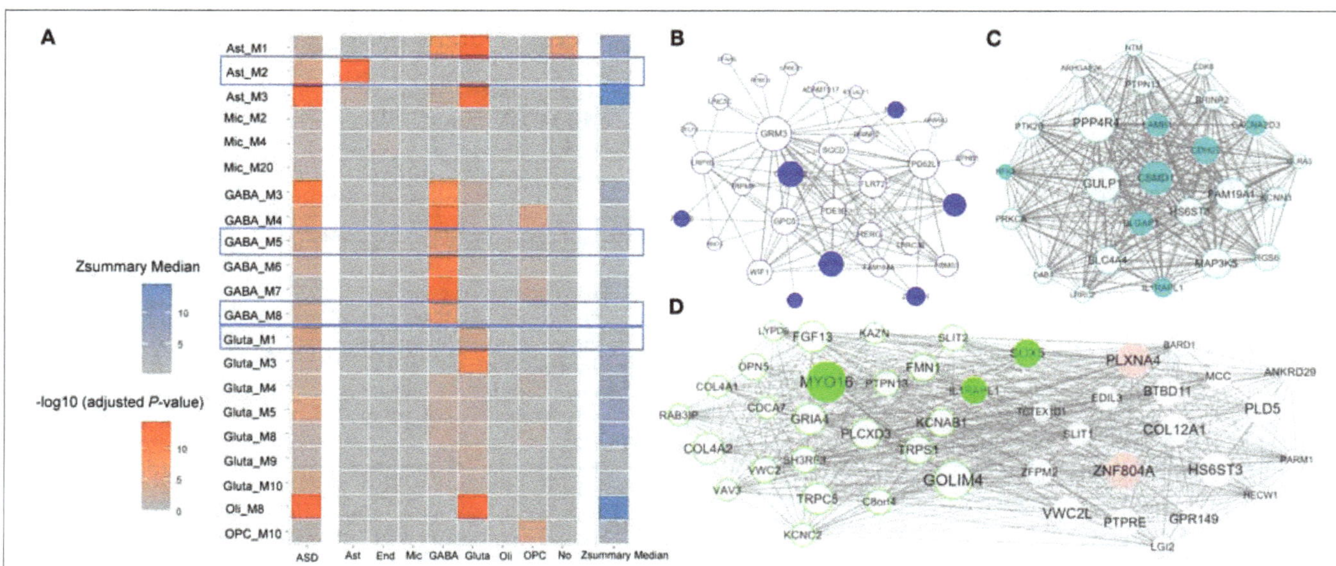

FIGURE 2 | (A) The enrichment of cell class-specific genes for ASD-associated gene modules along with medians of Zsummary. Each grid in the first column demonstrates the significance of enrichment of ASD candidate genes; each grid in the last column demonstrates the median of Zsummary; each grid in the other columns demonstrates the significance of enrichment of cell class-specific genes for each ASD-associated gene module. The cell class-specific ASD-associated gene modules are marked, which are Ast_M2, GABA_M5, GABA_M8, and Gluta_M1. The correlation networks between genes with top 50 module membership in cell class-specific ASD-associated gene modules were shown for **(B)** astrocytes, **(C)** glutamatergic neuron, and **(D)** GABAergic interneuron. The node size is proportional to the module membership of gene and the edge width is proportional to the entry of TOM between genes. SFARI ASD candidate genes from categories of S and 1–4 are filled with corresponding colors.

TABLE 1 | The identified functional cell class-specific ASD-associated gene modules and their enriched top three significant GO terms.

Cell class	Module ID	No. of genes	No. of ASD genes (*P*-value)	No. of cell class-specific genes (*P*-value)	Median of Zsummary	GO term
Ast	M2	123	20 (0.00012)	38 (6.22E-15)	1.67	GO: 0007411 axon guidance GO: 0097485 neuron projection guidance GO: 0002040 sprouting angiogenesis
GABA	M5	179	24 (0.00012)	30 (3.73E-06)	1.56	GO: 0098948 intrinsic component of postsynaptic specialization membrane GO: 0099634 postsynaptic specialization membrane GO: 0098936 intrinsic component of postsynaptic membrane
	M8	90	13 (0.00114)	20 (1.43E-06)	0.74	GO: 0005201 extracellular matrix structural constituent GO: 0015085 calcium ion transmembrane transporter activity GO:0015276 ligand-gated ion channel activity
Gluta	M1	345	39 (0.00010)	44 (0.00030)	1.83	GO: 0019902 phosphatase binding GO: 0051018 protein kinase A binding

The numbers of ASD candidate genes, cell class-specific genes and total genes in the module are shown along with FDR-corrected hypergeometric test P-values. For each module, the median of Zsummary values assessing the module preservation between the considered cell class and other cells is also listed. Ast, GABA, and gluta are short for astrocytes, GABAergic interneuron, and glutamatergic neuron.

using two types of signals, electrical and chemical signals. At an electrical synapse, ions flow directly between cells. At a chemical synapse, chemical signals, called as neurotransmitters, pass messages from the presynaptic neuron to the postsynaptic one. Glutamate and GABA (gamma-aminobutyric acid) are major excitatory and inhibitory neurotransmitters in brains respectively. Alterations of GABAergic neuron-associated extracellular matrix (Wang et al., 2018b), the glutamatergic neuron-associated protein kinase activity (Bemben et al., 2015) and the mutation or dysfunction of phosphatases (Gross, 2017) have been linked to ASD.

For the cell class-specific ASD-associated gene modules, we plotted the correlation networks between the genes with top 50 module membership values (**Figures 2B–D**). The genes with top module membership are informative for the networks, and may be used as potential therapeutic targets for ASD. For example, in modules GABA_M5 and GABA_M8 (**Figure 2D**), genes *MYO16* and *ZNF804A* with the largest module membership are of note. Indeed, more and more recent studies have shown the associations between them and ASD (Anitha et al., 2014; Liu et al., 2015; Zhang et al., 2019).

Comparison With Other Studies

To prove the effectiveness of our cell type-specific gene network-based analysis, we detected vulnerable cell types in ASD with EWCE (Skene and Grant, 2016) (**Supplementary Table 4**) using SFARI ASD genes from categories of S and 1–4, and our specificity matrices. Using our cell type-specific gene network-based analysis, four candidate cell cluster-specific ASD-associated gene modules were identified (**Supplementary Table 5**), including Inh L1-4 *LAMP5 LCP2*, Inh L1 *SST NMBR*, Astro L1-2 *FGFR3 GFAP*, and OPC L1-6 *PDGFRA*. Inh L1-4 *LAMP5 LCP2* and Inh L1 *SST NMBR* are cell clusters of GABAergic interneuron. From the result of EWCE, GABAergic interneuron is the most vulnerable cell type in ASD [also seen in Wang et al., 2018a], and Inh L1-4 *LAMP5 LCP2* and Inh L1 *SST NMBR* are also significant cell clusters (adjusted $P = 0.07$ and 0.001).

In addition, we found evidence from a recent single-nucleus transcriptomic study of ASD (Velmeshev et al., 2019) to validate our results. SFARI ASD genes were most overrepresented in L2/3 and L4 excitatory neurons, *VIP* and *SST*–expressing interneurons. Gene ontology analysis of differentially expressed genes identified in a cell type–specific way demonstrated that chemical synaptic transmission, axon guidance, neuronal migration, and GABA signaling were top dysregulated pathways. Besides, to assess if our identified cell class-specific ASD-associated gene modules can reemerge in the snRNA-seq dataset of ASD and controls, we used the expression data of protein-coding genes in this dataset to construct a gene co-expression network for each cell class using WGCNA. The module eigengene was associated with disease status to identify ASD-associated gene modules. We found that ASD-associated module denoted by blue constructed from excitatory neurons significantly includes the genes in Gluta_M1, ASD-associated modules denoted by yellow and brown constructed from inhibitory interneurons significantly include the genes in GABA_M5 and GABA_M8 (**Supplementary Figure 2**). The enriched functions in the blue module include protein serine/threonine kinase activity and negative regulation of phosphatase activity, the brown module is enriched with the functions of synaptic and postsynaptic membrane, integral and intrinsic component of synaptic and postsynaptic membrane, and ion gated channel activity, the yellow module is enriched with the functions of response to metal ion and metal ion transmembrane transporter activity. The results based on ASD snRNA-seq data validate the findings of our cell type-specific gene network-based analysis.

DISCUSSION

To identify the convergence of ASD pathology on common pathways, it is essential to understand the correlations among ASD candidate genes and study their shared molecular pathways. With the hypothesis that investigating functional relationships between ASD candidate genes in normal human brains may provide convergent mechanistic insight into the genetic heterogeneity of ASD, gene co-expression network was built based on normal human brain transcriptomic data sequenced by bulk RNA sequencing (Ben-David and Shifman, 2012; Mahfouz et al., 2015). The gene modules enriched with ASD candidate genes were analyzed for identifying the pathways which may be dysregulated in ASD. To depict the cell type heterogeneity of ASD, here we hypothesize further that different functions in different cell types may be dysregulated in ASD; investigating functional interactions between ASD candidate genes in different cell types in normal human brains may provide new insight into the genetic heterogeneity of ASD.

By conducting cell type-specific gene network-based analysis using human brain nucleus gene expression data, we identified cell type-specific ASD-associated gene modules, which were analyzed for studying dysregulated functions in ASD specific to cell types. Almost all enriched top GO terms in these cell type-specific ASD-associated gene modules are relevant to the corresponding cell types and have been proven to be associated with ASD. We found that different functions may be dysregulated in different human brain cell types, for instance, axon and neuron projection guidance in astrocytes; functions of postsynaptic membrane, extracellular matrix structural constituent and ion transmembrane transporter activity in GABAergic interneuron; functions of phosphatase binding and protein kinase A binding in glutamatergic neuron. By performing network visualization, we prioritize genes that may be used as potential therapeutic targets for ASD. In addition to using the definition of cell classes, we also used the classification of cell clusters to identify cell cluster-specific ASD-associated gene modules. Our findings provide new insights into the heterogeneity of ASD between different human brain cell types. Comparing with EWCE and single-cell transcriptomic study of ASD, it has been shown that cell type-specific gene network-based analysis is effective and can be applied to other kinds of complex diseases for identifying potential cell type-specific dysregulated molecular pathways, especially when the single-cell transcriptomic data of diseased samples is not available.

AUTHOR CONTRIBUTIONS

JG conceived and designed the study. JG, YL, and GJ conducted the analyses and wrote the manuscript.

FUNDING

This work has been supported by the National Natural Science Foundation of China (Nos. 61803320, 61573296, and 61871463), and the Fundamental Research Funds for the Central Universities in China (Xiamen University: 20720190022).

SUPPLEMENTARY MATERIAL

Supplementary Figure 1 | The identified functional ASD-associated gene modules and their enriched top five significant GO terms for cell classes of **(A)** astrocytes, **(B)** microglia, **(C)** GABAergic interneuron, **(D)** glutamatergic neuron, **(E)** OPC, and **(F)** oligodendrocytes.

Supplementary Figure 2 | The constructed gene co-expression modules using snRNA-seq data of ASD and controls for cell classes of **(A)** astrocytes, **(B)** excitatory neurons, and **(C)** inhibitory interneurons. The module eigengene was associated with disease status for showing the correlation coefficient and the FDR-corrected *P*-value. The constructed gene modules are also tested if they significantly include the genes in our identified cell class-specific ASD-associated gene modules (Ast_M2, Gluta_M1, GABA_M5, and GABA_M8). The FDR-corrected hypergeometric test *P*-values are shown.

Supplementary Table 1 | The gene co-expression modules built from each cell class. The module preservation statistics between gene modules built from each cell class and from other cell classes are also shown.

Supplementary Table 2 | The definition of cell classes and the calculated cell class specificity of genes.

Supplementary Table 3 | The definition of cell clusters and the calculated cell cluster specificity of genes.

Supplementary Table 4 | The result of EWCE for cell classes and clusters.

Supplementary Table 5 | The identified functional candidate cell cluster-specific ASD-associated gene modules and their enriched top five significant GO terms. The number of ASD candidate genes, cell cluster-specific genes and total genes in the module are shown along with FDR-corrected hypergeometric test *P*-values. Inh L1-4 *LAMP5 LCP2*: *LAMP5|LCP2*-expressing GABAergic interneuron; Inh L1 *SST NMBR*: *SST|NMBR*-expressing GABAergic interneuron; Astro L1-2 *FGFR3 GFAP*: *GFAP*-expressing astrocyte; OPC L1-6 *PDGFRA*: *PDGFRA*-expressing oligodendrocyte precursor cell.

REFERENCES

Allen, N. J., and Eroglu, C. (2017). Cell biology of astrocyte-synapse interactions. *Neuron* 96, 697–708. doi: 10.1016/j.neuron.2017.09.056

Anitha, A., Thanseem, I., Nakamura, K., Vasu, M. M., Yamada, K., Ueki, T., et al. (2014). Zinc finger protein 804A (ZNF804A) and verbal deficits in individuals with autism. *J. Psychiatry Neurosci.* 39, 294–303. doi: 10.1503/jpn.130126

Bemben, M. A., Nguyen, Q.-A., Wang, T., Li, Y., Nicoll, R. A., and Roche, K. W. (2015). Autism-associated mutation inhibits protein kinase C-mediated neuroligin-4X enhancement of excitatory synapses. *Proc. Natl. Acad. Sci. U.S.A.* 112, 2551–2556. doi: 10.1073/pnas.1500501112

Ben-David, E., and Shifman, S. (2012). Networks of neuronal genes affected by common and rare variants in autism spectrum disorders. *PLoS Genet.* 8:e1002556. doi: 10.1371/journal.pgen.1002556

Blackburn, D., Sargsyan, S., Monk, P. N., and Shaw, P. J. (2009). Astrocyte function and role in motor neuron disease: a future therapeutic target? *Glia* 57, 1251–1264. doi: 10.1002/glia.20848

Calvo, S. E., Clauser, K. R., and Mootha, V. K. (2016). MitoCarta2.0: an updated inventory of mammalian mitochondrial proteins. *Nucleic Acids Res.* 44, D1251–D1257. doi: 10.1093/nar/gkv1003

Ebrahimi-Fakhari, D., and Sahin, M. (2015). Autism and the synapse: emerging mechanisms and mechanism-based therapies. *Curr. Opin. Neurol.* 28, 91–102. doi: 10.1097/WCO.0000000000000186

Gilbert, J., and Man, H.-Y. (2017). Fundamental elements in Autism: from neurogenesis and neurite growth to synaptic plasticity. *Front. Cell. Neurosci.* 11:359. doi: 10.3389/fncel.2017.00359

Gross, C. (2017). Defective phosphoinositide metabolism in autism. *J. Neurosci. Res.* 95, 1161–1173. doi: 10.1002/jnr.23797

Gupta, S., Ellis, S. E., Ashar, F. N., Moes, A., Bader, J. S., Zhan, J., et al. (2014). Transcriptome analysis reveals dysregulation of innate immune response genes and neuronal activity-dependent genes in autism. *Nat. Commun.* 5:5748. doi: 10.1038/ncomms6748

Hodge, R. D., Bakken, T. E., Miller, J. A., Smith, K. A., Barkan, E. R., Graybuck, L. T., et al. (2019). Conserved cell types with divergent features in human versus mouse cortex. *Nature.* 573, 36–37.doi: 10.1038/s41586-019-1506-7

Langfelder, P., and Horvath, S. (2008). WGCNA: an R package for weighted correlation network analysis. *BMC Bioinformatics* 9:559. doi: 10.1186/1471-2105-9-559

Langfelder, P., Luo, R., Oldham, M. C., and Horvath, S. (2011). Is my network module preserved and reproducible? *PLoS Comput. Biol.* 7:e1001057. doi: 10.1371/journal.pcbi.1001057

Liu, Y. F., Sowell, S. M., Luo, Y., Chaubey, A., Cameron, R. S., Kim, H.-G., et al. (2015). Autism and intellectual disability-associated KIRREL3 interacts with neuronal proteins MAP1B and MYO16 with potential roles in neurodevelopment. *PLoS ONE* 10:e0123106. doi: 10.1371/journal.pone.0123106

Lun, A. T. L., McCarthy, D. J., and Marioni, J. C. (2016). A step-by-step workflow for low-level analysis of single-cell RNA-seq data with Bioconductor. *F1000Research* 5, 2122–2122. doi: 10.12688/f1000research.9501.2

Mahfouz, A., Ziats, M. N., Rennert, O. M., Lelieveldt, B. P., and Reinders, M. J. (2015). Shared pathways among autism candidate genes determined by co-expression network analysis of the developing human brain transcriptome. *J. Mol. Neurosci.* 57, 580–594. doi: 10.1007/s12031-015-0641-3

McKenzie, A. T., Wang, M., Hauberg, M. E., Fullard, J. F., Kozlenkov, A., Keenan, A., et al. (2018). Brain cell type specific gene expression and co-expression network architectures. *Scient. Rep.* 8:8868. doi: 10.1038/s41598-018-27293-5

Parikshak, N. N., Luo, R., Zhang, A., Won, H., Lowe, J. K., Chandran, V., et al. (2013). Integrative functional genomic analyses implicate specific molecular pathways and circuits in autism. *Cell* 155, 1008–1021. doi: 10.1016/j.cell.2013.10.031

Robinson, M. D., McCarthy, D. J., and Smyth, G. K. (2010). edgeR: a Bioconductor package for differential expression analysis of digital gene expression data. *Bioinformatics* 26, 139–140. doi: 10.1093/bioinformatics/btp616

Russo, F., Freitas, B., Pignatari, G., Fernandes, I., Sebat, J., Muotri, A., et al. (2017). Modeling the interplay between neurons and astrocytes in autism using human induced pluripotent stem cells. *Biol. Psychiatry* 83, 569–578. doi: 10.1016/j.biopsych.2017.09.021

Shannon, P., Markiel, A., Ozier, O., Baliga, N. S., Wang, J. T., Ramage, D., et al. (2003). Cytoscape: a software environment for integrated models of biomolecular interaction networks. *Genome Res.* 13, 2498–2504. doi: 10.1101/gr.1239303

Skene, N. G., and Grant, S. G. (2016). Identification of vulnerable cell types in major brain disorders using single cell transcriptomes and expression weighted cell type enrichment. *Front. Neurosci.* 10:16. doi: 10.3389/fnins.2016.00016

Velmeshev, D., Schirmer, L., Jung, D., Haeussler, M., Perez, Y., Mayer, S., et al. (2019). Single-cell genomics identifies cell type-specific molecular changes in autism. *Science* 364, 685–689. doi: 10.1126/science.aav8130

Voineagu, I., Wang, X., Johnston, P., Lowe, J. K., Tian, Y., Horvath, S., et al. (2011). Transcriptomic analysis of autistic brain reveals convergent molecular pathology. *Nature* 474, 380–384. doi: 10.1038/nature10110

Wang, P., Zhao, D., Lachman, H. M., and Zheng, D. (2018a). Enriched expression of genes associated with autism spectrum disorders in human inhibitory neurons. *Transl. Psychiatry* 8:13. doi: 10.1038/s41398-017-0058-6

Wang, T., Sinha, A. S., Akita, T., Yanagawa, Y., and Fukuda, A. (2018b). Alterations of GABAergic neuron-associated extracellular matrix and synaptic responses in Gad1-heterozygous mice subjected to prenatal stress. *Front. Cell. Neurosci.* 12, 284–284. doi: 10.3389/fncel.2018.00284

Willsey, A. J., Sanders, S. J., Li, M., Dong, S., Tebbenkamp, A. T., Muhle, R. A., et al. (2013). Coexpression networks implicate human midfetal deep cortical projection neurons in the pathogenesis of autism. *Cell* 155, 997–1007. doi: 10.1016/j.cell.2013.10.020

Yu, G., Wang, L.-G., Han, Y., and He, Q.-Y. (2012). clusterProfiler: an R package for comparing biological themes among gene clusters. *Omics* 16, 284–287. doi: 10.1089/omi.2011.0118

Zhang, L., Qin, Y., Gong, X., Peng, R., Cai, C., Zheng, Y., et al. (2019). A promoter variant in ZNF804A decreasing its expression increases the risk of autism spectrum disorder in the Han Chinese population. *Transl. Psychiatry* 9, 31–31. doi: 10.1038/s41398-019-0369-x

Permissions

All chapters in this book were first published by Frontiers; hereby published with permission under the Creative Commons Attribution License or equivalent. Every chapter published in this book has been scrutinized by our experts. Their significance has been extensively debated. The topics covered herein carry significant findings which will fuel the growth of the discipline. They may even be implemented as practical applications or may be referred to as a beginning point for another development.

The contributors of this book come from diverse backgrounds, making this book a truly international effort. This book will bring forth new frontiers with its revolutionizing research information and detailed analysis of the nascent developments around the world.

We would like to thank all the contributing authors for lending their expertise to make the book truly unique. They have played a crucial role in the development of this book. Without their invaluable contributions this book wouldn't have been possible. They have made vital efforts to compile up to date information on the varied aspects of this subject to make this book a valuable addition to the collection of many professionals and students.

This book was conceptualized with the vision of imparting up-to-date information and advanced data in this field. To ensure the same, a matchless editorial board was set up. Every individual on the board went through rigorous rounds of assessment to prove their worth. After which they invested a large part of their time researching and compiling the most relevant data for our readers.

The editorial board has been involved in producing this book since its inception. They have spent rigorous hours researching and exploring the diverse topics which have resulted in the successful publishing of this book. They have passed on their knowledge of decades through this book. To expedite this challenging task, the publisher supported the team at every step. A small team of assistant editors was also appointed to further simplify the editing procedure and attain best results for the readers.

Apart from the editorial board, the designing team has also invested a significant amount of their time in understanding the subject and creating the most relevant covers. They scrutinized every image to scout for the most suitable representation of the subject and create an appropriate cover for the book.

The publishing team has been an ardent support to the editorial, designing and production team. Their endless efforts to recruit the best for this project, has resulted in the accomplishment of this book. They are a veteran in the field of academics and their pool of knowledge is as vast as their experience in printing. Their expertise and guidance has proved useful at every step. Their uncompromising quality standards have made this book an exceptional effort. Their encouragement from time to time has been an inspiration for everyone.

The publisher and the editorial board hope that this book will prove to be a valuable piece of knowledge for researchers, students, practitioners and scholars across the globe.

List of Contributors

Lauren Rylaarsdam and Alicia Guemez-Gamboa
Department of Physiology, Feinberg School of Medicine, Northwestern University, Chicago, IL, United States

Elisa Ren, Stefania Trazzi, Claudia Fuchs, Giorgio Medici, Laura Gennaccaro, Manuela Loi, Giuseppe Galvani and Elisabetta Ciani
Department of Biomedical and Neuromotor Sciences, University of Bologna, Bologna, Italy

Vincenzo Roncacé
Department for Life Quality Studies, University of Bologna, Bologna, Italy

Keqiang Ye
School of Medicine, Emory University, Atlanta, GA, United States

Roberto Rimondini
Department of Biomedical and Clinical Sciences, University of Bologna, Bologna, Italy

Giorgio Aicardi
Department for Life Quality Studies, University of Bologna, Bologna, Italy
Interdepartmental Center "Luigi Galvani" for Integrated Studies of Bioinformatics, Biophysics and Biocomplexity, University of Bologna, Bologna, Italy

Mona Katrin Roesler, Franco Luis Lombino, Sandra Freitag, Jürgen R. Schwarz, Matthias Kneussel and Wolfgang Wagner
Department of Molecular Neurogenetics, Center for Molecular Neurobiology Hamburg, University Medical Center Hamburg-Eppendorf, Hamburg, Germany

Michaela Schweizer
Electron Microscopy Unit, Center for Molecular Neurobiology Hamburg, University Medical Center Hamburg-Eppendorf, Hamburg, Germany

Irm Hermans-Borgmeyer
Transgenic Animal Unit, Center for Molecular Neurobiology Hamburg, University Medical Center Hamburg-Eppendorf, Hamburg, Germany

Meng-Ping Wei and Chen Zhang
State Key Laboratory of Membrane Biology, School of Life Sciences, Peking University-IDG/McGovern Institute for Brain Research, Peking University, Beijing, China
Department of Neurobiology, Capital Medical University, Beijing, China

Tian-Jia Song, Xing-Yu Lan, Fu-Jun Zhai, Jia-Nan Wang, Shuo Yuan, Meng-Ying Jin, Yu-Fei Xie, Wan-Wen Dang, Ji-Sheng Han and Rong Zhang
Department of Neurobiology, School of Basic Medical Sciences, Peking University, Beijing, China
Neuroscience Research Institute, Peking University, Beijing, China
Key laboratory for Neuroscience, Ministry of Education/National Health and Family Planning Commission, Peking University, Beijing, China

Tobias M. Boeckers and Michael Schön
Institute for Anatomy and Cell Biology, Ulm University, Ulm, Germany

Pei-Wen Song and Mei-Hong Qiu
Department of Neurobiology, School of Basic Medical Sciences, Fudan University, Shanghai, China

Ya-Yue Song
School of Basic Medical Sciences, Tianjin Medical University, Tianjin, China

Song-Ping Han
Wuxi HANS Health Medical Technology Co., Ltd., Wuxi, China

Qiao Chen and You Qiao
Department of Rheumatology and Clinical Immunology, Peking Union Medical College Hospital, Chinese Academy of Medical Sciences & Peking Union Medical College, Beijing, China

Xin-jie Xu
Central Research Laboratory, Department of Scientific Research, Peking Union Medical College Hospital, Chinese Academy of Medical Sciences and Peking Union Medical College, Beijing, China

Xin You
Department of Rheumatology and Clinical Immunology, Peking Union Medical College Hospital, Chinese Academy of Medical Sciences & Peking Union Medical College, Beijing, China
Key Laboratory of Rheumatology and Clinical Immunology, Ministry of Education, Beijing, China
Autism Special Fund, Peking Union Medical Foundation, Beijing, China

Ying Tao
Institute of Artificial Intelligence, Ping An Technology (Shenzhen) Ltd., Beijing, China

Liming Shen, Kaoyuan Zhang, Junyan Ke, Xinqian Chen, Jing Lin, Cuihua Li, Javed Iqbal and Yuxi Zhao
College of Life Science and Oceanography, Shenzhen University, Shenzhen, China

Chengyun Feng and Yan Gao
Maternal and Child Health Hospital of Baoan, Shenzhen, China

Youjiao Chen
College of Life Science and Oceanography, Shenzhen University, Shenzhen, China
Xiang Ya Changde Hospital, Changde, China

Weibin Wang
School of Art, Shenzhen University, Shenzhen, China

Yangsik Kim
Graduate School of Medical Science and Engineering, Korea Advanced Institute of Science and Technology (KAIST), Daejeon, South Korea

Young Woo Noh and Kyungdeok Kim
Department of Biological Sciences, Korea Advanced Institute of Science and Technology (KAIST), Daejeon, South Korea

Esther Yang and Hyun Kim
Department of Anatomy, College of Medicine, Korea University, Seoul, South Korea

Eunjoon Kim
Department of Biological Sciences, Korea Advanced Institute of Science and Technology (KAIST), Daejeon, South Korea
Center for Synaptic Brain Dysfunctions, Institute for Basic Science (IBS), Daejeon, South Korea

Di Chen, Zongyan Li, Shengjun Xie, Yiwu Shi and Qian Chen
Institute of Neuroscience, Department of Neurology, The Second Affiliated Hospital of Guangzhou Medical University, Guangzhou, China

Keke Ren, Haiying Liu, Honghui Mao and Wenting Wang
Department of Neurobiology, School of Basic Medicine, Fourth Military Medical University, Xi'an, China

Huiming Mo
Department of Physiology, Medical College of Yan'an University, Yan'an, China

Mengmeng Wang, Xinyan Liu, Haifeng Zhang, Junjun Kang, Fei Wang, Yazhou Wang and Shengxi Wu
Department of Neurobiology, Institute of Neurosciences, School of Basic Medicine, Fourth Military Medical University, Xi'an, China

Yilin Hou
Department of Neurobiology, Institute of Neurosciences, School of Basic Medicine, Fourth Military Medical University, Xi'an, China
Department of Military Psychology, Fourth Military Medical University, Xi'an, China

Youyi Zhao
Department of Neurobiology, Institute of Neurosciences, School of Basic Medicine, Fourth Military Medical University, Xi'an, China
State Key Laboratory of Military Stomatology and National Clinical Research Center for Oral Diseases and Shaanxi Engineering Research, Department of Anethesiology, Center for Dental Materials and Advanced Manufacture, School of Stomatology, Fourth Military Medical University, Xi'an, China

Jing Chen
Department of Anatomy, School of Basic Medicine, Fourth Military Medical University, Xi'an, China

Xufeng Liu
Department of Military Psychology, Fourth Military Medical University, Xi'an, China

Razia Sultana, Amita Shrestha, Charles C. Lee and Olalekan M. Ogundele
Department of Comparative Biomedical Sciences, Louisiana State University School of Veterinary Medicine, Baton Rouge, LA, United States

Sara Schiavi, Antonia Manduca, Stefano Leone, Francesca Melancia and Viviana Trezza
Department of Science, Section of Biomedical Sciences and Technologies, University "Roma Tre", Rome, Italy

Daniela Iezzi, Carmen Carbone and Guido Mannaioni
Department of Neuroscience, Psychology, Drug Research and Child Health -NEUROFARBA-, Section of Pharmacology and Toxicology, School of Psychology, University of Florence, Florence, Italy

Michele Petrella
School of Pharmacy, University of Camerino, Camerino, Italy

Alessio Masi
Department of Neuroscience, Psychology, Drug Research and Child Health -NEUROFARBA-, Section of Pharmacology and Toxicology, School of Psychology, University of Florence, Florence, Italy
School of Pharmacy, University of Camerino, Camerino, Italy

Ziyi Wang
Division of Life Science, The Hong Kong University of Science and Technology, Clear Water Bay, Hong Kong

Yulong Cai, Hongyu Zhong, Xin Li, Rui Xiao, Lian Wang and Xiaotang Fan
Department of Developmental Neuropsychology, School of Psychology, Third Military Medical University, Chongqing, China

Jing Xu, Yong-lan Du, Jing-wei Xu, Ping-hong Hu, Tai-lin Liao, Qiang-qiang Xia and Junyu Xu
Department of Rehabilitation of the Children's Hospital, Zhejiang University School of Medicine, National Clinical Research Center for Child Health, Hangzhou, China
Department of Neurobiology, NHC and CAMS Key Laboratory of Medical Neurobiology, Zhejiang University School of Medicine, Hangzhou, China

Xiao-ge Hu
Key Laboratory of Tumor Molecular Diagnosis and Individualized Medicine of Zhejiang Province, Zhejiang Provincial People's Hospital, People's Hospital of Hangzhou Medical College, Hangzhou, China

Lin-fan Gu
Zhejiang University-University of Edinburgh Institute, Jiaxing, China

Xiu-mao Li
Department of Orthopaedics, The Second Affiliated Hospital, School of Medicine, Zhejiang University, Hangzhou, China

Qi Sun and Jian-hong Luo
Department of Neurobiology, NHC and CAMS Key Laboratory of Medical Neurobiology, Zhejiang University School of Medicine, Hangzhou, China

Jun Xia
Division of Life Science, The Hong Kong University of Science and Technology, Clear Water Bay, Hong Kong
Division of Biomedical Engineering, The Hong Kong University of Science and Technology, Clear Water Bay, Hong Kong
State Key Laboratory of Molecular Neuroscience, The Hong Kong University of Science and Technology, Clear Water Bay, Hong Kong

Jinting Guan
Department of Automation, Xiamen University, Xiamen, China
National Institute for Data Science in Health and Medicine, Xiamen University, Xiamen, China

Junyu Xu
Department of Neurobiology, Key Laboratory of Medical Neurobiology of the Ministry of Health of China, Collaborative Innovation Center for Brain Science, Zhejiang University School of Medicine, Hangzhou, China

Ori J. Lieberman
Division of Molecular Therapeutics, Department of Psychiatry, Columbia University Vagelos College of Physicians and Surgeons, New York, United States
Division of Movement Disorders, Department of Neurology, Columbia University Vagelos College of Physicians and Surgeons, New York, United States

Veronica Cartocci, Maya Molinari, Josep Carbonell, Miguel Bellés Broseta and Anders Borgkvist
Department of Neuroscience, Karolinska Institute, Stockholm, Sweden

Irena Pigulevskiy
Division of Movement Disorders, Department of Neurology, Columbia University Vagelos College of Physicians and Surgeons, New York, United States

Michael R. Post and David Sulzer
Division of Molecular Therapeutics, Department of Psychiatry, Columbia University Vagelos College of Physicians and Surgeons, New York, United States

Emanuela Santini
Division of Movement Disorders, Department of Neurology, Columbia University Vagelos College of Physicians and Surgeons, New York, United States
Department of Neuroscience, Karolinska Institute, Stockholm, Sweden

Miaoqi Huang, Chunmei Liang, Shengnan Li, Daji Guo, Yinghui Peng and Lei Shi
JNU-HKUST Joint Laboratory for Neuroscience and Innovative Drug Research, College of Pharmacy, Jinan University, Guangzhou, China

Jifeng Zhang, Bo Zhao and Guoqing Guo
Department of Anatomy, Medical College of Jinan University, Guangzhou, China

Yuyang Liu and Wei Liu
Shenzhen Key Laboratory for Neuronal Structural Biology, Biomedical Research Institute, Shenzhen Peking University - The Hong Kong University of Science and Technology Medical Center, Shenzhen, China

Yiping Lin
Department of Automation, Xiamen University, Xiamen, China

Guoli Ji
Department of Automation, Xiamen University, Xiamen, China
National Institute for Data Science in Health and Medicine, Xiamen University, Xiamen, China
Innovation Center for Cell Signaling Network, Xiamen University, Xiamen, China

Index